PWS-KENT Series in Computer Science

Payne, *Advanced Structured BASIC: File Processing with the IBM PC*

Payne, *Structured BASIC for the IBM PC with Business Applications*

Payne, *Structured Programming with QuickBASIC*

Pollack, *Effective Programming in Turbo Pascal*

Popkin, *Comprehensive Structured COBOL, Fourth Edition*

Radford/Haigh, *Turbo Pascal for the IBM PC*

Reynolds, *Program Design and Data Structures in Pascal*

Riley, *Advanced Programming and Data Structures Using Pascal*

Riley, *Data Abstraction and Structure, an Introduction to Computer Science II*

Riley, *Programming Using Turbo Pascal*

Riley, *Using MODULA-2*

Riley, *Using Pascal: An Introduction to Computer Science I*

Rojiani, *Programming in BASIC for Engineers*

Rood, *Logic and Structured Design for Computer Programmers, Second Edition*

Runnion, *Structured Programming in Assembly Language for the IBM PC*

Shelly/Cashman, *Introduction to Basic Programming*

Shelly/Cashman, *Introduction to Computer Programming: ANSI COBOL*

Shelly/Cashman, *Turbo Pascal Programming*

Skvarcius, *Problem Solving Using PASCAL: Algorithm Development and Programming Concepts*

Smith, *Design and Analysis of Algorithms*

Smith, *Introduction to Computers and Programming: Pascal*

Steward, *Software Engineering with Systems Analysis and Design*

Stubbs/Webre, *Data Structures with Abstract Data Types and Ada*

Stubbs/Webre, *Data Structures with Abstract Data Types and MODULA-2*

Stubbs/Webre, *Data Structures with Abstract Data Types and Pascal, Second Edition*

Suhy, *CICS using COBOL: A Structured Approach*

Wang, *An Introduction to ANSI C on UNIX*

Wang, *An Introduction to Berkeley UNIX*

Weinman, *FORTRAN for Scientists and Engineers*

Weinman, *VAX FORTRAN, Second Edition*

Worthington, *C Programming*

Programming Languages

Principles and Practice

Kenneth C. Louden
San Jose State University

PWS-KENT Publishing Company   *   **Boston**

PWS-KENT
Publishing Company

20 Park Plaza
Boston, Massachusetts 02116

For Margreth

Sponsoring Editors: *Tom Robbins* and *Michael J. Sugarman*
Production Editor: *Patricia Adams*
Manufacturing Coordinator: *Lisa Flanagan*
Cover and Interior Designer: *Patricia Adams*
Cover Artist: *The Image Bank/Michel Tcherevkoff*
Cover Printer: *John P. Pow Company, Inc.*
Printer/Binder: *Arcata Graphics/Martinsburg*

PWS-KENT Publishing Company is a division of Wadsworth, Inc.

Library of Congress Cataloging-in-Publication Data
Louden, Kenneth C.
Programming languages: principles and practice/Kenneth C. Louden.
p.   cm.
Includes bibliographical references and index.
ISBN 0-534-93277-0
1. Programming languages (Electronic computers) I. Title.
QA76.7.L68 1993
005.13—dc20   92-45605
CIP

 This book is printed on recycled, acid-free paper.

Printed in the United States of America.

1 2 3 4 5 6 7 8 9 10—97 96 95 94 93

Preface

This book is an introduction to the broad field of programming languages. It combines a general presentation of principles with considerable detail about many modern languages, including some of the newest functional and object-oriented languages. Unlike many introductory texts, it also contains significant material on implementation issues, the theoretical foundations of programming languages, and a large number of exercises, many of which have detailed answers in an appendix. All of these features make this text a useful bridge to compiler courses, and to the theoretical study of programming languages. However, it is specifically designed for use as a text in an advanced undergraduate programming languages survey course that covers most of the Programming Languages Requirements specified in the 1991 ACM/IEEE-CS Joint Curriculum Task Force Report, and the CS8 course of the 1978 ACM Curriculum.

Rather than focusing on a particular programming language, I use examples from the most widely known imperative languages, including **Pascal, C, Modula-2, Ada,** and **FORTRAN.** Also featured are some of the less widely known languages representing other language paradigms, such as **Scheme, ML, Miranda, C + +, Eiffel, Smalltalk,** and **Prolog.** Readers are not expected to know any one particular language. However, experience with at least one language is necessary. A certain degree of "computational sophistication," such as that provided by a course in data structures and a discrete mathematics course, is also expected.

Overview and Organization

In most cases each chapter is largely independent of the others, without artificially restricting the material in each. Cross references in the text allow the reader or instructor to fill in any gaps that might arise even if a particular chapter or section is skipped.

Chapter 1 is a survey of the concepts studied in later chapters, and introduces the different language paradigms with simple examples in typical languages.

Chapters 2 and 3 provide overviews of the history of programming languages and language design principles, respectively. Chapter 3 could well serve as a culminating chapter for the book, but I find it arouses interest in later topics when covered here.

Chapter 4 treats syntax in some detail, including the use of BNF, EBNF, and syntax diagrams. A brief section views recursive definitions (like BNF) as set equations to be solved, a view that recurs periodically throughout the text. One section is devoted to recursive-descent parsing and the use of parsing tools.

Chapters 5, 6, and 7 cover the central semantic issues of programming languages: declaration, allocation, evaluation; the symbol table and runtime environment as semantic functions; data types and type checking; and procedure activation and parameter passing. A final section in Chapter 7 is on exception handling.

Chapter 8 gives an overview of abstract data types, including language mechanisms and equational, or algebraic, specification. It also includes a section on separate compilation, and leads into the next chapter (on object-oriented programming) by discussing the limitations of abstract data type mechanisms.

Chapters 9, 10, and 11 address language paradigms, beginning with the object-oriented paradigm in Chapter 9. I use Simula67 to introduce the concepts in this chapter, which provides a gentle introduction using Algol-like syntax. Individual sections feature C++, Eiffel, and Smalltalk. Chapter 10 deals with the functional paradigm. One section covers the Scheme language in some detail, and there are additional sections on ML and Miranda. This chapter also includes introductions to the lambda calculus, the theory of recursive function definitions, and dynamic memory management. Chapter 11 is on logic programming, with an extended section on Prolog. One section is also devoted to equational languages such as OBJ.

Chapter 12 introduces the three principal methods of formal semantics: operational, denotational, and axiomatic. This is unique among introductory texts in that it gives enough detail to provide a real flavor for the methods.

Chapter 13 treats the major ways parallelism has been introduced into programming languages: coroutines, semaphores, monitors, and message passing, with examples from Modula-2, Ada, CSP, and Concurrent Pascal. A final section surveys recent efforts to introduce parallelism into LISP and Prolog.

Use as a Text

I successfully class-tested this text over a five-year period in my CS 152 classes at San Jose State University. This course is taken by upper division computer science majors and graduate students. I have taught the course using two completely different organizations, which could loosely be called the "principles" approach and the "paradigm" approach. Two suggested organizations of these approaches in a semester-long course are as follows:

The "principles" approach: Chapters 1, 4, 5, 6, 7, and 8. If there is extra time, Chapters 2 and 3.

The "paradigm" approach: Chapters 1, 9, 10, 11, and 13 (not necessarily in that order). If there is extra time, Chapters 2 and 3, or selected topics from Chapters 5, 7, and 8.

In a two-semester or two-quarter sequence it should be possible to cover most of the book.

A large number of exercises are at the end of each chapter, with selected answers in an appendix. Many of these are programming exercises (none extremely long) in languages discussed in the text. Conceptual exercises range from the short-answer type that test understanding of the material to longer essay-style exercises and challenging "thought" questions. A few moments' reflection should give the reader adequate insight into the potential difficulty of a particular exercise. Further knowledge can be gained by reading the answers, which I treat as an extension of the text and sometimes provide additional information beyond that required to solve the problem. Occasionally the answer to an exercise on a particular language requires the reader to consult a language reference manual or have knowledge of the language not specifically covered in the text.

One vexing issue in teaching a programming languages course is what specific languages to use for the programming exercises (which I consider essential in a programming languages course). Each instructor has his or her own favorite languages, and a text should not require the use of one language over another. This book lends itself to use with a broad mix of actual languages for programming projects.

ACKNOWLEDGMENTS

I would like to thank the many students in my CS 152 sections at San Jose State University for their direct and indirect contributions to this book. I also want to thank three of my colleagues at San Jose State, Michael Beeson, Cay Horstmann, and Vinh Phat, who read and commented on individual chapters. In addition, I thank my editors at PWS-KENT for their encouragement and assistance, particularly Tom Robbins and Patty Adams. A special thanks is owed to Marjorie Schlaiker, who first convinced me I should write this book. Finally, I thank my wife Margreth for her understanding, patience, and prodding during the long hours of work.

The following reviewers contributed useful suggestions: Ray Fanselau, *American River College*; Larry Irwin, *Ohio University*; Zane C. Motteler, *California Polytechnic State University*; Tony P. Ng, *University of Illinois-Urbana*; Rick Ruth, *Shippensburg University*; Ryan Stansifer, *University of North Texas*.

A quote from the preface to the *Concise Oxford Dictionary* edited by Henry W. Fowler impressed me many years ago:

"A dictionary-maker, unless he is a monster of omniscience, must deal with a great many matters of which he has no firsthand knowledge. That he has been guilty of errors and omissions in some of these he will learn soon after publication, sometimes with gratitude to his enlightener, sometimes otherwise."

I have tried to make this book as error-free as possible by testing most of the code myself. In a few cases, where language translators were not directly available to me, I relied on others, or my own reading of language manuals or research papers. I would be grateful to all readers willing to supply me with corrections of any errors that may have gone undetected.

K.C.L.

Contents

1 INTRODUCTION

How we communicate influences how we think, and vice versa. Similarly, how we program computers influences how we think about them, and vice versa. Over the last several decades a great deal of experience has been accumulated in the design and use of programming languages. Although there are still aspects of the design of programming languages that are not well understood, the basic principles and concepts now belong to the fundamental body of knowledge of computer science. A study of these principles is as essential to the programmer and computer scientist as the knowledge of a particular programming language such as C or Pascal. Without this knowledge it is impossible to gain the needed perspective and insight into the effect programming languages and their design have on the way we communicate with computers and the ways we think about computers and computation.

It is the goal of this text to introduce the major principles and concepts underlying all programming languages without concentrating on one particular language. Specific languages are used as examples and illustrations. These languages include Pascal, Modula-2, C, FORTRAN, Ada, LISP, and Prolog. It is not necessary for the reader to be familiar with all these languages, or even any of them, to understand the concepts being illustrated. At most the reader is required to be experienced in only one programming language and to have some general knowledge of data structures, algorithms, and computational processes.

In this chapter we will introduce the basic notions of programming languages and outline some of the basic concepts. We will also

1

briefly discuss the role of language translators. However, the techniques used in building language translators will not be discussed in detail in this book.

1.1 WHAT IS A PROGRAMMING LANGUAGE?

A definition often advanced for a programming language is "a notation for communicating to a computer what we want it to do."

But this definition is inadequate. Before the 1940s computers were programmed by being "hard-wired": switches were set by the programmer to connect the internal wiring of a computer to perform the requested tasks. This effectively communicated to the computer what computations were desired, yet switch settings can hardly be called a programming language.

A major advance in computer design occurred in the 1940s, when John von Neumann had the idea that a computer should not be "hard-wired" to do particular things, but that a series of codes stored as data would determine the actions taken by a central processing unit. Soon programmers realized that it would be a tremendous help to attach symbols to the instruction codes, as well as to memory locations, and **assembly language** was born, with instructions such as

```
LDA #2
STA X
```

But assembly language, because of its machine dependence, low level of abstraction, and difficulty in being written and understood, is also not what we usually think of as a programming language and will not be studied further in this text. (Sometimes, assembly language is referred to as a **low-level language** to distinguish it from the **high-level languages,** which are the subject of this text.) Indeed, programmers soon realized that a higher level of abstraction would improve their ability to write concise, understandable instructions that could be used with little change from machine to machine. Certain standard constructions, such as assignment, loops, and selections or choices, were constantly being used and had nothing to do with the particular machine; these constructions should be expressible in simple standard phrases that could be translated into machine-usable form, such as the Pascal for the previous assembly language instructions (indicating assignment of the value 2 to the location with name X)

```
X := 2
```

Programs thus became relatively machine independent, but the language still reflected the underlying architecture of the von Neumann model of a machine: an area of memory where both programs and data are stored and a separate central processing unit that sequentially executes instructions fetched from memory. Most modern programming languages still retain the flavor of this processor model of computation. With increasing abstraction, and with the development of new architectures, particularly parallel processors, came the realization that programming languages need not be based on any particular model of computation or machine, but need only describe computation or processing in general. This leads us to state the following definition.

> **Definition:** A **programming language** is a notational system for describing computation in machine-readable and human-readable form.

We will discuss the three key concepts in this definition.

Computation.   Computation is usually defined formally using the mathematical concept of a **Turing machine,** which is a kind of computer whose operation is simple enough to be described with great precision. Such a machine needs also to be powerful enough to perform any computation that a computer can, and Turing machines are known to be able to carry out any computation that current computers are capable of (though certainly not as efficiently). In fact, the generally accepted **Church's thesis** states that it is not possible to build a machine that is inherently more powerful than a Turing machine.

Our own view of computation in this text is less formal. We will think of computation as any process that can be carried out by a computer. Note, however, that computation does not mean simply mathematical calculation, such as the computation of the product of two numbers or the logarithm of a number. Computation instead includes *all* kinds of computer operations, including data manipulation, text processing, and information storage and retrieval. In this sense, computation is used as a synonym for processing of any kind on a computer. Sometimes a programming language will be designed with a particular kind of processing in mind, such as report generation, graphics, or database maintenance. Although such **special-purpose languages** may be able to express more general kinds of computations, in this text we will concentrate on the **general-purpose languages** that are designed to be used for general processing and not for particular purposes.

Machine readability.   For a language to be machine-readable, it must have a simple enough structure to allow for efficient translation. This is not something that depends on the notion of any particular machine, but is a general requirement that can be stated precisely in terms of definiteness and complexity of translation. First, there must be an **algorithm** to translate a language, that is, a step-by-step process that is unambiguous and finite. Second, the algorithm cannot have too great a complexity: most programming languages can be translated in time that is proportional to the size of the program. Otherwise, a computer might spend more time on the translation process than on the actual computation being described. Usually, machine readability is ensured by restricting the structure of a programming language to that of the so-called **context-free languages,** which are studied in Chapter 4, and by insisting that all translation be based on this structure.

Human readability.   Unlike machine readability, this is a much less precise notion, and it is also less understood. It requires that a programming language provide **abstractions** of the actions of computers that are easy to understand, even by persons not completely familiar with the underlying details of the machine. One consequence of this is that programming languages tend to resemble natural languages (like English or Chinese), at least superficially. This way, a programmer can rely on his or her natural understanding to gain immediate insight into the computation being described. (Of course, this can lead to serious misunderstandings as well.)

Human readability acquires a new dimension as the size of a program increases. (Some programs are now as large as the largest novels.) The readability of large programs requires suitable mechanisms for reducing the amount of detail required to understand the program as a whole. For example, in a large program we would want to localize the effect a small change in one part of the program would have—it should not require major changes to the entire program. This requires the collection of local information in one place and the prevention of this information from being used indiscriminately throughout the program. The development of such abstraction mechanisms has been one of the important advances in programming language design over the past two decades, and we will study such mechanisms in detail in Chapter 8.

Large programs also often require the use of large groups of programmers, who simultaneously write separate parts of the programs. This substantially changes the view that must be taken of a programming language. A programming language is no longer a way of describing computation, but it becomes part of a **software development environment** that promotes and enforces a software design methodology. Software development environments not only contain facilities for writing and translating programs in one or more programming languages, but also have facilities for manipulating program files, keeping records of changes, and performing debugging, testing, and analysis. Programming languages thus become part of the study of **software engineering.** Our view of programming languages, however, will be focused on the languages themselves rather than on their place as part of such a software development environment. A software engineering text can more adequately treat the design issues involved in integrating a programming language into a software development environment.

1.2   ABSTRACTIONS IN PROGRAMMING LANGUAGES

We have noted the essential role that abstraction plays in providing human readability of programs. In this section we briefly describe common abstractions that programming languages provide to express computation and give an indication of where they are studied in more detail in subsequent chapters. Programming language abstractions fall into two general categories: **data abstraction** and **control abstraction.** Data abstractions abstract properties of the data, such as character strings, numbers, or search trees, which is the subject of computation. Control abstractions abstract properties of the transfer of control, that is, the modification of the execution path of a program based on the situation at hand. Examples of control abstractions are loops, conditional statements, and procedure calls.

Abstractions also fall into **levels,** which can be viewed as measures of the amount of information contained in the abstraction. **Basic abstractions** collect together the most localized machine information. **Structured abstractions** collect more global information about the structure of the program. **Unit abstractions** collect information about entire pieces of a program.

In the following paragraphs we classify common abstractions according to the levels of abstraction, for both data abstraction and control abstraction.

1.2.1   Data Abstractions

Basic abstractions.   Basic data abstractions in programming languages abstract the internal representation of common data values in a computer. For example, integer data values are often stored in a computer using a two's complement representation, and standard operations such as addition and multiplication are provided. Similarly, a real, or floating-point, data value is usually provided. Locations in computer memory that contain data values are abstracted by giving them names and are called **variables.** The kind of data value is also given a name and is called a **data type.** Data types of basic data values are usually given the names of their corresponding mathematical values, such as **integer** and **real.** Variables are given names and data types using a **declaration,** such as the Pascal

```
var x: integer;
```

or the equivalent C declaration

```
int x;
```

In this example, x is established as the name of a variable and is given the data type *integer*. Data types are studied in Chapter 6 and declarations in Chapter 5.

Structured abstractions.   The **data structure** is the principal method for abstracting collections of data values that are related. For example, an employee record may consist of a name, address, phone number, and salary, each of which may be a different data type, but together represent the record as a whole. Another example is that of a group of items, all of which have the same data type and which need to be kept together for purposes of sorting or searching. A typical data structure provided by programming languages is the **array,** which collects data into a sequence of individually indexed items. Variables can be given a data structure in a declaration, as in the Pascal

```
a:  array  [1..10]  of  integer;
```

or the FORTRAN

```
INTEGER a(10)
```

which establish the variable *a* as containing an array of ten integer values. Data structures can also be viewed as new data types that are not internal, but are constructed by the programmer as needed. In many languages these types can also be given type names, just as the basic types, and this is done in a **type declaration,** such as the Pascal

```
type  intarray  =  array  [1..10]  of  integer;
```

Such data types are called **structured types.** The different ways of creating and using structured types are studied in Chapter 6.

Unit abstractions.   In a large program, it is useful and even necessary to collect all the information needed for the creation and use of a data type into one location and to restrict the access to the details of the data type. This ensures that changes in the structure of the data type do not affect large areas of the program and that programmers need not keep all the details of a data type in mind at all times. A programming language mechanism that provides this is called a **data encapsulation** or, more commonly, an **abstract data type** mechanism. Typical examples include the **module** of Modula-2 and the **package** of Ada. Abstract data type mechanisms are studied in Chapter 8.

1.2.2   Control Abstractions

Basic abstractions.   Typical basic control abstractions are those statements in a language that combine a few machine instructions into a more understandable abstract statement. We have already mentioned the **assignment statement** as a typical instruction that abstracts the computation and storage of a value into the location given by a variable, as for example,

```
x  :=  x  +  3
```

This assignment statement represents the fetching of the value of the variable x, adding the integer 3 to it, and storing it again in the location of x. Assignment is studied in Chapter 5.

Another typical basic control statement is the **goto** statement, which abstracts the jump operation of a computer or the transfer of control to a statement elsewhere in a program, such as the FORTRAN

```
        . . .
        GOTO 10
C       this part skipped
        . . .
C       control goes here
10      CONTINUE
        . . .
```

Goto statements today are considered too close to the actual operation of a computer to be a useful abstraction mechanism (except in special situations), so most modern languages provide only very limited forms of this statement. See Chapter 7 for a discussion.

Structured abstractions.   Structured control abstractions divide a program into groups of instructions that are nested within tests that govern their execution. Typical examples are selection statements, such as the **if-statement** of many languages, the **case-statement** of Pascal, and the **switch-statement** of C. For example, in the following Pascal code,

```
if x > 0.0 then
   begin
      numSolns := 2;
      r1 := sqrt(x);
      r2 := - r1;
   end
else
   begin
      numSolns := 0;
   end;
```

the three statements within the first begin-end pair are executed if $x > 0$, and the single statement within the second begin-end pair otherwise. Modula-2 goes one step farther in structured control, in that the opening of a group of nested statements is automatic and does not require a "begin":

```
IF x > 0.0 THEN
   numSolns := 2;
   r1 := sqrt(x);
   r2 := - r1;
ELSE
   numSolns := 0;
END;
```

(Note the required END keyword and the use of uppercase for keywords in Modula-2.)

One advantage of structured control structures is that they can be **nested** within other control structures, usually to any desired depth, as in the following Pascal code (which is a modification of the foregoing example):

```
if x > 0.0 then
  begin
    numSolns := 2;
    r1 := sqrt(x);
    r2 := - r1;
  end
else
  begin
    if x = 0.0 then
      begin
        numSolns := 1;
        r1 := 0.0;
      end
    else
      begin
        numSolns := 0;
      end;
  end;
```

or the Modula-2,

```
IF x > 0.0 THEN
  numSolns := 2;
  r1 := sqrt(x);
  r2 := - r1;
ELSE
  IF x = 0.0 THEN
    numSolns := 1;
    r1 := 0.0;
  ELSE
    numSolns := 0;
  END;
END;
```

Structured looping mechanisms come in many forms, including the **while,** and **for** loops of C, the **repeat** loops of Pascal, and the **loop-exit** mechanism of Modula-2. For example, the following program fragments, first in C and then Modula-2, both compute x to be the greatest common divisor of u and v using Euclid's algorithm (for example, the greatest common divisor of 8 and 20 is 4, and the greatest common divisor of 3 and 11 is 1):

```
/* C example */
x = u; y = v;
while (y > 0)
   {t = y;
    y = x % y; /* the integer mod operation in C */
    x = t;}

(* Modula-2 example *)
x := u; y := v;
LOOP
   IF y <= 0 THEN
     EXIT
   END;
   t := y;
   y := x MOD y;
   x := t
END;
```

Structured selection and loop mechanisms are studied in Chapter 7.

A further, powerful mechanism for structuring control is the **procedure,** sometimes also called a **subprogram** or **subroutine.** This allows a programmer to consider a sequence of actions as a single action and to control the interaction of these actions with other parts of the program. Procedure abstraction involves two things. First, a procedure must be defined by giving it a name and associating with it the actions that are to be performed. This is called **procedure declaration,** and it is similar to variable and type declaration, mentioned earlier. Second, the procedure must actually be called at the point where the actions are to be performed. This is sometimes also referred to as procedure **invocation** or procedure **activation.**

As an example, consider the sample code fragment that computes the greatest common divisor of integers u and v. We can make this into a procedure in Modula-2 with the following procedure declaration:

```
PROCEDURE gcd (u,v: INTEGER; VAR x: INTEGER);
VAR y,t: INTEGER;
BEGIN
   x := u; y := v;
   LOOP
     IF y <= 0 THEN
       EXIT
     END;
     t := y;
     y := x MOD y;
     x := t
   END;
END gcd;
```

In this declaration, u, v, and x have become **parameters** to the procedure, that is, things that can change from call to call. This procedure can now be **called** by simply naming it and supplying appropriate **actual parameters** or **arguments,** as in

```
gcd(8,18,d);
```

which gives d the value 2. (The parameter x is given the VAR label to indicate that its value is computed by the procedure itself and will change the value of the corresponding actual parameter of the caller.)

In FORTRAN, by contrast, a procedure is declared as a subroutine,

```
SUBROUTINE gcd (u,v,x)
      .   .   .
END
```

and is called using an explicit call-statement:

```
CALL gcd(a,b,L)
```

Procedure call is a more complex mechanism than selection or looping, since it requires the storing of information about the condition of the program at the point of the call and the way the called procedure operates. Such information is stored in a **runtime environment.** Procedure calls, parameters, and runtime environments are all studied in Chapter 7. (The basic kinds of runtime environments are also mentioned in Section 1.5 of this chapter.)

Unit abstractions.   Control can also be abstracted to include a collection of procedures that provide logically related services to other parts of a program and that form a **unit,** or stand-alone, part of the program. For example, a data management program may require the computation of statistical indices for stored data, such as mean, median, and standard deviation. The procedures that provide these operations can be collected into a program unit that can be translated separately and used by other parts of the program through a carefully controlled interface. This allows the program to be understood as a whole without needing to know the details of the services provided by the unit. Examples of unit abstractions include the module of Modula-2 and the package of Ada. Note that unit abstractions for data and for control are essentially the same.

One kind of control abstraction that does not fit into any one abstraction level is that of parallel programming mechanisms. Many modern computers have several processors or processing elements and are capable of processing different pieces of data simultaneously. A number of programming languages have included mechanisms that allow for the parallel execution of parts of programs, as well as providing for synchronization and communication among such program parts. Modula-2 has a mechanism for declaring **coroutines,** which are sequential, but independent, program segments (they are called **processes** in Modula-2). Ada provides the **task** mechanism for parallel execution. Ada's tasks are essentially a unit abstraction, while Modula-2's coroutines are structured (procedure-level) abstractions. Other languages provide different levels of parallel abstractions, even down to the statement level. Parallel programming mechanisms are surveyed in Chapter 13.

It is worth noting that almost all abstraction mechanisms are provided for human readability. If a programming language needs to describe only computation, then it needs only enough mechanisms to be able to describe all the computations that a Turing machine can perform. Such a language is called **Turing complete.** As the following property shows, Turing completeness can be achieved with very few language mechanisms:

> A programming language is Turing complete provided it has integer variables and arithmetic and sequentially executes statements, which include assignment, selection (if) and loop (while) statements.

1.3   COMPUTATIONAL PARADIGMS

Programming languages began by imitating and abstracting the operations of a computer. It is not surprising that the kind of computer for which they were written had a significant effect on their design. In most cases the computer in question was the von Neumann model mentioned in Section 1.1: a single central processing unit that sequentially executes instructions that operate on values stored in memory. Indeed, the result on Turing completeness of the previous section explicitly referred to sequential execution and the use of variables and assignment. These are typical features of a language based on the von Neumann model: variables represent memory values, and assignment allows the program to operate on these memory values.

A programming language that is characterized by these three properties—the sequential execution of instructions, the use of variables representing memory locations, and the use of assignment to change the values of variables—is called an **imperative** language, since its primary feature is a sequence of statements that represent commands, or imperatives. Sometimes such languages are also called **procedural** but this has nothing explicitly to do with the concept of procedures discussed earlier.

Most programming languages today are imperative. But it is not necessary for a programming language to describe computation in this way. Indeed, the requirement that computation be described as a sequence of instructions, each operating on a single piece of data, is sometimes referred to as the **von Neumann bottleneck,** since it restricts the ability of a language to indicate parallel computation, that is, computation that can be applied to many different pieces of data simultaneously, and nondeterministic computation, or computation that does not depend on order.[1] Thus it is reasonable to ask if there are ways to describe computation that are less dependent on the von Neumann model of a computer. Indeed there are, and these will be described shortly. Imperative programming languages therefore become only one **paradigm,** or pattern, for programming languages to follow.

Two alternative paradigms for describing computation come from mathematics. The **functional** paradigm comes from traditional mathematics and is based on the notion of a function. The **logic** paradigm is based on symbolic logic, which has been developed primarily in the last century. Each of these will be the subject of a subsequent chapter, but we will discuss them in a little more detail here.

Functional programming.   The functional paradigm bases the description of computation on the evaluation of functions or the application of functions to known values. For this reason, functional languages are sometimes called **applicative** languages. A functional programming language has as its basic mechanism the evaluation of a function, or the **function call.** This involves, besides the actual evaluation of functions, the passing of values as **parameters** to functions and the obtaining of the resultant values as **returned values** from functions. The functional paradigm involves no notion of variable or assignment to variables. Also, repetitive operations are not expressed by loops (which require control variables to terminate) but by **recursive** functions. Indeed the study of **recursive function theory** in mathematics has established the following property:

> A programming language is Turing complete if it has integer values, arithmetic functions on those values, and if it has a mechanism for defining new functions using existing functions, selection, and recursion.

It may seem surprising that a programming language can completely do away with variables and loops, but that is exactly what the functional paradigm does, and there may be advantages to doing so. We have already stated one: that the language becomes more independent of the machine model, with the possibility that such languages may be better suited to the machines of the future. Another is that, because functional programs resemble mathematics, it is easier to draw precise conclusions about their behavior. Exactly how this is possible is left to later chapters. We content ourselves here with one example of functional programming.

Let us return to the Modula-2 procedure to compute the greatest common divisor of two integers that we gave in the last section. A functional version of this procedure is as follows (in Modula-2 functions are also called procedures):

---

[1]Parallel and nondeterministic computations are related concepts. See Chapter 13.

```
PROCEDURE gcd (u,v: INTEGER): INTEGER;
BEGIN
  IF v = 0 THEN
    RETURN u;
  ELSE
    RETURN gcd(v,u MOD v);
  END;
END gcd;
```

Note that this code does not use any local variables or loops, but does use recursion (it calls itself with a different set of parameters). Note also the use of the RETURN statement to indicate the value returned by the function.

In an even more functionally oriented programming language, such as LISP, this function would be written as follows (here and throughout the book we use the Scheme dialect of LISP):

```
(define (gcd u v)
  (if (= v 0) u
      (gcd v (remainder u v))))
```

A few comments about this Scheme code may be worthwhile.

In LISP, programs are list expressions, that is, sequences of things separated by spaces and surrounded by parentheses, as in (+ 2 3). Programs are run by evaluating them as expressions, and expressions are evaluated by applying the first item in a list, which must be a function, to the rest of the items as arguments. Thus (gcd 8 18) applies the gcd function to parameters 8 and 18. Similarly 2 + 3 is written (+ 2 3), which applies the "+" function to the values 2 and 3.

In the definition of the gcd function we have used the if-then-else function, which is just called "if"—the "then" and "else" are dispensed with. Thus (if a b c) means "if a then b else c." Note that the "if" function represents control as well as the computation of a value: first a is evaluated and, depending on the result, either b or c is evaluated, with the resulting value becoming the returned value of the function. (This differs from the "if" statement of Pascal, C, or Modula-2, which does not have a value.)

Finally, LISP does not require a return-statement to indicate the value returned by a function. Simply stating the value itself implies that it is returned by the function.

Chapter 10 examines in detail Scheme and other functional programming languages.

Logic programming.   This language paradigm is based on symbolic logic. In a logic programming language, a program consists of a set of statements that describe what is true about a desired result, as opposed to giving a particular sequence of statements that must be executed in a fixed order to produce the result. A pure logic programming language has no need for control abstractions such as loops or selection. Control is supplied by the underlying system. All that is needed in a logic program is the statement of the properties of the computation. For this reason, logic programming is sometimes called **declarative programming,** since properties are declared, but no execution sequence is specified. (Since there is such a removal from the details of machine execution, logic programming languages are sometimes referred to as **very-high-level languages.**)

In the example of the greatest common divisor, we can state the properties of gcd in a form similar to that of a logic program as follows:

The gcd of u and v is u if $v = 0$.

The gcd of u and v is the same as the gcd of v and u mod v if v is > 0.

A number of logic programming languages have been developed in the past decade, but only one has become widely used: Prolog. The gcd statements given translate into Prolog as follows:

```
gcd(U,V,U)  : -  V=0.
gcd(U,V,X)  : -  V > 0,
                 Y is U mod V,
                 gcd(V,Y,X).
```

In Prolog, the form of a program is a sequence of statements, called **clauses,** which are of the form

```
a  : -  b,c,d
```

Such a clause roughly corresponds to the assertion that a is true if b and c and d are true. Unlike functional programming (and more like imperative programming), Prolog requires values to be represented by variables. However, variables do not represent memory locations as they do in imperative programming, but behave more as names for the results of partial computations, as they do in mathematics.

In the Prolog program, gcd has three parameters instead of two: the third represents the computed value, since gcd itself can only be true or false (that is, it can only succeed or fail). Note also the use of uppercase for variables. This is a standard convention for Prolog.

The first of the two clauses for gcd states that the gcd of U and V is U, provided V is equal to 0. The second clause states that the gcd of U and V is X, provided V is greater than 0, and that X is the result of the gcd of V and Y, where Y is equal to U mod V. (The "is" clause for Y is somewhat like assignment in an ordinary programming language and gives Y the value of U mod V.)

Details of Prolog and logic programming are treated in Chapter 11.

There is one more language paradigm that has gained much attention in recent years: **object-oriented programming.** It is based on the notion of an **object,** which can be loosely described as a collection of memory locations together with all the operations that can change the values of these memory locations. The standard simple example of an object is a variable, with operations to assign it a value and to fetch its value. In a sense, object-oriented programming is the opposite of functional programming: it concentrates on memory locations rather than values and functions. It represents computation as the interaction among, or communication between, a group of objects, each of which behaves like its own computer, with its own memory and its own operations. In many object-oriented languages, objects are grouped into **classes** that represent all the objects with the same properties. Classes are defined using declarations, much as structured types are declared in a language like C or Pascal. Objects are then created as particular examples, or **instances,** of a class.

In our running example of the greatest common divisor of two integers, the object-oriented view of the gcd is as an object that is created by supplying it with the information on which it depends, namely, the parameters u and v. The object can then be queried for its value, which is the result of computing the greatest common divisor of its initial values.

The language that introduced the notion of class and object was Simula67. A major role was played by Smalltalk in stimulating interest in the object-oriented paradigm, which has grown substantially in recent years. A number of newer languages, especially C++, have now become popular. We will give a solution to the gcd example in Simula, however, since it easy to read and understand:

```
class gcd(u,v);
integer u,v;
begin
  integer procedure value;
  begin
    if v = 0 then value := u
    else begin
      ref (gcd) x;
      x :- new gcd(v,u mod v);
      value := x.value;
    end;
  end value;
end gcd;
```

This class can be used by defining an object of the class as follows:

```
ref (gcd) z;
```

In this declaration the significance of the keyword "ref" is that z always is a location, or **reference.** At first there is no actual memory allocated to z; we must create, or **instantiate,** the object with the following assignment-like statement:

```
z  :-  new gcd(8,18);
```

Then we can ask z to tell us its value by calling the value procedure, as for example, in

```
y  :=  z.value;
```

Internally, the value procedure works in the case when v is not zero by creating locally yet another object of class gcd with the name x, giving it new initial data, and then asking for its value. (We examine object-oriented languages in more detail in Chapter 9.)

It needs to be stressed that, even though a programming language may exhibit most or all of the properties of one of the four paradigms just discussed, few languages adhere purely to one paradigm, but usually contain features of several paradigms. Indeed, as we saw, we were able to write a functional version of the gcd function in Modula-2, a language that is considered to be more of an imperative language. Nevertheless, it and most other modern imperative languages permit the definition of recursive functions, a mechanism that is generally considered to be functional. Similarly, the Scheme dialect of LISP, which is considered to be a functional language, does permit variables to be declared and assigned to, which is definitely an imperative feature. Scheme programs can also be written in an object-oriented style that closely approximates the object-oriented paradigm. Thus we can refer to a programming **style** as following one (or more) of the paradigms. In a language that permits the expression of several different paradigms, which one is used depends on the kind of computation desired and the requirements of the development environment.

1.4 *LANGUAGE DEFINITION*

A programming language needs a complete, precise description. As obvious as that sounds, in the past many programming languages began with only informal English descriptions. Even today most languages are defined by a **reference manual** in English, although the language in such manuals has become increasingly formalized. Such manuals will always be needed, but there has been increasing acceptance of the need for a formally precise definition of a programming language. Such definitions have, in a few cases, been completely given, but currently it is customary to give a formal definition only of parts of a programming language.

The importance of a precise definition for a programming language should be clear from its use to describe computation. Without a clear notion of the effect of language constructs, we have no clear idea of what computation is actually being performed. Moreover, it should be possible to reason mathematically about programs, and to do this requires formal verification or proof of the behavior of a program. Without a formal definition this is impossible.

But there are other compelling reasons for the need for a formal definition. We have already mentioned the need for machine or implementation independence. The best way to achieve this is through standardization, which requires an independent and precise language definition that is universally accepted. Standards organizations such as ANSI (American National Standards Institute) and ISO (International Standards Organization) have published definitions for several languages, including Pascal, FORTRAN, and C. The Ada programming language has been fixed by the U.S. Department of Defense, which requires every implementation to pass a rigorous test before it can use the name.

A further reason for a formal definition is that, inevitably in the programming process, difficult questions arise about program behavior and interaction. Programmers need an adequate reference to answer such questions besides the often-used trial-and-error process: it can happen that such questions need to be answered already at the design stage and may result in major design changes.

Finally, the requirements of a formal definition provide discipline during the design of a language. Often a language designer will not realize the consequences of design decisions until he or she is required to produce a clear definition.

Language definition can be loosely divided into two parts: **syntax,** or structure, and **semantics,** or meaning. We discuss each of these categories in turn.

Language syntax.   The syntax of a programming language is in many ways like the grammar of a natural language. It is the description of the ways different parts of the language may be combined to form other parts. As an example, the syntax of the if-statement in Pascal may be described in words as follows:

> An if-statement consists of the word "if" followed by a condition, followed by the word "then," followed by a statement, followed by an optional else part consisting of the word "else" and another statement.

The description of language syntax is one of the areas where formal definitions have gained acceptance, and the syntax of almost all languages is now given using **context-free grammars.** For example, a context-free grammar rule for the Pascal if-statement can be written as follows:

$$<\text{if-statement}> ::= \text{if } <\text{condition}> \text{ then } <\text{statement}>$$
$$[\text{else } <\text{statement}>]$$

An issue closely related to the syntax of a programming language is its **lexical structure.** This is similar to spelling in a natural language. The lexical structure of a programming language is the structure of the words of the language, which are usually called **tokens.** In the example of a Pascal if-statement, the words "if," "then," and "else" are tokens. Other tokens in programming languages include identifiers (or names), symbols for operations, such as " + " and "< = ," and special punctuation symbols such as the semicolon (";") and the period ("."").

In this book we shall consider syntax and lexical structure together, and a more detailed study is found in Chapter 4.

Language semantics.   Syntax represents only the surface structure of a language and thus is only a small part of a language definition. The semantics, or meaning, of a language is much more complex and difficult to describe precisely. Semantics involves a description of what happens during the execution of a program or program part. What is difficult about semantics is that the meaning of a particular mechanism may involve interactions with other mechanisms in the language.

To continue with our example of the Pascal if-statement, its semantics may be described in words as follows:

> An if-statement is executed by first evaluating its condition. If the
> condition evaluates to true, then the statement following the "then"
> is executed. If the condition evaluates to false, and there is an else
> part, then the statement following the "else" is executed.

This description in itself points out some of the difficulty in specifying semantics, even for a simple mechanism such as the if-statement. The description makes no mention of what happens if the condition evaluates to false, but there is no else part (presumably nothing happens; that is, the program continues at the point after the if-statement). It also does not specifically address the question of changes that may occur to variables or other entities during the evaluation of the condition. In fact, both the "then" statement and the "else" statement must inherit any such changes during their execution. Another question one may ask is whether there are other language mechanisms that may permit either the "then" statement or the "else" statement to be executed without the corresponding evaluation of the condition. If not, then the if-statement provides adequate protection from errors during execution, such as division by zero:

```
if x <> 0.0 then y := 1.0/x
```

Otherwise, additional protection mechanisms may be necessary.

The alternative to this informal description of semantics is to use a formal method. However, no generally accepted method, such as the use of context-free grammars for syntax, exists. Indeed, it is still not customary for a formal definition of the semantics of a programming language to be given at all. Nevertheless, several notational systems for formal definitions have been developed and are increasingly in use. These include **denotational semantics** and **axiomatic semantics.**

Language semantics are implicit in many of the chapters of this book, but semantic issues are more specifically addressed in Chapters 5 and 7. Chapter 12 discusses formal methods of semantic definition, including denotational and axiomatic semantics.

1.5   *LANGUAGE TRANSLATION*

For a programming language to be useful, it must have a **translator,** that is, a program that accepts other programs written in the language in question and that either executes them directly or transforms them into a form suitable for execution. A translator that immediately executes a program is called an **interpreter,** while a translator that changes a program into a form suitable for execution is called a **compiler.**

Interpretation is a one-step process, in which both the program and the input are provided to the interpreter, and the output is obtained:

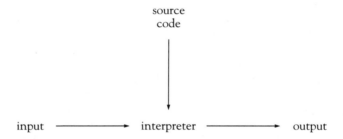

An interpreter can be viewed as a simulator for a machine whose "machine language" is the language being translated.

Compilation, on the other hand, is at least a two-step process: the original program (or **source program**) is input to the compiler, and a new program (or **target program**) is output from the compiler. This target program may then be executed, if it is in a form suitable for direct execution (i.e., in machine language). More commonly, the target language is assembly language, and the target program must be translated by an **assembler** into an object program, and then **linked** with other object programs, and **loaded** into appropriate memory locations before it can be executed. Sometimes the target language is even another programming language, in which case a compiler for that language must be used to obtain an executable object program.

The compilation process can be visualized as follows:

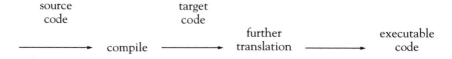

and

$$\begin{array}{c}
\text{executable} \\
\text{code} \\
\downarrow
\end{array}$$

input $\longrightarrow$ processor $\longrightarrow$ output

It is also possible to have translators that are intermediate between interpreters and compilers: a translator may translate a source program into an intermediate language and then interpret the intermediate language. Such translators could be called **pseudointerpreters,** since they execute the program without producing a target program, but they process the entire source program before execution begins.

It is important to keep in mind that a language is different from a particular translator for that language. It *is* possible for a language to be defined by the behavior of a particular interpreter or compiler (a so-called **definitional** translator), but this is not common (and even problematic, in view of the need for a formal definition discussed in the last section). More often, a language definition exists independently, and a translator may or may not adhere closely to the language definition (one hopes the former). When writing programs one must always be aware of those features and properties that depend on a specific translator and are not part of the language definition. There are significant advantages to be gained from trying to avoid nonstandard features as much as possible.

Both compilers and interpreters must perform similar operations when translating a source program. First, a **lexical analyzer,** or **scanner,** must translate the incoming characters into tokens. Then a **syntax analyzer** or **parser** must determine the structure of the sequence of tokens provided to it by the scanner. Finally, a **semantic analyzer** must determine enough of the meaning of a program to allow execution or generation of a target program to take place. Typically, these **phases** of translation do not occur separately but are combined in various ways. A language translator must also maintain a **runtime environment,** in which suitable memory space for program data is allocated, and that records the progress of the execution of the program. An interpreter usually maintains the runtime environment internally as a part of its management of the execution of the program, while a compiler must maintain the runtime environment indirectly by adding suitable operations to the target code. Finally, a language may also require a **preprocessor,** which is run prior to translation to transform a program into a form suitable for translation.

The properties of a programming language that can be determined prior to execution are called **static** properties, while properties that can be determined only during execution are called **dynamic** properties. This distinction is not very useful for interpreters, but it is for compilers: a compiler can *only* make use of the static properties of a language. Typical static properties of a language are its lexical and syntactic structure. In some languages, such as Pascal, C, and Ada, important semantic properties are also static: data types of variables are a significant example. (See Chapter 6.)

A programming language can be designed to be more suitable for interpretation or compilation. For instance, a language that is more dynamic, that is, has fewer static properties, is more suitable for interpretation and is more likely to be interpreted. On the other hand, a language with a strong static structure is more likely to be compiled. Historically, imperative languages have had more static properties and have been compiled, while functional and logic programming languages have been more dynamic and have been interpreted. Of course, a compiler or interpreter can exist for any language, regardless of its dynamic or static properties.

The static and dynamic properties of a language can also affect the nature of the runtime environment. In a language with **static allocation** only—all variables are assumed to occupy a fixed position in memory for the duration of the program's execution—a **fully static** environment may be used. For more dynamically oriented languages, a more complex **fully dynamic** environment must be used. Midway between these is the typical **stack-based** environment of languages like C and Pascal, which has both static and dynamic aspects. (Chapter 7 describes these in more detail.)

Efficiency may also be an issue in determining whether a language is more likely to be interpreted or compiled. Interpreters are inherently less efficient than compilers, since they must simulate the actions of the source program on the underlying machine. Compilers can also boost the efficiency of the target code by performing code improvements, or **optimizations,** often by making several **passes** over the source program to analyze its behavior in detail. Thus, a programming language that needs efficient execution is likely to be compiled rather than interpreted.

Situations may also exist when an interpreter may be preferred over a compiler. Interpreters usually have an interactive mode, so that the user can enter programs directly from a terminal and also supply input to the program and receive output using the interpreter alone. For example, a Scheme interpreter can be used to provide immediate input to a procedure as follows:

```
> (gcd 8 18)   ;; calls gcd with the values 8 and
               ;; 18
2              ;; the interpreter prints the
               returned value
```

By contrast, in Modula-2 the programmer must write out by hand the interactive input and output, as shown in Figure 1-1, so that the program may be compiled and run. This fact, plus the lack of the compilation step, makes an interpreter more suitable than a compiler in some cases for instruction and for program development. By contrast, a language

```
MODULE ModSample;

FROM InOut IMPORT WriteString,ReadInt,WriteInt,
  WriteLn;

PROCEDURE gcd ( u,v: INTEGER ) : INTEGER ;
BEGIN
  IF v = 0 THEN
    RETURN u;
  ELSE
    RETURN gcd(v,u MOD v);
  END;
END gcd;

VAR x,y: INTEGER;

BEGIN (* main program *)
  WriteString('Input two integers:');
  WriteLn;
  ReadInt(x);
  WriteLn;
  ReadInt(y);
  WriteLn;
  WriteString('The gcd of ');
  WriteInt(x,1);
  WriteString(' and ');
  WriteInt(y,1);
  WriteString(' is ');
  WriteInt(gcd(x,y),1);
  WriteLn;
END ModSample.
```

Figure 1-1   A Complete Modula-2 Program

can also be designed to allow **one-pass** compilation, so that the compilation step is efficient enough for instructional use (Pascal has this property).

An important property of a language translator is its response to errors in a source program. Ideally, a translator should attempt to correct errors, but this can be extremely difficult. Failing that, a translator should issue appropriate error messages. It is generally not enough to issue only one error message when the first error is encountered, though some translators do this for efficiency and simplicity. More appropriate is **error recovery,** which allows the translator to proceed with the translation, so that further errors may be discovered.

Errors may be classified according to the stage in translation at which they occur. Lexical errors occur during lexical analysis; these are generally limited to the use of illegal characters. An example in Pascal is

```
X# := 2
```

The character "#" is not a legal character in the language.

Misspellings such as "bigin" for "begin" are often not caught by a lexical analyzer, since it will assume that an unknown character string is an identifier, such as the name of a variable. Such an error will be caught by the parser, however. Syntax errors include missing tokens and malformed expressions, such as

```
if ScaleFactor <> 0 begin {missing 'then'}
```

or

```
Adjustment := Base + * ScaleFactor {missing
               operand}
```

Semantic errors can be either static (i.e., found prior to execution), such as incompatible types or undeclared variables, or dynamic (found during execution), such as an out-of-range subscript or division by zero.

A further class of errors that may occur in a program are **logic** errors. These are errors that the programmer makes that cause the program to behave in an erroneous or undesirable way. For example, the following Pascal fragment

```
x := u;
y := v;
while y > 0 do begin
    t := y;
    y := x * y;
    x := t;
end;
```

will cause an infinite loop during execution if u and v are 1. However, the fragment breaks no rules of the language and must be considered semantically correct from the language viewpoint, even though it does not do what was intended. Thus, logic errors are not errors at all from the point of view of language translation.

A language definition will often include a specification of what errors must be caught prior to execution (for compiled languages), what errors must generate a runtime error, and what errors may go undetected. The precise behavior of a translator in the presence of errors is usually unspecified, however.

Finally, a translator needs to provide user options for debugging, for interfacing with the operating system, and perhaps with a software development environment. These options, such as specifying files for inclusion, disabling optimizations, or turning on tracing or debugging information, are the **pragmatics** of a programming language translator. Occasionally, facilities for pragmatic directives, or **pragmas,** are part of the language definition. For example, in Ada the declaration

```
pragma LIST(ON);
```

turns on the generation of a listing by a compiler at the point it is encountered, and

```
pragma LIST(OFF);
```

turns listing generation off again.

1.6 LANGUAGE DESIGN

We have spoken of a programming language as a tool for describing computation; we have indicated that differing views of computation can result in widely differing languages but that machine and human **readability** are overriding requirements. It is the challenge of programming language design to achieve the power, expressiveness, and comprehensibility that human readability requires while at the same time retaining the precision and simplicity that is needed for machine translation.

Human readability is a complex and subtle requirement. It depends to a large extent on the facilities a programming language has for abstraction. A. N. Whitehead emphasized the power of abstract notation in 1911: "By relieving the brain of all unnecessary work, a good notation sets it free to concentrate on more advanced problems. . . . Civilization advances by extending the number of important operations which we can perform without thinking about them."

A successful programming language has facilities for the natural expression of the structure of data **(data abstraction)** and for the structure of the computational process for the solution of a problem **(control abstraction).** A good example of the effect of abstraction is the introduction of recursion into the programming language Algol60. C. A. R. Hoare, in his 1980 Turing Award Lecture, describes the effect his attendance at an Algol60 course had on him: "It was there that I first learned about recursive procedures and saw how to program the sorting method which I had earlier found such difficulty in explaining. It was there that I wrote the procedure, immodestly named QUICKSORT, on which my career as a computer scientist is founded."

The overriding goal of abstraction in programming language design is **complexity control.** A human being can retain only a certain amount of detail at once. To understand and construct complex systems, humans must control how much detail needs to be understood at any one time.

Abelson and Sussman, in their book *Structure and Interpretation of Computer Programs* [1985], have emphasized the importance of complexity control as follows: "We control complexity by building abstractions that hide details when appropriate. We control complexity by establishing conventional interfaces that enable us to construct systems by combining standard, well-understood pieces in a 'mix and match' way. We control complexity by establishing new languages for describing a design, each of which emphasizes particular aspects of the design and deemphasizes others."

In Chapter 3 we study additional language design issues that help to promote readability and complexity control.

Exercises

1. Translate the Modula-2 program of Figure 1.1 into one or more of the following languages (or into any language for which you have a translator): (a) Pascal, (b) C, (c) Ada, (d) FORTRAN, and (e) BASIC.

2. The following is a Pascal function that computes the number of (decimal) digits in an integer:

```
function numdigits( x: integer); integer;
var t,n: integer;
begin
  n := 1;
  t := x;
  while t >= 10 do begin
    n := n + 1;
    t := t div 10;
  end;
  numdigits := n;
end;
```

   Rewrite this function in functional style.

3. Write a numdigits function in any of the following languages (or in any language for which you have a translator): (a) Modula-2, (b) Scheme, (c) Prolog, (d) C, (e) Ada, (f) FORTRAN, and (g) BASIC.

4. Rewrite the numdigits function of Exercise 2 so that it will compute the number of digits to any base (such as base 2, base 16, base 8). You may do this exercise for any of the following languages or any other language for which you have a translator: (a) Pascal, (b) Modula-2, (c) Ada, (d) C, (e) FORTRAN, (f) Scheme, (g) Prolog, and (h) BASIC.

5. The functional and imperative versions of the gcd procedure in Modula-2 in this chapter actually have slightly different behaviors during execution. Describe the difference. Which version is better? Rewrite the other version so that it agrees with the better version.

6. The numdigits function of Exercise 2 will not work for negative integers. Rewrite it so that it will.

7. The following Pascal function computes the factorial of an integer:

```
function fact (n: integer) : integer;
begin
  if n <= 1 then fact := 1
  else fact := n * fact(n - 1);
end;
```

Rewrite this function into imperative style (i.e., using variables and eliminating recursion).

8. Write a factorial function in any of the following languages (or in any language for which you have a translator): (a) Modula-2, (b) Scheme, (c) Prolog, (d) C, (e) Ada, (f) FORTRAN, and (g) BASIC.

9. Factorials grow extremely rapidly, and overflow is soon reached in the factorial function of Exercise 7. What happens during execution when overflow occurs? How easy is it to correct this problem in Pascal? In any of the languages you have used in Exercise 8?

10. For any of the languages of Exercise 8, find where (if anywhere) it is specified in your translator manual what happens on integer overflow. Compare this, if possible, to the requirements of the language standard.

11. For any of the following languages, determine if strings are part of the language definition and whether your translator offers string facilities that are not part of the language definition: (a) Pascal, (b) Modula-2, (c) Ada, (d) C, (e) FORTRAN, and (f) Scheme.

12. Add explicit interactive input and output to the Scheme gcd function of Section 1.3 (that is, make it into a "compiler-ready" program).

13. Add explicit interactive input and output to the Prolog program for gcd in Section 1.3.

14. Based on Figure 1.1, list all the differences you see between Modula-2 and Pascal.

15. The following Modula-2 program differs from Figure 1.1 in that it contains a number of errors. Classify each error as to whether it is lexical, syntactic, static semantic, dynamic semantic, or logical:

```
MODULE ModSample?;

FROM InOut IMPORT WriteString,ReadInt,WriteInt,
    WriteLn;                                    continues
```

```
PROCEDURE gcd ( u,v: INTEGER ) : BOOLEAN;
BEGIN
  IF v > O THEN
  ELSE RETURN gcd(v,u MOD v)
END gcd

BEGIN (* main program *)
  WriteString('Input two integers:');
  WriteLn;
  ReadInt(x);
  WriteLn;
  ReadInt(y);
  WriteLn;
  WriteString('The gcd of ');
  WriteInt(x,1);
  WriteString(' and ');
  WriteInt(y,1);
  WriteString(' is ');
  WriteInt(gcd(x,y),1);
  WriteLn;
END.
```

16. Describe the syntax of the while-statement in Pascal.

17. Describe the semantics of the while-statement in Pascal.

18. Is it possible in any of the following languages to execute the statements inside an if-statement without evaluating the condition of the if: (a) Pascal, (b) C, (c) FORTRAN, and (d) Modula-2? Why or why not?

19. What are the reasons for the inclusion of many different kinds of loop statements in a programming language? (Address your answer in particular to the need for the repeat-, while-, and for-statements in Pascal.)

20. Given the following properties of a variable in Pascal, state which are static and which are dynamic, and why: (a) its value, (b) its data type, and (c) its name.

21. Given the following properties of a variable in Scheme, state which are static and which are dynamic, and why: (a) its value, (b) its data type, and (c) its name.

22. Prove that a language is Turing complete if it contains integer variables, integer arithmetic, assignment, and while-statements. (Hint: Use the characterization of Turing completeness stated on page 11, and eliminate the need for if-statements.)

23. Pick one of the following statements and argue both for and against it:
    (a) A programming language is solely a mathematical notation for describing computation.
    (b) A programming language is solely a tool for getting computers to perform complex tasks.

(c) A programming language should make it easy for programmers to write code quickly and easily.

(d) A programming language should make it easy for programmers to read and understand code with a minimum of comments.

24. Since most languages can be used to express any algorithm, why should it matter which programming language we use to solve a programming problem? (Try arguing both that it should and that it shouldn't matter.)

Notes and References

An early description of the von Neumann architecture and the use of a program stored as data to control the execution of a computer is in Burks, Goldstine, and von Neumann [1947]. A similar view of the definition of a programming language we have used is given in Horowitz [1984]. Human readability is discussed in Ghezzi and Jazayeri [1987], but with more emphasis on software engineering.

References for the major programming languages used as examples in this text are as follows. Standard Pascal is described in Cooper [1983]. FORTRAN is presented in many introductory texts, such as Koffman and Friedman [1990]. Ada is described by its reference manual (ANSI-1815A [1983]); standard texts for Ada include Barnes [1982] and Booch [1986]. A reference for the C programming language is Kernighan and Ritchie [1978]. (The new ANSI standard is described in Kernighan and Ritchie [1988].) Modula-2 is presented in Wirth [1988a], and described in detail in King [1988]. Gleaves [1984] provides an introduction to Modula-2 for Pascal programmers. Scheme is used as the language of choice in Abelson and Sussman [1985], where many programming issues are discussed, including complexity control using functional and object-oriented methods. The standard reference for Prolog is Clocksin and Mellish [1987]. The logic paradigm is discussed in Kowalski [1979], and the functional paradigm in Backus [1978]. The object-oriented language Simula67 is described in Birtwistle et al. [1973], Dahl and Nygaard [1966], and Lamprecht [1983]. Smalltalk is described in detail by Goldberg and Robson [1989]; introductory texts are Budd [1987] and Kaehler and Patterson [1986]. C++ is defined in Stroustrup [1986] and Ellis and Stroustrup [1990]; an introductory text is Lippman [1989].

The Turing completeness property for imperative languages stated on page 11 is proved in Böhm and Jacopini [1966]. The Turing completeness result for functional languages on page 12 can be extracted from results on recursive function theory in such texts as Hopcroft and Ullman [1979], Lewis and Papadimitriou [1981], and Mandrioli and Ghezzi [1987], where the role of Turing machines and Church's thesis in computation theory are discussed as well. Language translation techniques are described in Aho, Sethi, and Ullman [1986]. The quote from A. N. Whitehead in Section 1.6 is in Whitehead [1911], and Hoare's Turing Award Lecture quote is in Hoare [1981].

2 HISTORY

*P*rogramming languages describe computation for use by computers, particularly electronic digital computers with stored program capability. The history of programming languages is therefore tied to the evolution of these kinds of machines, which began in the 1940s. It is remarkable that the subject has developed so richly in such a few short years.

In the sections that follow we discuss the four decades of programming language history that followed the development of the modern computer, plus the one significant attempt to construct a mechanical general-purpose computer that predated this development. This is a very brief history that leaves out many interesting programming languages and developments. The interested reader is encouraged to consult the primary references at the end of the chapter and the further references contained in those.

There is, however, also a history of "programming languages" that developed independently of the existence of appropriate machines. This history is closely tied to the second important function of programming languages: the need to describe computation and algorithms for human use. It is also tied to the development of mathematics and mathematical notation. Two examples of this kind that appeared just before the development of the modern computer include the **Plankalkül** of Konrad Zuse and the **lambda calculus** of Alonzo Church. The second of these has had an important influence on functional programming languages and is studied further in Chapter 10.

But the need to describe computation goes back to early antiquity, for of course there was a need to calculate even then: sizes of land parcels, sums of money, amounts of property. It is interesting that one of the earliest uses of written human language was to describe computational methods for performing such calculations, something programming languages do so well today. In fact, right through the Greek flowering of mathematics, mathematical processes were seen primarily in terms of algorithms: how to calculate to get certain results.

Indeed, the stylized language used to describe algorithms on cuneiform tablets resembles very much a "programming language" in which sample data is used to describe a general computation. Here is an example of such a description, adapted from Knuth [1972]:

A cistern.
The length equals the height.
A certain volume of dirt has been excavated.
The cross-sectional area plus this volume comes to 120.
The length is 5. What is the width?
Add 1 to 5, getting 6.
Divide 6 into 120, obtaining 20.
Divide 5 into 20, obtaining the width, 4.
This is the procedure.

As mathematics developed, the description of algorithms became less important in relation to the theorems and proofs that became the primary content of modern mathematics. Mathematicians concentrated on the "what" rather than the "how." Now, however, with the expanding interest in computers and computation, there has been a renewed interest in computational mathematics and constructive methods, that is, algorithms that construct mathematical objects, as opposed to proofs that establish their properties without actual constructions.

2.1   EARLY HISTORY: THE FIRST PROGRAMMER

The first computers with stored programs and a central processor that executed instructions provided by users were built in the late 1940s by a team led by John von Neumann. "Real" programming could be said to date from these machines. Yet there were many previous machines that could be "programmed" in the sense that data could be supplied, usually in the form of cards or paper tape, that would affect what the machine did. One example is the Jacquard loom of the early 1800s, which automatically translated card patterns into cloth designs.

The first machine of this type devoted entirely to computation was invented by Charles Babbage in the 1830s and 1840s. "Programs" for his Analytical Engine consisted of a sequence of cards with data and operations. Although only parts of the machine were ever built,[1] several examples of the computations it could perform were developed by Ada Augusta, Countess Lovelace, a daughter of Lord Byron. For this reason, she is considered to be the first programmer, and the language Ada has been named after her.

Ada Lovelace had a remarkable and somewhat tragic life. Perhaps the most remarkable thing about her was her keen grasp of the significance of the concept of a computer, and particularly that of the stored program, building on the idea of the cards of the Jacquard loom:

> The distinctive characteristic of the Analytical Engine, and that which has rendered it possible to endow mechanism with such extensive faculties as bid fair to make this engine the executive right-hand of abstract algebra, is the introduction into it of the principle which Jacquard devised for regulating, by means of punched cards, the most complicated patterns in the fabrication of brocaded stuffs. . . . We may say most aptly, that the Analytical Engine weaves algebraical patterns just as the Jacquard loom weaves flowers and leaves. . . . In enabling mechanism to combine together general symbols in successions of unlimited variety and extent, a uniting link is established between the operations of matter and the abstract mental processes of the most abstract branch of mathematical science. A new, a vast, and a powerful language is developed for the future use of analysis, in which to wield its truths so that these may become of more speedy and accurate practical application for the purposes of mankind than the means hitherto in our possession have rendered possible. (Morrison and Morrison [1961], p. 252)

A further quote shows the extent to which she also understood the basic symbolic nature of computation, something that has been only slowly reunderstood in the modern computing community:

> Many persons who are not conversant with mathematical studies, imagine that because the business of the engine is to give its results in numerical notation, the nature of its processes must consequently be arithmetical and numerical, rather than algebraical and analytical. This is an error. The engine can arrange and combine its numerical quantities exactly as if they were letters or any other general symbols; and in fact it might bring out its results in algebraical notation, were provisions made accordingly. (Ibid., p. 273)

---

[1]Recently, Babbage's Difference Engine, a simpler computer than the Analytical Engine, but which was also never completed, was constructed at the National Museum of Science in London, England, from drawings he left. The success of this project indicates that the Analytical Engine, had it been built, would probably have worked—100 years before its electronic counterpart was invented.

2.2   THE 1950s: THE FIRST PROGRAMMING LANGUAGES

With the advent of general-purpose digital computers with stored pro-grams in the early 1950s, the task of programming became a significant challenge. Early programs were written directly in machine codes or se-quences of bit patterns. This soon gave way to assembly languages, which use symbols and mnemonics to express the underlying machine codes. However, assembly languages are highly machine dependent and are writ-ten using a syntax very unlike natural language. They are sometimes referred to as "low-level" languages.

The first high-level language was **FORTRAN,** developed between 1954 and 1957 by a team at IBM led by John Backus. It was designed primarily for scientific and computational programming, as its name im-plies (FORmula TRANslation), and its descendants are still dominant in scientific applications today. However, it has also been used for general-purpose programming, and many new features taken from other lan-guages have been added through the years (FORTRAN II, FORTRAN IV, FORTRAN66, FORTRAN77, FORTRAN90). The survival of FORTRAN has been at least partially due to the fact that compilers for it are still among the most efficient available, in that they produce very fast code. This was in fact a major goal of the initial design effort, since the general belief at the time was that translators for high-level languages would produce such inefficient code that writing programs in such lan-guages would be of little practical use. FORTRAN proved, at least par-tially, that this was not the case: though the machine code generated by a FORTRAN compiler was somewhat less efficient than what a human could produce directly, its speed was still comparable, and the modest sacrifice in execution efficiency was more than offset by the huge increase in the speed with which a program could be written using the higher-level language.

Since FORTRAN was the first high-level programming language, most of its features were new. Some of them have become standard in later languages. These include the array, loops controlled by an indexed variable, and a branching if-statement. Following FORTRAN, two other languages were developed that also had a major impact on programming and the use of computers: COBOL and Algol60.

COBOL (COmmon Business-Oriented Language) was developed by the U.S. Department of Defense (1959–1960) by a team led by Grace Hopper of the Navy. This language was quickly adopted by banks and corporations for large-scale record-keeping and other business applica-tions. It is perhaps still the most widely used programming language but has been largely ignored by the academic community. (Business schools offer courses on COBOL programming, but computer science departments generally do not.) This is partially due to the extreme wordiness of the language. (The design was supposed to permit nonprogrammers to read and understand programs, but it only complicated the syntax without providing true readability.) Complex algorithms are also extremely difficult to program in COBOL, and the language has added only a few new features to language design. However, those features are significant. Features that COBOL did pioneer were (1) the record structure for organizing data, (2) the separation of data structures from the execution section of a program, and (3) versatile formatting for output using "pictures," or examples of the desired format (still used in some database languages today).

Algol60 (ALGOrithmic Language) was developed by a committee (1958–1960) to provide a general, expressive language for describing algorithms, both in research and in practical applications. It is hard to overestimate the influence and importance of this language for future language development. Most of the current imperative languages are derivatives of Algol, including Pascal, C, Modula-2, and Ada. Research papers today still often use Algol or Algol-like syntax to describe algorithms, and there are still a number of compilers available. It achieved widespread practical acceptance in Europe for general programming tasks, but was rarely used outside of academic circles in the United States.

Algol60 introduced many concepts into programming, including free-format, structured statements, begin-end blocks, type declarations for variables, recursion, and call-by-value parameters. It also implicitly introduced the stack-based runtime environment for block-structured languages, which is still the major method for implementing such languages today. (See Chapter 7.) And it was the first to use Backus-Naur forms (BNF) notation to define syntax. (See Chapter 4.)

At the same time that these three languages were created, based on the standard von Neumann architecture of computers, other languages were being developed based on the mathematical concept of function. Two major examples of such languages are LISP and APL.

LISP (LISt Processor) was designed at MIT in the late 1950s by John McCarthy, based on general list structures and function application. It and its many variants are still in use today in many artificial intelligence applications. (Some common variants are MacLisp, UTLisp, Franz Lisp, and more recently Common LISP and Scheme.) It was based on a uniform data structure, the S-expression, and function application as the fundamental notion of computation. It pioneered general notions of computation and environment and introduced "garbage collection," or automatic reclamation of memory no longer in use, as a method of maintaining runtime storage allocation. Since it is based on a computational principle that is very different from the usual von Neumann architecture, it could not run efficiently on existing machines. However, machine architectures have been developed that are specifically designed to run LISP programs, and many practical decision-making systems have been written in LISP. Recent improvements in translation techniques and machine execution speed have made functional languages and functional techniques much more useful for general programming, and the influence of LISP has grown with time. Now almost all programming languages include features such as recursion that originated with LISP.

APL (A Programming Language) was designed by K. Iverson at Harvard University in the late 1950s and at IBM in the early 1960s as a language for programming mathematical computations, particularly those involving arrays and matrices. It is also functional in style and has a large set of operators that allow most iterations to be performed completely automatically. In the 1960s a version of APL was used as the basis for one of the first time-sharing systems, on an IBM 360. It is still in use today for some mathematical applications, but its major drawbacks are that it has no structuring and that it uses a Greek symbol set that requires the use of a special terminal. Programs written in APL are also extremely difficult to read.

It is interesting to note how rapidly programming languages developed in the short period 1955–1960. Three major imperative languages (FORTRAN, COBOL, Algol60) had come into existence, revolutionizing the view of computing and programming. All three are, in modified form, still in use today. And programming outside the von Neumann model, in particular, functional programming, had already begun with LISP, also still much in use today. The same can certainly not be said about the period to follow: the 1960s.

2.3   THE 1960s: AN EXPLOSION IN PROGRAMMING LANGUAGES

After the tremendous success of the first few programming languages, "everyone" tried to get into the act. The 1960s saw the development of literally hundreds of programming languages, each incorporating its designer's particular interests or concerns (some of these were so-called **special-purpose languages,** used for particular programming situations such as graphics, communications, report generation, etc.). Most of these languages have now vanished, and only a few had a significant effect on the development of programming languages. Figure 2-1 contains a list of some of the programming languages in existence in 1967.

Some of the designers involved in the original efforts of the 1950s began also to dream grandiosely of more general and universal languages, perhaps a "language to end all languages." In many ways such a project was the **PL/I** project at IBM: designed in 1963–1964 and intended for use with a new family of computers (the 360 family), it was supposed to combine all the best features of FORTRAN, COBOL, and Algol60 and to add concurrency and exception handling as well. Although it is still supported by IBM, it can be considered to be a failure: translators were difficult to write, slow, huge, and unreliable (at least in the beginning), and the language was difficult to learn and error prone to use, due to the large number of unpredictable interactions among language features. Some

ADAM	DIAMAG	MADCAP
AED	DIMATE	MAP
AESOP	DOCUS	MATHLAB
AIMACO	DSL	MATH-MATIC
ALGOL	DYANA	META
ALGY	DYNAMO	MILITRAN
ALTRAN	DYSAC	MIRFAC
AMBIT	FACT	NELIAC
AMTRAN	FLAP	OCAL
APL	FLOW-MATIC	OMNITAB
APT	FORMAC	OPS
BACIAC	FORTRAN	PAT
BASEBALL	FORTRANSIT	PENCIL
BASIC	FSL	PL/I
BUGSYS	GAT	PRINT
C-10	GECOM	QUIKTRAN
CLIP	GPL	SFD-ALGOL
CLP	GPSS	SIMSCRIPT
COBOL	GRAF	SIMULA
COGENT	ICES	SNOBOL
COGO	IDS	SOL
COLASL	IPL-V	SPRINT
COLINGO	IT	STRESS
COMIT	JOSS	STROBES
CORAL	JOVIAL	TMG
CORC	L	TRAC
CPS	LDT	TRANDIR
DAS	LISP	TREET
DATA-TEXT	LOLITA	UNCOL
DEACON	LOTIS	UNICODE
DIALOG	MAD	

Figure 2-1   Selected Languages from the 1967 Tower of Babel (Sammet [1969], pp. xi–xii. Adapted by permission of Prentice-Hall, Inc., Englewood Cliffs, N.J.)

consider PL/I to have been simply ahead of its time: a number of its features, such as concurrency and exception handling, were not well enough understood at the time. Yet a case could be made that it attempted to do too much, provide too many features, and satisfy too many users.

An analogous situation occurred with the development of Algol, but in a completely different direction. **Algol68** (1963–1968) attempted to improve on Algol60, not by incorporating many new features from different sources, but by creating a more expressive and theoretically completely consistent structure. It included a general-type system and adopted an expression orientation without arbitrary restrictions—a so-called completely **orthogonal** language. (See Chapter 3.) Moreover, in the interest of precision the Algol68 committee developed a new terminology with strict definitions to describe the language. Hence the language reference manual became almost unreadable to the average computer scientist or programmer. Although this language is still an extremely interesting example for its design consistency, type system, and runtime environment, it was rarely used, often maligned, and not readily available on popular computers.

Not all languages developed in the 1960s were failures, however. A few became widely used and made significant and lasting contributions to the development of programming languages. Such a language was, for example, **SNOBOL** (StriNg Oriented symBOlic Language, an intentionally humorous extreme of acronym building), developed in the early 1960s by R. Griswold at Bell Labs. It was one of the first string processing languages and in its revised form SNOBOL4 provides sophisticated and powerful pattern matching facilities.

Another influential language is **Simula67,** created by Kristen Nygaard and Ole-Johan Dahl at the Norwegian Computing Center in Oslo, Norway, during the period 1965–1967. It is based on an earlier language, Simula I, designed in the early 1960s, and includes Algol60 as a subset. Designed originally for simulations, it contributed fundamentally to the understanding of abstraction and computation through its introduction of the **class** concept fundamental to most object-oriented languages. Indeed, Simula67 can be called the first object-oriented language and is studied in Chapter 9.

A final example from the 1960s is the **BASIC** (Beginners All-purpose Symbolic Instruction Code) programming language. Initially designed in 1964 by John Kemeny and Thomas Kurtz at Dartmouth College, its original purpose was as a simple language for the new time-sharing systems of the time. It made a natural transition some ten years later to the new microcomputers, and it is still widely used in schools, businesses, and homes. BASIC is, in fact, not one language, but a family of languages. There are even two separate BASIC standards issued by ANSI: the 1978 "minimal BASIC" standard and the more elaborate 1988 version of full Standard BASIC, which dispenses with the line numbers of the earlier standard and adds structured control, variable declarations, and procedures. However, because of its simplicity the earlier version of BASIC continues to be in wide use as an instructional language and as a language for microcomputer applications despite its lack of modern language constructs.

2.4   THE 1970s: SIMPLICITY, ABSTRACTION, STUDY

After the turmoil of the 1960s, language designers returned to the "drawing boards" chastened and with a new appreciation for simplicity and consistency of language design. Niklaus Wirth in particular was, along with a few others, vigorous in his rejection of the Algol68 design. He and C. A. R. Hoare published **Algol-W** as a response, and then in 1971

Wirth described the programming language **Pascal,** which distilled the ideas of Algol into a small, simple, efficient, structured language that was intended for use in teaching programming. It was amazingly successful, gaining acceptance not only for instruction, but for many practical uses as well, despite its smallness and the omission of important practical features such as separate compilation, adequate string handling, and expandable input-output capabilities.

In 1972 another outgrowth of Algol was being designed by Dennis Ritchie at Bell Labs that was to become tremendously successful as well: the **C** programming language. C tries for simplicity in different ways from Pascal: by retaining and restricting the expression orientation, by reducing the complexity of the type system and runtime environment, and by providing more access to the underlying machine. For this latter reason, C is sometimes called a "middle-level" programming language, as opposed to a high-level language. This it shares with a number of other languages that are used for operating system programming, most notably BLISS (1971) and FORTH (1971). In part, the success of C has been due to the popularity of the Unix operating system with which it is associated, but it has been adapted to many other operating environments as well.

In themselves, C and Pascal have contributed few new concepts to programming language design. Their success has been principally due to their simplicity and overall consistency of design, perhaps as a result of having been designed by very small groups of people.

In the mid- and late 1970s language designers experimented extensively with mechanisms for data abstraction, concurrency, and verification (proving programs correct). Some of the more notable efforts include the following languages:

CLU.   Designed between 1974 and 1977 at MIT by a team led by Barbara Liskov, CLU aims for a consistent approach to abstraction mechanisms for the production of high-quality software systems. Abstraction mechanisms in CLU include data abstraction, control abstraction, and exception handling. In CLU, the **cluster** data abstraction mechanism is similar to the class construct of Simula. CLU also provides an **iterator** construct, which is a very general control abstraction. CLU's exception handling mechanism was carefully designed and became the basis for a similar facility in Ada (discussed shortly). Exception handling in CLU is studied briefly in Chapter 7 and the cluster mechanism in Chapter 8.

Euclid.   Designed by a committee based at the University of Toronto in 1976–1977, it extends Pascal to include abstract data types and aids program verification by suppressing aliasing and other undesirable programming features. Its principal goal was that of formal verification of programs, perhaps the first language to be so oriented. Euclid's data abstraction mechanism, the **module** (somewhat similar to the module of Modula-2), is studied briefly in Chapter 8.

Mesa.   Another experimental language designed by a team at the Xerox Palo Alto Research Center from 1976 to 1979, Mesa integrated a Pascal-like base language with a module facility, exception handling, and added mechanisms for concurrency, or parallel programming, to allow it to be used to write operating systems. (See Chapter 13 for a discussion of parallel programming.) Mesa's module facility strongly influenced the design of a similar mechanism in Modula-2 (discussed shortly).

2.5   THE 1980s: CONSOLIDATION AND NEW DIRECTIONS

Perhaps the single most important programming language event of the early 1980s was the advent of **Ada,** whose design was fixed in 1980 after a lengthy design effort by the Department of Defense. A group led by J. Ichbiah developed a number of carefully designed and interesting features, including an abstract data type mechanism (the **package**), a concurrency or parallel programming facility (the **task**), and exception handling.

Objections have been raised against the language, primarily based on its size and complexity. Some have called Ada the PL/I of the 1980s and predicted a similar fate for it. However, with the full economic power of the U.S. government behind it, and with the detail and care of its design, it is likely to remain influential and important through the end of the century. Indeed, although translators were slow to become available, its use is expanding.

The early 1980s also saw the development of a new language by Niklaus Wirth, **Modula-2.** Based on an earlier language, Modula, that was designed for constructing operating systems, Modula-2 was given its first definition in 1982, with subsequent revisions in 1985 and 1988. It is a general-purpose language that, like some of the experimental languages of the 1970s, attempts to correct perceived deficiencies in the design of Pascal as well as to add abstraction and partial concurrency facilities and permit better access to the underlying machine for system programming purposes. As in his design of Pascal, Wirth attempted to keep the language as small and simple as possible and, as a result, left out a number of features, including an exception handling mechanism. This, and a number of other design choices, has led some to criticize it, but its accessibility and additional features make it an attractive language for instructional purposes, and we use it for a number of examples in this book.

One major change in the 1980s over the 1970s was the renewed interest in functional programming and alternative language paradigms. Two new functional languages that had their origins already in the late 1970s are **Scheme** and **ML.** Scheme, a version of LISP, was developed from 1975 to 1978 by Gerald J. Sussman and Guy L. Steele, Jr., at MIT (like the original LISP). However, it did not become popular until the mid-1980s, with the publication of an influential book by Abelson and Sussman [1985]. Scheme provides a version of LISP that is more uniform than other versions and that was designed to resemble more closely the lambda calculus. Another version of LISP that appeared in the 1980s is **Common LISP,** which attempts to define a standard for the LISP family.

In another direction, the language ML (for metalanguage), was developed by Robin Milner at Edinburgh University beginning in 1978. ML is substantially different from previous functional languages in that it has a syntax more closely related to Pascal, and it also has a mechanism for type checking similar to Pascal, but much more flexible. A related language is **Miranda,** developed by David Turner at Manchester University (England) in 1985–1986. Scheme, ML, and Miranda are all studied in Chapter 10.

Many attempts to use mathematical logic more or less directly as a programming language have been made over the years, but the language **Prolog** has become the main practical example of logic programming. (See Chapter 11.) Developed by a group at Marseille led by A. Colmerauer beginning in 1972, it now has a number of good implementations and is being increasingly used in artificial intelligence and as a prototyping language. (It was the subject of much publicity a few years ago when it was chosen as the principal language of the so-called fifth-generation project of Japan.)

A similar attempt to translate set theory into a programming language by J. Schwartz at NYU has resulted in **SETL,** whose development also began in the 1970s. SETL has been used for prototyping and also to teach calculus and discrete mathematics, but has suffered from a lack of implementations.

The object-oriented view of programming, based on the class concept of Simula67, has also recently undergone a tremendous increase in popularity. The language **Smalltalk** was developed over the period 1972–1980 by Alan Kay, Dan Ingalls, and others at Xerox Corporation's Palo Alto Research Center. Smalltalk was designed to apply the object-oriented approach in a completely consistent way and is the purest example of an object-oriented language. Newer object-oriented languages include **C++,** developed by Bjarne Stroustrup, beginning in 1980, as an extension of the C language, and **Eiffel,** developed by Bertrand Meyer in the mid-1980s as a more Pascal-like, yet consistent, object-oriented language. These three languages, together with Simula67, are studied in more detail in Chapter 9.

Languages and generations.   A common game in the history of computers has been to classify different stages of development into "generations" of computer technology. This has been done for hardware for some time now, with so-called fourth- and fifth-generation architectures now in use. Languages have also been classified according to this scheme, with an attempt made to parallel the hardware development scheme.

Thus "first-generation" languages are essentially assembly languages, "second-generation" languages are the unstructured high-level languages, "third-generation" languages include most of the current procedural languages such as Pascal and C, and "fifth-generation" languages usually include the so-called very-high-level languages such as Prolog and SETL.

What about **fourth-generation** languages? Many language experts in the computer industry have emphasized these languages as a solution to the "software crisis" and lamented the fact that they tend to be ignored or downplayed in educational settings. Essentially the languages that are considered "fourth-generation" are those that have begun as command languages for database systems and have developed into languages on their own. They include powerful commands like FINDALL and SORT, which act on files of data or whole databases, and are usually embedded in an environment with many development tools such as editors, debuggers, and document preparation and control utilities. A common example of such a language is SQL (Structured Query Language). These languages do address the software crisis in data processing settings by allowing minimally trained programmers to write large-file applications quickly and in very few lines of code. However, they could perhaps more appropriately be classified as special-purpose languages for database applications, and they have made few contributions to the theory of language design.

2.6   THE FUTURE

In the 1960s some computer scientists dreamed of a single universal programming language that would meet the needs of all computer users. Attempts to design and implement such a language, however, resulted in frustration and failure. In the late 1970s and early 1980s a different dream emerged—a dream that programming languages themselves would become obsolete, that new **specification languages** would be developed that would allow computer users to just say what they wanted, and the system itself would find out how to implement the requirements. A succinct exposition of this view is contained in Winograd [1979]:

> Just as high-level languages enabled the programmer to escape from the intricacies of a machine's order code, higher level programming systems can provide help in understanding and manipulating complex systems and components. We need to shift our attention away from the detailed specification of algorithms, towards the description of the properties of the packages and objects with which we build. A new generation of programming tools will be based on the attitude that what we say in a programming system should be primarily declarative, not imperative: the fundamental use of a programming system is not in creating sequences of instructions for accomplishing tasks (or carrying out algorithms), but in expressing and manipulating descriptions of computational processes and the objects on which they are carried out. (Ibid., p. 393)

In a sense, he is just describing what logic programming languages and other "fifth-generation" languages attempt to do. But as we will see in Chapter 11, even though these languages can be used for quick prototyping, programmers still need to specify algorithms step by step when efficiency is needed. Little progress has been made in designing systems that can on their own construct algorithms to accomplish a set of given requirements.

Programming has thus not become obsolete. In a sense it has become even more important, since it now can occur at so many different levels, from assembly language to specification language. And with the development of faster, cheaper, and easier-to-use computers, the "software crisis" has if anything increased: there is a tremendous demand for more and better programs to solve a variety of problems. Perhaps this crisis is already being solved, but by organizational rather than strictly linguistic techniques: by greater reuse of existing code, by increasing the portability and reusability of code, and by mechanical systems such as syntax-directed editors to increase programmer productivity.

Where will programming language design be in the year 2000? The unfulfilled dreams of the past should make us modest and cautious in trying to answer such a question. It is impossible to predict with certainty the development of new programming languages. It will depend partially on hardware and architecture developments and partially on the interests of governments and large corporations. But it does not seem now as though there will be any really overwhelming new developments, but rather a steady process of increasing understanding and refinement, based primarily on existing languages.

Exercises

1. The Babylonian algorithm involving a cistern given at the beginning of this chapter expresses the solution to a particular algebraic equation.
   (a) Write down the equation and solve it for the width. Show how the Babylonian algorithm corresponds to your solution.
   (b) Write a procedure (in one or more languages) that implements the Babylonian algorithm, making the length and the sum of the area and volume into parameters to the procedure. Is your procedure easier to understand than the Babylonian description? Why?

2. Write out a description of Euclid's algorithm in the style of the Babylonian algorithm of the text.

3. Here is another algorithm in the Babylonian style:

   A rectangle.

   The perimeter is 2 less than the area.

The area is 20.

What are the dimensions?

Divide 2 into 20, giving 10.

Divide 2 into 2, giving 1.

Subtract 1 from 10, giving 9.

Multiply 9 by 9, giving 81.

Multiply 20 by 4, giving 80.

Subtract 80 from 81, giving 1.

Subtract 1 from 9, giving 8.

Divide 8 by 2, giving 4.

The width is 4.

Divide 20 by 4, giving 5.

The length is 5.

This is the procedure.

What famous mathematical formula is used by this algorithm? What special numeric requirement is necessary for this algorithm to work?

4. Pick a programming language you know or have heard of that was not mentioned in this chapter. Write a short report on its development, its major features, and its place in the history of programming languages.

5. Each of the following languages is historically related to a language or languages mentioned in this chapter. Determine and briefly describe this relationship.

   JOVIAL

   Euler

   BCPL

   Alphard

   HOPE

6. What does it mean for a language to "exist" at a particular time? Determine what criteria Sammet used for the languages in Figure 2.1. What criteria would you use?

7. Dates of origin of particular programming languages are difficult to determine and specify with precision. Give at least five different ways to specify the date of origin of a programming language. How is this related to your answer to Exercise 6?

8. One area of special-purpose languages that has been very active since the 1960s has been algebraic or formula manipulation languages. Write a brief report on the history of these languages, including the following languages: FORMAC, MATHLAB, REDUCE, Macsyma, Scratchpad, and Maple.

9. Here are some more "special-purpose" languages. Determine their area of specialty and briefly describe each: RPG, Pilot, APT, SPSS, GPSS, DCDL.

10. Language developments often occur as a result of or in step with new hardware or machine developments. Discuss one or more of the following hardware developments and its relationship to and effect on programming language development:

> Time sharing
>
> Personal computers
>
> Cheap, fast random access memory
>
> Disk drives
>
> Multiple processors
>
> Video display terminals

11. Many of the languages listed in the "1980s" section of this chapter were actually developed in the 1970s. Why is this? Is it justified? What, if anything, does this tell us about the recent development of programming languages?

12. In Backus et al. [1957] it is stated that FORTRAN was developed "to enable the programmer to specify a numerical procedure using a concise language like that of mathematics." But in Backus [1978], the author complains that languages like FORTRAN "lack useful mathematical properties" and proposes his FP language schema in part to make programming look more like mathematics. Thus, one interpretation of the history of programming languages is as a series of successive attempts to make programs look more and more like mathematics. Is this view supported by the historical overview given in this chapter? Why or why not?

13. A mathematical definition for the gcd of two numbers is often given as follows: x is the gcd of u and v if x divides both u and v, and given any other y that divides u and v, y divides x.
    (a) Discuss the difference between this definition and Euclid's algorithm (the algorithm of the gcd procedure of Chapter 1).
    (b) Is it possible to use this definition in a procedure to compute the gcd? Why or why not?
    (c) Based on this example, can you draw any conclusions about the relation of programming to mathematics? Explain.

14. Here is a quote from Gelernter and Jagannathan [1990], pp. 150–151:

> Programming after all is a kind of machine-building, not the derivation of formulas. No matter how great the superficial resemblance between a program and a mathematical derivation, the derivation has to be true, whereas the program has to work when you turn it on. It simply does not follow that by making a program look like a mathematical formula, programming takes on the characteristics of mathematics.

(a) Discuss the validity of this point of view.
(b) Discuss the relationship of this statement to the questions raised in Exercises 12 and 13.

Notes and References

Wexelblat [1981] is a collection of papers presented at an Association for Computing Machinery (ACM) conference on the history of programming languages in 1978. Many of the papers are by original designers of the languages discussed, and this book is still the primary reference on the history of many major languages.[2] (Articles by individual authors will also be mentioned in the following.) Sammet [1969] is an earlier book that discusses some of the same languages but with a focus on the details of the languages themselves. Another book that includes history with descriptions of a number of the languages mentioned is Birnes [1989]. Survey articles on programming language history include Wegner [1976], Sammet [1976], Rosen [1972], and Sammet [1972]. The early history of programming languages is discussed in Knuth and Trabb Pardo [1977].

Zuse's Plankalkül was developed in 1945 but did not appear until later (Zuse [1972]). A brief description of the Plankalkül is given in Sebesta [1989]. Ancient Babylonian algorithms are discussed in Knuth [1972]. For an introduction into constructive mathematics, that is, the mathematics of algorithmic computation, see Martin-Löf [1979] or Bridges and Richman [1987]. Charles Babbage and his machines are described in Morrison and Morrison [1961], which also contains the writings of Ada Lovelace. Biographies of Ada Lovelace include those by Stein [1985] and Moore [1977]. For an account of the construction of Babbage's Difference Engine at the National Science Museum in London, England, see Dane [1992].

The early history of FORTRAN is given in Backus [1981], of Algol60 in Naur [1981] and Perlis [1981], of LISP in McCarthy [1981], of COBOL in Sammet [1981], of Simula67 in Nygaard and Dahl [1981], of BASIC in Kurtz [1981], of PL/I in Radin [1981], of SNOBOL in Griswold [1981], and of APL in Falkoff and Iverson [1981]. References for languages more frequently used in this text are given at the end of Chapter 1; these include FORTRAN, Scheme, Pascal, Modula-2, Ada, C, C++, Simula67, Prolog, and Smalltalk. Articles and books on some of the other languages mentioned in this chapter are as follows: COBOL—Schneiderman [1985], Ashley [1980]; Algol60—Naur [1963a,b], Knuth [1967]; Algol68—Tanenbaum [1976]; Algol-W—Hoare and Wirth [1966]; APL—Iverson [1962]; SNOBOL—Griswold, Poage, and Polonsky [1971], Griswold and Griswold [1973]; CLU—Liskov et al. [1984], Liskov et al. [1977], Liskov and Snyder [1979]; Euclid—Lamp-

---

[2] A new conference is to be held in 1993.

son et al. [1981]; Mesa—Geschke, Morris, and Sattherthwaite [1977], Lampson and Redell [1980], Mitchell, Maybury, and Sweet [1979]; ML—Milner and Tofte [1990a], Milner, Tofte, and Harper [1990b], Mitchell and Harper [1988]; Miranda—Turner [1986]; and SETL—Schwartz et al. [1986].

An interesting perspective on the history of Prolog is given in Cohen [1988] and Kowalski [1988]. Some interesting languages not described in this chapter are Icon, a successor to SNOBOL which is described in Griswold and Griswold [1983]; Cedar, a successor to Mesa, described in Lampson [1983], Teitelman [1984], and Swinehart et al. [1986]; the "middle-level" languages BLISS (Wulf, Russell, and Habermann [1971]) and FORTH (Brodie [1981]); and AWK, described in Aho et al. [1988]. An interesting perspective on fourth-generation languages is given in Wexelblat [1984].

3 LANGUAGE DESIGN PRINCIPLES

*L*anguage design is one of the most difficult and poorly understood areas of computer science. In Chapter 1 we emphasized human readability and mechanisms for abstraction and complexity control as key requirements for a modern programming language. Judging a language by these criteria is difficult, however, since the success or failure of a language may depend on complex interactions among the language mechanisms.

Practical matters not directly connected to language definition also have a major effect on the success or failure of a language. This includes the availability, price, and quality of translators. Even politics, geography, timing, and markets have an effect. The C programming language has been a success at least partially because of the success of the Unix operating system, which promoted its use. PL/I, though in some ways a failure, has remained an important programming language because of its continuing support by IBM. And the language Ada has achieved instant influence because of its required use for many U.S. Defense Department projects.

Languages have been successes for as many different reasons as they have been failures. Language designers have noted the importance of the consistency of "feel" of a language and the uniformity of design concept that can be achieved when a language is designed by a single individual or a small group of individuals. This has been true, for example, with Pascal, C, Modula-2, APL, SNOBOL, and LISP. But languages designed by committees have also been successful: COBOL, the Algols, and Ada.

We mentioned in Chapter 2 the attempts to achieve even greater abstraction in programming languages—even to make programming obsolete with the use of specification languages and very-high-level constructs. None of these has succeeded, and we still find it necessary to specify algorithms and computation at a level considerably more detailed than the theorists had hoped. Why? A partial answer is that almost every programming application is different and requires different abstractions. Thus we must either provide suitable abstractions for particular situations with the design of the language or provide general facilities for the creation of these abstractions on demand. Thus programming language design depends heavily on the intended use and the requirements of this use. In this it is similar to programming itself—it is a goal-oriented activity.

Keeping the goal of the design in mind is particularly important for special-purpose languages, such as database languages, graphics languages, and real-time languages, since the particular abstractions for the application should be built into the language design. But it is true for general-purpose languages as well, where design goals can be less obvious. In most of the successful languages, particular design goals were constantly kept in mind during the design process. In FORTRAN it was efficiency of execution. In COBOL it was to provide an English-like nontechnical readability. In Algol60 it was to provide a block-structured language for describing algorithms. In Pascal it was to provide an extremely simple instructional language to promote top-down design.

Nevertheless, with all this in mind, it is still extremely difficult to say what good programming language design is. As a case in point, two language pioneers, Niklaus Wirth and C. A. R. Hoare offer somewhat conflicting advice on language design: Wirth [1974] advises us that simplicity is paramount, while Hoare [1973] emphasizes the design of individual language constructs. Others talk about "extensibility," "expressiveness," and other hazy-sounding qualities. In the sections that follow we will collect some general criteria and a list of more specific principles that can be an aid to the language designer. We will also give examples to emphasize good and bad choices. (Sometimes it will be necessary to read further sections of the book to understand fully the examples.)

3.1   HISTORY AND DESIGN CRITERIA

When programming languages began, there was one principal design criterion: **efficiency of execution.** (Machines were extremely slow, and program speed was a necessity; also, there was a generally held belief that language translators could not produce efficient executable code.) FORTRAN, for example, had as its most important goal the compactness and speed of the executable code. Indeed, the FORTRAN code was designed to resemble as much as possible the machine code that needed to be generated. Of course one could not forget that the whole reason for the existence of a high-level language was to make it easier to write than machine or assembly language. But this **writability**—the quality of a language that enables a programmer to use it to express a computation clearly, correctly, concisely, and quickly—was always subservient to efficiency. And the fact that programs should be readable by humans as well as machines was hardly appreciated, simply because programs at that time tended to be short, written by one or a few people, and rarely revised or updated except by their creators.

Both COBOL and Algol60 can be viewed as steps toward more general criteria than the efficiency of the generated code. The block structure and the availability of recursion in Algol60 made it more suitable for expressing algorithms in a logically clear and concise way, thus promoting even greater writability of the language. (We noted in Chapter 1 that C. A. R. Hoare understood how to express his QUICKSORT algorithm clearly only after learning Algol60.) But Algol60 was also designed as a language for communicating algorithms among people, not just from people to machines. Thus **readability**—the quality of a language that enables a programmer to understand and comprehend the nature of a computation easily and accurately—was also an important design goal. COBOL attempted to improve the readability of programs by trying to make programs look like ordinary written English. In a sense this was not a success, since it did not improve the ability of the reader to understand the logic or behavior of the program and, in fact, decreased the writability of programs by making them long and verbose. But human readability was perhaps for the first time a clearly stated design goal.

With the growing complexity of languages in the 1960s, language designers became aware of a greater need for abstraction mechanisms and for reducing the rules and restrictions programmers had to learn. Both of these were expressions of the need for complexity control. On the one hand, abstractions allow the programmer to control the complexity of a programming task. On the other hand, reducing the rules and restrictions of a language reduces the complexity of its definition and makes the language easier to use actually to solve the task. Simula67 had as a goal the provision of more powerful abstraction mechanisms, and Algol68 attempted to reduce the complexity of the language by being completely

general and **orthogonal:** the language features were designed to have as few restrictions as possible and be combinable in any meaningful way (see Section 3.3). Simula67's class concept was an innovation that influenced the abstraction mechanisms provided by many languages of the 1970s and 1980s. Algol68's generality and orthogonality, however, were less of a success. Wirth [1974] has pointed out that generality can in fact increase complexity even as it reduces the number of special rules, because extremely general constructs are more difficult to understand, their effects may be less predictable, and the underlying computational model is conceptually more difficult.

With the 1970s and early 1980s came a greater emphasis on simplicity and abstraction, as exhibited by Pascal, C, Euclid, CLU, Modula-2, and Ada. Attempts were also made to improve the reliability of programs by introducing mathematical definitions for constructs and providing a language with mechanisms that would permit a translator to prove the correctness of a program as it performed the translation. However, program proof systems have had limited success—due primarily to the added complexity they introduce, not only to the language design and the task of programming in the language, but to the translator itself.

In the 1980s interest continued in improving the logical or mathematical precision of languages, as well as attempting to make logic into a programming language itself. Interest in functional languages was rekindled with the development of ML and Miranda and the increasing popularity of Scheme. Also, interest in object-oriented languages grew enormously, particularly with the development of C++. Thus we see that the emphasis on different design goals has changed through the years both as a response to experience with previous language designs and as the nature of the problems addressed by computer science have changed. Still, readability, abstraction, and complexity control are issues that are involved in almost every design question.

3.2   EFFICIENCY

We want to list some of the more specific principles mentioned in the last section and give examples of good and bad design choices with respect to each. We start with the ubiquitous requirement that can apply in many different guises—efficiency.

This principle can encompass almost all the other principles in various forms. We usually think of efficiency of target code first: the language design should be such that a translator can generate **efficient executable code.** Sometimes this is referred to as **optimizability.** As an example, statically typed variables allow code to be generated that efficiently allocates and references them. As another example, in Pascal constants are restricted to explicit values only (expressions that need evaluation are not allowed), so that constant identifiers can be replaced by their values during translation (rather than execution), making the generated code shorter and faster.

A second kind of efficiency is **efficiency of translation:** Does the language design permit the source code to be translated efficiently, that is, quickly and by a reasonably sized translator? For example, does the language design allow a one-pass compiler to be written? This is the case in Pascal, since variables must be declared before they are used. In Modula-2, however, this restriction is dropped, so that a compiler must make a second pass over the code to resolve identifier references. Sometimes language designs include rules that are extremely difficult to check at translation time or even at execution time. One example of this is the rule in Algol68 that prohibits dangling reference assignments. Occasionally, language designers will try to escape such inefficiencies by allowing translators to fail to check such rules. Indeed, error checking in general can be a problematic efficiency issue, since to check for an error at translation time can cause the translator to be inefficient, while generating code to check the error during execution can cause the target code to be inefficient. On the other hand, ignoring error checking violates another design principle—**reliability**—the assurance that a program will not behave in unexpected or disastrous ways during execution.

There are many more views of efficiency than just these two, however. One is **implementability,** or the efficiency with which a translator can be written. This is related to efficiency of translation, but it is also a function of the complexity of the language definition. The success of a language can be impaired simply because it is too difficult to write a translator or because algorithms to perform the translation are not sufficiently well understood. One of the reasons Algol60 was not used more in the United States may have been that the stack-based structure needed for the runtime system was not widely known at the time. Type inference without declarations, as in the programming language ML, had to await the application of the unification algorithm to type inference. And the size and complexity of Ada has been a hindrance to the development of compilers and has impaired its availabiity and use. Occasionally, a language will even be designed with a requirement that cannot be met by a known method—the language is then untranslatable except by magic! Wirth [1974] states the principle of implementability particularly forcefully: "Language design is compiler construction."

Another view of efficiency is **programming efficiency:** How quickly and easily can programs be written in the language? This is essentially writability, as discussed earlier. One of the qualities involved in this is the **expressiveness** of the language: How easy is it to express complex processes and structures? And this is related to the power and generality of the abstraction mechanisms of the language. The conciseness of the syntax and the avoidance of unnecessary detail, such as variable declarations, are often considered to be important factors in this kind of efficiency as well. From this point of view, LISP and Prolog are ideal languages, since the syntax is extremely concise, no declarations are necessary, and many of the details of computations can be left to the runtime system. Of course, this can compromise other language principles, such as readability, efficiency of execution, and reliability.

Indeed, reliability can be viewed as an efficiency issue itself. A program that is not reliable causes many extra costs—modifications to isolate or remove the erroneous behavior, extra testing time, plus the time required to correct the effects of the erroneous behavior. If the program is extremely unreliable, it may even cause a complete waste of the development and coding time. This kind of efficiency is a resource consumption issue in software engineering. In this sense the efficiency with which software can be created depends on readability and **maintainability**—the ease with which errors can be found and corrected and new features added—while writability is less important. Software engineers estimate that much more time is spent on debugging and maintenance than on the original coding of a program. Thus readability and maintainability may ultimately be the most important efficiency issues of all.

3.3   GENERALITY, ORTHOGONALITY, UNIFORMITY

These three closely related concepts apply to programming language constructs, their interaction, and the concepts represented by the constructs. A language achieves **generality** by avoiding special cases in the availability or use of constructs and by combining closely related constructs into a single more general one. Orthogonality is a term borrowed from mathematics, where it means perpendicularity or in a completely independent direction. **Orthogonality** in a programming language means that language constructs can be combined in any meaningful way and that the interaction of constructs, or the context of use, should not cause unexpected restrictions or behavior. **Uniformity** means that similar things should look similar and have similar meanings and, inversely, that different things should look different.

We give next a series of examples of these three principles (mainly of constructs that violate them). The examples will also make clear that distinctions between the three are sometimes more a matter of viewpoint than actual substance.

Generality.   Here is a list of a few of the features in common programming languages that show a lack of generality:

- Pascal has procedure declarations and procedure value parameters, but no procedure variables. Thus the notion of procedure in Pascal lacks generality. This restriction is removed in Modula-2, but remains in Ada (where there are even no procedure parameters).

- Pascal has no variable-length arrays, so arrays lack generality. C and Ada do have variable-length arrays, and Modula-2 and FORTRAN have the ability to pass variable-length array parameters, but cannot define variable-length array types.

- In Pascal and Modula-2 the equality operator " = " can be applied only to scalars, pointers, and sets, but not to arrays or records. Thus the " = " operator lacks generality. A similar restriction applies in C. This restriction has been removed in Ada.

- In FORTRAN there is only one parameter passing mechanism, pass by reference. Algol68, on the other hand, has only one parameter passing mechanism—pass by value—but achieves generality by allowing a pointer to any object to be passed as a value. FORTRAN has no such facility.

- In FORTRAN named constants do not exist. In Pascal constants may not be expressions, while in Modula-2, constant expressions may not include function calls. Ada, however, has a completely general constant declaration facility (constants may even be dynamic quantities).

Generality can be a dangerous principle that runs counter to other principles. For example, it reduces the simplicity of a language and can make the language less readable and reliable. In Pascal, for instance, pointers are specifically restricted to reduce aliasing and insecurities, while in C they are permitted to be much more general.

Orthogonality.   Here the viewpoint is that language constructs should not behave differently in different contexts. Thus restrictions that are context dependent are nonorthogonalities, while restrictions that apply regardless of context are nongeneralities. Thus the nongenerality of constants in Modula-2 mentioned could be interpreted instead as a nonorthogonality of expressions: in constant declarations expressions can be only of restricted form. Similarly, the nongenerality of comparison for equality could be viewed as a nonorthogonality, since the applicability of " = " depends on the types of the values being compared. Here are some further examples of lack of orthogonality:

- In Pascal functions can return only scalar or pointer types as values. In C values of all data types except array types can be returned from a function (indeed arrays are treated in C differently from all other types). In Ada this nonorthogonality is removed.

- In Pascal file types have a special status and thus cause a number of nonorthogonalities. For example, files cannot be passed by value to procedures, and assignment to file variables is prohibited. In many other languages files are part of a (system dependent) library instead of the language definition, thus avoiding such nonorthogonalities.

- In Modula-2 strings can be assigned to string variables of greater length, but not vice versa; this is the only case in Modula-2 where assignment works for unequal-sized objects.

- In C there is a nonorthogonality in parameter passing: C passes all parameters by value except arrays, which are passed by reference.

Orthogonality was a major design goal of Algol68, and it remains the best example of a language where constructs can be combined in all meaningful ways.

Uniformity.   This principle focuses on the consistency of appearance and behavior of language constructs. Nonuniformities are of two types: similar things do not look similar or behave similarly, and dissimilar things actually look similar or behave similarly when they should not. Examples of nonuniformities include

- In Pascal repeat-statements open their own statement blocks, but while-statements and if-statements require begin-end pairs. Modula-2 and Ada rectify this nonuniformity.
- Case-statements in variant records in Pascal have a different syntax from case control statements. This situation has been rectified in Modula-2.
- Returned values from functions in Pascal look like assignments:

```
function f : boolean;
begin
  . . .
  f := true;
end;
```

Most languages use the return-statement for this operation. This is another case where different things should look different, but instead look confusingly alike. A similar situation occurs with the pointer operator "^" in Pascal: ^integer in a declaration means "pointer to integer," while x^ dereferences x, and means "thing pointed to." Modula-2 remedies this by using POINTER TO in declarations instead of ^.

- In Modula-2 and Pascal the semicolon is used as a statement separator as well as a declaration terminator:

```
procedure p; (* terminator *)
   var x: integer; (* terminator *)
    y: real; (* terminator *)
begin
   x := 0 ; (* separator *)
   y := 1.0
end; (* terminator *)
```

In C, the semicolon is used more consistently as a terminator.

Nonuniformities can in some cases be thought of as nonorthogonalities too, since nonuniformities occur in particular contexts and can be seen as interactions between constructs.

3.4   FURTHER LANGUAGE DESIGN PRINCIPLES

We have seen efficiency, generality, orthogonality, and uniformity as design principles in the previous sections. Further principles, some of which we have discussed briefly in Section 3.2, are the following:

Simplicity.   We have mentioned this principle already several times. It was one of the major design goals of Pascal, after experience with the complexity of Algol68 and PL/I. Simplicity is perhaps the major reason Pascal became so successful. Simplicity seems like an easy principle to achieve, but it is surprisingly difficult in practice. For one thing, generality, uniformity, and orthogonality are not simplicity. Algol68 is one of the most general, uniform, and orthogonal of languages, but it is not simple. Nor is simplicity merely a matter of very few basic constructs (though this does help): LISP and Prolog have only a few basic constructs but depend on a complex runtime system. On the other hand, overly simple programming languages can actually make the task of using them more complex. BASIC is a simple language, but the lack of some fundamental constructs, such as declarations and blocks, makes it much more difficult to program large applications. Pascal itself suffers from oversimplicity: it lacks good string handling, separate compilation, and reasonable input-output facilities, and it has many nonuniformities, such as the use of the assignment for function return. Perhaps it is worth repeating here the famous remark of Einstein:

> Everything should be made as simple as possible, but not simpler.

Oversimplicity makes the language cumbersome to use, lacking in expressiveness, and subject to too many restrictions.

Expressiveness.   We have mentioned this before as an aid to programming efficiency: expressiveness is the ease with which a language can express complex processes and structures. One of the original advances in expressiveness was the addition of recursion to programming languages (LISP and Algol60). LISP is also expressive in that both data and program can change during execution in arbitrary ways. This is especially useful in complex situations where the size and form of data may not be known. But as we have noted, expressiveness can conflict with simplicity: LISP, Prolog, and Algol68 are extremely expressive languages that are not simple—partially as a result of their expressiveness. Expressiveness is sometimes viewed as conciseness, which can also compromise simplicity. The

C language is expressive in this sense, yet many programmers do not find C expressions such as

```
while (*s++ = *t++);
```

easy to understand.[1]

Preciseness.   Sometimes called definiteness, preciseness is the existence of a precise definition for a language, so that the behavior of programs can be predicted. A precise language definition is an aid not only to reliability of programs but also to the reliability of translators: a precisely defined language will have more predictable translators, so that program behavior will not vary as much from machine to machine. One step in achieving preciseness is the publication of a language manual or report by the designer. Another is the adoption of a standard by a national or international standards organization such as the American National Standards Institute (ANSI) or the International Standards Organization (ISO). Published standards exist for many languages, including Common LISP, FORTRAN, Ada, Pascal, COBOL, and recently C. These are major assets for the usability of these languages. A language standard or reference manual, to be useful, must be not only as precise as possible but also comprehensible to most language users. The Algol68 designers, in attempting to gain greater precision, invented many new terms to describe the language. As a result the reference manual was extremely difficult to read, and the language lost acceptance.

Machine independence.   This principle is aided by a language definition that is independent of a particular machine. The primary method for achieving machine independence is the use of predefined data types that do not involve details of memory allocation or machine architecture. Unfortunately, these data types can never be entirely free from machine issues. For example, the real data type consists of numbers that may need infinite precision to specify exactly, while only finite precision can ever be implemented on a computer. Such questions of precision are difficult to specify in a completely machine-independent way. The design of a language must try therefore to isolate and identify whatever machine dependencies cannot be avoided, so that the programmer knows exactly where difficulties might arise. The use of the predefined constant maxint in Pascal is an example of a useful way of isolating a machine dependency. The Ada language contains many facilities for specifying the precision of floating point numbers and thus removing dependencies on the precision of the operations of a particular machine.

Security.   This principle promotes a language design that both discourages programming errors and allows errors to be discovered and re-

---

[1]A famous example of code used to copy one string to another. See Kernighan and Ritchie [1988], p. 105.

ported. Security is closely related to reliability and preciseness. It was this principle that led language designers to introduce types, type checking, and variable declarations into programming languages. The idea was to "maximize the number of errors that could not be made" (Hoare [1981]) by the programmer. In this it compromises both the expressiveness and conciseness of a language and puts the onerous task on the programmer of having to specify as many things as possible in the actual code. A debate still exists over the advisability of introducing many features that promote security into a language. LISP and Prolog programmers often feel that static type-checking and variable declarations cause major complications when attempting to program complex operations or provide "generic" utilities that work for a wide variety of data. On the other hand, in industrial, commercial, and defense applications, there is often a call for even greater security. Perhaps the real issue is how to design languages that are secure and yet allow for maximal expressiveness and generality. An example of an advance in this direction is the language ML, which is functional in approach, allows multityped objects, does not require declarations, and yet performs static type-checking.

Consistency with accepted notations and conventions.   A programming language should be easy to learn and understand for the experienced programmer. One aspect of this is that language design should incorporate as much as possible features and concepts that have become standard. Standard concepts such as program, function, and variables should be clearly recognizable. Standard forms for if-then-else and other control structures have evolved. Algol68 violates this principle in a number of ways—for example, in the use of the reserved word **mode** instead of **type.** White-space conventions can also be considered part of this design principle, since Algol60's free format has become the rule, FORTRAN notwithstanding. Blank lines should be allowed. Delimiters of reserved words and identifiers should make the program clear and readable. FORTRAN's ignoring of blanks can cause major problems in readability and security, as the following famous example shows:

```
DO 99 I = 1.10
```

Despite appearances this assigns the value 1.1 to the variable `D099I`. Such surprises are quite aptly referred to as violations of the **law of least astonishment:** things should not act or appear in completely unexpected ways.

Extensibility.   This principle advocates that there should be some general mechanism for the user to add features to a language. What one means by "add new features" varies, however, with one's point of view. It could mean simply to be able to define new data types, which most languages allow. At a different level it could mean to add new functions from a library, which many languages permit as well. It could also mean to be able to add keywords and constructs to the translator itself. In functional languages such as LISP, this is not too difficult, especially when, as in LISP, language constructs can be defined in terms of the language itself. Thus LISP is an extensible language in that it has a small number of built-in constructs, or **primitives,** and further operations are added to the environment as needed. In an imperative language, however, this is more difficult. The current trend in such languages is to settle for a little less than full extensibility: to permit the user to define new data types plus operations that apply to these types and to allow these operations to appear just as though they had been defined in the language in the first place.

As an example, the matrix data type can be added to Ada in such a way that matrix operations can be written just as ordinary integer or real operations. Given the declarations

```
type MATRIX is
     array ( INTEGER range <>, INTEGER range <> )
     of REAL;
function "+" (LEFT,RIGHT: MATRIX) return MATRIX;
A,B,C: MATRIX(1..10,1..10);
```

we can write

```
C := A + B;
```

The "+" operation is said then to be **overloaded.** (See Chapter 8 for more discussion.)

Restrictability. A language design should make it possible for a programmer to program usefully using a minimal knowledge of the language and a minimum number of language constructs. Thus the language design should promote the ability to define language subsets. This can be useful in two ways: first, a programmer need not learn the whole language to use it effectively; second, a translator writer could choose to implement only a subset if implementing the whole language is too costly or unnecessary. Of course, one could well ask, with an eye on simplicity: If one can program effectively using only a subset of the language, why not make the subset the whole language in the first place? For a general-purpose language it is difficult to decide what should be included and what should not, since different applications may require different facilities. For example, concurrency and exception handling may be of critical importance only for certain applications. Also, it is sometimes useful to have different versions of the same kind of constructs available—such as repeat-statements as well as while-statements—because of the greater expressiveness of each under certain circumstances. Strictly speaking, such **syntactic sugar** is unnecessary, but it may aid the understanding of a program. On the other hand, if there are ten or fifteen different ways of doing one thing, the complexity of the language increases substantially, with diminishing payoff in expressiveness.

Exercises

1. Give your own examples of features in any language that promote or violate the following design principles:

    Efficiency
    Expressiveness
    Maintainability
    Readability
    Reliability
    Security
    Simplicity
    Writability

2. Give your own examples to distinguish among the concepts of orthogonality, generality, and uniformity.

3. In Pascal, given a file variable f, f^ refers to the file buffer. Is this an example of a nonuniformity? Why or why not?

4. In Modula-2 and Ada there is a LOOP .. EXIT construct, and in PL/I there is a similar LOOP .. BREAK construct. No such construct exists in Pascal. Why do you think Wirth chose not to include one? Is this an example of any of the design principles?

5. In Pascal integers can be assigned to real variables, but not vice versa. What design principle does this violate? Would it be a good idea to allow reals to be assignable to integer variables? Why?

6. Choose a feature from a programming language of your choice that you think should be removed. Why should the feature be removed? What problems might arise as a result of the removal?

7. Choose a feature that you think should be added to a programming language of your choice. Why should the feature be added? What needs to be stated about the feature to specify completely its behavior and interaction with other features?

8. Redesign the syntax for defining variant records in Pascal or Modula-2 so that it doesn't use the **case** keyword. How do you deal with discriminants? Why did you choose the syntax you did? (See Chapter 6 for a discussion of variant records.)

9. In Ada the `end` reserved word must be qualified by the kind of block that it ends: `if ... then ... end if`, `loop ... end loop`, and so on. In Algol68 the END is replaced by writing a reserved word backward: `if ... then ... fi`, `while ... do ... od`, and so on. Discuss the effect these conventions have on readability, writability, and security. Compare the use of **ends** in Ada to that of Modula-2.

10. Should a language require the declaration of variables? Languages such as FORTRAN and BASIC allow variable names to be used without declarations, while Ada, Modula-2, Pascal, and C require all variables to be declared. Discuss the requirement that variables should be declared from the point of view of readability, writability, efficiency, security, and expressiveness.

11. Compare and contrast the views expressed in Hoare [1973], Hoare [1981], and Wirth [1974].

12. The semicolon was used as an example of a nonuniformity in Pascal and Modula-2. Discuss the use of the semicolon in C. Is its use entirely uniform?

13. Two opposing views on comments in programs could be stated as follows:
    (a) A program should always contain elaborate comments to make it readable and maintainable.
    (b) A program should be as much as possible self-documenting, with comments added sparingly only where the code itself might be unclear.
    Discuss these two viewpoints from the point of view of language design. What design features might aid one viewpoint but not the other? What might aid both?

14. Here are two more opposing statements:
    (a) A program should never run with error checking turned off. Turning off error checking after a program has been tested is like throwing away the life preserver when graduating from the pool to the ocean.
    (b) A program should always have error checking turned off after the testing stage. Keeping error checking on is like keeping training wheels on a bike after you've entered a race.
    Discuss (a) and (b) from the point of view of language design.

15. Discuss the following two views of language design:
    (a) Language design is compiler construction.
    (b) Language design is software engineering.

16. Two contrasting viewpoints on the declaration of comments in a programming language are represented by Ada and Modula-2: in Ada comments begin with adjacent hyphens and end with the end of a line:

    `-- this is an Ada comment`

In Modula-2 comments begin with "(∗" and proceed to a matching "∗)" (comments can be nested):

```
(* this is a (*Modula-2*) comment *)
```

Compare these two comment features with respect to readability, writability, and reliability.

17. The **principle of locality** maintains that variable declarations should come as close as possible to their use in a program. What language design features promote or discourage this principle? How well do Ada, Modula-2, C, and Pascal promote this principle?

18. Often a language can be much more easily learned and used if there exists a good symbolic runtime debugger. Compare the language systems you know with regard to the existence and/or quality of a debugger. Can you think of any language constructs that would aid or discourage the use of a debugger?

19. One of the major problems in programming language design is the lack of understanding of many human factors that affect language use, from psychology to human-machine interaction ("ergonomics"). One example of this is that programming errors made by humans are far from random, and language design should attempt to prevent the most common errors. Keep a record of the kinds of errors you have made most frequently in learning a new language, or look up the study by Ripley and Druseikis [1978] for the case of Pascal. How could the most common errors have been prevented by the language design?

20. Most programming languages now use the **free format** pioneered by Algol60: statements can begin anywhere and end not with the end of a line of text but with an explicit end symbol, such as a semicolon. By contrast FORTRAN and a few other languages use **fixed format**: statements must begin in a particular column and are ended by the physical end of the line, unless continuation marks are provided. Discuss the effect of fixed or free format on readability, writability, and security.

21. Here is a quote from D. L. Parnas [1985]: "Because of the very large improvements in productivity that were noted when compiler languages were introduced, many continue to look for another improvement by introducing better languages. Better notation always helps, but we cannot expect new languages to provide the same magnitude of improvement that we got from the first introduction of such languages. . . . We should seek simplifications in programming languages, but we cannot expect that this will make a big difference." Discuss.

22. A possible additional language design principle is **learnability,** that is, the ability of programmers to learn to use the language quickly and effectively. Describe a situation in which learnability may be an im-

portant requirement for a programming language to have. Describe ways in which a language designer can improve the learnability of a language.

23. In most language implementations the integer data type has a fixed size, which means that the maximum size of an integer is machine dependent. In some languages like Scheme, however, integers may be of any size, and so become machine independent. Discuss the advantages and disadvantages of making such "infinite-precision" integers a requirement of a language definition. Is it possible to also implement "infinite-precision" real numbers? Can real numbers be made machine independent? Discuss.

24. In Chapter 1 we discussed how the von Neumann architecture affected the design of programming languages. It is also possible for a programming language design to affect the design of machine architecture as well. Describe one or more examples of this.

Notes and References

Horowitz [1984] gives a list of programming language design criteria similar to the ones in this chapter, which he partially attributes to Barbara Liskov. For an extensive historical perspective on language design, see Wegner [1976] (this paper and the papers by Wirth [1974] and Hoare [1973] mentioned in this chapter are all reprinted in Horowitz [1987]). The unification algorithm for type-checking mentioned in Section 3.2 is described in Hindley [1969] and Milner [1978]. The language ML, which uses this algorithm to perform static type-checking without declarations, is described briefly in Chapter 10 and more extensively in Milner and Tofte [1990a], Milner, Tofte, and Harper [1990b], and Mitchell and Harper [1988]. The rationale for the design of Ada is discussed in Ichbiah et al. [1979], where many design principles are discussed. See also Hoare [1981] for some wry comments on designing languages, compilers, and computer systems in general.

4 SYNTAX

Syntax is the structure of a language. In Chapter 1 we noted the difference between the syntax and semantics of a programming language. In the early days of programming languages, both the syntax and semantics of a language were described by lengthy English explanations and many examples. While the semantics of a language are still usually described in English, one of the great advances in programming languages has been the development of a formal system for describing syntax that is now almost universally in use. In the 1950s Noam Chomsky developed the idea of context-free grammars, and John Backus, with contributions by Peter Naur, developed a notational system for describing these grammars that was used for the first time to describe the syntax of Algol60. These **Backus-Naur forms—BNFs** for short—have subsequently been used in the definition of many programming languages, including Pascal, Modula-2, C, and Ada. Indeed, every modern programmer and computer scientist needs to know how to read, interpret, and apply BNF descriptions of language syntax. These BNFs occur with minor textual variations in three basic forms: original BNF; extended BNF (EBNF), popularized by Niklaus Wirth; and syntax diagrams.

In Section 4.1, we briefly look at the lexical structure of programming languages. In Section 4.2 we introduce context-free grammars and their description in BNF. In Section 4.3 we describe the representation of syntactic structure using trees. In Section 4.4 we consider a few of the issues that arise in constructing BNFs for a programming language. EBNFs and syntax diagrams are introduced in Section 4.5. In Section 4.6 we discuss the basic technique of recursive-descent parsing and its close relationship to EBNF and syntax diagrams and briefly look at YACC, a standard tool for analyzing grammars and constructing parsers. Finally, in Section 4.7 we examine the sometimes hazy boundaries among the lexical, syntactic, and semantic structures of a programming language.

4.1   *LEXICAL STRUCTURE OF PROGRAMMING LANGUAGES*

The lexical structure of a programming language is the structure of its words, or **tokens.** Lexical structure can be considered separately from syntactic structure, but it is closely related to and, in some cases (depending on the design of the language), can be an inextricable part of syntax. Typically, the **scanning** phase of a translator collects sequences of characters from the input program into tokens, which are then processed by a **parsing** phase, which determines the syntactic structure.

Tokens generally fall into several distinct categories. Typical token categories include the following:

reserved words, sometimes called **keywords,** such as "begin," "if," and "while"

constants or **literals,** such as 42 (a numeric constant) or "hello" (a string constant)

special symbols, such as ";", "$<=$", or "$+$"

identifiers, such as x24, monthly__balance, or write

Reserved words are so named because an identifier cannot have the same character string as a reserved word. Thus, in Pascal, the following variable declaration is illegal because "if" is a reserved word:

```
var if: integer;
```

In some languages identifiers have a fixed maximum size, while in most newer languages identifiers can have arbitrary length. Occasionally, even when arbitrary-length identifiers are allowed, only the first six or eight characters are guaranteed to be significant. (This is guaranteed to be confusing to the programmer.)

A problem arises in determining the end of a variable-length token such as an identifier and in distinguishing identifiers from reserved words. As an example, the sequence of characters

```
doif
```

in a program could be either the two reserved words "do" and "if," or it could be the identifier doif. Similarly, the string x12 could be a single identifier or the identifier *x* and the numeric constant 12. To eliminate this ambiguity, it is a standard convention to use the **principle of longest substring** in determining tokens: at each point, the longest possible string of characters is collected into a single token. This means that doif and x12 are always identifiers. It also means that intervening characters, even blanks, can make a difference. Thus in most languages

```
do if
```

is not an identifier but becomes the two reserved words "do" and "if."

The format of a program can affect the way tokens are recognized. For example, as we just saw, the principle of longest substring requires that certain tokens be separated by **token delimiters** or **white space.** The end of a line of text can be doubly meaningful: it can be white space, and it can also mean the end of a structural entity. Indentation can also be used in a programming language to determine structure. A **free-format** language is one in which format has no effect on the program structure (other than to satisfy the principle of longest substring). Most modern languages are free format, but a few have significant format restrictions. Rarely is a language **fixed format,** in which all tokens must occur in prespecified locations on the page.

FORTRAN is the principal example of a language that violates many of the format and token conventions (perhaps its age is showing). In the last chapter we mentioned the following example in FORTRAN:

```
DO 99 I = 1.10
```

This statement is equivalent to the Pascal

```
DO99I := 1.10
```

In other words, it assigns the value 1.1 to the real variable DO99I. On the other hand, the FORTRAN

```
DO 99 I = 1,10
```

is equivalent to the Pascal

```
for I := 1 to 10 do
```

that is, it begins a loop by giving the bounds of the index *I*. Thus the first FORTRAN statement contains three tokens: an identifier, the assignment operator ("="), and the real constant 1.1. The second FORTRAN statement, on the other hand, contains seven tokens. The reason for this is that FORTRAN *ignores* spaces completely—they are removed before processing begins. Furthermore, FORTRAN has *no* reserved words at all: DO, WHILE, or any other word describing a structure can also be an identifier; the FORTRAN statement

```
WHILE = 2.2
```

is perfectly legal. In FORTRAN, the token structure and the syntax are inextricably entwined.

As a final example of lexical structure, we quote the description of the token conventions of the C language from the reference manual in Kernighan and Ritchie [1988]:

> There are six classes of tokens: identifiers, keywords, constants, string literals, operators, and other separators. Blanks, horizontal and vertical tabs, newlines, formfeeds, and comments as described below (collectively, "white space") are ignored except as they separate tokens. Some white space is required to separate otherwise adjacent identifiers, keywords, and constants. If the input stream has been separated into tokens up to a given character, the next token is the longest string of characters that could constitute a token.

Thus C adheres to the principle of longest substring.

4.2   CONTEXT-FREE GRAMMARS AND BNFs

We begin our description of grammars and BNFs with an example. In English, simple sentences consist of a noun phrase and a verb phrase followed by a period. We can express this as follows:

1. <sentence> ::= <noun-phrase> <verb-phrase>.

We must now, in turn, describe the structure of a noun phrase and a verb phrase:

2. <noun-phrase> ::= <article> <noun>

3. <article>   ::= a | the

4. <noun>   ::= girl | dog

5. <verb-phrase> ::= <verb> <noun-phrase>

6. <verb>   ::= sees | pets

Each of these grammar rules consists of a string enclosed in angle brackets "<>" (the name of the structure being described), followed by the symbol "::=", which can be read as "consists of" or "is the same as," and a sequence of other names and symbols. The angle brackets serve to distinguish the names of the structures from the actual words, or tokens, that may appear in the language. For example, in Pascal, "<program>"

will stand for a whole program structure, while the word "program" is the first token in every <program>:

$$\text{<program>} ::= \text{program} \ldots$$

The symbol ":: =" is a **metasymbol** that serves to separate the left-hand side from the right-hand side of a rule. The angle brackets are also metasymbols, as is the vertical bar "|", which means "or" or alternation. Thus rule 6 states that a verb is either the word "sees" or the word "pets." Sometimes a metasymbol is also an actual symbol in a language. In that case the symbol can be surrounded by quotes to distinguish it from the metasymbol. Often it is a good idea to do this for special symbols like punctuation marks, even when they are not also metasymbols. For example, rule 1 has a period in it. While a period is not part of any metasymbol described, it can easily be mistaken for one. Hence it might be better to write the rule as follows:

$$\text{<sentence>} ::= \text{<noun-phrase>} \text{<verb-phrase>} \text{`.'}$$

(Of course, now the quotes also become metasymbols.) Some authors also use italics and boldface to distinguish among symbols, metasymbols, and names.

Any legal sentence according to the foregoing grammar can be constructed as follows: we start with the symbol <sentence> and proceed to replace left-hand sides by alternatives of right-hand sides in the foregoing rules. This process creates a **derivation** in the language. Thus we could construct, or derive, the sentence "the girl sees a dog." as follows:

<sentence> ⟶	<noun-phrase> <verb-phrase>.	(rule 1)
⟶	<article> <noun> <verb-phrase>.	(rule 2)
⟶	the <noun> <verb-phrase>.	(rule 3)
⟶	the girl <verb-phrase>.	(rule 4)
⟶	the girl <verb> <noun-phrase>.	(rule 5)
⟶	the girl sees <noun-phrase>.	(rule 6)
⟶	the girl sees <article> <noun>.	(rule 2)
⟶	the girl sees a <noun>.	(rule 3)
⟶	the girl sees a dog.	(rule 4)

Conversely, we could start with the sentence "the girl sees a dog." and work backward through the derivation to arrive at <sentence> and so have shown that the sentence is legal in the language.

This simple grammar already exhibits most of the properties of programming language grammars. Note that not all legal sentences actually make sense: "the dog pets the girl." is one such. Note that there is also a subtle error: articles that appear at the beginning of sentences should be capitalized. Such a "positional" property is often hard to deal with using context-free grammars.

Here are some definitions for what we have seen. (We could give mathematically precise definitions, but we prefer a more informal approach.) A **context-free grammar** consists of a series of grammar rules as described: the rules consist of a left-hand side that is a single structure name, then the metasymbol "::=", followed by a right-hand side consisting of a sequence of items that can be symbols or other structure names. The names for structures (like <sentence>) are called **nonterminals,** since they are broken down into further structures. The words or token symbols are also called **terminals,** since they are never broken down. Grammar rules are also called **productions,** since they "produce" the strings of the language using derivations. Productions are in **Backus-Naur form** if they are as given using only the metasymbols "::=", "|", "<", and ">". (Sometimes parentheses are also allowed to group things together.)

In the foregoing example there are seven terminals ("girl," "dog," "sees," "calls," "the," "a," and "."), six nonterminals, and six productions. In general there as many productions in a context-free grammar as there are nonterminals, although one could eliminate the "|" metasymbol by writing each alternative separately, such as

<noun> ::= girl
<noun> ::= dog

in which case each nonterminal would correspond to as many productions as there are alternatives.

Why is such a grammar **context-free**? The simple reason is that the nonterminals appear singly on the left-hand sides of productions. This means that each nonterminal can be replaced by any right-hand side alternative, no matter where the nonterminal might appear. In other words, there is no **context** under which only certain replacements can occur. For example, in the grammar just discussed, it makes sense to use the verb "pets" only when the subject is "girl"; this can be thought of as a context-sensitivity. One could write out context-sensitive grammars by allowing "context strings" to appear on left-hand sides of the grammar rules, and some authors consider context-sensitivities to be syntactic issues. We shall adopt the view, however, that anything not expressible using context-free grammars is a semantic, not a syntactic issue. (Even some things that *are* expressible as context-free grammars are often better left to semantic descriptions, since they involve writing many extra productions; see Exercise 22.)

As an example of a context-sensitivity, we noted that articles that appear at the beginning of sentences in the preceding grammar should be capitalized. One way of doing this is to rewrite the first rule as

<sentence> ::= <beginning> <noun-phrase> <verb-phrase> '.'

and then add the context-sensitive rule:

<beginning> <article> ::= The | A

Now the derivation would look as follows:

<sentence> ⟶ <beginning> <noun-phrase>
          <verb-phrase>.   (new rule 1)

          ⟶ <beginning> <article> <noun>
             <verb-phrase>.   (rule 2)

          ⟶ The <noun> <verb-phrase>.
                              (new context-sensitive rule)

          ⟶ . . .

Context-free grammars have been studied extensively by formal language theorists and are now so well understood that it is natural to express the syntax of any programming language in BNF form. Indeed, doing so makes it easier to write translators for the language, since the parsing stage can be automated. (See Section 4.6.)

A typical simple example of the use of a context-free grammar in programming languages is the description of simple integer arithmetic expressions with addition and multiplication given in Figure 4-1.

<exp>   ::= <exp> + <exp> | <exp> • <exp>
          | (<exp>) | <number>

<number> ::= <number> <digit> | <digit>

<digit>   ::= 0 | 1 | 2 | 3 | 4 | 5 | 6 | 7 | 8 | 9

Figure 4-1   A Simple Arithmetic Expression Grammar

Note the recursive nature of the rules: an expression can be the sum or product of two expressions, each of which can be further sums or products. Eventually, of course, this process must stop by choosing the <number> alternative, or we would never arrive at a string of terminals.

Note also that the recursion in the rule for <number> is used to generate a repeated sequence of digits. For example, the number 234 is constructed as follows:

<number> ⟶ <number> <digit>
          ⟶ <number> <digit> <digit>
          ⟶ <digit> <digit> <digit>
          ⟶ 2 <digit> <digit>
          ⟶ 23 <digit>
          ⟶ 234

Figure 4-2 shows the beginning of a BNF description for Pascal.

<program>	::=	<program-heading> ';' <program-block> '.'
<program-heading>	::=	program <identifier> | program <identifier> '(' <program-parameters> ')'
<program-block>	::=	<block>
<program-parameters>	::=	<identifier-list>
<block>	::=	<label-declaration-part> <constant-definition-part> <type-definition-part> <variable-declaration-part> <procedure-and-function-declaration-part> <statement-part>
<label-declaration-part>	::=	label <label-list> ';' | <empty>
<label-list>	::=	<label-list> ',' <label> | <label>

. . .

. . .

Figure 4-2   Partial BNFs for Pascal (Adapted from Cooper [1983])

4.2.1 BNF Rules as Equations

An alternative way of explaining how BNF rules construct the strings of a language is as follows. Given a grammar rule such as

$$\text{<exp> ::= <exp> + <exp> | <number>}$$

(abstracted from Figure 4-1), let E be the set of strings representing expressions, and let N represent the set of strings representing numbers. The preceding grammar rule can be viewed as a **set equation**

$$E = E{+}E \cup N$$

where $E+E$ is the set constructed by concatenating all strings from E with the "$+$" symbol and then all strings from E and "$\cup$" is set union. Assuming that the set N has already been constructed, this represents a recursive equation for the set E. The *smallest set E satisfying this equation* can be taken to be the set defined by the grammar rule. Intuitively, this consists of the set

$$N \cup N{+}N \cup N{+}N{+}N \cup N{+}N{+}N{+}N \cup ..$$

and we could actually prove that this is the smallest set satisfying the given equation (see Exercise 40). Solutions to recursive equations appear frequently in formal descriptions of programming languages, and are a major object of study in the theory of programming languages, where they are called **least fixed points** (a term that will be explained later). We will see them again from time to time in later chapters (for example, in the definition of recursive data types, recursive functions, and formal semantics).

4.3   *PARSE TREES AND ABSTRACT SYNTAX TREES*

Syntax establishes structure, not meaning. But the meaning of a sentence (or program) must be related to its syntax. In English a sentence has a subject and a predicate, which are semantic notions, since the subject (the "actor") and the predicate (the "action") determine the meaning of the sentence. A subject generally comes at the beginning of a sentence and is given by a noun phrase. Thus, in the syntax of an English sentence, a noun phrase is placed first and is subsequently associated with a subject. Similarly, in the grammar for expressions, when we write

$$<exp> ::= <exp> + <exp>$$

we expect to add the values of the two right-hand expressions to get the value of the left-hand expression. This process of attaching the semantics of a construct to its syntactic structure is called **syntax-directed semantics.** We must therefore construct the syntax so that it reflects the semantics we will eventually attach to it as much as possible. (Syntax-directed semantics could just as easily have been called semantics-directed syntax.)

To make use of the syntactic structure of a program to determine its semantics we must have a way of expressing this structure as determined by a derivation. A standard method for doing this is with a **parse tree.** The parse tree describes graphically the replacement process in a derivation. For example, the parse tree for the sentence "the girl sees a dog." is as follows:

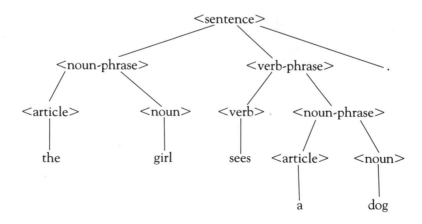

Similarly, the parse tree for the number 234 in the expression grammar is

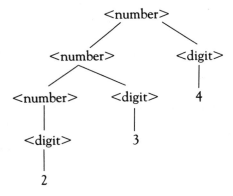

The parse tree is labeled by nonterminals at interior nodes and
terminals at leaves. All the terminals and nonterminals in a derivation
are included in the parse tree. But not all the terminals and nonterminals
may be necessary to determine completely the syntactic structure of an
expression or sentence. For example, the structure of the number 234
can be completely determined from the tree

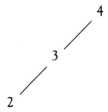

and a parse tree for 3 + 4 · 5 such as

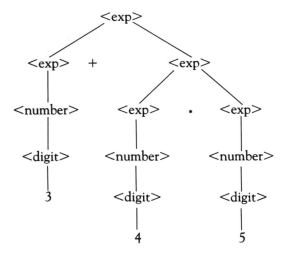

could be condensed to the tree

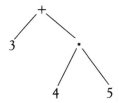

Such trees are called **abstract syntax trees** or just **syntax trees,** since they abstract the essential structure of the parse tree. Abstract syntax trees may also do away with terminals that are redundant once the structure of the tree is determined. For example, the grammar rule

<if-statement> :: = if <condition> then <statement>
else <statement>

gives rise to the parse tree

and the abstract syntax tree

It is possible to write out rules for abstract syntax in a similar way to the BNF rules for ordinary syntax, but we shall not do so here. Sometimes ordinary syntax is distinguished from abstract syntax by calling it **concrete syntax.**

A translator will often construct a syntax tree rather than a full parse tree because it is more concise and expresses the essentials of the structure.

4.4   AMBIGUITY, ASSOCIATIVITY, AND PRECEDENCE

Two different derivations can lead to the same parse tree: in the derivation for 234 in the last section we could have chosen to replace the <digit> nonterminals first:

<number> ⟶ <number> <digit>
⟶ <number> 4
⟶ <number> <digit> 4
⟶ <number> 34
. . .

but we would still have the same parse tree. However, different derivations can also lead to different parse trees. For example, if we construct 3 + 4 · 5 from the expression grammar of Figure 4-1, we can use the derivation

$$\langle exp \rangle \longrightarrow \langle exp \rangle + \langle exp \rangle$$
$$\longrightarrow \langle exp \rangle + \langle exp \rangle \cdot \langle exp \rangle$$

(replace the second $\langle exp \rangle$ with $\langle exp \rangle \cdot \langle exp \rangle$)

$$\longrightarrow \langle number \rangle + \langle exp \rangle \cdot \langle exp \rangle$$
$$\longrightarrow \dots$$

or the derivation

$$\langle exp \rangle \longrightarrow \langle exp \rangle \cdot \langle exp \rangle$$
$$\longrightarrow \langle exp \rangle + \langle exp \rangle \cdot \langle exp \rangle$$

(replace the first $\langle exp \rangle$ with $\langle exp \rangle + \langle exp \rangle$)

$$\longrightarrow \langle number \rangle + \langle exp \rangle \cdot \langle exp \rangle$$
$$\longrightarrow \dots$$

and these lead to two distinct parse trees:

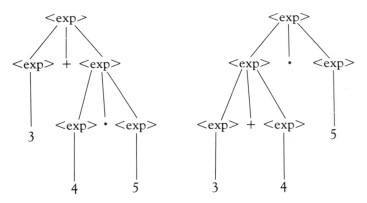

and two distinct abstract syntax trees:

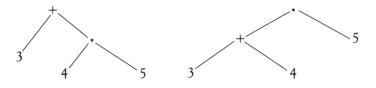

A grammar such as that in Figure 4-1, for which two distinct parse (or syntax) trees are possible for the same string is **ambiguous.** Ambiguous grammars present difficulties, since no clear structure is expressed. To be useful, either the grammar must be revised to remove the ambiguity, or a **disambiguating rule** must be stated to establish which structure is meant.

Which of the two parse trees is the correct one for the expression 3 + 4 · 5? If we think of the semantics to be attached to the expression, we can understand what this decision means. The first syntax tree implies that the multiplication operator "·" is to be applied to the 4 and 5 (resulting in the value 20), and this result is added to 3 to get 23. The second syntax tree, on the other hand, says to add 3 and 4 first (getting 7) and then multiply by 5 to get 35. Thus the operations are applied in a different order, and the resulting semantics are quite different.

If we take the usual meaning of the expression 3 + 4 · 5 from mathematics, we would choose the first tree over the second, since multiplication has precedence over addition. This is the usual choice in programming languages, although some languages (such as APL) make a different choice. How could we express the fact that multiplication should have precedence over addition? We could state a disambiguating rule separately from the grammar, or we could revise the grammar. The usual way to revise the grammar is to write a new grammar rule (called a "<term>") that establishes a "precedence cascade" to force the matching of the "·" at a lower point in the parse tree:

<exp> ::= <exp> + <exp> | <term>

<term> ::= <term> · <term> | (<exp>) | <number>

But we have not completely solved the ambiguity problem: the rule for an <exp> still allows us to parse 3 + 4 + 5 as either (3 + 4) + 5 or 3 + (4 + 5). In other words we can make addition either **right-** or **left-associative:**

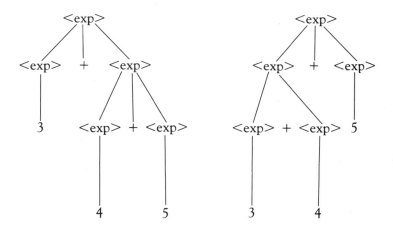

In the case of addition this does not affect the result, but if we were to include subtraction, it surely would: 8 − 4 − 2 = 2 if "−" is left-associative, but 8 − 4 − 2 = 6 if "−" is right-associative. What is needed is to replace the rule

<exp> ::= <exp> + <exp>

with either

$$\text{<exp>} ::= \text{<exp>} + \text{<term>}$$

or

$$\text{<exp>} ::= \text{<term>} + \text{<exp>}$$

The first rule is **left-recursive** while the second rule is **right-recursive.** A left-recursive rule for an operation causes it to left associate, as in the parse tree

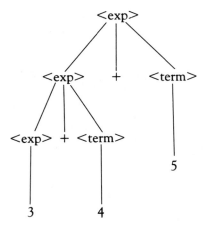

while a right-recursive rule causes it to right-associate:

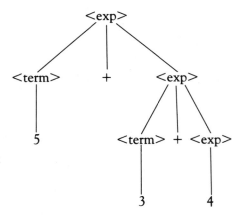

The revised grammar for simple arithmetic expressions that expresses both precedence and associativity is given in Figure 4-3.

The BNF for simple arithmetic expressions is now unambiguous (a proof of this requires more advanced techniques from parsing theory).

$$\begin{aligned}
&<exp> &&::= <exp> + <term> \mid <term> \\
&<term> &&::= <term> \cdot <factor> \mid <factor> \\
&<factor> &&::= (<exp>) \mid <number> \\
&<number> &&::= <number> <digit> \mid <digit> \\
&<digit> &&::= 0 \mid 1 \mid 2 \mid 3 \mid 4 \mid 5 \mid 6 \mid 7 \mid 8 \mid 9
\end{aligned}$$

Figure 4-3 Revised Grammar for Simple Arithmetic Expressions

Moreover, the parse tree corresponds to the semantics of the arithmetic operations as they are usually defined. Sometimes the process of rewriting a grammar to eliminate ambiguity causes the grammar to become extremely complex, and in such cases we prefer to state a disambiguating rule (see the if-statement discussion in Chapter 7).

4.5   *EBNFs AND SYNTAX DIAGRAMS*

We noted earlier that the grammar rule

$$<number> ::= <number> <digit> \mid <digit>$$

generates a number as a sequence of digits:

$$\begin{aligned}
<number> &\longrightarrow <number> <digit> \\
&\longrightarrow <number> <digit> <digit> \\
&\longrightarrow <number> <digit> <digit> <digit> \\
&\quad \cdot \;\; \cdot \;\; \cdot \\
&\longrightarrow <digit> \ldots <digit>
\end{aligned}$$
$$\text{(arbitrary repetitions of digit)}$$

Similarly, the rule

$$<exp> ::= <exp> + <term> \mid <term>$$

generates an expression as a sequence of terms separated by "$+$'s":

$$\begin{aligned}
<exp> &\longrightarrow <exp> + <term> \\
&\longrightarrow <exp> + <term> + <term> \\
&\longrightarrow <exp> + <term> + <term> + <term> \\
&\quad \cdot \;\; \cdot \;\; \cdot \\
&\longrightarrow <term> + \ldots + <term>
\end{aligned}$$

This situation occurs so frequently that a special notation for such grammar rules is adopted that expresses more clearly the repetitive nature of their structures:

$$<number> ::= <digit> \{<digit>\}$$

and

$$<\text{exp}> ::= <\text{term}> \{+ <\text{term}>\}$$

In this notation the curly brackets "{ }" stand for "zero or more repetitions of." Thus the rules express that a number is a sequence of one or more digits, and an expression is a term followed by zero or more repetitions of a "+" and another term. In this notation the curly brackets have become new metasymbols, and this notation is called **extended Backus-Naur form,** or **EBNF** for short.

This new notation obscures the left associativity of the "+" operator that is expressed by the left recursion in the original rule in BNF. We can get around this by simply assuming that any operator involved in a curly bracket repetition is left-associative. Indeed, if an operator were right-associative, the corresponding grammar rule would be right-recursive, and right-recursive rules are usually not written using curly brackets. (The reason for this is explained more fully in the next section.) This problem does point out a flaw in EBNF grammars: parse trees and syntax trees cannot be written directly from the grammar, but assumptions must be made about their structure. Therefore we will always use BNF to write parse trees.

A second common situation is for a structure to have an optional part, such as the optional else-part of an if-statement in Pascal, which is expressed in BNF as follows:

<if-statement> ::=
    if <condition> then <statement> |
    if <condition> then <statement> else <statement>

This is written more simply and expressively in EBNF as follows:

<if-statement> ::= if <condition> then <statement>
                   [else <statement>]

where the square brackets "[ ]" are new metasymbols indicating optional parts of the structure.

Another situation in which structures are optional occurs when a grammar rule includes the **empty string,** which is written as the new metasymbol ϵ (see Exercise 39), or as the nonterminal <empty>. For example, in Figure 4-2 the grammar rule

<label-declaration-part> ::= label <label-list> ';' | <empty>

establishes a label-declaration-part as optional. This is expressed in EBNF as

<label-declaration-part> ::= [label <label-list> ';']

Right-associative (binary) operators can also be written using these new metasymbols. For example, if "@" is a right-associative operator with BNF

$$<\text{exp}> ::= <\text{term}> @ <\text{exp}> | <\text{term}>$$

then this rule can be rewritten in EBNF as follows:

$$<exp> ::= <term> [@ <exp>]$$

For completeness, we write out the grammar of Figure 4-3 for simple arithmetic expressions in EBNF in Figure 4-4.

$$
\begin{aligned}
<exp> \quad &::= <term> \{+ <term>\} \\
<term> \quad &::= <factor> \{* <factor>\} \\
<factor> \quad &::= (<exp>) \mid <number> \\
<number> &::= <digit> \{<digit>\} \\
<digit> \quad &::= 0 \mid 1 \mid 2 \mid 3 \mid 4 \mid 5 \mid 6 \mid 7 \mid 8 \mid 9
\end{aligned}
$$

Figure 4-4   EBNF Rules for Simple Arithmetic Expressions

A useful graphical representation for a grammar rule is the **syntax diagram,** which indicates the sequence of terminals and nonterminals encountered in the right-hand side of the rule. For example, syntax diagrams for <noun-phrase> and <article> of our simple English grammar of Section 4.2 would be drawn as follows:

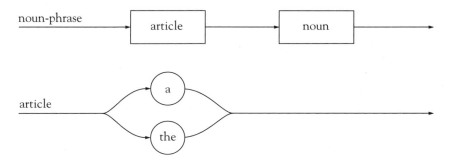

or, condensing the two into one diagram,

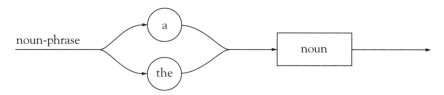

Syntax diagrams use circles or ovals for terminals and squares or rectangles for nonterminals, connecting them with lines and arrows to indicate appropriate sequencing. Syntax diagrams can also condense several productions into one diagram.

Syntax diagrams for the expression grammar in Figure 4-4 are given in Figure 4-5. Note the use of loops in the diagrams to express the repetition given by the curly brackets in the EBNFs.

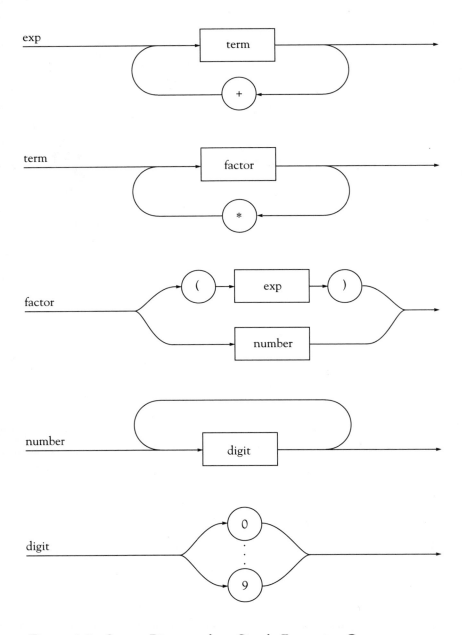

Figure 4-5   Syntax Diagrams for a Simple Expression Grammar

As an example of how to express the square brackets [ ] in syntax diagrams, we give the syntax diagram for the Pascal if-statement:

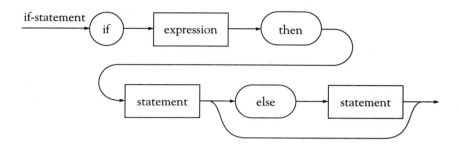

Syntax diagrams are always written from the EBNF, not the BNF, for reasons that are made clear in the next section. Thus the following diagram for <exp> would be *incorrect*:

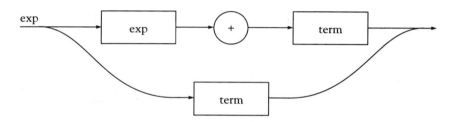

Examples of EBNFs and syntax diagrams for some of the grammar rules of Modula-2 are given in Figure 4-6.

<compilation-unit> ::= <definition-module> |
                         [IMPLEMENTATION] <program-module>
<definition-module> ::= DEFINITION MODULE <identifier> ';'
                         {<import-list>} {<definition>}
                         END <identifier> '.'
<program-module>   ::= MODULE <identifier>
                         [<module-priority>] ';' {<import-list>}
                         <block> <identifier> '.'

                         . . .

                         . . .

Figure 4-6a   Sample EBNFs for Modula-2 (Adapted from Wirth [1988a])

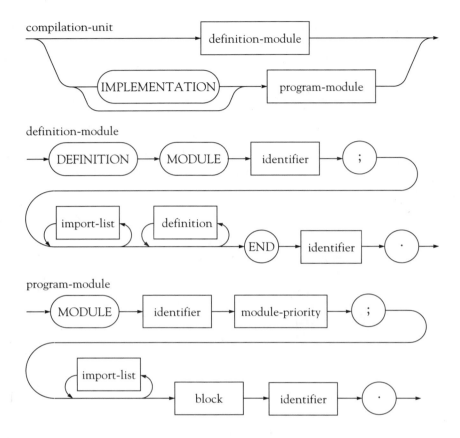

Figure 4-6b   Sample Syntax Diagrams for Modula-2 (Adapted from Wirth [1988a])

4.6 *PARSING TECHNIQUES AND TOOLS*

A grammar written in BNF, EBNF, or as syntax diagrams describes the strings of tokens that are syntactically legal in a programming language. The grammar thus also implicitly describes the actions that a parser must take to parse a string of tokens correctly, that is, construct, either implicitly or explicitly, a derivation or parse tree for the string. The simplest form of a parser is a **recognizer**—a program that accepts or rejects strings, based on whether they are legal strings in the language. More general parsers build parse trees (or, more likely, abstract syntax trees) and carry out other operations, such as calculating values for expressions.

Given a grammar in one of the three forms we have discussed, how does it correspond to the actions of a parser? One method of parsing attempts to match an input with the right-hand sides of the grammar rules. When a match occurs, the right-hand side is replaced by, or **reduced** to, the nonterminal on the left. Such parsers are **bottom-up** parsers, since they construct derivations and parse trees from the leaves to the root. They are sometimes also called **shift-reduce** parsers, since they shift tokens onto a stack prior to reducing strings to nonterminals. The other major parse method is **top-down:** nonterminals are expanded to match incoming tokens and directly construct a derivation. Both these parsing techniques can be automated; that is, a program can be written that will automatically translate a BNF description into a parser. Since bottom-up parsing is somewhat more powerful than top-down parsing, it is usually the preferred method for such **parser generators** (historically also called compiler compilers). One such parser generator in wide use is YACC (yet another compiler compiler), which we will study later in this section.

However, there is an older method for constructing a parser by hand from a grammar that is very effective and is still often used. Essentially, it operates by turning the nonterminals into a group of mutually recursive procedures whose actions are based on the right-hand sides of the BNFs; hence its name: **recursive-descent parsing.**

The right-hand sides are interpreted in the procedures as follows. Tokens are matched directly with input tokens as constructed by a scanner. Nonterminals are interpreted as calls to the procedures corresponding to the nonterminals.

As an example, in our simplified English grammar, procedures for <sentence>, <noun-phrase>, and <article> would be written as follows (in Pascal-like pseudocode):

```
procedure sentence;
begin
  nounPhrase;
  verbPhrase;
end;

procedure nounPhrase;
begin
  article;
  noun;
end;

procedure article;
begin
  if Token = 'a' then
    GetToken
  else if Token = 'the' then
    GetToken
  else Error;
end;
```

In this code we are using a global variable called Token to hold the current token as constructed by a scanner; the procedure GetToken of the scanner is called whenever a new token is desired. A match of a token corresponds to a successful test for that token, followed by a call to GetToken. Parsing starts with the variable Token already holding the first token, so a call to GetToken must precede the first call to the sentence procedure. We also assume there exists an Error procedure that aborts the parse. (Note that errors need only be detected when actual tokens are expected, as in the procedure for <article>. We could have checked for "a" or "the" in the procedure for <sentence>, but in this scheme it is unnecessary.)

If we apply this process to the BNF description of Figure 4-3, we encounter a problem with the left-recursive rules such as the one for an expression:

$$<exp> ::= <exp> + <term>$$

If we were to try to write this rule as a recursive-descent procedure, we would obtain

```
procedure exp;
begin
  exp;
  if Token = '+' then begin
    GetToken;
    term;
  end;
end;
```

Unfortunately, when this procedure is called, it causes an immediate infinite recursive loop. (This is "head recursion," which, unlike tail recursion, doesn't exist.) For this reason, language theorists have studied **left recursion removal** techniques. But a general technique is not needed here: if we write the rules in EBNF or as syntax diagrams, the left recursion is simply replaced by a loop (corresponding to the curly brackets of the EBNF). For example, the rule

$$<exp> ::= <term> \{+ <term>\}$$

in EBNF corresponds to the recursive-descent code:

```
procedure exp;
begin
  term;
  while Token = '+' do begin
    GetToken;
    term;
  end;
end;
```

Thus the curly brackets in EBNF represent left recursion removal by the use of a loop. Right-recursive rules, on the other hand, present no such problem in recursive-descent parsing, and the rule

$$<exp> ::= <term> @ <exp>$$

corresponds directly to the recursive-descent code

```
procedure exp;
begin
  term;
  if Token <> '@' then Error
  else begin
    GetToken;
    exp;
  end;
end;
```

There is a similar problem with BNF rules expressing optional constructs, such as the BNF for an if-statement:

$$<\text{if-statement}> ::= \text{if } <\text{condition}> \text{ then } <\text{statement}> \ | $$
$$\text{if } <\text{condition}> \text{ then } <\text{statement}>$$
$$\text{else } <\text{statement}>$$

This cannot be translated directly into code, since both alternatives begin with the same prefix. In EBNF, however, this is written with square brackets, and the common parts of the alternatives are "factored out":

$$<\text{if-statement}> ::= \text{if } <\text{condition}> \text{ then } <\text{statement}>$$
$$[\text{else } <\text{statement}>]$$

This corresponds directly to the recursive-descent code to parse an if-statement:

```
procedure ifStatement;
begin
  if Token <> 'if' then Error
  else begin
    GetToken;
    condition;
    if Token <> 'then' then Error
    else begin
      GetToken;
      statement;
      if Token = 'else' then begin
        GetToken;
        statement;
      end;
    end;
  end;
end;
```

This process of writing optional parts of BNF rules in EBNF by factoring out common prefixes and using square brackets is called **left factoring** and is necessary for recursive-descent parsing. Thus, EBNF rules or syntax diagrams correspond naturally to the code of a recursive-descent parser, and this is one of the main reasons for their use. In Figure 4-7 we give a sketch of a complete recursive-descent parser for the expression grammar of Figure 4-4.

In this method for converting a grammar into a parser, the resulting parser bases its actions only on the next available token in the input stream (stored in the Token variable in the code). This use of a single token to direct a parse is called **single-symbol lookahead,** and a parser that commits itself to a particular action based only on this lookahead is called a **predictive** parser (sometimes laboriously referred to as a top-down parser with single-symbol lookahead and no backtracking). Predictive parsers require that the grammar to be parsed satisfies certain conditions so that this decision-making process will work.

The first condition that predictive parsing requires is the ability to choose among several alternatives in a grammar rule. Suppose that a nonterminal A has the following alternatives:

$$A ::= \alpha_1 \mid \alpha_2 \mid \ldots \mid \alpha_n$$

(the α_i stand for strings of tokens and nonterminals). To decide which alternative to use, the tokens that begin each of the α_i must be different. Given a string α of tokens and nonterminals, we define **First(α)** to be the set of tokens that can begin the string α. For example, given the grammar rules

$$
\begin{aligned}
<factor> &::= (<exp>) \mid <number> \\
<number> &::= <digit> \{<digit>\} \\
<digit> &::= 0 \mid 1 \mid \ldots \mid 9
\end{aligned}
$$

we have

$$
\begin{aligned}
First((<exp>)) &= \{(\} \\
First(<number>) &= First(<digit>) \\
&= First(0) \cup First(1) \cup \ldots First(9) \\
&= \{0, \ldots, 9\}
\end{aligned}
$$

and then

$$
\begin{aligned}
First(<factor>) &= First((<exp>)) \cup First(<number>) \\
&= \{(, 0, 1, \ldots, 9\}
\end{aligned}
$$

The requirement that a predictive parser be able to distinguish between alternatives in a grammar rule can be stated in terms of First sets, as follows. Given the grammar rule

$$A ::= \alpha_1 \mid \alpha_2 \mid \cdots \mid \alpha_n$$

```
procedure exp;
begin
  term;
  while Token = '+' do begin
    GetToken;
    term;
  end;
end;

procedure term;
begin
  factor;
  while Token = '*' do begin
    GetToken;
    factor;
  end;
end;

procedure factor;
begin
  if Token = '(' then begin
    GetToken;
    exp;
    if Token = ')' then GetToken
    else Error
  end else number;
end;

procedure number;
begin
  digit;
  while Token in ['0'..'9'] do digit;
end;

procedure digit;
begin
  if Token in ['0'..'9'] then GetToken
  else Error;
end;

procedure parse;
begin
  GetToken;
  exp;
end;
```

Figure 4-7   Sketch of a Recursive-Descent Parser for Simple
Arithmetic Expressions

the First sets of no two alternatives can have any tokens in common; that is,

$$\text{First}(\alpha_i) \cap \text{First}(\alpha_j) = \varnothing \text{ for all } i <> j$$

($\varnothing$ denotes the empty set).

In the example of the grammar rule for a factor:

$$<\text{factor}> ::= (<\text{exp}>) \mid <\text{number}>$$

this condition for predictive parsing is satisfied, since

$$\text{First}((<\text{exp}>)) \cap \text{First}(<\text{number}>)$$
$$= \{(\} \cap \{0, \ldots, 9\} = \varnothing$$

There is a second condition for predictive parsing that arises when structures are optional. For example, to parse the grammar rule

$$<\text{exp}> ::= <\text{term}> [@ <\text{exp}>]$$

we must test for the presence of the token "@" before we can be sure that the optional part is actually present:

```
procedure exp;
begin
  term;
  if Token = '@' then begin
    GetToken;
    exp;
  end;
end;
```

However, if the token @ can also come after an expression, this test is insufficient: if @ is the next token in the input, it may be the start of the optional "@ <exp>" part, or it may be a token that comes after the whole expression. Thus the second requirement for predictive parsing is that, for any optional part, no token beginning the optional part can also come after the optional part.

We can formalize this condition in the following way. For any string α of tokens and nonterminals that appears on the right-hand side of a grammar rule, define **Follow(α)** to be the set of tokens that can follow α. The second condition for predictive parsing can now be stated in terms of Follow sets. Given a grammar rule in EBNF with an optional α,

$$A ::= \beta \: [\alpha] \: \sigma$$

we must have

$$\text{First}(\alpha) \cap \text{Follow}(\alpha) = \varnothing$$

As an example of the computation of Follow sets, consider the grammar of Figure 4-4. Follow sets for the nonterminals can be computed as follows. From the rule

$$\text{<factor>} ::= (\text{<exp>})$$

we get that the token ")" is in Follow(<exp>). Since <exp> can also comprise a whole expression, <exp> may be followed by the end of the input, which we indicate by the special symbol $. Thus Follow(<exp>) = {), $}. From the rule

$$\text{<exp>} ::= \text{<term>} \{+ \text{<term>}\}$$

we obtain that " + " is in Follow (<term>). Since a <term> also appears as the last thing in an <exp>, anything that follows an <exp> can also follow a <term>. Thus

$$\text{Follow(<term>)} = \{), \$, + \}$$

Finally, Follow(<factor>) = {), $, +, •} by a similar computation.

Note that the grammar of Figure 4-4 automatically satisfies the second condition for predictive parsing, since there are no optional struc-tures inside square brackets. A more instructive example comes from Figure 4-2 (a small part of a BNF grammar for Pascal), where the first two grammar rules are written as follows in EBNF:

<program> ::= <program-heading> ';' <program-block>'.'
<program-heading> ::= program <identifier> ['('<program-
                                              parameters>')']

The first grammar rule gives (with α = '(' <program-parameters> ')')

$$\text{Follow}(\alpha) = \{;\}$$

so that

$$\text{First}(\alpha) \cap \text{Follow}(\alpha) = \{ (\} \cap \{;\} = \varnothing$$

thus satisfying the second condition for predictive parsing.

The computation of First and Follow sets can also be useful in recursive-descent parsing to obtain appropriate tests. See Exercise 38.

We mentioned at the beginning of this section that the process of converting grammar rules into a parser can be automated; that is, a program can be written that will translate a grammar into a parser. Such parser generators or "compiler-compilers" take as their input a version of BNF or EBNF rules and generate an output that is a parser program in some language. This program can then be compiled to provide an exe-cutable parser. Of course, providing only a grammar to the parser generator will result in a recognizer. To get the parser to construct a syntax tree or perform other operations, we must provide operations or actions to be performed that are associated with each grammar rule, that is, a syntax-directed scheme.

One of the more common and popular of the parser generators is YACC, which is available on most Unix systems. Written by Steve Johnson in the mid-1970s, it generates a C program that uses a bottom-up algorithm to parse the grammar. The grammar is given in a BNF-like form, and associated actions are written in C. Figure 4-8 shows a complete

YACC description of a simple integer expression interpreter using the grammar of Figure 4-3 (Section 4.4). Note that it uses the original left-recursive BNF grammar: bottom-up parsers are not bothered by left recursion. The actions provided with the rules are simply to compute values rather than construct a syntax tree. The YACC convention for constructing such values is that the value of the left-hand side of a production is indicated by the symbol "$$," while the value of the nth symbol of the right-hand side is given by $n. Thus $1 + $3 represents the sum of the first and third symbols of the right-hand side of the rule

exp : exp '+' term

so that the value of exp and term on the right are added. Note the different conventions for metasymbols, nonterminals, and tokens.

YACC generates a procedure yyparse from the grammar, so we have to provide a main program that calls yyparse. YACC also assumes that tokens (aside from individual characters) are declared and are recognized by a scanner procedure called yylex. Thus we provide a yylex in C that does this. The procedures yylex and yyparse also communicate values via a global variable yylval. And an error procedure yyerror is needed to print error messages. Note that in Figure 4-8, NUMBER is declared as a token instead of being recognized by the grammar, and the value of a number is computed into yylval by yylex. See the next section for a discussion of scanner versus parser issues. In the Unix system it would also be possible to generate yylex automatically from a **scanner generator** such as LEX, but we will not study this here.

YACC is useful not only to the translator writer, it is also useful to the language designer: given a grammar, it provides a description of possible problems and ambiguities. However, to read this information we must have a more specific knowledge of bottom-up parsing techniques. The interested reader may consult the references at the end of this chapter.

4.7 LEXICS VERSUS SYNTAX VERSUS SEMANTICS

A context-free grammar includes a description of the tokens of a language by including the strings of characters that form the tokens in the grammar rules. For example, in the partial English grammar of Section 4.2, the tokens are the English words "a," "the," "girl," "dog," "sees," and "pets," plus the "." character, and in the simple integer expression grammar of Section 4.3 the tokens are the arithmetic symbols "+" and "∗," the parentheses "(" and ")," and the digits 0 through 9. Specific details of formatting, such as the white-space conventions mentioned in Section 4.1, are left to the scanner and need to be stated as lexical conventions separate from the grammar.

Some typical token categories, such as constants and identifiers, are not fixed sequences of characters in themselves, but are built up out

```
%{
#include <stdio.h>
#include <ctype.h>
%}

%token NUMBER

%%
command : exp {printf("%d\n",$1);}
          ; /* allows printing of the result */

exp : exp '+' term {$$ = $1 + $3;}
    | term {$$ = $1;}
    ;

term : term '*' factor {$$ = $1 * $3;}
     | factor {$$ = $1;}
     ;

factor : NUMBER {$$ = $1;}
       | '(' exp ')' {$$ = $2;}
       ;
%%

void main(void)
  {yyparse();}

int yylex(void)
{int c ;
  while((c = getchar()) == ' ');
  /* eliminates blanks */
  if (isdigit(c))
      {yylval = 0 ;
      while (isdigit(c))
            {yylval = 10*yylval + c - '0';
            c = getchar() ;}
      ungetc(c,stdin);
      return(NUMBER);}
  if (c == '\n') return 0;
  /* makes the parse stop */
  return(c);
}

void yyerror (char *s) /* allows for printing
  error message */
  {printf("%s\n",s);}
```

Figure 4-8   YACC Input for Simple Arithmetic Expressions

of a fixed set of characters, such as the digits 0..9. These token categories often have their structure defined by the grammar, as for example the grammar rules for <number> and <digit> in the expression grammar. However, it is possible to use a scanner to recognize these structures, since the full recursive power of a parser is not necessary, and the scanner can recognize them by a simple repetitive operation. This is more efficient—it makes the recognition of numbers and identifiers faster and simpler, and it reduces the size of the parser and the number of BNFs.

To express the fact that a number in the expression grammar should be a token rather than represented by a nonterminal, we rewrite the grammar of Figure 4-4 in Figure 4-9.

By making the string NUMBER uppercase in the foregoing grammar, we are saying that it is not a token to be recognized literally, but one whose structure is determined by the scanner. The structure of such tokens must then be specified as part of the lexical conventions of the language. A notation often used for this specification is that of **regular expressions** (see the notes and references). However, many language designers choose to include the structure of such tokens as part of the grammar, with the understanding that an implementor may include these in the scanner instead of the parser. Thus a description of a language using BNF, EBNF, or syntax diagrams may include not only the syntax but most of the lexical structure (or lexics) of a programming language as well. The boundary, therefore, between syntactic and lexical structure is not always clearly drawn but depends on the point of view of the designer and implementor.

The same is true for syntax and semantics. We have been taking the approach that syntax is anything that can be defined with a context-free grammar and semantics is anything that cannot. However, many authors include properties that we would call semantic as syntactic properties of a language. Examples include such rules as declaration before use for variables and no redeclaration of identifiers within a procedure. These are rules that are context-sensitive and cannot be written as context-free rules. Hence we prefer to think of them as semantic rather than syntactic rules.

Another conflict between syntax and semantics arises when languages require certain strings to be **predefined identifiers** rather than **reserved words.** Recall (from Section 4.1) that reserved words are fixed strings of characters that are tokens themselves and that cannot be used as identifiers. For example, the strings "begin," "end," "while," "do," and "procedure" are all reserved words in Pascal. However, the strings "true"

$$
\begin{aligned}
&\text{<exp>} \quad ::= \text{<term> } \{ + \text{ <term>} \} \\
&\text{<term>} \quad ::= \text{<factor> } \{ \cdot \text{ <factor>} \} \\
&\text{<factor>} ::= (\text{<exp>}) \mid \text{NUMBER}
\end{aligned}
$$

Figure 4-9   Numbers as Tokens in Simple Arithmetic

and "false" are not reserved words but are **predefined identifiers:** they are identifiers that have a fixed meaning in the language, but this meaning can be changed by redeclaring them within a program. To do so, however, would be extremely bad programming practice, since they may not have the usual semantics as Boolean constants with the usual values. Therefore it is probably better to make "true" and "false" syntactic entities—that is, reserved words—with corresponding fixed semantics.

Exercises

1. **(a)** The C programming language distinguishes character from string constants by using single quotes for characters and double quotes for strings. Thus, 'c' is the character c, while "c" is a string of length 1 consisting of the single character c. Why do you think this distinction is made? Is it useful?

    (b) Pascal, on the other hand, uses single quotes for both characters and strings (thus 'c' is either a character or string, depending on context). Discuss the advantages and disadvantages of these two approaches.

2. Devise a test in one or more of the following languages to determine if comments are considered white space: (a) Pascal, (b) C, (c) Modula-2, and (d) Ada. What is the result of performing your test?

3. Discuss the pros and cons of ignoring or requiring "white space" (i.e., blanks, end-of-lines, and tabs) when recognizing tokens.

4. Many programming languages (like Pascal) do not allow nested comments. Why is this requirement made? Modula-2 *does* allow nested comments. Why is this useful? Discuss the pros and cons for nesting of comments. What solution does Ada adopt?

5. In the simplified English grammar of Section 4.2 there are only finitely many legal sentences. How many are there? Why?

6. Translate the BNF rules of Figure 4-2 into (a) EBNF and (b) syntax diagrams.

7. Add subtraction and division to the (a) BNF, (b) EBNF, and (c) syntax diagrams of simple arithmetic expressions (Figures 4-3, 4-4, and 4-5). Be sure to give them the appropriate precedence.

8. Add the mod and power operation to (a) the arithmetic BNF or (b) EBNF. Use % for the mod operation and ^ for the power operation. Recall that mod is left-associative, like division, but that power is right-associative. (Thus $2 \char`\^ 2 \char`\^ 3 = 256$, not 64.)

9. Unary minuses can be added in several ways to the arithmetic expression grammar of Figure 4-3 or the grammar from Exercise 7. Revise the BNF and EBNF for each of the cases that follow so that it satisfies the stated rule:

    (a) At most one unary minus is allowed in each expression, and it must come at the beginning of an expression, so $-2 - 3$ is legal (and equals -5) and $-2 - (-3)$ is legal, but $-2 - -3$ is not.

    (b) At most one unary minus is allowed before a number or left parenthesis, so $-2 - -3$ is legal but $- -2$ and $-2 - - -3$ are not.

    (c) Arbitrarily many unary minuses are allowed before numbers and left parentheses, so everything above is legal, but, for example, $2 - + 3$ is not.

10. Draw parse trees and abstract syntax trees for the arithmetic expressions:

    (a) $((2))$

    (b) $3 + 4 \cdot 5 + 6 \cdot 7$

    (c) $3 \cdot 4 + 5 \cdot 6 + 7$

    (d) $3 \cdot (4 + 5) \cdot (6 + 7)$

    (e) $(2 + (3 + (4 + 5)))$

11. Finish writing the pseudocode for a recursive-descent recognizer for the English grammar of Section 4.2 that was begun in Section 4.6.

12. Translate the pseudocode of Exercise 11 into a working recognizer program in Pascal, C, Modula-2, or another programming language of your choice.

13. Revise the program of Exercise 12 so that it randomly *generates* legal sentences in the grammar. (This will require the use of a random number generator.)

14. Translate the pseudocode of Figure 4-7 into a working recognizer in a language of your choice.

15. Modify the program of Exercise 14 so that it actually calculates the result of the arithmetic expression.

16. Add subtraction and division to (a) the pseudocode of Figure 4-7 and (b) to your program of Exercise 14 or 15.

17. Add the mod and power operations as described in Exercise 8 to your program of any of the Exercises 14–16.

18. To eliminate the left recursion in the simple arithmetic grammar one might be tempted to write:

    $$<exp> ::= <term> + <term>$$

    Why is this wrong?

19. Add subtraction and division to the YACC program of Figure 4-8.

20. Add mod and power operations to the YACC program of Figure 4-8.

21. Capitalization of articles at the beginning of a sentence was viewed as a context-sensitivity in the text. However, in the simple English grammar of Section 4.2, capitalization can be achieved by adding only context-free rules. How would you do this?

22. It was stated in the chapter that it is not possible to include in the BNF description the rule that there should be no redeclaration of variables. Strictly speaking, this is not true if only finitely many variable names are allowed. Describe how one could include the requirement that there be no redeclaration of variables in the grammar for a language, if only finitely many identifiers are allowed. Why isn't it a good idea?

23. The text notes that it is more efficient to let a scanner recognize a structure such as an unsigned integer, which is just a repetition of digits. However, an expression is also just a repetition of terms and pluses:

$$<exp> ::= <term> \{ + <term> \}$$

Why can't a scanner recognize all expressions?

24. Rewrite the YACC description of Figure 4-8 to replace the token NUMBER by a grammar rule to be recognized by the parser. Be sure to include operations to compute the value of a number.

25. Write a BNF description for a statement-sequence as a sequence of statements separated by semicolons. (Assume that statements are defined elsewhere.) Then translate your BNF into EBNF and syntax diagrams.

26. Write a BNF description for a statement-sequence as a sequence of statements in which each statement is terminated by a semicolon. (Assume that statements are defined elsewhere.) Then translate your BNF into EBNF and syntax diagrams.

27. Pascal uses the semicolon as a statement separator (as in Exercise 25), but also allows a statement to be empty, so that the following is a legal Pascal program:

```
program huh;
begin
  ; ; ; ; ;
end.
```

Discuss the advantages and disadvantages of this.

28. (a) List the predefined identifiers in Pascal and describe their meanings.
    (b) List the predefined identifiers in Modula-2 and describe their meanings.
    (c) Does C have predefined identifiers? Explain.
    (d) Does Ada have predefined identifiers? Explain.

29. (a) One measure of the complexity of a language is the number of reserved words in its syntax. Compare the number of reserved words in C, Pascal, Ada, and Modula-2.

(b) One could argue that the preceding comparison is misleading because of the use of predefined identifiers in Pascal and Modula-2. Discuss the pros and cons of adding in the number of predefined identifiers in the comparison.

30. Here is a legal Pascal program:

```
program yecch;
var true,false: boolean;
begin
   true := 1 = 0;
   false := true;
   . . .
   . . .
end.
```

What values do true and false have in this program? What design principle does this violate? Is this program possible in Modula-2? Ada?

31. Is it possible to have a language without any reserved words? Discuss.

32. Some languages use format to distinguish the beginning and ending of structures, as follows:

```
if x = 0 then
   (* all indented statements here are part of
      the if *)
else
   (* all indented statements here are part of
      the else *)
(* statements that are not indented are outside
   the else *)
```

Discuss the advantages and disadvantages of this for (a) writing programs in the language, and (b) writing a translator. (This rule is sometimes called the **Offside rule;** it is used in Miranda; see Landin [1966].)

33. A number is defined in the grammar of Figure 4-3 using a left-recursive rule. However, it could also be defined using a right-recursive rule:

$$<number> ::= <digit> <number> \mid <digit>$$

Which is better, or does it matter? Why?

34. Given the following BNF:

$$<exp> ::= (<list>) \mid a$$
$$<list> ::= <list> , <exp> \mid <exp>$$

(a) Write EBNF rules and syntax diagrams for the language.
(b) Draw the parse tree for ((a,a),a,(a)).
(c) Write a recursive-descent recognizer for the language.

35. Compute First and Follow sets for the nonterminals of the grammar of Exercise 34.

36. Show that any left-recursive grammar rule does not satisfy the first condition for predictive parsing.

37. Show that the following grammar does not satisfy the second rule of predictive parsing:

$$<stmt> ::= <if\text{-}stmt> \mid other$$
$$<if\text{-}stmt> ::= if <stmt> [else <stmt>]$$

38. Given the following grammar in EBNF:

$$<exp> ::= (<list>) \mid a<list> ::= <exp> [<list>]$$

(a) Show that the two conditions for predictive parsing are satisfied.
(b) Write a recursive-descent recognizer for the language.

39. In Section 4.7 the definition of Follow sets was somewhat nonstandard. More commonly Follow sets are defined for nonterminals only rather than for strings, and optional structures are accommodated by allowing a nonterminal to become empty. Thus the grammar rule

$$<if\text{-}statement> ::= if <condition> then <statement> \mid$$
$$\qquad\qquad if <condition> then <statement> else <statement>$$

is replaced by the two rules

$$<if\text{-}statement> ::= if <condition> then <statement> <else\text{-}part>$$
$$<else\text{-}part> ::= else <statement> \mid \epsilon$$

where the symbol "ϵ" is a new metasymbol standing for the empty string. (The nonterminal $<empty>$ is used in place of ϵ in Figure 4-2.) A nonterminal A can then be recognized as optional if it either becomes ϵ directly, or there is a derivation beginning with A that derives ϵ. In this case we add ϵ to First(A). Rewrite the second condition for predictive parsing using this convention, and apply this technique to the grammars of Exercises 34 and 38.

40. Given the following grammar in BNF:

$$<string> := <string> <string> \mid a$$

let S be the set of all strings. Then S satisfies the recursive equation

$$S = SS \cup \{a\}$$

Show that the set $S = \{a, aa, aaa, aaaa, . . .\}$ is the smallest set satisfying the equation. [Hint: First show that S does satisfy the equation by showing set inclusion in both directions. Then show that, given any set S' that satisfies the equation, S' must be contained in S (this can be done using induction on the length of strings in S).]

41. According to Wirth [1976], data structures based on syntax diagrams can be used by a "generic" recursive-descent parser that will parse any set of grammar rules that satisfy the two conditions for predictive parsing. A suitable data structure is given by the following Pascal declaration:

```
type  ruleptr  =  ^rulerec;
      rulerec  =  record
         next,  other:  ruleptr;
         case  isToken:  boolean  of
               true:  (name:  Token);
               false:  (rule:  ruleptr);
      end;
```

The "next" field is used to point to the next item in the grammar rule, and the "other" field is used to point to alternatives given by the | metasymbol. Thus, the data structure for the grammar rule

<factor> ::= (<exp>) | <number>

from Figure 4.4 would look as follows:

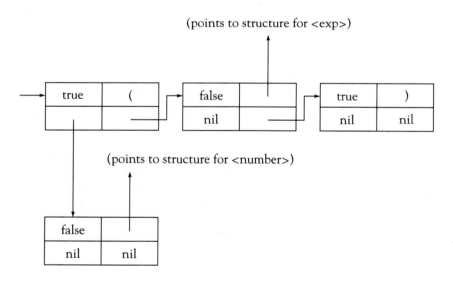

where the fields of the record structure are shown as follows:

isToken	name/rule
other	next

(a) Draw the data structures for the rest of the grammar rules in Figure 4.4. (Hint: For repetitive and optional structures you will need a special token to represent the empty string.)

(b) Write a generic parse procedure that uses these data structures to recognize an input string, assuming the existence of *GetToken* and *Error* procedures.

(c) Write a parser-generator that reads EBNF rules (either from a file or standard input) and generates the preceding data structures.

Notes and References

Many of the topics discussed in this chapter are treated in more detail in Aho, Sethi, and Ullman [1986]. EBNF and syntax diagrams are studied in Wirth [1976] and in Horowitz [1984]. Context-free grammars and regular expressions are studied in Hopcroft and Ullman [1979], Lewis and Papadimitriou [1981], and Mandrioli and Ghezzi [1987]. The original description of context-free grammars is in Chomsky [1956]. An early use of BNF in the description of Algol60 is in Naur [1963a]. A description of general algorithms to compute First and Follow sets, and to perform left recursion removal, are found in Aho, Sethi, and Ullman [1986] and also in Wirth [1976]. Our description of Follow sets is for EBNF grammars and is slightly nonstandard; see Exercise 39. YACC is described in more detail in Johnson [1975] and LEX in Lesk [1975].

5 BASIC SEMANTICS

In Chapter 1 we made the distinction between the syntax of a programming language—what the language constructs look like—and its semantics—what the language constructs actually do. In Chapter 4 we saw how the syntactic structure of a language can be precisely specified using context-free grammar rules in Backus-Naur form (BNF). In this chapter we will introduce the major features of the semantics of programming languages.

Specifying the semantics of a programming language is a more difficult task than is specifying syntax, as we might expect when we talk about meaning as opposed to form or structure. In Chapter 1 we noted that there are several ways to specify semantics:

1. *By a language reference manual.* This is the most common method. Experience with the use of English descriptions has made reference manuals clearer and more precise over the years, but they still suffer from the lack of precision inherent in natural language descriptions and also may have omissions and ambiguities.

2. *By a defining translator.* This has the advantage that questions about a language can be answered by experiment (as in chemistry or physics). A drawback is that questions about program behavior cannot be answered in advance—we must execute a program to discover what it does. Another drawback is that bugs and machine dependencies in the translator become parts of the language semantics, possibly unintentionally. Also, the translator may not be portable to all machines and may not be generally available.

3. *By a formal definition.* Such mathematical methods are precise, but are also complex and abstract, and require study to understand. Different formal methods are available, with the choice of method depending on its intended use. Perhaps the best formal method to use for the description of the translation and execution of programs is denotational semantics, which describes semantics using a series of functions.

In this chapter we will use an adaptation of informal description as it might occur in a manual, together with a simplified use of functions as in denotational descriptions. We will provide abstractions of the operations that occur during the translation and execution of programs in general, whatever the language, but will concentrate on the details of Algol-like languages, such as C, Pascal, Modula-2, and Ada. More formal methods of describing semantics are studied in Chapter 12.

5.1   ATTRIBUTES, BINDING, AND SEMANTIC FUNCTIONS

A fundamental abstraction mechanism in a programming language is the use of **names,** or **identifiers,** to denote language entities or constructs. In most languages, variables, procedures, and constants can have names assigned by the programmer. A fundamental step in describing the semantics of a language is to describe the conventions that determine the meaning of each name used in a program.

In addition to names, a description of the semantics of a programming language needs the concepts of **location** and **value.** Values are any storable quantities, such as the integers, the reals, or even array values consisting of a sequence of the values stored at each index of the array. Locations are places where values can be stored. Locations are like addresses in the memory of a computer, but we can think of them more abstractly than as the addresses of a particular computer. If necessary, we can think of locations being numbered by integers starting at 0 and going up to some maximum location number. Most of the time we will not need to be that specific.

The meaning of a name is determined by the properties, or **attributes** associated to the name. For example, the Pascal declaration

```
const n = 5;
```

makes n into a constant with value 5, that is, associates to the name n the two attributes const and "value 5." The Pascal declaration

```
var x: integer;
```

associates the attributes var and data type integer to the name x. The Pascal declaration

```
function f (n: integer): boolean;
begin
    . . .
end;
```

associates the attribute function to the name f and the following additional attributes:

1. The number, names, and data types of its parameters (in this case, one parameter with name n and data type integer)

2. The data type of its returned value (in this case, boolean)

3. The body of code to be executed when f is called (in this case, we have not written this code but just indicated it with three dots)

Declarations are not the only language constructs that can associate attributes to names. For example, the assignment

```
x := 2;
```

associates the new attribute "value 2" to the variable x. And, if y is a pointer variable[1] declared as

```
var y: ^integer;
```

the statement

```
new(y);
```

allocates memory for an integer variable, that is, associates a location attribute to it and assigns this location to y^, that is, associates a new value attribute to y.

The process of associating an attribute to a name is called **binding.** In some languages, constructs that cause values to be bound to names (such as the Pascal constant declaration earlier) are in fact called bindings rather than declarations.

An attribute can be classified according to the time during the translation/execution process when it is computed and bound to a name. This is called the **binding time** of the attribute. Binding times can be classified into two general categories, **static binding** and **dynamic binding.** Static binding occurs prior to execution, while dynamic binding occurs during execution. An attribute that is bound statically is a static attribute, while an attribute that is bound dynamically is a dynamic attribute.

Languages differ substantially in which attributes are bound statically

---

[1]Pointers are discussed more fully in Sections 5.4 and 5.6.

and which are bound dynamically. Often, functional languages have more dynamic binding than imperative languages. Binding times can also depend on the translator. Interpreters by definition perform all bindings dynamically, while compilers will perform many bindings statically. To make the discussion of attributes and binding independent of such translator issues, we usually refer to the binding time of an attribute as the earliest time that the language rules permit the attribute to be bound.

As examples of binding times, consider the previous examples of attributes. In the declaration

```
const  n  =  2;
```

the value 2 is bound statically to the name n, and in the declaration

```
var  x:  integer;
```

the data type integer is bound statically to the name x. A similar statement holds for the function declaration.

On the other hand, the assignment x := 2 binds the value 2 dynamically to x when the assignment statement is executed. And the statement

```
new(y);
```

dynamically binds a storage location to y^ and assigns that location as the value of y.

Binding times can be further refined into subcategories of dynamic and static binding. A static attribute can be bound during parsing or semantic analysis (translation time), during the linking of the program with libraries (link time), or during the loading of the program for execution (load time). For example, the body of an externally defined function will not be bound until link time, and the location of a Pascal global variable is bound at load time, since its location does not change during the execution of the program.

Names can be bound to attributes even prior to translation time. Predefined identifiers such as the Pascal data types boolean and char have their meanings (and hence attributes) specified by the language definition: data type boolean, for example, is specified as having the two values true and false. Some predefined identifiers, such as data type integer and constant maxint, have their attributes specified by the language definition *and* by the implementation. The language definition specifies that data type integer has values consisting of a subset of the integers and that maxint is a constant, while the implementation specifies the value of maxint and the actual range of data type integer.[2]

---

[2]This assumes that a program does not redefine the meanings of these names in a declaration. Redefinition is a possibility since these predefined identifiers are not reserved words.

Thus we have the following possible binding times for attributes of names:

Language definition time

Language implementation time

Translation time

Link time

Load time

Execution time

All binding times in this list, except for the last, represent static binding.

Bindings must be maintained by a translator so that appropriate meanings are given to names during translation and execution. A translator does this by creating a data structure to maintain the information. Since we are not interested in the details of this data structure, but only its properties, we can think of it abstractly as a function that expresses the binding of attributes to names. This function is a fundamental part of language semantics and is usually called the **symbol table.** Mathematically, the symbol table is a function from names to attributes, which we could write as SymbolTable : Names → Attributes or more graphically as

$$\text{Names} \xrightarrow{\quad\text{SymbolTable}\quad} \text{Attributes}$$

This function will change as translation and/or execution proceeds to reflect additions and deletions of bindings within the program being translated and/or executed. The symbol table will be studied in more detail in the next two sections.

A fundamental distinction exists between the way a symbol table is maintained by an interpreter and the way it is maintained by a compiler. A compiler can by definition compute only static attributes, since the program does not execute until after compilation is completed. Thus the symbol table for a compiler can be pictured as follows:

$$\text{Names} \xrightarrow{\quad\text{SymbolTable}\quad} \text{Static Attributes}$$

During the execution of a compiled program attributes such as locations and values must be maintained. A compiler generates code that maintains these attributes in data structures during execution. The memory allocation part of this process, that is, the binding of names to storage locations, is usually considered separately and is called the **environment:**

$$\text{Names} \xrightarrow{\quad\text{Environment}\quad} \text{Locations}$$

Finally, the bindings of storage locations to values is called the **memory,** since it abstracts the memory of an actual computer (sometimes it is also called the **store** or the **state**):

$$\text{Locations} \xrightarrow{\quad \text{Memory} \quad} \text{Values}$$

In an interpreter, on the other hand, the symbol table and the environment are combined, since static and dynamic attributes are both computed during execution. Usually, memory is also included in this function, and we have the following picture:

$$\text{Names} \xrightarrow{\quad \text{Environment} \quad} \text{Attributes}$$
$$\text{(including locations and values)}$$

5.2   DECLARATIONS, BLOCKS, AND SCOPE

Declarations are, as we have seen, a principal method for establishing bindings. Declarations may be **explicit** as in Pascal and many other languages, or they may be **implicit,** in which simply using the name of the variable causes it to be declared. Languages with implicit declarations usually have name conventions to establish other attributes. For example, FORTRAN does not require variable declarations for simple variables. All variables in FORTRAN that are not explicitly declared are assumed to be integer if their names begin with "I," "J," "K," "L," "M," or "N," and real otherwise. A similar convention holds in some BASICs, where variables ending in "%" are integer, variables ending in "$" are strings, and all others are real. Other languages with implicit declarations are APL and SNOBOL.

Declarations are usually associated with a particular language structure called a **block.** In Pascal, there are two kinds of blocks, the main program block and procedure/function blocks. The position of declarations in these blocks is illustrated schematically as follows:

```
program ex;

   . . .

   procedure p;                 }  declarations        declarations
      . . .                        of p                of ex
      . . .                                       }
   begin
      . . .
   end; (* p *)
   . . .                                                continues
```

```
continued
    begin (* main *)
        . . .
    end. (* ex *)
```

Declarations associated to e x are **global declarations,** while declarations associated to p are **declarations local to** p.

In Algol60 and Algol68, blocks also consist of sequences of statements surrounded by a begin-end pair.[3] The declarations are placed after the begin but before the first statement in the block, as in the following Algol60 example:

```
begin
   integer x;
   boolean y;
   x := 2;
   y := false;
   x := x + 1;
     . . .
end;
```

This general form of the block exists also in C, where blocks are surrounded by curly brackets:

```
void p(void)
{double r,z; /* the block of p */
     . . .
   {int x,y; /* another block */
      x = 2;
      y = 0;
      x += 1;
   }
     . . .
}
```

(The keyword **void** in the definition v o i d p (v o i d) indicates that p has no return value and no parameters.)

C also has an **external scope** that is not tied to any block, but that provides a scope that encloses all functions in a program. This external scope functions as a global scope, since in C the main program is just

---

[3]Sometimes Pascal statements surrounded by a begin-end pair are referred to as blocks. Strictly speaking, they are **compound statements,** not blocks, since declarations cannot be associated with them.

another function and has its own local scope separate from the rest of the program:

```
int x;
float y;
/* these are external to all functions
   and so global */

void main (void)
{int i,j; /* these are local to main */
   . . .
}
```

Ada combines Pascal's procedure and function declarations with Algol60-like blocks except that, unlike Algol60, the begin-end pair is preceded by the declarations with the reserved word **declare:**

```
declare x: INTEGER;
        y: BOOLEAN;
begin
  x := 2;
  y := 0;
  x := x + 1;
end;
```

Ada packages and tasks also contain declarations and thus form blocks.

In Modula-2 the blocks are modules and procedures, while in FORTRAN blocks are subroutine and function programs. (We shall see examples of these shortly.)

Declarations bind various attributes to names, depending on the kind of declaration. (We have seen examples of different attributes bound by declarations in the last section.) A declaration itself has an attribute that is determined by its position in the program. The **scope of a declaration** is the region of the program over which the bindings established by the declaration are maintained. We can also refer to the scope of the bindings themselves. Sometimes, by abuse of language, we refer to the scope of a name, but this is dangerous, since the same name may be involved in several different declarations, each with a different scope. For example, the following Pascal program contains two declarations of the name x, with different meanings and different scopes:

```
program ex;

procedure p;
var x: integer;
begin
   . . .
end;
```

continues

continued

```
procedure q;
var x: boolean;
begin
    . . .
end;

begin (* main *)
    . . .
end.
```

In a language like Pascal or C, where blocks can be nested (i.e., placed inside another block), the scope of a declaration is limited to the block in which it appears (and other blocks contained within it). Such languages are called **block structured,** and the kind of scope rules for blocks that we describe here is called **lexical scope,** since it follows the structure of the blocks as they appear in the written code. It is the standard scope rule in most languages (but see the next section for a discussion of a different scope rule).

Here is a simple example of scope in Pascal:

```
program ex;
var x: integer;

    procedure p;
    var y: boolean;
    begin
        . . .
    end; (* p *)

    procedure q;
    var z: real;
    begin
        . . .
    end; (* q *)

begin (* main of ex *)
    . . .  .
end. (* ex *)
```

In this program, the declarations of variable x and procedures p and q are associated to the main program block and thus are global. The declarations of y and z, on the other hand, are associated to the blocks of procedures p and q, respectively. They are **local** to these functions, and their declarations are valid only for p and q, respectively. Pascal has the further rule that the scope of a declaration begins at the point of the declaration itself (this is the so-called **declaration before use** rule), so that we can state the following basic scope rule in Pascal: the scope of a declaration extends from the point just after the declaration to the end of the block in which it is located.[4]

We repeat the Pascal example drawing arrows to indicate the scope of each declaration:

```
program ex;
var x: integer;

  procedure p;
    var y: boolean;
    begin
      . . .
    end; (* p *)

  procedure q;
    var z: real;
    begin
      . . .
    end; (* q *)

  begin (* main of ex *)
    . . .
  end. (* ex *)
```

Blocks in other Algol-like languages establish similar scope rules. For example, in the following Algol60 code,

```
A: begin
     integer x;
     boolean y;
     x := 2;
     y := false;
   B: begin
        integer a,b;
        if y then a := x
        else b := y;
      end;

      . . .
   end;
```

the scope of the declarations of x and y is all of block A (including block B), while the scope of the declarations of a and b is block B only.

Modula-2 has a block structure and scope rules similar to Pascal,

---

[4]Pascal's actual scope rule is more complicated, and we discuss a few of the complications later on in the chapter.

with two major differences. The first is that the scope of a variable or function declaration extends from the beginning of the block in which it appears, *not* just from the point of the declaration.[5] Thus Modula-2 does not adhere to the declaration before use rule:

```
MODULE Ex;

PROCEDURE p;
BEGIN
  x := 2; (* legal - global x defined below *)
END p;

VAR x: INTEGER;
BEGIN (* Ex *)
  . . .
END Ex.
```

The scope of the global variable x extends backward from its declaration to the beginning of module Ex.

The second major difference in scope rules between Modula-2 and Pascal is the use of local modules in Modula-2 to limit scope. Consider the following example:

```
MODULE A;
VAR x: INTEGER;

    PROCEDURE p;
    BEGIN

      . . .

    END p;

    MODULE B;
    VAR y: REAL;

        PROCEDURE q;
        BEGIN

          . . .

        END q;

      . . .

    END B;

  . . .

END A.
```

---

[5]Modula-2 also allows constant, variable, and procedure declarations to occur in any order, unlike Standard Pascal's rigid order (constants first, then type, variable, and procedure declarations, in that order).

The declarations of variable x and procedure p have scope extending over MODULE A *except* for MODULE B—references to x and p inside B are illegal. Correspondingly, references to y and q outside of B are also illegal. Local modules such as B in this example function as **scope boundaries**—no scopes cross these boundaries, with the exception of those explicitly exported or imported. An example of export and import is given in the following modification of the code, where procedure p is imported into module B and so can now be called from B; similarly, variable y is exported from B and so can be referenced in A:

```
MODULE A;
VAR x: INTEGER;

PROCEDURE p;
BEGIN
  . . .
END p;

    MODULE B;
    IMPORT p; (* p now available in B *)
    EXPORT y; (* y now available in A *)
    VAR y: REAL;

    PROCEDURE q;
    BEGIN
      . . .
    END q;

    END B;

BEGIN
  . . .
END A.
```

Scope in FORTRAN can be extended over several subroutines or functions in a somewhat similar way to Modula-2 export by the use of a COMMON declaration. Consider the following example of a FORTRAN program:

```
C     MAIN PROGRAM
      COMMON A
      A = 2.0
      B = 3.1
      CALL P
      END
```

continues

continued

```
SUBROUTINE P
COMMON A
B  =  A
A  =  A  +  1.0
RETURN
END
```

In this program, the main program and subroutine P are different scopes, so that variable B in the main program is not the same as variable B in P. On the other hand, the two COMMON statements establish the two variables with name A as the same, so A in P has the same value as A in the main program. Thus, at the end of the program, B still has value 3.1, while A has value 3.0. The use of COMMON in FORTRAN creates what is essentially a global variable. However, it works by identifying the locations of the variables listed in the COMMON statements, and this can have unusual effects. (See Section 5.6.)

One feature of block structure is that declarations in nested blocks take precedence over previous declarations. Consider the following example:

```
program ex;
var x: integer;

procedure p;
var x: boolean;
begin
  x := true; (* x p *)
  ...
end;

begin
  x := 2; (* global x *)
  ...
end.
```

The declaration of x in p takes precedence over the global declaration of x for the duration of p. Thus the global integer x cannot be accessed from within p. The global declaration of x is said to have a *scope hole* inside p. For this reason a distinction is sometimes made between the scope and the **visibility** of a declaration: visibility includes only those regions of a program where the bindings of a declaration apply, while scope includes scope holes (since the bindings still exist, but are hidden from view). (In Ada, such hidden declarations can still be accessed by using a scope qualifier similar to a record reference. Thus in Ada one could still refer to the global x inside p by writing ex.x. This is called **visibility by selection** in Ada.)

The bindings established by declarations are maintained by the symbol table. The way the symbol table processes declarations determines the scope of each declaration. In the next section we examine the way a symbol table can maintain scope in a block-structured language.

5.3   THE SYMBOL TABLE

A symbol table can be maintained by any number of data structures to allow for efficient access and maintenance of a table of names and attributes: hash tables, trees, and lists are some of the data structures that have been used. However, the maintenance of scope information in a lexically scoped language with block structure requires that declarations be processed in a stacklike fashion: on entry into a block, all declarations of that block are processed and the corresponding bindings added to the symbol table; then, on exit from the block, the bindings provided by the declarations are removed, restoring any previous bindings that may have existed. Without restricting our view of a symbol table to any particular data structure, we may nevertheless view the symbol table schematically as a collection of names, each of which has a stack of declarations associated to it, such that the declaration on top of the stack is the one whose scope is currently active.

To see how this works, consider the following Pascal program:

```
program symtabex;
var x: integer;
    y: boolean;
    procedure p;
    var x: boolean;

      procedure q;
      var y: integer;
      begin
        . . .
      end; (* q *)

    begin (* p *)
      . . .
    end; (* p *)

begin (* main *)
  . . .
end.
```

The names in program symtabex are x, y, p, and q, but x and y are associated with two different declarations with different scopes. Right after the processing of the variable declaration of p, the symbol table can be represented as follows:

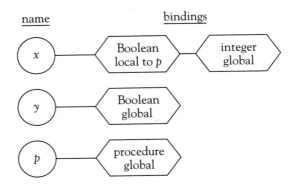

After the processing of the declarations of q, the symbol table becomes

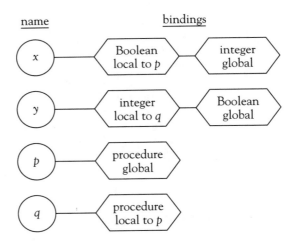

After the processing of the body of q, the bindings created by the declaration of y local to q are popped from the stack associated to the name y, and so during the processing of the body of p, the symbol table becomes

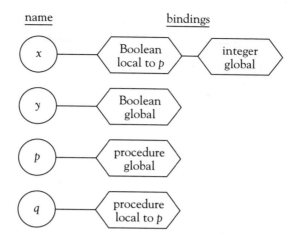

Finally, after the processing of the block of p, the bindings created by the declarations of x and q local to p are removed, and during the processing of the main program the symbol table becomes

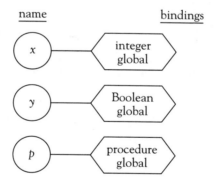

Note that this maintains the appropriate scope information, including the scope holes for the global declaration of x inside p and the global declaration of y inside q.

This representation of the symbol table assumes that the symbol table processes the declarations statically, that is, prior to execution. This is the case if the symbol table is managed by a compiler, and the bindings of the declarations are all static. But if the symbol table is managed in this same way, but dynamically, that is, during execution, then declarations are processed as they are encountered along an execution path through the program. This results in a different scope rule, which is usually called **dynamic scoping,** and our previous lexical scoping rule is sometimes called **static scoping.**

A simple example to show the difference between lexical and dynamic scope is the following, in Pascal syntax:

```
program ex;

var x: integer;

procedure p;
begin
  writeln(x);
end;

procedure q;
var x: integer;
begin
  x := 2;
  p;
end;

begin (* main *)
  x := 1;
  q;
end.
```

Using our previous method for representing the symbol table, the symbol table inside p has the following structure:

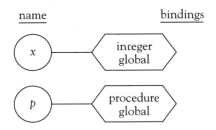

Thus the reference to x in the writeln statement of p is to the global x, and the program will print 1. This is a consequence of lexical scope. On the other hand, during the execution of the program, p is reached through q. The execution path is as follows:

```
main  -> call of q  -> call of p
```

If the symbol table processes declarations as they are encountered in this execution path, first the global declarations of main are processed, then the declarations of q, and finally the declarations of p (of which there are none). Thus, during the execution of p using dynamic scope, the symbol table is as follows:

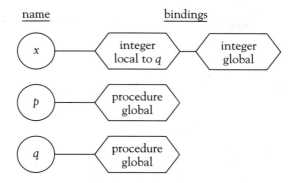

Now the reference to x inside the writeln statement of p refers to the local x inside q, since that was the last declaration of x to be processed by the symbol table. Thus the program would print 2 rather than 1.[6]

Languages that use dynamic scoping include APL, SNOBOL, and older versions of LISP. Almost all modern languages use lexical scoping. Indeed, dynamic scoping is now considered undesirable, for several reasons. The first, and perhaps foremost, is that under dynamic scoping, when a name is used in an expression or statement, the declaration that applies to that name cannot be determined by simply reading the program. Instead, the program must be executed, or its execution traced by hand, to find the applicable declaration. Second, dynamic scoping clashes with static typing of variables. For example, consider the following program:

```
program barfoo;
var x: integer;

procedure p;
begin
  x := ?? ;
end;

procedure q;
var x: boolean;
begin
  p;
end;                                              continues
```

---

[6]Of course, since Pascal uses lexical scope, we cannot actually execute this program this way. We are using Pascal syntax only as a convenience.

```
continued
    begin (* main *)
      p ;
      q ;
    end.
```

During execution, when p is called the first time (by the main program), any reference to x is to the global x, with data type integer. But when p is called the second time (from inside q), any reference to x is to the local x of q, with data type boolean. Thus x may have either boolean or integer data type inside p, and x cannot be given a unique static data type.

It may seem from this discussion that it is impossible to maintain lexical scope using an interpreter, since, by definition of an interpreter, the symbol table is maintained dynamically. This is not the case. However, maintaining lexical scope dynamically does require some extra structure and bookkeeping. Details on how this can be done are given in Chapter 7 in the discussion of environments and procedure calls.

5.4 ALLOCATION, EXTENT, AND THE ENVIRONMENT

Having considered the symbol table in some detail, we need also to study the environment, which maintains the binding of names to locations. Depending on the language, the environment may be constructed statically (at load time), dynamically (at execution time), or a mixture of the two. A language that uses a completely static environment is FORTRAN—all locations are bound statically. A language that uses a completely dynamic environment is LISP—all locations are bound during execution. Pascal, C, Modula-2, and other Algol-style languages are in the middle—some allocation is performed statically, while other allocation is performed dynamically.

Not all names in a program are bound to locations. In a compiled language, names of constants and data types may represent purely compile-time quantities that have no existence at load or execution time. For example, the Pascal constant declaration

```
const max = 10;
```

can be used by a compiler to replace all uses of max by the value 10. The name max is never allocated a location and, indeed, has disappeared altogether from the program when it executes.

Declarations can be used to construct the environment as well as the symbol table. In a compiler, the declarations are used to indicate what allocation code the compiler is to generate as the declaration is processed. In an interpreter, the symbol table and the environment are identified, so attribute binding by a declaration in an interpreter includes the binding of locations.

We will now discuss the varieties of allocation in block-structured languages and a little of the structure of the environment. We have already noted that allocation can be static or dynamic. Typically, global variables are allocated statically, since their meanings are fixed throughout the program. Variables local to blocks other than the program block, however, are allocated dynamically when execution reaches the block in question. In the last section we saw that in a block-structured language the symbol table uses a stacklike mechanism to maintain the bindings of a declaration. Similarly, the environment for a block-structured language binds locations to local variables in a stack-based fashion. To see how this takes place, consider the following Algol60 fragment with nested blocks:

```
A: begin
        integer x;
        boolean y;
        . . .
   B: begin
           real x;
           integer a;
           . . .
       end B;
       . . .
   C: begin
           boolean y;
           integer b;
           . . .
       D: begin
               integer x;
               real y;
               . . .
           end D;
           . . .
       end C;
       . . .
   end A;
```

During execution of this code, when each block is entered, the variables declared at the beginning of each block are allocated, and when each block is exited, those same variables are deallocated. If we view the environment as a linear sequence of storage locations, with locations allocated from the top in descending order, then the environment after the entry into A looks as follows (ignoring the size of each allocated variable),

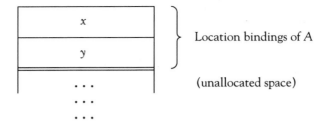

and the environment after entry into B is

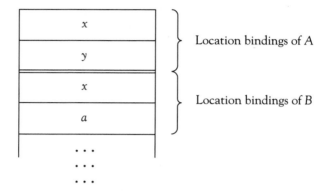

On exit from block B the environment returns to the environment as it existed just after the entry into A. Then, when block C is entered, the variables of C are allocated and the environment becomes

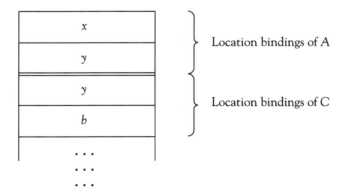

Notice that the variables y and b of block C are now allocated the same space that previously was allocated to the variables x and a of block B. This is okay, since we are now outside the scope of those variables, and they will never again be referenced.

Finally, on entry into block D, the environment becomes

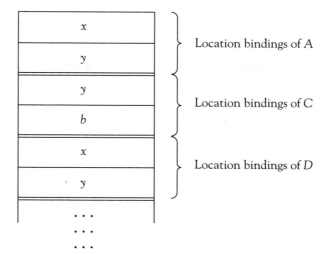

On exit from each block the location bindings of that block are successively deallocated, until, just prior to exit from block A, we have again recovered the original environment of A. In this way, the environment behaves like a stack. (Tradition has it that environments are drawn "upside down" from the usual way stacks are depicted.)

This behavior of the environment in allocating and deallocating space for begin-end blocks is relatively simple. Procedure and function blocks are more complicated. Consider the following procedure declaration in Pascal syntax:

```
procedure p;
var x: integer;
    y: real;
begin
   . . .
end; (* p *)
```

During execution, when this declaration is encountered, the block of p will not be executed, and the local variables x and y of p will not be allocated. Instead, the variables x and y will be allocated only when p is called. Also, each time p is called, new local variables will be allocated. Thus every call to p results in a region of memory being allocated in the environment. We refer to each call to p as an **activation** of p and the corresponding region of allocated memory as an **activation record.** A more complete description of the structure of activation records, and the information necessary to maintain them, is postponed to the discussion of procedures in Chapter 7.

It should be clear from these examples that, in a block-structured language with lexical scope, the same name may be associated with several different locations (though only one of these can be accessed at any one time). For instance, in the environment of the Algol60 block in the example, the name x is bound to two different locations during the execution of block D and the name y is bound to three different locations (though only the x and y of D are accessible at that time). We must therefore distinguish among a name, an allocated location, and the declaration that causes them to be bound. We will call the allocated location an **object.** That is, an object is an area of storage that is allocated in the environment as a result of the processing of a declaration. According to this definition, variables and procedures in Pascal are objects, but constants and data types are not (since type and constant declarations do not result in storage allocation).[7] The **lifetime** or **extent** of an object is the duration of its allocation in the environment. The lifetimes of objects can extend beyond the region of a program where they may be accessed. For example, in the Algol60 example, the declaration of integer x in block A defines an object whose lifetime extends through block B, even though the declaration has a scope hole in B, and the object is not accessible from inside B. Similarly, it is possible for the reverse to happen: an object can be accessible beyond its lifetime. (See Section 5.6.)

When pointers are available in a language, a further extension of the structure of the environment is necessary. A **pointer** is an object whose stored value is a reference to another object.

In Pascal the processing of the declaration

```
var  x:  ^integer;
```

by the environment causes the allocation of a pointer variable x. Although x is allocated by this declaration, it does not yet point to an allocated object. Indeed, x may have an undefined value, which could be any arbitrary location in memory. To permit the initialization of pointers that do not point to an allocated object, and to allow a program to determine whether a pointer variable points to allocated memory, Pascal contains the generic pointer value **nil,** which can be assigned to x to indicate that it does not yet point to an allocated object:

```
x  :=  nil;
```

Later, x can also be tested to determine if it has been allocated:

```
if  x  <>  nil  then  x^  :=  2  ;
```

For x to point to an allocated object, we must manually allocate it by the use of the **new** procedure. The call

```
new(x);
```

---

[7]This notion of object is not the same as that in object-oriented programming languages. See Chapter 9.

allocates a new integer variable and at the same time assigns its location to be the value of x. This new integer variable can be accessed by using the expression x^. The variable x is said to be **dereferenced** using the "^" operator. We can then assign integer values to x^ and refer to those values as we would with an ordinary variable, as in

```
x^ := 2;
writeln(x^);
```

x^ can be deallocated by calling the **dispose** procedure, as in

```
dispose(x);
```

In Modula-2, the situation is similar to Pascal, except that new and dispose procedures are not automatically available. Instead, procedures ALLOCATE and DEALLOCATE are imported from a library module Storage as follows:

```
MODULE StorageClient;
FROM Storage IMPORT ALLOCATE, DEALLOCATE;
    . . .
END StorageClient.
```

Inside a module that imports ALLOCATE and DEALLOCATE, an object pointed to by a pointer variable can be allocated and deallocated as follows:

```
TYPE IntPtr = POINTER TO INTEGER;
VAR x: IntPtr;
    . . .
ALLOCATE(x,SIZE(INTEGER));
    . . .
DEALLOCATE(x,SIZE(INTEGER));
```

(Some Modula-2 implementations also allow the use of NEW and DISPOSE in exactly the same way as Pascal, but they are interpreted as synonyms for the foregoing calls to ALLOCATE and DEALLOCATE, so these procedures must still be imported.)

In C the situation is similar, with the declaration

```
int * x;
```

creating an integer pointer variable x. To initialize x to a pointer that does not point to allocated space, we write

```
x = NULL;
```

(NULL is actually just a synonym for the number 0, which in C stands for the integer 0 and the nil pointer.)

To allocate an object and point x to it, we call the **malloc** function (for *memory allocation) and assign its returned value to x :

```
x = (int *) malloc(sizeof(int));
```

The malloc function returns the location it allocates and must be given the size of the data it is to allocate space for. This can be given in implementation-independent form using the **sizeof** function, which is given a data type and returns its (implementation-dependent) size. The malloc function must also be **cast** to the data type of the variable its result is being assigned to, by putting the data type in parentheses before the function. (Casts are explained in Section 6.7.)

When assigning to the object pointed to by x, the "*" is used to dereference x (like the "^" in Pascal, but on the other side):

```
*x = 2;
```

Finally, the **free** function is used in C to deallocate the object pointed to by x :

```
free(x);
```

To allow for arbitrary allocation and deallocation using new and dispose (or malloc and free), the environment must have an area in memory from which locations can be allocated in response to calls to new, and to which locations can be returned in response to calls to dispose. Such an area is traditionally called a **heap** (although it has nothing to do with the heap data structure). Allocation on the heap is usually referred to as **dynamic allocation,** even though allocation of local variables is also dynamic, as we have seen. To distinguish these two forms of dynamic allocation, allocation of local variables according to the stack-based scheme described earlier is sometimes called **stack-based** or **automatic,** since it occurs automatically under control of the runtime system. (A more appropriate term for pointer allocation using new and dispose might be manual allocation, since it occurs under "manual" programmer control.)

In a typical implementation of the environment, the stack (for automatic allocation) and the heap (for dynamic allocation) are kept at opposite ends of the memory available to a program, and each grows toward each other as new locations are allocated. Schematically, this layout of the environment looks as follows:

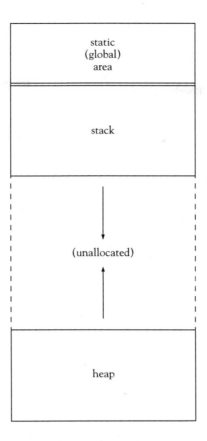

To summarize, in a block-structured language with pointers, there are three kinds of allocation in the environment: static (for global variables), automatic (for local variables), and dynamic (for pointers). These categories are also referred to as the **storage class** of the variable. Some languages, such as C, allow a declaration to specify a storage class as well as a data type. Typically, this is used in C to change the allocation of a local variable to static:

```
int f(void)
{static int x;
   . . .
}
```

Now x is allocated only once, and it has the same meaning (and value) in all calls to f. Algol68 also has storage class declarations, including stack and heap declarations.

We conclude this section with an extended example of the use of scope and extent to achieve certain properties of variables within a program.

Problem.   Write a function that returns a count of the number of times it is called.

Solution in Pascal.   Here is a solution in Pascal (together with some interesting code in the main program to test its behavior):

```
program count;
const n = 10; (* or any other positive integer *)
var pcount: integer; (* the no of times p is
                                          called *)
    i : integer;

function p: integer;
begin
  pcount := pcount + 1;
  p := pcount;
end;

begin (* main *)
  pcount := 0;
  for i := 1 to n do begin
    if p mod 3 <> 0 then writeln(p);
  end;
end.
```

A difficulty with this solution is that p cannot be written in a self-contained way; it depends on the global variable pcount, which must also be initialized in the main program. Indeed, pcount cannot be made local to p, as in

```
function p: integer;
var pcount: integer; (* wrong! *)
begin
  pcount := pcount + 1;
  p := pcount;
end;
```

because that would make pcount automatic, and its value would not be retained across calls to p (not to mention the problem of initializing pcount to 0).

Solution in Modula-2.   In Modula-2, as we have noted, the module is provided to limit scope. A module functions as a scope boundary, while retaining the extent characteristics of its surrounding block. Thus the counting program can be written with a better design in Modula-2:

```
MODULE Count;

FROM InOut IMPORT WriteCard, WriteLn;

    MODULE pcounter;
    EXPORT p;

    VAR pcount: CARDINAL;

    PROCEDURE p(): CARDINAL;
    BEGIN
      INC(pcount);
      RETURN pcount;
    END p;

    BEGIN (* pcounter *)
      pcount := 0;
    END pcounter;

  VAR i: CARDINAL;

BEGIN (* Count *)
  FOR i := 1 TO 10 DO
    IF p() MOD 3 <> 0 THEN
      WriteCard( p(), 1); WriteLn;
    END; (* IF *)
  END; (* FOR *)
END Count.
```

Procedure p is exported from the module pcounter since otherwise its scope would not extend to module Count. On the other hand, pcount is not exported, so it cannot be changed by Count.

Solution in C.   In C, the **static** storage class designator can be used to allow pcount to be put inside p, thus providing an even better solution:

```
int p(void)
{static int pcount = 0;
 return (pcount += 1);}

void main(void)
{int i;
 for (i=1;i<=10;i++)
    {if (p() % 3 != 0) printf("%d\n",p());}
}
```

In this solution, `pcount` cannot be referred to outside `p`, since it is local to `p`. However, `pcount` is allocated statically, and so retains its value across calls to `p`. (The initialization `p = 0` is also only performed once for static variables.)

5.5 VARIABLES AND CONSTANTS

5.5.1 Variables

A **variable** is an object whose stored value can change during execution. A variable can be thought of as being completely specified by its attributes, which include its name, its location, its value, and other attributes such as data type and size. A schematic representation of a variable can be drawn as follows:

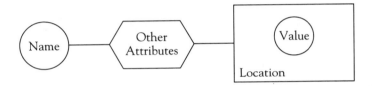

This picture singles out the name, location, and value of a variable as being its principal attributes. Often we will want to concentrate on these alone, and then we picture a variable in the following way:

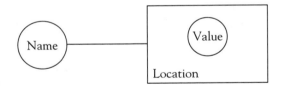

For want of a better term, we call this a **box-and-circle** diagram. The line drawn between the name and the location box can be thought of as representing the binding of the name to the location by the environment and the circle inside the box as representing the value bound by the memory, that is, the value stored at that location.

The principal way a variable changes its value is through the **assignment** statement $x := e$, where x is a variable name and e is an expression. The semantics of this statement are that e is evaluated to a value, which is then copied into the location of x. If e is a variable name, say, y, then the assignment

        x := y

can be viewed as follows (the double arrow stands for copying):

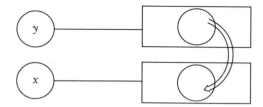

Since a variable has both a location and a value stored at that location, it is important to distinguish clearly between the two. However, this distinction is obscured in the assignment statement: y on the right-hand side stands for the value of y, while x on the left-hand side stands for the location of x. For this reason the value stored in the location of a variable is sometimes called its **r-value** (for right-hand side value), while the location of a variable is its **l-value** (for left-hand side value). Some languages, such as Algol68 and BLISS make a clearer distinction between r-values and l-values. Algol68 always considers a variable name to refer primarily to its location, or l-value. To access an r-value, a variable must be **dereferenced.** For example, the declaration

```
int x;
```

declares x to be a **reference** to an integer (called **ref int** mode in Algol68). To assign the value of x to another integer variable y, x is dereferenced as follows:

```
y := (int) x;
```

(The parenthesized type expression is a **cast;** see Chapter 6.) There is actually a rule that allows for **automatic dereferencing** as in Pascal, but it is still helpful to have the language make the distinction carefully.

In C a different approach is taken: dereferencing is assumed unless the operator "&" is given to fetch explicitly the location. Conversely, given an explicit location value, the operator "*" is provided to dereference it. Thus given the C declaration

```
int x;
```

&x is the address of x and *&x is the value of x. Also, C allows the mixing of expressions with assignments, where both the r-value and l-value of a variable are involved. Thus, to increment the integer x by 1, one can write either x = x + 1 or x += 1 (indicating that x is both added to 1 and reassigned).

In some languages a different meaning is given to assignment: locations are copied instead of values. In this case x := y has the result of binding the location of y to x instead of its value:

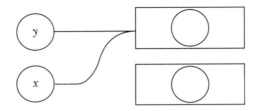

This is **assignment by sharing.** An alternative is to allocate a new location, copy the value of y, and bind x to the new location:

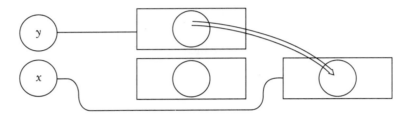

In both cases this interpretation of assignment is sometimes referred to as **pointer semantics** to distinguish it from the more usual semantics, which is sometimes referred to as **storage semantics.** A programming language that uses pointer semantics for assignment is SNOBOL. In some cases LISP also uses pointer semantics.

5.5.2   Constants

A **constant** is a language entity that has a fixed value for the duration of the program. A constant is like a variable, except that it has no explicit location, but a value only:

We sometimes say that a constant has **value semantics** instead of the storage semantics of a variable. This does not mean that a constant is not stored in memory. It is possible for a constant to have a value that is known only at execution time. In this case, its value must be stored in memory, but, unlike a variable, once this value is computed, it cannot change, and the location of the constant cannot be explicitly referred to by a program.

This notion of constant is **symbolic;** that is, a constant is essentially a name for a value. Sometimes representations of values, like the sequence of digits 42 or the representation of a character such as "a," are called constants. To distinguish them from the constants in a constant declaration, we sometimes refer to these representations of values as **literals.**

As we have noted, constants can be static or dynamic. A static constant is one whose value can be computed prior to execution, while a dynamic constant has a value that can be computed only during execution.

Pascal has only static constants. In fact, Pascal has the further restriction that only a literal can be used as the value of a constant in a constant declaration. Thus, in the declaration

```
const size  =  42;
      max  =  size  -  1;  (* illegal Pascal *)
```

the declaration of size is legal, but the declaration of max is illegal, since the value assigned to it is not a literal but an expression. Note that max is still a static constant. The only added complexity is that its value needs to be computed. Pascal makes this requirement to reduce the complexity of its compilers. A Pascal compiler can view constants as symbolic names for values that are given directly in the constant declaration, and all occurrences of the symbolic name in the program can therefore be immediately replaced by its value. For this reason, Pascal constants are sometimes referred to as **manifest constants.**

Modula-2 relaxes this restriction on constants, so that expressions may appear in constant declarations. For example, the following are all legal constant declarations in Modula-2:

```
CONST twoplusthree  =  2 + 3;
      size  =  42;
      max  =  size  -  1;
      a  =  twoplusthree  *  size DIV 5;
      e  =  2.7182836;
      x  =  1.0  /  e;
```

Constants in Modula-2 must still be static, however. Thus the declaration

```
CONST pi  =  4.0  *  arctan(1.0);
```

is illegal in Modula-2, since the code for the arctan function is not known at compile time (it is imported from a library module and linked after compilation). Indeed, Modula-2 restricts constant expressions so that they cannot contain function calls at all, even to predefined functions. Thus the following is also illegal in Modula-2:

```
CONST Null  =  CHR(0);
```

The reason for this is that CHR is not reserved and could be replaced by an unknown user-defined function.[8]

In Algol68 and Ada dynamic constants are allowed:

```
pi: constant FLOAT := 4.0 * arctan(1.0);
```

is a legal Ada constant. So is the following local constant declaration:

```
procedure Swap (x,y: in out INTEGER) is
   temp: constant INTEGER := x;
begin
  x := y;
  y := temp;
end Swap;
```

5.6   ALIASES, DANGLING REFERENCES, AND GARBAGE

This section describes several of the problems that arise with the naming and allocation conventions of programming languages, particularly the standard block-structured languages Pascal, Modula-2, Ada, and C. Language design solutions can be found to many of these problems—as opposed to programmer solutions, which are to avoid the problematic situations—and a few of these will be discussed.

5.6.1   Aliases

An alias occurs when the same object is bound to two different names at the same time. Aliasing can occur in several ways. One is during procedure call and is studied in Chapter 7. Another is through the use of pointer variables. A simple example in Pascal is given by the following code:

```
type intptr = ^integer;
var x,y: intptr;

begin
  new(x);
  x^ := 1;
```

---

[8]This has the unpleasant consequence that nonprinting characters cannot be written in constant declarations so Modula-2 offers a way out, allowing nonprinting characters to be represented by their ASCII values with a "C" placed at the end:

```
CONST Null = 0C;
      Return = 15C; (* Octal for CHR(13) *)
```

```
y := x; (* x^ and y^ now aliases *)
y^ := 2;
 writeln(x^);
end;
```

After the assignment of x to y, y^ and x^ both refer to the same variable, and the preceding code prints 2. We can see this clearly if we record the effect of the above code in our box-and-circle diagrams of Section 5.5, as follows.

After the declarations, both x and y have been allocated in the environment, but the values of both are undefined. We indicate that in the following diagram by shading in the circles indicating values:

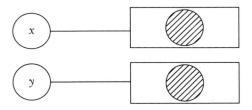

After the call to new (x), x^ has been allocated, and x has been assigned a value equal to the location of x^, but x^ is still undefined:

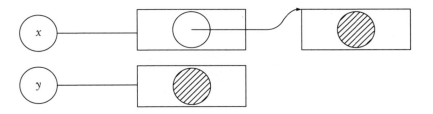

After the assignment x^ := 1, the situation is as follows:

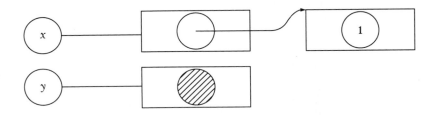

The assignment y := x now copies the value of x to y, and so makes y^ and x^ aliases of each other (note that x and y are not aliases of each other):

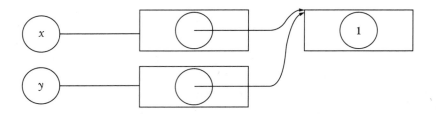

Finally, the assignment y ^ : = 2 results in the following diagram:

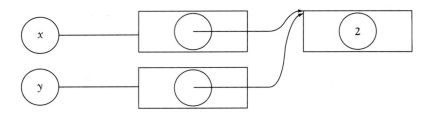

Aliases present a problem in that they cause potentially harmful **side effects.** For our purposes, we define a side effect of a statement to be any change in the value of a variable that persists beyond the execution of the statement.[9] From this definition, side effects are not all harmful, since an assignment is explicitly intended to cause one. However, side effects that are changes to variables whose names do not directly appear in the statement *are* potentially harmful in that the side effect cannot be determined from the written code. In the preceding example, the assignment y ^ = 2 also changed x ^, even though no hint of that change appears in the statement that causes it. One must instead read the previous code to discover that this is happening.

Aliasing due to pointer assignment is difficult to control and is one of the reasons that programming with pointers is so difficult. One language that does attempt to limit aliasing, not only by pointers, but throughout the language, is Euclid. See the references at the end of the chapter.

FORTRAN also provides an explicit mechanism for aliasing: the EQUIVALENCE statement. Thus

```
EQUIVALENCE X,Y
```

causes X and Y to be aliases of each other, so that an assignment to x causes an implicit assignment to y, and vice versa. In the early days of programming, the EQUIVALENCE statement was used to reduce the amount of memory needed for a large program by sharing memory locations among variables that were not used at the same time. Today the use of this statement would be considered poor design. COMMON statements in FORTRAN can also cause aliasing. See Exercise 3.

---

[9]Other definitions of side effect exist. See Exercise 22.

5.6.2   Dangling References

Dangling references are a second problem that can arise from the use of pointers. A dangling reference is a location that has been deallocated from the environment, but that can still be accessed by a program. Another way of stating this is that a dangling reference occurs if an object can be accessed beyond its lifetime in the environment.

A simple example of a dangling reference is a pointer that points to a deallocated object. In Pascal, the use of the `dispose` procedure can cause a dangling reference, as follows:

```
type intptr = ^integer;
var x,y: intptr;
  . . .
new(x);
  . . .
x^ := 2;
  . . .
y := x; (* y^ and x^ now aliases *)
dispose(x); (* y^ now a dangling reference *)
  . . .
writeln(y^); (* illegal! *)
```

In C, it is also possible for dangling references to result from the automatic deallocation of local variables when the block of the local declaration is exited. This is because C has an "address of" operator "&" that allows the location of any variable to be assigned to a pointer variable. Consider the following C code fragment:

```
{int * x;
 {int y;
  y = 2;
  x = &y;}
  /* *x is now a dangling reference */
}
```

When we exit the block in which y is declared in the code, the variable x contains the location of y, and the variable *x is an alias of y. But in the standard stack-based environment we described in Section 5.4, y has been deallocated on exit from the block. A similar example is the following C code:

```
int * dangle(void)
{int x;
 return &x;}
```

Whenever function `dangle` is called, it returns the location of its local automatic variable x, which has just been deallocated. Thus, after any assignment such as y = `dangle()`, the variable *y will be a dangling reference.

Pascal does not permit this kind of dangling reference, since it has no function equivalent to the "&" function of C. Modula-2 *does* have a similar function, called ADR. However, this and other low-level facilities can be used in a program only if they are explicitly imported from a SYSTEM module. Modules that import from SYSTEM are thus clearly marked as being inherently unsafe.

5.6.3 Garbage

One easy way to eliminate the dangling reference problem is simply to not perform any deallocation at all from the environment. This causes the third problem that we discuss in this section, namely, garbage. Garbage is memory that has been allocated in the environment but that has become inaccessible to the program.

A typical way for garbage to occur in Pascal is to fail to call dispose before reassigning a pointer variable:

```
var x: ^integer;
  . . .
new(x);
x := nil;
```

At the end of this code, the location allocated to x^ by the call to new(x) is now garbage, since x now contains the nil pointer, and there is no way to access the previously allocated object. A similar situation occurs when execution leaves the region of the program in which x itself is allocated, as in

```
procedure p;
var x: ^integer;
begin
  new(x);
  x^ := 2;
end;
```

When procedure p is exited, the variable x is deallocated and x^ is no longer accessible by the program. A similar situation occurs in other kinds of blocks, for example, in the following C fragment:

```
{...
  {int * x;
    x = (int *) malloc(sizeof(int));
    ...}
  /* *x no longer accessible here */
}
```

Garbage is a problem in program execution because it is wasted memory. However, an argument can be made that programs that produce garbage are less seriously flawed than programs that contain dangling references. A program that produces garbage may fail to run because it runs out of memory, but it is internally correct; that is, if it does not exceed available memory, it will produce correct results (or at least not be incorrect because of the failure to deallocate inaccessible memory). A program that accesses dangling references, on the other hand, may run but produce incorrect results, may corrupt other programs in memory, or may cause runtime errors that are hard to locate.

For this reason it is useful to remove the need to deallocate memory explicitly from the programmer (which, if done incorrectly, can cause dangling references), while at the same time automatically reclaiming garbage for further use. Language systems that automatically reclaim garbage are said to perform **garbage collection.**

We should note that the stack-based management of memory in the environment of a block-structured language can already be called a kind of simple garbage collection: when the scope of an automatic variable declaration is exited, the environment reclaims the location allocated to that variable by "popping" the memory allocated for the variable.

Historically, functional language systems, particularly LISP systems, pioneered garbage collection as a method for managing the runtime deallocation of memory. Indeed, in LISP, all allocation as well as deallocation is performed automatically. Object-oriented language systems also often rely on garbage collectors for the reclamation of memory during program execution. This is the case for Smalltalk, Simula67, and Eiffel (C + + is the notable exception, where the allocation and deallocation rules of C are retained).

Language design is a key factor in what kind of runtime environment is necessary for the correct execution of programs. Nevertheless, the language design itself may not explicitly state what kind of memory allocation is required. For example, the definition of Algol60 introduced block structure, and so implicitly advocated the use of a stack-based environment, without explicitly describing or requiring it. Definitions of LISP have also not mentioned garbage collection, even though a typical LISP system cannot execute reasonably without it.

One way for the designer of an Algol-like language to indicate the need for automatic garbage collection would be to include in the language definition a **new** procedure for pointers, but fail to include a corresponding **dispose** procedure. Simula67 takes this approach. So does Ada.

In Ada, a pointer variable is called an **access** variable and is defined as follows:

```
type intptr is access INTEGER;
x: intptr;
```

In Ada, the declaration of x automatically initializes it to **null,** and the object pointed to by x is allocated by the statement

```
x := new intptr;
```

Deallocation of x cannot be performed manually, however, unless we explicitly declare the type of x to be under programmer control, in the compiler directive

```
PRAGMA CONTROLLED(intptr);
```

Then, we must import the generic procedure UNCHECKED_DE-ALLOCATION and specialize it for use with intptr, as follows:

```
procedure DisposeIntptr is new
            UNCHECKED_DEALLOCATION(INTEGER,intptr);
```

(This is an example of the instantiation of a generic procedure in Ada, which is studied in Section 8.5.) Now x can be deallocated by the statement

```
DisposeIntptr(x);
```

Thus the design of Ada supports the use of a garbage collector, while at the same time allowing a programmer to use the more typical manual deallocation strategy of Pascal or C.

5.7 EXPRESSION EVALUATION

Programming languages often distinguish between **expressions** and **statements:** expressions, in their pure form, return a value and produce no side effects, that is, no change to program memory. Statements, on the other hand, are executed for their side effects and return no value. Sometimes expressions have side effects as well as return values, and there are languages that are **expression languages,** where language constructs return values and are executed both for these values and for side effects. C, Algol68, and functional languages like LISP are such languages. For example, in C the assignment x = y also returns the value of y, so that

```
x = (y = z)
```

assigns the value of z to both x and y. The same expression in Algol68 is x := (y := z). Note that in such languages, assignment can be considered to be a binary operator similar to arithmetic operators. In that case its precedence is usually lower than all such operators, and it is made right associative. Thus

```
x = y = z + w
```

in C assigns the sum of z and w to both x and y.

Expressions contain operators and operands. Operators are functions, and operands are arguments. Operators can be **predefined (built in)** or user defined. Operators can take one or more operands: an operator that takes one operand is called a **unary operator;** an operator that takes two is a **binary** operator. Operators can be written in **infix, postfix,** or **prefix** notation, corresponding to an inorder, postorder, or preorder traversal of the syntax tree of the expression. For example, the infix expression 3 + 4 · 5 with syntax tree (see Chapter 4)

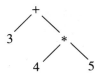

is written in postfix form as 3 4 5 · + and in prefix form as + 3 · 4 5.

Postfix and prefix forms have the advantage that parentheses are not necessary to express the order in which operators are applied, so operator precedence (see Chapter 4) is not required to disambiguate an unparenthesized expression. For instance, (3 + 4) · 5 is written in postfix form as 3 4 + 5 · and in prefix form as · + 3 4 5. Associativity of operators is also expressed directly in postfix and prefix form without the need for a rule. For example, the postfix expression 3 4 5 + + right associates and 3 4 + 5 + left associates the infix expression 3 + 4 + 5.

Most programming languages use prefix form for predefined unary operators and infix form for predefined binary operators, with specified associativity and precedence rules. However, user-defined functions can in these same languages often be written only in prefix form. For example, the Pascal function with declaration

```
function add(x,y: integer): integer;
```

must be applied using the following syntax:

```
c := add(a,b);
```

It cannot be written as c := a add b, as the predefined function "+" can.

A few languages such as Ada and Algol68 allow limited facilities for functions to be declared infix:

```
function "*" (a,b: MATRIX) return MATRIX is
    . . .
```

declares a matrix product in Ada as an infix operator having the same symbol as the usual multiplication, and it can be applied using the usual syntax for "*":

```
declare a,b,c: MATRIX;
   . . .
c := a * b;
```

Object-oriented languages such as Smalltalk and C++ also have mechanisms for allowing user-defined functions to be written in infix form.

LISP, however, uses prefix form consistently both for predefined and user-defined functions and requires expressions to be **fully parenthesized;** that is, all operators and operands must be enclosed in parentheses. This is because LISP operators can take variable numbers of arguments as operands. Thus 3 + 4 · 5 and (3 + 4) · 5 would look as follows in LISP:

```
(+ 3 (* 4 5))
(* (+ 3 4) 5)
```

Each programming language has rules for evaluating expressions. A common evaluation rule is that all operands are evaluated first and then operators are applied to them. This is called **applicative order evaluation,** or sometimes **strict** evaluation, and is the most common rule in programming languages. It corresponds to a bottom-up evaluation of the values at nodes of the syntax tree representing an expression. For example, the expression (3 + 4) · (5 − 6) is represented by the syntax tree

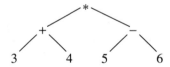

In applicative order evaluation, first the "+" and "−" nodes are evaluated to 7 and −1, respectively, and then the "·" is applied to get −7.

Let us also consider how this appears in terms of user-defined functions, written in prefix form. In Pascal syntax, the expression is

```
times(plus(3,4),minus(5,6))
```

Applicative order says evaluate the arguments first. Thus calls to plus(3,4) and minus(5,6) are made, which are also evaluated using applicative order. Then, the calls are replaced by their returned values, which are 7 and −1. Finally, the call

```
times(7,−1)
```

is made.

One question to be answered is in which order the subexpressions (3 + 4) and (5 − 6) are computed, or in which order the calls plus(3,4) and minus(5,6) are made. A natural order is left to right, corresponding to a left-to-right traversal of the syntax tree. However, many languages explicitly state that there is no specified order for the evaluation of arguments to user-defined functions, and the same is sometimes also true for predefined operators.

There are several reasons for this. One is that different machines may have different requirements for the structure of calls to procedures and functions. Another is that a translator may attempt to rearrange the order of computation so that it is more efficient. For example, consider the expression $(3 + 4) \cdot (3 + 4)$. A translator may discover that the same subexpression, namely, $3 + 4$, is used twice and will evaluate it only once. And in evaluating a call such as max(3,4+5), a translator may evaluate $4 + 5$ before 3 because it is more efficient to evaluate more complicated expressions first.

If the evaluation of an expression causes no side effects, then the expression will yield the same result, regardless of the order of evaluation of its subexpressions. Similarly, if the evaluation of the arguments of a function or procedure call causes no side effects, then the order of evaluation is immaterial. In the presence of side effects, however, the order of evaluation can make a difference. Consider, for example, the following Pascal program:

```
program sideEffect;
var x: integer;

function f: integer;
begin
  x := x + 1;
  f := x;
end;

function p(a,b: integer):integer;
begin
  p := b+a;
end;

begin
  x := 1;
  writeln(p(f,x));
end.
```

If the arguments of the call to p in the writeln statement are evaluated left to right, this program will print 4. If the arguments are evaluated right to left, the program will print 3. The reason is that a call to the function f has a side effect: it changes the value of the global variable x.

Similarly, in the C code

```
int f(int a, int b)
{return b+a;}

void main(void)
{int x,y;
 x = 1;
 y = f(x,x=x+1);}
```

the variable y will get the value 3 if the arguments to f are evaluated left to right and the value 4 if the sum is evaluated right to left.

In a language that explicitly states that the order of evaluation of arguments and/or expressions is unspecified, programs that depend on the order of evaluation for their results are incorrect, even though they may have predictable behavior for one or more translators.

The evaluation of an expression can sometimes be performed even without the evaluation of all its subexpressions. An interesting case is that of the Boolean, or logical, expressions. For example, the Boolean expressions

```
true or x
```

and

```
x or true
```

are true regardless of whether x is true or false. Similarly,

```
false and x
```

and

```
x and false
```

are clearly false regardless of the value of x. In a programming language one can specify that Boolean expressions are to be evaluated in left to right order, up to the point where the truth value of the entire expression becomes known and then the evaluation stops. A programming language that has this rule is said to possess **short-circuit evaluation** of Boolean or logical expressions.

Short-circuit evaluation has a number of benefits. One is that a test for the validity of an array index can be written in the same expression as a test of its subscripted value, as long as the range test occurs first:

```
if (i <= lastindex) and (a[i] = x) then ...
```

Without short-circuit evaluation, the test i <= lastindex will not prevent an error from occurring if i > lastindex, since the expression a[i] in the second part of the expression will still be computed. (This assumes, of course, that an out-of-range array subscript *will* produce an error.) Without short-circuit evaluation, the test must be written using nested if's:

```
if (i <= lastindex) then if (a[i] = x) then ...
```

Similarly, a test for a nil pointer can be made in the same expression as a dereference of that pointer, using short-circuit evaluation:

```
if (p <> nil) and (p^.data = x) then ...
```

Note that the order of the tests becomes important in short-circuit evaluation. Short-circuit evaluation will protect us from a runtime error if we write

```
if (x <> 0) and (y mod x = 0) then (* ok *)
```

but not if we write

```
if (y mod x = 0) and (x <> 0) then (* not ok! *)
```

In Pascal, the Boolean operators **and** and **or** are not short-circuit, but in Modula-2 AND and OR are short-circuit. In C the corresponding logical operators "&&" and "||" are also short-circuit. Ada has both short-circuit and non-short-circuit Boolean operators: the usual **and** and **or** operators are not short-circuit, while the corresponding short-circuit operators are written **and then** and **or else**:

```
if (i <= lastindex) and then (a(i) = x) then ...
```

Formally, we can define the short-circuit Boolean operators using a Boolean **if-then-else** operator as follows. The if-then-else operator has three arguments and is written

$$\text{if } a \text{ then } b \text{ else } c$$

It has the following semantics. First, a is evaluated. If the value of a is true, then b is evaluated and the value of b is the value of the expression. If the value of a is false, then c is evaluated, and the value of c is the value of the expression. We can now define the short-circuit Boolean operators, which we will call **cand** and **cor** (for conditional and and or) to distinguish them from the standard operators, as follows:

$$a \text{ cand } b = \text{if } a \text{ then } b \text{ else false}$$
$$a \text{ cor } b = \text{if } a \text{ then true else } b$$

Short-circuit Boolean operators are a special case of operators that **delay** evaluating their arguments. The general situation is called **delayed**

evaluation. In the case of the short-circuit operators, a cand b and a cor b both delay the evaluation of b until a is evaluated. Similarly, the Boolean if-then-else operator delays the evaluation of both b and c until a is evaluated.

One form of delayed evaluation that has important theoretical and practical consequences, especially for functional languages, is **normal order evaluation,** in which the evaluation of each argument or subexpression is delayed until it is actually needed in the computation of the result. One way of interpreting the normal order evaluation rule for functions is by textual substitution of the arguments into the body of the function.[10]

Consider the following example in Pascal syntax:

```
function sq(x: integer) : integer;
begin
  sq := x * x;
end;
```

If sq uses normal order evaluation for its argument, and if we call the sq function as follows,

```
sq(3+4)
```

this will have the result of substituting the expression $3 + 4$ into the code of sq without first evaluating it:

```
sq(3+4)  =  (3+4)*(3+4)
```

Only after this substitution is made will $3 + 4$ be evaluated. Note that this differs from applicative order evaluation in that $3 + 4$ is evaluated twice instead of once.

Exercises

1. Assume the language Pascal, C, or Modula-2. Give as precise binding times as you can for the following attributes, and give reasons for your answers:

---

[10]This interpretation is not accurate when the arguments contain names that may clash with local declarations of the function being called or when the meanings of the names can change between the place in the program where the expression is evaluated and the place where the function is declared. See the explanation of pass by name in Chapter 7.

(a) The number of significant digits of a real number
(b) The meaning of **char**
(c) The size of an array variable
(d) The size of an array parameter
(e) The location of a local variable
(f) The value of a constant
(g) The location of a function

2. Discuss the meaning of the following statement: early binding promotes security and efficiency, while late binding promotes flexibility and expressiveness.

3. In FORTRAN, global variables are created using a COMMON statement, but it is not required that the global variables have the same name in each subroutine or function. Thus, in the code

```
FUNCTION F
COMMON N
   . . .
END

SUBROUTINE S
COMMON M
   . . .
END
```

Variable N in function F and variable M in subroutine S share the same memory, so they behave as different names for the same global variable.
   (a) Compare this method of creating global variables to that of Pascal or C. How is it better? How is it worse?
   (b) Describe the difference between variables that are COMMON and variables that are EQUIVALENCEd.

4. In Pascal there is no distinction between global variables and those local to the main program. Is this distinction made in C? Modula-2? FORTRAN? Is such a distinction useful? Why or why not?

5. Compare the advantages and disadvantages of Pascal's declaration before use rule with Modula-2's rule that extends the scope of a declaration to the entire block, regardless of its position in the block.

6. Describe the bindings performed by a Pascal **forward** declaration. Why is such a declaration necessary?

7. Describe the bindings performed by a C **extern** declaration. Why is such a declaration necessary?

8. The C language makes a distinction between a **declaration** and a **definition**: a declaration binds data type but not location, while a definition binds both data type and location.
   (a) Is a **typedef** in C a declaration or a definition?
   (b) Is a Pascal type declaration a declaration or a definition?

(c) Is a Pascal variable declaration a declaration or a definition?

(d) Is a Pascal forward declaration a declaration or a definition?

9. Describe the scopes of the declarations in the following Pascal program. How would the scopes change using dynamic instead of static scoping? What does the program print in each case?

```pascal
program scope;
var a,b: integer;

function p: integer;
var a: integer;
begin
  a := 0; b := 1; p := 2;
end;

procedure print;
begin
  writeln(a); writeln(b); writeln(p);
end;

procedure q;
var b,p: integer;
begin
  a := 3; b := 4; p := 5; print;
end;

begin
  a := p;
  q;
end.
```

10. Using the organization of the symbol table described in the text, show the symbol table for the program of the previous exercise when the blocks of function p, procedure q, and the main program are processed (a) using static scope, and (b) using dynamic scope.

11. Describe the scopes of the declarations in the following C program. How would the scopes change using dynamic instead of static scoping? What does the program print in each case?

```c
int a,b;

int p(void)
{int a,p;
  /* point 1 */
  a = 0; b = 1; p = 2;
  return p;}
```

```
void print(void)
{printf("%d\n%d\n",a,b);}

void q(void)
{int b;
  /* point 2 */
  a = 3; b = 4;
  print();}

void main(void)
{/* point 3 */
  a = p();
  q();}
```

12. Show the symbol table for the program of the previous exercise at the points indicated by the comments (a) using static scope and (b) using dynamic scope.

13. Describe the scopes of the declarations of the following Modula-2 program:

```
MODULE M;
VAR x,y: INTEGER;

        MODULE N;
        IMPORT x; EXPORT z,w;
        VAR y,z: INTEGER;

                MODULE P;
                IMPORT x,y; EXPORT w;
                VAR z,w: INTEGER;
                . . .
                END P;

        . . .
        END N;

        MODULE Q;
        IMPORT y;
        VAR x,z,w: INTEGER;
        . . .
        END Q;
  . . .
  END M.
```

14. Describe the problem with dynamic scoping and static typing. Does a similar problem exist with static scoping and dynamic typing? Why?

15. Many programming languages, such as C, Modula-2, and Pascal, prohibit the same name to be redeclared in the same scope. Discuss the reasons for this rule.

16. Sometimes the symbol table is called the **static environment.** Discuss the validity of this viewpoint.

17. Is extent the same as dynamic scope? Why or why not?

18. An alternative organization for the symbol table in a block-structured language to that described in the text is to have only one stack. All declarations of all names are pushed onto this stack as they are encountered and popped when their scopes are exited. Then, given a name, its currently valid declaration is the first one found for that name in a top-down search of the stack.
    (a) Redo Exercise 10 with this organization for the symbol table.
    (b) Sometimes this organization of the symbol table is called **deep binding,** while the organization described in the text is called **shallow binding.** Discuss the reason for these terms. Should one of these organizations be required by the semantics of a programming language? Explain.

19. Execute the following Pascal program, and explain the resulting output:

```
program extent;

procedure p;
var y: integer;
begin
  writeln(y);
  y := 2;
end;

begin
  p; p;
end.
```

20. Execute the following C program and explain the resulting output:

```
void main(void)
{
  { int x;
    printf("%d\n",x);
    x = 1;
  }
  {int y;
    printf("%d\n",y);
  }
}
```

21. Explain the difference between aliasing and side effects.

22. A common definition of side effect is a change to a nonlocal variable or to the input or output made by a function or procedure. Compare this definition of side effect to the one in the text.

23. Given the following Pascal program, draw box-and-circle diagrams of the variables after the assignment to $x^{\wedge\wedge}$. Which variables are aliases of each other at that point? What does the program print?

```
program alias;
type
   intptr = ^integer;
   ptrptr = ^intptr;
var
   x: ptrptr;
   y: intptr;
   z: integer;
begin
   new(x);
   new(y);
   z := 1;
   y^ := 2;
   x^ := y;
   x^^ := z;
   writeln(y^);
   z := 3;
   writeln(y^);
   x^^ := 4;
   writeln(z);
end.
```

24. Explain the reason for the two calls to new in the previous exercise. What would be printed if the call to `new(x)` were left out? The call to `new(y)`?

25. A generalization of the notion of a constant in a programming language is that of a **single-assignment variable:** a variable whose value can be computed at any point but that can be assigned to only once, so that it must remain constant once it is computed. Discuss the usefulness of this generalization compared to constant declarations in Pascal, Modula-2, or Ada. How does this concept relate to that of a dynamic constant as discussed in Section 5.5?

26. In Ada, an object is defined as follows: "An object is an entity that contains a value of a given type." This is interpreted to mean that there are two kinds of objects: constants and variables. Compare this notion of object with that of Section 5.4.

27. Why is the following C code illegal:

```
{int x;
 &x = (int *) malloc(sizeof(int));
 ...}
```

28. Pointers in a programming language are generally used with records to define recursive, dynamic data structures such as lists and trees. In these cases, pointers always point to records, as in the following declaration of a linked list of integers:

```
type link = ^listrec;
     listrec = record
                   data: integer;
                   next: link;
               end;
```

Suppose we decided to restrict the declaration of pointers to pointers to records, so that the declaration

```
type ptr1 = ^integer;
```

is illegal but the declaration of link above remains legal. Discuss the advantages and disadvantages of such a restriction.

29. Rewrite the following infix expression in prefix and postfix and draw the syntax tree:

```
(3 - 4) / 5 + 6 * 7
```

30. Write a BNF description of (a) postfix arithmetic expressions and (b) prefix arithmetic expressions.

31. Modify the recursive descent parser for infix arithmetic expressions of Chapter 4 to translate infix expressions to postfix expressions.

32. In LISP the following unparenthesized prefix expression is ambiguous:

```
+ 3 * 4 5 6
```

Why? Give two possible parenthesized interpretations.

33. Some Pascal compilers use short-circuit evaluation of Booleans even though Standard Pascal defines the Boolean operators as non-short-circuit. Write a program to test your Pascal compiler for short-circuit evaluation of both **and** and **or**.

34. Examples were given in the text that show the usefulness of a short-circuit **and** operation. Give an example to show the usefulness of a short-circuit **or** operation.

35. Write a program to prove that short-circuit evaluation is used for (a) the logical operators of C and (b) the Boolean operators of Modula-2.

36. Write a program to determine the order of evaluation of function parameters in (a) Pascal, (b) Modula-2, and (c) C.

37. Test the following program on your FORTRAN compiler. Try to explain its behavior.

```
logical f
if (.false..and.(sqrt(-1.0).gt.0.0)) then
  print *,'ok'
else
  print *,'not-ok'
endif
if (.false..and.f()) then
  print *,'ok'
else
  print *,'not-ok'
endif
if (f().and.(sqrt(-1.0).gt.0.0)) then
  print *,'ok'
else
  print *,'not-ok'
endif
end
logical function f()
  print *,'in f!'
  f = .false.
end
```

38. We noted in Chapter 4 that the "+" operator is left associative, so that in the expression $a + b + c$, the expression $a + b$ is computed and then added to c. Yet we stated in Section 5.7 that an expression $a + b$ may be computed by computing b before a. Is there a contradiction here? Does your answer also apply to the subtraction operator?

39. Suppose we were to try write a short-circuit version of **and** in Pascal as the following function:

```
function cand (a,b: boolean) : boolean;
begin
  if a then cand := b else cand := false;
end;
```

(a) Why doesn't this work?
(b) Would it work if normal order evaluation were used? Why?

40. Describe one benefit of normal order evaluation. Describe one drawback.

41. Consider the expressions

```
(x <> 0) and (y mod x = 0)
```

and

```
(y mod x = 0) and (x <> 0)
```

In theory, both these expressions could have value false if x = 0.

(a) Which of these expressions has a value in Pascal?

(b) Which of these expressions has a value in Modula-2?

(c) Would it be possible for a programming language to require that both have values? Explain.

Notes and References

Most of the concepts in this chapter were pioneered in the design of Algol60 (Naur [1963a]), except for pointer allocation. Pointer allocation was, however, a part of the design of Algol68 (Tanenbaum [1976]). Some of the consequences of the design decisions of Algol60, including the introduction of recursion, may not have been fully understood at the time they were made (Naur [1981]), but certainly by 1964 full implementations of Algol60 existed, which used most of the techniques of today's translators (Randell and Russell [1964]). For more detail on these techniques, consult Chapter 7 and a compiler text such as Aho, Sethi, and Ullman [1986].

Structured programming, which makes use of the block structure in an Algol-like language, became popular some time later than the appearance of the concept in language design (Dahl, Dijkstra, and Hoare [1972]). For an interesting perspective on block structure, see Hanson [1981].

The distinction that C makes between definition and declaration, described in Exercise 8 is explained in detail in Kernighan and Ritchie [1988]. The effect of a declaration during execution, including its use in allocation, is called **elaboration** in Ada.

The notion of an object has almost as many definitions as there are programming languages. For different definitions than the one used in this chapter, see Exercise 26 and Chapter 9. The notions of symbol table, environment, and memory also change somewhat from language to language. For a more formal, albeit simple, example of an environment function, see Chapter 12. For a more detailed discussion of the theoretical representation of environments, see Meyer [1990]. For a more detailed description of environments in the presence of procedure calls, see Chapter 7.

Aliases and the design of the programming language Euclid, which attempts to remove all aliasing, are discussed in Popek et al. [1977] (see also Lampson et al. [1981]). Techniques for garbage collection and automatic storage management have historically been so inefficient that their use in imperative languages has been resisted. With modern advances, that may be changing. For example, the design of Ada promotes garbage collection, and some Algol-like object-oriented languages such as Modula-3 (Cardelli et al. [1989a,b]) and Eiffel (Meyer [1988]) require it. For an amusing anecdote on the early use of garbage collection, see McCarthy [1981, p. 183]. Garbage collection techniques are studied in Chapter 9.

Normal and applicative order evaluation is described in Abelson and Sussman [1985] and Wikström [1987]. We will see normal order evaluation again in Chapter 7 in the pass by name parameter passing mechanism of Algol60 and also in Chapter 10 when discussing delayed evaluation and the lambda calculus.

6 DATA TYPES

*E*very program uses data, either explicitly or implicitly, to arrive at a result. Data in a program is collected into data structures, which are manipulated by control structures that represent an algorithm. This is clearly expressed by the following pseudoequation (an equation that isn't mathematically exact but expresses the underlying principles),

$$\text{algorithms} + \text{data structures} = \text{programs}$$

which comes from the title of a book by Niklaus Wirth (Wirth [1976]). How a programming language expresses data and control largely determines how programs are written in the language. The present chapter studies the concept of data type as the basic concept underlying the representation of data in programming languages, while the next chapter studies control.

Data in its most primitive form inside a computer is just a collection of bits. A programming language could take this view as its basis and build up all data from it. This would in essence provide a virtual machine (that is, a simulation of actual hardware) as part of the definition of the language. But this would be complex and inefficient and would not provide the abstraction and machine independence that programming languages attempt to provide. Instead most programming languages provide a set of simple data entities, such as integers, reals, and Booleans, as well as mechanisms for constructing new data entities from these.

Such abstractions are an essential mechanism in programming

languages and contribute to almost every design goal: readability, writability, reliability, and machine independence. However, we should also be aware of the pitfalls to which such abstraction can lead. One is that machine dependencies are almost inevitably part of the implementation of these abstractions, and the language definition will often not address these because they are hidden in the basic abstractions.

An example of this is the **finiteness** of all data in a computer, which is masked by the abstractions. For example, when we speak of integer data we often think of integers in the mathematical sense as an infinite set: . . ., -2, -1, 0, 1, 2, . . ., but in a computer there is always a largest and smallest integer. Often this is ignored in the definition of a programming language, and it then becomes a machine dependency.

A similar situation arises with the precision of real numbers and the behavior of real arithmetic operations. This is a difficult problem for the language designer to address, since simple data types and arithmetic are usually built into hardware. A recent positive development has been the establishment by the Institute of Electrical and Electronics Engineers (IEEE) of a floating-point standard that attempts to reduce the dependency of real number operations on the hardware. It may be reasonable to include similar specifications in a programming language definition as well. So far, Ada is one of the few languages to do so.

Despite these problems, the use of abstraction to describe data contributes enormous power and usefulness to programming languages. Our viewpoint of data in programming languages will begin with the notion of **data type,** the basic abstraction mechanism, and the principal types and type constructors available in programming languages.

6.1   DATA TYPES AND TYPE INFORMATION

Program data can be classified according to their **types.** For example, the value -1 is of type integer, and 3.14159 is of type real. The inclusion of types into the definition of a programming language is important for reliability, readability, and maintainability: it allows the translator to determine whether the type of a value or object is correct (**type checking**), and it permits the programmer and the translator to draw conclusions about the ways in which values can be used and the operations that can be applied to them.

In Chapter 5 we saw that the types of variables are often associated with variables by a declaration, such as

```
var x: integer;
```

which assigns data type integer to the variable x. In a declaration like this, a type is just a name, which carries with it some properties, such as the kinds of values that can be stored, and the way these values are represented internally.

Since the internal representation is a system-dependent feature, from the abstract point of view, we can consider a type name to represent the possible values that a variable of that type can hold. Even more abstractly, we can consider the type name to be essentially identical to the set of values it represents, and we can state the following:

> **Definition 1.** A **data type** is a set of values.

A data type as a set can be specified in many ways: it can be explicitly listed or enumerated; it can be given as a subrange of otherwise known values; or it can be borrowed from mathematics, in which case the finiteness of the set in an actual implementation may be left vague or ignored. Set operations can also be applied to get new sets out of old (see Section 6.3).

EXAMPLE

Pascal has a predefined constant maxint that is system dependent and is the largest integer representable on the system. Thus integer type in Pascal includes the range 0..maxint and usually is (-maxint-1)..maxint, if the underlying representation is in two's complement form. On small computers two bytes are often used for storing integers, and then maxint = 32767 and the integers range from -32768 to 32767. In Modula-2 MAX and MIN predefined functions give the largest and smallest values of a data type, so that in this case MAX(INTEGER) = 32767 and MIN(INTEGER) = -32768. ∎

A set of values generally also has a group of operations that can be applied to the values. These operations are often not mentioned explicitly with the type, but are part of its definition. Examples include the arithmetic operations on integers or reals, successor and predecessor operations on enumerations, and field dereferencing operations on record types. These operations also have specific properties that may or may not be explicitly stated [e.g., succ(pred(x)) = x or x+y = y+x]. Thus we may want to revise our first definition to include explicitly the operations, as in the following definition:

> **Definition 2.** A **data type** is a set of values, together with a set of operations on those values having certain properties.

In this sense, a data type is actually a mathematical **algebra,** but we will not pursue this view here. (For a brief look at algebras, see the mathematics of abstract data types in Chapter 8.)

A programming language translator can make use of type information in several ways. It can check for the validity of operations and actions, thus providing improved error detection. For example, the division operator "/" may be limited to real values only, while truncated division (div) should be applied only to integers. Also assignment of values from variable to variable, such as

```
x := y
```

makes sense only when the types of x and y are the same or closely related in some sense.

A translator can also use type information to allocate space for variables. Indeed, efficient allocation of space is one of the major reasons to have type information available at translation time. Typical allocation schemes will be mentioned shortly with each individual type and type constructor.

Type information can be contained in a program either implicitly or explicitly. Implicit type information includes the types of constants and values, types that can be inferred from name conventions, and types that can be inferred from context. For example, the number 2 is implicitly an integer in most languages, TRUE is Boolean, and a variable I in FORTRAN is, in the absence of other information, an integer variable.

Explicit type information is primarily contained in **declarations.** Variables can be declared to be of specific types, such as

```
var x: array [1..10] of integer;
    b: boolean;
```

but in many languages it is also possible to give names to new types in a **type declaration:**

```
type intarray = array[1..10] of integer;
```

Some languages prefer to call these declarations **type definitions,** since they do not allocate actual space as do variable declarations. We will use the word **declaration** for both type and variable declarations.

The process a translator goes through to determine whether the type information in a program is consistent is called **type checking.** Type checking involves rules for determining when two types are the same: this is **type equivalence.** Algorithms for type equivalence are studied in Section 6.5. Type checking also uses rules for inferring types of language constructs from the available type information. The collection of these **type inference** rules, the type equivalence algorithm, and the methods used for constructing types are collectively referred to as a **type system.**

If a programming language definition requires all objects of a language to have well-defined types that can be determined statically, and specifies a complete set of rules for type equivalence and type inference that can be applied statically, then the language is said to be **strongly typed.** Taken literally, this definition means that all type errors in a strongly typed language can be determined at translation time. However, in most strongly typed languages, exceptions are made for conditions that are difficult or impossible to check at translation time, such as subrange bounds or record variants. Ada and Algol68 are strongly typed languages. Modula-2 and Pascal are usually considered to be strongly typed as well, even though there are a few loopholes. C has even more loopholes and so could be called a not so strongly typed language. Languages without complete static type systems—we could call them weakly typed (some authors may even call them "untyped")—include LISP, APL, SNOBOL, and BLISS.

Type checking rules will be examined in Section 6.6. Ways of relaxing type checking in strongly typed languages will be examined in Section 6.7. But first we want to study the basic types available in many languages and the common type constructors or ways of constructing new types from existing ones.

6.2 SIMPLE TYPES

Algol-like languages (Pascal, Algol68, C, Modula-2, Ada) all classify types according to a basic scheme, with minor variations. Unfortunately, the names used in different language definitions are often different, even though the concepts are the same. We will attempt to use a generic name scheme and then point out differences with some of the foregoing languages.

Every language comes with a set of **predefined types** from which all other types are constructed. These are generally specified using predefined identifiers such as `integer`, `real`, `boolean`, and `char`. Sometimes predefined numeric types with specified precision are included, such as `longreal`, `double`, `longint`, `short`, `shortreal`, and so on. Some languages have different formats for real types available, such as `fixed` and `float`. Sometimes special integer ranges are available as well, such as unsigned integers (C) or cardinals (Modula-2).

Predefined types are primarily **simple types:** types that have no other structure than their inherent arithmetic or sequential structure. All the foregoing types are simple. However, there are simple types that are not predefined: **enumerated types** and **subrange types** are also simple types.

Enumerated types are sets whose elements are named and listed explicitly. A typical example (in Pascal) is

```
type colors = (red, blue, green);
```

Enumerated types are not just sets, they are ordered sets: their elements are ordered in the order given in the declaration. Hence there are successor and predecessor operations. In the preceding example, succ(red) = blue. Note that pred(red) is undefined. (In Modula-2 INC and DEC are used to achieve the effect of succ and pred.)

Subrange types are contiguous subsets of simple types specified by giving a least and greatest element, as in the following Pascal declarations:

```
type digit = 0..9;
     byte = 0..255;
```

or the Modula-2 declarations (note the difference in bracket conventions):

```
TYPE digit = [0..9];
     byte = [0..255];
```

In these sample declarations, the simple type from which the subrange is taken is not stated: the **base type** of the subrange is implicit. In some languages the base type can be stated explicitly, as in the Ada declaration

```
subtype digit is INTEGER range 0..9;
```

or the equivalent Modula-2 declaration

```
TYPE digit = INTEGER [0..9];
```

In the absence of explicit base types, assumptions are made automatically about the base type, and this can lead to ambiguities and incompatibilities. See the discussion in Section 6.6 on implicit and overlapping types.

Subrange types are generally restricted to simple types for which successor and predecessor operations exist. These types are called **ordinal types** because of the discrete order that exists on the set. All the types we have mentioned so far are ordinal except those involving real numbers. Real numbers are ordered (i.e., $3.98 < 3.99$), but there is no successor or predecessor operation. Thus a subrange declaration such as

```
TYPE UnitInterval = [0.0..1.0];
```

is illegal in most languages.

Programming languages typically implement simple types by making use of types available in hardware, which usually include integers, unsigned integers, and reals. Typical implementations allocate two or four bytes for integers in two's complement form, four or eight bytes for reals in various formats, and one byte for Booleans and characters (Booleans commonly use only the low-order bit: 0 = FALSE, 1 = TRUE).[1] Enum-

---

[1] In a language like C, which does not have a predefined Boolean data type, different conventions are used. See Exercise 48.

erated types are often translated internally into unsigned integers and stored in the minimum number of bytes needed. Subranges can either be allocated the full space of their base type, or the translator can allocate the minimum number of bytes needed to store all the values.

6.3   TYPE CONSTRUCTORS

Since data types are sets, set operations can be used to construct new types out of existing ones. Such operations include Cartesian product, union, powerset, function set, and subset.

When applied to types these set operations are called **type constructors.** In a programming language all types are constructed out of the simple types using type constructors. In the previous section we have already seen a limited form of one of these constructors—the subset construction—in subrange types. There are also type constructors that do not correspond to mathematical set constructions. These include pointer and file types. In this section we will catalog and give examples of the common type constructors.

6.3.1   Cartesian Product

Given two sets U and V, we can form the Cartesian or cross product consisting of all ordered pairs of elements from U and V:

$$U \times V = \{(u, v) \mid u \text{ is in } U \text{ and } v \text{ is in } V\}$$

Cartesian products come with projection functions $p_1: U \times V \rightarrow U$ and $p_2: U \times V \rightarrow V$, where $p_1((u, v)) = u$ and $p_2((u, v)) = v$. This construction extends to more than two sets. Thus $U \times V \times W = \{(u, v, w) \mid u \text{ in } U, v \text{ in } V, w \text{ in } W\}$. There are as many projection functions as there are components.

In many languages the Cartesian product type constructor is available as the **record** construction. For example, in Modula-2 the declaration

```
TYPE IntBoolReal  =  RECORD
                 i :  INTEGER;
                 b :  BOOLEAN;
                 r :  REAL;
              END;
```

constructs the Cartesian product type INTEGER $\times$ BOOLEAN $\times$ REAL.

However, there is a difference between a Cartesian product and a record: the fields have names in a record, while in a product they are referred to by position. The projections in a record are given by the **field selector operation:** if x is a variable of type IntBoolReal, then x.i is the projection of x to the integers. Some authors therefore consider record types to be different from Cartesian product types. Indeed, most languages consider field names to be part of the type defined by a record. Thus

```
RECORD
    j : INTEGER;
    c : BOOLEAN;
    s : REAL;
END;
```

can be considered different from the record just defined, even though they represent the same Cartesian product set.

A typical allocation scheme for product types is sequential allocation according to the space needed by each component. Thus a variable of type IntBoolReal might be allocated seven bytes: the first two for an INTEGER, the third byte for a BOOLEAN, and the last four for a REAL. Sometimes the space must be allocated in even or word-size chunks, so an implementation might allocate eight bytes instead of seven.

6.3.2   Union

A second construction is the union of two types: it is formed by taking the set theoretic union of their sets of values. Union types come in two varieties: discriminated unions and undiscriminated unions. A union is **discriminated** if a **tag** or **discriminator** is added to each element field to distinguish which type the element is, that is, which set it came from. Discriminated unions are similar to disjoint unions in mathematics. Undiscriminated unions lack the tag, and assumptions must be made about the type of any particular element.

In Algol-like languages unions are often constructed using **variant records.** In Modula-2 the discriminated union of the types INTEGER and REAL can be given by the declaration

```
TYPE IntOrReal = RECORD
                    CASE IsInt: BOOLEAN OF
                        TRUE:  i : INTEGER|
                        FALSE: r : REAL
                    END;
                 END;
```

The tag field IsInt determines whether an element is INTEGER or REAL. Given a variable x of type IntOrReal, we can assign the integer value 0 to x as follows:

```
x.IsInt := TRUE;
x.i := 0;
```

An undiscriminated union is defined by the following:

```
TYPE IntOrReal = RECORD
                    CASE BOOLEAN OF
                        TRUE: i: INTEGER |
                        FALSE: r: REAL
                    END;
                END;
```

Note that the BOOLEAN type declaration in the CASE statement must still appear but the tag or field name is missing.

In C unions are given directly and are undiscriminated:

```
typedef union
    {int i;
    float r;} utype;
```

defines utype as the union of reals and integers, which may be accessed using the same dot notation as in Modula-2 or Pascal.

Algol68 has a similar declaration: ir = union (int, real) but insists that the type of an object be tested during execution to avoid illegal references. (This means that type attributes must be maintained during runtime, a fairly serious overhead.)

Unions are generally allocated space equal to the maximum of the space needed for individual variants, and variants are stored in overlapping regions of memory. Thus a variable of type IntOrReal (without the discriminant) might be allocated four bytes: the first two would be used for INTEGER variants, and all four would be used for a REAL variant. If a BOOLEAN tag field were added, five bytes would be needed.

6.3.3   Subset

In mathematics a subset can be specified by giving a rule to distinguish its elements, such as posint = $\{x \mid x$ an integer and $x > 0\}$. Similar rules can be given in programming languages to establish new types that are subsets of known types. By specifying a lower and upper bound, subranges of ordinal types can be declared in Pascal and Modula-2. Ada also allows the construction of subsets of array types by specifying a subrange for the index set. For example, with the Ada code

```
type digit is range 0..9;
type ar1 is array (digit) of INTEGER;
subtype ar2 is ar1 (2..5);
```

arrays of type ar2 have their indices restricted to the range 2 to 5. (Such subtypes of array types are called **slices.**)

Variant parts of records can also be fixed in this way. For example, in Ada the declaration of IntOrReal on page 161 would be written as follows (note the placement of the discriminant in the type name):

```
type IntOrReal(IsInt: BOOLEAN) is record
                    case IsInt is
                        when TRUE => i: INTEGER;
                        when FALSE => r: REAL;
                    end case;
        end record;
```

Now a subset type can be declared that fixes the variant part (which then must have the specified value):

```
subtype IRInt is IntOrReal(IsInt => TRUE);
subtype IRReal is IntOrReal(IsInt => FALSE);
```

Such subset types **inherit** operations from their parent types. Most languages, however, do not have ways in which a user can specify which operations are inherited and which are not. Instead operations are automatically or implicitly inherited. In Ada, for example, subtypes inherit all the operations of the parent type. It would be nice to be able to exclude operations that do not make sense for a subset type; for example, unary minus makes little sense for a value of type digit (page 162). Object-oriented languages *do* allow more control over such operations, and the subtype and inheritance mechanisms of object-oriented languages are more complex and more versatile than are the mechanisms discussed here (see Chapter 9).

6.3.4   Powerset

The powerset or set of all subsets is another common type constructor. An example in Modula-2 is

```
TYPE digit = [0..9];
     digitSet = SET OF digit;
```

In the construction SET OF t there are often restrictions on t: in Modula-2 and Pascal, for example, t can only be an ordinal type, and some translators have further restrictions on the size of t. SET OF INTEGER, for instance, is often not accepted, since the size of a variable of this type is quite large.

Sets are usually implemented as bit vectors: each possible member is present or absent according to whether its corresponding bit is 1 or 0. Thus the number of bytes required to allocate to a variable of type SET OF t is the cardinality of t divided by 8, rounded off to the nearest higher byte or word boundary. For example, a variable of type SET OF CHAR in a language using the ASCII character set would need 16 bytes of storage, since there are 128 ASCII characters.

6.3.5 Functions

The set of all functions $f: U \to V$ can give rise to a new type in two ways: as a **function type** or as an **array type.** When U is an ordinal type, the function f can be thought of as an **array** with **index type** U and **component type** V: if i is in U, then $f(i)$ is the ith component of the array, and the whole function can be represented by the sequence or tuple of its values $(f(low), \ldots, f(high))$, where low is the smallest element in U and $high$ is the largest. (For this reason, array types are sometimes referred to as **sequence types.**)

For example, in Modula-2 the declaration

```
TYPE digit = [0..9];
     digitToInt = ARRAY digit OF INTEGER;
```

represents functions from `digit` to `INTEGER` or ordered tuples of ten integers.

Often restrictions are placed on the size or description of the index ordinal type; for example, `ARRAY INTEGER OF INTEGER` sometimes causes an allocation error, especially on small machines.

In some languages the index range or even the index set can be left unspecified. In Modula-2, open-index array types can be used in the declaration of procedure and function parameters:

```
PROCEDURE FindLargest(a: ARRAY OF INTEGER):
  INTEGER;
VAR i: CARDINAL;
    max: INTEGER;
BEGIN
  max := a[0];
  FOR i := 1 TO HIGH(a) DO
    IF a[i] > max THEN
      max := a[i];
    END;(* IF *)
  END;(* FOR *)
  RETURN max;
END FindLargest;
```

declares a function that takes an array of integers as a parameter without specifying the index set. The function uses the predefined function `HIGH` to find the upper bound of the array; the lower bound is always assumed to be 0. If the actual index type was not in this range, it is mapped to it (any ordinal type permits this).

In Ada the declaration

```
type IntToInt is array (INTEGER range <>) of
  INTEGER;
```

creates an array type from a subrange of integers to integers. The brackets "<>" indicate that the precise subrange is left unspecified. Such a type can be used for parameters to procedures as in Modula-2; when a variable is declared, however, a range must be given:

```
table : IntToInt (-10..10);
```

Multidimensional arrays are also possible, as in the Modula-2 code:

```
TYPE IntMatrix = ARRAY digit,digit of INTEGER;
```

This can be viewed as a function from (digit × digit) to INTEGER.

Arrays are perhaps the most widely used type constructor, since their implementation can be made extremely efficient: space is allocated sequentially in memory, and indexing is performed by an offset calculation from the starting address of the array. In the case of multidimensional arrays, allocation is still linear, and a decision must be made about which index to use first in the allocation scheme: if x is of type IntMatrix, then x can be stored as x[0,0], x[0,1], x[0,2], ..., x[0,9], x[1,0], x[1,1], and so on (**row-major form**) or as x[0,0], x[1,0], x[2,0], ..., x[9,0], x[0,1], x[1,1] (**column-major form**).

General function and procedure types can also be created in some languages. For example, in Modula-2 the definition

```
TYPE intFunction = PROCEDURE (INTEGER): INTEGER;
```

defines a function type from integers to integers. (In Modula-2, similar to Algol60, the reserved word PROCEDURE is used for both functions and procedures.) In Pascal, function and procedure types exist only in parameters to other functions and procedures, and in some compilers even these are not implemented. As an example, the declaration

```
procedure p(function f(integer):integer,
              i: integer);
begin
  if f(i+1) = 0 then
  . . .
end;
```

has as its first parameter a function from the integers to the integers.

The format and space allocation of function variables depend on the size of the address needed to point to the code representing the function and on the runtime environment required by the language. See Chapter 7 for more details.

6.3.6   Pointers and Recursive Types

A type constructor that does not correspond to a set operation is the **reference** or **pointer** constructor, which constructs the set of all addresses of a specified type. In Modula-2 the declaration

```
TYPE IntPtr = POINTER TO INTEGER;
```

constructs the type of all addresses of integers. If x is a variable of type IntPtr, then it can be **dereferenced** to obtain a value of type integer: x^ := 10 assigns the integer value 10 to the location given by x. Of course, x must have previously been assigned a valid address; this is usually accomplished dynamically by a call to the allocation function NEW(x). (Pointer variables were discussed in Chapter 5.)

The same declaration as the foregoing in Pascal is

```
type IntPtr = ^integer;
```

where the reuse of the symbol "^" for both reference and dereference can be a little confusing (a violation of the principle of uniformity). In C the same problem exists, where the asterisk "*" is used instead of the "^" of Pascal. Thus, to declare a pointer to an integer in C, we write

```
int * x;
```

and to assign an integer value to the location pointed to by x, we write

```
* x = 10;
```

(Note the use of the "*" on the same side of x in both the declaration and assignment.)

• Pointers are most useful in the creation of **recursive types:** a type that uses itself in its declaration. Recursive types are extremely important in data structures and algorithms, since they naturally correspond to recursive algorithms, and represent data whose size and structure is not known in advance, but may change as computation proceeds. Two typical examples are lists and binary trees. Consider the following Modula-2-like declaration of lists of characters:

```
TYPE charlist = RECORD
                  data: CHAR;
                  next: charlist;
                END;
```

There is no reason in principle why such a recursive definition should be illegal; recursive functions have a similar structure. However, a close look at this declaration indicates a problem: any such data must contain an infinite number of characters. In the analogy with recursive functions, this is like a recursive function without a "base case," that is, a test to stop the recursion. For example, the function definition

```
PROCEDURE fact(n: INTEGER): INTEGER;
BEGIN
  RETURN fact(n−1) * n;
END;
```

lacks the test for small n and results in an infinite number of calls to fact (at least until memory is exhausted). We can remove this problem in the definition of charlist by providing a base case using a variant record:

```
TYPE charlist = RECORD CASE IsEmpty: BOOLEAN OF
                 TRUE: (* the empty list *) |
                 FALSE : data: CHAR;
                         next: charlist;
                 END; (* case *)
              END; (* record *)
```

If we view this as a definition for the set charlist, this can indeed be said to define such a set as a solution to the recursive equation:

$$\text{charlist} = \{\text{emptylist}\} \cup \text{CHAR} \times \text{charlist}$$

where "$\cup$" is union and $\times$ is Cartesian product. In Section 4.2.1 we described how BNF rules could be interpreted as recursive set equations that define a set by taking the smallest solution (or **least fixed point**). The current situation is entirely analogous, and one can show that the least fixed point solution of the preceding equation is

$$\{\text{emptylist}\} \cup \text{CHAR} \cup (\text{CHAR} \times \text{CHAR}) \cup$$
$$(\text{CHAR} \times \text{CHAR} \times \text{CHAR}) \cup \ldots$$

That is, a list is either the empty list or a list consisting of one character or a list consisting of two characters, and so on (see Exercise 7). Indeed, Scheme and other dialects of LISP allow lists to be written in exactly this way: "()" is the empty list, "('a')" is a list with one character, "('a' 'b')" is a list with two characters, and so on. (Scheme lists are actually a little more general, with different data types allowed as elements in a list; the statically typed functional languages ML and Miranda are closer to this description and have type declarations very similar to the preceding; see Chapter 10.)

There is still a major problem with this description of recursive types, and the preceding declaration of charlist is still not legal in Modula-2: a variable of type charlist has no fixed size and cannot be allocated prior to execution. This is an insurmountable obstacle to defining such a data type in a language without a fully dynamic runtime environment (see Chapter 7). The solution adopted in most procedural languages is to use pointers to allow manual dynamic allocation. Thus, in Modula-2 and Pascal, the direct use of recursion in type declarations is prohibited, but indirect recursive declarations through pointers is allowed, as in the following (now legal) Modula-2 declarations:

```
TYPE charlist = POINTER to charlistrec;
     charlistrec = RECORD
                     data: CHAR;
                     next: charlist;
                   END;
```

Note that this code violates the principle of declaration before use, since charlistrec is used before it is declared. This exception is made necessary by the type equivalence rules of Modula-2 and Pascal (see Section 6.5). In C this same declaration can be expressed somewhat more directly as follows:

```
typedef struct charlistrec
          {char data;
           struct charlistrec * next;}
             * charlist;
```

With these declarations each individual element in a list now has a fixed size, and they can be strung together to form a list of arbitrary size. In Modula-2, for example, the empty list is represented by the NIL pointer; the list containing the single character " 'a' " can be constructed as follows:

```
VAR cl: charlist;
    ...
NEW(cl);
cl^.data := 'a';
cl^.next := NIL;
```

and this can be changed to a list of two characters as follows:

```
NEW(cl^.next);
cl^.next^.data := 'b';
cl^.next^.next := NIL;
```

6.3.7   Other Type Constructors

Some languages have special type constructors in addition to the ones listed. An example is the Pascal **file type**:

```
type recfile = file of employeerec;
```

Pascal even has a predeclared file type text = file of char. Modula-2 has no specified file type; files are assumed to be system dependent, and their types will be imported from a library module. Ada takes a similar approach, except that the form of the file library is precisely specified.

An additional type that is predefined in some languages is the **string type,** that is, a sequence of characters of arbitrary length. Two approaches are possible: either there is a single string type with unspecified maximum length, or for each positive integer in some range a string type can be declared with that maximum length. For example, in PL/I the declaration

```
DCL  A  CHAR(80);
```

creates a variable A that is a string of length 80. Both Pascal and Modula-2 avoid the introduction of a special string type by specifying that strings are arrays of characters with certain index types. (Pascal's string types always have a lower bound of 1, as in array [1..n] of char, while Modula-2 strings always have a lower bound of 0, as in ARRAY [0..n] OF CHAR.) This has prompted some implementors to introduce their own string types, causing confusion and incompatibilities. Modula-2 has specific rules for handling character array types that make the picture a bit clearer. However, such string types are still limited in that there are no specifically string operations, such as concatenation, substring extraction, or the ability to grow or shrink dynamically.

Some languages include space allocation directives as a form of type constructor. Examples are the **packed** directive in Pascal and the **align** directive in C. It is questionable whether a language definition should include such directives. For one thing, they cause implementation dependencies. For another, a good translator should be able to optimize space allocation without the need for such directives. (Modula-2 does away with the packed directive of Pascal.)

Finally, it is often useful to be able to specify a "notype" type: a type that is distinct from all other types. Such a type could be thought of as a set containing a single value distinct from all other values. Such a type is the **void** type in C or Algol68 and the **unit** type of ML (see Section 10.4).

6.4   TYPE NOMENCLATURE IN *Pascal*-LIKE LANGUAGES

Although we have presented the general scheme of type mechanisms in Sections 6.2 and 6.3, various language definitions use different and confusing terminology to define similar things. In this section we give a brief description of the differences among several Algol-like languages.

6.4.1.   Pascal/Modula-2

An overview of Pascal types is given in Figure 6-1. The simple types correspond closely to our description. Types that are constructed using

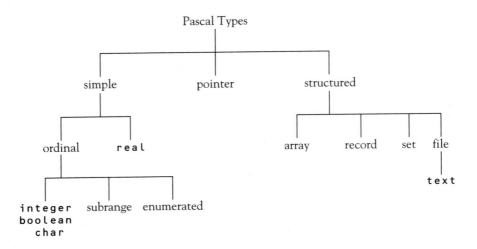

Figure 6.1   The Type Structure of Pascal

the constructors `array`, `record`, `set`, and `file` are called **structured types;** these are distinguished from both simple types and pointer types. Modula-2 has a similar type structure, with a few exceptions. There is a `CARDINAL` predefined ordinal type that is distinct from `INTEGER`. `CARDINAL`s begin at 0 and go up to some undefined maximum value that may be larger than the largest `INTEGER` (on many systems `INTEGER` = [−32768..32767] and `CARDINAL` = [0..65535]). Modula-2 has procedure types, which do not exist in Pascal, but there are no file types specified in the definition of Modula-2 (files are system-dependent features provided separately by each implementation). Pascal, on the other hand, has a predefined type `text` that is a structured type and is the same as `file of char`.

6.4.2   Ada

Ada has a rich set of types, a condensed overview of which is given in Figure 6-2. Simple types are called **scalar** types in Ada, and these are split into several overlapping categories. Ordinal types are called **discrete** types in Ada; numeric types comprise the real and integer types. Pointer types are called **access** types. Array and record types are called **composite** types. Files are dealt with as in Modula-2, except that the format of standard file facilities is given more precisely. There are no procedure or set types in Ada.

6.5   TYPE EQUIVALENCE

A major question involved in the application of types to type checking is that of **type equivalence:** When are two types the same? One way of

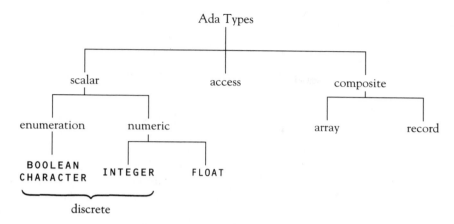

Figure 6-2   The Type Structure of Ada (somewhat simplified)

trying to answer this question is to compare the sets of values simply as sets. Two sets are the same if they contain the same values: for example, any type defined as the Cartesian product $A \times B$ is the same as any other type defined in the same way. On the other hand, if we assume type B is not the same as type A, then a type defined as $A \times B$ is not the same as a type defined as $B \times A$, since $A \times B$ contains the pairs (a,b) but $B \times A$ contains the pairs (b,a). This view of type equivalence is that two data types are the same if they have the same structure: they are built in exactly the same way using the same type constructors from the same simple types. This form of type equivalence is called **structural equivalence** and is one of the principal forms of type equivalence in programming languages.

EXAMPLE

In a Pascal-like syntax, the types `rec1` and `rec2` defined as follows are structurally equivalent, but `rec1` and `rec3` are not (the `boolean` and `integer` fields are reversed in the definition of `rec3`):

```
type
  range = 1..10;
  ar = array [range] of boolean;
  rec1 = record
    x: boolean;
    y: integer;
    z: ar;
  end;
  rec2 = record
    x: boolean;
    y: integer;
    z: array [1..10] of boolean;
  end;
  rec3 = record                              continues
```

continued

```
      x:  integer;
      y:  boolean;
      z:  ar;
   end;
```

Structural equivalence is relatively easy to implement (at least in the absence of recursive types; see Section 6.3.6) and provides all the information needed to perform error checking and storage allocation. It is used in such languages as Algol60, Algol68, FORTRAN, and COBOL. To check structural equivalence, a translator may represent types as trees and check equivalence recursively on subtrees (see Exercise 36). Questions still arise, however, in determining how much information is included in a type under the application of a type constructor. For example, are the two types

```
   t1  =  array  [−1..9]  of  integer;
   t2  =  array  [0..10]  of  integer;
```

structurally equivalent? Perhaps yes, if we were only concerned about the size of the index set; perhaps no, if one insists that the index sets must match. A similar question arises with respect to field names of records. If records are taken to be just Cartesian products, then, for example, the two records

```
   reca  =  record
      x:  boolean;
      y:  integer;
   end;
```

and

```
   recb  =  record
      a:  boolean;
      b:  integer;
   end;
```

should be structurally equivalent. However, in Algol68 they are not: structurally equivalent records must have the same field names.

In the case of dynamic arrays the further problem arises that the bounds of the index set are not known, and so the type obviously cannot include them. In fact, one might want to avoid the inclusion of the index type altogether in an array type, so that all arrays of integers would be equivalent. Thus

```
   array  [colors]  of  integer
```

and

```
array [0..maxint] of integer
```

would be equivalent. In Algol68 this is essentially the view taken: the dimension and component type of an array are part of its type, but not the index set. However, index sets are restricted to integers. In Ada the base type of the index set is also part of an array type, but not the bounds on the index. Thus the type

```
array (INTEGER range <>) of INTEGER
```

is an array of integers with integer indices.

A second and much stricter type equivalence algorithm is possible when types can be named in a type declaration: two named types are equivalent only if they have the same name. Since a name can refer only to a single type declaration, this is a stronger condition than structural equivalence. This type equivalence algorithm is called **name equivalence.** Name equivalence is available in Ada, but in few other programming languages.

EXAMPLE

In the following Pascal-like declaration,

```
type ar1 = array [1..10] of integer;
     ar2 = ar1;
     age = integer;
```

ar1 and ar2 are structurally equivalent but not name equivalent. Similarly, age and integer are structurally equivalent but not name equivalent. In Ada these declarations would look as follows (the "new" designation enforces the name equivalence):

```
type ar1 is array (1..10) of INTEGER;
type ar2 is new ar1;
type age is new INTEGER;                                        ∎
```

Name equivalence has its ambiguities as well. For instance, in a language with type declarations, it is usually still possible to use a type in a variable declaration without giving it a name, as in the following Pascal variable declaration:

```
var x: array [1..10] of integer;
    y: array [1..10] of integer;
```

(Similar declarations are possible in Ada.) The two array types of x and y are constructed directly and are not given names. Are they name equivalent? The standard answer is no—the question is resolved by considering such types to have internal names that are always different. But what about the following declaration:

```
var x,y: array [1..10] of integer;
```

Now x and y may or may not have the same type under name equivalence. (Ada resolves this situation by specifying that any combined declaration of variables be equivalent to declarations that are separate. Thus x and y are not type equivalent in Ada.)

Name equivalence and structural equivalence are the two extremes of type equivalence algorithms. However, they are rarely seen in pure form: programmers and language designers find it useful to define a number of situations where exceptions are made. These will be studied in more detail in the next section, where type checking is described. And, as we have noted, even the definitions are not always clear-cut in all situations, and various options are available to the language designer.

An important type equivalence algorithm that falls between name and structural equivalence is **declaration equivalence,** used in Pascal and Modula-2. In this algorithm, type names that lead back to the same original structure declaration by a series of redeclarations are considered to be equivalent types. For example, in the declarations

```
type
  t1 = array [1..10] of integer;
  t2 = t1;
  t3 = t2;
```

t1, t2, and t3 are all declaration equivalent, but not name equivalent. Similarly, in the example on the previous page, ar1 and ar2 are declaration equivalent, as are age and integer.

However, in the declaration

```
type ar3 = array [1..10] of integer;
     ar4 = array [1..10] of integer;
```

ar3 and ar4 are not declaration equivalent, since each is constructed separately in its own declaration. A simple way of viewing declaration equivalence is that each time a type constructor is applied, a new internal type name is constructed, which the programmer may or may not give an explicit name to.

Thus, in the Modula-2 declarations

```
TYPE t1 = ARRAY [1..10] OF INTEGER;
     t2 = t1;
     t3 = ARRAY [1..10] OF INTEGER;
```

```
VAR  x:  t1;
     y:  t2;
     z:  t3;
     w:  ARRAY  [1..10]  OF  INTEGER;
```

there are three different types with structure ARRAY [1..10] OF IN-
TEGER, namely, t1, t3, and the unnamed type of w (type t2 is the same
as t1 under declaration equivalence). Indeed, w can be type equivalent
to no other variable, since its type is not given a name and therefore
cannot be referred to again. Similarly, in the declaration

```
VAR  x,y:  ARRAY  [1..10]  OF  INTEGER;
```

x and y are declaration equivalent variables but cannot be equivalent to
any other variables.

    In the programming language C, a mixture of structural and dec-
laration equivalence is used: declaration equivalence for structures and
unions and structural equivalence for pointers and arrays.

6.6   TYPE CHECKING

Type checking, as we have said at the beginning of the chapter, is the
process a translator goes through to verify that all constructs in a program
make sense in terms of the types of its constants, variables, procedures,
and other entities. It involves the application of a type equivalence algorithm to expressions and statements, which can vary from strict to
permissive application.

    Type checking can be divided into **dynamic** and **static** checking: if
type information is maintained and checked at runtime, the checking is
dynamic. Interpreters by definition perform dynamic type checking. But
compilers can also generate code that maintains type attributes during
runtime in a table or as type tags in an environment. A LISP compiler,
for example, would do this. Dynamic type checking is required when the
types of objects can only be determined at runtime.

    The alternative to dynamic typing is static typing: the types of
expressions and objects are determined from the text of the program, and
type checking is performed by the translator before execution. In a strongly
typed language, all type errors must be caught before runtime, so these
languages must be statically typed. However, a language definition may
leave unspecified whether dynamic or static typing is to be used.

EXAMPLE 1

In Standard Pascal a distinction is made between errors that a translator
must detect (called **violations**) and those that may only be detected on
execution (called simply **errors**). Examples of type errors that are "errors"

instead of "violations" are accessing variant record fields that are not active and indexing an array with a value that is not in the index range. Since most type errors are "violations" instead of "errors," static type checking is required by the standard.   ■

EXAMPLE 2

C compilers apply static type checking during translation, but C is not really strongly typed since many type inconsistencies do not cause compilation errors but are automatically removed by compilers. Most modern compilers, however, have error level settings that do provide strong typing if it is desired.   ■

EXAMPLE 3

The Scheme dialect of LISP (see Chapter 10) is a weakly, dynamically typed language. There are no types in declarations. Variables and other symbols have no predeclared type, but take on the type of the value they possess at each moment of execution. Thus types in Scheme must be kept as explicit attributes of values. Internal type checking is restricted to generating errors for functions requiring certain values to perform their operations. For example, car and cdr require their operands to be lists: (car 2) generates an error. Types can be checked explicitly by the programmer, however, using predefined test functions. Types in Scheme include lists, symbols, atoms, and numbers. Predefined test functions include atom?, number?, and symbol?. (Such test functions are called predicates and always end in a question mark.)   ■

An essential part of type checking is **type inference,** where the types of expressions are inferred from the types of their subexpressions. Type checking rules (that is, when constructs are type correct) and type inference rules are often intermingled. For example, an expression *e1* + *e2* might be declared type correct if *e1* and *e2* have the same type, and that type has a "+" operation (type checking), and the result type of the expression is the type of *e1* and *e2* (type inference). In Pascal, this would mean that *e1* and *e2* are either sets of the same type or are of type integer or real or a subrange of integer. The result type is then the set type (if both are sets), real if either is real and integer otherwise.

As another example, in a function call, the types of the actual parameters or arguments must match the types of the formal parameters (type checking), and the result type of the call is the result type of the function (type inference).

Type checking and type inference rules have a close interaction with the type equivalence algorithm. For example, the Modula-2 declaration

```
PROCEDURE p(ar: ARRAY [1..max] OF INTEGER);
```

is an error under declaration equivalence, since no actual parameter can have the type of the formal parameter ar, and so a type mismatch will be declared on every call to p. As a result, the Modula-2 syntax restricts parameter declarations to type names rather than general type specifiers that include type constructors, so that we must write[2]

```
TYPE artype = ARRAY [1..max] OF INTEGER ;
    . . .
PROCEDURE p(ar: artype);
```

Exactly the same situation occurs in Pascal and Ada.

The process of type inference and type checking in statically typed languages is aided by explicit declarations of the types of variables, functions, and other objects. For example, if x and y are variables, the correctness and type of the expression x + y is difficult to determine prior to execution unless the types of x and y have been explicitly stated in a declaration. However, explicit type declarations are not an absolute requirement for static typing: the languages ML and Miranda, studied in Chapter 10, perform static type checking but do not require types to be declared. Instead, types are inferred from context using an inference mechanism that is more powerful than what we have described.

Type inference and correctness rules are often one of the most complex parts of the semantics of a language. Nonorthogonalities are hard to avoid in imperative languages such as Modula-2 and Ada. In the remainder of this section we will discuss major issues and problems in the rules of a type system.

6.6.1   Type Compatibility

Sometimes it is useful to relax type correctness rules so that the types of components need not be precisely the same according to the type equivalence algorithm. For example, we noted earlier that the expression e1 + e2 may still make sense even if the types of e1 and e2 are different subranges of integers. In such a situation, two different types that still may be correct when combined in certain ways are often called **compatible** types. In Modula-2 and Pascal, any two subranges of the same base type are compatible. (Of course, this can result in errors, as we shall see in Section 6.6.2.)

A related term, **assignment compatibility,** is often used for the type correctness of the statement x := e. Initially, this statement may be judged type correct when x and e have the same type. But this ignores a major difference: the left-hand side must be an l-value or address (see Chapter 5), while the right-hand side must be an r-value. Many languages solve this problem by requiring the left-hand side to be a variable name, whose address is taken as the l-value, and by automatically **dereferencing** variable names on the right-hand side to get their r-values. In Algol68

---

[2]An exception is the open array parameter declaration discussed in Section 6.3.5.

this is made more explicit by saying that the assignment is type correct if the type of the left-hand side (which may be an arbitrary expression) is ref t (an address of a value of type t), and the type of the right-hand side is t. Algol68 does permit automatic dereferencing to take place if the right-hand side is of type ref t. BLISS, however, requires explicit dereferencing: if y is a variable, we must write x : = . y with the period "." used as the dereference operator.

Assignment compatibility can be expanded to include other cases where both sides do not have the same type. For example, in Pascal, but not in Modula-2, the assignment x : = e is legal when e is of type integer and x is of type real: the integer value of e is converted to a real value and then stored in x. On the other hand, Modula-2 defines INTEGER and CARDINAL type to be assignment compatible, so that x : = e is type correct if x has type CARDINAL and e has type INTEGER, or vice versa. This kind of assignment compatibility is actually type conversion and is discussed in Section 6.7.

6.6.2 Overlapping Types

Types may overlap in that two types may contain values in common. For example, two subranges may overlap: integer subranges [- 5 . . 5] and [0 . . 1 0] overlap in the values 0..5. When the type correctness of expressions and statements is expanded through compatibility to include subranges of the same type, this can cause errors. Suppose for example that x has type [- 5 . . 5] and y has type [0 . . 1 0]. Then by compatibility, x : = y is type correct. But if y contains the value 6 when this statement is executed, an execution error (instead of a static type error) has occurred. Indeed in Pascal and Modula-2, subranges of the same type are assignment compatible, even if the subranges have no actual values in common. Error checking is postponed to a runtime range check. One could take the view that this compromises strong typing, or one could view subranges as not being separate types on their own. Thus a subrange is not a new type even if it is given a distinct name in a type declaration. An alternative strategy, used in Ada, is to make a distinction between a truly new type and a specification for dynamic range checking. In Ada a subrange declaration that implies range checking is called a **subtype,** while a subrange that becomes a new type on its own is called a **derived type.** For example, in

```
subtype digit is INTEGER range 0 . . 9;
type newdigit is new INTEGER range 0 . . 9;
```

the subtype digit is not a new type; elements of type digit will have their values checked at execution time. However, newdigit is a derived type different from digit and integer. Similar type checking questions arise with any subset type constructor.

6.6.3   Implicit Types

Types of basic entities such as constants and variables may not be given explicitly in a declaration. In this case the type must be inferred by the translator, either from context information or from standard rules. We could say that such types are **implicit,** since they are not explicitly stated in a program, though the rules that specify their types must be explicit in the language definition. As an example of such a situation in Modula-2, constants do not have explicit types, so rules must be stated in ambiguous cases. Particularly problematic are positive integers, sets, and strings. Modula-2 has both INTEGER and CARDINAL type, which overlap for positive integers. Is then a constant such as 3 or 42 an integer or a cardinal? The rule says they are "compatible" with either, and so can be thought of as having both types. This makes sense, since we would not want to worry about mixing numbers and variables of either integer or cardinal type in any expression—except that variables of cardinal and integer type cannot be mixed. On the other hand, string constants are considered to have a single implicit type ARRAY [0..length] OF CHAR (structurally equivalent to all such types), so that, given the declarations

```
CONST blanks = '     '; (* five blanks *)
VAR str1: ARRAY [1..5] OF CHAR;
    str2: ARRAY [0..4] OF CHAR;
```

the assignment

```
str1 := blanks;
```

generates a type error, but the assignment

```
str2 := blanks;
```

does not. Set constants, which are permitted in Modula-2, also cause problems: without explicit casting to a previously defined type (see Section 6.7), they are of the predefined type BITSET, which is implementation dependent.

A similar problem can arise with subset types. If the base type is not explicitly stated, an ambiguity can arise. For example, in Modula-2, is the subrange [0..9] a subset of INTEGER or CARDINAL? It could be either, but the language definition says it is CARDINAL. This problem can be avoided by explicitly giving the base type:

```
TYPE digit = INTEGER [0..9];
```

A similar solution exists in Ada.

6.6.4   Shared Operations

Types have a set of operations associated to them, usually implicitly. Often these operations are shared among several types or have the same name as other operations that may be different. For example, the operator "+" can be real or integer addition or set union. Such operators are said to be **overloaded,** since the same name is used for essentially different operations. (Overloaded operators are related to **polymorphic** operations—operations that can apply to a number of different types. Polymorphism and overloading are studied in more detail in Chapter 8.)

In the case of an overloaded operator, a translator must decide which operation is meant from the types of its operands. If the argument types of an overloaded operator are disjoint, then the translator can make an unambiguous choice of which operation is meant. But what happens when the types of the arguments of an overloaded operator are mixed or overlap? For example, which operation should be used for the expression 3.14 + 1? In some languages this causes the integer 1 to be converted to a real, and then real addition is applied; this is type **coercion,** which is discussed in more detail in Section 6.7. Strongly typed languages often insist that the types of the arguments of an operator be all the same, so that no conversion is involved. But this causes problems when types can overlap. For example, in Modula-2, if i is an integer and c is a cardinal, $i + c$ causes a type error, even though the result might be well-defined regardless of the interpretation. Moreover, expressions like $2 + 3$ can be thought of as having either CARDINAL or INTEGER type. (To make matters worse, CARDINAL and INTEGER variables are assignment compatible in Modula-2, even though they are not compatible in arithmetic expressions.)

6.6.5   Multiply-Typed Objects

Sometimes it is useful for compatibility to permit objects to have more than one type. We have already seen that nonnegative integers in Modula-2 have type INTEGER and CARDINAL. A similar example is the NIL pointer that is of any pointer type. For systems programming it is useful to have other pointers that can be of any pointer type. An example in Modula-2 is the ADDRESS type provided by a SYSTEM module, which is compatible with all pointers. Similarly a single character 'a' may be thought of as being of type character or type string in some languages.

6.7   TYPE CONVERSION

If variables I and J are of integer type, the statement

```
I := J + 2.718
```

could be interpreted in several ways. In a permissive language like C, addition can be performed for mixed types: J is converted to a real, and the type of the result of J + 2.718 is real. Then the real value is truncated to an integer and assigned to I. In a more strongly typed language like Modula-2, reals and integers cannot be mixed in arithmetic expressions, and reals cannot be assigned to integers, so the above statement would generate a type error. In Modula-2 the statement would have to be written

```
I := TRUNC (FLOAT(J) + 2.718)
```

where FLOAT and TRUNC are built-in functions.

In every programming language there is a need to convert one type to another under certain circumstances. Such **type conversion** can be built into the type system so that conversions are performed automatically, as in the C example. We refer to such automatic type conversion as **type coercion.** It is sometimes also referred to as **implicit** type conversion. Coercion has the benefit that the programmer does not have to write extra code to perform an obvious conversion, a contribution to the simplicity design goal. However, automatic transfers have unpleasant effects as well: they weaken type checking so that errors may not be caught. This compromises the strong typing and the reliability of the programming language. Automatic conversions can cause unpredictable behavior in that the programmer may expect a conversion to be done one way, while the translator actually performs a different conversion. A famous example in (early) PL/I is the expression

```
1/3 + 15
```

which is converted to the value 5.33333333333333 (on a machine with 15-digit precision). The leading 1 is lost by overflow because the language rules state that the precision of the fractional value must be maintained.

An alternative to coercion is the use of **type conversion functions:** functions that are built into the language or available from a library that convert values of one type to another. This is a form of **explicit** type conversion, since the conversion is explicitly stated in the code. Examples include the functions trunc and round in Pascal and TRUNC and FLOAT in Modula-2. String packages will also often include functions such as StringToInt and IntToString to convert strings of digits to values and vice versa:

```
StringToInt('012') = 12 and
IntToString(100) = '100'
```

Modula-2 also has a general type conversion function for ordinal types called the VAL function: it takes as its first argument a type and as its second a value, and returns a new value of the specified type. Thus, if

```
TYPE colors = (red, blue, green),
```

then

```
VAL(INTEGER,red) = 0
```

and

```
VAL(colors,1) = blue.
```

Functions that take type arguments can generalize type systems in other ways than just as type transfers; see Chapter 8 for a discussion.

A third way to perform type transfers is with a **cast:** a value or object of one type is preceded by a type name. This results in conversion to the named type. In Modula-2 casts are written as though they were functions: INTEGER(red) and colors(1) cause the same conversions to take place as with the VAL function earlier. In fact, in the definition of Modula-2 these are called type transfer functions. However, these are not functions in the usual sense. In their basic form, casts differ from type conversion functions in that they do not cause any conversion to be performed: the internal representation is simply reinterpreted as a value of the new type. Thus, for example, CARDINAL (−1) = 65535 in many Modula-2 implementations, since −1 is kept in two's complement form (as a two-byte value). In C, however, casts can result in implicit conversion being done:

```
(int) 3.14
```

truncates the real to 3, thus performing an actual conversion. In Modula-2 INTEGER(3.14) is illegal. In Ada, casts are written as functions as in Modula-2 but perform conversions as in C.

Casts are another kind of explicit type conversion and can be useful and even essential, depending on the type system of the language. In Modula-2, for example, set constants have implicit predefined type BITSET unless cast to another type. Hence it is impossible to assign a set constant to a set variable without the use of a cast:

```
TYPE colorset = SET OF colors;
VAR x: colorset;
. . .
x := colorset{red};
```

Trying to make the assignment x := {red}; will cause a type error in Modula-2, since the set constant {red} does not have type SET OF colors.[1]

In Algol68 casts can be used to achieve dereferencing. For example, if x is of type ref ref int (that is, a pointer whose value is a pointer

---

[1]Strictly speaking, this is a type specifier, not a cast, since parentheses are not used. However, the basic idea is the same.

to an integer) and y is of type ref int, then x := y makes x point
to y, but (ref int) x := (int) y copies the value of y into the
location that x points to.

In C, casts are recommended for use in allocating storage pointers,
since the standard allocators do not necessarily return pointers of the
appropriate type. Thus

```
int *ip;
ip = (int *) malloc(sizeof(int));
```

declares a variable ip of type pointer to integer and then allocates space
for an integer value, returning a pointer to char, which is then cast to
pointer to integer. Such casts are usually not enforced, however; C compilers generally permit automatic reinterpretation with considerable aban-
don (a hacker's delight, but a big problem for portability and reliability).
For example, if ch is a char, both ch = 0 and ch == 0 are allowed:
the first assigns the null character (represented by its integer ASCII value
0) to c; the second compares c to the null character.

A final method for converting values from one type to another is
provided by a loophole in the strong typing of some languages: undiscriminated unions can hold values of different types, and without a discriminant or tag a translator cannot distinguish values of one type from
another, thus permitting indiscriminate reinterpretation of values. Thus
the Modula-2 declaration

```
VAR x: RECORD CASE BOOLEAN OF
          TRUE: c: CHAR |
          FALSE: b: BOOLEAN
          END; (* case *)
       END (* record *);
```

and the statements

```
x.b := TRUE;
WriteInt(ORD(x.c),1);
```

would allow us to see the internal value used to represent the Boolean
value TRUE; in most implementations this will print 1.

Even in the case of the discriminated union

```
VAR x: RECORD CASE kind: BOOLEAN OF
          TRUE: c: CHAR |
          FALSE: b: BOOLEAN
          END; (* case *)
       END (* record *);
```

it is difficult to generate dynamic checks that would cause the following code to fail:

```
x.kind := FALSE;
x.b := TRUE;
x.kind := TRUE;
WriteInt(ORD(x.c),1);
```

Indeed, many compilers do not even generate code to check the discriminator value when alternative fields are accessed, so the same code as for the undiscriminated union will work for the discriminated as well.

In Ada, however, the use of unions to defeat type checking is prevented by requiring discriminators and prohibiting the reassignment of discriminator fields by themselves. For example, if

```
type CharBool(kind: BOOLEAN) is
    record case kind is
        when true => c: CHARACTER;
        when false => b: BOOLEAN;
        end case;
    end record;
```

then given the declarations

```
x: CharBool(TRUE);
y: CharBool;
```

the discriminant x.kind cannot be changed at all, since x is declared with a fixed value for the discriminant, and y.kind cannot be assigned by itself, but all fields of y must be assigned at once:

```
y := (kind => FALSE, b => FALSE);
y := (kind => TRUE, c => 'a');
```

Exercises

1. Compare the flexibility of the weak typing of LISP with the reliability of the strong typing of Ada or Modula-2. Think of as many arguments as you can both for and against strong typing as an aid to program design.

2. Look up the implementation details on the representation of data by your Pascal/Modula-2/Ada/C compiler and compare them to the sketches of typical implementations given in the text. Where do they differ? Where are they the same?

3. Assume a bit-vector representation for sets.
   (a) How many bytes must be allocated for a variable of type SET OF
        INTEGER, assuming two bytes are used to represent INTEGER?
   (b) How many bytes must be allocated for a variable of type SET OF
        INTEGER, assuming four bytes are used to represent INTEGER?
   (c) How many bytes are needed to represent a variable of type SET OF
        SET OF CHAR?

4. A statement in the text implied that in Pascal, Modula-2, and Ada the
predefined type Boolean is an ordinal type. What is the order? Is this
of any use to the programmer? Can you think of any reasons why Boolean
type *should* be an ordinal type?

5. In Pascal, the selection of the field of a record pointed to by a pointer
variable requires the use of the dereference operation "^" together with
the field selector operation ".". Thus, given the Pascal declarations

```
type node = record
        data: ...;
      end;
var x: ^node;
```

we must write x^. data to access the data field of the record pointed to
by x. In C, one writes this as (*x).data, but the operation –>
combines dereferencing and field selection, so x –> data can be used
instead. In Ada, the use of field selection automatically implies dereferencing, so only x.data needs to be written in this case. Discuss the
advantages and disadvantages of these three conventions.

6. Given the Pascal declarations

```
type rc = record
            data: integer;
            next: ^rc;
          end;
var x: ^rc;
```

the assignment x := x^. next generates a type error. Why? Does the
same thing happen in Modula-2? C? Ada?

7. Show that the set

{emptylist} ∪ CHAR ∪ (CHAR × CHAR) ∪

$\qquad\qquad\qquad$ (CHAR × CHAR × CHAR) ∪ ...

is the smallest solution to the set equation

$\qquad$ charlist = {emptylist} ∪ CHAR × charlist

(See page 167 and Chapter 4, Exercise 40.)

8. Consider the set equation

$$X \times \text{CHAR} = X$$

   (a) Show that any set X satisfying this equation must be infinite.
   (b) Show that any element of a set satisfying this equation must contain an infinite number of characters.
   (c) Is there a smallest solution to this equation?

9. Consider the following declaration in Modula-2 syntax:

```
TYPE chartree = RECORD
                    data: CHAR;
                    left,right : chartree;
                END;
```

   (a) Rewrite this declaration using a variant record to supply the base case of an empty chartree similar to the charlist declaration in Section 6.3.6.
   (b) Write a set equation for your declaration from part (a).
   (c) Describe a set that is the smallest solution to your equation of part (b).
   (d) Prove that your set in part (c) is the smallest solution.

10. Here are some type declarations in Pascal syntax:

```
type ptr1  = ^rec1;
     ptr2  = ^rec2;
     rec1  = record
                 data: integer;
                 next: ptr2;
             end;
     rec2  = record
                 data: integer;
                 next: ptr1;
             end;
```

   Should these be allowed? Are they allowed? Why?

11. (a) What is the difference between a subtype and a derived type in Ada?
    (b) What Pascal type declaration is the following Ada declaration equivalent to?

```
subtype New_Int is INTEGER;
```

    (c) What Pascal type declaration is the following Ada declaration equivalent to?

```
type New_Int is new INTEGER;
```

12. The Modula-2 report (Wirth [1988a]) gives the following type rules for the expression $e1 = e2$: the $=$ relation applies to the basic types INTEGER, CARDINAL, BOOLEAN, CHAR, REAL, to enumerations, and to subrange types. It also applies to sets and pointers. Discuss the reasons for these rules. Are there any ambiguities?

13. Describe the type rules for the C equality operator $==$. Compare them to the Modula-2 rules given in the previous exercise.

14. Suppose we want to define an if-then-else expression that performs the test and then evaluates either to the value of the then-part or to the value of the else-part, depending on the value of the test. For example, the expression

    ```
    if 1 = 2 then 'a' else 'b'
    ```

    should evaluate to the character 'b'. What type correctness and type inference rules should apply to such an if-then-else expression? Is it possible to define such an expression with an optional else-part? Why?

15. The C language has an if-the-else expression similar to the one described in the previous exercise, except that "if e1 then e2 else e3" is written

    ```
    e1 ? e2 : e3
    ```

    Describe the type correctness and inference rules for this expression in C.

16. Write a program to test whether your Modula-2 or Pascal compiler actually tests the discriminant of a variant record when a variant field is accessed.

17. Given the type

    ```
    IntPtr = POINTER TO INTEGER
    ```

    write a Modula-2 procedure that will print out the address held by any variable of type IntPtr. You will need to use a variant record and look up the format for addresses on your machine. Do not use any features imported from the SYSTEM module or other features outside the language definition. Use your procedure to determine the internal form of the NIL pointer.

18. Do the previous exercise in Pascal for the type

    ```
    IntPtr = ^integer.
    ```

19. Suppose we used the following Modula-2 code in an attempt to print out the internal value of TRUE used by an implementation:

```
VAR x: RECORD CASE BOOLEAN OF
            TRUE: i: INTEGER |
            FALSE: b: BOOLEAN
          END; (* case *)
        END (* record *);
  . . .
x.b := TRUE;
WriteInt(x.i,1);
```

(a) What implementation dependencies may cause this code to fail?

(b) Is it possible to rewrite the code to eliminate these implementation dependencies? If so, write out the new code. If not, explain why not.

20. The chapter makes no mention of the initialization problem for variables: When a program starts running, are variables automatically set to some initial value? Discuss the problems you might encounter in writing an initialization requirement for a language definition. Can initial values always be associated with every type? Should initial values be programmer defined? Should they be associated with types or variables?

21. Test your Modula-2 or Pascal compiler to see what initializations are performed. Are pointers always set to NIL? What about predefined types? What about structured types?

22. Ada and C, unlike Pascal and Modula-2, allow explicit initialization of variables. Compare the facilities in these two languages.

23. Here are some type and variable declarations in Pascal syntax:

```
type
  range = -5..5;
  table1 = array [range] of char;
  table2 = table1;
var
  x,y: array [-5..5] of char;
  z: table1;
  w: table2;
  i: range;
  j: -5..5;
```

State which variables are type equivalent under (a) structural equivalence, (b) name equivalence, and (c) declaration equivalence and why. Be sure to identify those cases that are ambiguous from the information at hand.

24. Write some code to test your answer to Exercise 23(c) in (a) Modula-2, and (b) Pascal. What does the result tell you about subranges?

25. Here are some type and variable declarations in Pascal syntax:

```
type
  rec1 = record
    x: integer;
    case boolean of
    true: (y:char);
    false: (z:boolean);
  end;
  rec2 = rec1;
  rec3 = record
    x: integer;
    case b:boolean of
    true: (y:char);
    false: (z:boolean);
  end;
var
  a,b: rec1;
  c: rec2;
  d: rec3;
```

State which variables are type equivalent under (a) structural equivalence, (b) name equivalence, and (c) declaration equivalence and why. Be sure to identify those cases that are ambiguous from the information at hand.

26. Compare the syntax of the variant record case declaration with the case statement and discuss the differences from the point of view of design criteria in (a) Modula-2 and (b) Pascal.

27. Compare the syntax of the variant record case declaration of Modula-2 to that of Pascal. Explain why the syntax of Modula-2 allows more than one variant part in a record declaration, while the syntax of Pascal restricts a record declaration to one variant part at the end of the declaration.

28. Show how to use multiple type declarations to get more than one variant part in a record declaration in Pascal.

29. Can an undiscriminated union in C, Modula-2, or Pascal be used to convert integers to reals and vice versa? Why or why not?

30. The C language includes a **union** type constructor distinct from a **struct,** while Pascal and Modula-2 incorporate the union type into the **record** structure using the **case** construct. From one point of view, C's approach is better, since it distinguishes separate concepts. But from a practical point of view, the C mechanism causes an extra difficulty that limits its use. Describe the difficulty.

31. State which operations are implicitly created with the set type constructor in (a) Modula-2 and (b) Pascal.

32. State which operations are implicitly created with the file type constructor in Pascal.

33. The MOD operation is shared in Modula-2 between INTEGER and CARDINAL data types. Is the operation different for arguments of the two different types? If not, why not? If so, can a Modula-2 compiler always determine which operation is meant? Explain.

34. Some Pascal extensions contain an **anytype** type declaration that serves to create LISP-like variables that assume their types from the values they store during execution. Describe the design of such a language extension, and some of the uses it might be put to. What problems do you foresee in implementing the design?

35. In a language in which "/" can mean either integer or real division and that allows coercions between integers and reals, the expression $I + J/K$ may yield different results. Describe how this can happen. Which interpretation does FORTRAN use? Which does C use? Which interpretation is better?

36. Data types can be kept as part of the syntax tree of a program and checked for structural equivalence by a simple recursive algorithm. For example, the type

```
RECORD
   x: REAL;
   y: ARRAY [1..10] OF INTEGER;
END;
```

might be kept as the tree

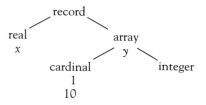

Describe a tree node structure that could be used to express the types of Pascal or Modula-2 as trees. Write out a TypeEqual function in pseudocode that would check structural equivalence on these trees.

37. How could the trees of the previous exercise represent recursive types? Modify your TypeEqual function to take recursive types into account.

38. The language C uses structural type equivalence for arrays and pointers, but declaration equivalence for structs and unions. Why do you think the language designers did this? Does it cause any problems for the programmer? Explain.

39. Compare the BNFs for type declarations in Pascal with the type tree of Figure 6-1. To what extent is the tree a direct reflection of the syntax?

40. Draw a type tree for Modula-2 similar to the trees for Pascal and Ada in Figures 6-1 and 6-2. Be sure to include all the predefined types.

41. Draw a type tree for C similar to the trees for Pascal and Ada in Figures 6-1 and 6-2.

42. What operations would you consider necessary for a string data type? How well do arrays of characters support these operations?

43. Suppose we decided to call a string a `file of char` in Pascal. How well would this support string operations?

44. Test your Pascal compiler to determine whether type

    ```
    array [integer] of char;
    ```

    is legal. Is type

    ```
    array [char] of integer
    ```

    legal?

45. Given the following Modula-2 declarations,

    ```
    VAR i: INTEGER; c: CARDINAL;
    ```

    let us assume that `INTEGER` data type is from -32768 to 32767 and `CARDINAL` is from 0 to 65535. Which of the following assignments cause a runtime error and which do not? Why?

    ```
    c := 50000;
    i := c;
    i := INTEGER(c);
    i := VAL(INTEGER,c);
    ```

46. In Modula-2, casts can be applied only when the data type being cast to has the same size in memory as the data type being cast from. Thus, if c is a `CARDINAL`, `INTEGER(c)` is legal but `REAL(c)` and `CHAR(c)` are not. Why is this restriction made?

47. The conversion rules for an arithmetic expression such as $e1 + e2$ in (pre-ANSI) C are stated in Kernighan and Ritchie [1978] as follows:

    First, any operands of type `char` or `short` are converted to `int`, and any of type `float` are converted to `double`. Then, if either operand is `double`, the other is converted to `double` and that is the type of the result.

Otherwise, if either operand is long, the other is converted to long and that is the type of the result.

Otherwise, if either operand is unsigned, the other is converted to unsigned and that is the type of the result.

Otherwise, both operands must be int, and that is the type of the result.

Given the following expression in C, assuming x is an unsigned with value 1, describe the type conversion that occur during evaluation and the type of the resulting value. What is the resulting value?

```
'0' + 1.0 * (-1 + x)
```

48. In C there is no boolean data type. Instead, comparisons such as a == b and a <= b return the integer value 0 for false and 1 for true. On the other hand, the if-statement in C considers any nonzero value of its condition to be equivalent to true. Is there an advantage to doing this? Why not allow the condition a <= b to return *any* nonzero value if it is true?

49. The text mentions in Section 6.2 that a subrange can be allocated more efficiently if it is packed into the minimum space necessary to store its values. For example, the subrange 0..7 could be stored in just three bits instead of the full allocated space of its integer base type. This creates type conversion problems, however, since now values of the subranges 0..7 and 1..8 are stored differently and cannot be directly copied to each other or to an integer variable. Explain how these conversions can be done. Is it possible for a translator to insert code to perform these?

Notes and References

Data type systems in Algol-like languages such as Pascal, C, Modula-2, and Ada seem to suffer from excessive complexity and many special cases. In part, this is because a type system is trying to balance two opposing design goals: expressiveness and security. That is, a type system tries to make it possible to catch as many errors as possible while at the same time allowing the programmer the flexibility to create and use as many types as are necessary for the natural expression of an algorithm. Algol68 escapes from this complexity somewhat by using structural equivalence, but this weakens the effectiveness of type names in distinguishing different uses of the same structure. Ada has perhaps the most consistent system, albeit containing many different ideas and hence extremely complex. An interesting variant on traditional type systems is that of Modula-3, an object-oriented modification of Modula-2 that uses structural equivalence for ordinary data and name equivalence for objects (Cardelli et al. [1989a,b]; Nelson [1991]). A similar idea works for ML and Miranda (Chapter 10): structural equivalence is used except for specially constructed types, including abstract types (with protection of internal data, Chapter 8) and concrete (ML) or algebraic (Miranda) types.

One frustrating aspect of the study of type systems is that language reference manuals rarely state the underlying algorithms explicitly. Instead, the algorithms must be inferred from a long list of special rules, a time-consuming investigative task. There are also few references that give detailed overviews of language type systems. Two that do have considerable detail are Cleaveland [1986] and Bishop [1986]. A lucid description of Pascal's type system can be found in Cooper [1983], most of which applies to Modula-2 as well. For a study of type polymorphism and overloading, see Cardelli and Wegner [1985].

The IEEE floating-point standard, mentioned in Section 6.2, appears in IEEE [1985].

7 CONTROL

In Chapter 6 we discussed the abstraction of data through the use of data types. In this chapter we discuss the abstraction of control through the use of structured control and procedures.

Control structures began in programming languages as GOTOs, which are simple imitations of the jump statements of assembly language, transferring control directly, or after a test, to a new location in the program. With Algol60 came the improvement of **structured control,** in which control statements transfer control to and from sequences of statements that are (at least in principle) **single-entry, single-exit,** that is, those that enter from the beginning and exit from the end. Examples of such single-entry, single-exit constructs are the **blocks** of Algol60, Algol68, C, and Ada, which may also include declarations, and which we studied in Chapter 5. The compound statements of Pascal and the statement sequences of Modula-2 also qualify as single-entry, single-exit (these do not contain declarations).[1]

Structured programming led to an enormous improvement in the readability and reliability of programs, and structured control constructs are part of most major languages today. Some languages do away with GOTOs altogether, although a debate rages to this day on the utility of GOTOs within the context of structured programming. In this chapter

---

[1]All these languages contain certain relaxations of the single-entry, single-exit property of these constructs, but the principle of controlling entry and exit points remains.

we will first discuss structured control mechanisms; then we will review the use of the GOTO statement.

Extending the idea of the block is the procedure or function as a block whose execution is deferred and whose interfaces are clearly specified. These too are structures with clearly defined entries and exits.

The final topic discussed in this chapter is a situation where transfers of control must be preempted: exception handling. This is a more complex situation, because exceptions cause the normal flow of control to be disturbed.

7.1   GUARDED COMMANDS AND CONDITIONALS

The most typical form of structured control is execution of a group of statements only under certain conditions. This involves making a Boolean, or logical, test before entering a sequence of statements. The well-known **if-then-else** construct is the most common form of this construct. The various ways such a conditional can be introduced will be discussed shortly.

First, however, we want to describe a general form of conditional statement that encompasses all the various conditional constructs: the **guarded if** statement introduced by E. W. Dijkstra:

```
i f  B1  –>  S1
  |  B2  –>  S2
  |  B3  –>  S3
       . . .
  |  Bn  –>  Sn
 f i
```

The semantics of this statement are as follows: the B_i's are all Boolean expressions, called the **guards,** and the S_i's are statement sequences. If one of the B_i's evaluates to true, then the corresponding statement sequence S_i is executed. If more than one of the B_i's is true, then one and only one of the corresponding S_i's is selected for execution. If none of the B_i's is true, then an error occurs.

There are several interesting features in this description. First, it does not say that the first B_i that evaluates to true is the one chosen. Thus the guarded if introduces **nondeterminism** into programming, a feature that becomes very useful in concurrent programming (Chapter 13). Second, it leaves unspecified whether all the guards are evaluated.

Thus, if the evaluation of a B i has a side effect, the result of the execution of the guarded if may be unknown. Of course, the usual deterministic implementation of such a statement would sequentially evaluate the B i's until a true one is found, whence the corresponding S i is executed and control is transferred to the point following the guarded statement.

The two major ways that programming languages implement conditional statements like the guarded if are as if-statements and case-statements.

7.1.1   If-statements

The basic form of the if-statement is as given in the Pascal extended Backus-Naur form (EBNF) rule, with an optional "else" part:

<if-statement> ::= if <Boolean-expression> then <statement>
                   [else <statement>]

where <statement> can be either a single statement or a sequence of statements surrounded by a begin-end pair:

```
if x <> 0.0 then y := 1.0/x
else begin
  x := 2.0;
  y := 1.0/z;
end;
```

This form of the if (which also exists in Algol60 and C) has a problem, however: it is ambiguous in the syntactic sense described in Chapter 4. Indeed, the statement

```
if B1 then if B2 then S1 else S2
```

has two different parse trees according to the BNF:

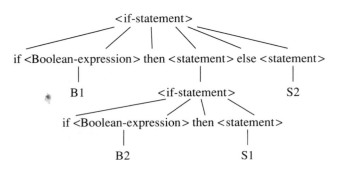

and

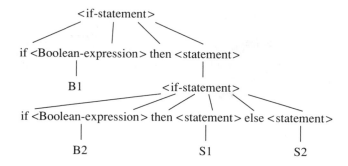

This ambiguity is called the **dangling-else** problem. In Pascal and Algol60 the syntax does not tell us whether an e l s e after two if-statements is to be associated with the first or second i f. Pascal solves this problem by stating a **disambiguating rule:** the e l s e is to be associated with the closest i f that does not already have an e l s e part. This rule is also referred to as the **most closely nested rule** for if-statements. It states that the second parse tree is the correct one.

The dangling-else problem is somewhat questionable language design from two points of view: it makes us state a new rule to describe what is essentially a syntactic feature, and it makes the interpretation of the if-statement by the reader more difficult; that is, it violates the readability design criterion. As an illustration, if we want actually to associate the e l s e with the first i f in the preceding statement, we would have to write either

```
if B1 then begin if B2 then S1 end else S2
```

or

```
if B1 then if B2 then S1 else else S2
```

There are other ways to solve the dangling-else than by using a disambiguating rule. In fact, it is possible to write out BNF rules that specify the association precisely, but these rules are complex (see Exercise 9). A better way is to use a **bracketing keyword** for the if-statement, such as the Algol68 rule:

<if-statement> ::= if <Boolean-expression> then <statement>
　　　　　　　　　　[else <statement>] fi

The i f spelled backward closes the if-statement and removes the ambiguity, since we must now write either

```
if B1 then if B2 then S1 fi else S2 fi
```

or

```
if B1 then if B2 then S1 else S2 fi fi
```

to decide which if is associated to the else part. This also removes the necessity of using a begin-end pair to open a new sequence of statements: the if-statement can open its own sequence of statements and thus becomes fully structured:

```
if x > 0.0 then
    y := 1.0/x;
    done := true;
else
    x := 1.0;
    y := 1.0/z;
    done := false;
fi
```

A similar approach is taken in Ada, where the two reserved words end if close an if-statement; in FORTRAN77, where the bracketing keyword is ENDIF; and in Modula-2, where the bracketing keyword is just END:

```
IF x > 0.0 THEN
    y := 1.0/x;
    done := true;
ELSE
    x := 1.0;
    y := 1.0/z;
    done := false;
END
```

A problem with the Modula-2 solution, however, is that the reserved word END is used to terminate many other structures as well, so the syntax does not allow us to associate easily the END with the structure that it terminates. The Algol68 and Ada solutions are a little better.

An extension of the if-statement simplifies things when there are many alternatives. Multiple elses would have to be written in Modula-2 as

```
IF B1 THEN
    S1
ELSE
    IF B2 THEN
        S2
    ELSE
```

```
        IF B3 THEN
            S3
        ELSE
            S4
        END
    END
END
```

with many ENDs piled up at the end to close all the IFs. Instead the ELSE IF is compacted into a new reserved word ELSIF that opens a new sequence of statements at the same level:

```
IF B1 THEN
    S1
ELSIF B2 THEN
    S2
ELSIF B3 THEN
    S3
ELSE
    S4
END
```

Ada has the same construct, and in Algol68 the elsif is called elif.

7.1.2   Case-statements

The case-statement was invented by C. A. R. Hoare as a special kind of guarded if, where the guards, instead of being Boolean expressions, are ordinal values that are selected by an ordinal expression. In Modula-2 this looks like

```
CONST n = 5;
VAR x: [1..10];

CASE x-1 OF
    0 :
        y := 0;
        z := 2;
|   2, 3..n:
        y := 3;
        z := 1;
|   7,9:
        z := 10;
ELSE
        (* do nothing *)
END (* case *)
```

Note that cases can be constants, constant expressions, or constant ranges or lists of these. (Standard Pascal leaves ranges out of its definition of the case-statement.) The catch-all ELSE part is optional, but if a case occurs that is not listed, and there is no ELSE part, an error occurs. Also, the same value cannot be part of two case specifiers.

Most modern languages have a case-statement similar to that of Modula-2, with similar restrictions (no overlapping cases, an error if an unspecified case occurs). Pascal omits the catch-all else, forcing all cases to be listed. (Most implementations add it, however, as either an else or an otherwise.) Algol68 has a similar structure, but the selectors are limited to integer values. Also in Algol68, the case list need not be exhaustive: if a case occurs that is not listed, control passes to the statement after the case-statement rather than an error occurring.

C has a variation on the case-statement, called the **switch**-statement:

```
switch (x-1)
{case 0 :
    y = 0;
    z = 2;
    break;
 case 2:
 case 3:
 case 4:
 case 5:
    y = 3;
    z = 1;
    break;
 case 7:
 case 9:
    z = 10;
    break;
 default:;
    /* do nothing */
}
```

As in Algol68, cases can only be integer-valued. They must also be listed individually. And a break must be used to exit the statement unless the programmer wants to continue executing all the remaining statements. This allows cases to be lumped together as in the list of the cases 2 through 5, but it also means that the break must be used to terminate each separate case.

If constructs and other selectors can be expressions that return values as well as statements. In this case type restrictions apply, since there must be an inferable result type for the expression. For example, in Algol68, the expression

```
if B then exp1 else exp2 fi
```

returns either the value of e x p 1 or e x p 2, depending on the value of B, and so e x p 1 and e x p 2 must have either the same type or compatible types, so that a common result type can be returned.

In C there is a conditional expression in addition to the conditional statement. The conditional expression is

```
e1 ? e2 : e3
```

where e 1 is evaluated; if it is nonzero, e 2 is evaluated and its value returned as the value of the expression; otherwise, the value of e 3 is returned. The expressions e 2 and e 3 must, of course, have compatible types. The type of the result is determined by the type conversion rules of C.

7.2   *LOOPS AND VARIATIONS ON WHILE*

Loops and their use to perform repetitive operations, especially using arrays, have been one of the major features of computer programming since the beginning—computers were in a sense invented to make the task of performing repetitive operations easier and faster. A general form for a loop construct is given by the corresponding structure to Dijkstra's guarded if, namely, the **guarded do:**

```
do   B1  -> S1
   | B2  -> S2
   | B3  -> S3
        . . .
   | Bn  -> Sn
 od
```

This statement is repeated until all the B i 's are false. At each step, one of the true B i 's is selected nondeterministically, and the corresponding S i is executed.

A standard form of loop construct, which is essentially a guarded do with only one guard (thus eliminating the nondeterminism), is the while-loop of Algol68,

```
while B do S od
```

or the while-loop of Modula-2,

```
WHILE B DO S END
```

In these statements B is a Boolean expression that is evaluated first. If it is true, then the statement (or block, or statement sequence) S is executed. Then B is evaluated again, and so on. Note that if B is false to begin with, then S is never executed. Some languages have an alternative statement that ensures that S is executed at least once. In Pascal this is the **repeat**-statement (Modula-2 has an identical statement):

```
repeat S until B
```

Of course, this is exactly equivalent to the following code,

```
S;
while not B do S
```

so the repeat-statement is "syntactic sugar" (a language construct that is completely expressible in terms of other constructs). But it does express a common situation.

The while and repeat constructs have the property that termination of the loop can occur at only one point and that S cannot be exited at intermediate points, unless extra Boolean variables are introduced and tested in B. Sometimes it is helpful to be able to exit a loop from arbitrary points inside it. A more general form of loop is therefore sometimes included in languages, such as the LOOP-EXIT of Modula-2:

```
LOOP
   ...
   IF B1 THEN EXIT END;
   ...
   IF B2 THEN EXIT END;
   ...
END; (* loop *)
```

A LOOP-EXIT statement can have arbitrarily many exits within its body. A LOOP-EXIT statement may also contain no EXIT statement at all, in which case it loops forever. In PL/I and C a break is used instead of EXIT (exit is used in C to cause execution of the entire program to terminate). A loop with exits can be simulated by a while- or repeat-statement. For example, the foregoing loop with two exits could be written as

```
Done1 := FALSE;
Done2 := FALSE;
REPEAT
   ...
   IF B1 THEN Done1 := TRUE
   ELSE
      ...
      IF B2 THEN Done2 := TRUE
      ELSE
         ...
      END (* if B2 *)
   END (* if B1 *)
UNTIL Done1 OR Done2;
```

but this is far less readable than the code with the LOOP statement. It also involves the introduction of the extra Boolean variables Done1 and Done2. In this sense, single-entry, single-exit statements like repeat- and while-statements are less "powerful" than are loops with multiple exits. But, as we noted in Chapter 1, they are not strictly necessary to perform any computation: given any one loop construct, all the others are "syntactic sugar."

A common special case of a looping construct is the **for-loop,** as in the Modula-2,

```
FOR I := 0 TO 2*Nmax STEP 2 DO
   . . .
END;
```

or the DO loop of FORTRAN,

```
DO 20 I = 0,2*Nmax
   . . .
20 CONTINUE
```

In the Modula-2 loop, I is a **control variable.** The loop is executed by first evaluating the **bound expressions** (0 and 2*Nmax, in this case), setting I to the first bound and incrementing I by the STEP expression (in this case, 2) after each execution of the loop. This form of loop is often included in languages because it can be more effectively optimized than other loop constructs. For example, the control variable (and perhaps the final bound) can be put into registers, allowing extremely fast operations. Also, many processors have a single instruction that can both increment a register, test it, and branch, so that the loop control and increment can occur in a single machine instruction. To gain this efficiency, however, many restrictions must be placed on a for-statement. Most of the restrictions involve the control variable I. Typical restrictions are the following:

- The value of I cannot be changed within the body of the loop.
- The value of I is undefined after the loop terminates.
- I must be of restricted type and may not be declared in certain ways, for example, as a parameter to a procedure, or as a record field, or perhaps it must even be a local variable.

Some languages restrict control variables to integer type. Others such as Pascal and Modula-2 allow any ordinal type. Ada goes one step farther and has the loop define its own control variable whose type is determined from the bound expressions and which is not available outside the loop.

Further questions about the behavior of loops include

- Are the bounds evaluated only once? If so, then the bounds may not change after execution begins.

- If the lower bound is greater than the upper bound, is the loop executed at all? Most modern languages perform a bound test at the beginning rather than the end of the loop, so the loop behaves like a while-loop. Some older FORTRAN implementations, however, have loops that always execute at least once.

- Is the control variable value undefined even if a GOTO or EXIT statement is used to leave the loop before termination? Some languages permit the value to be available on "abnormal termination," but not otherwise.

- What translator checks are performed on loop structures? Some language definitions do not insist that a translator catch assignments to the control variable, which can cause unpredictable results.

Some languages, such as CLU, have a general form of for-loop construct that involves a new language object, called an **iterator**. Abstractly, an iterator must provide for the definition of control variables, an iteration scheme for these control variables (that is, a way of assigning a new value given its current value), and a facility for making termination tests. Thus an iterator becomes something like a new type declaration (and can be put into the scheme of abstract data types in Chapter 8). An example taken from Liskov et al. [1977] is

```
numcount = proc (s:string) returns (int);
  count: int = 0;
  for c: char in stringchars(s) do
    if numeric(c) then
      count := count +1;
    end;
  end;
  return (count);
end numcount;

stringchars = iter (s: string) yields (char);
  index: int := 1;
  limit: int := string$size(s);
  while index <= limit do
    yield (string$fetch(s,index))
    index := index + 1;
  end;
end stringchars;
```

The iterator is stringchars. Iterators are defined like functions with a returned value (in this case, char). However, the effect of calling an iterator is as follows.

The first time an iterator is called, the values of its parameters are saved. The iterator then commences to execute, until it reaches a **yield-**statement, when it suspends execution and returns the value of the expression in the yield. Upon subsequent calls it resumes execution after the yield, suspending whenever it reaches another yield, until it exits, whence the loop from which it is called also is terminated.

7.3   *THE GOTO CONTROVERSY*

GOTOs are still the mainstay of a number of programming languages, such as FORTRAN and BASIC. For example, the FORTRAN code

```
10  IF (A(I).EQ.0) GOTO 20
    . . .
    I = I + 1
    GOTO 10
20  CONTINUE
```

is the FORTRAN77 equivalent to the Pascal:

```
while a[i] <> 0 do begin
    . . .
    i := i + 1;
end;
```

Ever since a famous letter by E. W. Dijkstra in 1968, GOTOs have been considered suspect, since they can so easily lead to unreadable "spaghetti" code:

```
    IF (X.GT.0) GOTO 10
    IF (X.LT.0) GOTO 20
    X = 1
    GOTO 30
10  X = X + 1
    GOTO 30
20  X = -X
    GOTO 10
30  CONTINUE
```

The GOTO statement is very close to actual machine code. As Dijkstra pointed out, its "unbridled" use can compromise even the most careful language design and lead to undecipherable programs. Dijkstra proposed that its use be severely controlled or even abolished. This unleashed one of the most persistent controversies in programming, which still rages today. One group argues that the GOTO is indispensable for efficiency and even for good structure. Another argues that it can be useful under carefully limited circumstances. A third argues that it is an anachronism that should truly be abolished henceforth from all computer languages.

We do not want to try to give all the arguments used in this controversy; perhaps just one example will suffice of a situation where many have argued for the use of a GOTO, in a deeply nested structure to return to the outermost level (this is legal Pascal code):

```
if ok then begin
  while not done do begin
    . . .
    while not found do begin
      . . .
      if disaster then goto 99;
      . . .
    end; (* while not found *)
  end; (* while not done *)
end; (* if ok *)
. . .
99: . . .
```

In such cases it may be well to ask whether some other construct might achieve the same effect and thus eliminate even the few places where the GOTO does simplify the code. For example, many languages provide EXIT or BREAK statements to allow the transfer of control to the end of a statement sequence from arbitrary points within it:

```
LOOP
  . . .
  IF done THEN
    EXIT;
  END; (* if *)
  . . .
END; (* loop *)
```

is an example from Modula-2, where control is transferred by the EXIT statement to the statement following the END of the LOOP. This would perhaps satisfy most of the situations given by the previous Pascal example.

If, however, a language has many situations in which GOTOs are seen as necessary for the clarity of the code, it may be that the language has not included enough structured control structures. For instance, in the FORTRAN example simulating the while-statement, the GOTO was necessary only because FORTRAN77 failed to include a WHILE statement.

One can also take the view that the GOTO should remain, but with severe restrictions on its use. As an example, in Pascal the rules governing the use of the GOTO imply that a GOTO cannot be used to jump into a sequence of statements that the GOTO statement is not a part of. Thus the following is a legal GOTO in Pascal,

```
1: readln(i);
   if i < j then begin
     Search(i,j);
     if error then goto 1;
   end; (* if *)
```

but the following is not:

```
if ok then goto 1
else begin
  readln(i);
  1: Search(i,j);
end; (* if *)
```

Similar rules apply in Ada. These rules are supposed to encourage the use of GOTOs to enhance the structure of a program rather than to destroy it. Indeed, in languages where structured control mechanisms are not available, the GOTO can be used to simulate them, as in the FORTRAN77 simulation of a while-loop. A few languages, like Modula-2, have taken the extreme form of Dijkstra's position and abolished the GOTO altogether.

7.4   PROCEDURES AND PARAMETERS

A procedure is a mechanism in a programming language for abstracting a group of actions or computations. The group of actions is called the **body** of the procedure, and the body of the procedure is represented as a whole by the name of the procedure. A procedure is declared by specifying its name, its **parameters,** and its body, as in the following Pascal procedure declaration:

```
procedure intswap (var x,y: integer);
var t: integer;
begin
  t := x;
  x := y;
  y := t;
end;
```

Procedure intswap swaps the values of its parameters x and y, using a local variable t.

A procedure is **called** or **activated** by stating its name, together with **arguments** to the call, which correspond to its parameters:

```
intswap(a,b);
```

A call to a procedure transfers control to the beginning of the body of the called procedure (the **callee**). When execution reaches the end of the body, control is returned to the **caller.** In some languages, control can be returned to the caller before reaching the end of the callee's body by using a **return-statement.** Pascal contains no return-statement, but Modula-2 does:

```
PROCEDURE intswap (VAR x,y: INTEGER) ;
VAR t: INTEGER;
BEGIN
  IF x = y THEN
    RETURN;
  END;
  t := x;
  x := y;
  y := t;
END intswap;
```

In some languages, such as FORTRAN, to call a procedure one must also include the keyword CALL, as in

```
CALL INTSWAP(A,B)
```

(In FORTRAN, procedures are called **subroutines.**)

A programming language may make a distinction between procedures, which carry out their operations by changing their parameters or nonlocal variables, and **functions,** which appear in expressions and compute **returned values.** Functions may or may not also affect their parameters and nonlocal variables. In Pascal, a function is declared using the keyword function but is nothing more than a procedure with a returned value:

```
function intswap (var x,y: integer): boolean;
var t: temp;
begin
  t := x;
  x := y;
  y := t;
  intswap := true;
end;
```

The assignment to intswap in the last statement of its body is not really variable assignment but establishes a returned value for the function (in this case always the constant Boolean value true). In Pascal this statement can appear at any point in the body of the function and does not imply that the function returns to its caller at that point. Thus the following is semantically equivalent to the previous code:

```
function intswap (var x,y: integer): boolean;
var t: temp;
begin
   intswap := true;
   t := x;
   x := y;
   y := t;
end;
```

Pascal functions and procedures are single-entry, single-exit constructs, like structured control statements in Pascal: they always execute their bodies entirely and return only at the end.

In Modula-2, like Pascal, functions are also just procedures with returned values, and this fact is emphasized by declaring them as procedures:

```
PROCEDURE intswap (VAR x,y: INTEGER) : BOOLEAN;
VAR t: INTEGER;
BEGIN
   t := x;
   x := y;
   y := t;
   RETURN TRUE;
END intswap;
```

In Modula-2, however, returned values are established by a RETURN statement, which also transfers control back to the caller. Thus the RETURN statement in the foregoing Modula-2 code must be placed last.

In some languages, there are only functions. Functional languages in particular have this property (see Chapter 10). In some languages, such as C, a procedure is distinguished from a function by returning a **null** or **void** value:

```
void intswap (int*x,int*y)
/* x and y are pointers to integers */
{int t = *x;
    *x = *y;
    *y = t;}
```

(The use of x and y as pointers in the code will be explained later in this section.)

In some languages, procedure and function declarations are written in a form similar to constant declarations, using an equal sign, as in the following Algol68 procedure declaration, which defines an intswap procedure exactly as the original Pascal (or C) code:

```
proc intswap = (ref int x,y) void:
begin
  int t := x;
  x := y;
  y := t
end;
```

Note the declaration of the parameters in parentheses after the " = " sign and the return value void after the parentheses.

The use of an equal sign to declare procedures is justified, because a procedure declaration gives the procedure name a meaning that remains constant during the execution of the program. We could say that a procedure declaration creates a constant procedure value and associates a symbolic name—the name of the procedure—with that value.

In the following discussion we will make no distinction between procedures and functions, but we will consider them both to be aspects of the same mechanism in a programming language.

A procedure communicates with the rest of the program through its parameters and also through **nonlocal references,** that is, references to variables declared outside of its own body. The **scope rules** that establish the meanings of nonlocal references were introduced in Chapter 5. In the remainder of this section, we will first review the semantics of blocks, as described in that chapter, emphasizing the difference between procedure and nonprocedure blocks. We will then study procedure parameters as mechanisms for communicating with the rest of the program. The structure of the environment necessary to maintain the communication and control links during procedure calls is discussed in the next section.

7.4.1   Procedure Semantics

A procedure is a block whose declaration is separated from its execution. In Chapter 5, we saw examples of blocks in C and Algol60 that are not procedure blocks; these blocks are always executed immediately when they are encountered. For example, in Algol60, blocks A and B in the following code are executed as they are encountered:

```
A:begin
    integer x,y;
    . . .
    x := y*10;
    B:begin
        integer i;
        i := x div 2;
        . . .
    end B;
end A;
```

In Chapter 5 we saw that the **environment** determines the allocation of memory and maintains the meaning of names during execution. In a block-structured language, when a block is encountered during execution, it causes the allocation of local variables and other objects corresponding to the declarations of the block. This memory allocated for the local objects of the block is called the **activation record** of the block, and the block is said to be **activated** as it executes under the bindings established by its activation record. As blocks are entered during execution, control passes from the activation of the surrounding block to the activation of the inner block. When the inner block exits, control passes back to the surrounding block, and the activation record of the inner block is released, returning to the environment of the activation record of the surrounding block.

For example, in the preceding Algol60 code, during execution x and y are allocated in the activation record of block A:

x
y

Activation record of A

When block B is entered, space is allocated in the activation record of B:

x
y
i

Activation record of A

Activation record of B

When B exits, the environment reverts to the activation record of A. Thus the activation of B must retain some information about the activation from which it was entered.

In the preceding code, block B needs to access the variable x declared in block A. A reference to x inside B is a **nonlocal** reference, since x is not allocated in the activation record of B, but in the activation record of the surrounding block A. This, too, requires that B retain information about its surrounding activation.

Now consider what would happen if B were a procedure called from A instead of a block entered directly from A. Suppose, for the sake of a concrete example, that we have the following situation, which we give in Pascal syntax:

```
program envex;
var x: integer;
```

continues

continued

```
procedure B;
var i: integer;
begin
  i := x div 2;
  . . .
end; (* B *)

procedure A;
var x,y: integer;
begin
  . . .
  x := y*10;
  B;
end; (* A *)

begin
  A;
end. (* envex *)
```

B is still entered from A, and the activation of B must retain some information about the activation of A so that control can return to A on exit from B. But there is now a difference in the way nonlocal references are resolved: under the **lexical scoping** rule (see Chapter 5), the x in B is the global x of the program, not the x declared in A. In terms of activation records, we have the following picture:

The activation of B must retain information about the global environment, since the nonlocal reference to x will be found there instead of in the activation record of A. This is because the global environment is the **defining environment** of B, while the activation record of A is the **calling environment** of B. (Sometimes the defining environment is called the **static environment** and the control environment the **dynamic environment**.) For blocks that are not procedures, the defining environment and the calling environment are always the same. By contrast a procedure has different calling and defining environments. Indeed, a procedure can have any number of calling environments during which it may retain the same defining environment.

The actual structure of the environment that keeps track of defining and calling environments will be discussed in the next section. What we are interested in in this section is the way an activation of a block **communicates** with the rest of the program.

Clearly, a nonprocedure block communicates with its surrounding block via nonlocal references: lexical scoping allows it access to all the variables in the surrounding block that are not redeclared in its own declarations. By contrast, under lexical scoping, a procedure block can communicate *only* with its defining block via references to nonlocal variables. It has no way of directly accessing the variables in its calling environment. In the sample Pascal code, procedure B cannot directly access the local variable x of procedure A. Nevertheless, it may need the value of x in A to perform its computations.

The method of communication of a procedure with its calling environment is through **parameters.** A **parameter list** is declared along with the definition of the procedure, as in

```
function gcd(u,v: integer):integer;
begin
  if v = 0 then gcd := u
  else gcd := gcd(v, u mod v)
end;
```

where u and v are **parameters** to the function gcd. They do not take on any value until gcd is called, when they are replaced by the **arguments** from the calling environment, as in

```
z := gcd(x+y,10);
```

In this call to gcd, the parameter u is replaced by the argument $x + y$, and the parameter v is replaced by the argument 10. To emphasize the fact that parameters have no value until they are replaced by arguments, parameters are sometimes called **formal parameters,** while arguments are called **actual parameters.**

A call to a procedure such as gcd binds the arguments to the parameters of the procedure declaration, while at the same time transferring control to the body of the procedure. How these bindings are interpreted depends on the **parameter passing mechanisms** used for the call. We will discuss four of the most important parameter passing mechanisms in the rest of this section: pass by value, pass by reference, pass by value-result, and pass by name. Some variations on these will be discussed in the exercises.

7.4.2 Parameter Passing Mechanisms

Pass by Value. In this mechanism, the arguments are expressions that are evaluated at the time of the call, and their values become the values of the parameters during the execution of the procedure. In its simplest form, this means that value parameters behave as constant values during the execution of the procedure, and one can interpret **pass by value** as replacing all the parameters in the body of the procedure by the values of its arguments. For instance, we can think of the call gcd(10,2+3) of the preceding gcd function as executing the body of gcd with u replaced by 10 and v replaced by 5:

```
if 5 = 0 then gcd := 10
else gcd := gcd(5, 10 mod 5)
```

This form of pass by value is the default in Ada (such parameters may also be explicitly declared as in parameters). Pass by value is also the default mechanism in Pascal and Modula-2 and is essentially the only parameter passing mechanism in C and Algo168. However, in these languages a slightly different interpretation of pass by value is used: the parameters are viewed as local variables of the procedure, with initial values given by the values of the arguments in the call. Thus, in Pascal and Modula-2, value parameters may be assigned to, just as with local variables (but cause no changes outside the procedure), while Ada in parameters may not be assigned to.

One question not resolved by pass by value is the order of the evaluation of the parameters. In the absence of side effects, the order is immaterial, and many language definitions state that any result that depends on the order of evaluation is an error. A few languages insist on left-to-right or right-to-left order. (Evaluation order for expressions, including function calls, was discussed in Section 5.7.)

Pass by Reference.   Here the arguments must be variables with allocated locations. Instead of passing the value of a variable, pass by reference passes the location of the variable, so that the parameter becomes an **alias** for the argument and any changes made to the parameter occur to the argument as well. In FORTRAN, pass by reference is the only parameter passing mechanism. In Pascal and Modula-2, pass by reference can be achieved with the use of the VAR keyword (note that this is a nonuniformity in that VAR is used for two rather unrelated things, variable declarations and pass by reference):

```
procedure refer(var x:integer);
begin
  x := x + 1;
end;
```

After a call to refer(a), the value of a has increased by 1, so that a side effect has occurred. Multiple aliasing is also possible, such as in the code

```
var a: integer;
   . . .
procedure ack(var x,y: integer);
begin
   x := 2;
   y := 3;
   a := 4;
end;


   . . .


ack(a,a);
```

Inside procedure a c k after the call, the identifiers x, y, and a all refer to the same variable, namely, the variable a.

C and Algol68 can achieve pass by reference by passing a reference or location explicitly. C uses the operator "&" to indicate the location of a variable and the operator "*" to dereference a pointer. Thus

```
void refer (int*x)
{*x += 1; /* adds 1 to *x */}


   . . .


int a;


   . . .


refer(&a);
```

has the same effect as the previous Pascal code. C has the further quirk, however, that arrays are always passed by reference (arrays are "pointer constants"):

```
void p(int x[])
{x[0] = 1;}


   . . .


int a[10];


   . . .


p(a);
```

has the effect of assigning the value 1 to a[0].

In Algol68 pointers are indicated by a **ref** type (for reference). Thus, in the following code,

```
proc refer = (ref int x) int:
begin
  x := x + 1
end;

begin
  int x := 1;
  refer(x)
end
```

x ends up with the value 2, since x has type ref int and value equal to its location, so the location of x is passed to procedure refer. On the other hand, the following code is illegal in Algol68, since parameter x has only a value and cannot be assigned to:

```
proc p = (int x) int:
begin
  x := x + 1
end;
```

Pass by Value-Result. This mechanism achieves a similar result to pass by reference, except that no actual alias is established: the value of the argument is copied and used in the procedure, and then the final value of the parameter is copied back out to the location of the argument when the procedure exits. Thus this method is sometimes known as copy-in, copy-out—or copy-restore. This is the mechanism of the Ada in out parameter. (Ada also has simply an out parameter, which has no initial value passed in; this could be called **pass by result**).

Pass by value-result is only distinguishable from pass by reference in the presence of aliasing. Thus, in the following code,

```
procedure p(x,y: integer);
begin
  x := x + 1;
  y := y + 1;
end;

begin
  a := 1;
  p(a,a);
end.
```

a has value 3 after p is called if pass by reference is used, while a has the value 2 if pass by value-result is used.

Issues left unspecified by this mechanism, and possibly differing in different languages or implementations, are the order in which results are copied back to the arguments and whether the locations of the arguments are calculated only on entry and stored or whether they are recalculated on exit.

Ada has a further quirk: its definition states that i n o u t parameters may actually be implemented as pass by reference and any computation that would be different under the two mechanisms (thus involving an alias) is an error.

Pass by Name.   This is the most difficult of the parameter passing mechanisms to understand. It is essentially the same as the normal order evaluation described in Chapter 5. It is used in Algol60, but fell into disuse after that, especially after complex interactions with other language constructs, particularly arrays and assignment, were discovered. Recently, pass by name has enjoyed a resurgence of interest in functional languages, where it is called **delayed evaluation** (see Chapter 10). The idea of pass by name is that the argument is not evaluated until its actual use (as a parameter) in the called program. Thus the name of the argument, or its textual representation at the point of call, replaces the name of the parameter it corresponds to. As an example, in the code

```
procedure p(x);
begin
   x := x + 1;
end;
```

if a call such as p (a [i]) is made, the effect is of evaluating a [i] := a [i] + 1. Thus, if i were to change before the use of x inside p, the result would be different from either pass by reference or pass by value-result:

```
var  i: integer;
     a: array [1..10] of integer;

procedure p(x);
begin
   i := i + 1;
   x := x + 1;
end;

begin
   i := 1;
   a[1] := 1;
   a[2] := 2;
   p(a[i]);
end.
```

has the result of setting a[2] to 3 and leaving a[1] unchanged. The interpretation of pass by name is as follows. The text of an argument at the point of call is viewed as a function in its own right, which is evaluated every time the corresponding parameter name is reached in the code of the called procedure. However, the argument will always be evaluated in the environment of the caller, while the procedure will be executed in its defining environment. To see how this works, consider the following example, in Pascal syntax:

```
program test;
var  i:  integer;

function p(y:integer):  integer;
var  j:  integer;
begin
  j  :=  y;
  i  :=  i  +  1;
  p  :=  j  +  y;
end;  (*  p  *)

procedure q;
var  j:  integer;
begin
  i  :=  0;
  j  :=  2;
  writeln(p(i+j));
end;  (*  q  *)

begin  (*  main  *)
  q;
end.
```

The argument i+j to the call to p from q is evaluated every time the parameter y is encountered inside p. The expression i+j is, however, evaluated as though it were still inside q, so in the first statement of p it produces the value 2. Then, in the third statement, since i is now 1, it produces the value 3 (the j in the expression i+j is the j of q, so it hasn't changed, even though the j inside p has). Thus, if pass by name is used for the parameter y of p in the program, the program will print 5.

Historically, the interpretation of pass by name arguments as functions to be evaluated during the execution of the called procedure was expressed by referring to the arguments as **thunks.** Presumably, the image was of little machines that "thunked" into place each time they were needed.

Pass by name is problematic when side effects are desired. Consider the intswap procedure we have discussed before:

```
procedure intswap (x,y: integer);
var t: integer;
begin
   t  := x;
   x  := y;
   y  := t;
end;
```

Suppose that pass by name is used for the parameters x and y and that we call this procedure as follows,

```
intswap(i,a[i])
```

where i is an integer index and a is an array of integers. The problem with this call is that it will function as the following code:

```
t  := i;
i  := a[i];
a[i]  := t;
```

Note that by the time the address of a [i] is computed in the third line, i has been assigned the value of a [i] in the previous line, and this will not assign t to the array a subscripted at the original i, unless i = a [i].

Despite these problems, pass by name can be a powerful mechanism in certain circumstances. One of the earliest examples of this power is called **Jensen's device** after its inventor J. Jensen. Jensen's device uses pass by name to apply an operation to an entire array, as in the following example, in Pascal syntax:

```
function sum (a,index,lower,upper: integer) :
                                        integer;
var temp: integer;
begin
   temp  := 0;
   for index  := lower to upper do
   temp  := temp + a;
   sum  := temp;
end;
```

If a and index are pass by name parameters, then in the following code

```
var x: array[1..10] of integer;
     i,xtotal: integer;
   . . .
xtotal  := sum(x[i],i,1,10);
```

the call to sum computes the sum of all the elements x [1] through x [10].

7.4.3 Type Checking of Parameters

In strongly typed languages, procedure calls must be checked so that the arguments agree in type and number with the parameters of the procedure. This means, first of all, that procedures may not have a variable number of parameters and that rules must be stated for the type compatibility between parameters and arguments. In the case of pass by reference, parameters usually must have the same type, but in the case of pass by value, this can be relaxed to assignment compatibility (Chapter 6), as is done in Modula-2, Pascal, and Ada.

7.5 PROCEDURE ENVIRONMENTS, ACTIVATIONS, AND ALLOCATION

In this section we want to give a little more detail on how information can be computed and maintained in an environment during procedure calls. We already saw in Chapter 5 and in the last section that the environment for a block-structured language with lexical scope can be maintained in a stack-based fashion, with an activation record created on the environment stack when a block is entered and released when the block is exited. We also saw how variables declared locally in the block are allocated space in this activation record.

In this section we want to see how this same structure can be extended to procedure activations, in which the defining environment and the calling environment differ, and we want to study the kinds of information necessary to maintain this environment correctly. A clear understanding of this **execution model** is often necessary to understand fully the behavior of programs, since the semantics of procedure calls are embedded in this model.

We also want to show that this stack-based environment is no longer adequate to deal with procedure variables and the dynamic creation of procedures and that languages with these facilities, particularly the functional languages of Chapter 10, are forced to use a more complex fully dynamic environment with garbage collection.

But, first, by way of contrast, we want to give a little more detail about the fully static environment of FORTRAN, which is quite simple, yet completely adequate for that language. We emphasize that the structures that we present here are only meant to illustrate the general scheme. Actual details implemented by various translators may differ substantially from the general outlines given here.

7.5.1 Fully Static Environments

In a language like FORTRAN, all memory allocation can be performed at load time, and the locations of all variables are fixed for the duration of program execution. Functions and procedures (or subroutines) cannot be nested, and recursion is not allowed. Thus all the information associated with a function or subroutine can be statically allocated. Each procedure or function has a fixed **activation record,** which contains space for the local variables and parameters, and possibly the return address for proper return from calls. Global variables are defined by COMMON statements, and are determined by pointers to a common area. Thus the general form of the runtime environment for a FORTRAN program with subroutines S1 ... Sn is as follows:

COMMON area
Activation record of main program
Activation record of S1
Activation record of S2
etc.

Each activation record, moreover, is broken down into several areas:

space for local variables
space for passed parameters
return address
temporary space for expression evaluation

When a call to a procedure S occurs, the parameters are evaluated, and their locations (using pass by reference) are stored in the parameter space of the activation record of S. Then the current instruction pointer is stored as the return address, and a jump is performed to the instruction pointer of S. When S exits, a jump is performed to the return address. If S is a function, special arrangements must be made for the returned value; often it is returned in a special register, or space can be reserved for it in the activation record of the function or the activation record of the caller.

As an example, consider the following FORTRAN program:

```
REAL TABLE(10),MAXVAL
READ *, TABLE(1),TABLE(2),TABLE(3)
CALL LRGST(TABLE,3,MAXVAL)
PRINT *, MAXVAL
END

SUBROUTINE LRGST (A,SIZE,V)
INTEGER SIZE
REAL A(SIZE),V
INTEGER K
V = A(1)
DO 10 K = 1,SIZE
IF (A(K).GT.V) V = A(K)
10 CONTINUE
RETURN
END
```

The environment of this program would look as follows, where we have added pointers indicating location references that exist immediately after the call to LRGST from the main program:

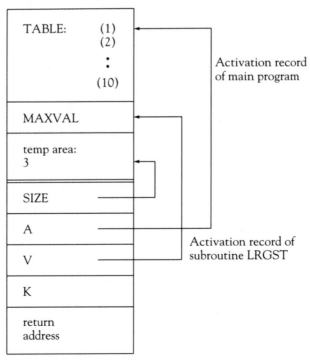

7.5.2   Stack-Based Runtime Environments

In a block-structured language with recursion, such as Pascal and other Algol-like languages, activations of procedure blocks cannot be allocated statically, since a procedure may be called again before its previous activation is exited, and so a new activation must be created on each procedure entry. As we have seen, this can be done in a stack-based manner, with a new activation record created on the stack every time a block is entered and released on exit.

What information must be kept in the environment to manage a stack-based environment? As with the fully static environment of FORTRAN, space in an activation needs to be allocated for local variables, temporary space, and a return pointer. However, several additional pieces of information are required. First, a pointer to the current activation must be kept, since each procedure has no fixed location for its activation record, but the location of its activation record may vary as execution proceeds. This pointer to the current activation must be kept in a fixed location, usually a register, and it is called the **environment pointer** or **ep,** since it points to the current environment.

The second piece of information that needs to be kept in a stack-based environment is a pointer to the activation record of the block from which the current activation was entered. In the case of a procedure call, this is the activation of the caller. The reason this piece of information is necessary is that, when the current activation is exited, the current activation record needs to be removed (i.e., popped) from the stack of activation records. This means that the ep must be restored to point to the previous activation, and this can be done only if the old ep, which pointed to the previous activation record, is retained in the new activation record. This stored pointer to the previous activation record is called the **control link,** since it points to the activation record of the block from which control passed to the current block and to which control will return.

A simple example is the following, in Pascal syntax:

```
program envex;

procedure p;
begin
   . . .
end;

procedure q;
begin
   . . .
   p;
end;
```

continues

continued

```
begin (* main program *)
   q;
end.
```

At the beginning of execution of the program, there is just a global area allocated, and the ep points there:

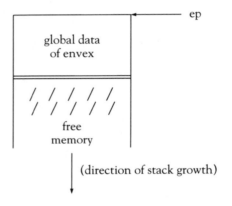

After the call to q, an activation record for q has been added to the stack, the ep now points to the activation record of q, and q has stored the old ep as its control link:

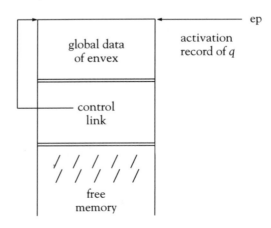

When p is called inside q, a new frame is added for p. Thus, after the call to p from within q, the activation stack looks as follows:

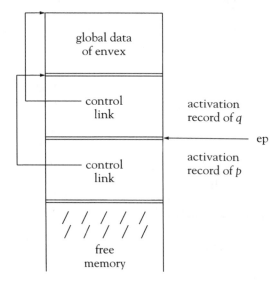

Now when p is exited, the activation record of p is returned to free memory, and the ep is restored from the control link of the activation record of p, so that it points to the activation record of q again. Similarly, when q is exited, the ep is restored to point to the global data area, and the original environment of the main program is recovered.

With this new requirement, the fields in each activation record need to contain the information in Figure 7-1.

Consider now how the environment pointer can be used to find variable locations. Local variables are allocated in the current activation record, which is pointed to by the ep. Since the local variables are allocated using the declarations of the block, each time the block is entered the same declarations are processed, and each variable can be allocated the same position in the activation record relative to the beginning of the record.[2] This position is called the **offset** of the local variable. Each local variable can be found using its fixed offset from the location pointed to by the ep.

Consider the following additions to our previous example:

```
program envex;
var x: integer;
```

continues

---

[2]This assumes that each variable has a constant size. Variable-length arrays are an exception to this requirement. See Exercise 27.

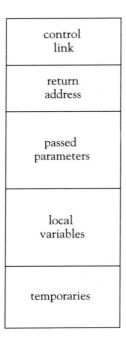

Figure 7-1   An Activation Record

continued

```
procedure p( y: integer);
var i: integer;
    b: boolean;
begin
  i := x;
  . . .
end;

procedure q (a: integer);
var x: integer;
begin
  . . .
  p(1);
end;

begin (* main program *)
  q(2);
end.
```

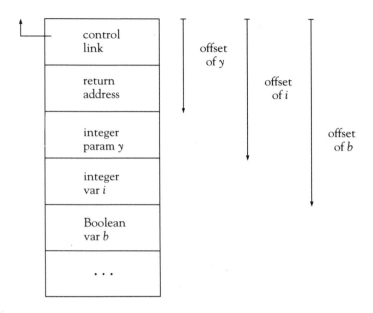

Figure 7-2   An Activation Record of p

Any activation record of p will have a format such as Figure 7-2. Each time p is called, the parameter y and the local variables i and b will be found in the same place relative to the beginning of the activation record.

Now consider the case of nonlocal references, such as the reference to x in p indicated in the foregoing code. How is x found? One idea would be to follow the control link to the activation record of q, but this would find the x local to q. This would achieve dynamic scope rather than lexical scope. To achieve lexical scope, a procedure such as p must maintain a link to its **lexical** or **defining environment.** This link is called the **access link,** since it provides access to nonlocal variables. In the example p is a global procedure, so its defining environment is the global environment, or global data area, and the access link for p is the ep when p is defined; that is, it points to the global data area. To satisfy this requirement, each activation record needs a new field, the access link field, and the complete picture of the environment for our example (after the call to p in q) is as follows:

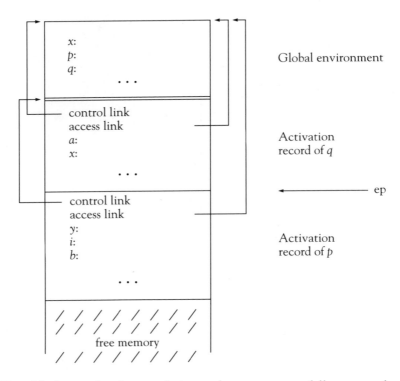

When blocks are deeply nested, it may be necessary to follow more than one access link to find a nonlocal reference. For example, in the program

```
program ex;
var  x:  ... ;

    procedure p;
    . . .
        procedure q;
        begin (* q *)
          . . .
            writeln(x);
        end; (* q *)

    begin (* p *)
      . . .
    end; (* p *)

begin (* main *)
  . . .
end.
```

to access x from inside q requires following the access link in the activation record of q to its defining environment, which is an activation record of p, and then following the access link of p to the global environment.

This process is called **access chaining,** and the number of access links that must be followed corresponds to the difference in nesting levels, or **nesting depth,** between the accessing environment and the defining environment of the variable being accessed.

With this organization of the environment, the semantics of a procedure must include not only the code for the body of the procedure (which is to be executed when it called), but also the defining environment of the procedure, which is used to resolve nonlocal references under lexical scope rules. Thus a function or procedure in a language like Pascal must be represented by a pair of pointers: the code or instruction pointer, which we denote by ip, and the access link, or environment pointer of its defining environment, which we denote by ep. We write this pair of pointers as <**ep,ip**> and refer to it as the **closure** of the procedure, because it fixes the environment under which the procedure executes, and resolves all references to nonlocal names.

We finish this section with an example of a program with nested procedures and a diagram of its environment at one point during execution (Figures 7-3 and 7-4). Note in the diagram that the nested procedure show has two different closures, each corresponding to the two different activations of p in which show is defined.

7.5.3   Dynamically Computed Procedures and Fully Dynamic Environments

The stack-based runtime environment shown is completely adequate for almost all block-structured languages with lexical scope. Indeed, in a language like C, which does not have nested procedures, an even simpler

```
program lastex;

    procedure p(n: integer);

        procedure show;
        begin
            if n > 0 then p(n-1);
            writeln(n);
        end;

    begin (* p *)
        show;
    end; (* p *)

begin (* main *)
    p(1);
end.
```

Figure 7-3   A Pascal Program with Nested Procedures

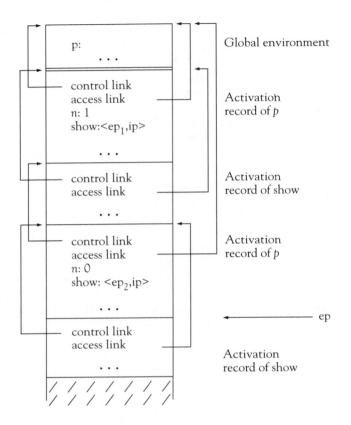

Figure 7-4   Environment of lastex During the Second Call to show

environment is possible (see Exercise 31). The use of closures for procedures makes this environment suitable for languages with parameters
that are themselves procedures, as long as these parameters are value
parameters: a procedure that is passed to another procedure is passed as
a closure (an <ep,ip> pair), and when it is called, its access link is the
ep part of its closure. An example of a language for which this organization
is necessary is Standard Pascal.

A stack-based environment does have its limitations, however, which
we already noted in Chapter 5. For instance, any procedure that can
return a pointer to a local object, either by returned value or through a
pass by reference parameter, will result in a **dangling reference** when the
procedure is exited, since the activation record of the procedure will be
deallocated from the stack. The simplest example of this is when the
address of a local variable is returned, as for instance in the C code:

```
int * dangle(void)
{int x;
 return &x;}
```

An assignment `addr = dangle()` now causes `addr` to point to an unsafe location in the activation stack. The same situation can be achieved in Modula-2 by importing the `ADR` function from the `SYSTEM` module:

```
FROM SYSTEM IMPORT ADR;

TYPE IntPtr = POINTER TO INTEGER;

PROCEDURE Dangle(): IntPtr;
VAR x: INTEGER;
BEGIN
    RETURN (ADR(x));
END Dangle;
```

This can also happen in C, but it cannot happen in Pascal, since the address of a local variable is unavailable. One might attempt to specify in the language definition that such an action is an error (Algol68 does this), but checking statically for such an error is usually not possible, and the overhead of performing a runtime check is significant. Thus most languages leave this as an error that will not be caught, either during translation or execution. In practice, it is easy for programmers who have an understanding of the environment to avoid this error.

A more serious situation occurs if the language designer wishes to extend the expressiveness and flexibility of the language by allowing procedures to be dynamically created, that is, allowing procedures to be returned from other procedures via returned value or reference parameters. This kind of flexibility is usually desired in a functional or object-oriented language, and in such a language, procedures become what are called **first-class values:** no "arbitrary" restrictions apply to their use. In such a language, a stack-based environment cannot be used, since the closure of a locally defined procedure will have an ep that points to the current activation record. If that closure is available outside the activation of the procedure that created it, the ep will point to an activation record that no longer exists. Any subsequent call to that procedure will have an incorrect access environment.

Consider the following example, in which we may reasonably want a procedure to create another procedure. We write this example in Modula-2, since Modula-2 has procedure types and parameters, and so can express the situation quite well (this example is adapted from Abelson and Sussman [1985]):

```
TYPE WithdrawProc = PROCEDURE (INTEGER) :
    INTEGER;

PROCEDURE MakeNewBalance(InitBalance: INTEGER):
    WithdrawProc;
VAR CurrentBalance: INTEGER;
```

continues

continued

```
      PROCEDURE Withdraw (Amt: INTEGER): INTEGER;
      BEGIN
        IF Amt <= CurrentBalance THEN
            CurrentBalance := CurrentBalance - Amt;
        ELSE
            Error('Insufficient Funds!');
        END;
        RETURN CurrentBalance;
      END Withdraw;

  BEGIN (* MakeNewBalance *)
      CurrentBalance := InitBalance;
      RETURN Withdraw;
  END MakeNewBalance;
```

We now might want to make two different accounts from which to withdraw, one with an initial balance of 500 and the other with an initial balance of 100 dollars:

```
VAR Withdraw1,Withdraw2: WithdrawProc;

Withdraw1 := MakeNewBalance(500);
Withdraw2 := MakeNewBalance(100);
```

The problem is that in a stack-based environment, the activation records in which both these functions were created have disappeared: each time MakeNewBalance returns, the local environment of MakeNewBalance is released.

Pascal does not have this problem, since there are no procedure variables (procedures can only be value parameters). In C all procedures are global, so again this problem cannot arise. Modula-2 has a rule that also prohibits this from occurring: only globally defined procedures can be parameters to and return values from other procedures.

Nevertheless, we may want to be able to do things just like this in a language in which functions and procedures are first class values; that is, no nongeneralities or nonorthogonalities should exist for functions and procedures. Such a language, for example, is LISP. What kind of environment would we need to allow such constructs?

Now it is no longer possible for the activation record of procedure MakeNewBalance to be removed from the environment, as long as there are references to any of its local objects. Such an environment is **fully dynamic** in that it deletes activation records only when they can no longer be reached from within the executing program. Such an environment must perform some kind of automatic reclamation of unreachable storage. Two standard methods of doing so are **reference counts** and **garbage collection;** see Chapter 10 for more detail.

This situation also means that the structure of the activations be-comes treelike instead of stacklike: the control links to the calling en-vironment no longer necessarily point to the immediately preceding activation. For example, in the two calls to `MakeNewBalance`, the two activations remain, with their control links both pointing at the global environment:

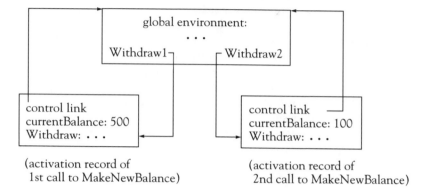

(activation record of   (activation record of
1st call to MakeNewBalance)   2nd call to MakeNewBalance)

Each activation of `MakeNewBalance` can disappear only if `Withdraw1` or `Withdraw2` are reassigned or themselves disappear.

This is the model under which Scheme and other functional lan-guages execute. See the chapter on functional programming (Chapter 10) for more detail.

7.6   EXCEPTION HANDLING

So far all the control mechanisms we have studied have been **explicit:** at the point where a transfer of control takes place, there is a syntactic indication of the transfer. For example, in a **while**-loop, the loop begins with the keyword `while`. In a procedure call, the called procedure with its arguments is named at the point of call. There are situations, however, where transfer of control is **implicit:** the transfer is set up at a point in the program before any actual transfer takes place. At the point where the transfer actually occurs, there is then no syntactic indication that control will transfer at that point.

Such a situation is **exception handling:** the control of error con-ditions or other unusual events during the execution of a program. Ex-ception handling involves the declaration of both exceptions and exception handlers. An **exception** is any unexpected or infrequent event. When an exception occurs, it is said to be **raised** or **signaled.** Typical examples of exceptions include runtime errors, such as out-of-range array subscripts or division by zero. In interpreted languages exceptions can also include static errors, such as syntax and type errors. (These errors are not excep-tions for compiled languages, since a program containing them cannot be executed.) But exceptions need not be restricted to errors: an exception can be any unusual or infrequent event, such as an end of file, end of page, bad input, or even a timeout. An **exception handler** is a procedure or code sequence that is designed to be executed when a particular exception is raised and that is supposed to make it possible for normal execution to resume.

Exception handling is an attempt to imitate in a programming language the features of a hardware interrupt or error trap, in which the processor transfers control automatically to a location that is specified in advance according to the kind of error or interrupt. It is reasonable to try to build such a feature into a language, since it is often unacceptable for a program to allow the underlying machine or operating system to take control. This usually means that the program is aborted, or "crashes." Programs that exhibit this behavior fail the test of **robustness,** which is part of the design criteria of security and reliability: a program must be able to recover from errors and continue execution. In this section we will present only a brief view of this topic. The interested reader may consult the references at the end of the chapter for more information.

It is helpful in designing an exception handling facility to recall how exceptions can be dealt with in a language without such facilities. Exception conditions in such languages have to be found before an error occurs, and this assumes it is possible to test for them in the language. One can then attempt to handle the error at the location where it occurs, as in the following Modula-2 code:

```
IF y = 0 THEN
    WriteString('Error: denominator is zero!');
    WriteLn;
ELSE
    ratio := x DIV y;
END;
```

Or, if the error occurs in a procedure, one can either pass an error condition back to the caller, as in the Modula-2 code

```
TYPE ErrorKind = (OutOfInput, BadChar, Normal);
. . .
PROCEDURE GetNumber (VAR error: ErrorKind,
                     VAR result: CARDINAL);
VAR ch: CHAR;
BEGIN
    IF AtEOF(Input) THEN
        error := OutOfInput;
        RETURN;
    END;
    Read(ch);
    IF NOT Digit(ch) THEN
```

```
            error := BadChar;
            RETURN;
        END;
        error := Normal;
        (* continue to compute *)
        . . .
    END GetNumber;
```

or, alternatively, one could pass an exception handling procedure into the procedure as a parameter,

```
    TYPE ErrorKind = (OutOfInput, BadChar, Normal);
         ErrorProc = PROCEDURE (ErrorKind);
    . . .
    VAR value: CARDINAL;
    . . .
    PROCEDURE Handler (error: ErrorKind);
    BEGIN
        . . .
    END Handler;
    . . .
    PROCEDURE GetNumber (Handle: ErrorProc;
                             VAR result: CARDINAL);
    VAR ch: CHAR;
    BEGIN
      IF AtEOF(Input) THEN
         Handle(OutOfInput);
         RETURN;
      END;
      Read(ch);
      IF NOT Digit(ch) THEN
         Handle(BadChar);
         RETURN;
      END;
      (* continue to compute *)
      . . .
    END GetNumber;
    . . .
    . . .
    GetNumber(Handler,value);
    . . .
```

Explicit exception testing makes a program more difficult to write, since the programmer must test in advance for all possible exceptional conditions. We would like to make this task easier by declaring exceptions in advance of their occurrence and specifying what a program is to do if an exception occurs. In designing such a facility we must consider the following questions:

Exceptions. What exceptions are predefined in the language? Can they be disabled? Can user-defined exceptions be created? What is their scope?

Exception handlers. How are they defined? What is their scope? What default handlers are provided for predefined exceptions? Can they be replaced?

Control. How is control passed to a handler? Where does control pass after a handler is executed? What runtime environment remains after an error handler executes?

The environment under which execution continues after an exception is sometimes called the **continuation** of the exception. An exception handling mechanism that resumes the execution at the point where the exception occurred is said to follow the **resumption model** for exceptions, while a mechanism that causes the block in which the exception occurred to terminate execution is said to follow the **termination model.**

One simple but usable exception handling mechanism is that provided by the BASIC programming language. The statement

```
ON ERROR GOTO 100
```

sets the transfer of control on any error to line number 100. At line number 100 an error handler is written, which ends with one of three types of RESUME statements: RESUME by itself transfers control back to the beginning of the line where the error occurred, RESUME NEXT transfers control to the line following the line where the error occurred, and RESUME with a line number transfers control to the specified line. The error handler can test for the kind of error that had occurred by consulting the value of the predefined variable ERR. It can also test for the line where the error occurred with the predefined variable ERL. Finally, ON ERROR GOTO 0 turns off error handling; if it is executed in the error handler before a RESUME, it ends the execution of the program and transfers control to the system.

BASIC's exception handling is rudimentary because it is lacking in a number of features. Only one error handler can exist at any one time; it is not bound to any specific error but must handle all potential errors. Only predefined errors can be handled, and these cannot be disabled; no user-defined errors can be declared.

BASIC also lacks nested scopes and activation records: there is no block structure, and all variables are global. Thus exception handling is also global, and there is no particular continuation structure that must be provided.

Block-structured languages need more complex exception handling mechanisms. Block-structured languages with exception handling include PL/I, Mesa, CLU, Eiffel, C++, ML, and Ada. We will describe Ada's approach to exceptions and mention how PL/I and CLU, the two major forerunners of Ada's exception handling mechanism, differ from Ada.

Ada has both predefined exceptions and user-defined exceptions. Predefined exceptions are as follows:

CONSTRAINT__ERROR: This includes subrange constraints and array index constraints.

NUMERIC__ERROR: This includes overflow and division by zero.

PROGRAM__ERROR: This includes errors that occur during the dynamic processing of a declaration.

STORAGE__ERROR: This is caused by the failure of dynamic memory allocation.

TASKING__ERROR: This occurs during concurrency control.

The user can also define exceptions using the reserved word **exception** in a declaration:

```
SINGULAR: exception;
```

The declaration of an exception follows the same static scope rules as other declarations.

Exception handlers in Ada are associated with blocks and are declared at the end of a block:

```
begin
  . . .
-- normal code goes here
  . . .
exception
  when SINGULAR | NUMERIC__ERROR =>
    PUT("matrix is singular");
  when others => PUT("fatal error"); raise ERROR;
end;
```

The syntax of the exception part of a block is similar to that of the case-statement. The handler for each exception is the code sequence designated by the choice for that exception.

When an exception is raised in Ada, the handler for the exception in the current block is executed, after which the block is exited. (Thus Ada follows the termination model for exceptions.) If the block has no exception part, or if no handler for the exception exists, the block is exited, and the exception is reraised in the controlling block in the execution path. Thus, if the block is a procedure, the control link is followed to find the block in which to reraise the exception. Exceptions are therefore **propagated dynamically** up the stack of activation records, and exception handlers observe dynamic scope rules.

In the case of a user-defined exception, the system cannot automatically raise the exception; it must instead be raised manually using a **raise**-statement. For example, in the code here, the catch-all user-defined exception ERROR is raised for all errors except SINGULAR and NUMERIC__ERROR.

If an exception is raised for which no handler is found in the dynamic chain, a PROGRAM_ERROR is raised by the system, and execution is aborted. Predefined exceptions can, however, be disabled by a PRAGMA compiler directive. For example,

```
pragma SUPPRESS(RANGE_CHECK);
```

will cause the suppression of all CONSTRAINT_ERROR exceptions that are raised as a result of a range check.

As an example of Ada exception handling, we rewrite the Modula-2 program at the beginning of this section in Ada:

```
BadChar, Fatal_Error: exception;
. . .

function GetNumber () return UNSIGNED_INTEGER is
   ch: char;
begin
   GET(InFile,ch);
   if not Digit(ch) then
     raise BadChar;
   end if;
   -- continue to compute
   . . .
exception
   when End_Of_File | Bad_Char raise;
   when others raise Fatal_Error;
end GetNumber;
```

Note the use of raise by itself for End_Of_File and Bad_Char. This reraises each exception in the calling procedure.

PL/I is similar to Ada in that exceptions are propagated dynamically. However, in PL/I, exceptions are associated to statements rather than blocks, and control is passed back to the beginning of the statement in which the exception was raised instead of exiting a block. (Thus PL/I follows the resumption model for exceptions.) Alternatively, a GOTO statement can be used in a handler to pass control essentially anywhere in a program, in a similar fashion to BASIC.

CLU, on the other hand, is similar to Ada in that exceptions are associated with procedure blocks. However, in CLU exceptions cannot be handled by the procedure in which they are raised, and exceptions cannot be propagated: CLU insists that exceptions be handled by the calling procedure. If the caller has no handler for the raised exception, the program fails. On the other hand, exceptions can be manually propagated from within an error handler (as in the ERROR example in Ada earlier). CLU also differs from Ada in that it permits parameters to be passed to an error handler, much as in a normal procedure call.

1. Pascal insists that a sequence of statements be surrounded by a begin-end pair in structured statements such as while-statements:

   <while-stmt> ::= while <cond> do <statement>

   <statement> ::= <simple-stmt> | <compound-stmt>

   <simple-stmt> ::= <while-stmt> | ...

   <compound-stmt> ::= begin <stmt-sequence> end

   <stmt-sequence> ::= <stmt-sequence> ';' <statement> | ϵ

   (The symbol ϵ in the last grammar rule stands for the empty string.)

   Suppose that we eliminated the begin-end in compound statements and wrote the grammar as follows:

   <while-stmt> ::= while <cond> do <stmt-sequence>

   <stmt-sequence> ::= <stmt-sequence> ';' <statement> | ϵ

   <statement> ::= <while-stmt> | ...

   Show that this grammar is ambiguous. What can be done to correct it without going back to the Pascal convention?

2. Some versions of Pascal have a default case for the case-statement given by the new keyword otherwise, instead of using else (as Modula-2 does). Describe the advantages and disadvantages of using otherwise instead of else in a case-statement. What design principles apply here?

3. Show how to imitate a while-statement in Pascal with a repeat-statement.

4. Show how to imitate both a REPEAT statement and a WHILE statement with LOOP-EXIT statements in Modula-2.

5. We saw in this chapter (and in Exercise 14 of Chapter 6) that it makes sense to have an if-expression in a language.
   (a) Does it make sense to have a while-expression; that is, can a while-expression return a value?
   (b) Does it make sense to have a repeat-expression?
   (c) We have noted that C and Algol68 both have if-expressions. Do either of these languages have a while-expression? A repeat-expression?

6. Show how to write repeat and loop-exit statements in FORTRAN77 using GOTO statements.

7. Compare and contrast the syntax of the case-statement in Pascal, Modula-2, and Ada.

8. An important difference between the semantics of the case-statement in Pascal and Algol68 is that an unlisted case causes a runtime error in Pascal, while in Algol68, execution "falls through" to the statement following the case-statement. Compare these two conventions with respect to the design principles of Chapter 3. Which principles apply?

9. (From Aho, Hopcroft, and Ullman [1986]) The problem with the dangling else in Pascal or Algol60 can be fixed by writing more complicated syntax rules. One attempt to do so might be as follows:

<stmt> ::= if <cond> then <stmt> | <matched-stmt>

<matched-stmt> ::= if <cond> then <matched-stmt>

else <stmt> | <other-stmt>

   (a) Show that this grammar is still ambiguous.
   (b) How can it be fixed so that the grammar expresses the most closely nested rule unambiguously?

10. Describe the effect of the FORTRAN "spaghetti code" on page 205. Write Pascal or Modula-2 statements without GOTOs that are equivalent to the FORTRAN code.

11. Clark [1973] humorously describes a "come from" statement as a replacement for the GOTO statement:

```
10 J = 1
11 COME FROM 20
12 PRINT *, J
   STOP
13 COME FROM 10
20 J = J + 2
```

This sample program in FORTRAN syntax prints 3 and stops. Develop a description of the semantics of the COME FROM statement. What problems might a translator have generating code for such a statement?

12. Rubin [1987] used the following example to "prove" that GOTOs are essential to clear and concise code:

```
for i := 1 to n do begin
  for j := 1 to n do
    if x[i,j] <> 0 then goto reject;
  writeln('First all-zero row is: ',i);
  break;
reject:
end;
```

This program is supposed to find the first zero row in a matrix x[1..n,1..n], with n >= 1.

(a) Rewrite this program using only LOOP-EXITs as in Modula-2.

(b) Rewrite it in Pascal using only while-statements.

(c) Do you agree with Rubin? Why or why not?

13. Test each of the following Pascal code fragments with a translator of your choice (or rewrite it into another language and test it) and explain its behavior:

(a)

```
n := 3;
for i := 1 to n do begin
  writeln('i = ',i);
  n := 2;
end;
```

(b)

```
for i := 1 to 3 do begin
  writeln('i = ',i);
  i := 3;
end;
```

14. Give the output of the following program (written in Pascal syntax) using the four parameter passing methods discussed in Section 7.4:

```
program params;
var i: integer;
    a: array[1..2] of integer;

procedure p(x,y: integer;);
begin
  x := x + 1;
  i := i + 1;
  y := y + 1;
end;

begin
  a[1] := 1;
  a[2] := 1;
  i := 1;
  p(a[i],a[i]);
  writeln(a[1]);
  writeln(a[2]);
end.
```

15. Give the output of the following program using the four parameter

passing methods of Section 7.4:

```
program partwo;
var i: integer;
    a: array[0..2] of integer;

procedure swap(x,y: integer);
begin
  x := x + y;
  y := x - y;
  x := x - y;
end;

begin
  i := 1;
  a[0] := 2;
  a[1] := 1;
  a[2] := 0;
  swap(i,a[i]);
  writeln(i);
  writeln(a[0]);
  writeln(a[1]);
  writeln(a[2]);
  swap(a[i],a[i]);
  writeln(a[0]);
  writeln(a[1]);
  writeln(a[2]);
end.
```

16. FORTRAN has the convention that all parameter passing is by reference. Nevertheless it is possible to call subroutines with expressions as arguments, as in

```
CALL P(X,X+Y,2)
```

(a) Explain how this can be implemented using pass by reference.

(b) Explain how one can use this mechanism to pass a variable X by value in FORTRAN.

(c) Suppose that subroutine P is declared as follows

```
SUBROUTINE P(A)
INTEGER A
PRINT *, A
A = A + 1
RETURN
END
```

and is called from the main program as follows:

```
CALL P(1)
```

In some FORTRAN systems this will cause a runtime error. In others, no runtime error occurs, but if the subroutine is called again with 1 as its argument, it may print the value 2. Explain how both behaviors might occur.

17. Ada has the rule that i n parameters (passed by value) are read-only; that is, they cannot be used as local variables. Thus the following code is illegal in Ada:

```
procedure p (x: in INTEGER) is
begin
  x := x + 1;
end p;
```

Discuss this rule with respect to the design criteria of Chapter 3.

18. Ada restricts the parameters in a function declaration to be i n parameters. Why is this?

19. A variation on pass by name is **pass by text,** in which the arguments are evaluated in delayed fashion, just as in pass by name, but each argument is evaluated in the environment of the called procedure, rather than in the calling environment. Show that pass by text can have different results than pass by name.

20. The Algol60 definition states the following **substitution rule** for pass by name:

1. Any formal parameter . . . is replaced, throughout the procedure body, by the corresponding actual parameter, after enclosing this latter in parentheses wherever syntactically possible. Possible conflicts between identifiers inserted through this process and other identifiers already present within the procedure body will be avoided by suitable systematic changes of the formal or local identifiers involved.
2. Finally the procedure body, modified as above, is inserted in place of the procedure statement and executed. If the procedure is called from a place outside the scope of any nonlocal quantity of the procedure body the conflicts between the identifiers inserted through this process of body replacement and the identifiers whose declarations are valid at the place of the procedure statement or function designator will be avoided through suitable systematic changes of the latter identifiers. (Naur [1963a], p. 12)

(a) Give an example of an identifier conflict as described in rule 1.
(b) Give an example of an identifier conflict as described in rule 2.
(c) Carry out the replacement process described in these two rules on the t e s t program on page 218.

21. (a) Write a function that uses Jensen's device and pass by name to compute the scalar product of two vectors declared as a r r a y [1..n] of integer.

(b) Rewrite the s um procedure on page 219 in Pascal, using a function parameter for the parameter a to imitate pass by name.

22. The text did not discuss the scope of parameter declarations inside function or procedure declarations.

(a) Describe the scope of the declaration of x in the following procedure:

```
procedure p (x: integer);
var y,z: integer;
begin
   . . .
end;
```

(b) State whether the following procedure declarations are legal, and give reasons:

```
procedure p (p: integer);
begin
   . . .
end;

procedure p (x: integer);
var x: integer;
begin
   . . .
end;
```

23. Draw the stack of activation records for the following program after each procedure call. Show the control and access links, and fill in the local names in each activation. Describe how each referenced name is found during the execution of the program.

```
program act;
var x: integer;

procedure p;
var r: real;
begin
   . . .
   writeln(r);
   writeln(x);
end;

procedure q;
var x: real;

   procedure r;
   begin
```

```
    x  :=  1;
    p;
  end;

begin
  r;
  p;
end; (*  q  *)

begin (*  main  *)
  . . .
  p;
  q;
end.
```

24. Draw the stack of activation records as in the previous exercise for the following program after the second call to procedure b:

```
program env;

procedure a;

  procedure b;
    procedure c;
    begin
      a;
    end;
    begin (*  b  *)
      c;
    end; (*  b  *)

  begin (*  a  *)
    b;
  end; (*  a  *)

begin
  a;
end.
```

25. The following program contains a function parameter. Draw the stack of activation records after the call to x in p. What does the program print?

```
program params;

procedure p(function x(n: integer):integer);
var m: integer;
begin                                        continues
```

continued

```
    m := 3;
    writeln(x(2));
end; (* p *)

procedure q;
var m: integer;

    function f(n: integer): integer;
    begin
      f := m + n;
    end;

begin
  m := 0;
  p(f);
end; (* q *)

begin (* main *)
  q;
end.
```

26. FORTRAN allows the passing of variable-length arrays, as in the following examples:

```
SUBROUTINE P(A,I)
INTEGER I
REAL A(*)
...

SUBROUTINE Q(B,N)
INTEGER N,B(N)
...
```

Does this cause any problems for the activations of P and Q, which in FORTRAN must have fixed size and location?

27. Some FORTRAN implementations use pass by value-result rather than pass by reference. Would this affect your answer to the previous exercise? Why?

28. In both Modula-2 and C, variable-length arrays can be passed to procedures, as in the following Modula-2 declaration, where a is a variable-length array:

```
PROCEDURE FindMax (a: ARRAY OF INTEGER; VAR Max:
    INTEGER);
```

How does this affect the need for all variables to be at fixed offsets within an activation record? Describe a way around this problem.

29. In C, blocks that are not procedures, but have variable declarations, such as

```
{int i;
  for (i=1; i<n; i++) a[i] = i;}
```

can be allocated a stack frame just as procedures. What fields in the activation are unused or redundant in this case? Can such blocks be implemented without a new stack frame?

30. Suppose we disallowed recursion in Pascal. Would it be possible to construct a fully static environment for the language? Is the same true for C?

31. Describe why C does not need access links in the activation records of its runtime environments. How do C functions find nonlocal variables?

32. (a) Describe how, in a language without procedure parameters, the environment pointer of a procedure closure does not need to be stored with the procedure, but can be computed when the procedure is called.
    (b) Describe how Modula-2 can also compute a procedure closure when the procedure is called, even though the language has procedure parameters.

33. Suppose we wanted to state a rule that would make the C dangling reference created by the following function illegal:

```
int * dangle(void)
{int x;
 return &x;}
```

Suppose we decided to make the following statement: the address of a local variable cannot be a returned value and cannot be assigned to a nonlocal variable.
    (a) Can this rule be checked statically?
    (b) Does this rule solve the problem of dangling references created by the use of a stack-based environment?

34. The following program has a function that has another function as its returned value, and so needs a fully dynamic runtime environment as described in Section 7.5.3. Draw a picture of the environment when g is called inside b. What should this program print?

```
program ret;

function a(): function (integer): integer;
var m: integer;

  function addm( n: integer): integer;
  begin
```
continues

continued
```
      return (n + m);
   end;

begin
  m := 0;
  return addm;
end; (* a *)

procedure b (g: function (integer): integer);
begin
  writeln(g(2));
end; (* b *)

begin (* main *)
  b(a());
end.
```

35. It was noted that Ada, unlike PL/I, cannot return control after an exception to the statement in which the exception occurred. Nevertheless, this behavior can be simulated using an extra block. Show how this can be done.

36. It was noted that CLU allows parameters to be passed to exception handlers, while Ada does not. Can you think of an example where this might be useful or even necessary?

37. Rewrite the simple arithmetic expression parser of Chapter 4 so that it uses exception handling (in simulated form if not available in the language you are using).

38. Describe a method for implementing Ada exception handling in a stack-based runtime environment.

39. Write a BASIC program to determine what happens in your system if an error occurs during the execution of an error handler (i.e., before the execution of a RESUME but after the occurrence of an error). What do you think ought to happen?

40. Does BASIC follow the resumption model or the termination model for exceptions?

41. Can an Ada exception be propagated outside the scope of its definition? If not, why not? If so, how can it be handled?

42. Does the Modula-2 program on page 235 follow the resumption model or the termination model for exceptions? Could it be rewritten to follow the other model?

Notes and References

Dijkstra's guarded if and guarded do commands are described in Dijkstra [1975]. Hoare describes his design of the case-statement in Hoare [1981]. The iterators of CLU are described in Liskov et al. [1977] and Liskov et al. [1984]. Dijkstra's famous letter on the GOTO statement appears in Dijkstra [1968a]. A recent letter by Rubin [1987] rekindled the argument, which continued in the letters of the *Communications of the* ACM throughout most of 1987. Dijkstra's letter, however, was not the earliest mention of the problems of the GOTO statement. Naur [1963b] also comments on their drawbacks. For the disciplined use of GOTOs, see Knuth [1974]. For an amusing takeoff on the GOTO controversy, see Clark [1973] and Exercise 11.

Structures of runtime environments are described in more detail in Aho, Sethi, and Ullman [1986]. Closures of procedures with nonlocal references are related to closures of lambda expressions with free variables; see Section 10.6. The expression of the semantics of procedures as an environment binding as well as a code binding is important for many languages, including Pascal. C and Modula-2 escape the need for a procedure parameter or variable to have an environment pointer by restricting the procedures involved to global procedures (C has no nested procedures at all).

Exception handling in general is studied in Goodenough [1975]. Exception handling in CLU is described and comparisons with other languages are given in Liskov and Snyder [1979]. See also Liskov et al. [1984]. Exception handling in Ada is discussed in Booch [1986] and in Luckam and Polak [1980]. Exception handling in PL/I is described in McLaren [1977]. Exception handling in C++ is described in Ellis and Stroustrup [1990]. Exception handling in Eiffel is described in Meyer [1992]. Exception handling in ML is described in Sethi [1989], Milner and Tofte [1990a], and Milner, Tofte, and Harper [1990b]. A control structure related to exceptions is the **continuation** of the Scheme dialect of LISP. For a description of this mechanism see Springer and Friedman [1989] and Friedman, Haynes, and Kohlbecker [1985].

8 ABSTRACT DATA TYPES

*I*n Chapter 6 we defined a data type as a set of values with certain operations on those values. Data types were divided into the predefined types of a language and user-defined types. Predefined types such as integer and real are designed to insulate the user of a language from the implementation of the data type, which is machine dependent. These data types can be manipulated by a set of predefined operations, such as the arithmetic operations, whose implementation details are also hidden from the user. Their use is completely specified by predetermined semantics, which are either explicitly stated in the language definition or are implicitly well known (like the mathematical properties of the arithmetic operations).

User-defined types, on the other hand, are built up from data structures created using the built-in types and type constructors of the language. Their structures are visible to the user, and they do not come with any operations other than the accessing operations of the data structures themselves (such as the field selection operation on a record structure). One can, of course, define functions to operate on these data structures, but with the standard procedure or function definitions available in most programming languages, these user-defined

250

functions are not directly associated with the data type, and the implementation details of the data type and the operations are visible throughout the program.

It would be very desirable to have a mechanism in a programming language to construct data types that would have as many of the characteristics of a built-in type as possible. Such a mechanism should provide the following:

1. A method for defining a data type and at the same time operations on that type. The definitions should all be collected in one place, and the operations should be directly associated with the type. The definitions should not depend on any implementation details. The definitions of the operations should include a specification of their semantics.

2. A method for collecting the implementation details of the type and its operations in one place, and of restricting access to these details by programs that use the data type.

A data type constructed using a mechanism satisfying some or all of these two criteria is often called an **abstract data type** (or **ADT** for short). Note, however, that there is nothing really more abstract about such a type than a usual built-in type. It is just a more comprehensive way of creating user-defined types than the usual type declaration mechanism of Algol-like languages.

Criteria 1 and 2 promote three design goals that data types were originally introduced to assist with: modifiability, reusability, and security. Modifiability is enhanced by interfaces that are implementation independent, since changes can be made to an implementation without affecting its use by the rest of the program. Reusability is enhanced by standard interfaces, since the code can be reused by different programs. Security is enhanced by protecting the implementation details from arbitrary modification by other parts of a program.

Some authors, rather than using criteria 1 and 2, refer to **encapsulation** and **information hiding** as the essential properties of an abstract data type mechanism. Encapsulation refers to the collection of all definitions related to a data type in one location and restricting the use of the type to the operations defined at that location. Information hiding refers to the separation of implementation details from these definitions and the suppression of these details in the use of the data type. Since encapsulation and information hiding are sometimes difficult to separate in practice, we will use criteria 1 and 2 as our basis for studying abstract data types.

Confusion can sometimes result from the failure to distinguish a **mechanism** for constructing types in a programming language that has the foregoing properties, with the **mathematical concept** of a type, which is a conceptual model for actual types. This second notion is sometimes also called an abstract data type, or abstract type. Such mathematical models are often given in terms of an **algebraic specification,** which can be used to create an actual type in a programming language using an abstract data type mechanism with the foregoing properties.

Even more confusion exists over the difference between abstract data types and so-called **object-oriented programming,** the subject of the next chapter. Object-oriented programming emphasizes the capability of language entities to control their own use during execution and to share operations in carefully controlled ways. In an object-oriented programming language the primary language entity is the object, that is, something that occupies memory and has state. But these objects also are active: they control access to their own memory and state. This can include types, which control access to themselves in declarations and operations. In this sense, an abstract data type mechanism lends itself to the object-oriented approach, since information about a type is localized and access to this information is controlled. But abstract data type mechanisms do not provide the level of active control that represents true object-oriented programming. See Section 8.7 and the next chapter for more details.

In the sections that follow we will first describe a method for specifying abstract data types and introduce some standard abstract data type mechanisms in programming languages. Examples will be given from Modula-2, Ada, Euclid, and CLU. We will also discuss the relationship of abstract data types to polymorphism and separate compilation and will survey some of the limitations of these mechanisms. In the last section we discuss the mathematics of abstract data types.

8.1   THE ALGEBRAIC SPECIFICATION OF ABSTRACT DATA TYPES

As an example of an abstract data type we will use the **complex** data type, which is not a built-in data type in most programming languages.

Mathematically, complex numbers are well-known objects and are extremely useful in practice, since they represent solutions to algebraic equations. Complex numbers are usually represented as a pair of real numbers (x, y) in Cartesian coordinates, which is written as $x + iy$, where i is a symbol representing the complex number $\sqrt{-1}$. x is called the "real" part, and y is called the "imaginary" part. In fact, there are other representations for complex numbers, for example, as polar coordinates (r, θ). In defining complex numbers, we shouldn't need to specify their representation, but only the operations that apply to them. These include the usual arithmetic operations "$+$," "$-$," "$*$," and "$/$". Also needed is a way of creating a complex number from a real and imaginary part and functions to extract the real and imaginary part from an existing complex number.

A general specification of a data type needs to include the name of the type and the names of the operations, including a specification of their parameters and returned values. This is the **syntactic specification** of an abstract data type. In a language-independent specification, it is appropriate to use the function notation of mathematics for the operations of the data type: given a function f from set X to set Y, X is the domain, Y is the range, and we write $f: X \rightarrow Y$. For the complex data type, a syntactic specification looks like this:

type complex **imports** real

operations:

$+$	: complex $\times$ complex $\rightarrow$ complex
$-$	: complex $\times$ complex $\rightarrow$ complex
$*$	: complex $\times$ complex $\rightarrow$ complex
$/$	: complex $\times$ complex $\rightarrow$ complex
$-$	: complex $\rightarrow$ complex
makecomplex	: real $\times$ real $\rightarrow$ complex
realpart	: complex $\rightarrow$ real
imaginarypart	: complex $\rightarrow$ real

Note that the dependence of the complex data type on an already existing data type, namely, real, is made explicit by the "imports real" clause. (Do not confuse this imports clause with the IMPORT statement in Modula-2; see Exercise 34.) Note also that the negative sign is used for two different operations: subtraction and negation. Indeed the usual names are used for all the arithmetic operations. Some means must eventually be used to distinguish these from the arithmetic operations on the integers and reals.

The preceding specification, however, lacks any notion of semantics: What properties must the operations actually possess? For example, $z * w$ might be defined to be always 0! In mathematics, the semantic properties of functions are often described by **equations** or **axioms**. In the case of arithmetic operations, examples of axioms are the associative, commutative, and distributive laws (in the equations that follow, x, y, and z are assumed to be variables of type complex; that is, they can take on any complex value):

$$x + (y + z) = (x + y) + z \; (\bullet \text{ associativity of } + \bullet)$$
$$x \bullet y = y \bullet x \qquad\qquad\quad (\bullet \text{ commutativity of } \bullet \bullet)$$
$$x \bullet (y + z) = x \bullet y + x \bullet z \; (\bullet \text{ distributivity of } \bullet \text{ over } + \bullet)$$

Axioms such as these can be used to define the semantic properties of complex numbers, or the properties of the complex data type can be **derived** from those of the real data type by stating properties of the operations that lead back to properties of the real numbers. For example, complex addition can be based on real addition by giving the following properties:

$$realpart(x+y) = realpart(x) + realpart(y)$$
$$imaginarypart(x+y) = imaginarypart(x) + imaginarypart(y)$$

The appropriate arithmetic properties of the complex numbers can then be proved from the corresponding properties for reals.

A complete algebraic specification of type complex combines syntax, variables, and equational axioms:

type complex **imports** real

operations:

$+$	: complex $\times$ complex $\rightarrow$ complex
$-$	: complex $\times$ complex $\rightarrow$ complex
$\bullet$	: complex $\times$ complex $\rightarrow$ complex
$/$	: complex $\times$ complex $\rightarrow$ complex
$-$	: complex $\rightarrow$ complex

makecomplex : real $\times$ real $\rightarrow$ complex
realpart : complex $\rightarrow$ real
imaginarypart : complex $\rightarrow$ real

variables: x,y,z: complex; r,s: real

axioms:
  $realpart(makecomplex(r,s)) = r$
  $imaginarypart(makecomplex(r,s)) = s$
  $realpart(x+y) = realpart(x) + realpart(y)$
  $imaginarypart(x+y) = imaginarypart(x) + imaginarypart(y)$
  $realpart(x-y) = realpart(x) - realpart(y)$
  $imaginarypart(x-y) = imaginarypart(x) - imaginarypart(y)$
  $\cdots$
    $\ldots$ ($\bullet$ more axioms $\bullet$)

Such a specification of a type is called an **algebraic specification** of an abstract data type. It provides a concise specification of a data type and its associated operations, and the equational semantics give a clear indication of implementation behavior, often containing enough information to allow coding directly from the equations. Finding an appropriate set of equations, however, can be a difficult task. Some indications of how this can be done are given in the paragraphs that follow.

Remember the difference in the foregoing specification between **equality** as used in the axioms and the **arrow** of the syntactic specification of the functions. Equality is of function values, while the arrows separate domain and range of the functions.

A second example of an algebraic specification of an abstract data type is the following specification of a queue:

type queue(element) **imports** boolean

operations:

create:	$\rightarrow$ queue
enqueue:	queue $\times$ element $\rightarrow$ queue
dequeue:	queue $\rightarrow$ queue
front:	queue $\rightarrow$ element
empty:	queue $\rightarrow$ boolean

variables: q: queue; x: element

axioms:
empty(create) = true
empty(enqueue(q,x)) = false
front(create) = error
front(enqueue(q,x)) = if empty(q) then x else front(q)
dequeue(create) = error
dequeue(enqueue(q,x)) = if empty(q) then q else
$\qquad\qquad\qquad\qquad$ enqueue(dequeue(q),x)

This specification exhibits several new features. First, the data type queue is **parametrized** by the data type element, which is left unspecified. Such a type parameter can be replaced by any type and is indicated by placing its name inside parentheses, just as a function parameter would be. Second, there is an operation create that has no specified domain: intuitively, create is a function with no parameters that constructs and initializes a queue. Mathematically, such an operation always returns the same value, and so is called a **constant** of the abstract data type. Third, there are now axioms that specify error values, such as

$$front(create) = error$$

Such axioms can be called **error axioms,** and they provide limitations on the application of the operations. The actual error value of an error axiom is unspecified. Finally, the equations are specified using an if-then-else function, whose semantics are as follows:

$$\text{if true then } a \text{ else } b = a$$
$$\text{if false then } a \text{ else } b = b$$

Note also that the dequeue operation as specified does not return the front element of the queue, as in most implementations: it simply throws it away. Abstractly, this is simpler to handle and does not take away any functionality of the queue, since the front operation can extract the front element before a dequeue operation is performed.

The equations specifying the semantics of the operations in an algebraic specification of an abstract data type can be used not only as a specification of the properties of an implementation, and as a guide to the code for an implementation, but can also be used to prove specific properties about objects of the type. For example, the following applications of axioms shows that dequeuing from a queue with one element leaves an empty queue:

empty(dequeue(enqueue(create,x))) = empty(create)

$$\text{(by the sixth axiom above)}$$
$$= \text{true}$$
$$\text{(by the first axiom)}$$

How do we find an appropriate axiom set for an algebraic specification? In general, this is a difficult question. One can, however, make some judgments about what kind and how many axioms are needed by looking at the syntax of the operations. An operation that maps to the data type being defined is called a **constructor,** while an operation that maps to another data type is called an **inspector.** In the queue example, create, enqueue, and dequeue are constructors, while front and empty are inspectors. Some of the constructors reduce the amount of information available; these can be called **destructors.** The operation **dequeue** is a destructor because it removes the front element from a queue. Inspector operations can also be broken down into **predicates,** which return Boolean values, and **selectors,** which return non-Boolean values. Thus front is a selector, and empty is a predicate.

In general, one needs one axiom for each combination of an inspector with a nondestructive constructor and one axiom for each combination of a destructor with a nondestructive constructor. For the queue example, the axiom combinations are

empty(create)
empty(enqueue(q,x))
front(create)
front(enqueue(q,x))
dequeue(create)
dequeue(enqueue(q,x))

According to this scheme, there should be six rules in all, and that is in fact the case.

As a final example of an algebraic specification of an abstract data type, we give a specification for the **stack** abstract data type, which has many of the same features as the queue ADT:

type stack(element) **imports** boolean

operations:

create	:	$\rightarrow$ stack
push	: stack $\times$ element	$\rightarrow$ stack
pop	: stack	$\rightarrow$ stack
top	: stack	$\rightarrow$ element
empty	: stack	$\rightarrow$ boolean

variables: s: stack; x: element

axioms:
empty(create) = true
empty(push(s,x)) = false
top(create) = error
top(push(s,x)) = x
pop(create) = error
pop(push(s,x)) = s

In this case, the operations create and push are nondestructive constructors, the pop operation is a destructor, the top operation is a selector, and the empty operation is a predicate. By our proposed scheme, therefore, there should again be six axioms.

8.2   ABSTRACT DATA TYPES IN Modula-2

In Modula-2, the specification and implementation of an abstract data type are separated into a DEFINITION MODULE and an IMPLEMENTA- TION MODULE. For the type COMPLEX described in the previous section, a Modula-2 specification module would look like this:

```
DEFINITION MODULE ComplexNumbers;

TYPE COMPLEX; (* opaque type - see below *)

PROCEDURE Add (x,y: COMPLEX): COMPLEX;
PROCEDURE Subtract (x,y: COMPLEX): COMPLEX;
PROCEDURE Multiply (x,y: COMPLEX): COMPLEX;
PROCEDURE Divide (x,y: COMPLEX): COMPLEX;
PROCEDURE Negate (z: COMPLEX): COMPLEX;
PROCEDURE MakeComplex (x,y: REAL): COMPLEX;
```

continues

continued

```
PROCEDURE RealPart (z: COMPLEX) : REAL;
PROCEDURE ImaginaryPart (z: COMPLEX) : REAL;

END ComplexNumbers.
```

A Modula-2 DEFINITION MODULE contains only definitions or declarations, and only the declarations that appear in the DEFINITION MODULE are **exported,** that is, are usable by other modules. The incomplete type specification of type COMPLEX in the DEFINITION MODULE is called an **opaque type;** the details of its declaration are hidden in an implementation module and are not usable by other modules.

A corresponding IMPLEMENTATION MODULE in Modula-2 for the DEFINITION MODULE is as follows:

```
IMPLEMENTATION MODULE ComplexNumbers;

FROM Storage IMPORT ALLOCATE;

TYPE COMPLEX = POINTER TO ComplexRecord;
     ComplexRecord = RECORD
        re, im: REAL;
     END;

PROCEDURE Add (x,y: COMPLEX): COMPLEX;
VAR t: COMPLEX;
BEGIN
  NEW(t);
  t^.re := x^.re + y^.re;
  t^.im := x^.im + y^.im;
  RETURN t;
END Add;

PROCEDURE Subtract (x,y: COMPLEX): COMPLEX;
(* similar to add *)
  . . .

PROCEDURE Multiply (x,y: COMPLEX): COMPLEX;
VAR t: COMPLEX;
BEGIN
  NEW(t);
  t^.re := x^.re * y^.re - x^.im * y^.im;
  t^.im := x^.re * y^.im + x^.im * y^.re;
  RETURN t;
END Multiply;
```

```
(* similarly for divide and negate *)
   . . .
PROCEDURE MakeComplex (x,y: REAL): COMPLEX;
VAR t: COMPLEX;
BEGIN
   NEW(t);
   t^.re := x;
   t^.im := y;
   RETURN t;
END MakeComplex;

PROCEDURE RealPart (z: COMPLEX) : REAL;
BEGIN
   RETURN z^.re;
END RealPart;

PROCEDURE ImaginaryPart (z: COMPLEX) : REAL;
BEGIN
   RETURN z^.im;
END ImaginaryPart;

END ComplexNumbers.
```

Note that in this implementation, type COMPLEX was defined to be a pointer to a record instead of a record itself. This is a limitation of opaque types in Modula-2: opaque types can only be scalar or pointer types; they may not be structured types. This also means that MakeComplex has to include a call to NEW to allocate space for a new complex number, and this in turn requires that ALLOCATE be imported from a system Storage module. (The compiler converts a call to NEW to a call to ALLOCATE.)

Another module in Modula-2 uses type COMPLEX by **importing** it and its functions from the ComplexNumbers module:

```
MODULE ComplexUser;

IMPORT ComplexNumbers;

VAR x,y,z: ComplexNumbers.COMPLEX;
   . . .
BEGIN
   x := ComplexNumbers.MakeComplex(1.0,2.0);
   y := ComplexNumbers.MakeComplex(-1.0,1.0);
      . . .
   z := ComplexNumbers.Multiply(x,y);
      . . .
END ComplexUser.
```

A module such as ComplexUser that imports from module ComplexNumbers is called a **client** of ComplexNumbers, and ComplexNumbers is the **provider** of the imported services.

The IMPORT clause in MODULE ComplexUser imports all items exported by the ComplexNumbers DEFINITION MODULE. These items must be **qualified** by the name of the module, so that Add becomes ComplexNumbers.Add and type COMPLEX becomes ComplexNumbers.COMPLEX. An alternative to this is to use a **dereferencing** clause. In Modula-2, the dereferencing clause is the FROM clause:

```
MODULE ComplexUser;

FROM ComplexNumbers IMPORT
  COMPLEX,Multiply,MakeComplex;
VAR x,y,z: COMPLEX;
  . . .
BEGIN
  x := MakeComplex(1.0,2.0);
  y := MakeComplex(-1.0,1.0);
  . . .
  z := Multiply(x,y);
  . . .
END ComplexUser.
```

When a FROM clause is used, imported items must be listed by name in the IMPORT statement, and no other items (either imported or locally declared) may have the same names as those imported.

The separation of a module into a DEFINITION MODULE and an IMPLEMENTATION MODULE in Modula-2 supports the first principle of an abstract data type mechanism: it allows the data type and operation definitions to be collected in one place (the DEFINITION MODULE) and associates the operations directly with the type via the MODULE name.

The use of an opaque type in a DEFINITION MODULE supports the second principle of an abstract data type mechanism: the details of the COMPLEX data type implementation are separated from its declaration and are hidden in an IMPLEMENTATION MODULE together with the implementation of the operations. Further, a client is prevented from using any of the details in the IMPLEMENTATION MODULE. Thus, in the following module, all uses of z are illegal:

```
MODULE BadClient;
FROM Storage IMPORT ALLOCATE;
FROM ComplexNumbers IMPORT COMPLEX, MakeComplex;

VAR z: COMPLEX;
    x: REAL;
```

```
BEGIN
  NEW(z); (* illegal *)
  z^.re := 1.0; (* also illegal *)
  . . .
  x := z^.re (* illegal too *)
  . . .
END BadClient.
```

Clients are required to manipulate data of type COMPLEX using only the operations provided.

Since the DEFINITION MODULE is independent of any of the details of the IMPLEMENTATION MODULE, the implementation can be rewritten without affecting any use of the module by clients. For example, the representation of complex numbers could be changed to polar coordinates without requiring any changes to clients:

```
IMPLEMENTATION MODULE ComplexNumbers;
  . . .


TYPE COMPLEX = POINTER TO ComplexRecord;
     ComplexRecord = RECORD
         radius, angle: REAL;
     END;
  . . .


PROCEDURE MakeComplex (x,y: REAL): COMPLEX;
VAR t: COMPLEX;
BEGIN
  NEW(t);
  t^.radius := sqrt(x*x+y*y);
  IF x=0 THEN t^.angle := PI/2.0
  ELSE t^.angle := arctan(y/x); END;
  RETURN t;
END MakeComplex;


PROCEDURE RealPart (z: COMPLEX) : REAL;
BEGIN
  RETURN z^.radius * cos(z^.angle);
END RealPart;


PROCEDURE ImaginaryPart (z: COMPLEX) : REAL;
BEGIN
  RETURN z^.radius * sin(z^.angle);
END ImaginaryPart;


END ComplexNumbers.
```

8.3   ABSTRACT DATA TYPES IN Ada

Ada has a mechanism similar to Modula-2, except that it calls a module a **package,** which is divided into a package **specification** and a package **body.** A package specification in Ada for type COMPLEX is as follows:

```
package ComplexNumbers is

    type COMPLEX is private;

    function Add (x,y: in COMPLEX) return COMPLEX;
    function Subtract (x,y: in COMPLEX) return
        COMPLEX;
    function Multiply (x,y: in COMPLEX) return
        COMPLEX;
    function Divide (x,y: in COMPLEX) return
        COMPLEX;
    function Negate (z: in COMPLEX) return COMPLEX;
    function MakeComplex (x,y: in FLOAT) return
        COMPLEX;
    function RealPart (z: in COMPLEX) return FLOAT;
    function ImaginaryPart (z: in COMPLEX) return
        FLOAT;

private
    type COMPLEX is
        record
            re, im: FLOAT;
        end record;

end ComplexNumbers;
```

Ada allows the designation of a section at the bottom of a package specification as **private:** any declarations given in this section are inaccessible to a client. Type names, however, can be given in the public part of a specification and designated as private. This corresponds to the Modula-2 opaque type, except that an actual type declaration must be given in the private part of the specification in Ada. This violates criterion 2 for abstract data type mechanisms, since the specification is still dependent on actual implementation details, even though clients are prevented from using these details. This problem can be partially removed in Ada by using pointers (which Modula-2 needs anyway for its opaque types), and so a specification in Ada more equivalent to the Modula-2 one is as follows:

```
package ComplexNumbers is

  type COMPLEX is private;

-- functions as before

private
  type ComplexRecord;
-- incomplete type defined in package body
  type COMPLEX is access ComplexRecord;

end ComplexNumbers;
```

A corresponding implementation for this package specification is as follows:

```
package body ComplexNumbers is

type ComplexRecord is record
        re, im: FLOAT;
      end record;

function Add (x,y: in COMPLEX) return COMPLEX is
t: COMPLEX;
begin
  t := new ComplexRecord;
  t.re := x.re + y.re;
  t.im := x.im + y.im;
  return t;
end Add;
 ...

function MakeComplex (x,y: in FLOAT) return
  COMPLEX is
t: COMPLEX;
begin
  t := new ComplexRecord'(re => x, im => y);
  return t;
end MakeComplex;

function RealPart (z: in COMPLEX) return FLOAT
  is
begin
  return z.re;
end RealPart;                              continues
```

continued

```
function ImaginaryPart (z: in COMPLEX) return
  FLOAT is
begin
  return z.im;
end ImaginaryPart;

end ComplexNumbers;
```

Note that pointers are automatically dereferenced in Ada by the dot notation and that fields can be assigned during allocation using the apostrophe attribute delimiter (the single quote in MakeComplex).

A client program can use the ComplexNumbers package by including a with clause at the beginning of the program:

```
with ComplexNumbers;

procedure ComplexUser is
  z,w: ComplexNumbers.COMPLEX;
  . . .
begin
  z := ComplexNumbers.MakeComplex(1.0,0.0);
  . . .
  w := ComplexNumbers.Add(z,z);
  . . .
end ComplexUser;
```

The with statement in Ada has the same function as the IMPORT statement in Modula-2. As in Modula-2, all entities from the package must be referred to using the package name as a qualifier. Ada also has an analogous statement to the FROM statement in Modula-2 to dereference a package name automatically. In Ada, however, this statement is separate from the with statement. It is the use statement:

```
with ComplexNumbers;
use ComplexNumbers;
procedure ComplexUser is
  z,w: COMPLEX;
  . . .
begin
  z := MakeComplex(1.0,0.0);
  . . .
  w := Add(z,z);
  . . .
end ComplexUser;
```

8.4 ABSTRACT DATA TYPES IN OTHER LANGUAGES

Historically, abstract data type mechanisms began with Simula67 and made significant progress in the 1970s through language design experiments at universities and research centers. Among the languages that have contributed significantly to abstract data type mechanisms in Ada, Modula-2, and other contemporary languages are the languages CLU, Euclid, Modula (the predecessor to Modula-2), Mesa, and Cedar. To indicate how abstract data type mechanisms have developed, we sketch briefly the approaches to abstract data types taken by Euclid and CLU. A discussion of Simula67 is contained in the next chapter (on object-oriented programming).

8.4.1 Euclid

In the Euclid programming language, modules are types, so a complex number module is declared as a type:

```
type ComplexNumbers = module
     exports(COMPLEX, Add, Subtract, Multiply,
        Divide, Negate, MakeComplex, RealPart,
        ImaginaryPart)
     type COMPLEX = record
        var re, im: real
     end COMPLEX

     procedure Add (x,y: COMPLEX,
        var z: COMPLEX) =
     begin
        z.re := x.re + y.re
        z.im := x.im + y.im
     end Add

     procedure MakeComplex (x,y: real,
        var z:COMPLEX) =
     begin
        z.re := x
        z.im := y
     end MakeComplex

        . . .

     end ComplexNumbers
```

To be able to declare complex numbers, however, we need an actual object of type ComplexNumbers—a module type in itself does not exist as an object. Thus we must declare

```
var C: ComplexNumbers
```

and then we can declare

```
var z,w: C.COMPLEX
```

and apply the operations of C:

```
C.MakeComplex(1.0,1.0,z)
C.Add(z,z,w)
```

Note that this implies that there could be two different variables of type ComplexNumbers declared and thus two different sets of complex numbers:

```
var C1,C2: ComplexNumbers
var x: C1.COMPLEX
var y: C2.COMPLEX

C1.MakeComplex(1.0,0.0,x)
C2.MakeComplex(0.0,1.0,y)        (* x and y cannot be
                                    added together *)
```

When module types are used in a declaration, this creates a variable of the module type, or **instantiates** the module. In Euclid two different instantiations of ComplexNumbers can therefore exist simultaneously, unlike Modula-2 or Ada, where modules are not types, but are objects on their own, with a single instantiation of each. (Ada does have a kind of package, the generic package, which can have different instantiations; see Section 8.5.)

8.4.2   CLU

In CLU, abstract data types are defined using the **cluster** mechanism. In the case of complex numbers, the data type COMPLEX can be defined directly as a cluster:

```
COMPLEX = cluster is Add, Multiply,....,
          MakeComplex, RealPart, ImaginaryPart
  rep = struct [re,im: real]
  Add = proc (x,y: cvt) returns (cvt)
        return
        (rep${re: x.re+y.im,
         im: x.im+y .im})
```

```
end Add

   . . .

MakeComplex = proc (x,y: real) returns (cvt)
        return (rep${re:x,im:y})
end MakeComplex

RealPart = proc (x: cvt) returns (real)
        return (x.re)
end RealPart


   . . .


end COMPLEX
```

The principal difference of this abstraction mechanism from the previous ones is that the data type COMPLEX is defined directly as a cluster. However, when we define

```
x,y: COMPLEX
```

we do not mean that they should be of the cluster type, but of the representation type within the cluster (given by the **rep** declaration). Thus a cluster in CLU really refers to two different things: the cluster itself and its internal representation type. Of course, the representation type must be protected from access by the outside world, so the details of the representation type can be accessed only from within the cluster. This is the purpose of the cvt declaration (for **convert**), which converts from the external (opaque) type COMPLEX to the internal rep type and back again. cvt can be used only within the body of a cluster.

Clients can use the functions from COMPLEX in a similar manner to other mechanisms:

```
x := COMPLEX$MakeComplex(1.0,1.0)
x := COMPLEX$Add(x,x)
```

Note the use of the "$" to qualify the operations instead of the dot notation used in Ada and Modula-2.

8.5 OVERLOADING AND POLYMORPHISM

It is often desirable to apply the same, or similar, operations to objects of different types. This can take the form of the sharing of a name among several essentially different, but conceptually related operations. Thus the arithmetic operations of addition and subtraction for integers and reals usually have the same names ("+" and "−") even though the actual implementation of the two operations is substantially different, because of the different internal representations of the two types. A translator can distinguish between the two operations, or **disambiguate** them, by looking at the number and type of the supplied arguments.

In other cases it is useful to be able to define operations that apply essentially without change to many different types. Such an operation is, for example, the swap operation:

```
procedure swap (var x,y: anytype);
var temp: anytype;
begin
  temp := x;
  x := y;
  y := temp;
end;
```

Further examples include the assignment operation ": =" (on which the swap operation depends) and the comparison operations " =" and "<>." Many languages also have input and output operations that can take parameters of several different types, and even different numbers of parameters. Pascal, for example, has write and writeln procedures that can take any number of parameters of various types:

```
writeln('count=',i,' type=',ch);
```

Operations that can accept values of arbitrary types are called **polymorphic** (Greek for "having multiple forms"), while different operations that share the same name are called **overloaded.** In practice, this distinction is sometimes a little obscure: while polymorphic code is in principle capable of being shared by objects of different types, in practice translators often generate distinct code for each type. Conceptually, the primary difference is that overloaded functions can apply only to a finite set of distinct types that are known in advance, while polymorphic functions can potentially apply to any type, which is not known in advance. To emphasize this distinction, overloading is sometimes called **ad hoc polymorphism,** while true polymorphism is referred to as **parametric polymorphism** (because a **type parameter** must in general be supplied).

Data types, as well as functions, can be polymorphic in the parametric sense: a data type specification may depend on another type that may be arbitrary. We have already seen an example of this in Section 8.1 with the algebraic specification of the data type queue, which may store elements of an arbitrary type.

Abstract data type mechanisms in programming languages should be designed to handle both overloading and parametrization. In the context of ADT mechanisms, we should note the following further distinction between overloading and parametrization: overloading is a problem for *clients*, which may import operations with the same name from several different ADTs, while parametric polymorphism is a problem for *providers*, which must deal with the question of an unspecified type.

Modern languages are more and more providing facilities for overloading and parametrization. Modula-2, unfortunately, provides no such facilities. Ada, however, does provide some facilities, and we describe the Ada approach in the following. We also provide some additional remarks about ML, another language that allows parametric polymorphism and that is studied in somewhat more detail in Chapter 10. Somewhat different opportunities for polymorphism are provided by object-oriented languages, and these are described in the next chapter.

8.5.1   Overloading

The sample mechanisms in Sections 8.2 and 8.3 of introducing a new numeric type COMPLEX in Modula-2 and Ada, although they satisfy the criteria stated at the beginning of the chapter for abstract data type mechanisms, nevertheless do not make the type COMPLEX as usable as the built-in types—the operations must still be written as functions or procedures in prefix notation:

```
z := Add(x,y);
z := Negate(z);
```

We really would like to write

```
z := x + y;
```

and

```
z := -z;
```

To do this, the "+" and "−" operations must be overloaded, and the language must allow the use of infix instead of prefix form. In Ada we achieve this by using the appropriate symbols in quotes in the function definitions:

```
function "+" (x,y: in COMPLEX) return COMPLEX;
function "-" (x: in COMPLEX) return COMPLEX;
```

Now we can use these operations in either prefix or infix form after a use statement:

```
with ComplexNumbers;
use ComplexNumbers;
procedure ComplexUser is
  z,w: COMPLEX;
    . . .
```

continues

continued

```
begin
  z := MakeComplex(1.0,0.0);
  ...
  w := "+"(z,z);
  w := z + z
    -- the same as the previous operation
  ...
end ComplexUser;
```

If we do not dereference the package name, then prefix form is necessary:

```
with ComplexNumbers;
use ComplexNumbers;
procedure ComplexUser is
  z,w: COMPLEX;
  ...
begin
  z := MakeComplex(1.0,0.0);
  ...
  w := "+"(z,z);
  w := z + z
    -- the same as the previous operation
  ...
end ComplexUser;
```

Ada does not restrict overloading to predefined infix functions, however. Procedure and function names can be overloaded either by importing them from different packages or by using the same name in different declarations, as long as a translator can tell which declaration is meant by the types and number of the arguments. For example, one can declare two swap procedures as follows:

```
procedure swap (x,y: in out FLOAT) is
temp: FLOAT := x;
begin
  x := y;
  y := temp;
end swap;

procedure swap (x,y: in out COMPLEX) is

temp: COMPLEX := x;
begin
  x := y;
  y := temp;
end swap;
```

Now swap can be called with either FLOAT or COMPLEX parameters:

```
a,b: FLOAT;
z,w: COMPLEX;
swap(a,b); -- first swap meant
swap(z,w); -- second swap meant
```

The use of infix form in Ada, however, is restricted to the existing arithmetic operations. Also, when an infix operator is overloaded, it inherits the precedence and associativity rules of its namesake operation (unlike prefix form, infix form is ambiguous unless it is fully parenthesized; see Chapter 4).

8.5.2   Parametrized Abstract Data Types

We have already given two examples of parametrized abstract data types— queues and stacks—in Section 8.1. As we noted there, the name of the type parameter is written in the algebraic specification in parentheses after the name of the type and is left otherwise unspecified, as for example, the element parameter in the specification of the queue ADT:

type queue(element) . . .

Parametrized types are extremely common—many types that contain data are not restricted to specific kinds of data but can contain data of almost any type, and the operations, such as enqueue and front, can be defined for more than one type, thus becoming polymorphic. An abstract data type mechanism should allow us to define such parametrized abstract data types without having to specify the actual type of the parameter until the abstract data type is used by a client. In Ada such a facility does exists, while in Modula-2 no such mechanism is available, and it must be imitated with other mechanisms. We briefly study parametrized abstract data types in these two languages.

In Ada, a package that implements such a parametrized abstract data type is called a **generic package** (the reader should be warned that the term "generic" is used in the literature in other senses as well):

```
generic
  type ELEMENT is private;
package Stacks is
  type STACK(Size: POSITIVE) is private;
  function Create return STACK;
  function Push (S: in STACK; x: in ELEMENT)
    return STACK;
  function Pop (S: in STACK) return STACK;
  function Top (S: in STACK) return ELEMENT;
  function Empty (S: in STACK) return BOOLEAN;
private
  type store is array (POSITIVE range <>) of
                                          ELEMENT;
```

continues

continued

```
      type STACK(Size: POSITIVE) is record
        top: INTEGER
        data: Store (1..Size)
      end record;
    end Stacks;
```

Such a generic package cannot be used, however, until the actual type ELEMENT is specified. This specification of a generic parameter is called **instantiation** in Ada (similar to the instantiation of a Euclid module in Section 8.4). The generic stack package could, for example, be instantiated to real or integer stacks by the following declarations:

```
    package IntStacks is new Stacks(INTEGER);
    package RealStacks is new Stacks(FLOAT);
```

Only after instantiation can we make actual use of a generic package as follows:

```
    -- declarations of variables
    SI: IntStacks.STACK(100);
    SR: RealStacks.STACK(20);
      . . .
    SI := IntStacks.Create;
    SR := RealStacks.Create;
    SI := IntStacks.Push(SI,23);
    SR := RealStacks.Push(SR,7.1);
      . . .
```

One can also dereference the package names with a use clause, thereby overloading the operation names:

```
    use IntStacks,RealStacks;
      . . .
    SI := Push(SI,10); -- SI is an IntStack
    SR := Push(SR,2.7); -- SR is a RealStack
```

Ada also permits other objects, such as procedures and functions, to be generic. The polymorphic swap procedure mentioned could, for example, be implemented as an Ada generic procedure:

```
    generic
      type ELEMENT is private;
    procedure swap (x,y: in out ELEMENT) is
      temp: ELEMENT := x;
    begin
      x := y;
      y := temp;
    end swap;
```

Each use of swap for a particular type would then have to be preceded by an instantiation for that type:

```
procedure intswap is new swap(INTEGER);
   . . .
intswap(i,j);
```

Sometimes a type parameter in a package must itself have particular operations available before it is suitable for use in a parametrized ADT. For example, elements in an ordered structure such as a binary search tree or ordered list must have an available order relation. In Ada it is possible to specify this requirement using additional declarations in the generic part of a package declaration:

```
generic
   type ELEMENT is private;
   with function LessThan (x,y: ELEMENT) return
      BOOLEAN;
package OrderedList is
   . . .
end OrderedList;
```

Now an OrderedList package can be instantiated only by providing a suitable LessThan function, as in

```
type IntOrderedList is
   new OrderedList (INTEGER,"<");
```

Such a requirement could be called **constrained parametrization.** Without explicit constraints in Ada, no operations are assumed for the type parameter except equality, inequality, and assignment. (This is the content of the keyword private in the declaration of type element; see the discussion on limited private types in Section 8.7.)

As we have noted, in Modula-2 no mechanism exists for parametrizing modules. However, such a mechanism can be simulated in a rudimentary way by importing the necessary information from a separate module:

```
DEFINITION MODULE StackElem;

TYPE Element; (* opaque type *)

END StackElem.

DEFINITION MODULE Stacks;

FROM StackElem IMPORT Element;
TYPE STACK; (* opaque type *)
```

continues

continued

```
PROCEDURE Create (): STACK;
PROCEDURE Push (S: STACK; x: Element): STACK;
PROCEDURE Pop (S: STACK): STACK;
PROCEDURE Top (S: STACK): Element;
PROCEDURE Empty (S: STACK) : BOOLEAN;

END Stacks.
```

Of course, each time a new type for Element is used, a complete copy of the Element and Stacks modules must be made (and renamed). Thus this is really just a textual substitution process similar to a macro facility (and a manual one at that!). Other ad hoc methods are possible in Modula-2, but they all use system-dependent features and are potentially unsafe. We do not study them here.

Other approaches to polymorphism than those of Ada are possible. Indeed, dynamically typed languages such as LISP and Prolog have no trouble admitting polymorphism—it is a natural part of such languages, since the types of objects vary dynamically and depend only on their current values, not on a prespecified declaration.

It is a subject of recent research what kind of polymorphism is best that would also allow strong static type checking while providing maximum flexibility. One approach would be to permit variables to be declared to be of type "type" and then to perform an analysis of the kinds of values each type variable may contain. Such an approach is taken in the programming language **Russell** (see the notes at the end of the chapter). Unfortunately, this results in rather complex type-checking algorithms.

A different approach is taken in the language **ML**. In ML, functions are written as they are in LISP, without a type specification, such as the following length function for any list type with null and tail operations:

```
fun length(lis) =
    if null(lis) then 0
    else length(tail(lis))+1;
```

A translator then collects type information based on information contained in the body of the function and applies this information to the uses of the function. This is a more extensive kind of type inference than is usually available, and in the case of ML, the major algorithm used is a pattern matching algorithm called **unification**. For example, the length function can be statically determined to be type correct and return the type integer by an ML translator, with the parameter "lis" remaining an arbitrary list type. See Chapter 10 for more on the language ML.

8.6   MODULES AND SEPARATE COMPILATION

The Modula-2 module and the Ada package represent a compromise approach to an abstract data type mechanism. Indeed, modules and packages are not types in themselves but are mechanisms for general complexity control, which allow the division of a large program into pieces that can be managed individually, and whose interfaces are controlled. Stated another way, a module is a provider of services that are collected into a protected unit suitable for separate compilation and inclusion into a library. Thus modules and packages are designed not just as a mechanism for abstract data types, but also as a mechanism for separate compilation.

As an example, take the case of a compiler. This is a large program that can be split into several pieces corresponding to the phases described in Chapter 1. As a program it could be split into several modules under the control of a main module:

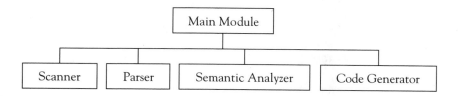

The structure of the program is actually a little more complicated than this. The different modules need to communicate via global variables, which must be placed in their own module. Also a symbol table must be generated and maintained. And an error handler must offer error recovery facilities. For purposes of this example, however, we are going to ignore everything except the scanner, the parser, and the global variables, so we have a program with the following approximate structure:

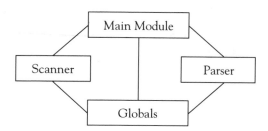

A skeleton for this program in Modula-2 might be as follows (comment lines of asterisks indicate separation into different files):

```
MODULE Main;
FROM Globals IMPORT SyntaxTree;
```
continues

continued

```
    FROM Parser IMPORT Parse;
      . . .
    BEGIN
      (* call parser to generate syntax tree *)
      Parse(SyntaxTree);
      (* call other phases, such as semantic analyzer
         and code generator *)
      . . .
    END Main.

    (****************************************)
    DEFINITION MODULE Scanner;

    PROCEDURE NewToken();

    END Scanner.

    (****************************************)
    IMPLEMENTATION MODULE Scanner;
    FROM Globals IMPORT TokenType, Token;

    PROCEDURE GetChar(): CHAR;
    BEGIN
      . . .
    END GetChar;

    PROCEDURE NewToken();
    VAR ch: CHAR;
    BEGIN
      REPEAT
        ch := GetChar();
        . . .
      UNTIL ...;
      Token.kind := ...;
      Token.strVal := ...;
      . . .
    END NewToken;

    END Scanner.

    (****************************************)
    DEFINITION MODULE Parser;
    FROM Globals IMPORT TreeType;

    PROCEDURE Parse(VAR tree: TreeType);
```

```
END Parser.

(* * * * * * * * * * * * * * * * * * * * * * * * * * * * * * * * * * * * *)
IMPLEMENTATION MODULE Parser;
FROM Globals IMPORT TokenType, TreeType,
  Token,...;
FROM Scanner IMPORT NewToken;

PROCEDURE ParseProgram(): TreeType;
BEGIN
  IF Token.kind = tProgram THEN
    NewToken();
    ...
  END; (* if *)
END ParseProgram;

(* etc... *)

PROCEDURE Parse(VAR tree: TreeType);
BEGIN
  NewToken();
  tree := ParseProgram();
END Parse;

END Parser.

(* * * * * * * * * * * * * * * * * * * * * * * * * * * * * * * * * * * * *)
DEFINITION MODULE Globals;
CONST MaxStrLen = 80;
TYPE
  StrType = ARRAY [0..MaxStrLen-1] OF CHAR;
  TokenType = (tUnknown, tProgram, ...);
  TreeType = POINTER TO TreeRecord;
  TreeRecord = RECORD
                 ...
               END;
VAR
  Token: RECORD
           kind: TokenType;
           StrVal: StrType;
         END;
  SyntaxTree: TreeType;

END Globals.

(* * * * * * * * * * * * * * * * * * * * * * * * * * * * * * * * * * * * *)
IMPLEMENTATION MODULE Globals;                      continues
```

```
continued
    BEGIN
      (* Only initialization here *)
      Token.kind := tUnknown;
      Token.strVal := "";
      SyntaxTree := NIL;
      . . .
    END Globals.
```

These modules are all providers of services, among which can be types, variables, procedures, or even constants. Each of the modules is capable of separate compilation. A DEFINITION MODULE is compiled to essentially a symbol table. Each DEFINITION MODULE must be compiled prior to its associated IMPLEMENTATION MODULE. Other restrictions on the order of compilation are implied by the IMPORT lists that establish dependencies among the modules: if A imports from B then B must be compiled before A. These dependencies can be expressed as a graph. In the case of the compiler program, the dependencies exhibited by the given code would result in the **compilation dependency graph** of Figure 8-1 (A → B means A imports from B):

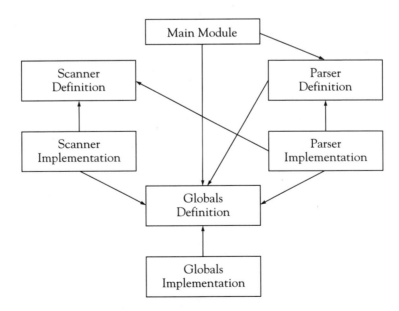

Figure 8-1   Compilation Dependency Graph for the Sample Program

Note that DEFINITION MODULEs and IMPLEMENTATION MOD-ULEs can have different dependencies. For there to exist a correct compilation order, there must not be any circular dependencies in the graph. Thus the dependency graph must be **acyclic,** and a correct compilation order is given by any sequence in which all modules are compiled before their predecessors. Such an order for a directed acyclic graph is called a **topological sort.**

For example, here are two correct compilation orders for the graph for our sample program:

GLOBALS.DEF	SCANNER.DEF
SCANNER.DEF	GLOBALS.DEF
PARSER.DEF	SCANNER.MOD
MAIN.MOD	PARSER.DEF
GLOBALS.MOD	PARSER.MOD
SCANNER.MOD	MAIN.MOD
PARSER.MOD	GLOBALS.MOD

Now a language translator can get involved in maintaining a library of separately compiled modules. Whenever a new module is compiled, or an old one recompiled, the compiler can check the dependencies to see which other modules might be affected and recompile them as well.

It is also possible for each module to have a main block of code that must be executed before any of its clients can be executed. For example, in the following skeleton code, the main block of MODULE A must be executed before that of MODULE B:

```
DEFINITION MODULE A;
   . . .
(* services provided by A *)
   . . .
END A.


(* * * * * * * * * * * * * * * * * * * * * * * * * * * * * * * * * * * * *)


IMPLEMENTATION MODULE A;
   . . .
(* implementation of services of A *)
   . . .

BEGIN
(* Main block of A - must be executed once before
    any clients are executed *)
END A.


(* * * * * * * * * * * * * * * * * * * * * * * * * * * * * * * * * * * * *)
```

continues

continued

```
MODULE B;
IMPORT A: (* B is a client of A *)
    . . .
BEGIN
(* Main block of B - must be executed after that
   of A *)
END B.
```

This requirement means that a linker must also link the object code of the separately compiled modules in such a way that the main blocks of each module are scheduled for execution according to a topological sort of the dependency graph: main blocks of separately compiled modules are executed only once, before the block of the main module is executed, and each must be executed before any of the services provided by that module are accessed.

The dependency graph for the linker is a little different from that of the compiler, however: the object modules combine the information from both the definition module and the implementation module, and so the dependencies for both modules are combined in the link dependency graph. In the compiler example, the link dependency graph is shown in Figure 8-2.

The link dependency graph must also be acyclic for there to exist a correct order for scheduling the execution of the initialization sections of the separately compiled modules. In the case of our compiler example, a correct initialization order would be

GLOBALS
SCANNER
PARSER
MAIN

corresponding to a topological sort of the link dependency graph. However, it is not always true that an acyclic compile dependency graph will

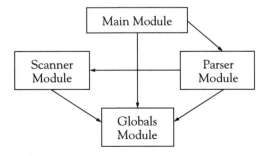

Figure 8-2   Link Dependency Graph for the Sample Program

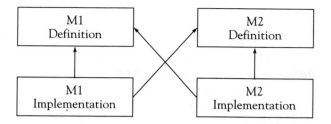

Figure 8-3 Compilation Dependencies

result in an acyclic link dependency graph. For example, the modules M1 and M2, which have acyclic compile dependencies, have a cycle in their link dependencies:

```
DEFINITION MODULE M1;
VAR X1: INTEGER;
END M1.


(**************************************)
IMPLEMENTATION MODULE M1;
FROM M2 IMPORT X2;
BEGIN
  X1 := X2;
END M1.


(**************************************)
DEFINITION MODULE M2;
VAR X2: INTEGER;
END M2.


(**************************************)
IMPLEMENTATION MODULE M2;
FROM M1 IMPORT X1;
BEGIN
  X2 := X1;
END M2.
```

The compilation and link dependency graphs for the example are shown in Figures 8-3 and 8-4.

Figure 8-4 Link Dependencies

For these modules there is no order of execution of the initialization sections that is correct. In other examples there may still be an execution order that is correct, but a linker may not be able to find it. In practice, linkers will generally adopt an ad hoc scheduling for the execution of initialization sections rather than declaring an error. For example, a linker could resolve circularities by simply using the reverse of the order of the import lists in the client modules. Thus, in the example, if a main module imports M1 and M2 as follows, M1 will be initialized before M2:

```
MODULE Main;

FROM M2 IMPORT X2;
FROM M1 IMPORT X1;

BEGIN
   . . .
END Main.
```

In Ada, separate compilation facilities are similar to those of Modula-2: package specification sections can be in separate files from their implementation sections. Ada has a more general facility, however, in that any function can be compiled separately using the **separate** declaration:

```
package A is
   . . .
   function f(x: FLOAT) return FLOAT;
   . . .
end A;

package body A is
   procedure g(y,z: FLOAT) is begin ... end g;
   function f(x: FLOAT) return FLOAT is separate;
   . . .
end A;
```

In the example, the code for function f is in a separate file from the body of package A:

```
separate(A)
function f(x: FLOAT) return FLOAT is
begin
   -- implementation of f is here
   . . .
   g(x,x);
   . . .
end f;
```

The declaration separate(A) indicates that, although f is compiled separately, it is a part of package A and thus has access to other parts of A, such as the procedure g. In Ada terminology, f is a **subunit** of A.

Abstract data type mechanisms in programming languages use separate compilation facilities to meet protection and implementation independence requirements. The specification part of the ADT mechanism is used as an interface to guarantee consistency of use and implementation. But ADT mechanisms are used to create types and associate operations to types, while separate compilation facilities are providers of services, which may include variables, constants, or any other programming language entities. Thus compilation units are in one sense more general than ADT mechanisms. But at the same time they are less general, in that the use of a compilation unit to define a type does not identify the type with the unit, and thus is not a true type declaration. Furthermore, units are static entities—they retain their identity only before linking, which can result in allocation and initialization problems, as described in Section 8.6. Thus the use of separate compilation units such as modules or packages to implement abstract data types is a compromise in language design—but a useful one, as it reduces the implementation question for ADTs to one of consistency checking and linkage.

8.7   PROBLEMS WITH ABSTRACT DATA TYPE MECHANISMS

Modula-2, Ada, and a number of other languages have drawbacks to their abstract data type mechanisms. Many of these are corrected by object-oriented languages, but before we study object-oriented languages (in the next chapter), it will be helpful to point out some of the drawbacks to the mechanisms studied in Sections 8.2, 8.3, and 8.4. (We have already mentioned a few of these.) Not all languages suffer from all the drawbacks listed, but Modula-2 suffers from most of them and is a good example to keep in mind.

8.7.1   Modules Are Not Types

In Ada and Modula-2 difficulties arise because a module must export a type as well as operations. It would be helpful instead to define a module to **be a type.** Then there is no need to arrange to protect the implementation details of the type with an ad hoc mechanism such as opaque or private declarations; the details are all contained in the implementation section of the type.

Euclid is an example of a language that takes this approach, and this simplifies the definition of many abstract data types, for example, that of a stack:

```
type IntStack = module
  exports(push,pop,top,empty)
  var StackRec = record
      . . .
  procedure push (x: integer) =
    imports(var StackRec)
      . . .
  end push

  procedure pop =
    imports(var StackRec)
      . . .
      etc.
end IntStack
```

Now a stack variable contains its own data and operations, which are completely within the module and not visible to clients:

```
var S,T: IntStack; ...
  S.push(20);
  T.push(10);
  S.pop;
```

This also means that no create procedure need be exported, since the module can initialize itself at declaration time (see Section 8.7.3).

In Modula-2 it is also possible to define a module that contains its own data structure hidden in its implementation part, but such modules cannot be created on demand. This brings up a second problem associated with modules.

8.7.2 Modules Are Static Entities

If we need only one stack in Modula-2, we could write, in a similar fashion to Euclid,

```
DEFINITION MODULE IntStack;

PROCEDURE Push (value: INTEGER);
PROCEDURE Pop ();
PROCEDURE Top (): INTEGER;
PROCEDURE Empty(): BOOLEAN;

END IntStack.

IMPLEMENTATION MODULE IntStack;
CONST Size = 100;
VAR data: ARRAY [1..Size] OF INTEGER;
    top: [0..Size];
```

```
PROCEDURE Push (value: INTEGER);
BEGIN
  INC(top);
  data[top] := value;
END Push;

PROCEDURE Pop ();
BEGIN
  DEC(top);
END Pop;

PROCEDURE Top (): INTEGER;
BEGIN
  RETURN data[top];
END Top;

PROCEDURE Empty(): BOOLEAN;
BEGIN
  RETURN top = 0;
END Empty;
BEGIN
  top := 0; (* Initialization - executed once *)
END IntStack.
```

But each new stack would need a new module, which must be copied manually from this one. This is because modules are static: they cannot be created on demand, and the initialization code for a module is only executed once.

8.7.3   Modules That Export Types Do Not Adequately Control Operations on Variables of Such Types

In the Modula-2 and Ada examples of data type COMPLEX in Sections 8.2 and 8.3, variables of type COMPLEX were pointers that had to be allocated and initialized by calling the procedure MakeComplex. But the exporting module cannot guarantee that this procedure is called before the variables are used; thus correct allocation and initialization cannot be ensured. Even worse, because complex numbers are pointers in the sample implementations, copies can be made and deallocations performed outside the control of the module, without the user being aware of the consequences, and without the ability to return the deallocated memory to available storage. For instance, in

```
z := MakeComplex(1.0,0.0);
x := MakeComplex(-1.0,0.0);
x := z;
```

the last assignment has the effect of making z and x point to the same allocated storage and leaves the original value of x as garbage in memory. Indeed, the implementation of type COMPLEX as a pointer type gives variables of this type pointer semantics, subject to problems of sharing and copying (see Chapter 5).

Even if we were to rewrite the implementation of type COMPLEX as a record instead of a pointer (which would wipe out some encapsulation and information hiding in both Modula-2 and Ada), we would not regain much control. In that case, the declaration of a variable of type COMPLEX would automatically perform the allocation, and calling MakeComplex would perform initialization only. Still, we would have no guarantee that initializations would be properly performed, but at least assignment would have the usual storage semantics, and there would be no unexpected creation of garbage or side effects.

Part of the problem comes from the use of assignment. Indeed, when x and y are pointer types, x := y performs assignment by sharing the object pointed to by y, with resulting potential unwanted side effects. This is another example of an operation that a module exporting types has no control of. Similarly, the comparison x = y tests pointer equality, identity of location in memory, which is not the right test when x and y are complex numbers:

```
x  := MakeComplex(1.0,0.0);
y  := MakeComplex(1.0,0.0);
(* now a test of x = y returns false *)
```

We could write procedures Equal and Assign and add them to the exported operations, but, again, there would be no guarantee that they would be appropriately applied by a client.

In Ada, however, there is a mechanism for controlling the use of equality and assignment: the use of a **limited private type:**

```
package ComplexNumbers is

    type COMPLEX is limited private;

    -- operations, including assignment and equality
    . . .
    function Equal(x,y: in COMPLEX) return BOOLEAN;
    procedure Assign(x: out COMPLEX;
                     y: in COMPLEX);

private
    type ComplexRec;
    type COMPLEX is access ComplexRec;

end ComplexNumbers;
```

Now clients are prevented from using the usual ": = " and " = " operations, and the package body can ensure that equality is performed appropriately and that assignment deallocates garbage and/or copies values instead of pointers. Indeed, the " = " (and, implicitly, the inequality "/ = ") operator can be overloaded as described in Section 8.5, so the same infix form can be used after redefinition by the package. Assignment, however, cannot be overloaded in Ada. And there is still no automatic initialization and deallocation.

8.7.4   Modules Do Not Always Adequately Represent How They Depend on Imported Types

For example, a stack uses assignment of elements to store and retrieve elements from memory. And a binary search tree or priority queue needs an order relation and equality test. But the use of such operations may not be made explicit:

```
MODULE PriorityQueues;
FROM Elem IMPORT Element;

TYPE PriQueue; (* opaque type *)

PROCEDURE Create (VAR p: PriQueue);
PROCEDURE Insert (VAR p: PriQueue, x: Element);
PROCEDURE DeleteMin (VAR p: PriQueue; VAR x:
   Element);
(* Comparison operator < needed for type Element
   for Insert and DeleteMin operations *)
END PriorityQueues.
```

In an Ada generic package, however, there is a mechanism for controlling the operations needed for a type parameter, at least to a certain extent. See the discussion on parametrized types in Section 8.5.

8.7.5   Module Definitions Include No Specification of the Semantics of the Provided Operations

In the algebraic specification of an abstract data type, equations are given that specify the behavior of the operations. Yet in almost all languages no specification of the behavior of the available operations is required. Some experiments have been conducted with systems that require semantic specification and then attempt to determine whether a provided implementation agrees with its specification, but such languages and systems are still unusual and experimental.

One example of a language that does allow the specification of semantics is Eiffel, which is one of the object-oriented languages that we study in the next chapter. In Eiffel, semantic specifications are given by preconditions, postconditions, and invariants. Preconditions and post-conditions establish what must be true before and after the execution of a procedure or function. Invariants establish what must be true about the internal state of the data in an abstract data type. For more on such conditions, see Chapter 12 on formal semantics. For more on Eiffel, see the next chapter.

A brief example of the way Eiffel establishes semantics is as follows. In a queue ADT as described in Section 8.1, the enqueue operation is defined as follows in Eiffel:

```
enqueue (x:element) is
require
  not full
ensure
  if old empty then front = x
  else front = old front;
  not empty
end; -- enqueue
```

The **require** section establishes preconditions—in this case, to execute the enqueue operation correctly, the queue must not be full (this is not part of the algebraic specification as given in Section 8.1; see Exercise 23). The **ensure** section establishes postconditions, which in the case of the enqueue operation are that the newly enqueued element becomes the front of the queue only if the queue was previously empty and that the queue is now not empty. These requirements correspond to the algebraic axioms

```
front(enqueue(q,x)) = if empty(q) then x else
                         front(q)
empty(enqueue(q,x)) = false
```

of Section 8.1.

In most languages we are confined to giving indications of the semantic content of operations inside comments.

8.8 THE MATHEMATICS OF ABSTRACT DATA TYPES

In the algebraic specification of an abstract data type, a data type, a set of operations, and a set of axioms in equational form are specified. Nothing is said, however, about the actual existence of such a type—such a type is still hypothetical until an actual type is constructed that meets all the requirements. Such an actual type is a set with operations on the set of the appropriate form that satisfy the given equations. A set and operations that meet the specification is a **model** for the specification. Given an algebraic specification, it is possible for no model to exist, or many models. Therefore, it is necessary to distinguish an actual type—a model—from a potential type—an algebraic specification. Potential types are called **sorts,** and potential operations are called **signatures.** Thus a sort is the name of a type, which is not yet associated to any actual set of values. Similarly, a signature is the name of an operation, which exists only in theory, having no actual operation yet associated to it. A model is then an actualization of a sort and its signatures and is called an **algebra** (since it has operations).

For this reason, algebraic specifications are often written using the sort-signature terminology:

sort queue(element) **imports** boolean

signatures:
    create: $\rightarrow$ queue
    enqueue: queue $\times$ element $\rightarrow$ queue
    dequeue: queue $\rightarrow$ queue
    front: queue $\rightarrow$ element
    empty: queue $\rightarrow$ boolean

axioms:
    empty(create) = true
    empty(enqueue(q,x)) = false
    front(create) = error
    front(enqueue(q,x)) = if empty(q) then x else front(q)
    dequeue(create) = error
    dequeue(enqueue(q,x)) = if empty(q) then q else
                                enqueue(dequeue(q),x)

Given a sort, signatures, and axioms, we would, of course, like to know that an actual type exists for that specification. In fact, we would like to be able to construct a *unique* algebra for the specification that we would then take to be *the* type represented by the specification.

How does one construct such an algebra? A standard mathematical method is to construct the **free algebra of terms** for a sort and signatures and then to form the **quotient algebra** of the equivalence relation generated by the equational axioms. The free algebra of terms consists of all the legal combinations of operations. For example, the free algebra for sort queue(integer) and signatures create, enqueue, dequeue, front, and empty has terms such as the following:

                create
                enqueue(create,2)
                enqueue(enqueue(create,2),1)
                dequeue(enqueue(create,2))
                dequeue(enqueue(enqueue(create,2), -1))
                dequeue(dequeue(enqueue(create,3),1))
                etc.

Note that the axioms for a queue imply that some of these terms are actually equal, for example,

$$\text{dequeue(enqueue(create,2))} = \text{create}$$

In the free algebra, however, all terms are considered to be different; that is why it is called free. In the free algebra of terms, no axioms are true. To make the axioms true, and so to construct a type that models the specification, we need to use the axioms to reduce the number of distinct elements in the free algebra. The two distinct terms create and dequeue(enqueue(create,2)) need to be identified, for example, in order to make the axiom

$$\text{dequeue(enqueue}(q,x)) = $$
$$\text{if empty}(q) \text{ then } q \text{ else}$$
$$\text{enqueue(dequeue}(q),x)$$

hold. This can be done by constructing an **equivalence relation** $==$ from the axioms: "$==$" is an equivalence relation if it is symmetric, transitive, and reflexive:

if $x == y$ then $y == x$ (symmetry)

if $x == y$ and $y == z$ then $x == z$ (transitivity)

$x == x$ (reflexivity)

It is a standard task in mathematics to show that, given an equivalence relation $==$ and a free algebra F there is a unique, well-defined algebra $F/==$ such that $x = y$ in $F/==$ if and only if $x == y$ in F. The algebra $F/==$ is called the quotient algebra of F by $==$. Furthermore, given a set of equations, such as the axioms in an algebraic specification, there is a unique "smallest" equivalence relation making the two sides of every equation equivalent and hence equal in the quotient algebra. It is this quotient algebra that is usually taken to be "the" data type defined by an algebraic specification. This algebra has the property that the only terms that are equal are those that are provably equal from the axioms. Thus, in the queue example,

$$\text{dequeue(enqueue(enqueue(create,2),3))} = $$
$$\text{enqueue(dequeue(enqueue(create,2)),3)} = \text{enqueue(create,3)}$$

but enqueue(create,2) $<>$ enqueue(create,3).

For mathematical reasons (coming from category theory and universal algebra), this algebra is called the **initial algebra** represented by the specification, and using this algebra as the data type of the specification results in what are called **initial semantics.**

How do we know whether the algebra we get from this construction really has the properties of the data type that we want? The answer is that we don't, unless we have written the "right" axioms. In general, axiom systems should be **consistent** and **complete.** Consistency says that the axioms should not identify terms that should be different. For example, empty(create) = true and empty(create) = false are inconsistent axioms, because they result in false = true; that is, false and true become identified in the initial semantics. Consistency of the axiom system says that the initial algebra is not "too small." Completeness of the axiom system, on the other hand, says that the initial algebra is not "too big"; that is, elements of the initial algebra that should be the same aren't. (Note that adding axioms identifies more elements, thus making the initial algebra "smaller" while taking away axioms makes it "larger.") A further useful, but not as critical, property for an axiom system is for it to be **independent:** no axiom is implied by other axioms. For example, front(enqueue(enqueue(create,x),y)) = x is redundant because it follows from other axioms:

$$\text{front(enqueue(enqueue(create,}x\text{),}y\text{))} = \text{front(enqueue(create,}x\text{))}$$

since front(enqueue(q,y)) = front(q) for q = enqueue(create,x), by the third axiom on page 289 applied to the case when $q <>$ create, and then

$$\text{front(enqueue(create,}x\text{))} = x$$

by the same axiom applied to the case when q = create.

Deciding on an appropriate set of axioms is in general a difficult process. In Section 8.1 we gave a simplistic method based on the classification of the operations into constructors, destructors, and inspectors. Such methods, while useful, are not foolproof and do not cover all cases. Moreover, dealing with errors causes extra difficulties, which we do not study here.

Initial semantics for algebraic specifications are unforgiving because, if we leave out an axiom, we can in general get many values in our data type that should be equal but aren't. More forgiving semantics are given by an approach that assumes that any two data values that cannot be distinguished by inspector operations must be equal. An algebra that expresses such semantics is called (again for mathematical reasons) a **final algebra,** and the associated semantics are called **final semantics.**

A final algebra is also essentially unique, and can be constructed by means similar to the initial algebra construction. To see the difference between these two definitions, we take the example of an integer array abstract data type. An algebraic specification is as follows:

type IntArray **imports** integer

operations:
    create: → IntArray
    insert: IntArray × integer × integer → IntArray
    extract: IntArray × integer → integer

variables: A: IntArray; i,j,k: integer;

axioms:
    extract(create,i) = 0
    extract(insert(A,i,j),k) = if $i=k$ then j else extract(A,k)

This array data type is essentially ARRAY [INTEGER] OF INTEGER (in Modula-2 syntax): $insert(A,i,j)$ is like $A[i] := j$, and $extract(A,i)$ is like getting the value $A[i]$. There is a problem, however: in initial semantics, the arrays

$$insert(insert(create,1,1),2,2)$$

and

$$insert(insert(create,2,2),1,1)$$

are not equal! (There is no rule that allows us to switch the order of inserts.) Final semantics, however, tells us that two arrays must be equal if all their values are equal:

$A = B$ if and only if for all integers i $extract(A,i) = extract(B,i)$.

This is an example of the **principle of extension** in mathematics: two things are equal precisely when all their components are equal. It is a natural property and is likely to be one we want for abstract data types, or at least for the IntArray specification. To make the final and initial semantics agree, however, we must add the axiom:

$$insert(insert(A,i,j),k,m) = insert(insert(A,k,m),i,j)$$

In the case of the queue algebraic specification, the final and initial semantics already agree, so we don't have to worry: given two queues p and q,

$p = q$ if and only if $p = create$ and $q = create$
        or $front(p) = front(q)$ and $dequeue(p) = dequeue(q)$

Exercises

1. Discuss how the following languages meet or fail to meet criteria 1 and 2 for an abstract data type mechanism on page 251:
   (a) Modula-2
   (b) Ada
   (c) Euclid
   (d) CLU

2. In the algebraic specification of the complex abstract data type in Section 8.1, axioms were given that base complex addition and subtraction on the corresponding real operations. Write similar axioms for (a) multiplication, and (b) division.

3. An alternative to writing axioms relating the operations of complex numbers to the corresponding operations of their real and imaginary parts is to write axioms for all the usual properties of complex numbers, such as associativity, commutativity, and distributivity. What problems do you foresee in this approach?

4. Finish writing the implementation of MODULE ComplexNumbers in Section 8.2.

5. Finish writing the implementation of package ComplexNumbers in Section 8.3.

6. Use your implementation of Exercise 4 or 5 to compute the roots of a quadratic equation $ax^2 + bx + c = 0$. (a, b, and c may be assumed to be either real or complex.)

7. Write an implementation for the queue abstract data type of Section 8.1 using an Ada generic package.

8. A **double-ended queue**, or **deque**, is a data type that combines the actions of a stack and a queue. Write an algebraic specification for a deque abstract data type assuming the following operations: create, empty, front, rear, addfront, addrear, deletefront, deleterear.

9. Which operations of the complex abstract data type of Section 8.1 are constructors? Which are inspectors? Which are destructors? Which are selectors? Which are predicates? Based on the suggestions in Section 8.1, how many axioms should you have?

10. Write the axioms for an algebraic specification for an abstract data type SymbolTable with the following operations:

    create: → SymbolTable
    enter: SymbolTable × name × value → SymbolTable
    lookup: SymbolTable × name → value
    isin: SymbolTable × name → boolean

11. Which operations of the SymbolTable abstract data type in Exercise 10 are constructors? Which are inspectors? Which are destructors? Which are selectors? Which are predicates? Based on the suggestions in Section 8.8, how many axioms should you have?

12. Write an algebraic specification for an abstract data type string; think up appropriate operations for such a data type and the axioms they must satisfy. Compare your operations to standard string operations in a language of your choice.

13. Write an algebraic specification for an abstract data type bstree (binary search tree) with the following operations:

create: $\rightarrow$ bstree

make: bstree $\times$ element $\times$ bstree $\rightarrow$ bstree

empty: bstree $\rightarrow$ boolean

left: bstree $\rightarrow$ bstree

right: bstree $\rightarrow$ bstree

data: bstree $\rightarrow$ element

isin: bstree $\times$ element $\rightarrow$ boolean

insert: bstree $\times$ element $\rightarrow$ bstree

What does one need to know about the element data type in order for a bstree data type to be possible?

14. Write Modula-2 or Ada implementations for the specifications of Exercises 8, 10, 12, and 13.

15. The text mentioned that a function with no parameters is a constant. Thus the create function, which is a part of many specifications, is a constant. Mathematically, such a function must always return the same value. Why? Implementations of such functions in a programming language may not return the same value, however. Why? Does this cause problems in satisfying the axioms in an implementation? Discuss.

16. Describe the Boolean data type using an algebraic specification.

17. Show using the axioms for a queue on page 255 that the following are true:
    (a) front(enqueue(enqueue(create,x),y)) = x
    (b) front(enqueue(dequeue(enqueue(create,x)),y)) = y
    (c) front(dequeue(enqueue(enqueue(create,x),y))) = y

18. A delete operation in a SymbolTable (see Exercise 10),

$$\text{delete: SymbolTable} \times \text{name} \rightarrow \text{SymbolTable}$$

might have two different semantics, as expressed in the following axioms:

delete(enter(s,x,v),y) = if $x=y$ then s else
$\qquad\qquad$ enter(delete(s,y),x,v)

or

delete(enter(s,x,v),y) = if $x=y$ then delete(s,x) else
$\qquad\qquad$ enter(delete(s,y),x,v)

(a) Which of these is more appropriate for a symbol table in a translator for a block-structured language with static scoping? In what situations might the other be more appropriate?
(b) Rewrite your axioms of Exercise 7 to incorporate each of these two axioms.

19. Ada requires generic packages to be instantiated with an actual type before the package can be used. By contrast, some other languages allow for the use of a type parameter directly in a declaration as follows:

```
x: STACK(INTEGER);
```

Why do you think Ada did not adopt this approach?

20. **(a)** Show how overloading of operations in Modula-2 could be imitated by providing a procedure with a parameter of an enumerated type.
    (b) Why can't parametric polymorphism be imitated in this way?

21. The use of an opaque type in Modula-2 in general requires the export of `Assign` and `Equal` procedures. Why? Write `Assign` and `Equal` procedures for the `ComplexNumbers` module of the text.

22. One could complain that the error axioms in the stack and queue algebraic specifications given in this chapter are unnecessarily strict, since for at least some of them, it is possible to define reasonable nonerror values. Give two examples of such axioms. Is it possible to eliminate all error values by finding nonerror substitutes for error values? Discuss.

23. In the algebraic specification of a stack or a queue, no mention was made of the possibility that a stack or queue might become full:

$$\text{full: stack} \rightarrow \text{boolean}$$

Such a test requires the inclusion of another operation, namely,

$$\text{size: stack} \rightarrow \text{integer}$$

and a constant

$$\text{maxsize:} \rightarrow \text{integer}$$

Write out a set of axioms for such a stack.

24. The Ada package specification of a generic stack in Section 8.5.2 had the size as a parameter to the declaration of a variable of type `STACK`. An alternative would be to make the size into a generic parameter of the package. Discuss the pros and cons of these two methods.

25. Does the C language contain an ADT mechanism through its separate compilation facility? Explain.

26. Describe how error axioms in an abstract data type specification might be handled in Modula-2 or Ada. Would it be appropriate to make them into exceptions? Discuss.

27. An implementation of abstract data type bstree of Exercise 13 is unsafe if it exports all the listed operations: a client can destroy the order property by improper use of the operations. Which operations should be exported and which should not? Discuss the problems this creates, if any.

28. Could a compiler discover a circularity in the link dependency graph of a collection of modules?

29. Should a linker complain if it discovers a circularity in link dependencies? When might such a circularity not matter? Can you think of a situation in which such a circularity might be useful?

30. Can the integers be used as a model for the Boolean data type? How do the integers differ from the initial algebra for this data type?

31. A **canonical form** for elements of an algebra is a way of writing all elements in a standard, or canonical, way. For example, the initial algebra for the queue algebraic specification has the following canonical form for its elements:

$$\text{enqueue(enqueue(. . .enqueue(create}, a_1). . .,a_{n-1}),a_n)$$

Show that any element of the initial algebra can be put in this form, and use the canonical form to show that the initial and final semantics of a queue are the same.

32. Given the following algebraic specification

type Item **imports** boolean

operations:
   create: $\rightarrow$ Item
   push: Item $\rightarrow$ Item
   empty: Item $\rightarrow$ boolean

variables: s: Item;

axioms:
   empty(create) = true
   empty(push(s)) = false

show that the initial and final semantics of this specification are different. What axiom needs to be added to make them the same?

33. Exercise 3 noted that abstract data type complex may need to have all its algebraic properties, such as commutativity, written out as axioms. This is not necessary if one uses the principle of extension (page 292) and assumes the corresponding algebraic properties for the reals. Use the principle of extension and the axioms of Exercise 2 to show the commutativity of complex addition.

34. In the algebraic specification of the abstract data type complex in Section 8.1, the type real was imported, but in the Modula-2 DEFINITION MODULE ComplexNumbers in Section 8.2, it was not. On the other hand, in the algebraic specification of the stack abstract data type in Section 8.1, the type element was a parameter, while in the Modula-2 DEFINITION MODULE in Section 8.5 it was imported. Explain.

Notes and References

The earliest language to influence the development of abstract data types was Simula67, which introduced abstract data types in the form of classes. Since classes are closely related to object-oriented programming, which is the subject of the next chapter and which can be viewed as an extension of abstract data types, Simula67 is treated in detail there instead of this chapter. The algebraic specification of abstract data types described in Section 8.1 was pioneered by Guttag [1977] and Goguen, Thatcher, and Wagner [1978], who also developed the initial algebra semantics described in Section 8.8. The alternative final algebra semantics described there was developed by Kamin [1983]. A good general reference for abstract data type issues, including mathematical issues discussed in Section 8.8, is Cleaveland [1986]. More examples of ADT specification and implementation in Modula-2 (Section 8.2) can be found in King [1988]. More details on ADT specification and implementation in Ada (Section 8.3) can be found in Booch [1986] and Barnes [1982]. CLU examples (Section 8.4) can be found in Liskov [1984]. Euclid examples (Section 8.4) can be found in Lampson et al. [1981]. Other languages with interesting abstract data type mechanisms are Mesa (Mitchell, Maybury, and Sweet [1979]; Geschke, Morris, and Satterthwaite [1977]) and Cedar (Lampson [1983], Teitelman [1984]). A survey of overloading and polymorphism (Section 8.5) can be found in Cardelli and Wegner [1985]. The language ML, mentioned in Section 8.5 and described in a little more detail in Section 10.4, is treated in Wikström [1987]; Mitchell and Harper [1988]; Milner, Tofte, and Harper [1990]; and Milner and Tofte [1991]. The language Russell, with an interesting polymorphic type system (and also mentioned in Section 8.5), is described in Demers, Donahue, and Skinner [1978] and Donahue and Demers [1985]. Separate compilation as a specific language issue (Section 8.6) has been dealt with less as a theoretical question in language design and more as an issue in language pragmatics. One text that does discuss it is Marcotty and Legard [1986]. More on the properties of directed acyclic graphs and topological sorts (used in Section 8.6 to describe compilation dependencies) can be found in Aho, Hopcroft, and Ullman [1983].

9 OBJECT-ORIENTED PROGRAMMING LANGUAGES

Object-oriented programming languages began in the 1960s with the Simula project, an attempt to design a programming language that extends Algol60 in a way suitable for performing computer simulations of real-world situations. One of the central ideas of this project was to incorporate into the language the notion of an object, which, similar to a real-world object, is an entity with certain properties, and with the ability to react in certain ways to events. A program then consists of a set of objects, which can vary dynamically, and which execute by acting and reacting to each other, in much the same way that a real-world process proceeds by the interaction of real-world objects. These ideas were incorporated into the general-purpose language Simula67, which is still today a useful (and used) language.

Simula67's influence took two different directions during the 1970s. The first was the development of abstract data type mechanisms, which we have studied in the last chapter. The second was the

development of the object paradigm itself, which considers a program
to be a collection of interacting independent objects. The primary rep-
resentative of this direction of development was the Dynabook Project,
which culminated in the language Smalltalk-80, the first language to
incorporate the object paradigm in a thorough and consistent way.

Since then, the two directions of Simula67's influence have begun to converge again, with improvements in abstract data type mechanisms that more closely adopt the object paradigm, and with the
design of languages with objects emphasizing efficiency and reuse
rather than specifically adhering to the object paradigm for its own
sake.

Beginning in the mid-1980s, **object-oriented programming,** not
only as a language paradigm, but also as a methodology for program
design, has experienced an explosion in interest and activity, much as
structured programming and top-down design did in the early 1970s.
Nowadays almost every language has some form of structured constructs, such as the if-then-else statement, as well as procedural abstraction, and it is well known that it is possible to apply structured
programming principles even in a relatively unstructured language like
FORTRAN. Similarly, the ideas of object-oriented programming can
be applied, at least to a certain extent, in non-object-oriented languages. Nevertheless, the real power of the technique comes only in a
language with true object-oriented constructs, so that it can definitely
be considered to be a language paradigm in its own right (unlike structured versus nonstructured languages) and take its place among the
other major paradigms—imperative, functional, and logic programming.

In the following sections we shall introduce the major concepts of
object-oriented programming, using Simula67 (or Simula for short) as
our primary example. The concepts we will cover include the notions
of object and class as a pattern for objects, inheritance of operations as
a tool for code reuse and the maintenance of control over dependencies, and the dynamic nature of operations as an essential feature of
reuse. We will also study three languages in addition to Simula as major examples of the object-oriented paradigm: C++, Eiffel, and Smalltalk. Finally, we will look briefly at some issues of object-oriented
design and techniques for implementation of object-oriented language
features.

9.1 *SOFTWARE REUSE AND INDEPENDENCE*

Object-oriented programming languages address themselves to two issues in software design: the need to reuse software components as much as possible and the need to maintain the independence of different components. In the last chapter we saw that abstract data type mechanisms can aid the independence of software components by separating interfaces from implementations and by controlling dependencies through import lists. In theory, abstract data type mechanisms should also provide for the reuse of software components. It turns out, however, that in practice each new programming problem tends to require a slightly different version of the services provided by a module. What is needed are different ways of varying the services a module offers to clients, while at the same time retaining control over access to those services. In this section we explore the principal ways that the services of software components can be varied and the ways that access to these services can be controlled. These can then be used to evaluate the versatility and effectiveness of an object-oriented mechanism in the subsequent sections.

There are five basic ways that a software component can be modified for reuse: extension, restriction, redefinition, abstraction, and "polymorphization," each of which we discuss in turn.

1. *Extension of the data and/or operations.* As an example of this kind of modification, consider a queue with operations create, enqueue, dequeue, front, and empty (as in Chapter 8). In a particular application, it may be necessary to extend the operations of a queue so that elements can be removed from the rear of the queue and added to the front of the queue. Such a data structure is called a double-ended queue or deque, with new operations addfront and deleterear. These two new operations need to be added to the basic queue structure without necessarily changing the underlying implementation data. As another example of modification by extension, a window is defined on a computer screen as a rectangle specified by its four corners, with operations that may include translate, resize, display, and erase. A text window can be defined as a window with some added text to be displayed. Thus a text window extends a window by adding data, without necessarily changing the operations to be performed.

2. *Restriction of the data and/or operations.* This is essentially the opposite operation from the previous one. For example, if a double-ended queue is available, an ordinary queue can be obtained by restricting the operations, eliminating addfront and deleterear. More commonly, both queues and double-ended queues can be obtained from a general list structure by restricting the kinds of insertions and deletions available. Similarly (but less commonly), a new structure may be obtained by dropping a data item, while preserving the operations. For ex-

ample, a rectangle has both a length and a width, but a square has length equal to width, so one piece of data can be dropped in creating a square. Restriction is a mechanism that is rarely seen in programming languages (perhaps because it is more natural to extend than restrict programs), and we will not see specific mechanisms for it in the languages we study. Nevertheless it is worth stating as a mechanism, since it does occasionally arise in practice as a contrast to extension.

3. *Redefinition of one or more of the operations.* Even if the operations of a new data item remain essentially the same, it may be necessary to redefine some of them to accommodate new behavior. For example, a text window may have the same operations on it as a general-purpose window, but the display operation needs redefinition in order to display the text in the window as well as the window itself. Similarly, if a square is obtained from a rectangle, an area or perimeter function may need to be redefined to take into account the reduced data needed in the computation.

   In several areas in computing (such as the windows examples), the basic structure of each application is so similar to others that software developers have begun using **application frameworks** that provide basic services in object-oriented form and that are used by software developers through redefinition and reuse to provide specific services for each particular application. Such reuse technology promises to provide new major speedups in software development.

4. *Abstraction, or the collection of similar operations from two different components into a new component.* For example, a circle and a rectangle are both objects that have position and that can be translated and displayed. These properties can be combined into an abstract object called a figure, which has the common features of circles, rectangles, triangles, and so on. Specific examples of a figure are then forced to have each of these common properties.

5. *"Polymorphization," or the extension of the type of data that operations can apply to.* We have already seen examples of this in the previous chapter as two kinds of polymorphism: overloading and parametrized types. Extending the types that an operation applies to can also be viewed as an example of abstraction, where common operations from different types are abstracted and collected together. A good example might be that of a print function, which should be applicable to any variable as long as its value is printable. (Indeed, the Pascal write function is polymorphic in this sense, even though polymorphism is not an available mechanism within the language.) We might call such variables printable-objects and define a print procedure for all printable-objects.

   Design for reuse is not the only goal of object-oriented languages. Restricting access to internal details of software components is another. As we have seen in Chapter 8, this requirement is necessary to ensure that clients use components in a way that is independent of the implementation details of the component and that any changes to the implementation of a component will have only a local effect.

The two goals of restricting access and modifiability for reuse can sometimes be mutually incompatible. For example, to add operations to a queue, one needs access to the internal implementation details of the queue data structure. Access restriction can also be complementary to the need for modification, since it forces operations to be defined in an abstract way, which may make it easier to modify their implementation without changing the definition.

Control over access can take several forms. One way is to list explicitly all operations and data that are accessible to clients in an export list (as in the Euclid example in Chapter 8). A second is to list those properties of a component that are inaccessible in a private part, as in Ada. Most explicit of all is to insist that public and private entities both be explicitly declared.

Implicit export is another possibility, as with the Modula-2 DEFI-NITION MODULE, where all entities declared in the definition part of a module are implicitly exported.

It may also be possible to declare parts of a software component to be partially accessible, that is, accessible to some but not all outside components. This can be done either by explicitly naming of the outside components or by implicitly allowing access to a group of components.

Correspondingly, clients may be required to declare explicitly their use of a component by an import list, as in Modula-2. Or they may be able to use a component implicitly, which must then be located automatically by the language system or by instructions to an interface checker and linker.

Mechanisms for restricting access to internal details go by several names. Some authors call them encapsulation mechanisms, while others refer to them as information hiding mechanisms. As we noted in the last chapter, both of these terms are somewhat confusing. We shall instead refer in this chapter to **protection mechanisms.**

9.2   OBJECTS, CLASSES, AND METHODS

In this section we study the basic components of an object-oriented programming language: objects, classes, and methods. This terminology is taken primarily from Simula and Smalltalk and is somewhat unusual for those familiar only with imperative or functional languages, so part of the goal of this section is to relate these terms to more commonly known language constructs.

In Chapter 5 we gave a definition for an **object** as something that occupies memory and has (modifiable) state. This is essentially what an object is in an object-oriented language, but with some modification. First, the state of an object in an object-oriented language is primarily

internal, or **local** to the object itself. That is, the state of an object is represented by local variables declared as part of the object and inaccessible to components outside the object. Second, each object includes a set of functions and procedures through which the local state can be accessed and changed. These are called **methods,** but they are similar to ordinary procedures and functions, except that they can automatically access the object's data (unlike the "outside world") and therefore can be viewed as containing an implicit parameter representing the object itself. Calling a method of an object is sometimes called **sending the object a message.** We shall use the terminology "invoke a method" or "call a method" in this chapter.

Objects can be declared by creating a pattern for the local state and methods. This pattern is called a **class,** and it is essentially just like a data type. Indeed, in many object-oriented languages, a class *is* a type and is incorporated into the type system of the language in more or less standard ways (as described in Chapter 6). Objects are then declared to be of a particular class exactly as variables are declared to be of a particular type in a language like C or Pascal. An object is said to be an **instance** of a class (a terminology related to the instantiation of Ada generic packages or the instantiation of variables by allocating them appropriate memory locations). The local variables representing an object's state are called **instance variables.**

We pause to consider an example in Simula. Consider the complex data type, which was described as an abstract data type in Chapter 8 and implemented there using the mechanisms of the Modula-2 module and the Ada package. In Simula the type complex can be defined as a class as follows:

```
class COMPLEX (x,y);
      real x,y;
begin
  real re,im;
  real procedure RealPart;
  begin
    RealPart := re;
  end RealPart;
  real procedure ImaginaryPart;
  begin
    ImaginaryPart := im;
  end ImaginaryPart;
  procedure Add(y); ref (COMPLEX) y;
  begin
    re := re + y.RealPart;
    im := im + y.ImaginaryPart;
  end Add;
    . . .
  comment - initialization code;                    continues
```

continued

```
 re := x;
 im := y;
end COMPLEX;
```

Instance variables for class COMPLEX are re and im.[1] Methods are RealPart, ImaginaryPart, Add, and other operations not included in the foregoing declaration for brevity's sake. Note that, in the code for Add, the RealPart and ImaginaryPart methods of the parameter y are accessed using a dot notation just like the record field reference of Pascal or C. Note also that the instance variables of the "current instance" to which Add belongs are accessed directly by the Add procedure.

In this definition of class COMPLEX, we have provided methods RealPart and ImaginaryPart to fetch the values of the instance variables re and im. Alternatively, we could access re and im directly (this is permissible in Simula, since protection mechanisms were a later addition; see Exercise 11). However, as we described in Chapter 8, this would make the use of the class dependent on the way local data is stored. Using methods to fetch and store local data is a standard feature of object-oriented programming that makes the use of a class independent of the internal representation of the data (as long as clients use only these methods). For example, we could rewrite the class COMPLEX to use polar coordinates without changing any of the method interfaces as follows (see the similar example in Section 8.2):

```
class COMPLEX (x,y);
      real x,y;
begin
  real radius,angle;
  real procedure RealPart;
  begin
    RealPart := radius * cos(angle);
  end RealPart;
  real procedure ImaginaryPart;
  begin
    ImaginaryPart := radius * sin(angle);
  end ImaginaryPart;
    . . .
  comment - initialization code;
  radius := sqrt(x*x + y*y);
  if x = 0.0 then angle := pi / 2.0
  else angle := arctan(y/x);
end COMPLEX;
```

---

[1]Simula allows the use of the parameters x and y as instance variables, but for consistency in this example, we shall not do so.

Instances of class COMPLEX are created in Simula as pointers, or references:

```
ref (COMPLEX) z;
ref (COMPLEX) w;
. . .
z  :-  new COMPLEX (1.0,1.0);
w  :-  new COMPLEX (1.0,0.0);
```

Note how this mechanism separates the declaration of the variables z and w from the creation (or instantiation) of COMPLEX objects via the **new** statements (":−" is pointer assignment in Simula). Note also that initialization of the objects z and w occurs at the same time as allocation, so that after these statements, z.re = 1.0, z.im = 1.0, w.re = 1.0, and w.im = 0.0. In many object-oriented languages, objects are implicitly reference or pointer types, so that initialization can be explicitly controlled during allocation and so that assignment is by sharing (that is, pointer semantics are maintained as described in Chapter 5).

Methods for the objects z and w can be invoked after allocation by using the usual dot notation. For example,

```
z.Add(w) ·
```

adds w to z and stores the result in z (so z.RealPart = 2.0 and z.ImaginaryPart = 1.0). This mechanism for creating and operating on complex numbers causes difficulties for representing binary operations. For example, to write z := x + y, we would have to create z, copy the values of x's instance variables to it, and add y:

```
z  :-  new COMPLEX(x.RealPart,x.ImaginaryPart);
z.Add(y);
```

This makes binary operations look peculiar, with one parameter singled out as the current instance. There are good points to this mechanism, however. No MakeComplex procedure is necessary, since the call to new can immediately assign values. And the association of the operations with the objects themselves has the advantage of giving each object more direct control.

Classes can refer to themselves in their definition. Consider, for example, the Simula definition of a class of linkable objects, which contain a link field to an object of the same class:

```
class linkableObject;
begin
  ref (linkableObject) link;
  ref (linkableObject) procedure next;
  begin                                              continues
```

continued

```
      next  :-  link;
    end next;
    procedure linkto (p); ref(linkableObject) p;
    begin
      link :- p;
    end linkto;
    link :- none
  end linkableObject;
```

In this example, link is an instance variable of type ref
(linkableObject), which is initialized to the null object (the reserved
word none in Simula). The methods next and linkto allow fetching
and assignment of the link variable. The statement

```
  x  :- new linkableObject
```

creates x as a pointer to a storage location with a single link field
initialized to the null pointer:

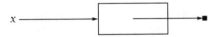

Alternatively, one could define a linkableObject that is initialized to point to itself:

```
  class linkableObject;
  begin
    ref (linkableObject) link;
    ref(linkableObject) procedure next;
    . . .
    link :- this linkableObject
  end linkableObject;
```

Now x :- new linkableObject creates the following picture:

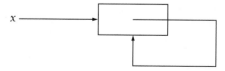

Note the use of the expression this linkableObject to refer explicitly
to the current object, a useful tool in self-referential structures.
  The concepts of class and object can be thought of as generalizing
the notion of record or structure type and variable, respectively. Indeed,

in a language with procedure and function types, such as Modula-2, the foregoing class definitions can be imitated as follows:

```
TYPE COMPLEX = POINTER TO ComplexRecord;
     ComplexRecord = RECORD
        re,im : REAL;
        RealPart : PROCEDURE (): REAL;
        . . .
        Add : PROCEDURE (x: COMPLEX);
        . . .
     END;

TYPE linkableObject = POINTER TO LinkRecord;
     LinkRecord = RECORD
        link: linkableObject;
        next: PROCEDURE (): linkableObject;
        linkto: PROCEDURE (p: linkableObject);
     END;
```

There are major differences, however. For example, there is no initialization of the record fields in Modula-2. (In particular, the PROCEDURE fields need to be explicitly assigned values of global procedures.) There is also no way for a variable of type COMPLEX or linkableObject to refer to itself. Indeed, the Add procedure cannot be defined in Modula-2 as it was in Simula (see Exercise 7). There are also no protection mechanisms available to limit access to the fields of a record. Further differences are in the treatment of method functions, as discussed in Section 9.4. Nevertheless, some object-oriented languages (such as C++) do treat classes as a form of record declaration.

9.3   INHERITANCE

Inheritance is the major mechanism in object-oriented languages that allows the sharing of data and operations among classes. A class B can **inherit** some or all of the instance variables and methods of another class A by declaring that class in its definition. In Simula this is done by listing A before B:

```
A class B;
begin
   . . .
end B;
```

In Simula, B inherits all the instance variables and methods of A, and B is called a **subclass** of A and A a **superclass** of B. This can be confusing, however (see the discussion that follows). We will adopt the terminology of C++ and call B a **derived class** and A a **base class.**

Consider the example from Section 9.1 of a deque as an extension of a queue that adds the operations addfront and removerear. A deque can inherit from a queue in Simula as follows (for simplicity we assume that the data stored is integer):

```
class queue;
begin
  comment ***instance variables of queue
    here***;
  procedure enqueue (x); integer x; begin ...
    end enqueue;
  procedure dequeue; begin ... end dequeue;
  integer procedure front; begin ... end front;
  boolean procedure empty; begin ... end empty;
  comment ***initialization code for queue
    here***;
end queue;

queue class deque;
begin
  procedure addfront (x); integer x; begin ...
    end addfront;
  procedure deleterear; begin ...
    end deleterear;
end deque;
```

Now whenever we create a deque, all six operations are available (four from queue and the two added operations). A deque is an **extension** of the class queue. In some languages, when a derived class includes all the operations of its base class, the derived type is said to be a **subtype,** and objects of the derived class obey the **subtype principle:**

An object of a subtype may be used anywhere its supertype is legal.

For example, if we define the following objects in Simula,

```
ref (queue) q;
ref (deque) d;
```

and then create a deque,

```
d :- new deque;
```

it is now possible to assign d to q:

```
q :- d;
```

Now q.dequeue and d.dequeue perform exactly the same operation. The difference is that d.deleterear is a legal operation, but q.deleterear is not (see Exercise 8).

To state this another way, inheritance that obeys the subtype principle expresses the **is-a** relation: if A is a subclass of B, then every object belonging to A also belongs to B, or every A "is a" B.

In Simula, since there are no protection mechanisms for methods or instance variables, all methods are available to derived classes, and derived classes are always subtypes (this a justification for the use of the terms subclass and superclass). In other languages, however, inheritance can be a more general concept, since it is possible to restrict access to methods and data of a base class. In this case the subtype principle may no longer hold.

As another example of how inheritance promotes reuse, consider the situation of a graphics object that can be a circle or a rectangle. We might define these as follows:[2]

```
class point(x,y);
real x,y;
begin
   . . .
end point;

class circle(center,radius);
ref (point) center;
real radius;
begin
  real procedure area;
  begin
    area := pi*radius*radius
  end area;
  . . .
end circle;

class rectangle (center,width,height);
ref (point) center;
real width,height;
begin
  real procedure area;
  begin
    area := width*height
  end area;
  . . .
end rectangle;
```

---

[2]In the following Simula code, class parameters are also used as instance variables.

Both circle and rectangle have things in common, namely, a point object (pointed to by center) describing its location and the method area. Indeed, every closed figure will have these same properties, and we may abstract them as follows:

```
class closedFigure(center);
ref (point) center;
virtual:
      real procedure area;
begin
    . . .
end closedFigure;
```

Now the area method has become **virtual,** that is, a method that is always available for objects of the class but that is given different implementations for different derived classes. In the case of area, it cannot be given a general implementation for closedFigure, but an implementation must be deferred until a derived class is defined with enough properties to enable the area to be determined. Indeed, virtual methods are sometimes called **deferred,** and a class that has a deferred method is called a **deferred class.** The advantage to defining virtual or deferred methods is not only to consolidate code, but also to make it a requirement that any closedFigure have an area function, that is, to ensure that any object that is derived from closedFigure has an area.

To complete the example of closedFigure, we define area in the two derived classes circle and rectangle:

```
closedFigure class circle(radius);
real radius;
begin
  real procedure area;
  begin
    area := pi*radius*radius
  end area;
  . . .
end circle;

closedFigure class rectangle(width,height);
real width, height;
begin
  real procedure area;
  begin
    area := width*height
  end area;
  . . .
end rectangle;
```

Now given the following declarations and initializations,

```
ref (point) x,y;
ref (closedFigure) f;
ref (rectangle) s;
ref (circle) c;

x  :- new point(0.0,0.0);
y  :- new point(1.0,-1.0);
s  :- new rectangle(x,1.0,1.0);
c  :- new circle(y,1.0);
f  :- s;
f.area;
f  :- c;
f.area;
```

the first call to f.area calls the appropriate method of s (and returns a value of 1.0), while the second call to f.area calls the appropriate method of c (and returns a value of pi). Note that inheritance causes the initialization parameters (and instance variables) to accumulate in Simula. Indeed, to create a rectangle we must state three parameters in the expression new rectangle (x, 1.0, 1.0). The first parameter x is to initialize the location of the rectangle as a closedFigure, while the two additional parameters initialize the length and width of the rectangle.

Inheritance establishes a parent-child dependency relationship between base classes and derived classes, so that the class inheritance relationship can be viewed as an **inheritance graph.** For example, the graphical figures in the example have the following inheritance graph (the arrows point from derived class to base class):

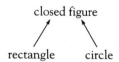

A more detailed inheritance graph along these same lines might be the following:

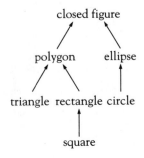

In each of the cases we have examined, the inheritance graph is a tree. This situation is called **single inheritance,** since each derived class can inherit from only one base class. It is also possible to have **multiple inheritance,** in which a class may inherit from two or more base classes. Newer object-oriented languages such as Eiffel and C++ provide multiple inheritance.[3] In a language with multiple inheritance, inheritance graphs can be directed acyclic graphs instead of being restricted to trees.

As an example of multiple inheritance, consider the classes COMPLEX and linkableObject from Section 9.2. (For purposes of the example, we adapt the syntax of Simula to allow multiple inheritance, even though it is not an actual part of the language.) A linkableObject as defined in Section 9.2 contains no data other than a link to another linkableObject. To link together objects that contain complex numbers (for example, in a queue of complex numbers), we can create a new class linkableComplex that is derived from both linkableObject and COMPLEX:

```
COMPLEX, linkableObject
  class linkableComplex;
begin
  . . .
end linkableComplex;
```

Now an object of class linkableComplex can appear anywhere an object of class linkableObject or COMPLEX can appear. In particular, if x and y are two objects of class linkableComplex, then it is possible both to link them and add them:

```
x.Add(y);
y.linkto(x);
```

Multiple inheritance can be useful, but it is also a source of complications. One complication is that methods may be inherited in more than one way. For example, a method from class A is inherited by class D in two different ways in the following inheritance graph:

---

[3]All four object-oriented languages in this book have undergone some revisions and/or later additions. In particular, C++ originally did not contain multiple inheritance, and Eiffel had not added the storage semantics option for objects. The descriptions in this chapter have tried consistently to follow one reference for each language. For Simula this is Birtwistle [1973], for C++ it is Ellis and Stroustrup [1990], for Eiffel it is Meyer [1992], and for Smalltalk it is Goldberg and Robson [1989].

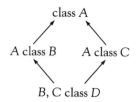

This creates difficulties in resolving references to methods. For instance, what happens if B, but not C, redefines a method of A? (C++ and Eiffel handle this problem in completely different ways.) In Smalltalk and Simula, the original languages are restricted to single inheritance because of such complications.

Inheritance provides many opportunities for polymorphism, since any method that applies to a base class can apply to a subclass as well. For example, in an object-oriented language one might choose to define both integers and reals as derived classes of a class number:

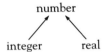

Now addition can be defined as a virtual method of class number, which acquires different implementations in derived classes integer and real.

As another example of polymorphism, consider the case of a queue of linkable objects, with several possible data items, all of which are derived from linkableObject (just as in the example of linkableComplex):

```
COMPLEX,linkableObject class linkableComplex;
begin
  . . .
end linkableComplex;

linkableObject class linkableReal(data);
real data;
begin
  . . .
end linkableReal;

linkableObject class linkableInt(data);
integer data;
begin
  . . .
end linkableInt;

class queue;
```

continues

```
continued
    begin
      ref (linkableObject) rear;
      comment -- uses a circular list
              -- with rear.next = front;

      ref (linkableObject) procedure front;
      begin
        front :- rear.next;
      end front;

      procedure enqueue(x); ref (linkableObject) x;
      begin
        ...
      end enqueue;
      ...
      etc.
      ...
    end queue;
```

Now any objects of the classes linkableComplex, linkable-
Real, and linkableInt can be inserted into a queue object:

```
ref (queue) q;
ref (linkableReal) r;
ref (linkableInt) i;
ref (linkableComplex) c;

q :- new queue;
r :- new linkableReal(1.0);
i :- new linkableInt(0);
c :- new linkableComplex(1.0,-1.0);
q.enqueue(r);
q.enqueue(i);
q.enqueue(c);
```

This mechanism for polymorphism does contain a drawback, however. If we want to perform an operation on the front of the queue,

```
ref (linkableObject) x;
x :- q.front;
    ... perform some operation on x...
```

we now do not know if x is linkableReal, linkableComplex, or
linkableInt, and we may want to invoke methods that are particular
to one or the other subclass. In this case, class membership may need to
be explicitly tested, and some object-oriented languages provide mech-

anisms for doing this. For example, Simula provides the **is** relation, which is a test on class membership:

```
if x is linkableReal then ...
else if x is linkableInt then ...
```

9.4 DYNAMIC BINDING

One of the principal features that distinguishes classes in an object-oriented language from modules or packages in a language like Modula-2 or Ada is the dynamic nature of classes versus the static nature of modules. This is visible already in the fact that objects from a class are allocated storage in a fully dynamic way, usually on a "heap."

Depending on the language, this dynamic allocation of objects may be under the manual control of the programmer (as in the Pascal `new` and `dispose` operations), or it may be fully automatic (as in most functional languages such as LISP, ML, or Miranda), or it may be a hybrid of the two. Allocation schemes for specific languages are mentioned in the next sections, and allocation strategies are studied in Section 9.9 and in Section 10.6, where the main techniques for fully dynamic storage allocation are surveyed. We note here only that Simula uses a hybrid scheme where the allocation (and initialization) of objects is under programmer control through the use of the `new` expression, but that there is no corresponding `dispose`. Instead, objects are reclaimed automatically, either by exiting their scopes (in a stack-based fashion) or by some form of garbage collection (Section 10.6).

However, the dynamic nature of classes goes beyond the allocation and deallocation of objects. Methods can also vary dynamically, and in this lies much of the power of the object-oriented approach. We have already seen one example of this in the last section, in which the `area` method of class `closedFigure` is declared to be virtual and is defined differently for each derived class. Then the appropriate area method is invoked for each object of `closedFigure`, depending dynamically on which derived class the object belongs to. Such methods are said to obey **dynamic binding,** and dynamic binding is one of the main sources of the power of an object-oriented language.

In the preceding example, the `area` method was in fact undefined for the class `closedFigure`, so it was necessary for appropriate methods of derived classes to be invoked. Dynamic binding can also occur when a method is **redefined** in a derived class.

Consider for example a class `borderedRectangle` that is derived from rectangle and that redefines the virtual method `area` to include the extra area covered by the border:

```
rectangle class borderedRectangle (border);
real border;                                        continues
```

continued

```
begin
  real procedure area;
  begin
    area := (width+2.0*border)*(height+
             2.0*border);
  end area;
   . . .
end square·
```

Now any rectangle object that is actually a borderedRectangle will call the new area procedure. For example, with the declarations

```
rectangle r;
r :- new borderedRectangle;
 . . .
 . . .
r.area
 . . .
```

the call to r.area will compute the area according to the new area function.

It is possible to offer both static and dynamic binding of methods in an object-oriented language. For instance, in Simula, if a method is not first declared virtual, static binding applies instead of dynamic binding. As an example, if area had not been declared a virtual method of closedFigure, the redefinition of area in square would not apply in the call to r.area.

As another example, consider the following class definitions:

```
class A;
begin
  virtual procedure p;
end A;

A class B;
begin
  procedure p;
  begin
    . . .
  end p;

  procedure q;
  begin
    . . .
  end q;
```

```
procedure f;
begin
   p;
end f;

procedure g;
begin
   q;
end g;

end B;

B class C;
begin
   procedure p;
   begin

      . . .
   end p;

   procedure q;
   begin

      . . .
   end q;

end C;
```

Now if x is an object of C,

```
C x;
x :- new C;
```

then a call x . f will invoke the p procedure of C, while a call x . g will invoke the q procedure of B. The procedure p is dynamically bound, while the procedure q is statically bound.

Object-oriented languages that adhere strictly to the object-oriented paradigm offer only dynamic binding. Languages that represent more of a compromise between the object-oriented paradigm and standard imperative languages (these include Simula and C++) offer a choice, with one choice as the default. Indeed, in Simula the default is static binding, with dynamic binding offered by the **virtual** declaration.

In fact, the use of the virtual declaration in Simula confuses two issues, namely, dynamic binding and the definition of a method that may not have an implementation in the base class. (Such a method was a r e a in class c l o s e d F i g u r e.) A method that has no definition in a class is more aptly referred to as a **deferred** or **abstract** method, while the term **virtual** would perhaps more appropriately be reserved for methods to which dynamic binding applies.

A further issue in the use of dynamic binding in an object-oriented language is how to determine which method to invoke during execution. Superficially, it appears that during execution the runtime environment must check the class to which each object belongs to determine which method is meant. This, in turn, requires dynamic typing of variables, which can cause significant runtime overhead. However, it is possible to offer dynamic binding while retaining static typing. See Section 9.9 for more detail.

9.5 C++

In the last sections we have used the first object-oriented language, Simula67, as our sample language while discussing the basic concepts of object-oriented languages. In this and the following two sections, we survey three other object-oriented languages—C++, Eiffel, and Small-talk—and discuss the differences in terminology and available features of each. The examples we will use are the ones that have featured strongly in our previous discussions: complex numbers, queues, closed figures, and linkable objects.

C++ was developed by Bjarne Stroustrup at AT&T Bell Labs (where C was developed) in an attempt to add Simula-like classes to C. It is a compromise language in that it contains the C language as a subset (as Simula67 contains Algol60 as a subset). C++ was also designed to be an efficient, practical language, developing out of the needs of its users. As such it has become the most-used object-oriented language in the few years since its introduction in 1985. Since the first reference manual was published in 1986, a number of new features have been added, including multiple inheritance. The latest version is described in Ellis and Stroustrup [1990], which has become the base document for a future American National Standards Institute (ANSI) standard. It is this document that we follow in our next discussion.

C++ contains class and object declarations similar to those of Simula. Instance variables and methods are both called **members** of a class: instance variables are referred to as **data members,** and methods are referred to as **member functions.** One basic difference between C++ and most other object-oriented languages is that objects are not automatically pointers or references. Indeed, except for inheritance and dynamic binding of member functions, the class data type in C++ is identical to the struct (or record) data type.

In C++ three levels of protection are provided for class members: public, private, and protected. **Public** members are those accessible to clients and inherited by derived classes. **Protected** members are inaccessible to clients but are still inherited by derived classes. **Private** members are accessible neither to clients nor to derived classes. In a class declaration the default protection is private, while in a struct declaration the default is public.

In C++, initialization of objects is given explicitly in the declaration of a class by declaring a **constructor** function, which has the same name as that of the class. Constructor functions are automatically called when an object is allocated space in memory, and actual parameters to the constructor function are specified at that time (similar to Simula's initialization of instance variables). C++ also has a **destructor** function, which like a constructor has the same name as the class, but is preceded by the special symbol "~" (sometimes used in logic to mean "not"). Destructors are automatically called when an object is deallocated, but they must be provided by the programmer and so represent a manual approach to memory deallocation. Thus C++ has no automatic memory allocation or deallocation requirements—memory management is the same as for C, but dynamic allocation on the heap uses standard procedures new and delete similar to Pascal's new and dispose, as opposed to the malloc and free of C.

A class declaration in C++ does not always contain the implementation code for all member functions. Member functions can be implemented outside the declaration by using the **scope resolution operator** indicated by a double colon "::" after the class name. It is called the "scope resolution operator" because it causes the scope of the class declaration to be reentered. Member functions that *are* given implementations in a class declaration are automatically assumed to be **inline** (that is, a compiler may replace the function call by the actual code for the function).

As an example of the foregoing features, let us write out the code for a queue data type in C++, using a circular linked list implementation. We first must write out the declaration for linkableObject, as follows:

```
class linkableObject
{private:
   linkableObject* link;
 public:
   linkableObject (void) {link = 0;}
   linkableObject (linkableObject* p)
     {link = p;}
   linkableObject * next(void) {return link;}
   void linkto(linkableObject* p) {link = p;}
};
```

This declares a linkableObject with a link field as a pointer to a linkableObject (but so far no data) and a constructor function that initializes the link field. Note that there are actually two constructor functions. The first has no parameters and initializes the link field to the null pointer 0. The second has one parameter (a pointer to a linkableObject) that is used to initialize the link field. C++ allows such overloading, where the compiler can distinguish which function is meant by the number and type of the parameters. Constructor functions are declared without a return value.

If we want to create a pointer to a linkableObject, we can do so using the two different parameter conventions given by the two declarations of the constructor. For example,

```
linkableObject* p = new linkableObject;
linkableObject* q = new linkableObject(p);
```

creates two linkableObjects, pointed to by p and q. The first call to new has no parameters, so the first form of the constructor for linkableObject is called implicitly, and so p → link is set to 0. The second call to new has p as a parameter, and the implicit call to the second constructor form sets q → link to p.

Note that in C++, variables can be declared at any point in a program. Thus linkableObject* p = ... creates the pointer variable p (as a pointer to a linkableObject) and assigns it a value simultaneously.

We now define a queue of linkableObjects as follows:

```
class queue
{protected:
    linkableObject* rear;
  public:
    queue (void) {rear = 0;}
    int empty (void) {return rear == 0;}
    void enqueue (linkableObject* item);
    void dequeue (void);
    linkableObject* front(void)
      {return rear->next();}
    ~queue(void);
};

void queue::enqueue (linkableObject* item)
{if (empty()) {rear = item;
               rear->linkto(item);}
 else {item->linkto(rear->next());
       rear->linkto(item);
       rear = item;}
}

void queue::dequeue (void)
{linkableObject* temp = front();
 if (temp == rear) rear = 0;
 else rear->linkto(temp->next());
}

queue::queue(void)
{linkableObject* temp = rear;
 if (temp == 0) return;
 do {linkableObject* temp2 = temp;
```

```
        temp = temp->next();
        delete temp2;}
while (temp != rear);
}
```

This example shows the use of the scope resolution operator "::" to allow member functions to have their implementation given outside the declaration of a class. The preceding code also illustrates the existence of a destructor (called ~queue), which frees all linkableObjects if a queue object is released from memory (such as on exit from a local scope). Note that the member functions empty and front are inline functions, and calls to them are replaced by the actual code for the functions. Note also the use of the **protected** keyword to allow access to the rear pointer for derived classes, but not for clients.

We can now create linkableObjects and put them in and take them off a queue as follows:

```
queue q;
linkableObject* x = new linkableObject;
q.enqueue(x);
q.enqueue(new linkableObject);
linkableObject* y = q.front(); // now y is x
q.dequeue();
q.dequeue(); // q is now empty
```

A class deque can inherit the operations of queue and provide the extra operations addfront and deleterear using the following declaration:

```
class deque : public queue
{public:
    void addfront (linkableObject* x);
    void deleterear (void);
};
```

The use of the keyword **public** before the base class queue of derived class deque is to indicate that all access to members of queue remains as declared in queue. Thus all public members of queue remain public in deque and similarly for protected members (private members are unavailable in any case). In other words, the subclass relationship holds for deque. C++ also allows private derivation, as for example,

```
class B : private A {...};
```

Now class B has private access to the public and protected members of A, but must reexport any members it wishes to make public, as in the following example:

```
class stack : private queue
{public:
   queue::empty; // adjust access - no type info
   void pop (void) {dequeue();}
   // rename dequeue as pop
   ...};
```

Inheritance can be used to insert actual data into a queue object, as in the following code:

```
class linkableInt : public linkableObject
{private:
   int item;
 public:
   int data(void) {return item;}
   void setdata(int x) {item = x;}
};
...
queue q;
linkableInt* x = new linkableInt;
x->setdata(42);
q.enqueue(x);
...
```

This is a use of inheritance to achieve polymorphism, as described in Section 9.3. C++ also provides a limited direct mechanism for defining parametrized classes using a **template** mechanism. For example, a "generic" queue can be defined in C++ as follows:

```
template<class T> class queue
{protected:
   class linkable : public linkableObject
   {private:
      T item;
    public:
      T data(void) {return item;}
      void setdata(T x) {item = x;}
   };
   linkable* rear;
 public:
   queue (void) {rear = 0;}
   int empty (void) {return rear == 0;}
   void enqueue (T item);
   void dequeue (void);
   T front(void)
      {return ((linkable*)rear->next())->data();}
   ~queue(void);
};
```

Now a queue of integers can be declared as follows:

```
queue<int> q ;
```

Templates in C++ are essentially a macro substitution mechanism, so separate copies of all template code are made for each application.

Dynamic binding of member functions is provided in C++ using the keyword **virtual** (not quite the same as its use in Simula, as we will indicate shortly). For example, if we want to redefine an area function for a square derived from a rectangle, we would do so as follows:

```
class rectangle
{private:
   double length,width;
 public:
   virtual double area(void)
   {return length*width;};
   ...};

class square : public rectangle
{public:
   double area(void) {return width*width;};
      // redefines rectangle::area dynamically
   ...};
```

Of course, what we really want in this example is a deferred area function in a deferred class closedFigure, and this can be achieved in C++ by the use of a so-called **pure virtual declaration** (deferred classes are called **abstract classes** in C++):

```
class closedFigure // an abstract class
{public:
   virtual double area(void) = 0 ;
               // pure virtual
      ...};

class rectangle : public closedFigure
{private:
   double length,width;
 public:
   double area(void) {return length*width;}
   ...};

class circle : public closedFigure
{private
   double radius;
 public:
   double area(void) {return pi*radius*radius;}
   ...};
```

The 0 in the pure virtual declaration indicates that the function is null at that point, that is, has no body (and cannot be called). Thus a virtual declaration in C++ indicates a function that is dynamically bound during execution, while a pure virtual function is one that is not only dynamically bound but that *must* be given a meaning in derived classes, since it is not given a body to execute in the class in which it is declared. (In Simula the virtual declaration corresponds to a pure virtual declaration in C++; that is, no function in Simula can be dynamically bound without first being declared abstractly.)

C++ offers multiple inheritance using a comma-separated list of base classes, as in

```
class C : public A, private B {...};
```

Multiple inheritance in C++ ordinarily creates separate copies of each class on an inheritance path. For example, the declarations

```
class A {...};
class B : public A {...};
class C : public A {...};
class D : public B, public C {...};
```

provides any object of class D with *two* separate copies of objects of class A, and so creates the following inheritance graph:

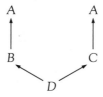

We may call this **repeated** inheritance. To get a single copy of an A in class D, one must declare the inheritance using the **virtual** keyword:

```
class A {...};
class B : virtual public A {...};
class C : virtual public A {...};
class D : public B, public C {...};
```

This achieves the following inheritance graph:

This can be called **shared** inheritance. Resolution of operator conflicts created by multiple (shared) inheritance (see Section 9.3) is explored in Exercise 17.

As a final example in C++, we offer the following declaration of a complex number class:

```
class COMPLEX
{private:
   double re,im;
 public:
   COMPLEX(double r = 0, double i = 0)
   {re = r; im = i;}
   double realpart(void) {return re;}
   double imaginarypart(void) {return im;}
   COMPLEX operator- (void)
   {return COMPLEX(-re, -im);}
   COMPLEX operator+ (COMPLEX y)
   {return COMPLEX(re+y.realpart(),
                         im+y.imaginarypart());}
   COMPLEX operator- (COMPLEX y)
   {return COMPLEX(re-y.realpart(),
                         im-y.imaginarypart());}
   COMPLEX operator* (COMPLEX y)
   {return COMPLEX
          (re*y.realpart()-im*y.imaginarypart(),
           im*y.realpart()+re*y.imaginarypart());}
   COMPLEX operator/ (COMPLEX y)
   {...}
};
```

This declaration includes a couple of new features of C++. First, the `complex` constructor function is declared with default values given for its parameters. This allows COMPLEX objects to be created with 0, 1, or 2 parameters (and avoids the need to create different overloaded constructors, as we did in the example of `linkableObject`):

```
COMPLEX i (0.0,1.0); // i constructed as (0,1)
COMPLEX y; // y constructed as default (0,0)
COMPLEX x (1.0); // x constructed as (1,0)
```

Class COMPLEX also has arithmetic functions that overload the standard arithmetic operators " + ," " − ," " * ," and "/" using the keyword **operator** before the operator symbol, as for example,

```
COMPLEX operator+ (COMPLEX y) {...}
```

This definition also permits the use of " + " in its standard infix binary form, so that

```
y = x.operator+(i);
```

and

```
y = x + i;
```

have identical meanings. This corrects the problem in object-oriented languages of having to write binary operators in unary form as described in Section 9.2. However, this can only be done for a fixed set of predefined operators in C++, and the newly defined operators must follow the same precedence and associativity rules that their predefined namesakes obey.

Note also in the code that the COMPLEX operators call the COMPLEX constructor directly, as in the statement

```
return COMPLEX(re+y.realpart(),
               im+y.imaginarypart());
```

This has the effect of allocating new (temporary) space for a complex value, from which the data members are copied in an assignment. Thus pointer semantics are avoided in this case, but at a cost in complexity of translated code (see Exercise 33).

Finally, C++ uses a similar terminology to Simula to name the current instance of a class directly, but without the class qualification:

```
class linkableObject;
{private:
   linkableObject* next;
 public:
   linkableObject (void); {next = this;}
 ...};
```

(Compare this code to the Simula code on page 306.)

9.6 *Eiffel*

Eiffel was developed in the mid-1980s by Bertrand Meyer. It has a Pascal-like syntax, but it is not based on any previous language, and it has perhaps the most consistent design of any of the Pascal-like object-oriented languages. Among its features are built-in semantic specifications using preconditions, postconditions, and invariants (see Section 12.5 for a discussion) and an exception-handling facility that is integrated with its object-oriented design. We shall not study these aspects of Eiffel, however, but will concentrate on its basic object-oriented design.

In Eiffel, there are only classes and objects. There are no programs or procedures. A "program" in Eiffel is called a **system,** and a system consists of a set of objects that interact. A system has a **root,** or main object, that is created at the beginning of execution and that begins the creation and interaction of all other objects in the system.

In Eiffel instance variables of an object are called **attributes** and methods are called **routines,** which can be procedures or functions. Attributes and routines together are called **features.**

There is only one structured type in Eiffel—the class. Thus classes are not extensions of record or structure types, as in C++ or Simula, but represent the only mechanism for structuring data and code.

Objects in Eiffel are created by explicitly calling a creation routine (unlike the implicit calls of C++). The simplest form of creation call has two exclamation points:

```
!!x
```

This causes a default creation to occur, which allocates storage for x and gives default initial values to all attributes. Default initializations are provided for all basic data types (including objects, which are initialized to Void, the null object). Additional initializations can be provided manually by writing a user-defined creation procedure in the definition of a class.

Like Simula, objects in Eiffel are implicitly references (i.e., pointers), unless a class is specifically declared to be **expanded,** in which case the usual storage semantics of records holds. Unlike Simula, however, there are predefined procedures that permit the overriding of pointer semantics. These routines are copy, which copies fields from one allocated object to another; clone, which allocates new storage as well as making a copy; and equal, which tests equality of field values (rather than pointer equality). Although allocation of memory for objects occurs explicitly with a call to a creation routine, there is no corresponding manual deallocation, such as the delete operation in C++. Reclaiming storage in Eiffel is automatic and requires the use of a garbage collector. On the other hand, type checking in Eiffel is static (like C++): all class declarations represent static types, which can be checked at compile time.

We redo our standard example of a linkableObject in Eiffel to illustrate these properties:

```
class linkableObject
feature {NONE}
  link: linkableObject;
feature
  next: linkableObject is
  do
    Result := link
  end; -- next
  linkto (p: linkableObject) is
  do                                        continues
```

continued

```
      link := p;
   end; -- linkto
end; -- class linkableObject

class queue -- uses a circular list of
   linkableObjects
feature {NONE}
   rear: linkableObject;
feature
   empty: BOOLEAN is
      do
         Result := rear = Void
              -- Result indicates returned value
      end; -- empty
   front : linkableObject is
      do
         Result := rear.next
      end; -- front
   enqueue (item: linkableObject) is
      do
         if empty then
            rear := item;
            rear.linkto(item)
         else
            item.linkto(rear.next);
            rear.linkto(item);
            rear := item
         end
      end; -- enqueue
   dequeue is
      local temp: linkableObject
      do
         temp := front;
         if temp = rear then
            rear.Forget --sets rear to Void
         else
            rear.linkto(temp.next)
         end
      end; -- dequeue
end; -- class queue
```

This code uses, as before, a pointer to the rear of a queue, which is the only attribute of a queue. Features include the usual operations, all of which are defined within the feature section of the class declaration. Note that there are actually two feature sections; this is to provide protection for the rear attribute and will be described shortly.

Features of an object are accessed using the usual dot notation. There are a few other differences from typical Pascal-like code, which include the use of the keyword `local` to introduce local variables in routines and the use of the predefined variable `Result` to indicate returned values.

We illustrate the use of this code with the following sample declarations and statements:

```
-- declarations:

q: queue;
x,y: linkableObject;


-- statements:

!!q; -- automatically initializes q.rear to Void
!!x; -- automatically initializes x.next to Void
!!y; -- automatically initializes y.next to Void
q.enqueue(x);
q.enqueue(y);
y := q.front; -- now y is x, but
        -- the old value of y is still in the queue
q.dequeue;
q.dequeue; -- q is now empty
```

Inheritance in Eiffel uses an **inherit** clause:

```
class deque
inherit queue
feature
  addfront (x: linkableObject) is do ... end;
  deleterear is do ... end;
end; -- class deque
```

Derived classes are called **descendants,** and base classes are called **ancestors.** In Eiffel, protection of features occurs by supplying qualifiers to the `feature` declaration. No qualifiers implies public export. The qualifier `{NONE}` implies no export (i.e., the same as a `private` declaration in C++). For example, in the declaration of class `queue`, the feature declaration

```
feature {NONE}
  rear: linkableObject;
```

indicates that `rear` is not exported. It is also possible to protect a feature from clients while allowing access by descendants (like the C++ `protected` declaration). This is done by qualifying the `feature` declaration with the class name itself:

```
class A
feature {A}
-- allows access to x by all instances of A
-- including descendants
  x: ... ;
  ...
end; -- class A
```

Features in descendant classes may be redefined, but every redefined feature must be declared as such in a **redefines** clause. Redefined features obey dynamic binding in Eiffel. In other words, all routines behave as virtual routines. It is, however, possible to retain features of ancestors that have been redefined by renaming them in a **renames** clause. Here are some illustrations:

```
-- the following shows how routines can be
-- renamed and reexported by a descendant
class stack
inherit deque -- from the above code
  rename front as top, addfront as push, dequeue
    as pop;
  export
  {NONE} enqueue, deleterear;
      -- these are not exported
  {ANY} top,push,pop;
      -- these are exported to all clients
  end
  ...

end; -- class stack

-- the following two class declarations show
-- how a single routine can be redefined
-- (and which will follow dynamic binding)

class rectangle
feature {NONE}
  length, width: REAL;
feature
  area : REAL is
    do Result := length * width end;
  ...
end; -- class rectangle

class square
inherit rectangle
  redefine area
```

```
      end
feature
   area : REAL is
   do
      Result := width * width
   end; -- area
   . . .
end; -- class square
```

It is also possible to have deferred (or abstract) classes in Eiffel using a **deferred** clause, as follows:

```
deferred class closedFigure
feature
   . . .
   area : REAL is
      deferred
   end; -- area
   . . .
end; -- class closedFigure

class circle
inherit closedFigure
feature {NONE}
   radius: REAL;
feature
   . . .
   area : REAL is
      do
         Result := pi * radius * radius
   end; -- area
end; -- class circle

class rectangle
inherit closedFigure
feature {NONE}
   length,width: REAL;
feature
   area : REAL is
      do Result := length * width
   end; -- area
   . . .
end; -- class rectangle
```

In this code, the deferred routine area must be defined in all descendants of closedFigure (unless the descendant itself is deferred). Note that area does not need to appear in a redefine statement in circle, since it is deferred at that point and, therefore, has not yet been defined.

In Eiffel, it is also possible to have parametrized or generic classes, as in the following example (which follows the C++ example in the last section):

```
class queue[T]
feature
  . . .
  empty: BOOLEAN is
    do ... end;
  enqueue (item: T) is
    do ... end;
  dequeue is
    do ... end;
  front : T is
    do ... end;
end; -- class queue[T]
```

Objects of parametrized types are declared by including a type parameter:

```
realq : queue[REAL];
figureq : queue[closedFigure];
```

Multiple inheritance is also available in Eiffel using the following syntax:

```
class A
inherit
  B rename ... redefine ...end ;
  C rename ... redefine ...end ;
  D rename ... redefine ...end ;
  . . .
feature
  . . .
end; -- class A
```

Unlike C++, the default is **shared** inheritance rather than **repeated** inheritance. That is, a feature inherited from a single ancestor is always considered the same regardless of the number of inheritance paths. Thus the inheritance scheme

```
class A ...;
class B ... inherit A ...
class C ... inherit A ...
class D ... inherit B ... ; inherit C ...
```

results in one copy of A being included in every object of class D, as long
as no feature of A is redefined or renamed in B or C:

On the other hand, repeated inheritance, in which several copies
of an ancestor are contained in a descendant, can be obtained by renaming. For example, the declarations

```
class A ...;
class B ... inherit A ...
class C ... inherit A ...
class D ...
inherit B rename ... ;
    -- rename every feature f of A as B_f
inherit C rename ... ;
    -- rename every feature f of A as C_f
```

result in the following inheritance graph:

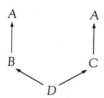

Finally, we present an Eiffel class for complex numbers:

```
class COMPLEX
creation
    makeComplex -- a nondefault creation feature
feature {NONE}
    re,im: REAL; -- not exported
feature
    makeComplex (x,y: REAL) is
        do
            re := x;
            im := y
        end; -- makeComplex
    realpart : REAL is
        do Result := re end;                        continues
```

continued

```
imaginarypart : REAL is
   do Result := im end;
add (y: COMPLEX) is
   do
      re := re+y.realpart;
      im := im+y.imaginarypart
   end;  -- add
subtract (y: COMPLEX) is
   do
      re := re-y.realpart;
      im := im-y.imaginarypart
   end;  -- subtract
negate is
   do
      re := -re;
      im := -im
   end;  -- negate
multiply (y: COMPLEX) is
   local r, i: REAL
   do
      r := re*y.realpart - im*y.imaginarypart;
      i := im*y.realpart + re*y.imaginarypart;
      re := r;
      im := i
   end;  --multiply
divide (y: COMPLEX) is ...
end;  -- class COMPLEX
```

This class can be used in the following way to add two COMPLEX objects
and store the result in a third COMPLEX object:

```
x,y,z: COMPLEX;
...
!!x.makeComplex(1.0,1.0);  -- make an x
!!y.makeComplex(2.0,-1.0);  -- make a y
z := clone(x);  -- z gets a copy of x
z.add(y);
-- z is now x + y; x and y have not changed
```

In this code we have explicitly called the makeComplex creation
feature. The class COMPLEX needs this creation feature, since without it
a COMPLEX object would be initialized with re = 0.0 and im = 0.0,
and there would be no way to change these attributes, since they are not
exported. (Indeed, in Eiffel, if one or more explicit creation features are
declared, it is no longer possible to use the default creation mechanism
!!x.)

We have also used the `clone` predefined procedure in the code, which is like assignment, only with storage semantics. If we had written `z := x`, `z` and `x` would share memory, and so a change to `z` would have the undesirable effect of also changing `x`.

We note further that the code has operations that compute their results by changing the state of the current object rather than by returning a new object with the computed value. This is in keeping with the sketch and discussion of the complex implementation in Simula in Section 9.2, but differs from the implementation presented earlier for C++. It is possible to write code in Eiffel that looks and behaves more like standard arithmetic (as does the C++ code). Indeed, Eiffel allows operators to be declared as infix operators, so we could have declared addition as

```
infix "+" (y: COMPLEX) : COMPLEX is
  do
    . . .
    -- now we must create a new COMPLEX object to
    -- return as result
  end; -- infix "+"
```

Addition can then be written as `z := x + y`. See Exercise 33 for further discussion of the different approaches to class `COMPLEX`.

Finally, we mention Eiffel's convention for self-reference within a class declaration, corresponding to the use of `this` in Simula and C++. Eiffel instead uses a predefined `Current` variable to indicate the current instance, as follows:

```
class linkableObject
creation make
feature {NONE}
  next: linkableObject;
feature
  make is
  do
    next := Current; -- set next to point here
  end;
  . . .
end;
```

9.7 Smalltalk

Smalltalk arose out of a research project, called the Dynabook Project, begun by Alan Kay at Xerox Corporation's Palo Alto Research Center in the early 1970s. Influenced by both Simula and LISP, a series of stages marked its development, with its principal early versions being Smalltalk-

72 and Smalltalk-76. The final version is Smalltalk-80, and we will use the name Smalltalk as a synonym for Smalltalk-80. Other major contributors to the design of Smalltalk were Adele Goldberg and Daniel Ingalls.

Of all the object-oriented languages, Smalltalk has the most thorough and consistent approach to the object-oriented paradigm. In Smalltalk, almost every language entity is an object, including constants such as numbers and characters. Thus Smalltalk can be said to be **pure** object oriented in almost the same sense that a language can be called pure functional (see Chapter 10).

However, because the Smalltalk language has a somewhat unusual syntax, and because it is intimately connected to (and has no separate existence from) the Smalltalk runtime system, it is difficult to present just language issues in Smalltalk without getting into a lengthy discussion of the interactive runtime system, especially the **user interface,** through which programs are created and executed. We will, however, try to give some of the flavor of the language, in the following way. We will first give a brief overview of the Smalltalk system. Then we will discuss a few central language features. We will finish the discussion with two of the standard examples we have been using in other sections, namely, complex numbers and queues.

Smalltalk was innovative not only from the language point of view, but also in that, from the beginning, it was envisioned as a complete system for a powerful personal workstation, such as those that have only become available in the 1980s. The user interface was also novel in that it included a windowing system with menus and a point-and-click device, or mouse, before such systems became common for personal computers. (It had in fact a major influence on the development of such systems.)

Smalltalk as a language is interactive and dynamically oriented. All classes, objects, and methods are created by interaction with the system, using windows and screen templates provided by the system. New classes are entered into a class dictionary, and the interaction of objects is also managed by the system. The Smalltalk system comes with a large hierarchy of preexisting classes, and each new class must be a subclass of an existing class. The class hierarchy is a tree, since Smalltalk-80 has only single inheritance. The base or parent class of each class is called its **superclass** in Smalltalk. There is only one class that has no superclass—it is the root of the class hierarchy—and its name is **Object.** (In Smalltalk, class names begin with uppercase letters, while object and method names begin with lowercase letters.) Every class (other than Object itself) is a subclass of class Object. A sketch of the Smalltalk class tree is given in Figure 9-1.

A class is specified in Smalltalk by giving its superclass, its instance variables, and its methods at appropriate places within the Smalltalk system. There is no specific syntax for the layout of a class definition. All methods of a class are available to clients. In other words, there is no export or privacy control of methods in Smalltalk. However, access

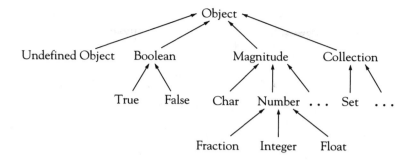

Figure 9-1   Simplified Smalltalk Class Hierarchy

to instance variables is restricted to methods: instance variables may not be accessed directly by clients. This provides adequate protection, since the state of an object can be changed only by invoking a method of that object.[4] It also means that enough methods must be supplied for clients to query an object about the values of its instance variables and to modify those variables suitably.

Method names are called **selectors** in Smalltalk, and they are divided into categories: **unary** selectors correspond to operations without parameters, and **keyword** selectors correspond to operations with parameters. A **message,** or method invocation, in Smalltalk consists of the name of an object followed by the method selector and parameter names, if any. Dot notation is not used.

A couple of examples should make clear how object methods are invoked in Smalltalk. The C++ function call to a `queue` object `q`,

```
q.front()
```

would correspond to the Smalltalk,

```
q  front
```

and the C++ call,

```
q.enqueue(x)
```

would correspond to the Smalltalk

```
q  enqueue: x
```

In Smalltalk parlance, `front` is a **unary selector,** and `enqueue:` is a **keyword selector.** (Note the necessary colon at the end of a keyword

---

[4]This is true of Eiffel as well.

selector.) The reason that method names are called keyword selectors is that, when a method takes several parameters, keywords must separate all the parameters. Thus the Smalltalk message

```
table  insert:  anItem at:  anIndex
```

means the same as the C++ (or Simula or Eiffel) call:

```
table.insert(anItem,anIndex)
```

In other words, the full name of the insert method in Smalltalk is actually insert:at:, and the suffix at: must separate the two parameters. Note also the use of anItem and anIndex as parameter names to achieve some resemblance to an English sentence. A name such as anItem is by convention any object from class Item. Parameters do not have their class explicitly given in a message selector.

Actually, there is one other category of selector: **binary selectors,** which are used for binary operations and must consist of one or two nonalphabetic characters. A good example is the name " + ," which is a binary selector for the addition operation. Thus the expression

```
2  +  3
```

in Smalltalk means the same as 2. + (3) and is a message to the object 2 requesting that it add 3 to itself. And

```
2  +  3  +  4
```

is a message to the result of the message 2 + 3 requesting that 4 be added to it, thus achieving the sum (2 + 3) + 4.

We will now give the definition of the class LinkableObject in Smalltalk, similar to the linkableObject example of previous sections (remember that class names in Smalltalk must begin with an uppercase letter). Since Smalltalk has no direct syntax for class and method definitions, but uses screen windows, we will simply list the class, its superclass, its instance variables, and its methods, as follows:

```
Class name:  <name>
Superclass:  <name>
Instance variables:  <list-of-names>
Methods:  <name>
              <implementation>
          <name>
              <implementation>
```

Instance variables, like parameters, do not get types in Smalltalk as they do in a statically typed language, since Smalltalk, like LISP, is dynamically typed (and the only typing is class membership; see Exercise 16).

Here now is the example of linkableObject in Smalltalk:

```
Class name: LinkableObject
Superclass: Object
Instance variables: link
Methods: next
         ↑ link
         linkTo: anObject
         link <- anObject
```

In the declarations of methods next and linkTo, the symbol ↑ means "return this value" in Smalltalk, like return in C or C++ or Result := . . . in Eiffel. If no return value is specified, then the method returns the current object. The symbol <- is assignment in Smalltalk, like := in Pascal or = in C.

Now an object of class LinkableObject can be created as follows:

```
x <- LinkableObject new
```

This sends the unary message new to the class LinkableObject, returning a new object of the class, which is then assigned to x. It also initializes the instance variable link to the nil object. Note that new is a **class method:** it is sent to the class LinkableObject. Smalltalk views classes themselves as objects of a "metaclass" Class. Fortunately, metaclass Class has a default new method that LinkableObject inherits. If, however, extra initialization is required, then the definition of a new class must contain a redefinition of this class method, as well as the instance methods, such as next and linkTo:. For example, the following class method definition would initialize a new instance of LinkableObject to point to the parameter aLinkableObject:

```
new: aLinkableObject
   ↑ (self new) linkTo: aLinkableObject
```

In this code, self refers to the current object, just as this does in Simula or C++ and Current in Eiffel. The message self new selects the existing new class method of class aLinkableObject (without parameters) and returns a reference to a linkableObject with its link field initialized to nil. This new linkableObject is then sent the message linkTo: aLinkableObject, which reassigns the link field to aLinkableObject.

This definition of new: will always apply when sent to LinkableObject, since dynamic binding of methods is always observed in Smalltalk.

Now let us look at a definition of class Queue in Smalltalk:

```
Class name: Queue

Superclass: Object

Instance variables: rear

Methods:

  empty
    ↑ rear == nil
  front
    ↑ rear next
  enqueue: aLinkableObject
   self empty
     ifTrue:  [rear <- aLinkableObject.
               rear linkTo: rear]
     ifFalse: [aLinkableObject linkTo: rear next.
               rear linkTo: aLinkableObject.
               rear <- aLinkableObject]
  dequeue
   | temp |
   temp <- front.
   (rear == temp)
      ifTrue: [rear <- nil]
      ifFalse: [rear linkTo: (temp next)]
```

There are a couple of new features in this code. First, local variables within a method body are declared within vertical bars, as in

```
| temp |
```

(Note again that variables are untyped.) Second, the period "." is used to separate statements, instead of the semicolon of Pascal-like languages. Third, the operator "==" (a binary selector) tests for identity of objects, returning an object of class True if it succeeds and False otherwise.

Finally, the code contains examples of a Smalltalk **block,** which is a code sequence surrounded by square brackets [. . .]. A block represents "unevaluated code," much as a pass by name parameter does in Algol60 (see Chapter 7). When an object is passed a block, it may choose to evaluate it by sending it the **value** message. This allows Smalltalk to handle control in a purely object-oriented fashion: the class True responds to the message ifTrue: by evaluating the passed block, and False responds to ifTrue: by doing nothing. Conversely, True does nothing when sent the message ifFalse:, while False evaluates the passed block. In other words, we can visualize class True as having the following method definitions,

```
ifTrue: aBlock
  ↑ aBlock value
ifFalse: aBlock
  ↑ nil
```

and similarly for class False. Note, finally, in the code for class Queue that a message must always have a target object, even if an object is passing the message to itself. Thus a queue can find out if itself is empty by sending the message

```
self empty
```

This is different from C++, Eiffel, and Simula.

As an example of the use of class Queue, we translate the demonstration code for Eiffel (page 329) into Smalltalk:

```
q <- Queue new.
x <- LinkableObject new.
y <- LinkableObject new.
q enqueue: x.
q enqueue: y.
y <- q front.
"now y == x"
q dequeue.
q dequeue.
"now q is empty"
```

Finally, we present an implementation of a class Complex similar to that of previous sections:

```
Class name: Complex
Superclass: Object
Instance variables: re im
Methods:
  realPart
    ↑ re
  imagPart
    ↑ im
  setReal: x
    re <- x
  setImag: y
    im <- y
  + y
    ↑ (COMPLEX new setReal: (re + (y realPart)))
                  setImag: (im + (y imagPart))
  ... etc.
```

This class can be used as follows:

```
x <- (COMPLEX new setReal: 1.0) setImag: 1.0.
y <- (COMPLEX new setReal: 1.0) setImag: -1.0.
z <- x + y.
```

9.8 DESIGN ISSUES IN OBJECT-ORIENTED LANGUAGES

In this section we survey a few of the issues surrounding the introduction of object-oriented features into a programming language and summarize the different approaches taken in the four languages we have studied.

Object-oriented features represent at their heart dynamic rather than static capabilities (such as the dynamic binding of methods to objects), so one aspect of the design of object-oriented languages is to introduce features in such a way as to reduce the runtime penalty of the extra flexibility. In a dynamically oriented (and usually interpreted) language like Smalltalk, this is less important, but in languages like C++, Eiffel, and Simula, the runtime penalty of their object-oriented features over the non-object-oriented features of their cousins (such as C and Algol) is an important aspect of their overall design.

One feature promoting efficiency has already been mentioned in the section on C++: member functions whose implementations are included in the class definition are automatically inline functions in C++. This avoids the penalty of function call during execution.

Other issues that arise in connection with the efficient design of object-oriented languages involve the proper organization of the runtime environment as well as the ability of a translator to discover optimizations. Discussion of such implementation issues is delayed until the next section.

We note also that this section discusses design issues only as they relate to overall language design, not program design. Object-oriented design of programs to take maximum advantage of an object-oriented language is not within the scope of this book, but involves complex software engineering issues. Several of the references at the end of the chapter contain more information on these issues.

9.8.1 Classes Versus Types

The introduction of classes into a language with data types means that classes must be incorporated in some way into the type system. There are several possibilities, three of which we catalog.

1. Classes could be specifically excluded from type checking. Objects would then become typeless objects, whose class membership would

be maintained separately from the type system—generally at runtime using a tagging mechanism. This method of adding classes to an existing language is the simplest and has been used in a few languages, such as Objective-C (see the references at the end of the chapter).

2. Classes could become type constructors, thus making class declarations a part of the language type system. This is the solution adopted by C++ and a number of other languages that add object-oriented facilities to an existing language. In C++ a class is just a different form of record, or structure, type. In this case, the assignment compatibility of objects of descendant classes to objects of ancestor classes must be incorporated into the type-checking algorithms. Specifically, if x is an object of a descendant class of the class of object y, then type checking must permit the assignment y : = x but must flag the assignment x : = y as an error. This complicates the type-checking algorithm.

3. Classes can also simply *become* the type system. That is, all other structured types are excluded from the language. This is the approach of many languages designed from the beginning as object-oriented, such as Smalltalk and Eiffel. (Simula also uses the class as the basic type structure—the array is the only other structured type.) In Eiffel, for example, there are five basic predefined types: BOOLEAN, INTEGER, CHARACTER, REAL, and DOUBLE. All other types, including arrays and strings, must be defined as classes. This makes inheritance into *the* basic structure for type checking. It also means that, under static typing, the validity of all object assignments can be checked prior to execution, even though exact class membership is not known until execution time.[5]

9.8.2   Inheritance Versus Import

In object-oriented programming clients are clearly distinguished from descendants. Clients import features of a class, but internal details of the class information are protected from use by clients. (As noted in Chap-

---

[5]There are always a few situations where a program benefits from knowing exact class membership during execution, and this involves a kind of "dynamic typing." For example, in Eiffel there is a **reverse assignment attempt**

```
x  ?=  y ;
```

that is statically valid when x is an object of a subclass of the class of y. During execution this assignment works only if y actually is an object of (a subclass of) the class of x. In Simula a comparable mechanism is the **is** test, described on page 315. C++ uses casts to obtain the same effect (but without error checking). (See the code on page 322 and Exercise 34).

ter 8, this property is sometimes referred to as **information hiding.**) Descendants, on the other hand, inherit access not only to the features of a class, but to their implementations as well. (This is referred to as the **open-closed principle** in Meyer [1988].) Thus inheritance is a naturally less secure process than is import.

Some languages therefore provide mechanisms for the control of access to class features and internals by descendants as well as clients. An example is C++, where members that are not declared public (exported) or protected (inherited but not exported) are automatically private (available neither to clients nor to descendants). Eiffel has a similar mechanism, but with the opposite convention (the default is "public"). Some versions of Simula have a similar mechanism (see Exercise 11).

C++ also has a mechanism that allows a class to open up details of its implementation to another class or function: the other class or function is listed by the class as a **friend.** For example, in a C++ implementation of a complex data type, the problem arises that a binary operation such as addition acquires an unusual syntax when written as a method of class COMPLEX, namely,

```
x.operator+(y)
```

(Fortunately, C++ does allow the substitute syntax x + y.) An alternative solution (and the only one in some earlier C++ implementations) is to declare the "+" operation outside the class itself as a friend (so that it can access the internal data of each COMPLEX object) as follows:

```
class COMPLEX
   {private:
      double re,im;
    public:
      friend COMPLEX operator+(COMPLEX,COMPLEX);
      ...};

COMPLEX operator+(COMPLEX x, COMPLEX y)
{return COMPLEX (x.re+y.re,x.im+y.im);}
```

Eiffel has a somewhat similar mechanism (see Exercise 21). Other languages have fewer options for control of access to internal features of a class. Smalltalk, for example, has no explicit access control mechanisms; all methods are automatically exported, instance variables cannot be exported, and subclasses always have access to all details of superclasses.

We should also note that none of the object-oriented languages studied in this chapter have an **import** clause for clients. Instead, classes are made available to clients by locating them in a library, which is known or made available to the translator by the system, and clients import class features simply by using them.

9.8.3   Inheritance Versus Polymorphism

Non-object-oriented languages frequently provide some form of polymorphism as a limited way for programs to reuse code. For example, as we have seen in Chapters 7 and 8, Ada allows for the reuse (overloading) of the name of a function or procedure if a translator can distinguish the different forms of the operation through type checking of parameters. Ada also allows for the definition of generic types using a type parameter (parametrization), such as a stack of (unspecified) elements.

Object-oriented languages, on the other hand, have less need of explicit polymorphic facilities, since inheritance and dynamic binding provide a mechanism for implicit polymorphism. This is particularly true for overloading, since calling a method of an object automatically chooses the method based on the class of the current object. For example, the expression

```
x + y
```

in Smalltalk, C++, and Eiffel is interpreted as x. + (y), that is, calling the "+" function of the class of x with parameter y. If x and y are of class COMPLEX, this will naturally be complex addition, while if x and y are real, real addition will result. (The case of a mixed expression when x is complex and y is real, or vice versa, is an important one, but we will not study it here.)

Parametrized types, however, are somewhat more difficult to imitate using inheritance. In the case of a linked list of unspecified items, we have shown in previous examples how to obtain polymorphism by defining a class linkableObject that incorporates the properties needed for making linked lists and then making all actual data elements be derived classes of this class (pages 313 and 314). The problem with this solution is that a linked list may still contain objects of many different subclasses, and thus no uniformity of features can be assumed for stored items. To a certain extent, this can be corrected by defining abstract classes that collect needed operations, but this substantially increases the complexity of the solution (see Exercises 33 and 38).

For this reason, object-oriented languages frequently still include a mechanism for parametrizing classes. This is true of both C++ and Eiffel, as examples in the sections on these languages have shown. One important aspect of parametrization is that a parametrized type should enable its code be shared among different parametrized uses, instead of having essentially the same code duplicated for each use. (See Exercise 43.)

9.9   IMPLEMENTATION ISSUES IN OBJECT-ORIENTED LANGUAGES

In this section we discuss a few of the issues encountered when implementing an object-oriented language, and we present several methods that allow object-oriented features to be implemented in an efficient way. Since these are primarily issues of efficient code generation by a compiler, they are less applicable to a dynamic, primarily interpreted language such as Smalltalk.

9.9.1   Implementation of Objects and Methods

Typically, objects are implemented exactly as record structures would be in C or Pascal, with instance variables representing data fields in the record. For example, an object of the following class (using Simula syntax),

```
class point;
begin
  real x,y;
  procedure moveto(dx,dy);
  begin
    x := x+dx;
    y := y+dy;
  end moveto;
    . . .
end point;
```

could be allocated space for its instance variables x and y just as the record

```
record
  x: real;
  y: real;
end;
```

by allocating space for x and y sequentially in memory:

space for x
space for y

An object of a derived class can be allocated as an extension of the preceding data object, with new instance variables allocated space at the end of the record. For example, given the declaration (again in Simula syntax),

```
point class circle;
begin
  real radius;
  real procedure area;
  begin
    area := pi*r*r;
```

```
end area;
end circle;
```

an object of class circle could be allocated as follows:

Point part:	space for x
	space for y
Circle part:	space for radius

Now the instance variables x and y inherited by any circle object from point can be found at the same offset from the beginning of its allocated space as for any point object. Thus the location of x and y can be determined statically, even without knowing the exact class of an object—just that it belongs to a descendant class of point.

Methods can also be implemented as ordinary functions. Methods do differ from functions in two basic ways. The first is that a method can directly access the data of the current object of the class. For example, the moveto method of class point changes the internal state of a point by assigning to the instance variables x and y. To implement this mechanism, one simply views a method as a function with an implicit extra parameter, which is a pointer that is set to the current instance at each call. For example, the moveto method of class point given can be viewed as implicitly declared in the following way

```
procedure moveto(p,dx,dy);
ref (point) p; real dx,dy;
```

and each call z.moveto(dx,dy) would be interpreted by the translator as moveto(z,dx,dy). Note that, as before, the instance variables of the object pointed to by p can be found by static offset from p, regardless of the actual class membership of the object at the time of execution.

A more significant problem arises with the dynamic binding of methods during execution, since this certainly does depend on the class membership of the current object when the call is made. This is dealt with in the next subsection.

9.9.2   Inheritance and Dynamic Binding

In the implementation of objects that we have described, only space for instance variables is allocated with each object; allocation of methods is not provided for. This works as long as methods are completely equivalent to functions, and the location of each is known at compile time, as is the case for ordinary functions in an imperative language.

A problem arises with this implementation when dynamic binding is used for methods, since the precise method to use for a call is not known except during execution. A possible solution is to keep all "virtual" methods (i.e., those for which dynamic binding applies—we use the C++ terminology here) as extra fields in the record structures allocated for each object. For example, given the following declaration (again in Simula syntax, but with the keyword "virtual" indicating dynamic binding):

```
class A;
real x,y;
procedure f;
virtual procedure g;
  . . .
end A;

A class B;
real z;
procedure f;
virtual procedure h;
  . . .
end B;
```

an object a of class A would be allocated space as follows:

space for x
space for y
space for g

while an object b of class B would be allocated space as follows:

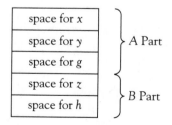

Here space for procedures contains code pointers (and perhaps environment pointers, see Chapter 7) that can be copied from an initialization table for each class when an object is created. Now an assignment a : – b would make a point to the structure of b, and a call to a . g would find the g of b at the (statically fixed) offset from the beginning of a's record.

The problem with this is that each object structure must maintain a list of all virtual functions available at that moment, and this list could be very large, thus wasting considerable space. Indeed, in object-oriented languages, it is likely for most methods to be "virtual" in the C++ sense, that is, have redefinitions in descendant classes. Indeed, in Eiffel, there is no "virtual" declaration. All methods are capable of redefinition by descendant classes (but see Exercise 22).

An alternative to this expensive strategy is to maintain a table of virtual methods for each class at some central location, such as the global storage area, that can be statically loaded with code pointers and have a single pointer to this table stored in each object structure. Such a table is called a **virtual method table** or VMT, and the previous declarations of classes A and B with objects a and b would result in the following allocation picture:

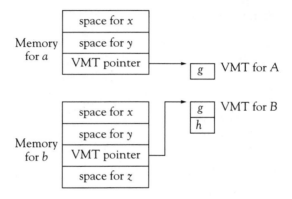

Now a call to each virtual method is achieved by an extra indirection through the VMT pointer. And an object assignment a : - b would just make a's VMT pointer point to the VMT for class B, thus ensuring that B's virtual methods will be called.

Note that neither of these implementation possibilities requires that the inheritance graph be maintained during execution. In fact, as we have seen in the previous section, compatibility of assignments such as a : - b can be viewed purely as a type-checking issue and can be determined statically by a compiler. It is, however, possible to maintain an inheritance graph at runtime and to resolve virtual method calls by a search of this graph. (See Exercise 42.)

9.9.3   Allocation and Initialization

Object-oriented languages can maintain a runtime environment in the traditional stack/heap fashion of Pascal or C as described in Chapter 7. For example, this is true of C++, Eiffel, and Simula. (Simula does have the added complication of coroutines; see Chapter 13.) Within such an environment it is possible to allocate objects either on the stack or the heap, but since objects are generally dynamic in nature, it is more common for them to be allocated on the heap than the stack. Indeed, Eiffel (as its default) and Simula both view objects implicitly as pointers, which must be allocated on the heap as well as initialized (the stack being reserved for maintaining the call structure and local variables). In Eiffel allocation involves the explicit call to a creation procedure, while in Simula a call to new will also execute the main block of a class definition as initialization code.

C++, on the other hand, permits an object to be allocated either directly on the stack or as a pointer. In the case of stack allocation, the compiler is responsible for the automatic generation of constructor calls on entry into a block and destructor calls on exit, while in the case of heap allocation of pointers, explicit calls to new and delete cause constructor and destructor calls to be scheduled. This means that C++ can maintain exactly the same runtime environment as C, but with the added burden to the compiler that it must schedule the constructor and destructor calls, as well as create and maintain locations for temporary objects. (See Exercise 33.)

Eiffel and Simula, on the other hand, have no explicit deallocation routines, but require the use of a garbage collector to return inaccessible storage to the heap. The execution overhead and added runtime complexity of such a requirement are significant, but techniques such as incremental garbage collection can be used to reduce the penalty. See Section 10.6 for a further discussion.

During the execution of initialization code, it is often necessary to execute the initialization code of an ancestor class before current initializations are performed. A simple example of this is when instance variables defined in an ancestor need to be allocated space before they can be used in the initialization of a descendant. In C++ and Simula the calls to initialization code of ancestors are scheduled automatically by a compiler. This can cause problems similar to the compile and link dependency problems described in Section 8.6. Indeed, in C++ (and Simula), initialization code is performed according to the topological sort of the dependency graph determined by the order in which parent classes are listed in each derived class declaration. In Eiffel, by contrast, no implicit call to a parent class's creation routine is made. If a call is needed, the programmer must supply it manually (and hence supply an order in which the initializations occur).

Exercises

1. Describe how object-oriented programming languages solve the problems with abstract data type mechanisms listed in Section 8.7.

2. Describe the differences in the definitions of an object in object-oriented

languages and an object as given in Chapter 5. Is it possible for an entity to be an object under one definition but not the other? Why?

3. Describe the difference between inheritance and import.

4. Describe the difference between inheritance and overloading.

5. Give an example to show that protection and modifiability can be mutually conflicting requirements.

6. How does dynamic binding support reuse? Protection?

7. Why is it not possible for a class such as complex numbers to be adequately imitated by a Modula-2 record type?

8. If x is an object of class A and y is an object of a class B that is derived from A, after the assignment x : − y, why is x.m illegal when m is a method of B but not A? Why does this not violate the subtype principle?

9. Describe the differences among the protection mechanisms of (a) C++, (b) Eiffel, and (c) Smalltalk.

10. (Snyder [1986]) A problem exists in the relationship of the subtype principle to private inheritance in C++.
    (a) Describe the problem.
    (b) Does Eiffel have the same problem?
    (c) Can you think of a way of revising either the subtype principle or protection mechanisms in C++ to avoid it?

11. Some newer versions of Simula have the following protection mechanism. An instance variable or method declared **protected** is unavailable to clients. A variable or method can also be declared **hidden,** which makes it unavailable to descendants.
    (a) Compare these to the mechanisms of C++.
    (b) Should a derived class be able to make an unprotected inherited feature protected? Why?
    (c) Should a derived class be able to make a protected inherited feature hidden? Why?
    (d) Should the reverse of (b) and (c) also be possible? Why?

12. Why is it not possible to create an object of an abstract class? Does this mean that variables of abstract class types cannot be declared? Explain.

13. Should deferred methods always be dynamically bound?

14. Describe the two meanings of the keyword **virtual** in Simula discussed in the text.

15. Describe the two meanings of the keyword **virtual** in C++ discussed in the text.

16. What is the difference between a type and a class?

17. Suppose class D inherits from both classes B and C, and classes B and C both inherit a method m from class A, but B redefines m. If d is an object of class D, then d.m could be either B.m or A.m.

(a) Describe how Eiffel solves this problem.

(b) Is there an equivalent C++ solution? (You will need to consult a C++ reference such as Ellis and Stroustrup [1990]).

18. During the initialization of objects, it is possible that initialization routines of ancestor classes may need to be called. Under multiple inheritance this can result in questions about the order of initializations and the duplication of initializations. Describe these problems and outline a possible solution.

19. A print procedure is a good candidate for a dynamically bound method. Why?

20. Given the following code in a Simula-like language,

```
class A;
procedure p;
begin
  print('x');
end p;
  . . .
end A;

A class B;
procedure p;
begin
  print('y');
end p;
  . . .
end B;

ref (A) a;
ref (B) b;

a :- b;
a.p;
```

what does the call a.p print? Why?

21. In Eiffel a class can **selectively export** a feature to another class by appending a list of targets to a feature clause in the class declaration. For example, in

```
class linkableObject
feature {linkedStructure}
  next: linkableObject;
end;
```

only the class linkedStructure can access the next field of a linkableObject. Compare this Eiffel mechanism to the friend mechanism of C++ described in Section 9.8. Use the C++ friend mechanism to imitate this code.

22. In Eiffel there is no declaration by the programmer whether a method will need to be dynamically bound or not during execution (like the C++ "virtual").
    (a) Does this mean that all methods must be assumed "virtual" in the runtime environment? Why?
    (b) Is it possible to obtain static binding in Eiffel?

23. Describe how the expression 2 + 3 · 4 is evaluated in Smalltalk.

24. Describe how Smalltalk accommodates multiple messages in the same expression, as in for example,

    `(q enqueue: x) enqueue: y`

25. Write a Smalltalk implementation for the class `False`.

26. On page 339 we mentioned that `new` is a "class method" rather than an "object method" in Smalltalk. What is the difference between these two kinds of methods?

27. The following question refers to the definition of the method `new:` on page 339. Explain how the expression

    `(self new) linkTo: aLinkableObject`

    is evaluated.

28. **(a)** If we try to redefine a `new` method in Smalltalk that initializes linkable objects to point to themselves as in the Simula code on page 306, we might try the following:

    ```
    new
        ↑ (self new) linkTo: self
    ```

    This will not work. Why?
    (b) Suggest a way of writing a correct `new` method.

29. Similar to the `ifTrue` and `ifFalse` messages described on pages 340–341, Smalltalk has `whileTrue` and `whileFalse` messages.
    (a) To what class should these messages apply? What parameters should they have?
    (b) Write an implementation of `whileTrue`. (Hint: Use `ifTrue`.)

30. In Modula-2 one can use imported features of a module by using the FROM <module-name> IMPORT <feature-list> statement described in Chapter 8. Is this a reasonable mechanism to want in an object-oriented language? Why?

31. On page 313, the class `linkableComplex` is declared as inheriting from class COMPLEX. Why? Is there a better way?

32. Suppose we wanted to define a sortedList class that would store linkableObjects in sorted order. Show how to define an abstract class comparableObject that can be used to force any object stored in a sortedList to have a comparison operation.

33. The implementations of class COMPLEX in Simula and Eiffel (pages 303 and 333) have operations that work by side effect on the state of the current object, while the C++ and Smalltalk implementations (pages 325 and 341) return new objects as the results of the operations.
    (a) Describe the consequences of this difference.
    (b) Rewrite the C++/Smalltalk implementation to agree with the others.
    (c) Rewrite the Simula/Eiffel implementation to agree with the others.

34. (a) The C++ template for a parametrized queue contains a piece of questionable code, namely, that a pointer to a linkableObject is cast to type linkable * in the code for front. Why was this cast necessary? Is it dangerous?
    (b) One way of removing the problem described in (a) is to make linkableObject itself into a template. Write out the declarations of linkableObject and queue using this idea.
    (c) A different solution to the problem in (a) is to make linkableObject into an abstract class, defining enough pure virtual methods to deal with stored data. Write out the declarations of linkableObject and queue using this idea.
    (d) How does either solution (b) or (c) affect the generality of the implementation? Which is better?

35. Suppose we have a queue containing data of different classes. Introduce printLinkable and printList methods into the declarations of linkableObject and linkedList to allow for printing of a list.

36. A class gcd with a single method value was written in Chapter 1 in Simula. Write a similar class definition in (a) C++, (b) Eiffel, and (c) Smalltalk.

37. Write a class definition for a factorial class in (a) Simula, (b) C++, (c) Eiffel, and (d) Smalltalk.

38. An alternative to the inheritance graph for geometric figures on page 311, which interprets inheritance as **specialization,** is to turn the graph upside down and interpret inheritance as **generalization.** For example, if we define square as follows,

```
class square;
begin
  ref (point) center;
  real side;
```

```
real procedure area; comment- assumed virtual
begin
  area := side*side; end area;
  . . .
end class square;
```

we could define a rectangle by extending square as follows:

```
square class rectangle;
begin
  real height;
  real procedure area;
  begin
    area := side*height;
  end area;
  . . .
end rectangle;
```

Describe the advantages of this view of inheritance. Describe its disadvantages. Which is preferable?

39. On page 349 the allocated space for an object of class B included a VMT pointer field, which was located after the space for inherited instance variables x and y, but before instance variable z. Why was this? Is there an advantage to not having the VMT pointer allocated at the beginning of each object?

40. In the example on pages 348 and 349, space for objects of class A and B did not include a field for procedure f. Why? How is f found?

41. Multiple inheritance causes complications for the description of the allocation of objects in Section 9.9. Try to extend the mechanism described there so that it will handle multiple inheritance.

42. Instead of having a VMT for each class that includes all available dynamically bound methods for that class, it is possible to store only newly defined methods for each class and include pointers to parent classes in the VMT.
    (a) Give details on method invocation and VMT layout using this structure.
    (b) What are the advantages and disadvantages of this implementation method?

43. In the use of a parametrized class definition, runtime savings are achieved only if the same code for methods can be used, regardless of the parameter. If the size of the parameter's data can vary arbitrarily, this creates a problem for the compiler. What is it? Describe why code reuse for parametrized types is easier in Eiffel and Simula than it is in C++.

44. Assuming the following C++ declarations,

```
class A {public:
  int a;
  virtual void f(void);
  virtual void g(void);};
class B: public A
{public:
   int b;
   void f(void);
   void h(void);};
class C: public B
{public:
   int c;
   void g(void);};
```

draw the VMT of each class and the layout of memory for an object of each class.

45. Meyer [1988] distinguishes overloading from parametric polymorphism as follows (Ibid., p. 38): "Overloading is a facility for client programmers: it makes it possible to write the same client code when using different implementations of a data structure provided by different modules. Genericity [parametrization] is for module implementors: it allows them to write the same module code to describe all instances of the same implementation of a data structure, applied to various types of objects." Discuss this view of polymorphism.

Notes and References

A good general reference for object-oriented programming techniques is Meyer [1988], where an earlier version of Eiffel is also described; the version of Eiffel used here is described in Meyer [1992]. Simula is described in Birtwistle [1973]. Dahl and Nygaard [1966] and Lamprecht [1983] are other references. C++ is described in Stroustrup [1986] and Ellis and Stroustrup [1990]. A useful introduction to C++ is Lippman [1989]. Smalltalk is described in Goldberg [1984] and Goldberg and Robson [1989]. Budd [1987] describes an interesting implementation of a subset of Smalltalk without the graphics-user interface. A gentle introduction to the user interface and programming in Smalltalk is given in Kaehler and Patterson [1986].

Other interesting object-oriented languages that are not studied here are described in the following references. Modula-3 is a Modula-2 derivative with object-oriented extensions (Cardelli et al. [1989a,b], Nelson [1991], Cardelli et al. [1992]). Objective C is an extension of C with object-oriented features designed by Cox [1984, 1986]. Two object-oriented extensions of Pascal are described in Tesler [1985] and Turbo [1988]. Object-oriented versions of LISP include CLOS (Gabriel, White, and Bobrow [1991]; Bobrow et al. [1988]); Loops (Bobrow and Stetik [1983]), and Flavors (Moon [1986]). Oberon (Wirth [1988b,c]) is an attempt to design a minimal language with significant object-oriented features.

Many papers on recent research, as well as reports on object-oriented programming techniques, have appeared in OOPSLA [1986–1990]. An interesting application of object-oriented techniques to the sieve of Eratosthenes in C++ is given in Sethi [1989].

10 FUNCTIONAL PROGRAMMING

The functional approach to programming, and functional programming languages, provide a substantially different view of programming than do the more traditional imperative programming languages. Functional programming has a number of distinct advantages over imperative programming, which have traditionally made it popular for artificial intelligence, mathematical proof systems, and logic applications. These include the uniform view of programs as functions, the treatment of functions as data, the limitation of side effects, and the use of automatic memory management. A functional programming language has as a result great flexibility, conciseness of notation, and simple semantics.

The major drawback has traditionally been the inefficiency of execution of functional languages. Because of their dynamic nature, such languages historically were interpreted rather than compiled, with a resulting substantial loss in execution speed. Even when compilers became available, the speedups obtained were inadequate. Recently, however, advances in compilation techniques for functional languages, plus the development of hardware architectures specifically designed for their needs, have made them more attractive for general programming (although efficiency is still a problem), and their semantic simplicity and orthogonality of design have made them a reasonable alternative for teaching computer science. Even more, functional constructs have crept into almost all programming languages, and functional techniques are becoming more and more widely used in the general computer community. Functional programming is therefore likely to play an increasingly important role in computer science and computing.

In this chapter, we review the concept of a function and how programs can be viewed as functions. We give a brief introduction to functional techniques using Modula-2 (showing that you do not need a "functional" language to do functional programming). We then survey three modern functional languages—Scheme, ML, and Miranda—and discuss some of their properties. Following that, we give a somewhat more mathematical look at function definition, including the definition of recursive functions, and a short introduction to lambda calculus, the underlying mathematical model for functional languages. Finally, we review the most common dynamic memory management techniques for functional languages. (These are also used by some object-oriented languages as well; see the previous chapter.)

10.1   PROGRAMS AS FUNCTIONS

A program is a description of a specific computation. If we ignore the details of the computation—the "how" of the computation—and focus on the result being computed—the "what" of the computation—then a program becomes simply a "black box" for obtaining output from input. From this point of view, a program is essentially equivalent to a mathematical function:

> **Definition:** A *function* is a rule that associates to each x from some set X of values a unique y from another set Y of values. In mathematical terminology, if f is the name of the function, we write
>
> $$y = f(x)$$
>
> or
>
> $$f: X \rightarrow Y$$

The set X is called the **domain** of f, while the set Y is called the **range** of f. The x in $f(x)$, which represents any value from X, is called the **independent variable,** while the y from the set Y, defined by the equation $y = f(x)$, is called the **dependent variable.** Sometimes f is not defined for all x in X, in which case it is called a **partial function** (and a function that *is* defined for all x in X is called **total**).

We can think of programs, procedures, and functions in a programming language as all being represented by the mathematical concept of a function. In the case of a program, x represents the input and y represents the output. In the case of a procedure or function, x represents the parameters and y represents the returned values. In either case we can refer to x as "input" and y as "output." Thus the functional view of programming makes no distinction between a program, a procedure, and a function. It always makes a distinction, however, between input and output values.

In programming languages we must also distinguish between **function definition** and **function application:** the former is a declaration describing how a function is to be computed using **formal** parameters (see Chapter 7), while function application is a **call** to a declared function using **actual parameters,** or **arguments.** In mathematics a distinction is often not clearly made between a "variable" and a parameter: the term "independent variable" is often used for both actual and formal parameters. For example, in mathematics one writes

$$\text{square}(x) = x \cdot x$$

for the definition of the squaring function and then frequently applies the function to a variable x representing an actual value:

$$\text{Let } x \text{ be such that square}(x) = 2 \ . \ . \ .$$

In mathematics, variables always stand for actual values, while in imperative programming languages, variables refer to memory locations as well as values. In mathematics there is no concept of memory location, or l-values of variables, so that a statement such as

$$x := x + 1$$

makes no sense. The functional view of programming must therefore eliminate the concept of variable, except as a name for a value. This also eliminates assignment as an available operation. Thus, in functional programming, there are no variables, only constants, parameters, and values.

Practically speaking, this view of functional programming is referred to as **pure functional programming.** Most functional programming languages retain some notion of variable and assignment, and so are "impure," but it is still possible to program effectively using the pure approach—indeed, as we noted in Chapter 1, pure functional programming is Turing complete in that any computation may be described using functions alone.

One consequence of the lack of variables and assignment in functional programming is that there also can be no loops. Indeed, a loop must have a control variable that is reassigned as the loop executes, and this is not possible without variables and assignment. How do we write repeated operations in functional form? Recursion is the essential feature. For example, in Chapter 1 we noted that the procedure

```
PROCEDURE gcd (u,v: INTEGER; VAR x: INTEGER);
VAR y,t: INTEGER;
BEGIN
  x := u; y := v;
  LOOP
    IF y = 0 THEN EXIT; END;
    t := y;
    y := x MOD y;
    x := t
  END;
END gcd;
```

can be written instead without variables and assignment in the following recursive functional form:

```
PROCEDURE gcd (u,v: INTEGER): INTEGER;
BEGIN
  IF v = 0 THEN
    RETURN u;
  ELSE
    RETURN gcd(v,u MOD v);
  END; (* if *)
END gcd;
```

This second form is close to the (recursive) mathematical definition of the function as

$$\gcd(u, v) = \begin{cases} u \text{ if } v = 0 \\ \gcd(v, u \bmod v) \text{ if } v <> 0 \end{cases}$$

Another consequence of the lack of variables and assignment is that there is no notion of the internal state of a function: the value of any function depends only on the values of its parameters, and not on any previous computations, including calls to the function itself. The value of any function also cannot depend on the order of evaluation of its parameters, a fact that has been proposed as a reason to use functional programming for concurrent applications. The property of a function that its value depends only on the values of its parameters is called **referential transparency.** For example, the gcd function is referentially transparent since its value depends only on the value of its parameters. On the other hand, a function rand, which returns a (pseudo)random value, cannot be referentially transparent since it depends on the state of the machine (and previous calls to itself). Indeed, a referentially transparent function with no parameters must always return the same value and, thus, is no different from a constant.

The lack of variables and the referential transparency of functional programming make the semantics of functional programs particularly straightforward: there is no state, since there is no concept of memory locations with changing values (a memory location would imply the existence of a variable). The runtime environment associates names to values only (not memory locations), and once a name enters the environment, its value can never change. Such a notion of semantics is sometimes called **value semantics,** to distinguish it from the more usual storage semantics or pointer semantics. Indeed, the lack of local state in functional programming makes it in a sense the opposite of object-oriented programming, where computation proceeds by changing the local state of objects.

Finally, in functional programming we must be able to manipulate functions in arbitrary ways, without arbitrary restrictions—functions must be general language objects. In particular, functions must be viewed as values themselves, which can be computed by other functions and which can also be parameters to functions. We express this generality of functions in functional programming by saying that functions are **first-class values.**

As an example, one of the essential operations on functions is **composition.** Mathematically, the composition operator "o" is defined as follows: if $f: X \rightarrow Y$ and $g: Y \rightarrow Z$, then $g \circ f: X \rightarrow Z$ is given by $(g \circ f)(x) = g(f(x))$.

Composition is itself a function that takes two functions as parameters and produces another function as its returned value. Such functions are sometimes called **higher-order functions.**

We summarize the qualities of functional programming languages and functional programs as follows:

1. All programs and procedures are functions and clearly distinguish incoming values (parameters) from outgoing values (results).

2. There are no variables or assignments—variables are replaced by parameters.

3. There are no loops—loops are replaced by recursive calls.

4. The value of a function depends only on the value of its parameters and not on the order of evaluation or the execution path that led to the call.

5. Functions are first-class values.

10.2   FUNCTIONAL PROGRAMMING IN A PROCEDURAL LANGUAGE

Functional programming style and techniques can to a surprising extent be used in an imperative language like Modula-2, Pascal, or Ada. This approach is being used more and more widely in imperative programming, for the same reasons that functional languages themselves are increasing in use: the simplicity of the semantics and the resultant clarity of the programs.

The basic requirement for functional programming in any language is the availability of recursion and a suitably general function mechanism. We have already seen examples of writing procedures in functional style in languages like Modula-2, C, and Pascal in Chapter 1 and the last section.

As a further example of functional-style programming, consider a function that returns the sum of integers between i and j:

$$\text{sum}(i, j) = i + (i + 1) + \cdots + (j - 1) + j$$

This is usually written in a procedural language as a loop (here in Modula-2):

```
PROCEDURE sum(i,j: INTEGER) : INTEGER;
VAR k,temp: INTEGER;
BEGIN
  temp := 0;
  FOR k := i TO j DO
    temp := temp + k;
  END;
  RETURN temp;
END sum;
```

This can be written in functional style as

```
PROCEDURE sum(i,j: INTEGER) : INTEGER;
BEGIN
  IF i > j THEN
    RETURN 0;
  ELSE
    RETURN i + sum(i+1,j);
  END;
END sum;
```

A typical problem in functional-style programming is the cost of performing all loops by recursion. Even with modern processors, which substantially reduce the overhead of a procedure call, recursive implementations are slower than those that use standard loops. There is, however, one form of recursion that is easy to discover during translation, that can be easily converted internally to a standard loop structure, and that is **tail recursion,** where the last operation in a procedure is to call itself with different arguments. For example, the functional version of the gcd procedure on page 361 is tail recursive and can be automatically converted by a translator into a loop by reassigning the parameters and starting over, as indicated by the following code:

```
PROCEDURE gcd(u,v: INTEGER): INTEGER;
VAR t1,t2: INTEGER; (* temps introduced by
  translator *)
BEGIN
  LOOP
    IF v = 0 THEN RETURN u;
    ELSE
      t1:= v ; t2 := u MOD v; (* reassign
        parameters *)
      u := t1; v := t2;
    END; (* if *)
  END; (* loop *)
END gcd;
```

(Compare this to the previous nonrecursive version of the gcd procedure.)

Unfortunately, many simple uses of recursion for looping are not tail recursive—the sum procedure earlier, for example, is not. As a consequence, functional programmers have invented techniques for converting functions into tail-recursive ones, with so-called **accumulating parameters** that are used to precompute operations performed after the recursive call, and to pass the results to the recursive call. As an example, we rewrite the sum procedure using an accumulating parameter:

```
PROCEDURE sum1(i,j, sumSoFar: INTEGER) : INTEGER;
BEGIN
  IF i > j THEN
    RETURN sumSoFar;
  ELSE
    RETURN sum1(i+1,j,sumSoFar+i);
  END;
END sum1;
```

Now the original sum procedure can be written as a single call to sum1 by initializing the accumulating parameter (sum1 is called a **helping procedure**):

```
PROCEDURE sum (i,j: INTEGER) : INTEGER;
BEGIN
  RETURN sum1(i,j,0);
END sum;
```

Lest one think that languages like Pascal, C, Modula-2, or Ada can be used to write perfectly pure functional programs, we note that procedural languages contain a number of restrictions that make it difficult or impossible to translate all programs into this style. In particular, the following restrictions are common in procedural languages:[1]

1. Structured values such as arrays and records cannot be returned values from functions.

2. There is no way to build a value of a structured type directly.

3. Functions are not first-class values, so higher-order functions cannot be written.

To understand how these restrictions can affect our ability to program in functional style (and how the functional methods can be simulated using occasional procedural constructs), we consider two examples: a sorting program and the composition higher-order function described earlier.

In functional style a sort procedure needs to return a sorted array given an input array. In a language like Ada, where arrays can be returned as values of functions, we can write (assuming the data to be sorted are integers)

```
function IntSort(A: in INTARRAY) return INTARRAY
  is
-- type INTARRAY is array (INTEGER range <>) of
-- INTEGER;
begin
  . . .
end IntSort;
```

In Pascal, however, an array or other structured type cannot be the returned value of a function. Some Modula-2 compilers also have this restriction, and in any case in Modula-2 a function cannot return an array with unspecified size, as in the Ada code. Instead, the IntSort function must be declared as follows:

```
PROCEDURE IntSort (A: ARRAY OF INTEGER;
                   VAR B: ARRAY OF INTEGER);
BEGIN
  . . .
END IntSort;
```

This definition imitates the functional style by using a VAR parameter to return the value of the function. The more common procedural

---

[1]This is somewhat less true as time goes on. For example, both C and Ada permit structured values to be returned from functions. Ada also allows the direct construction of structured values (at least in limited form). And C and Modula-2 have function variables and parameters. Nevertheless, such languages continue to have significant restrictions in these areas.

form for this procedure is the following:

```
PROCEDURE IntSort (VAR A: ARRAY OF INTEGER);
BEGIN
   . . .
END IntSort;
```

While this form may be more efficient, it violates the rule of functional programming that the input to a function should always be distinguished from its output. In fact, this form of the sort procedure destroys the original values of the array A.

Even when a language can return values of arbitrary types from a function, it may not be possible to construct these values without the use of a local variable. In Pascal, for example, there are value constructors for strings and sets but not for arrays or records: single quotes can be used to construct a string value (an element with implicit type `packed array [1..len] of char`), such as

```
str := 'hello, world!';
```

and square brackets "[" and "]" can be used to construct a set, as in

```
S := [0,1,2];
```

In Ada there *is* an array constructor that uses parentheses and lists of values to construct an array value directly from its component values. However, restrictions apply, so that the sort procedure still needs to be written with a local temporary to construct the sorted array:

```
function IntSort(A: in INTARRAY) return INTARRAY
   is
-- type INTARRAY is array (INTEGER range <>) of
-- INTEGER;
temp: INTARRAY(A'FIRST..A'LAST);
begin
   . . .
   return temp;
end IntSort;
```

The third restriction in the list—the non-first-classness of functions in procedural languages—is a little more difficult to overcome by using such simple expedients. In Modula-2 functions are more available than in Ada or Pascal, since there are function types and function variables. It is still not possible to define a higher-order function such as composition, however, although we can attempt a definition as follows:

```
TYPE ProcType = PROCEDURE(INTEGER):INTEGER;

PROCEDURE Compose (g,f: ProcType;
                       VAR h: ProcType);
    PROCEDURE Comp(x: INTEGER): INTEGER;
    BEGIN
        RETURN g(f(x));
    END Comp;

BEGIN
    h := Comp;
END Compose;
```

The Compose procedure is syntactically legal in Modula-2, but is a semantically illegal use of functions, since only global functions can be assigned to VAR parameters of procedures. This restriction is necessary because of the stack-based runtime environment in Modula-2, which would deallocate the frame of Compose after it executes, thus destroying the values of the parameters f and g, which still need to be accessed when h is called. To make such a function possible, it is necessary to retain the activation of Compose as long as the function Comp can be called, and this requires a fully dynamic runtime environment as described in Section 7.6.4. In Section 10.8 we will study methods for maintaining such environments.

As a final example of functional programming in a procedural language, let us consider a function for computing the maximum value in an array:

```
PROCEDURE IntArrayMax
    (a: ARRAY OF INTEGER; Low,High: INTEGER) :
        INTEGER;
VAR i: INTEGER;
    temp: INTEGER;
BEGIN
    temp := a[Low];
    FOR i := Low+1 TO High DO
        IF temp < a[i] THEN
            temp := a[i]
        END;
    END;
    RETURN temp;
END IntArrayMax;
```

To convert this into a functional-style program, we must eliminate the local variables i and temp, the loop, and the assignments. We do this by using the Low parameter as an index and recursion to perform the loop. We also need to introduce an IntMax procedure to simplify the computation of the maximum of two integer values. The following two procedures result:

```
PROCEDURE IntMax (x,y: INTEGER): INTEGER;
BEGIN
  IF x < y THEN RETURN y
  ELSE RETURN x
  END;
END IntMax;

PROCEDURE IntArrayMax (a: ARRAY OF INTEGER;
                       Low,High: INTEGER)  :
                       INTEGER;
BEGIN
  IF Low = High THEN RETURN a[Low]
  ELSE
    RETURN IntMax(a[Low],
                  IntArrayMax (a,Low+1,High))
  END;
END IntArrayMax;
```

10.3   *Scheme: A DIALECT OF LISP*

In the late 1950s and early 1960s, a team at MIT led by John McCarthy developed the first language that contained many of the features of modern functional languages. Based on ideas from mathematics, in particular the lambda calculus of Church, it was called LISP (for LISt Processor) because its basic data structure is a list. LISP first existed as an interpreter on an IBM 704 and incorporated a number of features that, strictly speaking, are not aspects of functional programming per se but that have been closely associated with functional languages because of the enormous influence of LISP. These include

1. The uniform representation of programs and data using a single general data structure—the list

2. The definition of the language using an interpreter written in the language itself—called a **metacircular interpreter**

3. The automatic management of all memory by the runtime system

Unfortunately, no single standard evolved for the LISP language, and many different LISP systems have been created over the years. In addition, the original version of LISP and many of its successors did not have a uniform treatment of functions as first-class values and used dynamic scoping for nonlocal references. Recently, however, two dialects of LISP have become standard that use static scoping and give a more uniform treatment of functions: Common LISP, developed by a committee in the early 1980s, and Scheme, developed by a group at MIT in the late 1970s. In the following we will use the Scheme dialect of LISP.

10.3.1   The Elements of Scheme

All programs and data in Scheme are expressions, and expressions are of two varieties: atoms and lists (actually, there is a slightly more general form of list, called an S-expression, but we will ignore this complication in the following discussion). Atoms are like the constants and identifiers of a procedural language: they include numbers, strings, names, functions, and a few other constructs we will not mention here. A list is simply a sequence of expressions separated by spaces and surrounded by parentheses. Thus the syntax of Scheme is particularly simple:

<expression> ::= <atom> | <list>

<atom> ::= <number> | <string> | <identifier> | ...

<list> ::= '(' <expression-sequence> ')'

<expression-sequence> ::= <expression> <expression-sequence>
                                      | <empty>

Some examples of Scheme expressions are the following:

```
42                          —a number
"hello"                     —a string
(2.1 2.2 3.1)               —a list of numbers
a                           —an identifier
hello                       —another identifier
(+ 2 3)                     —a list consisting of the identifier
                               "+" and two numbers
(* (+ 2 3) (/ 6 2))         —a list consisting of an identifier
                               followed by two lists
```

Since programs in Scheme are expressions, and programs need to be executed or evaluated, the semantics of Scheme are given by an **evaluation rule** for expressions. The standard evaluation rule for Scheme expressions is as follows:

1. Constant atoms, such as numbers and strings, evaluate to themselves.

2. Identifiers are looked up in the current environment and replaced by the value found there. (The environment in Scheme is essentially a dynamically maintained symbol table that associates identifiers to values.)

3. A list is evaluated by evaluating the first expression in the list. This expression must evaluate to a function. This function is then applied to the evaluated values of the rest of the list.

We can apply these rules to the sample Scheme expressions as follows: 42 and "hello" evaluate to themselves; a and hello are looked up in the environment and their values returned; (+ 2 3) is evaluated by looking up the value of " + " in the environment—it returns a function value, namely, the addition function, which is predefined—and then applying the addition function to the values of 2 and 3, which are 2 and 3 (since constants evaluate to themselves). Thus the value 5 is returned. Similarly, (* (+ 2 3) (/ 6 2)) evaluates to 15. The list (2.1 2.2 3.1), on the other hand, cannot be evaluated, since its first expression 2.1 is a constant that is not a function. This list does not represent a Scheme program and results in an error if evaluation is attempted.

The Scheme evaluation rule implies that all expressions in Scheme must be written in prefix form. It also implies that the value of a function (as an object) is clearly distinguished from a call to the function: the function value is represented by its name, while a function call is surrounded by parentheses. (A similar situation exists in Modula-2 and C.) Thus a Scheme interpreter would show behavior similar to the following:

```
> +
#PROCEDURE PLUS

> (+)
0 ; a call to the + procedure with no
  ; arguments
```

A comparison of some expressions in Modula-2 and Scheme is given in Table 10-1.

The Scheme evaluation rule represents **applicative order evaluation** as discussed in Chapter 5: all subexpressions are evaluated first, so that the expression tree is evaluated from leaves to root. Thus the Scheme expression (* (+ 2 3) (+ 4 5)) is evaluated by first evaluating the two additions and then evaluating the resultant expression (* 5 9), as indicated by a bottom-up traversal of the expression tree

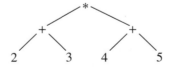

Table 10.1 Some Expressions in Modula-2 and Scheme

Modula-2	Scheme
3 + 4 * 5	(+ 3 (* 4 5))
(a=b) AND (a<>0)	(and (= a b) (<> a 0))
gcd (10,35)	(gcd 10 35)
gcd	gcd
read()	(read)

This corresponds to the evaluation of (2 + 3) * (4 + 5) in a language like Pascal, where expressions are written in infix form.

A special position in Scheme is occupied by the empty list ( ), which cannot be evaluated as a list, since there is no first item. The empty list is considered to be both a list and an atom, which evaluates to itself. A synonym for ( ) is n i l. The empty list does extra duty by representing the Boolean value f a l s e (much as the integer 0 represents f a l s e in the C language). The constant value t r u e is usually referred to by the name #T or T.

Since all Scheme constructs are expressions, we need expressions that govern the control of execution. Loops are provided by recursive call, but selection must be given by explicit functions. The basic functions that do this are the i f function, which is like an if-then-else construct, and the c o n d function, which is like a c a s e or e l s i f construct (c o n d stands for **condition**):

```
(if (= a 0)              ;   if  a=0  then
      0                  ;         return 0
    (/ 1 a))             ;   else  return 1/a

(cond ((= a 0) 0)        ;   if  a=0  then  return 0
      ((= a 1) 1)        ;   elsif  a=1  then  return 1
      (T (/ 1 a)))       ;   else  return 1/a
```

The semantics of the expression (if <exp1> <exp2> <exp3>) are that <exp1> is evaluated first; if the value of <exp1> is the Boolean value true, then <exp2> is evaluated and its value returned by the if expression; otherwise, <exp3> is evaluated and returned. In Scheme the "else" part must always be present, and the keyword e l s e is suppressed.

Similarly, the semantics of (cond <exp1> . . . <expn>) are that each <expi> must be a pair of expressions: <expi> = (<fst> <snd>). Each expression <expi> is considered in order, and the first part of it is evaluated. If <fst> evaluates to true, then <snd> is evaluated, and its value is returned by the c o n d expression. If no condition evaluates to true, then n i l is the returned value of the c o n d expression.

Notice that neither the i f nor the c o n d function obeys the standard evaluation rule for Scheme expressions: if they did, all of their arguments would be evaluated each time, regardless of their values, which would render them useless as control mechanisms. Instead, the arguments to such control procedures are **delayed** until the appropriate moment. Delayed evaluation is related to pass by name parameter passing, discussed in Chapter 7, while ordinary Scheme functions use pass by value. Delayed evaluation is an important issue in functional programming, and it is discussed further in Section 10.5. Functions in Scheme and LISP that use delayed evaluation are called **special forms.**

Two other important special forms are the q u o t e function and the l e t function. The q u o t e function simply prevents the evaluation of its argument. It is used to write list constants, since otherwise the evaluation rule would try to evaluate a list as a function call. Thus, if we were to write (see page 374 for a definition of c a r)

```
>  (car (1  2  3))
```

the Scheme interpreter would print an error message, since the first element in the list (1 2 3) is not a function. To pass the list (1 2 3) directly to a function without evaluation, one uses the q u o t e function

```
>  (car (quote (1  2  3)))
1
```

or its abbreviation

```
>  (car '(1  2  3))
1
```

The l e t function allows values to be given temporary names within an expression:

```
>  (let ((a  2)  (b  3))  (+  a  b))
5
```

The first expression in a l e t is a **binding list,** which associates names to values. In this binding list of two bindings, a is given the value 2 and b the value 3. The names a and b can then be used for their values in the second expression, which is the body of the l e t and whose value is the returned value of the l e t.

To complete the process of creating a Scheme program, we must also have a way of declaring functions, or entering them into the environment, so that they may be called. This is done using the d e f i n e function (which is also a special form). There are two ways of using define, either to define names directly by giving their values, as in

```
(define a  2)
(define emptylist  ())
```

or by defining a function name (with its parameters) and then giving the function body:

```
(define (gcd u  v)  ;    function name and parameters
        (if (=  v  0)
            u                               ;function body
            (gcd v  (remainder u  v))))
```

Given these definitions, we can then refer to the values of a, e m p t y l i s t, and g c d and also call the function g c d:

```
> a
2

> emptylist
( )

> gcd
#PROCEDURE gcd

> (gcd 25 10)
5
```

The gcd function implements Euclid's algorithm in Scheme. To use the function we could simply "load" the function into the environment by evaluating the define expression and then entering the parameter values directly into a call from within the interpreter as in the evaluation of (gcd 25 10), or we could provide a further function with input and output operations to ask the user explicitly for values, as we would need to do in a compiled program. To finish this example of Scheme programming, we provide such an outer-level I/O function.

Scheme has two basic built-in I/O functions: read and display (princ is the more usual function in other LISPs). The read function has no parameters—it returns whatever value the keyboard provides:

```
> read
#PROCEDURE READ

> (read)
234  ; user types this
234  ; the read function returns this

> (read)
"hello, world"
"hello, world"
```

The display function similarly prints its parameter to the screen:

```
> (display "hello, world")
hello, world

> (display 234)
234
```

Here is an outer-level function to go with the gcd function just defined (note that `define` and `let` allow sequences of expressions in their bodies; this is also true of `cond` alternatives:

```
(define (euclid)
    (display "enter two integers:")
    (newline) ; goes to next line on screen
    (let ((u (read)) (v (read)))
        (display "the gcd of ")
        (display u)
        (display " and ")
        (display v)
        (display " is ")
        (display (gcd u v))
        (newline)))
```

10.3.2   Data Structures in Scheme

In Scheme as with other LISPs, the basic data structure is the list; all other structures must be put into the form of lists. This is not hard, as a list can represent an array, record, or any other data. For example, the following is a list representation of a binary search tree:

("horse" ("cow" () ("dog" () ())) ("zebra" ("yak" () ()) ()))

A node in this tree is a list of three items (`name left right`), where `name` is a string, and `left` and `right` are the child trees, which are also lists. Thus the given list represents the following tree:

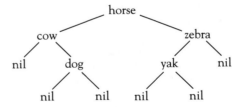

To use lists effectively we must have an adequate set of functions that operate on lists. Scheme has many predefined list functions, but the basic functions that are common to all LISP systems are the selector functions `car` and `cdr`, which compute the head and the tail of a list, and the constructor function `cons`, which adds a new head to an existing list. Thus, if `L` is the list (1 2 3), then

```
> (car L)
1
> (cdr L)
(2 3)
> (cons 4 L)
(4 1 2 3)
```

The names c a r and c d r are a historical accident. The first machine that LISP was implemented on was an IBM 704, and addresses or pointers were used to represent lists in such a way that the head of a list was the "Contents of the Address Register," or car, and the tail of a list was the "Contents of the Decrement Register," or cdr. This historical accident persists in all modern LISPs, partially because of the normal resistance to change by programmers, but more important because of another accident: because of the single letter difference in the names of the operations, repeated applications of both can be combined by combining the letters "a" and "d" between the "c" and the "r." Thus (c a r (c d r L)) becomes (c a d r L), (c d r (c d r L)) becomes (c d d r L), and (c a r (c d r (c d r L))) becomes (c a d d r L). For clarity, however, we will avoid these abbreviations.

The view of a list as a pair of values represented by the c a r and the c d r has also continued to be useful as a representation or visualization of a list. According to this view a list L is a pointer to a "box" of two pointers, one to its car and the other to its cdr.

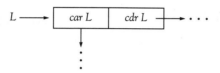

This "box notation" for a simple list such as (1 2 3) is as follows:

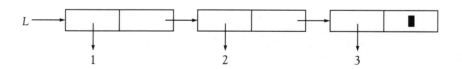

(The symbol ■ in the box at the end stands for the empty list.)
For a more complicated example, see Figure 10-1.

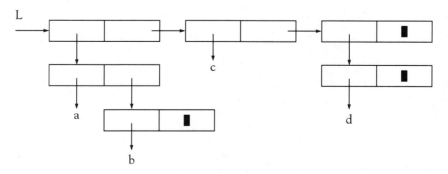

Figure 10-1   Box Notation for the List L = ((a b) c (d))

A box diagram is useful for interpreting the list operations: the car operation represents following the first pointer, while the cdr operation represents following the second pointer. Thus, for the L of Figure 10-1, (car (car L)) = a, (cdr (car L)) = (b), and (car (cdr (cdr L)) = (d).

All the basic list manipulation operations can be written as functions using the primitives car, cdr, and cons. For example, an append operation that returns the appended list of two lists can be written as follows:

```
(define (append L M)
  (if (null? L) M
      (cons (car L) (append (cdr L) M))))
```

and a reverse operation is as follows:

```
(define (reverse L)
  (if (null? L) ()
      (append (reverse (cdr L)) (list (car L)))))
```

In the reverse function we use the primitive function list, which makes an item into a list:

```
> (list 2)
(2)

> (list '(a b))
((a b))
```

The use of the list function is necessary, since append needs both its parameters to be lists.

Finally, we offer the example of the use of car and cdr to access the elements of a binary search tree defined as a list with structure (data leftchild rightchild):

```
(define (leftchild B) (car (cdr B)))

(define (rightchild B) (car (cdr (cdr B))))

(define (data B) (car B))
```

Now we can write a tree traversal program as follows:

```
(define (traverse B)
  (cond ((null? B) ())
        (T (traverse (leftchild B))
           (display (data B))
           (traverse (rightchild B)))))
```

10.3.3   Programming Techniques in Scheme

Programming in Scheme, as in any functional language, relies on recursion to perform loops and other repetitive operations. One standard technique for applying repeated operations to a list is to "cdr down and cons up"— meaning we apply the operation recursively to the tail of a list and then collect the result with the cons operator by constructing a new list with the current result. An example is the append procedure. Another example is a procedure to square all the members in a list of numbers:

```
(define (sqr-lis L)
  (if (null? L) ()
      (cons (* (car L) (car L)) (sqr-lis
       (cdr L)))))
```

An example of a loop that is not applied to a list is a procedure that simply prints out the squares of integers from 1 to n:

```
(define (print-sqrs low high)
  (cond ((> low high) ())
        (T (display (* low low))
           (newline)
           (print-sqrs (+ 1 low) high))))
```

A call to (print-sqrs 1 100) will generate the desired result.

In the print-sqrs example we had to use the extra parameter low to control the recursion, just as a loop index controls repetition. At the end of the last section we noted that, in such cases, tail-recursive procedures are preferred because of the relative ease with which translators can optimize them into actual loops. In fact, the print-sqrs function is tail recursive. In Scheme, however, the language goes one step farther: the language *defines* tail recursion as equivalent to a loop in a procedural language. That is, a Scheme compiler or interpreter *must* perform tail recursion more efficiently than a standard call. This means that in Scheme one should program as much as possible using tail-recursive procedures.

In the last section we also demonstrated the technique of using an accumulating parameter to turn a non-tail-recursive procedure into a tail-recursive one. As an example in Scheme, we apply this technique to the sqr-lis function by defining a helping procedure sqr-lis1 with an extra parameter to accumulate the intermediate result:

```
(define (sqr-lis1 L listsofar)
  (if (null? L) listsofar
      (sqr-lis1 (cdr L)
        (append listsofar (list (* (car L)
         (car L)))))))
```

Now we define sqr−lis as a call to sqr−lis1 with nil as its first accumulated value:

```
(define (sqr−lis L) (sqr-lis1 L ()))
```

Similarly, for reverse one defines reverse1 and reverse as follows:

```
(define (reverse1 L listsofar)
       (if (null? L) listsofar
           (reverse1 (cdr L) (append listsofar
                                     (list (car L)))))))
(define (reverse L) (reverse1 L ()))
```

10.3.4   Higher-Order Functions

Since functions are first-class values in Scheme, we can write functions that take other functions as parameters and functions that return functions as values. (Such functions are called higher-order functions.)

To give a simple example of a function with a function parameter, we can write a function apply-to-all that applies another function to all the elements in a list and then pass it the sqr function to get the sqr-lis example:

```
(define (apply−to−all f L)
(if (null? L) ()
    (cons (f (car L)) (apply-to-all f (cdr L)))))

(define (sqr x) (* x x))

(define (sqr−lis L) (apply−to−all sqr L))
```

Here is an example of a function that has a function parameter and also returns a function value:

```
(define (make−double f)
  (define (doublefn x) (f x x))
  doublefn)
```

This function assumes that f is a function with two parameters and creates the function that repeats the parameter x in a call to f. The function value doublefn returned by make−double is created by a local define and then written at the end to make it the returned value of make−double. Note that x is not a parameter to make−double itself but to the function created by make−double.

We can use make-double to get both the sqr function and the double function (a function that doubles its numerical value):

```
(define sqr (make-double *))
(define double (make-double +))
```

The symbols "*" and "+" are the names for the multiplication and addition functions. Their values—which are function values—are passed to the make-double procedure, which in turn returns function values that are assigned to the names sqr and double. Note that we are using here the simple form of the define, which just assigns computed values rather than defining a function with a given body. Just as

```
(define a 2)
```

assigns the value 2 to the name a, the expression

```
(define sqr (make-double *))
```

assigns the function value returned by make-double to the name sqr.

Indeed, we have until now always used the function version of define to create functions with a given name. Scheme also has a way of creating function values directly, without having to give them a name. The expression that creates a function value in Scheme is called a **lambda expression**—the word *lambda* is the name of the Greek symbol "λ" and is borrowed from lambda calculus (Section 10.7).

A lambda expression has the following form

```
(lambda param-list body)
```

and can be used to define functions directly, as in

```
(define sqr (lambda (x) (* x x)))
```

or

```
(define gcd (lambda (u v)
             (if (= v 0) u
                (gcd v (remainder u v)))))
```

Thus the second version of define is just a different way of writing the first version:

```
(define (sqr x) (* x x))
```

is completely equivalent to

```
(define sqr (lambda (x) (* x x)))
```

Lambda expressions can also be used directly, without giving a name to the function value, as in

```
((lambda (x) (* x x)) 2)
```

This applies the function constructed by the lambda expression—the square function—directly to 2, returning the value 4. The same process can be applied to construct function parameters directly:

```
(define (square-lis L)
    (apply-to-all
        (lambda (x) (* x x)) L))
```

In this example, the square function is constructed by a lambda expression right in the call to apply-to-all.

We can also use lambdas in let expressions to assign local names to functions. For example, the following code represents a local construction and application of the square function:

```
(let ((sqr (lambda (n) (* n n))))
    (display (sqr (read))))
```

Unfortunately, the let cannot be used to define recursive functions, since let bindings cannot refer to themselves or each other. Thus the following code will generate an error:

```
(let ((fact (lambda (n) (if (= n 0) 1 (* n
                                (fact (- n 1)))))))
    (display (fact (read))))
```

For such situations there is a different construct, called letrec, that is just like a let, except that it allows arbitrary recursive references within the binding list:

```
(letrec
    ((fact (lambda (n) (if (= n 0) 1 (* n (fact
                                (- n 1)))))))
    (display (fact (read))))
```

Finally, we can also use lambdas to return constructed function values in higher-order functions, thus making the use of a local define unnecessary. For example, the make-double function can be written as follows:

```
(define (make-double f)
    (lambda (x) (f x x)))
```

The composition function for two functions with a single parameter can be written using a lambda to construct the returned value, as follows:

```
(define (compose g f)
  (lambda (x) (g (f x))))
```

As we have noted at the end of Section 10.2 and in Chapter 7, this ability of functional languages, including Scheme, to return function values from higher-order functions, means that the runtime environment of functional languages is more complicated than the stack-based environment of a standard block-structured procedural language. Indeed, since the activation record of a function cannot in general be returned to free storage on exit from a call without causing dangling references, activations must be retained until all references to them have disappeared. Returning activations to free storage then requires the use of automatic memory management techniques, such as **garbage collection,** which are studied in Section 10.8.

As a final example of a higher-order function, we can rewrite the example of Section 7.6.4 of a make-new-balance function with a local variable that persists after the call that allocates it:

```
(define (make-new-balance balance)
  (lambda (amount)
    (if   (< balance amount) "Insufficient funds"
        (set! balance (- balance amount)))))
```

This function uses the nonfunctional construct set!, which is Scheme's assignment function. Its use signals that balance is being used as a variable instead of as an (unchangeable) value parameter. Every call to make-new-balance creates a new environment that persists as long as its local state, represented by the variable balance, is accessible through its returned function value:

```
> (define withdraw1 (make-new-balance 100))
withdraw1

> (define withdraw2 (make-new-balance 100))
withdraw2

> (withdraw1 20)
80

> (withdraw2 50)
50

> (withdraw1 20)
60

> (withdraw2 60)
Insufficient funds
```

Persistent local environments in Scheme can be used to control the scope of variables and the access to those variables. In the preceding example the variable `balance` cannot be changed except by calling the function returned by the `make-new-balance` function. Thus Scheme can encapsulate functions and variables in local environments. This is no longer functional programming, since it uses variables and assignments. It is really object-oriented programming, and such methods can be used in Scheme to achieve implementations of abstract data types (although Scheme does not have facilities for separating specification from implementation).

10.4 ML AND *Miranda:* FUNCTIONAL PROGRAMMING WITH STATIC TYPING

ML and Miranda are two recently developed functional programming languages that are quite different from versions of LISP, such as Scheme. First, they have a more Algol-like syntax, which avoids the use of many parentheses. Second, they are strongly typed: the type of every expression is determined before execution, and types can be checked for consistency. While traditional LISP programmers may dislike the constraints of a strong type system, there are significant advantages: the language is more secure, in that more errors can be found prior to execution, especially important in instructional settings and for good software engineering. There is also the efficiency to be gained by being able to predetermine size and allocation requirements. Also, ML and Miranda have a significant advantage over traditional strongly typed languages such as Pascal and C: they do not insist that *all* types be declared by the programmer, but they contain a **type inference system,** so that types can be inferred from available information by the translator. Both languages also allow polymorphism, where expressions can under certain circumstances range over a set of types.

ML (for MetaLanguage) began in the late 1970s as part of a system for proving the correctness of programs: the Edinburgh Logic for Computable Functions (LCF) system developed by a team led by Robin Milner. Milner also developed a strong typing inference system based on a pattern matching method called **unification,** a principle that is also used in Prolog (see Chapter 11). The current Standard ML is a combination of the earlier language and the HOPE language, developed by Rod Burstall, also at Edinburgh. ML is a language with a semantics like Scheme in that it has static scoping and an applicative order evaluation rule. Unlike Scheme it is strongly typed, has type declarations, and has a module facility.

Miranda is a language developed by David Turner based on the languages SASL and KRC. It has a type system very similar to, and based on, that of ML, but Miranda differs from ML in a number of essential ways. First, Miranda is a pure functional language in the sense of Section 10.1: there are no variables and no assignments. Second, Miranda uses a different evaluation rule than either Scheme or ML, called **lazy evaluation,** which is a kind of delayed evaluation, and is studied in more detail in Section 10.5. Third, the language contains a powerful method for expressing iterated lists of values, called list comprehensions.

In the following paragraphs we will give a brief overview of these two languages to reveal some of their flavor and to indicate in more detail their differences from Scheme, and from each other.

10.4.1   ML

In ML the basic program is, as in Scheme, a function declaration. As a first example we give the factorial function in ML:

```
> fun fact n = if n = 0 then 1
                            else n * fact(n-1);
val fact = fn: int -> int
```

The reserved word fun in ML introduces a function declaration. The identifier immediately after fun is the name of the function, and the names of the parameters follow, up to the equal sign. After the equal sign is the body of the function.

The ML system responds to a declaration by returning the data type of the value defined. In this example, fact is a function, so ML responds that the value of fact is fn, with type int -> int, which means that fact is a function from integers to integers. Indeed, we could have given type declarations for the type of fact and the type of its parameter as follows:

```
> fun fact (n: int): int = if n = 0 then 1
                            else n * fact(n-1);
val fact = fn: int -> int
```

The ML system, however, can deduce the types of n and fact from the expression in the body after the "=". How ML does this is indicated later.

Once a function has been declared it can be called as follows:

```
> fact 5;
120 : int
```

ML responds with the returned value and its type. ML has essentially the same evaluation rule as Scheme: fact must evaluate to a function; then 5 is evaluated, and its type must agree with the parameter type of the function. The function is then called and its returned value printed together with its type. ML, however, does not need a quote as in Scheme to prevent evaluation, since data is distinct from programs. There is also almost no need for parentheses in ML, as the system can determine the meaning of items based solely on their position.

ML also has the equivalent of a lambda expression in Scheme, except that the reserved word fn is used in place of lambda:

```
> val sqr = fn x: int => x * x;
val sqr = fn : int -> int
```

This definition of sqr is equivalent to the following:

```
> fun sqr x: int = x * x; (* int declares the
                                  type of sqr *)
```

Function expressions can also be applied directly, as in Scheme:

```
> (fn x: int => x * x) 2
4 : int
```

Note that the type declaration of sqr as an int function is necessary, since x could also be real or any other type with an operation named "*". Without the type declaration ML responds as follows:

```
> fun sqr x = x * x;
Unresolvable overloaded identifier: x
```

The function cannot be defined because the system cannot tell whether to use real or integer multiplication for "*", since the type of x cannot be deduced from the available information. Alternative type declarations for the sqr function are also possible:

```
> fun sqr (x: int) = x * x
            (* declares x to be of type int *)
> fun sqr (x: int): int = x * x;
            (* declares both x and sqr to be int *)
```

In the case of recursive functions, the additional reserved word rec (for "recursive") must be used when using a function expression, since the name of the function must be known before the body is processed. Thus we must write for the fact function:

```
> val rec fact = fn n => if n = 0 then 1
                                  else n * fact(n−1);
val fact = fn : int -> int
```

Declarations using the fun keyword are automatically assumed to be recursive.

ML, unlike Scheme and other LISPs, complains if the type of an expression disagrees with its expected type:

```
> sqr 2.5;
Type Clash in: sqr 2.5
Looking for a:  int
I have found a: real
```

ML will also not automatically convert types:

```
> fun realsqr x: real = x * x;
val realsqr = fn : real -> real

> realsqr 2;
Type Clash in: realsqr 2
Looking for a:  real
I have found a: int

> realsqr (real 2);
4.0 : real
```

As an example of a slightly more complicated function in ML, here is Euclid's algorithm (gcd):

```
> fun gcd (n,m) : int = if m = 0 then n
                               else gcd (m, n mod m) ;
val gcd -> fn : int * int -> int
  (* this type is explained below *)

> gcd (15,10);
5 : int
```

Data Structures in ML.   Unlike Scheme, ML has a rich set of data-types, from enumerated types to records to lists. We will give only the briefest overview of this rich type structure.

Lists in ML are written using brackets and commas:

```
> [1,2,3];
[1,2,3] : int list
```

Elements in a list must all have the same type: the preceding list is a list of integers and so has the type int list.

There is a constructor operation (similar to cons in LISP) given by a double colon:

```
> 1 :: [2,3];
[1,2,3] : int list
```

If we want to collect together data of different types in ML we cannot use lists: [1,2.5] is an error, since it combines an integer and a real number. We must instead use a **tuple:**

```
> (1,2.5);
(1,2.5) : int*real
```

Tuples are just Cartesian product types, as discussed in Chapter 6, hence the notation int•real. In a function definition where there is more than one parameter, such as the gcd function, we can use a tuple to collect the parameters together:

```
> fun gcd (u,v) : int = ...;
```

gives the type int•int -> int for gcd.

ML also has enumerated types, which can be defined in a datatype declaration:

```
> datatype direction = north | east | south | west;
```

The vertical bar is used for alternative values in the declaration and the names, such as north and east, are called **value constructors.** ML views such a declaration as the creation of **patterns to be matched,** and ML has a built-in pattern matcher similar to that of Prolog (Chapter 11). This pattern matcher can be used to program functions as the following example shows:

```
> fun heading north = 0.0 |
      heading east   = 90.0 |
      heading south  = 180.0 |
      heading west   = 270.0 ;
val heading = fn : direction -> real
```

We could have used patterns to define functions of existing data types as well—for example,

```
> fun gcd (u,0) : int = u |
      gcd (u,v) : int = gcd (v,u mod v);
```

Patterns can also be used to retrieve the head and tail of a list (like car and cdr in LISP):

```
> fun hd (a::x) = a
> fun tl (a::x) = x
```

An ML system will give information on whether cases overlap or are incomplete. For example, if we had given the incomplete definition

```
> fun heading north = 0.0 |
      heading east   = 90.0 |
      heading south  = 180.0 ;
```

then ML will issue a warning such as "patterns not exhaustive."

Similarly, if patterns overlap, ML will give a warning. For example in the definition of g c d using patterns, the first and second patterns overlap. In this case ML will use the first pattern that matches, which is exactly what we want.

Recursive types such as binary search trees are also declared using patterns:

```
> datatype bst = empty | node of string*bst*bst;
```

An example of a node of a binary search tree is n o d e (" d o g " , e m p t y , emp t y).

We can define d a t a, l e f t c h i l d, and r i g h t c h i l d functions by pattern matching. For example,

```
> fun leftchild node(s,l,r) = l;
val leftchild = fn : bst -> bst
```

Note that this does not define l e f t c h i l d of emp t y. Since there is no l e f t c h i l d of emp t y, this should cause an error, and to give a complete definition of l e f t c h i l d, we use the **exception** mechanism of ML (see Section 7.7 for exception handling mechanisms):

```
> exception leftchild;
```

```
> fun leftchild empty = raise leftchild |
      leftchild node(s,l,r) = l;
```

A traversal function for binary search trees that prints out the string nodes is as follows:

```
> fun traverse empty = {} |
     traverse node (s,l,r) =
              (traverse l ;
               output (std_out,s);
               traverse r)
```

Here we have used a couple of new symbols. "{ }" refers to a **unit** type that has only one value. It is used when the returned value of the function is immaterial and is similar to the v o i d type of C. We have also written a sequence of operations in the t r a v e r s e function by using parentheses and semicolons: (op1; ... ;opn) represents the sequence of instructions o p 1, ... , o p n.

Type Inference and Type Checking in ML.   ML is strongly typed in that every expression has a static type, and these types are checked by an ML translator prior to execution. But ML allows some of the types in an expression to be **type variables** in that the type of a subexpression can be undetermined and depend on the actual type supplied during execution. For example, the hd and tl functions defined earlier can apply to any list type. ML considers these functions to have a type variable that is the base type of the list:

```
> hd
val hd = fn : 'a list -> 'a

> tl
val tl = fn : 'a list -> 'a list
```

The symbol "'a" in the preceding types is a type variable. ML prints type variables as "'a", "'b", "'c", and so on. A function whose type contains type variables is **polymorphic,** as described in Chapter 8, in that the type variables refer to fixed but arbitrary types, which are replaced by actual types when the functions are applied. There can be more than one type variable in a type expression. For example, the function fst that returns the first element in a tuple of length 2 is defined as follows:

```
> fun fst (x,y) = x;
val fst = fn : 'a * 'b -> 'a
```

ML uses pattern matching to resolve type variables during execution. For example, if the hd function is applied to the int list [1,2,3]:

```
> hd [1,2,3];
1: int
```

to get the type of the result to be int, ML matches int list with 'a list in the type of hd, thus matching 'a with int. Then the type variable 'a is replaced with int in the result type of hd:

```
hd        : 'a list -> 'a
[1,2,3] : int list (* 'a = int *)
hd [1,2,3] = 1 : int
```

ML also uses pattern matching to determine statically the type of functions with incomplete type information given in declarations. This process is called **type inference.** The information from ML's type inference process is then also used to perform static type checking of expressions. As an example, consider how ML determines the type of the factorial function

```
> fun fact n = if n = 0 then 1
                              else n * fact (n-1);
val fact = fn : int -> int
```

ML first assigns type variables to n and f a c t:

```
n     : 'a
fact : 'a -> 'b
```

Then the i f expression is type-checked, which requires that the first expression n = 0 be Boolean and that the types of the result expressions match. Now n = 0 is indeed a Boolean expression, but is only type correct if n is an integer. Thus type variable 'a = i n t and we get

```
n     : int
fact : int -> 'b
```

Then the types of the result expressions are determined and compared: 1 is an integer, and n * f a c t (n − 1) is an integer, since n is an integer. Thus the result type of f a c t must also be i n t, giving 'b = i n t. Thus the complete expression is type correct with 'a = i n t and 'b = i n t.

By contrast, the function definition

```
> fun sqr x = x * x;
```

does not have a well-defined type, since the multiplication on the right-hand side forces x to be of type r e a l or i n t, so s q r is either of type f n : i n t -> i n t or f n : r e a l -> r e a l. s q r cannot be of type f n : 'a -> 'a, since 'a could be any type, while the definition of s q r requires 'a to be r e a l or i n t. Thus s q r does not have a well-defined type according to the ML type system.

As a second example of type inference using pattern matching, consider the following function definition, which itself uses pattern matching:

```
> fun mkpairs [] = [] |
      mkpairs (x::y) = (x,x) :: (mkpairs y);
```

This function takes a list of arbitrary elements and returns a list of pairs of the elements of the given list:

```
> mkpairs [1,2,3];
[(1,1), (2,2), (3,3)] : (int*int) list
```

ML determines the type of mkpairs as follows. From the first expression for mkpairs,

```
mkpairs [] = []
```

ML concludes that mkpairs takes a list as a parameter and returns a list as its result. Thus, so far, it infers that the type of mkpairs is

```
'a list -> 'b list
```

From the second expression for mkpairs,

```
mkpairs (x::y) = (x,x) :: (mkpairs y);
```

it concludes that x must be of type 'a and that (x, x) must be of type 'b. Pattern matching then gives the result

```
'b = 'a * 'a
```

and ML infers that the type of mkpairs is

```
'a list -> ('a * 'a) list
```

10.4.2   Miranda

Miranda is a functional language that has adopted many of the features of ML, particularly the type system and pattern matching. Miranda has, however, no variables or assignment, and so is completely referentially transparent, unlike practically every other functional language, including ML and Scheme. Miranda also uses a different evaluation rule called lazy evaluation, which is studied in the next section.

Function declarations in Miranda are called **scripts,** and they resemble declarations in ML using pattern matching:

```
fact 0 = 1
fact n = n * fact (n-1)
```

This defines fact to be a partial function, since it is not defined for n < 0. (In Miranda there is no need for a fun symbol before the declaration, since Miranda distinguishes expressions from definitions by having all definitions stored in a script file.)

In Miranda one can also give function definitions using **guards,** which are Boolean expressions that control the applicability of a definition:

```
fact n = 1, if n = 0
fact n = n * fact (n-1), if n > 0
```

The guards in the foregoing declarations are n = 0 and n > 0. They are separated from the body of the declaration by a comma and the reserved word if and always come after the body.

Miranda has lists, such as [1,2,3], and tuples, such as (1,2) as data types, similar to ML. Some functions on lists and tuples are

```
len [] = 0
len (hd:tl) = 1 + len tl
reverse [] = []
reverse (hd:tl) = reverse tl ++ [hd]

take 0 l = []
take n [] = []
take n (hd:tl) = hd : take (n-1) tl

fst (a,b) = a
snd (a,b) = b
```

In the foregoing, the notation (hd:tl) is a pattern that stands for a list whose head (or car) is hd and whose tail (or cdr) is tl. Thus, if (hd:tl) = [1,2,3], then hd = 1 and tl = [2,3]. The "++" function is concatenation of lists, so that [1,2]++[3,2] = [1,2,3,2]. And the take function returns the first n items in a list:

```
take 3 [1,2,3,4] = [1,2,3]
take 1 [1,2,3,4] = [1]
```

Miranda has strong typing with type variables like ML, except that symbols for type variables in Miranda are *, **, ***, . . . instead of the ML notation 'a, 'b, 'c, ... Miranda also condenses all numeric types into one type num. Thus a square function

```
sqr x = x * x
```

is legal in Miranda but not in ML. Here are Miranda types for some of the foregoing functions:

```
sqr :: num -> num
fact :: num -> num
len :: [*] -> num
reverse :: [*] -> [*]
fst :: (*,**) -> *
snd :: (*,**) -> **
```

Miranda has special list constructors similar to mathematical set constructors, called list comprehensions. A list comprehension has the syntax [body | qualifiers], indicating the set of body satisfying qualifiers. A typical example is

```
evens n = [i | i <- [1..n]; i mod 2 = 0]
```

which represents the even integers between 1 and n. This says that e v e n s n consist of the items i, where i is taken from the set [1 . . n], and i mod 2 = 0. Another example is

```
factors  n  =  [i | i <- [1..n div 2]; n mod i = 0]
```

As an example of how programs can be made extremely compact using list comprehensions, we give the example of QUICKSORT in Miranda:

```
qsort [] = []
qsort (a:l) = qsort [x | x <- l; x <= a] ++
              [a] ++ qsort [x | x <- l; x > a]
```

10.5   *DELAYED EVALUATION*

An important problem that arises in the design and use of functional languages is the distinction between "ordinary" functions and special forms. As we have already noted, in a language with an applicative order evaluation rule, such as Scheme and ML, all parameters to user-defined functions are evaluated at the time of a call, even though it may not be necessary to do so—or even wrong to do so.

Typical examples that we have mentioned before are the Boolean functions a n d and o r and the i f function. In the case of the a n d function, the Scheme expression (a n d a b) or the infix expression a a n d b in a language like Pascal, need not evaluate the parameter b if a evaluates to false. This is called short-circuit evaluation of Boolean expressions, and it is an example of the usefulness of delayed evaluation. In the case of the i f function, it is not a case of just usefulness, but of necessity: for the expression (i f a b c) in Scheme to have the proper semantics, the evaluation of b and c must be delayed until the result of a is known, and based on that, either b or c is evaluated, but never both. For this reason, an i f function cannot be written as a standard user-defined function in Scheme, ML, or Pascal. It also means that Scheme and ML must distinguish between two kinds of predefined functions, those that use standard evaluation and those that do not (the special forms). This compromises the uniformity and extendibility of these languages, since programmers cannot use standard mechanisms to extend the language.

A possible argument for restricting function evaluation to applicative order evaluation is that the semantics (and the implementation) are simpler. Consider the case of a function call in which one parameter may have an undefined value, such as in the Scheme expression (a n d (= 1 0) (= 1 (/ 1 0))) or its Pascal equivalent (1 = 0) a n d (1 = 1 d i v 0). In this case delayed evaluation can lead to a well-defined result, even though subexpressions or parameters may be undefined. Functions with this property are called **nonstrict,** and languages with the property that functions are strict are easier to implement. In essence, strict languages satisfy a strong form of the GIGO principle (garbage in, garbage out), in that they will consistently fail to produce results when given incomplete or malformed input, while nonstrict languages may nevertheless produce a (possibly faulty) result. Strictness also has an important simplifying effect on formal semantics (formal semantics are discussed in Chapter 12).

Nevertheless, as we have seen, nonstrictness can be a desirable property. It is interesting to note that the language Algol60 included delayed evaluation in its pass by name parameter passing convention, discussed in Chapter 7. According to pass by name evaluation, a parameter is evaluated only when it is actually used in the code of the called procedure. Thus the function

```
function p(x: boolean; y: integer): integer;
begin
  if x then p := 1
  else p := y;
end;
```

will, using pass by name evaluation, return the value 1 when called as p(true,1 div 0), since y is never reached in the code of p, and so the value of y—the undefined expression 1 div 0—will never be computed.

In a language that has function values, it is possible to delay the evaluation of a parameter by putting it inside a function "shell" (a function with no parameters). For example, in Modula-2, we can achieve the same effect as pass by name in the previous example by writing

```
TYPE IntProc = PROCEDURE (): INTEGER;
PROCEDURE DivByZero () : INTEGER;
BEGIN
  RETURN 1 DIV 0 ;
END DivByZero;

PROCEDURE p(x: BOOLEAN; y: IntProc) : INTEGER;
BEGIN
  IF x THEN RETURN 1;
  ELSE RETURN y();
  END;
END p;
```

and calling p(TRUE,DivByZero). (Sometimes such "shell" procedures as DivByZero are referred to as **pass by name thunks,** or just thunks, for somewhat obscure historical reasons.) In Scheme and ML, this process of surrounding parameters with function shells is even easier, since the lambda and fn function value constructors can be used directly, as in the following Scheme definition:

```
(define (p x y) (if x 1 (y)))
```

which can be called as follows:

```
(p #T (lambda () (/ 1 0)))
```

Note that the code of p must change to reflect the function parameter y — y must be surrounded by parentheses to force a call to y. Otherwise the function itself and not its value will be returned.

Indeed, Scheme has two functions that do precisely what we have been describing. The special form delay delays the evaluation of its arguments and returns an object that can be thought of as a lambda "shell," or **promise** to evaluate its arguments. The corresponding procedure force causes its parameter, which must be a delayed object, to be evaluated. Thus the function p would be written as

```
(define (p x y) (if x 1 (force y)))
```

and called as

```
(p #T (delay (/ 1 0)))
```

Inefficiency results from delayed evaluation when the same delayed expression is repeatedly evaluated. For example, in the delayed version of the square procedure,

```
(define (delayed-sqr x) (* (force x) (force x)))
```

the parameter x will be evaluated twice in the body of delayed-sqr, which is inefficient if x is a complicated expression. In fact, Scheme has an improvement to pass by name built into the force function. Scheme uses a **memoization** process, where the value of a delayed object is stored the first time the object is forced, and then subsequent calls to force simply return the previous value rather than recomputing it. (This kind of parameter evaluation is sometimes referred to as **pass by need.**)

Pass by name delayed evaluation is helpful in that it allows parameters to remain uncomputed if not needed and permits special forms such as if and cond to be defined as ordinary functions. However, pass by name is not able to handle more complex situations where only parts of each parameter are needed in a computation. Consider the following simple example of a take procedure that returns the first n items of a list (this procedure was described earlier in Miranda):

```
(define (take n L)
  (if (= n 0) ()
      (cons (car L) (take (- n 1) (cdr L)))))
```

If we write a version in which the computation of L is delayed,

```
(define (take n L)
  (if (= n 0) ()
      (cons (car (force L)) (take (- n 1)
                                  (cdr (force L))))))
```

then a call (take 1 (delay) L) will force the evaluation of the entire list L, even though we are interested in the very first element only. This can be disastrously inefficient if L happens to be a very long list produced by a list generation procedure such as

```
(define (intlist m n)
  (if (> m n) () (cons m (intlist (+ 1 m) n))))
```

Now a call (take 1 (delay (intlist 2 100))) will still construct the entire list (2..100) before taking the first element to produce the list (2). What is needed is a delay in the second parameter to cons in intlist as well:

```
(define (intlist m n)
  (if (> m n) () (cons m (delay (intlist
                                  (+ 1 m) n))))))
```

so that taking (cdr (cons m (delay ...))) returns a delayed object to the recursive call to take. Thus we have the following sequence of events in this computation, where each delayed object is represented by the computation it "promises" to perform enclosed in quotes:

1. The call (take 1 (delay (intlist 2 100))) causes the delayed object "(intlist 2 100)" to be passed as L to

```
(cons (car (force L)) (take (- 1 1)
                            (cdr (force L))))
```

2. The first call to (force L) in the cons causes L to be evaluated to

```
(cons 2 ((delay (intlist (+ 1 2) 100))))
```

which causes the construction of the list with head 2 and tail the delayed object "(intlist (+ 1 2) 100)."

3. The car of (force L) returns 2 from the cons, leaving the following expression to be evaluated:

```
(cons 2 (take (- 1 1) (cdr (force L))))
```

4. The call to (take (− 1 1) (cdr (force L))) causes (− 1 1) to be evaluated to 0, and the cdr of (force L) to be evaluated to the delayed object "(intlist (+ 1 2) 100)" as constructed in step 2. Then the expression (take 0 "(intlist (+ 1 2) 100)") is evaluated, which returns the empty list () without forcing the evaluation of (intlist (+ 1 2) 100).

5. The result of (cons 2 ()) is finally evaluated, returning the list (2). Thus the rest of the integer list is never computed.

The scenario we have just described is called **fully lazy evaluation,** or just lazy evaluation for short. It can be achieved in a functional language without explicit calls to delay and force by requiring the runtime environment to evaluate expressions according to the following rules:

1. All arguments to user-defined functions are delayed.

2. All bindings of local names in let and letrec expressions are delayed.

3. All arguments to constructor functions (such as cons) are delayed.

4. All arguments to other predefined functions, such as the arithmetic functions "+," "∗," and so on are forced.

5. All function-valued arguments are forced.

6. All conditions in selection functions such as if and cond are forced.

These rules allow operations on long lists to compute only as much of the list as is necessary. It is also possible to include potentially infinite lists in languages with lazy evaluation, since the "infinite" part will never be computed, but only as much of the list as is needed for a particular computation. To express the potentially infinite nature of such lists, lists that obey lazy evaluation rules are often called **streams.** A stream can be thought of as a partially computed list whose remaining elements can continue to be computed up to any desired number. Streams are an important issue in functional programming: to eliminate side effect completely, one has to introduce input and output into functional languages as streams, and both Scheme and ML have ad hoc stream constructions (besides the manual delay and force procedures mentioned earlier), which we do not study here.

An example of a functional language with fully lazy evaluation is Miranda. Miranda can represent infinite lists by recursive definitions such as

```
nats i = i : nats (i+1)
```

which defines the natural numbers as a stream beginning with i (the : operator is Miranda for cons). Such a recursive definition would cause an immediate recursive loop in a language without lazy evaluation. It works as follows in Miranda: for each successive number i + 1, i + 2 that is required by a computation, the call to nats(i+1), nats(i+2), and so on is forced and is then immediately delayed again at the next recursive call. Thus nats 0 is the list beginning with 0, which can also be written in Miranda using the abbreviated notation [0..].

Such infinite lists cannot be printed out, of course, but any finite part can. The take function is available for extracting any piece of an infinite list:

```
take 4 [0..] = [0,1,2,3]
```

Lazy evaluation permits a style of functional programming that allows us to separate a computation into pieces, consisting of procedures that generate streams and other procedures that modify streams, without worrying about the efficiency of each step. Procedures that generate streams are called **generators,** and procedures that modify streams are called **filters,** and we will call this style of programming **generator-filter programming.** For example, the intlist procedure in a previous Scheme example is a generator, and the take procedure is a filter.

A famous problem in functional programming that requires generator-filter programming is the **same-fringe** problem for lists. Two lists have the same fringe if they contain the same non-null atoms in the same order, or to put it another way, when written as trees, their non-null leaves taken in left-to-right order are the same. For example, the lists ((2 (3)) 4) and (2 (3 4 ())) have the same fringe. To determine whether two lists have the same fringe, we must **flatten** them to just lists of their atoms:

```
(define (flatten L)
   (cond ((null? L) ())
         ((atom? L) (cons L ()))
         (#T (append (flatten (car L)) (flatten
            (cdr L))))))
```

In the case of both lists in the previous paragraph, flatten returns the list (2 3 4). Flatten can be viewed as a filter, which then can be used as the input to the samefringe procedure, as follows:

```
(define (eqlist? L M)
   (or (and (null? L) (null? M))
       (and (eq? (car L) (car M)) (eqlist? (cdr L)
          (cdr M)))))

(define (samefringe L M) (eqlist? (flatten L)
                                   (flatten M)))
```

The problem with this computation under the usual Scheme evaluation rule is that flatten will produce complete lists of the atoms of L and M, even if L and M differ already in their first fringe elements. Lazy evaluation, on the other hand, will compute only enough of the flattened lists as necessary before their elements disagree. (Of course, if the lists actually do have the same fringe, the entire lists must be processed.)

A similar situation arises when using the sieve of Eratosthenes to compute prime numbers. In this method, a list of consecutive integers from 2 is generated, and each successive remaining number in the list is used to cancel out its multiples in the list. Thus, beginning with the list (2 3 4 5 6 7 8 9 10 11), we first cancel multiples of 2, leaving the list (2 3 5 7 9 11). Then we cancel the multiples of 3, giving (2 3 5 7 11), and now we cancel all remaining multiples of 5, 7, and 11 (of which there are none) to obtain the list of primes from 2 to 11 as (2 3 5 7 11). Each cancellation step can be viewed as a filter on the list of the previous cancellation step. Using lazy evaluation and list comprehensions in Miranda, we obtain the extremely compact and efficient program that can compute any number of primes from 2 using the take filter ("$\sim =$" is Miranda for "not equal" in this code):

```
sieve (p : l) = p : sieve [n | n <- l ;
                                n mod p ~= 0]

primes = sieve [2..]
```

Now take 10 primes returns the list [2, 3, 5, 7, 11, 13, 17, 19, 23, 27]. Indeed, the list comprehension [n | n <- l ; p(n)] in Miranda can be viewed as a filter of the list l by the predicate p(n)—only those elements of l remain for which p(n) is true.

Why don't all functional languages use delayed evaluation? Part of the answer is contained in the remarks at the beginning of this section: it complicates the semantics of the language. In practical terms, this translates into an increased complexity in the runtime environment that must maintain the evaluation rules 1–6 listed earlier. But there is another reason: because of the interleaving of delays and forces, it is difficult to write programs with side effects, in particular, programs with variables that change as computation proceeds. In a way, this is similar to the synchronization problem for shared memory in parallel processing (studied in Chapter 13). Indeed, delayed evaluation has been described as a form of parallelism, with delay as a form of process suspension, and force a kind of process continuation (see the exercises of Chapter 13 for a little more in this vein). The principal point is that side effects, in particular variables and assignment, do not mix well with lazy evaluation. This is in part the reason that Miranda is purely functional, with no variables or assignment, and why Scheme and ML are strict languages, with some ad hoc stream and delayed evaluation facilities.

10.6 THE MATHEMATICS OF FUNCTIONAL PROGRAMMING I: RECURSIVE FUNCTIONS

In Section 10.1 we stated that a function f is a rule that associates to each element of a domain set X a unique element of a range set Y, and we write $f : X \rightarrow Y$. An alternative view is that f defines a collection of pairs of elements (x, y) of X and Y with the property that $y = f(x)$ and that each x is contained in at most one pair of such elements. (If (x, y) is such a pair and so is (x, y'), then $y = f(x)$ and $y' = f(x)$, so $y = y'$ and the pairs are the same.)

Thus a function can be viewed as a **set of pairs** (x, y) such that $y = f(x)$ or as a subset of the Cartesian product $X \times Y$:

$$f \equiv \{(x, y) \in X \times Y \mid y = f(x)\}$$

where $\equiv$ means "is equivalent to" and $\in$ means "is contained in."

Viewing a function as a set has certain advantages for the study of the definition of functions in programming languages. In particular, there are two standard methods for defining sets. First, we can list all its elements. Thus, for example,

$$\text{digit} = \{0, 1, 2, 3, 4, 5, 6, 7, 8, 9\}$$

represents the set of all digits. This method of set definition is sometimes called **definition by extension.** It is possible to define functions this way also. For example, the function on the set of digits that adds one to each digit (wrapping around at 9 in a modulo fashion) can be defined as follows:

$$\{(0,1), (1,2), (2,3), (3,4), (4,5), (5,6), (6,7), (7,8), (8,9), (9,0)\}$$

In a program this would be an unusual way of defining functions, since it would need to be a giant case-statement taking up many lines of code. Instead, the more common definition of a function is by a **formula** or **property.** For example, a formula expressing the definition of the previous function would be

$$f(x) = (x + 1) \bmod 10$$

or in set terminology

$$f \equiv \{(x, y) \in \text{digit} \times \text{digit} \mid y = (x + 1) \bmod 10\}$$

Definition by formula is sometimes called **definition by comprehension.**

In a purely functional language the body of a function given in its definition typically represents an equation that gives its definition by comprehension. For example, in the Miranda function definition

```
square x = x * x
```

we are saying that the square function is given as the set

$$\text{square} \equiv \{(x, y) \in \text{num} \times \text{num} \mid y = x \cdot x\}$$

Now let us consider recursive functions. The first thing to note is that the recursion can be thought of as purely part of the equation representing the definition of the function, as in the recursive definition of the factorial function:

$$\text{fact } n = \text{if } n = 0 \text{ then } 1 \text{ else } n \cdot \text{fact } (n-1)$$

Nothing in this equation expresses anything about the nature of the runtime environment required to implement it, or even that the use of fact on the right-hand side represents a call, while the left-hand side represents a definition. Thus, to be mathematically precise, we speak of a **recursive definition** rather than a recursive function.

Can we give a mathematical meaning to a recursive definition? In Chapters 4 and 6 we saw that recursive definitions of language syntax and data types were common and could be represented as particular solutions to certain recursive set equations. But functions are also sets, so we might expect that the same kind of theory would apply in this case too. And indeed it does, but with complications. If we want to write the equation for the fact function in set form, we must rewrite the right-hand side in terms of sets. One way to do this is to realize that the expression if $n = 0$ then 1 else $n \cdot f(n - 1)$ represents the union of two functions. The then-part represents the function $\{(0,1)\}$, that is, the function with the value 1 at 0, and no other values. The else-part represents the function $f'(n) = n \cdot f(n - 1)$, which takes the value of f at $n - 1$ and multiplies it by n. For example, if $f = \{(0,1), (1,2)\}$ (i.e., f has the two values $f(0) = 1$ and $f(1) = 2$), then

$$\begin{aligned}
f' &= \{(n, n \cdot f(n - 1)) \mid n - 1 \in \text{domain of } f\} \\
&= \{(n, n \cdot f(n - 1)) \mid n - 1 = 0 \text{ or } n - 1 = 1\} \\
&= \{(n, n \cdot f(n - 1)) \mid n = 1 \text{ or } n = 2\} \\
&= \{(1, 1 \cdot f(1 - 1)), (2, 2 \cdot f(2 - 1))\} \\
&= \{(1, 1 \cdot 1), (2, 2 \cdot 2)\} = \{(1,1), (2,2)\}
\end{aligned}$$

and the expression if $n = 0$ then 1 else $n \cdot f(n - 1)$ is the function represented by the set $\{(0,1) \cup \{(1,1), (2,2)\} = \{(0,1), (1,1), (2,2)\}$. With this interpretation, the set equation for fact is

$$\text{fact} = \{(0,1)\} \cup \text{fact}'$$

where $\text{fact}'(n) = n \cdot \text{fact}(n - 1)$ is constructed as outlined.

There is another interpretation of the function equation, however, that is based on higher-order functions (and that is more common in the theoretical literature). We think of the left-hand and right-hand sides of the equation as representing possibly two different functions f and g:

$$f(n) = \text{if } n = 0 \text{ then } 1 \text{ else } n \cdot g(n - 1)$$

Now the right-hand side of the equation has two parameters, namely, n and g. We can think of this as defining a higher-order function H as follows:

$$H(g)(n) = \text{if } n = 0 \text{ then } 1 \text{ else } n \cdot g(n - 1)$$

(The use of the name H is traditional for this function; see the next section.) Thus H is a function that takes a function as a parameter and returns a new function; that is, H is a higher-order function.

Now consider the factorial function. The definition of fact implies that:

$$H(\text{fact})(n) = \text{fact}(n)$$

or that $H(\text{fact}) = \text{fact}$. Thus the factorial function is a **fixed point** of the function H. Of course, this equation for H contains the same information as the set equation, and as with previous such equations in Chapters 4 and 6, we want the **smallest solution** to this equation to be the chosen definition of the fact function. For this reason, recursive function definitions are said to have **least-fixed-point semantics,** and fact is taken to be the least fixed point of the function H.

How can a least fixed point solution be constructed for fact? If we go back to the equation

$$\text{fact} \equiv \{(0,1)\} \cup \text{fact}'$$

we can see a way of building up fact as a set. Start with a function with no values at all, that is, the empty set $\varnothing$. Call this function fact_0. Then consider fact_0'. This function can have no values either, since it is based on the domain of fact. Now we construct a new function fact_1 using the equation, as follows:

$$\text{fact}_1 = \{(0,1)\} \cup \text{fact}_0' = \{(0,1)\} \cup \varnothing = \{(0,1)\}$$

We now have a function fact_1 that has one value, namely, $\text{fact}_1(0) = 1$. Now let us compute fact_1' from fact_1:

$$
\begin{aligned}
\text{fact}_1' &= \{(n, n \cdot \text{fact}(n - 1)) \mid n - 1 \in \text{domain of fact}_1\} \\
&= \{(n, n \cdot f(n - 1)) \mid n - 1 = 0\} \\
&= \{(n, n \cdot f(n - 1)) \mid n = 1\} \\
&= \{(1, 1 \cdot 1)\} = \{(1, 1)\}
\end{aligned}
$$

Finally, $\text{fact}_2 = \{(0,1)\} \cup \text{fact}_1' = \{(0,1)\} \cup \{(1,1)\} = \{(0,1), (1,1)\}$. We now have a function with two points! Continuing in this way we get

$$\text{fact}_3 = \{(0,1), (1,1), (2,2)\}$$

and

$$\text{fact}_4 = \{(0,1), (1,1), (2,2), (3,6)\}$$

The fact function is now the union of all these partial fact functions:

$$\text{fact} = \text{fact}_0 \cup \text{fact}_1 \cup \text{fact}_2 \cup \ \ldots$$

It is possible to show that this is indeed a smallest solution to the given set equation.

Note that the fact function we have constructed does indeed represent exactly those values of the fact function that would be computed by a series of recursive calls. Indeed, the definition we used gave fact only as a partial function with domain equal to the set of integers $>= 0$ (if a negative value is passed to fact, an infinite recursive loop results). It is possible to find a fixed point for the equation for fact that is defined for more values. For example, if we define $\text{fact}(n)$ as usual for $n >= 0$, and fact(n) = 0 for all $n < 0$, then fact still satisfies the equation

$$\text{fact}(n) = \text{if } n = 0 \text{ then } 1 \text{ else } n \cdot \text{fact}(n - 1)$$

This is the reason for taking the least fixed point solution to this equation: the least solution has exactly those function values that will be constructed by a runtime system implementing recursive calls.

10.7 THE MATHEMATICS OF FUNCTIONAL PROGRAMMING II: LAMBDA CALCULUS

Lambda calculus was invented by Alonzo Church as a mathematical formalism for expressing computation by functions, similar to the way a Turing machine is a formalism for expressing computation by a computer. In fact, lambda calculus can be used as a model for (purely) functional programming languages in much the same way that Turing machines can be used as models for procedural programming languages (see Chapter 1). Thus it is an important result for functional programming that lambda calculus as a description of computation is equivalent to Turing machines. This implies the result that was stated in Chapter 1, namely, that a purely functional programming language (no variables and no assignment) with an if-then-else construct and recursion is Turing complete—any computation performed by a Turing machine can be described by such a language.

It is useful for anyone interested in functional programming to have at least some knowledge of lambda calculus, since many functional languages, including LISP, ML, and Miranda, have been based on lambda calculus, and since lambda calculus provides a particularly simple and clear view of computation. Therefore, we offer this section as a basic introduction to the subject. For those with more than a superficial interest in functional programming, we recommend consulting one of the texts listed at the end of the chapter.

The essential construct of lambda calculus is the **lambda abstraction:**

$$(\lambda x. + 1\ x)$$

This can be interpreted exactly as the lambda expression

$$(\text{lambda } (x)\ (+\ 1\ x))$$

in Scheme, namely, as representing an unnamed function of the parameter x that adds 1 to x. Note that, like Scheme, expressions such as (+ 1 x) are written in prefix form.

The basic operation of lambda calculus is the **application** of expressions such as the lambda abstraction. The expression

$$(\lambda x. + 1\ x)\ 2$$

represents the application of the function that adds 1 to x to the constant 2. Lambda calculus expresses this by providing a **reduction rule** that permits 2 to be substituted for x in the lambda (and removing the lambda), yielding the desired value:

$$(\lambda x. \; + \; 1 \; x) \; 2 \Rightarrow (+ \; 1 \; 2) \Rightarrow 3$$

The syntax for lambda calculus is very simple:

$$
\begin{aligned}
<\text{exp}> ::= \; & <\text{constant}> \\
& | \; <\text{variable}> \\
& | \; (<\text{exp}> \; <\text{exp}>) \\
& | \; (\lambda \; <\text{variable}> . \; <\text{exp}>)
\end{aligned}
$$

Constants in this grammar are numbers like "0" or "1" and certain pre-defined functions like "+" and "·." Variables are names like x and y. The third rule for expressions represents function application ($f \; x$) as noted earlier. The fourth rule gives lambda abstractions.

Variables in lambda calculus are not like variables in a programming language—they do not occupy memory, since lambda calculus has no concept of memory. Lambda calculus variables correspond instead to function parameters as in purely functional programming. The set of constants and the set of variables are not specified by the grammar. Thus it is more correct to speak of many **lambda calculi.** Each specification of the set of constants and the set of variables describes a particular lambda calculus. Lambda calculus without constants is called *pure* lambda calculus.

Parentheses are included in the rules for function application and lambda abstraction to avoid ambiguity, but by convention may be left out, in case no ambiguity results. Thus, according to our grammar, we should have written $(\lambda x.((+ \; 1) \; x))$ for $(\lambda x. \; + \; 1 \; x)$ and $((\lambda x.((+ \; 1) \; x) \; 2)$ for $(\lambda x. \; + \; 1 \; x) \; 2$. However, no ambiguity results from the way they were written.

The variable x in the expression $(\lambda x.E)$ is said to be **bound** by the lambda. The **scope** of the binding is the expression E. An occurrence of a variable outside the scope of any binding of it by a lambda is a **free occurrence.** An occurrence that is not free is a **bound** occurrence. Thus, in the expression $(\lambda x.E)$, all occurrences of x in E are bound. For example, in the expression

$$(\lambda x. \; + \; y \; x)$$

x is bound and y is free. If we try to apply the function specified by this lambda abstraction, we substitute for x, but we have no way of determining the value of y:

$$(\lambda x. \; + \; y \; x) \; 2 \Rightarrow (+ \; y \; 2)$$

The variable y is like a nonlocal reference in the function—its value must be specified by an external environment.

Different occurrences of a variable can be bound by different lambdas, and some occurrences of a variable may be bound, while others are free. In the following expression

$$(\lambda x. \; + \; ((\lambda y.((\lambda x. \; \cdot \; x \; y) \; 2)) \; x) \; y)$$

the occurrence of x after the · is bound by a different lambda than the outer x. Also the first occurrence of y is bound, while the second occurrence is free. In fact, applying the functions defined by the lambdas gives the following reduction:

$$(\lambda x. \; + \; ((\lambda y.((\lambda x. \; \cdot \; x \; y) \; 2)) \; x) \; y) \Rightarrow$$
$$(\lambda x. \; + \; ((\lambda y.(\cdot \; 2 \; y)) \; x) \; y) \Rightarrow$$
$$(\lambda x. \; + \; (\cdot \; 2 \; x) \; y)$$

When reducing expressions that contain multiple bindings with the same name, care must be taken not to confuse the scopes of the bindings— sometimes renaming is necessary (discussed shortly).

One apparent problem with lambda calculus as a representation of functions is that each lambda abstraction binds only one variable. It appears that lambda calculus can only describe functions of a single variable. For example, to express the gcd function we might be tempted to write

$$(\lambda n \; m. \; \text{if} \; m \; = \; 0 \; \text{then} \; n \; \text{else} \; . \; . \; .)$$

What we really need to do is to bind each of n and m with its own lambda:

$$(\lambda n.(\lambda m. \; . \; . \; .))$$

This can be viewed as defining a function of the variable n that has as its value a function of the variable m, that is, a higher-order function. In other words n and m can be applied separately to achieve the desired result. This process of splitting multiple parameters into single parameters to higher-order functions is called **currying,** after H. B. Curry, the logician who popularized its use.

As a simple example of currying, consider the addition function "+". It is a function of two variables, but considering it as a curried function, each variable can be supplied separately: the expression $(+ \; 2)$ has as its value a function that adds 2 to any value—$((+ \; 2) \; 3) = (+ \; 2 \; 3) \Rightarrow 5$. "+" can therefore be viewed as a function of a single integer variable that returns as its value a function from an integer to an integer. Indeed, this is precisely how Miranda views the "+" function:[2]

```
+ : :  n u m  - >  n u m  - >  n u m
```

In Miranda all functions are **fully curried** unless parentheses are specified to indicate a Cartesian product. Thus the definition

```
gcd  n  m  =  n ,  if  m  =  0
          =  gcd  m  ( n  mod  m ) ,  otherwise
```

---

[2]ML by contrast views the + operator as applying to a pair, so the type of + is $num \; \cdot \; num \; - > \; num$. The situation is slightly complicated by the use of infix form. In ML x op y is interpreted as op (x, y), while in Miranda it is interpreted as op x y.

makes gcd into a curried function, so that we can apply each parameter separately:

```
gcd  ::  num  ->  num  ->  num
```

By contrast, our definition in Section 10.4 used the Cartesian product, indicated by the parentheses around the parameters:

```
gcd (n, m) = n, if m = 0
    else gcd (m, n mod m), otherwise
```

This represents an "uncurried" version of the gcd function:

```
gcd  ::  (num, num)  ->  num
```

We can view lambda calculus as modeling functional programming by considering a lambda abstraction as a function definition and the juxtaposition of two expressions as function application. As a model, however, lambda calculus is extremely general. For example, nothing prevents us in lambda calculus from applying a function to itself or even defining a function that takes a function parameter and applies it to itself: (x x) and (λx. x x) are legal expressions in lambda calculus. A more restrictive form of lambda calculus, called the **typed lambda calculus,** includes the notion of data type from programming languages, thus reducing the set of expressions that are allowed. We will not consider the typed lambda calculus further.

Since lambda calculus is so general, however, very precise rules must be given for transforming expressions, such as substituting values for bound variables. These rules have historical names, such as "alpha-conversion" and "beta-conversion." We will give a short overview to show the kinds of operations that can occur on lambda expressions.

The primary method for transforming lambda expressions is by **substitution,** or **function application.** We have seen a number of examples of this already: ((λx. + x 1) 2) is equivalent to (+ 2 1) by substituting 2 for x and eliminating the lambda. This is exactly like a call in a programming language to the function defined by the lambda abstraction, with 2 substituted for x as a value parameter. Historically, this process has been called **beta-reduction** in lambda calculus. One can also view this process in reverse, where (+ 2 1) becomes ((λx. + x 1) 2), in which case it is called **beta-abstraction. Beta-conversion** refers to either beta-reduction or beta-abstraction and establishes the equivalence of the two expressions. Formally, beta-conversion says that ((λx.E) F) is equivalent to E[F/x], where E[F/x] is E with all free occurrences of x in E replaced by F.

Care must be taken in beta-conversion when F contains variable names that occur in E. Consider the expression

$$((\lambda x.(\lambda y. + x\ y))\ y)$$

The first occurrence of y is bound, while the second is free. If we were to replace x by y blindly, we would get the incorrect reduction $(\lambda y. + y\ y)$. This is called the **name capture** problem. What we have to do is change the name of y in the inner lambda abstraction so that the free occurrence will not conflict, as follows:

$$((\lambda x.(\lambda y. + x\ y))\ y) \Rightarrow ((\lambda x.(\lambda z. + x\ z))\ y) \Rightarrow (\lambda z. + y\ z)$$

Name change is another available conversion process in lambda calculus, called **alpha-conversion:** $(\lambda x.E)$ is equivalent to $(\lambda y.E[y/x])$, where as before, $E[y/x]$ stands for the expression E with all free occurrences of x replaced by y. (Note that if y is a variable that already occurs in E there can be trouble similar to the substitution problem just discussed; see Exercise 41.)

Finally, there is a conversion that allows for the elimination of "redundant" lambda abstractions. This conversion is called **eta-conversion.** A simple example is the expression $(\lambda x. (+ 1\ x))$. Since $+$ is curried, the expression $(+ 1)$ is a function of one argument, and the expression $(+ 1\ x)$ can be viewed as the application of the function $+ 1$ to x. Thus $(\lambda x. (+ 1\ x))$ is equivalent to the function $(+ 1)$ without the lambda abstraction. In general, $(\lambda x.(E\ x))$ is equivalent to E by eta-conversion, as long as E contains no free occurrences of x. As a further example of eta-conversion, we have

$$(\lambda x.(\lambda y.(+ x\ y))) \Rightarrow (\lambda x.(+ x)) \Rightarrow +$$

which is to say that the first expression is just another notation for the $+$ function.

The order in which beta-reductions are applied to a lambda expression can have an effect on the final result obtained, just as different evaluation orders can make a difference in programming languages. In particular, it is possible to distinguish applicative order evaluation (or pass by value) from normal order evaluation (or pass by name). For example, in the following expression

$$((\lambda x. \cdot x\ x)\ (+ 2\ 3))$$

we could either use applicative order, replacing $(+ 2\ 3)$ by its value and then applying beta-reduction, as in

$$((\lambda x. \cdot x\ x)\ (+ 2\ 3)) \Rightarrow ((\lambda x. \cdot x\ x)\ 5) \Rightarrow (\cdot 5\ 5) \Rightarrow 25$$

or we could apply beta-reduction first and then evaluate, giving normal order evaluation:

$$((\lambda x. \cdot x\ x)\ (+ 2\ 3)) \Rightarrow (\cdot\ (+ 2\ 3)\ (+2\ 3)) \Rightarrow (\cdot 5\ 5) \Rightarrow 25$$

Normal order evaluation is a kind of **delayed** evaluation, since the evaluation of expressions is done only after substitution.

Normal order evaluation can have a different result than applicative order. A striking example is when parameter evaluation gives an undefined result. If the value of an expression does not depend on the value of the parameter, then normal order will still compute the correct value, while applicative order will also give an undefined result.

For example, consider the lambda expression $((\lambda x.\ x\ x)\ (\lambda x.\ x\ x))$. Beta-reduction on this expression results in the same expression all over again. Thus beta-reduction goes into an "infinite loop," attempting to reduce this expression. If we use this expression as a parameter to a constant expression, as in

$$((\lambda y.\ 2)\ ((\lambda x.\ x\ x)\ (\lambda x.\ x\ x)))$$

then using applicative order, we get an undefined result, while using normal order we get the value 2, since it does not depend on the value of the parameter y.

Functions that can return a value even when parameters are undefined are said to be **nonstrict,** while functions that are always undefined when a parameter is undefined are **strict.** In lambda calculus notation, the symbol $\perp$ represents an undefined value, and a function f is strict if it is always true that $(f\ \perp) = \perp$. Thus applicative order evaluation is strict, while normal order evaluation is nonstrict.

Normal order reduction is significant in lambda calculus in that expressions can always be reduced using normal order to a normal form that cannot be reduced further. This is the content of the famous **Church-Rosser theorem.** The equivalence of expressions can then be determined by reducing them using normal order and comparing their normal forms. This has practical applications for translators of functional languages, too, since a translator can use normal forms to replace one function by an equivalent but more efficient function.

Finally, in this brief overview of lambda calculus, we wish to show how lambda calculus can model recursive function definitions in exactly the way we have treated them in the previous section. Consider the following definition of the factorial function:

$$\text{fact} = (\lambda n.\ (\text{if}\ (n=0)\ 1\ (\cdot\ n\ (\text{fact}\ (-\ n\ 1)))))$$

We remove the recursion by creating a new lambda abstraction as follows:

$$\text{fact} = (\lambda F.\lambda n.\ (\text{if}\ (n=0)\ 1\ (\cdot\ n\ (F\ (-\ n\ 1)))))\ \text{fact}$$

In other words, the right-hand side can be viewed as a lambda abstraction, which, when applied to fact, gives fact back again.

If we write this abstraction as

$$H = (\lambda F.\lambda n.\ (\text{if}\ (n = 0)\ 1\ (\cdot\ n\ (F\ (-\ n\ 1)))))$$

then the equation becomes

$$\text{fact} = H\ \text{fact}$$

or that fact is a **fixed point** of H. In the last section we constructed a least-fixed-point solution by building up a set representation for the function. However, in the lambda calculus, lambda expressions are primitive;

that is, we cannot use sets to model them. Thus, to define a recursive function fact in the lambda calculus, we need a function Y for constructing a fixed point of the lambda expression H. Y needs therefore to have the property that $Y\ H$ = fact or $Y\ H$ = $H\ (Y\ H)$. Such a Y can indeed be defined by the following lambda expression:

$$Y = (\lambda\ h.\ (\lambda\ x.\ h\ (x\ x))\ (\lambda\ x.\ h\ (x\ x))).$$

Y is called a **fixed-point combinator,** a combinator being any lambda expression that contains only bound variables. Such a Y actually constructs a solution that is in some sense the "smallest." Thus one can refer to the **least-fixed-point semantics** of recursive functions in lambda calculus, as well as in the ordinary set-based theory of functions.

10.8   DYNAMIC MEMORY MANAGEMENT FOR FUNCTIONAL LANGUAGES

An essential feature of the runtime environment for a functional language is efficient automatic allocation and deallocation of memory. In procedural languages, the automatic allocation and deallocation of storage occurs only for activation records on a stack. This is a relatively easy process: space is allocated for an activation record when a procedure is called and deallocated when the procedure is exited. Fully dynamic allocation, such as for pointer variables, is manual and occurs in a "heap" through programmer calls to allocation and deallocation procedures such as Pascal's new and dispose.

By contrast, in a language with first-class function values, however, a stack-based system cannot be used, since references to a procedure's local environment can persist even after the procedure has been exited. An example of this, in both this chapter and Chapter 7, was the make-new-balance procedure that returns a function that performs "bank account withdrawals," thus requiring the continued existence of make-new-balance's activation in memory. The use of a stack-based environment would cause this function to fail. Since functional languages such as Scheme, Miranda, and ML are languages with first-class function values, a more general runtime environment is needed for them. Object-oriented languages such as Smalltalk also fall into this category, and the following discussion applies to them as well.

One might attempt to solve this problem by using a very simple approach: simply do not deallocate any memory once it has been allocated! This means that every call to a function creates a new activation record in memory, but on exit this memory is not deallocated. This method has two advantages: it is correct, and it is easy to implement. While this method actually can work for small programs, functional and object-oriented languages have the property that large amounts of memory are dynamically allocated, for several reasons: symbol tables are usually retained during execution, processing occurs primarily by function call, and the internal representation of data uses pointers and requires a substantial amount of indirection and memory overhead. Thus performing no deal-location causes memory to be very quickly exhausted.

In fact, this method *has* been used in conjunction with virtual memory systems, since the address space for such systems is almost inex-haustible. This only pushes off the basic problem, however, since it causes the swap space of the operating system to become exhausted and can cause a serious degradation of performance due to page faults. These topics are beyond the scope of this book, but at least serve to point out that there is a strong interaction between memory management and operating system issues.

Automatic memory management actually falls into two categories: the **reclamation** of previously allocated but no longer used storage, some-times called **garbage collection,** and the **maintenance** of the free space available for allocation. Maintenance is a little more straightforward than is reclamation, so we discuss it first.

10.8.1   Maintaining Free Space

Generally, a contiguous block of memory is provided by the operating system for the use of an executing program. The free space within this block is maintained by a list of free blocks. One way to do this is via a linked list, such as the circular list in the following figure, indicating the total available space, with allocated blocks shaded and free blocks blank:

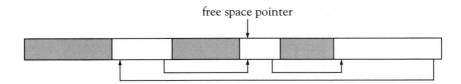

free space pointer

When a block of a certain size needs to be allocated, the memory manager searches the list for a free block with enough space, and then adjusts the free list to remove the allocated space, as in the following picture:

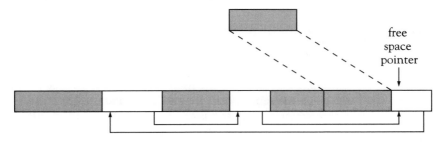

free space pointer

When memory is reclaimed, blocks are returned to the free list. For example, if the light-shaded areas are storage to be reclaimed,

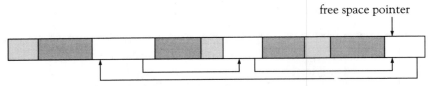

then the new free list after reclamation would look as follows:

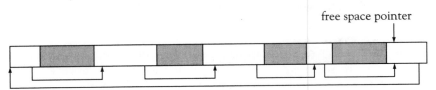

When blocks of memory are returned to the free list, they must be joined with immediately adjacent blocks to form the largest contiguous block of free memory. This process is called **coalescing.** In the preceding example, the small block freed in the middle of the memory area was coalesced with the free block adjacent to it on the right. Even with coalescing, however, a free list can become **fragmented,** that is, consist of a number of small-sized blocks. When this occurs, it is possible for the allocation of a large block to fail, even though there is enough total space available to allocate it. To prevent this, memory must occasionally be **compacted** by moving all free blocks together and coalescing them into one block. For example, the five blocks of free memory in the previous diagram could be compacted as follows:

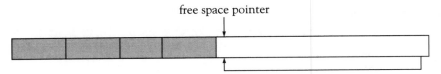

Compaction involves considerable overhead, since the locations of most of the allocated quantities will change and data structures and tables in the runtime environment will have to be modified to reflect these new locations.

10.8.2 Reclamation of Storage

Recognizing when a block of storage is no longer referenced, either directly or indirectly through pointers, is a much more difficult task than is the maintenance of the free list itself. Historically, two main methods have been used: reference counting and mark and sweep.

Reference counting is an "eager" method of storage reclamation, in that it tries to reclaim space as soon as it is no longer referenced. Each block of allocated storage contains an extra count field, which stores the number of references to the block from other blocks. Each time a reference is changed, these reference counts must be updated. When the reference count drops to zero, the block can be returned to the free list. In theory this seems like a simple and elegant solution to the problem, but in fact it suffers from serious drawbacks. One obvious one is the extra memory that it takes to keep the reference counts themselves. Even more serious, the effort to maintain the counts can be fairly large. For example, when making an assignment, which we will model by a Pascal-like pointer assignment $p := q$, first the old value of p must be followed, and its reference count decremented by one. If this reference count should happen to drop to zero, it is not sufficient simply to return it to free storage, since it may itself contain references to other storage blocks. Thus reference counts must be decremented recursively. Finally, when q is copied to p, its reference count must be incremented. A pseudocode description of assignment would therefore look as follows:

```
procedure assign(p,q);

  procedure decrement(p);
  begin
    p^.refcount := p^.refcount - 1;
    if p^.refcount = 0 then begin
      for all fields r of p^ that are pointers do
        decrement(r);
      deallocate(p^);
    end; (* if *)
  end; (* decrement *)

begin (* assign *)
  decrement(p);
  copy q to p;
  q^.refcount := q^.refcount + 1;
end; (* assign *)
```

However, the overhead to maintain reference counts is not the worst flaw of this scheme. Even more serious is that circular references can cause unreferenced memory to never be deallocated.

For example, consider a circular list such as

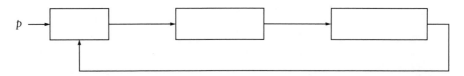

If p is deallocated, the reference count of the block pointed to by p will drop from 2 to 1. The entire list will never be deallocated at all!

The standard alternative to reference counts is **mark and sweep.** This method is a "lazy" method, in that it puts off reclaiming any storage until the allocator runs out of space, at which point it looks for all storage that can be referenced and moves all unreferenced storage back to the free list. It does this in two passes. The first pass follows all pointers recursively, starting with the current environment or symbol table, and marks each block of storage reached. This process requires an extra bit of storage for the marking. A second pass then sweeps linearly through memory, returning unmarked blocks to the free list.

This method, unlike reference counts, has no difficulty freeing blocks with circular references. However, it also requires extra storage, and it suffers from another serious problem: the double pass through memory causes a significant delay in processing, sometimes as much as a few seconds, each time the garbage collector is invoked—which can be every few minutes. This is clearly unacceptable for many applications involving interactive or immediate response. However, many modern LISP and Smalltalk implementations still suffer from this problem.

A bookkeeping improvement can be made by splitting available memory into two halves and allocating storage only from one half at a time. Then during the marking pass, all reached blocks are immediately copied to the second half of storage not in use. This means that no extra mark bit is required in storage, and only one pass is required. It also performs compaction automatically. Once all reachable blocks in the used area have been copied, the used and unused halves of memory are interchanged, and processing continues. However, this does little to improve processing delays during storage reclamation.

Recently, a method has been invented that reduces this delay significantly. Called **generation scavenging,** it adds a permanent storage area to the reclamation scheme of the previous paragraph. Allocated objects that survive long enough are simply copied into permanent space and are never deallocated during subsequent storage reclamations. This means that the garbage collector needs to search only a very small section of memory for newer storage allocations, and the time for such a search is reduced to a fraction of a second. Of course, it is possible for permanent memory still to become exhausted with unreachable storage, but this is a much less severe problem than before, since temporary storage tends to disappear quickly, while storage that stays allocated for some time is small and tends to persist anyway. This process has been shown to work very well, especially with a virtual memory system.

Exercises

1. The following Modula-2 procedure computes the power a^b, where a is an integer and b is a cardinal:

```
PROCEDURE Power (a: INTEGER; b: CARDINAL):
  INTEGER;
VAR temp: INTEGER;
    I: CARDINAL;
BEGIN
  temp := 1;
  FOR I := 1 TO b DO
    temp := temp * a;
  END;
  RETURN temp;
END Power;
```

(a) Rewrite this procedure in functional form.
(b) Rewrite your answer to (a) using an accumulating parameter to make it tail recursive.

2. A function that returns the maximum value of a 0-ended list of integers input from a user is given by the following Modula-2 procedure:

```
PROCEDURE ReadMax (): INTEGER;
VAR max,x: INTEGER;
BEGIN
  ReadInt(x); WriteLn;
  IF x = 0 THEN (* do nothing *)
  ELSE
    max := x;
    ReadInt(x); WriteLn;
    WHILE x <> 0 DO
      IF x > max THEN
        max := x;
      END; (* if *)
      ReadInt(x); WriteLn;
    END; (* while *)
    RETURN max;
  END; (* else *)
END ReadMax;
```

Rewrite this procedure as much as possible in functional style using tail recursion (the ReadInt procedure prevents a complete removal of variables).

3. Recursive sorts are easier to write in functional style than others. Two recursive sorts are Quicksort and Mergesort. Write functional versions of these two sorts in a procedural language of your choice (e.g., Pascal, C, Ada, Modula-2), using an array of integers as your basic data structure.

4. It is possible to write nonrecursive programs that implement recursive algorithms using a stack, but at the cost of extra complexity (a necessary overhead of using a nonrecursive language like FORTRAN). Write

nonrecursive versions of Quicksort and Mergesort. Discuss the difficulties of the added complexity. Which of the two sorts is easier to implement nonrecursively? Why?

5. State which of the following functions are referentially transparent, and give reasons:
   (a) The factorial function.
   (b) A function that returns a number from the keyboard.
   (c) A function p that counts the number of times it is called (see the problem at the end of Section 5.4).

6. Is a function that has no side effects referentially transparent?

7. The binomial coefficients are a frequent computational task in computer science. They are defined as follows for $n >= 0$, $0 <= k <= n$ (! is factorial and $0! = 1$):

$$B(n, k) = \frac{n!}{(n - k)!\, k!}$$

   (a) Write a procedure using a loop to compute $B(n, k)$. Test your program on $B(10, 5)$.
   (b) Use the following recurrence and the fact that $B(n, 0) = 1$ and $B(n, n) = 1$ to write a functional procedure to compute $B(n, k)$:

$$B(n, k) = B(n - 1, k - 1) + B(n - 1, k)$$

   Test your program on $B(10,5)$.
   (c) Can you write a more efficient program than your program of (b) and still preserve the functional style? (Hint: Think of pass by need memoization as discussed in Section 10.5.)

8. The following functional programming exercises can be solved in any of the languages studied in the text (Scheme, ML, Miranda) or in a functional language of your choice (a few have already been given solutions in the chapter, and these are indicated in parentheses):
   (a) Write a tail-recursive procedure to compute the length of an arbitrary list.
   (b) Write a procedure that computes the maximum and minimum of a list of integers.
   (c) Write a procedure that collects integers from the user until a 0 is encountered and returns them in a list in the order they were input.
   (d) Use your procedures of (b) and (c) to write a program to input a 0-ended list of integers, print the list in the order entered, and print the maximum and minimum of the list.
   (e) Write Quicksort for a list of integers (Miranda, page 392).
   (f) Write Mergesort for a list of integers.
   (g) A Pythagorean triple is a tuple of integers (x, y, z) such that $x \cdot x + y \cdot y = z \cdot z$. Write a procedure with a parameter n to print all Pythagorean triples such that $1 <= x <= y <= z <= n$.
   (h) Write a function to square a list of numbers (Scheme, page 377).

(i) Write a make-double higher-order function (Scheme, page 378).

(j) Write a higher-order function twice that takes as a parameter a function of one argument and returns a function that represents the application of that function to its argument twice. Given the usual definition of the sqr function, what function (in Scheme syntax) is (twice (twice sqr))?

(k) Write a higher-order function inc-n that takes an integer n as a parameter and returns an nth increment function, which increments its parameter by n. Thus, in Scheme syntax, ((inc-n 3) 2) = 5 and ((inc-n -2) 3) = 1.

9. Many procedures we have seen are not tail recursive but "almost" so, in that the recursive call comes just before an arithmetic operation, which is the last operation in the procedure. For example, factorial and length of a list are almost tail recursive in this sense. Describe a general pattern for turning an almost tail-recursive procedure into a loop, in the same way a tail-recursive procedure can be so transformed, as described in Section 10.1. Can a translator recognize almost tail recursion as easily as tail recursion? How might it do so?

10. Draw box diagrams for the following lists:

```
((((a))))
(1 (2 (3 4)) (5))
((a ()) ((c) (d) b) e)
```

11. Use the box diagrams of the last exercise to compute the following for each list for which they make sense:

```
(car (car L))
(car (cdr L))
(car (cdr (cdr (cdr L))))
(cdr (car (cdr (cdr L))))
```

12. Represent the following elements as car/cdr expressions of the lists of Exercise 8:

a of the first list
3 of the second list
c of the third list

13. Scheme's basic data structure is actually a little more general than the lists described in this chapter. Indeed, since the car of a list can be a list or an atom, it is also possible for the cdr to be an atom as well as a list. In the case when the cdr is not a list, the resulting structure is called a **pair** or **S-expression** instead of a list and is written (a . b), where a is the car and b is the cdr. Thus (cons 2 3) = (2 . 3), and (cdr '(2 . 3)) = 3. The list (2 3 4) can then be written in pair notation as (2 . (3 . (4 . ()))). Discuss any advantages you can think of to having this more general data structure.

14. The function reverse described in the text reverses only the "top level" of a list: if L = ((a b) c (d e)) then (reverse L) = ((d e) c (a b)). Write a Scheme function deep-reverse that also reverses all sublists: (deep-reverse L) = ((e d) c (b a)).

15. Write a Scheme list representation for the binary search tree:

16. Write an insert procedure in Scheme for the binary search tree data structure described in Section 10.3.2.

17. Try to write a tail-recursive version of the append function in Scheme. What problems do you encounter? Can you think of a list representation that would make this easier?

18. Scheme has two functions that test equality of values: eq? and equal?. The first tests identity of memory location, while the second tests "structural equality," that is, identity of structure. Use these two versions of equality to show that Scheme uses pointer semantics for assignment, as described in Section 5.5.

19. Here is a definition of a new if function in Scheme:

```
(define (my-if a b c) (if a b c))
```

Why won't this function work? Will a similar function written in ML work? In Miranda?

20. The Scheme let expression is actually syntactic sugar for a lambda that is immediately applied to a set of arguments.
    (a) Rewrite (let ((x 2) (y 3)) E) as a lambda application.
    (b) Can a letrec be given a similar interpretation?
    (c) Why is the following let binding not legal (assuming a is not in the environment of the let):

```
(let ((a 2) (b (+ 1 a))) ... )
```

    (d) How could it be made legal, using a similar interpretation to that of (a)?

21. (a) Give an algebraic specification for the ADT List with the following operations, and with properties as in Scheme: car, cdr, cons, null?, makenull.
    (b) Write a Modula-2 MODULE to implement the ADT of (a).
    (c) Use the MODULE of (b) to write a "tiny Scheme" interpreter in Modula-2, that is, an interpreter that has only the ADT list functions as available operations and only has numbers as atoms.

22. In Section 10.3.4 we defined the make-double higher-order function in Scheme. What functions are returned by (make-double -) and (make-double /)?

23. The Scheme make-new-balance function defined in Section 10.3.4 used a local variable and assignment (set!) to keep and reset the value of the account balance, thus violating functional programming principles. Rewrite the definition of make-new-balance to eliminate the nonfunctional features. Discuss the effect this has on protection.

24. (a) Give an example to show that Scheme does not curry its functions.
    (b) Write a Scheme higher-order function that takes a function of two parameters as its parameter and returns a curried version of the function.

25. List the ML types for all the functions in Exercise 6.

26. Write an ML function that determines the length of any list. Show how an ML system can determine the type of the length function using pattern matching.

27. List the Miranda types for all the functions in Exercise 6.

28. Write Miranda list comprehensions for the following lists: (a) all integers that are squares, (b) all Pythagorean triples (see Exercise 6), and (c) all perfect numbers (a perfect number is the sum of all of its proper factors).

29. Write functions to test whether ML and Scheme use short-circuit evaluation for Boolean expressions. Does the text already imply the answer to this question for Miranda?

30. When a function is defined using pattern matching in ML, the text mentions that an ML system may complain if cases are left out of the definition. Such missing cases imply the function is partial. Discuss the advantages and disadvantages of requiring all functions to be total in a programming language.

31. The fact function defined in this chapter for ML and Scheme is in fact partial, yet an ML translator will not discover this. Why?

32. ML and Miranda do not have general list structures like Scheme, but require the elements in a list to have all the same data type. Why is this? What data structure in a procedural language do such lists imitate?

33. Write a Scheme program to show that the Scheme procedures force and delay actually use pass by need memoization.

34. Write a sieve of Eratosthenes in Scheme or ML using generators and filters, similar to the Miranda version in Section 10.5. Rewrite the Scheme version to use force and delay.

35. Rewrite the Scheme intlist function in Section 10.5 so that it takes only a lower bound as a parameter and produces a stream of integers from that point on: (intlist 5) = (5 6 7 8 ...).

36. Miranda list comprehensions are actually compact expressions for generator-filter programs as described in Section 10.5. For example, the list comprehension

```
evens = [n | n <- [2..]; n mod 2 = 0]
```

is equivalent to a generator procedure that produces the stream of integers beginning with 2 (represented by [2..]) and sends its output to the selector procedure of the predicate n mod 2 = 0 that passes on the list whose elements satisfy the predicate. Write a Scheme procedure that uses force and delay to produce the stream of even integers in a similar generator-filter style.

37. Rewrite the flatten and eqlist Scheme procedures of Section 10.5 to use force and delay.

38. (From Abelson and Sussman [1985]) Define a delayed version of the apply-to-all procedure from Section 10.3.4 as follows:

```
(define (apply-to-all f L)
  (if (null? L) ()
      (cons (f (car (force L))) (apply-to-all
                                  (cdr (force L))))))
```

Now define a show procedure that prints a value and returns the same value:

```
(define (show x) (display x) (newline) x)
```

Finally, define a delayed list as follows:

```
(define L (delay (apply-to-all show (delay
  (intlist 1 100)))))
```

where intlist is the delayed version from Section 10.5. What will the Scheme interpreter print when given the following expressions to evaluate in the order given (take is also the delayed version in Section 10.5):

```
> (take 5 L)
... some output here

> (take 7 L)
... some more output here
```

(Hint: The answer depends on whether Scheme uses pass by need or not. See Exercise 33.)

39. Show that the fact function as computed in Section 10.6 is the smallest solution to the set equation fact $= \{(0,1)\} \cup$ fact$'$.

40. (a) Write out the definition of the higher-order function H as described in Section 10.6 for the recursive definition of the gcd function.
    (b) Give a mathematical description of the sets gcd_0, gcd_1, and gcd_2 in the least-fixed-point construction as described in Section 10.6.

41. Write lambda calculus expressions for the higher-order functions twice and inc-n. (See Exercise 6.)

42. Assume sqr $= (\lambda x.\ .\ x\ x)$ in lambda calculus. Show the steps in an applicative order and normal order reduction of the expression (twice (twice sqr)).

43. Give applicative and normal order reductions for the following lambda expressions. State which steps use which conversions and which variables are bound and which are free.
    (a) $(\lambda x.((\lambda y.(\cdot\ 2\ y))\ (+\ x\ y)))\ y$
    (b) $(\lambda x.\lambda y.(x\ y))\ (\lambda z.(z\ y))$

44. It is a surprising fact in lambda calculus that lists can be expressed as lambda abstractions. Indeed, the list constructor cons can be written as $(\lambda x.\ \lambda y.\ \lambda f.\ f\ x\ y)$. With this definition one can write car as $(\lambda z.\ z\ (\lambda x.\ \lambda y.\ x))$ and cdr as $(\lambda z.\ z\ (\lambda x.\ \lambda y.\ y))$. Show that using these definitions the usual formulas (car (cons a b)) $= a$ and (cdr (cons a b)) $= b$ are true.

45. (From Abelson and Sussman [1985]) It is also possible to express the integers as lambda abstractions:

    zero $= \lambda f.\lambda x.x$
    one $= \lambda f.\lambda x.(f\ x)$
    two $= \lambda f.\lambda x.(f\ (f\ x))$
    ...

    These are called Church numbers, after Alonzo Church.
    (a) Given the following definition of the successor function:

    $$\text{successor} = \lambda n.\lambda f.\lambda x.(f\ ((n\ f)\ x))$$

    show that (successor zero) $=$ one and (successor one)$=$ two.
    (b) Generalize (a) to any Church number.
    (c) Define addition and multiplication for Church numbers.
    (d) Write out an implementation of your lambda expressions in (b) as procedures in a functional language, and write an output procedure that shows they are correct.

46. Use the lambda expression for H on page 407 and the property that the fact function is a fixed point of H to show that fact $1 = 1$.

47. We noted that the fixed-point combinator Y can itself be written as the lambda abstraction $(\lambda h.\ (\lambda x.\ h\ (x\ x))\ (\lambda x.\ h\ (x\ x)))$. Show that this expression for Y does indeed give it the property that $Y\ H = H\ (Y\ H)$.

48. Write Pascal, C, or Modula-2 declarations for the maintenance of a free list of memory as (a) a circular singly linked list, and (b) a noncircular doubly linked list. Write procedures to deallocate a block using both of these data structures, being sure to coalesce adjacent blocks. Compare the ease of coalescing blocks in each case.

49. Show how compaction of memory can be accomplished by using a table to maintain an extra level of indirection, so that when a block of storage is moved, only one pointer needs to be changed.

50. In Section 10.8 a method of mark and sweep garbage collection was described in which memory is split into two sections, only one of which is used for allocation between calls to the garbage collector. It was claimed in the text that this eliminates the need for extra space to mark memory that has been previously seen. Describe how this can be accomplished.

51. In the generation-scavenging method of garbage collection, it is still necessary eventually to reclaim "permanently" allocated storage after long execution times. It has been suggested that this could be made to interfere the least with execution by scheduling it to be performed "off-line," that is, during periods when the running program is waiting for input or other processing. For this to be effective, the garbage collector must have a good interface with the operating system, especially if virtual memory is in use. Describe as many operating system issues as you can think of in this approach.

Notes and References

There are quite a few books on functional programming. We list only a few here that are directly related to the languages and issues discussed in the chapter. For an overview of functional programming languages, including historical perspectives, from a somewhat different viewpoint from this chapter, see Hudak [1989]. Abelson and Sussman [1985] is a good reference for much of this chapter, as well as for the Scheme language (Section 10.3). The bank balance example in Section 10.3.4 is adapted from that book, as are a couple of the exercises. Springer and Friedman [1989] is another good reference for functional programming techniques and for Scheme. The definition of Scheme is published in Rees and Clinger [1986].

Functional programming with the ML language (Section 10.4.1) is treated in Milner and Tofte [1991] and Milner, Tofte, and Harper [1990], where the definition of Standard ML is given; see also Wikström [1987] and Mitchell and Harper [1988]. The Miranda language (Sections 10.4.2 and

10.5) is presented in Bird and Wadler [1988], Turner [1986], and Peyton Jones [1987]. Underlying ideas are presented in Turner [1982]. Delayed evaluation is studied in Henderson [1980]; parts of Section 10.5 are adapted from that reference. Unification and the type inference algorithm used in ML and Miranda are studied in Hindley [1969] and Milner [1978]; examples of such type inference are presented in Aho, Sethi, and Ullman [1986].

Interest in functional programming increased dramatically following the ACM Turing Award lecture of Backus [1978], in which he describes a general framework for functional programming, called FP. A significant modern version of LISP not discussed in this chapter is Common LISP, which is described in Steele [1982] and defined in Steele [1984]. The explanation of least-fixed-point semantics of recursive functions in Section 10.6 was inspired by Meyer [1990]. The lambda calculus (Section 10.7) began with Church [1941] and is studied in Curry and Feys [1958]. Overviews of lambda calculus are presented in Peyton Jones [1987] and Meyer [1990]. The use of normal forms in compiling Miranda is discussed in the former reference, and parts of the presentation in Section 10.7 are patterned after that text.

A history of the lambda calculus and the Church-Rosser theorem is given in Rosser [1982]. Currying is apparently originally due not to Curry but to Schönfinkel [1924]. Dynamic memory management (Section 10.8) is treated in more detail in Horowitz and Sahni [1984] and Aho, Hopcroft, and Ullman [1983]. Generation scavenging is discussed in Ungar [1984]. Other techniques are treated in Moon [1984]. An overview of memory management, particularly with regard to list allocation is in Sethi [1989]. A survey of traditional methods of garbage collection is in Cohen [1981].

Traditionally, functional programming has been thought to be highly inefficient because of its reliance on function call and dynamic memory management. Advances in algorithms, such as the generation-scavenging method, and advances in translation techniques make this less true. Some references dealing with these issues are Steele [1977] and Gabriel [1985]. Using recursive calls to do functional programming in a procedural language is also less expensive than one might imagine, and the techniques in Section 10.1 are usable in practice. An example of this is discussed in Louden [1987].

11 LOGIC PROGRAMMING

Logic as the science of reasoning and proof has existed since the time of the philosophers of ancient Greece. Mathematical or symbolic logic as the theory of mathematical proofs began with the work of George Boole and Augustus De Morgan in the middle of the 1800s. Since then logic has become a major mathematical discipline, and has played a significant role in the mathematics of the twentieth century, particularly with respect to the famous incompleteness theorems of Kurt Gödel. (See the Notes and References.)

Logic is closely associated with computers and programming languages in a number of ways. First, computer circuits are designed with the help of Boolean algebra (named after George Boole), and Boolean expressions and data are almost universally used in programming languages to control the actions of a program. (See Chapters 5 and 6.)

Logical statements have also been used to describe the semantics of programming language constructs: such semantics are called **axiomatic semantics** and are studied in Chapter 12. Logical statements can also be used as formal specifications for the required behavior of programs, and together with the axiomatic semantics of the language they can be used to prove the correctness of a program in a purely mathematical way.

In a different direction, computers have been used as tools to implement the principles of mathematical logic, and programs have been written that will construct proofs of mathematical theorems using the principles of logic. Such **automatic deduction systems** or **automatic theorem provers** turn proofs into computation. Experience with such programs in the 1960s and 1970s led to the major realization that the reverse is also true: computation can be viewed as a kind of proof. Thus logical statements, or at least a restricted form of them, can be viewed as a programming language and executed on a computer, given a sophisticated enough interpretive system. This work, primarily by Robinson, Colmerauer, and Kowalski (see the Notes and References), led to the programming language Prolog. The development of efficient Prolog interpreters in the late 1970s, particularly at the University of Edinburgh, Scotland, resulted in a tremendous increase in interest in logic programming systems. Prolog remains today the most significant example of a logic programming language, although a number of attempts have been made to design more powerful logic programming systems, in particular equational systems that use equations instead of logic to describe computation.

In the following sections we will first give a brief introduction to mathematical logic and the way logic can be used as a programming language. Next we turn our attention to a description of Prolog and the techniques of writing Prolog programs. We also give a brief description of the principles behind the operation of a Prolog system, and some of the weaknesses of these systems. Finally, we describe some attempts to extend Prolog to equational systems.

11.1 LOGIC AND LOGIC PROGRAMS

To describe what is meant by logic programming, we need to know a little bit about mathematical logic. The kind of logic used in logic programming is the **first-order predicate calculus,** which is a way of formally expressing **logical statements,** that is, statements that are either true or false.

EXAMPLE 1
The following English statements are logical statements:

> 0 is a natural number.
> 2 is a natural number.
> For all x, if x is a natural number, then so is the successor of x.
> -1 is a natural number.

A translation into predicate calculus is as follows:

natural(0).
natural(2).
For all x, natural(x) $\rightarrow$ natural(successor(x)).
natural(-1). ∎

Among these logical statements, the first and third statement can be viewed as **axioms** for the natural numbers: statements that are assumed to be true and from which all true statements about natural numbers can be proved. Indeed, the second statement can be **proved** from these axioms, since 2 = successor(successor(0)) and natural(0) $\rightarrow$ natural(successor(0)) $\rightarrow$ natural(successor(successor(0))). The fourth statement, on the other hand, cannot be proved from the axioms and so can be assumed to be false.

First-order predicate calculus classifies the different parts of such statements as follows:

1. *Constants.* These are usually numbers or names. Sometimes they are called atoms, since they cannot be broken down into subparts. In Example 1, 0 is a constant.

2. *Predicates.* These are names for functions that are true or false, like Boolean functions in a program. Predicates can take a number of arguments. In Example 1, the predicate natural takes one argument.

3. *Functions.* First-order predicate calculus distinguishes between functions that are true or false—these are the predicates—and all other functions, like successor in Example 1, which represent non-Boolean values.

4. *Variables that stand for as yet unspecified quantities.* In Example 1, x is a variable.

5. *Connectives.* These include the operations and, or, and not, just like the operations on Boolean data in programming languages. Additional connectives in predicate calculus are implication "$\rightarrow$" and equivalence "$\longleftrightarrow$." These are not really new operations: $a \rightarrow b$ means that b is true whenever a is, and this is equivalent to the statement b or not a. (See Exercise 1.) Also $a \longleftrightarrow b$ means the same as $(a \rightarrow b)$ and $(b \rightarrow a)$.

6. *Quantifiers.* These are operations that introduce variables. In Example 1, "for all" is the quantifier for x; it is called the **universal quantifier.** There is also the **existential quantifier** "there exists" as in the following statement:

there exists x, natural(x).

This statement means that there exists an x such that x is a natural number. A variable introduced by a quantifier is said to be **bound** by the quantifier. It is possible for variables also to be **free,** that is, not bound by any quantifier.

7. *Punctuation symbols.* These include left and right parentheses, the comma, and the period. (Strictly speaking, the period isn't necessary,

but we include it since most logic programming systems use it.) Parentheses are used to enclose arguments and also to group operations. Parentheses can be left out based on common conventions about the precedence of connectives, which are usually assumed to be the same as in most programming languages. (Thus the connectives in order of decreasing precedence are not, and, or, →, and ↔.)

In predicate calculus, arguments to predicates and functions can only be **terms,** that is, combinations of variables, constants, and functions. Terms cannot contain predicates, quantifiers, or connectives. In Example 1, terms that appear include constants 0, −1, 2, the variable x, and the term successor(x) consisting of the function successor with argument x. Some examples of additional terms that can be written are successor(0) and successor(successor(successor(x))).

EXAMPLE 2

The following are logical statements in English:

A horse is a mammal.

A human is a mammal.

Mammals have four legs and no arms, or two legs and two arms.

A horse has no arms.

A human has arms.

A human has no legs.

A possible translation of these statements into first-order predicate calculus is as follows:

mammal(horse).
mammal(human).
for all x, mammal(x) →
       legs(x,4) and arms(x,0) or legs(x,2) and arms(x,2).
arms(horse,0).
not arms(human,0).
arms(human,2).
legs(human,0).   ■

In this example, the constants are the integers 0, 2, and 4 and the names horse and human. The predicates are mammal, arms, and legs. The only variable is x, and there are no functions.

As in the previous example, we might consider the first five statements to be axioms—statements defining true relationships. Then, as we shall see shortly, arms(human,2) becomes provable from the axioms. It is also possible to prove that legs(human,2) is true, so the last statement is false, given the axioms.

Note that we have used precedence to leave out many parentheses in the preceding statements, so that, for example, when we write

legs(x,4) and arms(x,0) or legs(x,2) and arms(x,2)

we mean the following:

$$(\text{legs}(x,4) \text{ and } \text{arms}(x,0)) \text{ or } (\text{legs}(x,2) \text{ and } \text{arms}(x,2)).$$

In addition to the seven classes of symbols described, first-order predicate calculus has **inference rules:** ways of deriving or proving new statements from a given set of statements.

EXAMPLE 3

A typical inference rule is the following:

From the statements $a \rightarrow b$ and $b \rightarrow c$, one can derive the statement $a \rightarrow c$, or written more formally,

$$\frac{(a \rightarrow b) \text{ and } (b \rightarrow c)}{a \rightarrow c}$$ ∎

Inference rules allow us to construct the set of all statements that can be derived, or proved, from a given set of statements: these are statements that are always true whenever the original statements are true. For example, the first five statements about mammals in Example 2 allow us to derive the following statements:

> legs(horse,4).
> arms(horse,0).
> legs(human,2).
> arms(human,2).

Stated in the language of logic, if we take the first five statements of Example 2 to be axioms, then the preceding four statements become **theorems.** Notice that proving these statements from the given statements can be viewed as the computation of the number of arms and legs of a horse or a human. Thus the set of statements in Example 2 can be viewed as representing the potential computation of all logical consequences of these statements.

This is the essence of logic programming: a collection of statements are assumed to be axioms, and from them a desired fact is derived by the application of inference rules in some automated way. Thus we can state the following definition:

> *Definition:* A *logic programming language* is a notational system for writing logical statements together with specified algorithms for implementing inference rules.

The set of logical statements that are taken to be axioms can be viewed as the **logic program,** and the statement or statements that are to be derived can be viewed as the "input" that initiates the computation. Such inputs are also provided by the programmer and are called **queries** or **goals.** For example, given the set of axioms of Example 2, if we wanted to know how many legs a human has, we would provide the following query,

Does there exist a y such that y is the number of legs of a human?

or, in predicate calculus,

there exists y, legs(human,y)?

and the system would respond with something like

yes: $y = 2$

For this reason, logic programming systems are sometimes referred to as **deductive databases,** databases consisting of a set of statements and a deduction system that can respond to queries. Notice that these are different from ordinary databases, since they contain not only facts like mammal(human) or natural(0), but also more complex statements like $natural(x) \rightarrow natural(successor(x))$, and the system can answer not only queries about facts but also queries involving such implications.

In a pure logic programming system, nothing is said about *how* a particular statement might be derived from a given set of statements. The specific path or sequence of steps that an automatic deduction system chooses to derive a statement is the **control problem** for a logic programming system. The original statements represent the logic of the computation, while the deductive system provides the control by which a new statement is derived. This property of logic programming systems led Kowalski to state the logic programming paradigm as the pseudoequation

$$algorithm = logic + control$$

as a contrast to Niklaus Wirth's expression of procedural programming as

$$algorithms + data\ structures = programs$$

(See the Notes and References.) Kowalski's principle points out a further feature of logic programming: since logic programs do not express the control, operations (in theory at least) can be carried out in any order or simultaneously. Thus logic programming languages are natural candidates for parallelism.

Unfortunately, automated deduction systems have difficulty handling all of first-order predicate calculus. First, there are too many ways of expressing the same statements, and second, there are too many inference rules. As a result, most logic programming systems restrict themselves to a particular subset of predicate calculus, called Horn clauses, that we will briefly study.

11.2   *Horn CLAUSES*

A **Horn clause** (named after their inventor Alfred Horn) is a statement of the form

$$a_1 \text{ and } a_2 \text{ and } a_3 \ldots \text{ and } a_n \rightarrow b$$

where the a_i are only allowed to be simple statements involving no connectives. Thus there are no "or" connectives and no quantifiers in Horn clauses. The Horn clause here says that a_1 through a_n imply b or that b is true if all the a_i are true. b is called the **head** of the clause, and the $a_1, \ldots, a_n$ the **body** of the clause. In the Horn clause, the number of a_i's may be 0, in which case the Horn clause has the form

$$\rightarrow b$$

Such a clause means that b is always true, that is, b is an axiom and is usually written without the connective $\rightarrow$. Such clauses are sometimes also called **facts.**

Horn clauses can be used to express most, but not all, logical statements. Indeed, there is an algorithm that can perform a reasonable translation from predicate calculus statements to Horn clauses, but it is beyond the scope of this book to describe. (See the Notes and References.) The basic idea is to remove "or" connectives by writing separate clauses and to treat the lack of quantifiers by assuming that variables appearing in the head of a clause are universally quantified, while variables appearing in the body of a clause (but not in the head) are existentially quantified.

EXAMPLE 4

The following statements from Example 1 are written in first-order predicate calculus:

> natural(0).
> for all x, natural(x) $\rightarrow$ natural(successor(x)).

These can be very simply translated into Horn clauses by dropping the quantifier:

> natural(0).
> natural(x) $\rightarrow$ natural(successor(x)).   ∎

EXAMPLE 5

Consider the logical description for the Euclidian algorithm to compute the greatest common divisor of two positive integers u and v:

The gcd of u and 0 is u.

The gcd of u and v, if v is not 0, is the same as the gcd of v and the remainder of dividing v into u.

> Translating this into first-order predicate calculus gives

> for all u, gcd(u,0,u).

> for all u, for all v, for all w,
> not zero(v) and gcd(v,u mod v,w) $\rightarrow$ gcd(u,v,w).

(Remember that gcd(u,v,w) is a predicate expressing that w is the gcd of u and v.)

To translate these statements into Horn clauses, we need again only drop the quantifiers:

gcd(u,0,u).
not zero(v) and gcd(v,u mod v, w) $\rightarrow$ gcd(u,v,w).   ∎

EXAMPLE 6

The foregoing examples contain only universally quantified variables. To see how an existentially quantified variable in the body may also be handled, consider the following statement:

x is a grandparent of y if x is the parent of someone who is the parent of y.

Translating this into predicate calculus, we get

for all x, for all y,
(there exists z, parent(x,z) and parent(z,y))
$\rightarrow$ grandparent(x,y).

As a Horn clause this is expressed simply as

parent(x,z) and parent(z,y) $\rightarrow$ grandparent(x,y).   ∎

EXAMPLE 7

To see how or connectives are handled, consider the following statement:

For all x, if x is a mammal then x has two or four legs.

Translating in predicate calculus, we get

for all x, mammal(x) $\rightarrow$ legs(x,2) or legs(x,4).

This may be approximated by the following Horn clauses:

mammal(x) and not legs(x,2) $\rightarrow$ legs(x,4).
mammal(x) and not legs(x,4) $\rightarrow$ legs(x,2).   ∎

In general, the more connectives that appear to the right of a "$\rightarrow$" connective in a statement, the harder it is to translate into a set of Horn clauses. (See Exercise 8.)

Horn clauses are of particular interest to automatic deduction systems such as logic programming systems, because they can be given a **procedural interpretation.** If we write a Horn clause in reverse order

$$b \leftarrow a_1 \text{ and } a_2 \text{ and } a_3 \ldots \text{ and } a_n$$

we can view this as a definition of procedure b: the body of b is given by the body of the clause, namely, the operations indicated by the a_i's. This is very similar to the way context-free grammar rules were interpreted as procedure definitions in recursive descent parsing in Chapter 4. There is more than a passing similarity here, since logic programs can be used to directly construct parsers. (See the Notes and References.) In fact, the parsing of natural language was one of the motivations for the original development of Prolog. The major difference between parsing and logic programming is that in pure logic programming, the order in which the a_i are called is not specified.

Nevertheless, most logic programming systems are deterministic in that they perform the calls in a certain prespecified order, usually left to right, which is exactly the order indicated by context-free grammar rules. The particular kind of grammar rules used in Prolog programs are called **definite clause grammars.**

Horn clauses can also be viewed as **specifications** of procedures rather than strictly as implementations. For example, we could view the following Horn clause as a specification of a sort procedure:

$$sort(x,y) \leftarrow permutation(x,y) \text{ and } sorted(y).$$

This says that (assuming that x and y are lists of things) a sort procedure transforms list x into a sorted list y such that y is a permutation of x. To complete the specification, we must of course supply specifications for what it means for a list to be sorted and for a list to be a permutation of another list. The important point is that we may think of the Horn clause as not necessarily supplying the algorithm by which y is found, given an x, but only the properties such a y must have.

With the foregoing procedural interpretation in mind, most logic programming systems not only write Horn clauses "backward," but also drop the and connectives between the a_i and just separate them with commas. Thus the greatest common divisor clauses in Example 5 would appear as follows:

$$gcd(u,0,u).$$
$$gcd(u,v,w) \leftarrow \text{ not } zero(v), gcd(v,u \text{ mod } v,w).$$

This is beginning to look suspiciously like a more standard programming language expression for the gcd, such as

$$gcd(u,v) = \text{ if } v = 0 \text{ then } u \text{ else } gcd(v,u \text{ mod } v).$$

From now on we will write Horn clauses in this form.

There is the question of the scope of the variables in a procedural interpretation of Horn clauses. As with procedure definitions in a block-structured language, the assumption is that all variables are local to each "call" of the procedure. Indeed, variables used in the head can be viewed as "parameters," while variables used only in the body can be viewed as "local temporaries." This is only an approximate description, as the algorithms used to implement the "execution" of Horn clauses treat variables in a more general way, as we will see in Section 11.3.

We haven't yet seen how queries or goal statements can be expressed as Horn clauses. In fact, a query is exactly the "opposite" of a fact—a Horn clause with no head:

$$mammal(human) \leftarrow . \quad \text{— a fact}$$
$$\leftarrow mammal(human). \quad \text{— a query or goal}$$

A Horn clause without a head could also include a sequence of queries separated by commas:

$$\leftarrow \text{mammal}(x), \text{legs}(x,y).$$

Why queries correspond to Horn clauses without heads should become clear when we understand the inference rule that logic programming systems apply to derive new statements from a set of given statements, namely, the resolution rule or principle studied next.

11.3   RESOLUTION AND UNIFICATION

Resolution is an inference rule for Horn clauses that is especially efficient. Resolution says that if we have two Horn clauses, and we can match the head of the first Horn clause with one of the statements in the body of the second clause, then the first clause can be used to replace its head in the second clause by its body. In symbols, if we have Horn clauses

$$a \leftarrow a_1, \ldots, a_n.$$
$$b \leftarrow b_1, \ldots, b_m.$$

and b_i matches a, then we can infer the clause

$$b \leftarrow b_1, \ldots, b_{i-1}, a_1, \ldots, a_n, b_{i+1}, \ldots, b_m.$$

The simplest example of this is when there are only single statements in the body of the Horn clauses, such as in

$$b \leftarrow a.$$

and

$$c \leftarrow b.$$

Then resolution says that we may infer the following clause:

$$c \leftarrow a.$$

This is precisely the inference rule that we gave in Example 3 in Section 11.1.

Another way of looking at resolution is to combine left- and right-hand sides of both Horn clauses and then cancel those statements that match on both sides. Thus, for the simplest example,

$$b \leftarrow a.$$

and

$$c \leftarrow b.$$

give

$$b, c \leftarrow a, b.$$

and canceling the b,

$$b, c \leftarrow a, b.$$

gives

$$c \leftarrow a.$$

Now we can see how a logic programming system can treat a goal or list of goals as a Horn clause without a head. The system attempts to apply resolution by matching one of the goals in the body of the headless clause with the head of a known clause. It then replaces the matched goal with the body of that clause, creating a new list of goals, which it continues to modify in the same way. The new goals are called **subgoals.** In symbols, if we have the goal

$$\leftarrow a.$$

and the clause $a \leftarrow a_1, \ldots , a_n$, then resolution replaces the original goal a by the subgoals

$$\leftarrow a_1, \ldots, a_n.$$

If the system succeeds eventually in eliminating all goals—thus deriving the empty Horn clause—then the original statement has been proved.

EXAMPLE 8

The simplest case is when the goal is already a known fact, such as

$$\text{mammal(human).}$$

and one asks whether a human is a mammal:

$$\leftarrow \text{mammal(human).}$$

Using resolution, the system combines the two Horn clauses into

$$\text{mammal(human)} \leftarrow \text{mammal(human).}$$

and then cancels both sides to obtain

$$\leftarrow.$$

Thus the system has found that indeed a human is a mammal and would respond to the query with "Yes."   ■

EXAMPLE 9

A slightly more complicated example is the following. Given the rules

$$\text{legs}(x,2) \leftarrow \text{mammal}(x), \text{arms}(x,2).$$
$$\text{legs}(x,4) \leftarrow \text{mammal}(x), \text{arms}(x,0).$$
$$\text{mammal(horse).}$$
$$\text{arms(horse,0).}$$

if we supply the query

$$\leftarrow \text{legs(horse,4).}$$

then applying resolution using the second rule, we get

$$\text{legs}(x,4) \leftarrow \text{mammal}(x), \text{arms}(x,0), \text{legs}(\text{horse},4).$$

Now, to cancel the statements involving the predicate legs from each side, we have to match the variable x to horse, so we replace x by horse everywhere in the statement:

$$\text{legs}(\text{horse},4) \leftarrow \text{mammal}(\text{horse}), \text{arms}(\text{horse},0), \text{legs}(\text{horse},4).$$

and cancel to get the subgoals

$$\leftarrow \text{mammal}(\text{horse}), \text{arms}(\text{horse},0).$$

Now we apply resolution twice more using the facts mammal(horse) and arms(horse,0) and cancel:

$$\text{mammal}(\text{horse}) \leftarrow \text{mammal}(\text{horse}), \text{arms}(\text{horse},0).$$
$$\leftarrow \text{arms}(\text{horse},0).$$
$$\text{arms}(\text{horse},0) \leftarrow \text{arms}(\text{horse},0).$$
$$\leftarrow.$$

Since we have arrived at the empty statement, our original query is true. ∎

Example 9 demonstrates an additional requirement when we apply resolution to derive goals: to match statements that contain variables, we must set the variables equal to terms so that the statements become identical and can be canceled from both sides. This process of pattern matching to make statements identical is called **unification,** and variables that are set equal to patterns are said to be **instantiated.** Thus, to implement resolution effectively, we must also provide an algorithm for unification. A very general unification algorithm does exist, but most logic programming systems use a weaker algorithm that we discuss in Section 11.4.

EXAMPLE 10

To show in more detail the kind of unification that takes place in a logic programming language, consider the greatest common divisor problem (Example 6):

$$\text{gcd}(u,0,u).$$
$$\text{gcd}(u,v,w) \leftarrow \text{not zero}(v), \text{gcd}(v,u \bmod v,w).$$

Now given the goal

$$\leftarrow \text{gcd}(15,10,x).$$

resolution fails using the first clause (15 does not match 0), so using the second clause and unifying $\text{gcd}(u,v,w)$ with $\text{gcd}(15,10,x)$ gives

$$\text{gcd}(15,10,x) \leftarrow \text{not zero}(10), \text{gcd}(10,15 \bmod 10,x), \text{gcd}(15,10,x).$$

Assuming that the system knows that zero(10) is false, so that not zero(10) is true, and simplifying 15 mod 10 to 5, we cancel gcd (15,10,x)

from both sides and obtain the subgoal

$$\leftarrow gcd(10,5,x).$$

Note that this is just another goal to be resolved like the original goal. This we do by unification as before, obtaining

$$gcd(10,5,x) \leftarrow not\ zero(5),\ gcd(5,10\ mod\ 5,x),\ gcd(10,5,x).$$

and so get the further subgoal

$$\leftarrow gcd(5,0,x).$$

Now this matches the first rule

$$gcd(u,0,u).$$

so instantiating x to 5 results in the empty statement, and the system will reply with something like

$$Yes: x = 5$$

Resolution and unification have performed the computation of the greatest common divisor of 10 and 15 using Euclid's algorithm! ■

There is one other problem that must be solved before a working resolution implementation can be achieved. To achieve efficient execution a logic programming system must apply a fixed algorithm that specifies (1) the order in which the system attempts to resolve a list of goals and (2) the order in which clauses are used to resolve goals. As an example of (1), consider the goal

$$\leftarrow legs(horse,4).$$

In Example 9 this led to the two subgoals

$$\leftarrow mammal(horse),\ arms(horse,0).$$

A logic programming system must now decide whether to try to resolve mammal(horse) first or arms(horse,0) first. In the example given, both choices lead to the same answer, but, as we shall see in the examples that follow, the order can have a significant effect on the answers found.

The order in which clauses are used can also have a major effect on the result of applying resolution. For example, given the Horn clauses

$$ancestor(x,y) \leftarrow parent(x,z),\ ancestor(z,y).$$
$$ancestor(x,x).$$
$$parent(amy,bob).$$

if we provide the query

$$\leftarrow ancestor(x,bob).$$

there are two possible answers: $x = bob$ and $x = amy$. If the assertion $ancestor(x,x)$ is used, the solution $x = bob$ will be found. If the clause $ancestor(x,y) \leftarrow parent(x,z),\ ancestor(z,y)$ is used, the solution $x = amy$ will be found. Which one is found first, or even if any is found, can depend on the order in which the clauses are used, as well as the order in which goals are resolved.

Logic programming systems using Horn clauses and resolution with prespecified orders for (1) and (2) therefore violate the basic principle that such systems set out to achieve: that a programmer need worry only about the logic itself, while the control (the methods used to produce an answer) can be ignored. Instead, a programmer must always be aware of the way the system produces answers. It is possible to design systems that will always produce all the answers implied by the logic, but they are (so far) too inefficient to be used as programming systems.

11.4   THE LANGUAGE Prolog

Prolog is the most widely used logic programming language. Prolog uses Horn clauses and implements resolution using a strictly linear "depth-first" strategy and a unification algorithm described in more detail shortly. Although no standard Prolog exists, the Prolog developed in the late 1970s and early 1980s at the University of Edinburgh has become some-what of a de facto standard, and we will use that as a basis for our description. Other Prolog systems (particularly Turbo Prolog) differ substantially from this. We discuss the essential features of Prolog in the sections that follow.

11.4.1   Notation and Data Structures

Prolog uses almost the identical notation developed earlier for Horn clauses, except that the implication arrow "$\leftarrow$" is replaced by a colon followed by a dash, "$:-$". Thus the sample ancestor program from the previous section would be written in Prolog syntax as follows:

```
ancestor(X,Y) :- parent(X,Z), ancestor(Z,Y).
ancestor(X,X).
parent(amy,bob).
```

and Example 4 would be written as follows:

```
natural(0).
natural(successor(X)) :- natural(X).
```

Note that the variables X and Y are written in uppercase. Prolog distinguishes variables from constants and names of predicates and functions by using uppercase for variables and lowercase for constants and names. It is also possible in most Prolog systems to denote a variable by writing an underscore before the name, as in ancestor(_x,_x).

In addition to the comma connective that stands for "and," Prolog uses the semicolon ";" for "or." However, the semicolon is rarely used in programming, since it is not a standard part of Horn clause logic.

Basic data structures are terms like `parent(X,Z)` or `successor(successor(0))`. Prolog also includes lists as a basic data structure, which uses square brackets (like ML and Miranda): the list consisting of items x, y, and z is written as `[x,y,z]`.

It is also possible to specify the head and tail of a list using a vertical bar: `[H|T]` means that H is the first item in the list and T is the tail of the list. Thus, if `[H|T] = [1,2,3]`, then H = 1 and T = `[2,3]`. It is also possible to write as many terms as one wishes before the bar: `[X,Y|Z]` = `[1,2,3]` gives X = 1, Y = 2, and Z = `[3]`. The empty list is denoted by `[]` and does not have a first element.

Prolog has a number of standard predicates that are always built in, such as `not`, `=`, and the I/O operations `read`, `write`, and `nl` (for newline). One anomaly in Prolog is that the "less than or equal to" operator is usually written "`=<`" instead of "`<=`" (perhaps because the latter is too easily confused with implication).

11.4.2   Execution in Prolog

There exist compilers for Prolog, but most systems are run as interpreters. A Prolog program consists of a set of Horn clauses in Prolog syntax, which is usually entered from a file and stored in a dynamically maintained database of clauses. Once a set of clauses has been entered into the database, goals can be entered either from a file or from the keyboard to begin execution. Thus, once a Prolog system has begun to execute, it will provide the user with a prompt for a query, such as

```
?- _
```

EXAMPLE 11

If the clauses

```
ancestor(X,Y) :- parent(X,Z), ancestor(Z,Y).
ancestor(X,X).
parent(amy,bob).
```

have been entered into the database, then the following queries would cause the indicated response:

```
?- ancestor(amy,bob).
yes

?- ancestor(bob,amy).
no

?- ancestor(X,bob).
X = amy ->_
```

In the last query there are two answers. Most Prolog systems will find one answer and then wait for a user prompt before printing more answers. If the user supplies a semicolon at the underscore (meaning "or"), then Prolog continues to find more answers:

```
?- ancestor(X,bob).
X = amy  ->;
X = bob

?- _
```

A carriage return usually cancels the continued search.   ∎

11.4.3   Arithmetic

Prolog has built-in arithmetic operations and an arithmetic evaluator. Arithmetic terms can be written either in the usual infix notation or as terms in prefix notation: 3 + 4 and +(3, 4) mean the same thing. However, Prolog cannot tell when to consider an arithmetic term as a term itself (that is, strictly as data), or when to evaluate it. Thus

```
?- write(3+5).
3+5
```

To force the evaluation of an arithmetic term, a new operation is required: the is built-in predicate. Thus, to get Prolog to evaluate 3 + 5, we need to write

```
?- X is 3+5, write(X).
X = 8
```

A further consequence of this is that two arithmetic terms may not be equal as terms even though they have the same value:

```
?- 3+4 = 4+3.
no
```

To get equality of values we must force evaluation using is, for example, by writing the predicate

```
valequal(Term1,Term2) :- X is Term1, Y is Term2,
                          X = Y.
```

We would then get

```
?- valequal(3+4,4+3).
yes
```

Now we can see how to write Euclid's algorithm for the greatest common divisor from Example 10 in Prolog. We wrote this algorithm in generic Horn clauses as

$$gcd(u,0,u).$$
$$gcd(u,v,w) \leftarrow not\ zero(v),\ gcd(v,u\ mod\ v,w).$$

In Prolog this translates to

```
gcd(U,0,U).
gcd(U,V,W) :- not(V=0), R is U mod V, gcd(V,R,W).
```

The middle statement R is U mod V is required to force evaluation of the mod operation.

11.4.4   Unification

Unification is the process by which variables are instantiated, or allocated memory and assigned values, so that patterns match during resolution. Unification is the process of making two terms "the same" in some sense. The basic expression whose semantics is determined by unification is equality: in Prolog the goal s = t attempts to unify the terms s and t. It succeeds if unification succeeds and fails otherwise. Thus we can study unification in Prolog by experimenting with the effect of equality:

```
?- me = me.
yes

?- me = you.
no

?- me = X.
X = me

?- f(a,X) = f(Y,b).
X = b
Y = a

?- f(X) = g(X)
no

?- f(X) = f(a,b)
no

?- f(a,g(X)) = f(Y,b)
no

?- f(a,g(X)) = f(Y,g(b)).
X = b
Y = a
```

From these experiments we can formulate the following unification algorithm for Prolog:

1. A constant unifies only with itself: me = me succeeds but me = you fails.
2. A variable that is uninstantiated unifies with anything and becomes instantiated to that thing.
3. A structured term (i.e., a function applied to arguments) unifies with another term only if it has the same function name and the same number of arguments, and the arguments can be unified recursively. Thus f(a, X) unifies with f(Y, b) by instantiating X to b and Y to a.

A variation on case 2 is when two uninstantiated variables are unified:

```
?- X = Y.
X = _23
Y = _23
```

The number printed on the right-hand side—in this case, 23—will differ from system to system and indicates an internal memory location set aside for that variable. Thus unification causes uninstantiated variables to share memory, that is, become aliases of each other.

We can use unification in Prolog to get very short expressions for many operations. As examples, let us develop Prolog programs for the list operations **append** and **reverse**. We note again that because Prolog allows a list to be represented by a term such as [X|Y], where X and Y are variables, there is no need for a built-in function to return the head of a list or the tail of a list: just setting [X|Y] = [1,2,3] with uninstantiated variables X and Y returns the head as X and the tail as Y by unification. Similarly, there is no need for a list constructor like the cons operation of LISP: if we want to add 0, say, to the list [1,2,3], we simply write [0|[1,2,3]], as for example,

```
:- X = [0|[1,2,3]].
X = [0,1,2,3]
```

However, we could, if we wanted, write the following clause

```
cons(X,Y,L) :- L = [X|Y].
```

and then use it to compute heads, tails, and constructed lists, depending on how we instantiate the variables on the left-hand side:

```
?- cons(0,[1,2,3],A).
A = [0,1,2,3]

?- cons(X,Y,[1,2,3]).
X = 1
Y = [2,3]
```

Thus we can use variables in a term as either input or output parameters, and Prolog clauses can be "run" backward as well as forward—something the procedural interpretation of Horn clauses did not tell us!

Indeed, unification can be used to shorten clauses such as `cons` further. Since the " = " operator is there only to force unification, one can let resolution cause the unification automatically by writing the patterns to be unified directly in the parameters of the head. Thus the following definition of cons has precisely the same meaning as the previous definition:

```
cons(X,Y,[X|Y]).
```

The appearance of the pattern [X|Y] in place of the third variable automatically unifies it with a variable used in that place in a goal. This process could be referred to as **pattern-directed invocation.** The functional languages ML and Miranda studied in Chapter 10 have a similar mechanism.

Now let's write an append procedure:

```
append(X,Y,Z) :- X = [], Y = Z.
append(X,Y,Z) :- X = [A|B], Z = [A|W],
                 append(B,Y,W).
```

The first clause states that appending any list to the empty list just gives that list. The second clause states that appending a list whose head is A and tail is B to a list Y gives a list whose head is also A and whose tail is B with Y appended.

Rewriting this using pattern-directed invocation, we get the following extremely concise form:

```
append([],Y,Y).
append([A|B],Y,[A|W]) :- append(B,Y,W).
```

This `append` can also be "run" backward and can even find all the ways to append two lists together to get a specified list:

```
?- append(X,Y,[1,2]).
X = []
Y = [1,2]  ->;

X = [1]
Y = [2]  ->;

X = [1,2]
Y = []
```

Prolog does this by first using the first clause and matching X to the empty list [] and Y to the final list. Then it continues the search for solutions by using the second clause, matching X to [A|B] and setting up the subgoal append(B,Y,W) with W = [2,3]. This begins the search over again with B in place of X, so B is first matched with [ ] and Y with [2,3], giving X = [1|[]] = [1]. Then B is matched with a new [A|B] by the second clause, and so on.

Finally, in this section we give a Prolog definition for the reverse of a list:

```
reverse([],[]).
reverse([H|T],L) :- reverse(T,L1),
                    append(L1,[H],L).
```

11.4.5   Prolog's Search Strategy

Prolog applies resolution in a strictly linear fashion, replacing goals left to right and considering clauses in the database in top-to-bottom order. Subgoals are also considered immediately once they are set up. This search strategy can be viewed as a depth-first search on a tree of possible choices.

To see this, consider the following clauses:

```
(1) ancestor(X,Y) :- parent(X,Z), ancestor(Z,Y).
(2) ancestor(X,X).
(3) parent(amy,bob).
```

Given the goal ancestor(X,bob), Prolog's search strategy is left to right and depth first on the following tree of subgoals. Edges are labeled by the number of the clause used by Prolog for resolution, and instantiations of variables are written in curly brackets.

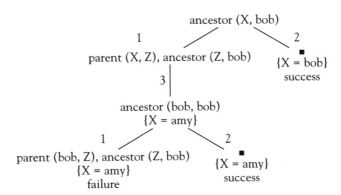

Leaf nodes in this tree occur either when no match is found for the leftmost clause or when all clauses have been eliminated, thus indicating success. Whenever failure occurs, or the user indicates a continued search with a semicolon, Prolog **backtracks** up the tree to find further paths to a leaf, releasing instantiations of variables as it does so. Thus, in the tree shown, after the solution X = amy is found, if backtracking is initiated this instantiation of X will be released, and the new path to a leaf with X = bob will be found.

This depth-first strategy is extremely efficient, since it can be implemented in a stack-based or recursive fashion using an approach similar to that of a stack of activation records as described in Chapter 7. However, it means also that solutions may not be found if the search tree has branches that have infinite depth. For example, suppose we had written the clauses in a slightly different order:

```
(1)  ancestor(X,Y) :- ancestor(Z,Y), parent(X,Z).
(2)  ancestor(X,X).
(3)  parent(amy,bob).
```

Now Prolog will go into an infinite loop attempting to satisfy ances-tor(Z,Y), continually reusing the first clause. Of course, this is a result of the "left-recursive" way the first clause was written and the fact that no other clauses precede it, but in true logic programming, the order of the clauses should not matter. Indeed, a logic programming system that adopts breadth-first instead of depth-first search will always find solutions if there are any. Unfortunately, breadth-first search is far more expensive than is depth first, so few logic programming systems use it. Prolog always uses depth-first search.

11.4.6   Loops and Control Structures

We can use the depth-first search with backtracking of Prolog to perform loops and repetitive searches. What we must do is force backtracking even when a solution is found. We do this with the built-in predicate fail. As an example, we can get Prolog to print all solutions to a goal such as append without needing to give semicolons to the system as follows. Define the predicate

```
printpieces(L) :- append(X,Y,L),
                  write(X),
                  write(Y),
                  nl,
                  fail.
```

Now we get the following behavior:

```
?- printpieces([1,2]).
[ ][1,2]
[1][2]
[1,2][ ]
no
```

Backtracking on failure forces Prolog to write all solutions at once.

We can also use this feature to get repetitive computations. For example, the following clauses generate all integers $>= 0$ as solutions to the goal `num(X)`:

```
(1)  num(0).
(2)  num(X)  :-  num(Y), X is Y+1 .
```

The search tree is displayed next. In this case, it has an infinite branch to the right. (The different uses of Y from clause (2) in the tree are indicated by adding quotes to the variable name.)

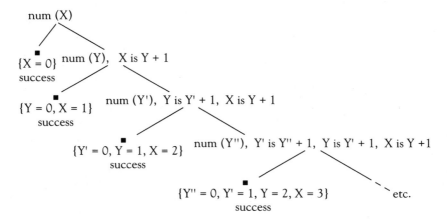

Now we could try to generate the integers from 1 to 10, say, by writing

```
writenum(I,J)  :-  num(X),
                   I =< X,
                   X =< J,
                   write(X),
                   nl,
                   fail.
```

and giving the goal `writenum(1,10)`. Unfortunately, this will go into an infinite loop after X = 10, generating ever-larger integers X even though X =< 10 will never succeed.

What is needed is some way of stopping the search from continuing through the whole tree. Prolog has an operator to do this: the **cut**, usually written as an exclamation point. The cut "freezes" the choice made when it is encountered. If a cut is reached on backtracking, the search of the subtrees of the parent node of the node containing the cut stops, and the search continues with the "grandparent" node. In effect, the cut "prunes" the search tree of all other siblings to the right of the node containing the cut.

EXAMPLE 12

Consider the tree representing the goal ancestor(X,bob). If we rewrite the clauses using the cut as follows:

```
(1)  ancestor(X,Y) :- parent(X,Z), !,
                                 ancestor(Z,Y).
(2)  ancestor(X,X).
(3)  parent(amy,bob).
```

then only the solution X = amy will be found, since the branch containing X = bob will be pruned from the search:

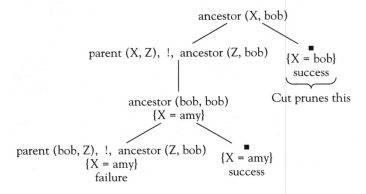

If we place the cut as follows,

```
(1)  ancestor(X,Y) :- !, parent(X,Z),
                             ancestor(Z,Y).
(2)  ancestor(X,X).
(3)  parent(amy,bob).
```

then no solutions at all will be found:

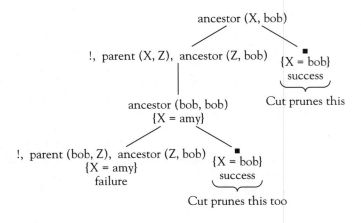

On the other hand, with the cut placed as follows,

```
(1)  ancestor(X,Y)  :-  parent(X,Z),  ancestor(Z,Y).
(2)  ancestor(X,X)  :-  !.
(3)  parent(amy,bob).
```

both solutions will still be found, since the right subtree of ances-
tor(X,bob) is not pruned (in fact nothing at all is pruned in this
example).

The cut can be used as an efficiency mechanism to reduce the
number of branches in the search tree that need to be followed. The cut
also allows us to solve the problem of the infinite loop in the program
to print numbers between I and J. The following is one solution:

```
num(0).
num(X)  :-  num(Y),  X  is  Y+1  .
writenum(I,J)  :-  num(X),
                   I  =<  X,
                   X  =<  J,
                   write(X),  n1,
                   X  =  J,  !,
                   fail.
```

In this code, X = J will succeed when the upper bound J is reached,
and then the cut will cause backtracking to fail, halting the search for
new values of X.

The cut can also be used to imitate if-then-else constructs in procedural and functional languages. To write a clause such as

$$D = \text{if } A \text{ then } B \text{ else } C$$

we write the following Prolog:

```
D  :-  A,  !,  B.
D  :-  C.
```

Note that we could have achieved almost the same result without
the cut,

```
D  :-  A,  B.
D  :-  not(A),  C.
```

but this is subtly different, since A is "executed" twice. Of course, if A
has no side effects, then the two forms are equivalent. Nevertheless, the
cut does improve the efficiency.

Finally, we give a longer program that uses most of the features
discussed so far. It is a program to compute primes using the sieve of
Erastosthenes and is adapted from an example in Clocksin and Mellish
[1987]):

```
primes(Limit,Ps)  :- integers(2,Limit,Is),
                           sieve(Is,Ps).
integers(Low,High,[Low|Rest])  :-
               Low =< High,  !,  M is Low+1,
               integers(M,High,Rest).
integers(Low,High,[]).
sieve([],[]).
sieve([I|Is],[I|Ps])  :- remove(I,Is,New),
                           sieve(New,Ps).
remove(P,[],[]).
remove(P,[I|Is],[I|Nis])  :-
        not(0 is I mod P),  !,  remove(P,Is,Nis).
remove(P,[I|Is],Nis)  :-
        0 is I mod P,  !,  remove(P,Is,Nis).
```

11.5   PROBLEMS WITH LOGIC PROGRAMMING

The original goal of logic programming was to make programming into a specification activity—to allow the programmer to specify only the properties of a solution and to let the language system provide the actual method for computing the solution from its properties. Logic programming languages, and Prolog in particular, have only partially met this goal. Instead, the nature of the algorithms used by logic programming systems, such as resolution, unification, and depth-first search, have introduced many pitfalls into the specifics of writing programs, which a programmer must be aware of to write efficient, or even correct, programs. We have mentioned this occasionally, but we want now to collect some of these problems together, including a number of problems that have not yet been mentioned. The problems we will discuss are the "occur-check" problem in unification, problems with negation (the not operator), the limitations of Horn clauses in logic, and the need for control information in a logic program.

11.5.1   The Occur-Check Problem in Unification

The unification algorithm used by Prolog is actually incorrect: when unifying a variable with a term, Prolog does not check whether the variable itself occurs in the term it is being instantiated to. This is the "occur-check" problem. The simplest example is expressed by the following clause:

```
is_own_successor  :- X = successor(X).
```

This will be true if there exists an X for which X is its own successor. However, even in the absence of any other clauses for successor, Prolog still answers "yes"; that is, any X will do! That this is incorrect becomes apparent only if we make Prolog try to print out such an X, as with

```
is_own_successor(X) :- X = successor(X).
```

Now Prolog will respond with an infinite loop:

```
?- is_own_successor(X).
X = successor(successor(successor(successor(
    successor(successor(successor(successor(
    successor(successor(successor(successor(
    successor(successor(successor(successor(
    successor(successor(successor(successor(
    successor(successor(successor(successor(
    successor(successor(successor(successor(
    successor(successor(successor(successor....
```

The reason is that unification has constructed X as a circular structure indicated by the following picture:

X is finite, but the attempt to print X is infinite. Thus what should be logically false now becomes a programming error.

Why doesn't Prolog's unification contain a check for such occurrences? The answer is that unification without the occur-check can be relatively easily implemented in an efficient way, while efficient algorithms that include the occur-check are more complex. (For a discussion, see Lloyd [1984, p. 23].)

11.5.2   Negation as Failure

All logic programming systems have the basic property that something that cannot be proved to be true is assumed to be false. This is called the **closed-world assumption.** We saw an example of this already in Example 1, where we noted that, since natural(-1) cannot be proved from the axioms for the predicate "natural," it is assumed to be false. This property of logic programming, together with the way negation is implemented, results in further surprises in the behavior of logic programs.

How can one implement the not operator in logic programming? The straightforward answer is that the goal not(X) succeeds whenever the goal X fails. This is what is meant by "negation as failure." As a simple example, consider the following program consisting of one clause:

```
parent(amy,bob).
```

If we now ask,

```
?- not(mother(amy,bob)).
```

the answer is yes, since the system does not know that amy is female, and that female parents are mothers. If we were to add these facts to our program, not(mother(amy,bob)) would no longer be true.

The foregoing property of logic programs—that adding information to a system can reduce the number of things that can be proved—is called **nonmonotonic reasoning** and is a consequence of the closed-world assumption. Nonmonotonic reasoning has been the subject of considerable study in logic programming and artificial intelligence. (See the Notes and References.)

A related problem is that failure causes instantiations of variables to be released by backtracking, so that after failure, a variable may no longer have an appropriate value. Thus, for example, not(not(X)) does not have the same result as X itself (we assume the fact human(bob) in this example):

```
?- human(X).
X=bob

?- not(not(human(X))).
X  = _23
```

The goal not(not(human(X))) succeeds because not(human(X)) fails, but when not(human(X)) fails, the instantiation of X to bob is released, causing X to be printed as an uninstantiated variable.

A similar situation is shown by the following:

```
?- X=0, not(X=1).
X=0

?- not(X=1), X=0.
no
```

The second pair of goals fails because X is instantiated to 1 to make X=1 succeed, and then not(X=1) fails. The goal X=0 is never reached.

11.5.3 Horn Clauses Do Not Express All of Logic

Not every logical statement can be turned into Horn clauses. In particular, statements involving quantifiers may not be expressible in Horn clause form. A simple example is the following:

$$p(a) \text{ and (there exists } x, \text{ not}(p(x))).$$

We can certainly express the truth of $p(a)$ as a Horn clause, but the second statement cannot be written in Horn clause form. If we try to do so in Prolog, we might try something like:

```
p(a).
not(p(b)).
```

but the second statement will result in an error (trying to redefine the not operator). Perhaps the best approximation would be simply the statement p(a). Then the closed-world assumption will force not(p(X)) to be true for all X not equal to a, but this is really the logical equivalent to

$$p(a) \text{ and (for all } x, \text{not}(x = a) \rightarrow \text{not}(p(a))).$$

which is not the same as the original statement.

11.5.4   Control Information in Logic Programming

We have already talked about the cut as a useful, even essential, explicit control mechanism in Prolog. But because of its depth-first search strategy, and its linear processing of goals and statements, Prolog programs also contain implicit information on control that can easily cause programs to fail.

One example is the ancestor program used earlier:

```
ancestor(X,Y) :- parent(X,Z), ancestor(Z,Y).
ancestor(X,X).
parent(amy,bob).
```

If we accidentally wrote the right-hand side of the first clause backward, as

```
ancestor(X,Y) :- ancestor(Z,Y), parent(X,Z).
```

we would immediately get into an infinite loop: Prolog will try to instantiate the variable Z to make ancestor true, causing an infinite descent in the search tree using the first clause. On the other hand, if we changed the order of the clauses to

```
ancestor(X,X).
ancestor(X,Y) :- ancestor(Z,Y), parent(X,Z).
parent(amy,bob).
```

the search will now find both solutions X = amy and X = bob to the query ancestor(amy, X), but will still go into an infinite loop searching for further (nonexistent) solutions.

A similar situation exists if we write the clauses for the program to generate natural numbers in reverse order:

```
num(X) :- num(Y), X is Y+1 .
num(0).
```

Now the goal num(X) will go into an infinite loop. Nothing at all will be generated.

A more complicated logical question is the representation of algorithmic logic using Horn clauses. We mentioned in Section 11.3 that a specification for a sorting procedure could be given as follows, for two lists S and T:

```
sort(S,T)  :-  permutation(S,T),  sorted(T).
```

We can now give specifications for the meaning of permutation and sorted in Prolog syntax:

```
sorted([]).
sorted([X]).
sorted([X,Y|Z])  :-  X  =<  Y,  sorted([Y|Z]).

permutation([],[]).
permutation(X,[Y|Z])  :-  append(U,[Y|V],X),
                          append(U,V,W),
                          permutation(W,Z).
```

This represents a mathematical definition for what it means for a list of numbers to be sorted in increasing order, but as a program, it represents almost the slowest sort in the world: permutations of the unsorted list are generated until one of them happens to be sorted!

In the best of all possible worlds, one would want a logic programming system to accept the mathematical definition of a property and *find* an efficient algorithm to compute it. Of course, in Prolog or any other logic programming system, we cannot only provide specifications in our programs, we must also provide algorithmic control information. Thus, in the gcd program of Example 10, we specified explicitly the steps used by Euclid's algorithm instead of providing a mathematical definition of the greatest common divisor. Similarly, to get a reasonably efficient sorting program in Prolog, we must specify the actual steps an algorithm must take to produce the result. For example, a quicksort program in Prolog is as follows (adapted from Clocksin and Mellish [1987]):

```
qsort([],[]).
qsort([H|T],S)  :-  partition(H,T,L,R),
                    qsort(L,L1),
                    qsort(R,R1),
                    append(L1,[H|R1],S),
partition(P,[A|X],[A|Y],Z)  :-  A  <  P,
                                partition(P,X,Y,Z).
partition(P,[A|X],Y,[A|Z])  :-  A  >=  P,
                                partition(P,X,Y,Z).
partition(P,[],[],[]).
```

In this program, the standard method of partitioning is shown by the clauses for the predicate `partition`, and the two recursive calls to `qsort` in the second clause are readily evident. Thus, in specifying sequential algorithms such as sorting, Prolog is not so different from imperative or functional programming as one might think.

There is, however, one useful aspect to being able to execute a specification for a property, even if it is not acceptable as an algorithm for computing that property: it lets us test whether the specification is correct. Prolog has in fact been used successfully as a basis for running such specifications during the design of a program. (See the Notes and References.)

11.6   EXTENDING LOGIC PROGRAMMING: EQUATIONAL SYSTEMS

One of the principal features of a logic programming language is that it can be used to write executable specifications for a programming system. Such specifications can be tested to verify that they are not only correct, but that they adequately represent the user's requirements. Thus logic programming languages can be used as **rapid prototyping systems** for software development.

Unfortunately, the Horn clause logic of Prolog, or even predicate calculus, is not able to express the kinds of specifications that have been developed for a major area of programming, namely, the specification of abstract data types. In Chapter 8 we described the algebraic specification of abstract data types as developed by Goguen and Guttag, which uses equations to specify the behavior of the data type. For example, the specification of a stack of integers from that chapter is written as follows (we restrict ourselves here to integer stacks for simplicity):

type intstack **imports** boolean, integer

operations:

> create: $\rightarrow$ intstack
> push: intstack $\times$ integer $\rightarrow$ intstack
> pop: intstack $\rightarrow$ intstack
> top: intstack $\rightarrow$ integer
> empty: intstack $\rightarrow$ boolean

variables: s: intstack; x: integer

axioms:

> top(create) $=$ error
> top(push(s,x)) $=$ x
> pop(create) $=$ error
> pop(push(s,x)) $=$ s

empty(create) = true
empty(push(s,x)) = false

The equations given in the axiom section completely define the behavior of the functions given in the operations section. It would be nice if these **equational specifications** could be written directly in a logic programming language.

However, Prolog and other Horn clause systems do not accept equations as rules, so an algebraic specification cannot be translated directly into Prolog. It *is* possible to give an approximate translation of some specifications into Prolog. For example, the intstack specification can be approximated by the following Prolog clauses:

```
intstack(create).
intstack(push(S,X)) :- intstack(S), integer(X).
pop(push(S,X),S) :- intstack(push(S,X)).
top(push(S,X),X) :- intstack(push(S,X)).
empty(create).
```

These clauses essentially define an intstack to be of the form push(push(push(...push(create,Xn)...,X3),X2),X1), where all the Xi are integers. They rely on the closed-world assumption to make top(create,X), pop(create,S), and empty(push(S,X)) false. A similar translation scheme could be used for other equational specifications in which the data type could be put into a standard form, such as the sequence of push applications (such a form was called a canonical form in Chapter 8).

It would be much better, however, if the equational specifications could be written directly in a logic programming language, and this has been a partial motivation for the development and study of **equational logic** programming languages, such as the **OBJ** language developed by Goguen and the **Equation Interpreter Project** of O'Donnell. (See the Notes and References.) Equational logic languages allow the axioms for an abstract data type to be interpreted directly, or with small modifications, by the language system, without any underlying assumptions about the representation of such data types. Inference rules for such systems generally include the usual properties of equality, such as reflexivity, symmetry, and transitivity. Equational logic systems allow for the specification of a data type to be tested directly for consistency and applicability for a particular purpose.

Here, for example, is an OBJ specification for the intstack abstract data type:

```
obj STACK_OF_INT is
  protecting INT .
  sorts Stack NeStack .
  subsorts NeStack < Stack .
  op empty :  -> Stack .
```

```
op push : Int Stack -> NeStack .
op top_ : NeStack -> Int .
op pop_ : NeStack -> Stack .
var I : Int .
var S : Stack .
eq: top push(I,S) = I .
eq: pop push(I,S) = S .
jbo
```

(The need for two types, nonempty stack = NeStack and ordinary stack = Stack comes from the error conditions in the algebraic specification.)

Equational logic programming languages have been difficult to implement, since the algorithms for inference are complex and inefficient. Thus equational systems are still restricted to a few experimental implementations that have not been widely used.

Exercises

1. A standard method for analyzing logical statements is the truth table: assigning truth values to elementary statements allows us to determine the truth value of a compound statement, and statements with the same truth tables are logically equivalent. Thus the statement "p and not p" is equivalent to "false" by the following truth table:

p	not p	p and not p	false
false	true	false	false
true	false	false	false

Use truth tables to show that $p \rightarrow q$ is equivalent to (not p) or q (remember that $p \rightarrow q$ is false only if p is true and q is false).

2. A **tautology** is a statement that is always true, no matter what the truth values of its components. Use a truth table to show that false $\rightarrow p$ is a tautology for any statement p.

3. A **refutation system** is a logical system that proves a statement by assuming it is false and deriving a contradiction. Show that Horn clause logic with resolution is a refutation system. (Hint: The empty clause is assumed to be false, so a goal $\leftarrow a$ is equivalent to $a \rightarrow$ false. Show this is equivalent to not(a).)

4. Write the following statements in the first-order predicate calculus:

If it is raining or snowing, then there is precipitation.

If it is freezing and there is precipitation, then it is snowing.

If it is not freezing and there is precipitation, then it is raining.

It is snowing.

5. Write the statements in Exercise 4 as Prolog clauses, in the order given. What answer does Prolog give when given the query "Is it freezing?" The query "Is it raining?" Why? Can you rearrange the clauses so that Prolog can give better answers?

6. Write the following mathematical definition of the greatest common divisor of two numbers in first-order predicate calculus: the gcd of u and v is that number x such that x divides both u and v, and, given any other number y such that y divides u and v, then y divides x.

7. Translate the definition of the gcd in Exercise 6 into Prolog. Compare its efficiency to Euclid's algorithm as given in Section 11.4.3.

8. Write the following statement as Prolog clauses:

Mammals have four legs and no arms, or two arms and two legs.

9. Add the statement that a horse is a mammal and that a horse has no arms to the clauses of Exercise 8. Can Prolog derive that a horse has four legs? Explain.

10. Write Prolog clauses to express the following relationships, given the parent relationship: grandparent, sibling, cousin.

11. Write a Prolog program to find the last item in a list.

12. Write a Prolog program to find the maximum and minimum of a list of numbers.

13. Write a Prolog program that reads numbers from the standard input until a 0 is entered, creates a list of the numbers entered (not including the 0), and then prints the list in the order entered, one number per line. (`read(X)` can be used to read integer X from the input if the integer is entered on its own line and is terminated by a period.)

14. Write a Prolog program that will sort a list of integers according to the mergesort algorithm.

15. Compare the Prolog program for quicksort on page 450 with the Miranda version on page 392. What are the differences? What are the similarities?

16. Prolog shares some features with functional languages like Scheme, ML, and Miranda, studied in Chapter 10. Describe two major similarities. Describe two major differences.

17. In Prolog it is possible to think of certain clauses as representing tail recursion, in which the final term of a clause is a recursive reference, and a cut is written just before the final term. For example, the `gcd` clause

```
gcd(U,V,W) :- not(V=0), R is U mod V, !,
              gcd(V,R,W).
```

can be viewed as being tail recursive. Explain why this is so.

18. Write a Prolog program to print all Pythagorean triples (x, y, z) such that $1 <= x <= y <= z <= 100$. ((x, y, z) is a Pythagorean triple if $x \cdot x + y \cdot y = z \cdot z$.)

19. Write Prolog clauses for a member predicate: `member(X,L)` succeeds if X is a member of the list L (thus `member(2,[2,3])` succeeds but `member(1,[2,3])` fails). What happens if you use your clauses to answer the query `member(X,[2,3])`? The query `member(2,L)`? Draw search trees of subgoals as in Section 11.4.5 to explain your answers.

20. Write a Prolog program to compute the factorial of a natural number $n = 1 \cdot 2 \cdot \cdots \cdot (n-1) \cdot n$. Draw the search tree of subgoals that Prolog uses to compute the factorial of 4.

21. Write tail-recursive versions of the programs of Exercises 19 and 20 (see Exercise 17).

22. Draw search trees of subgoals and explain Prolog's responses based on the trees for the following goals:
    (a) `gcd(15,10,X)`. (See Section 11.4.3.)
    (b) `append(X,Y,[1,2])`. (See Section 11.4.4.)

23. Rewrite the Prolog clauses for Euclid's algorithm in Section 11.4.3 to use the cut instead of the test `not(V = 0)`. How much does this improve the efficiency of the program? Redraw the search tree of Exercise 22(a) to show how the cut prunes the tree.

24. Explain using a search tree why the cut in the following program has no effect on the solutions found to the query `ancestor(X, bob)`. Does the cut improve the efficiency at all? Why?

```
ancestor(X,Y) :- parent(X,Z), ancestor(Z,Y).
ancestor(X,X) :- !.
parent(amy,bob).
```

25. If we use cuts to improve the efficiency of the Prolog append program, we would write

```
append([],Y,Y) :- !.
append([A|B],Y,[A|W]) :- append(B,Y,W).
```

Now given the goal `append(X,Y,[1,2])` Prolog only responds with the solution X=[], Y=[1,2]. Explain using a search tree.

26. Rewrite the sieve of Erastosthenes Prolog program in Section 11.4.6 to remove all the cuts. Compare the efficiency of the resulting program to the original.

27. Explain the difference in Prolog between the following two definitions of the sibling relationship:

```
sibling1(X,Y) :- not(X=Y), parent(Z,X),
                 parent(Z,Y).
sibling2(X,Y) :- parent(Z,X), parent(Z,Y),
                 not(X=Y).
```

Which definition is better? Why?

28. Given the following Prolog clauses,

```
ancestor(X,Y) :- ancestor(Z,Y), parent(X,Z).
ancestor(X,X).
parent(amy,bob).
```

explain using a search tree of subgoals why Prolog fails to answer when given the goal ancestor(X,bob).

29. Given the following Prolog clauses:

```
ancestor(X,X).
ancestor(X,Y) :- ancestor(Z,Y), parent(X,Z).
parent(amy,bob).
```

explain Prolog's response to the query ancestor(amy,X) using a search tree of subgoals.

30. What is wrong with the following Prolog specification for a sort procedure:

```
sort(S,T) :- sorted(T), permutation(S,T).
```

Why?

31. Given only the following Prolog clause:

```
human(bob).
```

Prolog will respond as follows:

```
?- human(X).
X = bob

?- not(human(X)).
no
```

Why did Prolog respond to the last goal as it did? Is Prolog saying that there are no X that are not human, that is, that all X are human? Why?

32. The following is a possible implementation of a for-loop construct in Prolog, similar to the statement f o r I : = L t o H in Pascal:

```
for(I,I,I)  :- !.
for(I,I,H)  .
for(I,L,H)  :- L1 is L + 1,
                  for(I,L1,H).
```

Using this definition, we can repeat operations over I, such as printing all integers between L and H as follows:

```
printint(L,H)  :- for(I,L,H), write(I),  nl,  fail.
```

Explain how backtracking causes the f o r predicate to behave like a loop.

33. In the brief explanation of the difference between free and bound variables in Section 11.1, the details about potential reuse of names were ignored. For example, in the statement

$$a(x) \rightarrow \text{there exists } x,\ b(x)$$

the x in b is bound, while the x in a is free. Thus the **scope of a binding** must be properly defined to refer to a subset of the uses of the bound variable. Develop scope rules for bindings from which it can be determined which uses of variables are free and which are bound.

34. Compare the definition of free and bound variables in logical statements with the definition of free and bound variables in the lambda calculus (Chapter 10). How are they similar? How are they different?

35. The occur-check was dropped from Prolog because simple algorithms are inefficient. Describe using the a p p e n d clauses (page 440) why the occur-check can be inefficient.

36. We have seen that Prolog can have difficulties with infinite data sets, such as that produced by the clauses

```
int(0).
int(X)  :- int(Y), X is Y + 1 .
```

and with self-referential terms such as

```
X = [1|X]
```

which causes an occur-check problem. In Miranda (Chapter 10) infinite data constructions such as the foregoing are possible using delayed evaluation. Does delayed evaluation make sense in Prolog? Can you think of any other ways infinite data structures might be dealt with?

37. Give a Prolog implementation for the following intqueue abstract data type specification similar to the specification for an intstack in Section 11.6:

type intqueue **imports** boolean, integer

operations:

> create: → intequeue
> enqueue: intqueue × integer → intqueue
> dequeue: intqueue → intqueue
> front: intqueue → integer
> empty:intqueue → boolean

variables: q:intqueue; x: integer

axioms:

> empty(create) = true
> empty(enqueue(q,x)) = false
> front(create) = error
> front(enqueue(q,x)) = if empty(q) then x else front(q)
> dequeue(create) = error
> dequeue(enqueue(q,x)) =
> > if empty(q) then q else enqueue(dequeue(q),x)

38. Kowalski [1988] makes the following statement about his pseudoequation A(lgorithm) = L(ogic) + C(ontrol): "With Prolog we have a fixed C and can improve A only be improving L. Logic programming is concerned with the possibility of changing both L and C." Explain why he says this. Explain why it is not completely true that Prolog cannot change C.

39. In Chapter 10 we described a unification method used by ML and Miranda to perform type inference. Compare this unification with the unification of Prolog. Are there any differences?

40. Unification can be described as a substitution process that substitutes more specific values for variables so that equality of two expressions is achieved. For example, in Prolog the lists [1|Y] = [X] can be unified by substituting 1 for X and [ ] for Y. It is possible for different substitutions to cause equality. For instance, if [1|Y] is unified with X, one could set X = [1] and Y = [ ], or one could set X = [1|Y] and leave Y uninstantiated. This latter substitution is **more general** than the first because the additional substitution Y = [ ] transforms the first into the second. A substitution is a **most general unifier** of two expressions if it is more general than every other substitution that unifies the two expressions. Why does the unification algorithm of Prolog produce a most general unifier? Would it be useful for a logic programming language

to have a unification algorithm that does not produce a most general unifier? Why?

Notes and References

Logic programming arose out of work on proof techniques and automated deduction. The resolution principle was developed by Robinson [1965], and Horn clauses were invented by Horn [1951]. Kowalski [1979b] gives a general introduction to logic and the algorithms used in logic programming, such as unification and resolution. Lloyd [1984] gives a mathematical treatment of general unification techniques and negation as failure.

The early history of the development of Prolog is discussed in a pair of companion articles by Kowalski [1988] and Cohen [1988]. Both mention the importance of the first interpreters developed by Alain Colmerauer and Phillipe Roussel in Marseilles and the later systems written by David Warren, Fernando Pereira, and Luis Pereira in Edinburgh. Kowalski [1979a] introduced the famous formulation of Prolog's basic strategy as "Algorithm = Logic + Control" and gives a detailed account of how computation can be viewed as theorem proving, or "controlled deduction." (Niklaus Wirth's formulation of procedural programming "Algorithms + Data Structures = Programs" is the title of Wirth [1976] and is discussed in Chapters 1 and 6.)

Clocksin and Mellish [1987] is a basic reference for Prolog programming. Some of the examples in this chapter are based on examples in that text. Another reference for programming techniques in Prolog is Sterling and Shapiro [1986].

Davis [1982] describes how Prolog can be used as a runnable specification in the design of a software system. Warren [1980] shows how Prolog can be used in language translation and compilers. Clocksin and Mellish [1987] provide a chapter on the use of Prolog to parse grammars and a chapter on relation of logic programming to logic, in particular the translation of statements in predicate calculus into Horn clauses. For an approach to infinite data structures in Prolog (Exercise 36), see Colmerauer [1982].

Nonmonotonic reasoning, mentioned in Section 11.5.2, is the subject of considerable recent research. See Lukaszewicz [1990] for an introduction to the field and Ginsberg [1987] for a collection of papers. The Equation Interpreter Project mentioned in Section 11.6 is described in O'Donnell [1985]. The OBJ language also discussed in that section has undergone several revisions. For a description of OBJ3, see Goguen et al. [1988]. The example of the integer stack specification in Section 11.6 is in OBJ2 and is taken from Goguen and Meseguer [1987], where references to earlier versions of OBJ can also be found.

12 FORMAL SEMANTICS OF PROGRAMMING LANGUAGES

*I*n Chapters 5 through 7 we discussed the semantics, or meaning, of programs from an informal, or descriptive, point of view. Historically, this has been the usual approach, both for the programmer and the language designer, and it is typified by the language reference manual, which explains language features based on an underlying model of execution that is more implied than explicit.

Over the last 20 years, however, many computer scientists have emphasized the need for a more mathematical description of the behavior of programs and programming languages. The advantages of such a description are to make the definition of a programming language so precise that programs can be **proven** correct in a mathematical way and that translators can be **validated** to produce exactly the behavior described in the language definition. In addition, the work of producing such a precise specification aids the language designer in discovering inconsistencies and ambiguities.

Attempts to develop a standard mathematical system for providing precise semantic descriptions of languages have not met with complete acceptance, so there is no single method for formally defining semantics. Instead, there are a number of methods that differ in the formalisms used and the kinds of intended applications. No one method can be considered universal, although the denotational method described in Section 12.2 has been recently gaining more acceptance as the most rigorous method. Nevertheless, most languages are still specified in a somewhat informal way. Formal semantic descriptions are more often supplied after the fact, and only for a part of the language. Also, the use of formal definitions to prove correct program behavior has been confined primarily to academic settings, although it appears that formal methods will play a more significant role in the future. The purpose of this chapter is to survey the different methods that have been developed and to give a little flavor of their potential application.

Three principal methods that have been developed by researchers to describe semantics formally are

1. *Operational semantics.* This method defines a language by describing its actions in terms of the operations of an actual or hypothetical machine. Of course, this requires that the operations of the machine used in the description also be precisely defined, and for this reason a very simple hypothetical machine is often used that bears little resemblance to an actual computer. Indeed, the machine we use for operational semantics in Section 12.2 is more of a mathematical model, namely, a "reduction machine," which is a collection of permissible steps in reducing programs by applying their operations to values. It is similar in spirit to the notion of a Turing machine, in which actions are precisely described in a mathematical way.

2. *Denotational semantics.* This approach uses mathematical functions on programs and program components to specify semantics. Programs are translated into functions about which properties can be proved using the standard mathematical theory of functions.

3. *Axiomatic semantics.* This method applies mathematical logic to language definition. Assertions, or predicates, are used to describe desired outcomes and initial assumptions for programs. Language constructs are associated to **predicate transformers** that create new assertions out of old ones, reflecting the actions of the construct. These transformers can be used to prove that the desired outcome follows from the initial conditions. Thus this method of formal semantics is aimed specifically at correctness proofs.

All these methods are syntax directed in that the semantic definitions are based on a context-free grammar or Backus-Naur Form (BNF) rules as studied in Chapter 4. Formal semantics must then define all properties of a language that are not specified by the BNF.

These include static properties such as static types and declaration before use, which a translator can determine prior to execution. Although some authors consider such static properties to be part of the syntax of a language rather than its semantics, formal methods can describe both static and dynamic properties, and we will continue to view the semantics of a language as everything not specified by the BNF.

In the sections that follow we will give an overview of each of these approaches to formal semantics. To make the differences in approach clearer, we will use a sample small language as a standard example. We first give a description of the syntax and informal semantics of this language.

12.1 A SAMPLE SMALL LANGUAGE

The basic sample language that we will use throughout the chapter is a version of the integer expression language used in Chapter 4 and elsewhere. BNF rules for this language are given in Figure 12-1.

<exp> ::= <exp> '+' <term> | <exp> '−' <term> | <term>
<term> ::= <term> '•' <factor> | <factor>
<factor> ::= '(' <exp> ')' | <number>
<number> ::= <number> <digit> | <digit>
<digit> ::= '0' | '1' | '2' | '3' | '4' | '5' | '6' | '7' | '8' | '9'

Figure 12-1 Basic Sample Language

The semantics of such arithmetic expressions are particularly simple: the value of an expression is a complete representation of its meaning. Thus 2 + 3 • 4 means the value 14, and (2 + 3) • 4 means 20. Since this language is a little too simple to demonstrate adequately all the aspects of the formal methods, we add complexity to it in two stages, as follows.

In the first stage, we add variables, statements, and assignments, as given by the grammar in Figure 12-2.

A program in the extended language consists of a list of statements separated by semicolons, and a statement is an assignment of an expression to an identifier. The grammar of Figure 12-1 remains as before, except that identifiers are added to factors:

<factor> ::= '(' <exp> ')' | <number> | <identifier>

<program> ::= <stmt-list>
<stmt-list> ::= <stmt> ';' <stmt-list> | <stmt>
<stmt> ::= <identifier> ':=' <exp>
<identifier> ::= <identifier> <letter> | <letter>
<letter> ::= 'a' | 'b' | 'c' |. . .| 'z'

Figure 12-2   First Extension of the Sample Language

The semantics of such programs are now represented not by a single value, but by a set of values corresponding to identifiers whose values have been defined, or bound, by assignments. For example, the program

```
a  := 2+3;
b  := a*4;
a  := b−5
```

results in the bindings $b = 20$ and $a = 15$ when it finishes, and so the set of values representing the semantics of the program is $\{a = 15, b = 20\}$. Such a set is essentially a function from identifiers ($=$ strings of lowercase letters according to the foregoing grammar) to integer values, with all identifiers that have not been assigned a value undefined. For the purposes of this chapter we will call such a function an **environment,** and we will write

$$Env\colon \text{Identifier} \to \text{Integer} \cup \{undef\}$$

to denote a particular environment Env. For example, the Env function given by the program example can be defined as follows:

$$Env(I) = \begin{cases} 15 & \text{if } I = a \\ 20 & \text{if } I = b \\ undef & \text{otherwise} \end{cases}$$

The operation of looking up the value of an identifier I in an environment Env is then simply described by function evaluation $Env(I)$. The operation of adding a new value binding to Env can also be defined in functional terms. We will use the notation $Env \,\&\, \{I = n\}$ to denote the adding of the new value n for I to Env. In terms of functions,

$$(Env \,\&\, \{I = n\})(J) = \begin{cases} n & \text{if } J = I \\ Env(J) & \text{otherwise} \end{cases}$$

Finally, we also need the notion of the **empty environment,** which we will denote by Env_0:

$$Env_0(I) = undef \text{ for all } I$$

This notion of environment is particularly simple and differs from what we called the environment in Chapters 5 and 7. Indeed, an environment as defined here incorporates both the symbol table and state functions from Chapter 5. We note that such environments do not allow pointer values, do not include scope information, and do not permit aliases. More complex environments require much greater complexity and will not be studied here.

The second extension to our sample language will be the addition of "if" and "while" control statements to the first extension. Statements can now be of three kinds, and we extend their definition accordingly (see Figure 12-3).

<stmt> ::= <assign-stmt> | <if-stmt> | <while-stmt>
<assign-stmt> ::= <identifier> ':=' <exp>
<if-stmt> ::= 'if' <exp> 'then' <stmt-list>
         'else' <stmt-list> 'fi'
<while-stmt> ::= 'while' <exp> 'do' <stmt-list> 'od'

Figure 12-3   Second Extension of the Sample Language

The syntax of the if-statement and while-statement borrow the Algol68 convention of writing reserved words backward—thus od and fi—to close statement blocks rather than using the begin and end of Pascal and Algol60.

The meaning of an <if-stmt> is that <exp> should be evaluated in the current environment. If it evaluates to an integer greater than 0, then <stmt-list> is executed. If not, <stmt-list> is skipped. The meaning of a <while-stmt> is similar: as long as <exp> evaluates to a quantity greater than 0, <stmt-list> is repeatedly executed. Note that these semantics are nonstandard!

Here is an example of a program in this language:

```
n := 0 - 5;
if n then i := n else i := 0 - n fi;
fact := 1;
while i do
   fact := fact * i;
   i := i - 1
od
```

The semantics of this program are given by the (final) environment $\{n = -5, i = 0, fact = 120\}$.

Loops are the most difficult of the foregoing constructs to give formal semantics for, and in the following we will not always give a complete solution. These can be found in the references at the end of the chapter.

Formal semantic methods frequently use a simplified version of syntax from that given. Since the parsing step can be assumed to have already taken place, and since semantics are to be defined only for syntactically correct constructs, an ambiguous grammar can be used to define semantics. Further, the nonterminal symbols can be replaced by single letters, which may be thought to represent either strings of tokens or nodes in a parse tree. Such a syntactic specification is sometimes called **abstract syntax.** An abstract syntax for our sample language (with extensions) is the following:

$$P ::= L$$
$$L ::= L_1 \ ';' \ L_2 \ | \ S$$
$$S ::= I \ ':=' \ E$$
$$\quad | \ 'if' \ E \ 'then' \ L_1 \ 'else' \ L_2 \ 'fi'$$
$$\quad | \ 'while' \ E \ 'do' \ L \ 'od'$$
$$E ::= E_1 \ '+' \ E_2 \ | \ E_1 \ '-' \ E_2 \ | \ E_1 \ '\cdot' \ E_2$$
$$\quad | \ '(' \ E_1 \ ')' \ | \ I \ | \ N$$
$$N ::= N_1 \ D \ | \ D$$
$$D ::= '0' \ | \ '1' \ | \ . \ . \ . \ | \ '9'$$
$$I ::= I_1 \ A \ | \ A$$
$$A ::= 'a' \ | \ 'b' \ | \ . \ . \ . \ | \ 'z'$$

Here the letters stand for syntactic entities as follows:

P : Program
L : Statement-list
S : Statement
E : Expression
N : Number
D : Digit
I : Identifier
A : Letter

To define the semantics of each one of these symbols, we define the semantics of each right-hand side of the abstract syntax rules in terms of the semantics of their parts. Thus syntax-directed semantic definitions are recursive in nature. This also explains why we need to number the letters on the right-hand sides when they represent the same kind of construct: each choice needs to be distinguished.

We note finally that the tokens in the grammar have been enclosed in quotes. This becomes an important point when we must distinguish between the symbol '+' and the operation of addition on the integers, or +, which it represents. Similarly, the symbol '3' needs to be distinguished from its value, or the number 3.

We now survey the different formal semantic methods.

12.2   OPERATIONAL SEMANTICS

Operational semantics define the semantics of a programming language by specifying how an arbitrary program is to be executed on a machine whose operation is completely known.

We have noted in the introduction that there are many possibilities for the choice of a defining machine. The machine can be an actual computer, and the operational semantics can be specified by an actual translator for the language written in the machine code of the chosen machine. Such **definitional interpreters** or **compilers** have in the past been de facto language definitions (FORTRAN and C were originally examples). However, there are drawbacks to this method: the defining translator may not be available to a user, the operation of the underlying computer may not be completely specified, and the defining implementation may contain errors or other unexpected behavior.

By contrast, operational semantics can define the behavior of programs in terms of an **abstract machine** that does not need to exist anywhere in hardware, but that is simple enough to be completely understood and to be simulated by any user to answer questions about program behavior.

In principle, an abstract machine can be viewed as consisting of three parts: a program, a control, and a store or memory.

An operational semantic specification of a programming language specifies how the control of this abstract machine reacts to an arbitrary program in the language to be defined, and in particular, how storage is changed during the execution of a program.

The particular form of abstract machine that we will present is that of a **reduction machine,** whose control operates directly on a program to reduce it to its value. For example, given the expression $(3 + 4) \cdot 5$, the control of the reduction machine will reduce it to its value using the following sequence of steps:

$$(3 + 4) \cdot 5 => (7) \cdot 5 \quad \text{—3 and 4 are added to get 7}$$
$$=> 7 \cdot 5 \quad \text{—the parentheses around 7 are dropped}$$
$$=> 35 \quad \text{—7 and 5 are multiplied to get 35}$$

To specify the operational semantics of our sample language, we give **reduction rules** that specify how the control reduces the constructs of the language to a value. These reduction rules are given in a mathematical notation similar to logical inference rules, which we now briefly discuss.

12.2.1 Logical Inference Rules

Inference rules in logic are written in the following form:

$$\frac{\text{premise}}{\text{conclusion}}$$

That is, the premise, or condition, is written first; then a line is drawn, and the conclusion, or result, is written. This indicates that whenever the premise is true, the conclusion is also true. As an example, we can express the commutative property of addition as the following inference rule:

$$\frac{a + b = c}{b + a = c}$$

In logic, such inference rules are used to express the basic rules of propositional and predicate calculus. As an example of an inference rule in logic, the transitive property of implication is given by the following rule:

$$\frac{a \rightarrow b,\ b \rightarrow c}{a \rightarrow c}$$

This says that if a implies b and b implies c, then a implies c.

Axioms are inference rules with no premise—they are always true. An example of an axiom is $a + 0 = a$ for integer addition. This can be written as an inference rule with an empty premise:

$$\frac{}{a + 0 = a}$$

More often, this is written without the horizontal line:

$$a + 0 = a$$

12.2.2   Reduction Rules for Integer Arithmetic Expressions

We use the notation of inference rules to describe the way the control operates to reduce an expression to its value. We base the rules on the abstract syntax for in our sample language expressions:

$$
\begin{aligned}
E ::= &\ E_1 \ '+' \ E_2 \\
     &|\ E_1 \ '-' \ E_2 \\
     &|\ E_1 \ '\cdot' \ E_2 \\
     &|\ '(' \ E_1 \ ')' \\
     &|\ N \\
N ::= &\ N_1\, D \mid D \\
D ::= &\ '0' \mid '1' \mid . . . \mid '9'
\end{aligned}
$$

For the time being we can ignore the storage, since this grammar does not include identifiers. We use the following notation: E, E_1, and so on are used to denote expressions that have not yet been reduced to values; V, V_1, and so on will stand for integer values; $E => E_1$ states that expression E reduces to expression E_1 by some reduction rule. Reduction rules for expressions are the following, each of which we will discuss in turn.

(1) We collect all the rules for reducing digits to values in this one

rule, all of which are axioms:

$$
\begin{aligned}
\text{`0'} &=> 0 \\
\text{`1'} &=> 1 \\
\text{`2'} &=> 2 \\
\text{`3'} &=> 3 \\
\text{`4'} &=> 4 \\
\text{`5'} &=> 5 \\
\text{`6'} &=> 6 \\
\text{`7'} &=> 7 \\
\text{`8'} &=> 8 \\
\text{`9'} &=> 9
\end{aligned}
$$

(2) We collect the rules for reducing numbers to values in this one rule, which are also axioms:

$$
\begin{aligned}
V \text{ `0'} &=> 10 \cdot V \\
V \text{ `1'} &=> 10 \cdot V + 1 \\
V \text{ `2'} &=> 10 \cdot V + 2 \\
V \text{ `3'} &=> 10 \cdot V + 3 \\
V \text{ `4'} &=> 10 \cdot V + 4 \\
V \text{ `5'} &=> 10 \cdot V + 5 \\
V \text{ `6'} &=> 10 \cdot V + 6 \\
V \text{ `7'} &=> 10 \cdot V + 7 \\
V \text{ `8'} &=> 10 \cdot V + 8 \\
V \text{ `9'} &=> 10 \cdot V + 9
\end{aligned}
$$

(3) $\qquad V_1 \text{ `+'} V_2 => V_1 + V_2$

(4) $\qquad V_1 \text{ `−'} V_2 => V_1 - V_2$

(5) $\qquad V_1 \text{ `·'} V_2 => V_1 \cdot V_2$

(6) $\qquad \text{`('} V \text{`)'} => V$

(7) $\qquad \dfrac{E => E_1}{E \text{ `+'} E_2 => E_1 \text{ `+'} E_2}$

(8) $\qquad \dfrac{E => E_1}{E \text{ `−'} E_2 => E_1 \text{ `−'} E_2}$

(9) $\qquad \dfrac{E => E_1}{E \text{ `·'} E_2 => E_1 \text{ `·'} E_2}$

(10) $\qquad \dfrac{E => E_1}{V \text{ `+'} E => V \text{ `+'} E_1}$

(11) $\qquad \dfrac{E => E_1}{V \text{ `−'} E => V \text{ `−'} E_1}$

(12) $\qquad \dfrac{E => E_1}{V \text{ `·'} E => V \text{ `·'} E_1}$

(13)
$$\frac{E \Rightarrow E_1}{\text{'(' } E \text{ ')'} \Rightarrow \text{'(' } E_1 \text{ ')'}}$$

(14)
$$\frac{E \Rightarrow E_1 \ , \ E_1 \Rightarrow E_2}{E \Rightarrow E_2}$$

Rules 1 through 6 are all axioms. Rules 1 and 2 express the reduction of digits and numbers to values: '0' $\Rightarrow$ 0 states that the **character** '0' (a syntactic entity) reduces to the **value** 0 (a semantic entity). Rules 3, 4, and 5 say that whenever we have an expression that consists of two values and an operator symbol, we can reduce that expression to a value by applying the appropriate operation whose symbol appears in the expression. Rule 6 says that if an expression consists of a pair of parentheses surrounding a value, then the parentheses can be dropped.

The remainder of the reduction rules are inferences that allow the reduction machine to combine separate reductions together to achieve further reductions. Rules 7, 8, and 9 express the fact that, in an expression that consists of an operation applied to other expressions, the left subexpression may be reduced by itself and that reduction substituted into the larger expression. Rules 10 through 12 express the fact that, once a value is obtained for the left subexpression, the right subexpression may be reduced. Rule 13 says that we can first reduce the inside of an expression consisting of parentheses surrounding another expression. Finally, rule 14 expresses the general fact that reductions can be performed stepwise (sometimes called the **transitivity rule** for reductions).

Let us see how these reduction rules can be applied to a complicated expression to derive its value. Take, for example, the expression 2 • (3 + 4) − 5. To show each reduction step clearly, we surround each character with quotes within the reduction steps.

We first reduce the expression 3 + 4 as follows:

$$
\begin{aligned}
\text{'3' '+' '4'} &\Rightarrow 3 \text{ '+' '4'} &&\text{(Rules 1 and 7)} \\
&\Rightarrow 3 \text{ '+' } 4 &&\text{(Rules 1 and 10)} \\
&\Rightarrow 3 + 4 = 7 &&\text{(Rule 3)}
\end{aligned}
$$

Hence by rule 14, we have '3' '+' '4' $\Rightarrow$ 7. Continuing,

$$
\begin{aligned}
\text{'(' '3' '+' '4' ')'} &\Rightarrow \text{'(' 7 ')'} &&\text{(Rule 13)} \\
&\Rightarrow 7 &&\text{(Rule 6)}
\end{aligned}
$$

Now we can reduce the expression 2 • (3 + 4) as follows:

$$
\begin{aligned}
\text{'2' '•' '(' '3' '+' '4' ')'} &\Rightarrow 2 \text{ '•' '(' '3' '+' '4'')'} &&\text{(Rules 1 and 9)} \\
&\Rightarrow 2 \text{ '•' } 7 &&\text{(Rule 12)} \\
&\Rightarrow 2 • 7 = 14 &&\text{(Rule 5)}
\end{aligned}
$$

And, finally,

$$
\begin{aligned}
\text{'2' '•' '(' '3' '+' '4' ')' '−' '5'} &\Rightarrow 14 \text{ '−' '5'} &&\text{(Rules 1 and 8)} \\
&\Rightarrow 14 \text{ '−' } 5 &&\text{(Rule 11)} \\
&\Rightarrow 14 − 5 = 9 &&\text{(Rule 4)}
\end{aligned}
$$

We have shown that the reduction machine can reduce the expression $2 \cdot (3 + 4) - 5$ to 9, which is the value of the expression.

12.2.3   Environments and Assignment

We want to extend the operational semantics of expressions to include environments and assignments, according to the following abstract syntax:

$$P ::= L$$
$$L ::= L_1 \text{ ';' } L_2 \mid S$$
$$S ::= I \text{ ':=' } E$$
$$E ::= E_1 \text{ '+' } E_2 \mid E_1 \text{ '-' } E_2 \mid E_1 \text{ '·' } E_2$$
$$\mid \text{ '(' } E_1 \text{ ')' } \mid I \mid N$$
$$N ::= N_1 D \mid D$$
$$D ::= \text{ '0' } \mid \text{ '1' } \mid \ldots \mid \text{ '9' }$$
$$I ::= I_1 A \mid A$$
$$A ::= \text{ 'a' } \mid \text{ 'b' } \mid \ldots \mid \text{ 'z' }$$

To do this we must include the effect of assignments on the storage of the abstract machine. Our view of the storage will be the same as in other sections; that is, we view it as an environment that is a function from identifiers to integer values (including the undefined value):

$$Env: \text{ Identifier} \rightarrow \text{Integer} \cup \{undef\}$$

To add environments to the reduction rules, we need a notation to show the dependence of the value of an expression on an environment. We use the notation $<E \mid Env>$ to indicate that expression E is evaluated in the presence of environment Env. Now our reduction rules change to include environments. For example, rule 7 with environments becomes

$$(7) \qquad \frac{<E \mid Env> \; => \; E_1 \mid Env>}{<E \text{ '+' } E_2 \mid Env> \; => \; <E_1 \text{ '+' } E_2 \mid Env>}$$

This states that if E reduces to E_1 in the presence of environment Env, then $E \text{ '+' } E_2$ reduces to $E_1 \text{ '+' } E_2$ in the same environment. Other rules are modified similarly. The one case of evaluation that explicitly involves the environment is when an expression is an identifier I:

$$(15) \qquad \frac{Env(I) \; = \; n}{<I \mid Env> \; => \; <n \mid Env>}$$

This states that if the value of identifier I is n in environment Env, then I reduces to n in the presence of Env.

It remains to add assignment statements and statement sequences to the reduction rules. First, statements must reduce to environments instead of integer values, since they create and change environments. Thus we have

$$(16) \qquad <I := n \mid Env> \; => \; Env \; \& \; \{I = n\}$$

which states that the assignment of the value n to I in environment Env reduces to a new environment where I is equal to n.

The reduction of expressions within assignments proceeds via the following rule:

(17) $$\frac{<E \mid Env> \; => \; <E_1 \mid Env>}{<I := E \mid Env> \; => \; <I := E_1 \mid Env>}$$

A statement sequence reduces to an environment formed by accumulating the effect of each assignment:

(18) $$\frac{<S \mid Env> \; => \; Env_1}{<S \text{ ';' } S_1 \mid Env> \; => \; <S_1 \mid Env_1>}$$

Finally, a program is a statement sequence that has no prior environment; it reduces to the effect it has on the empty starting environment:

(19) $$S \; => \; <S \mid Env_0>$$

(recall that $Env_0(I) =$ undef for all identifiers I).

We leave the rules for reducing identifier expressions to the reader; they are completely analogous to the rules for reducing numbers (see Exercise 4).

Let us use these rules to reduce the following sample program to an environment:

```
a  := 2+3;
b  := a*4;
a  := b-5
```

To simplify the reduction, we will suppress the use of quotes to differentiate between syntactic and semantic entities. First, by rule 19, we have

$a := 2 + 3; b := a \cdot 4; a := b - 5 =>$
$<a := 2 + 3; b := a \cdot 4; a := b - 5 \mid Env_0>$

Also, by rules 3, 17, and 16,

$<a := 2 + 3 \mid Env_0> =>$
$<a := 5 \mid Env_0> =>$
$Env_0 \; \& \; \{a = 5\} = \{a = 5\}$

Then, by rule 18,

$<a := 2 + 3; b := a \cdot 4; a := b - 5 \mid Env_0> =>$
$<b := a \cdot 4; a := b - 5 \mid \{a = 5\}>$

Similarly, by rules 15, 9, 5, 17, and 16,

$<b := a \cdot 4 \mid \{a = 5\}> => <b := 5 \cdot 4 \mid \{a = 5\}> =>$
$<b := 20 \mid \{a = 5\}> => \{a = 5\} \; \& \; \{b = 20\} = \{a = 5, b = 20\}$

Thus, by rule 18,

$<b := a \cdot 4; a := b - 5 \mid \{a = 5\}> =>$
$<a := b - 5 \mid \{a = 5, b = 20\}>$

Finally, by a similar application of the rules, we get

$$\langle a := b - 5 \mid \{a = 5, b = 20\}\rangle =>$$
$$\langle a := 20 - 5 \mid \{a = 5, b = 20\}\rangle =>$$
$$\langle a := 15 \mid \{a = 5, b = 20\}\rangle =>$$
$$\{a = 5, b = 20\} \& \{a = 15\} = \{a = 15, b = 20\}$$

and the program reduces to the environment $\{a = 15, b = 20\}$.

12.2.4 Control

It remains to add the if- and while-statements to our sample language, with the following abstract syntax:

$$S ::= \text{'if'} \; E \; \text{'then'} \; L_1 \; \text{'else'} \; L_2 \; \text{'fi'}$$
$$\mid \text{'while'} \; E \; \text{'do'} \; L \; \text{'od'}$$

Reduction rules for if-statements are the following:

(20)
$$\frac{\langle E|Env\rangle => \langle E_1|Env\rangle}{\langle \text{'if'} \; E \; \text{'then'} \; L_1 \; \text{'else'} \; L_2 \; \text{'fi'} \mid Env\rangle =>}$$
$$\langle \text{'if'} \; E_1 \; \text{'then'} \; L_1 \; \text{'else'} \; L_2 \; \text{'fi'} \mid Env\rangle$$

(21)
$$\frac{V > 0}{\langle \text{'if'} \; V \; \text{'then'} \; L_1 \; \text{'else'} \; L_2 \; \text{'fi'} \mid Env\rangle => \langle L_1 \mid Env\rangle}$$

(22)
$$\frac{V \le 0}{\langle \text{'if'} \; V \; \text{'then'} \; L_1 \; \text{'else'} \; L_2 \; \text{'fi'} \mid Env\rangle => \langle L_2 \mid Env\rangle}$$

Reduction rules for while-statements are as follows:

(23)
$$\frac{\langle E \mid Env\rangle => \langle V \mid Env\rangle, V \le 0}{\langle \text{'while'} \; E \; \text{'do'} \; L \; \text{'od'} \mid Env\rangle => Env}$$

(24)
$$\frac{\langle E \mid Env\rangle => \langle V \mid Env\rangle, V > 0, \langle L \mid Env\rangle => Env_1}{\langle \text{'while'} \; E \; \text{'do'} \; L \; \text{'od'} \mid Env\rangle =>}$$
$$\langle \text{'while'} \; E \; \text{'do'} \; L \; \text{'od'} \mid Env_1\rangle$$

Note that the last rule is recursive. It states that if, given environment Env, the expression E evaluates to a positive value, then execution of the while-loop under Env reduces to an execution of the while-loop under the new environment formed by executing the body L of the loop under Env.

As an example, let us reduce the while-statement of the program

```
n := 0 - 3;
if n then i := n else i := 0 - n fi;
fact := 1;
while i do
  fact := fact * i;
  i := i - 1
od
```

to its environment value. The environment at the start of the while-loop is $\{n = -3, i = 3, \text{fact} = 1\}$. Since $<i \mid \{n = -3, i = 3, \text{fact} = 1\}>$ $=> <3 \mid \{n = -3, i = 3, \text{fact} = 1\}>$ and $3 > 0$, rule 24 applies, so we must compute the environment resulting from the application of the body of the loop to the environment $\{n = -3, i = 3, \text{fact} = 1\}$:

$<\text{fact} := \text{fact} \cdot i \mid \{n = -3, i = 3, \text{fact} = 1\}> =>$
$<\text{fact} := 1 \cdot i \mid \{n = -3, i = 3, \text{fact} = 1\}> =>$
$<\text{fact} := 1 \cdot 3 \mid \{n = -3, i = 3, \text{fact} = 1\}> =>$
$<\text{fact} := 3 \mid \{n = -3, i = 3, \text{fact} = 1\}> =>$
$\{n = -3, i = 3, \text{fact} = 3\}$

and

$<\text{fact} := \text{fact} \cdot i ; i := i - 1 \mid \{n = -3, i = 3, \text{fact} = 1\}> =>$
$<i := i - 1 \mid \{n = -3, i = 3, \text{fact} = 3\}> =>$
$\{n = -3, i = 2, \text{fact} = 3\}$

so

$<\text{while } i \text{ do} \ldots \text{od} \mid \{n = -3, i = 3, \text{fact} = 1\}> =>$
$<\text{while } i \text{ do} \ldots \text{od} \mid \{n = -3, i = 2, \text{fact} = 3\}>$

Continuing in this way, we get

$<\text{while } i \text{ do} \ldots \text{od} \mid \{n = -3, i = 2, \text{fact} = 3\}> =>$
$<\text{while } i \text{ do} \ldots \text{od} \mid \{n = -3, i = 1, \text{fact} = 6\}> =>$
$<\text{while } i \text{ do} \ldots \text{od} \mid \{n = -3, i = 0, \text{fact} = 6\}> =>$
$\{n = -3, i = 0, \text{fact} = 6\}$

so the final environment is $\{n = -3, i = 0, \text{fact} = 6\}$.

12.3   DENOTATIONAL SEMANTICS

Denotational semantics use functions to describe the semantics of a programming language. A function describes semantics by associating semantic values to syntactically correct constructs. A simple example of such a function is a function that maps an integer arithmetic expression to its value, which we could call the *Val* function:

$$Val : \text{Expression} \longrightarrow \text{Integer}$$

For example, $Val(2 + 3 \cdot 4) = 14$ and $Val((2 + 3) \cdot 4) = 20$. The domain of a semantic function such as *Val*, is a **syntactic domain.** In the case of *Val* it is the set of all syntactically correct integer arithmetic expressions. The range of a semantic function is a **semantic domain,** which is a mathematical structure. In the case of *Val*, the set of integers is the semantic domain. Since *Val* maps the syntactic construct $2 + 3 \cdot 4$ to the semantic value 14, $2 + 3 \cdot 4$ is said to **denote** the value 14. This is the origin of the name denotational semantics.

A second example may be useful before we give denotational semantics for our sample language from Section 12.1. In many programming languages a program can be viewed as something that receives input and produces output. Thus the semantics of a program can be represented by a function from input to output, and a semantic function for programs would look like this:

$$P : \text{Program} \longrightarrow (\text{Input} \longrightarrow \text{Output})$$

The semantic domain to which P maps programs is a set of functions, namely, the functions from Input to Output, which we represent by Input $\longrightarrow$ Output, and the semantic value of a program is a function. For example, if p represents the Pascal program

```
program identity;
var x: integer;
begin
  read(x);
  write(x);
end.
```

that inputs an integer and outputs the same integer, then p denotes the identity function f from integers to integers: $P(p) = f$, where f: Integer $\longrightarrow$ Integer is given by $f(x) = x$.

Very often semantic domains in denotational descriptions will be function domains, and values of semantic functions will be functions themselves. To simplify the notation of these domains, we will often assume that the function symbol "$\longrightarrow$" is right associative and leave off the parentheses from domain descriptions. Thus

$$P : \text{Program} \longrightarrow (\text{Input} \longrightarrow \text{Output})$$

becomes

$$P : \text{Program} \longrightarrow \text{Input} \longrightarrow \text{Output}$$

In the following we will give a brief overview of a denotational definition of the semantics of a programming language and then proceed with a denotational definition of our sample language from Section 12.1.

A denotational definition of a programming language consists of three parts:

1. A definition of the **syntactic domains,** such as the sets Program and Expression, on which the semantic functions act.

2. A definition of the **semantic domains** consisting of the values of the semantic functions, such as the sets Integer and Integer $\longrightarrow$ Integer.

3. A definition of the semantic functions themselves (sometimes called **valuation functions**).

We will consider each of these parts of the denotational definition in turn.

12.3.1   Syntactic Domains

Syntactic domains are defined in a denotational definition using notation that is almost identical to the abstract syntax described in Section 12.1. The sets being defined are listed first with capital letters denoting elements from the sets. Then the grammar rules are listed that recursively define the elements of the set. For example, the syntactic domains Number and Digit are specified as follows:

$$D: \text{Digit}$$
$$N: \text{Number}$$

$$N ::= N\,D \mid D$$
$$D ::= \text{`0'} \mid \text{`1'} \mid . \ . \ . \mid \text{`9'}$$

A denotational definition views the syntactic domains as sets of syntax trees whose structure is given by the grammar rules. Semantic functions will be defined recursively on these sets, based on the structure of a syntax tree node.

12.3.2   Semantic Domains

Semantic domains are the sets in which semantic functions take their values. These are sets like syntactic domains, but they also may have additional mathematical structure, depending on their use. For example, the integers have the arithmetic operations " $+$ ", " $-$ ", and " $\cdot$ ". Such domains are **algebras,** which need to be specified by listing their functions and properties. A denotational definition of the semantic domains lists the sets and the operations but usually omits the properties of the operations. These can be specified by the algebraic techniques studied in Chapter 8, or they can simply be assumed to be well known, as in the case of the arithmetic operations on the integers. A specification of the semantic domains also lists only the basic domains without specifically including domains that are constructed of functions on the basic domains.

Domains sometimes need special mathematical structures that are the subject of **domain theory** in programming language semantics. In particular, the term "domain" is sometimes reserved for an algebra with the structure of a complete partial order. Such a structure is needed to define the semantics of recursive functions and loops. See the references at the end of the chapter for further detail on domain theory.

An example of a specification of a semantic domain is the following specification of the integers:

Domain v: Integer $= \{\ldots, -2, -1, 0, 1, 2, \ldots\}$

Operations

$\quad +$: Integer $\times$ Integer $\longrightarrow$ Integer
$\quad -$: Integer $\times$ Integer $\longrightarrow$ Integer
$\quad \cdot$: Integer $\times$ Integer $\longrightarrow$ Integer

In this example we restrict ourselves to the three operations " $+$ ", " $-$ ", and " $\cdot$ ", which are the only operations represented in our sample language. In the foregoing notation the symbols " v: " in the first line indicate that the name v will be used for a general element from the domain, that is, an arbitrary integer.

12.3.3   Semantic Functions

A semantic function is specified for each syntactic domain. Each semantic function is given a different name based on its associated syntactic domain. A common convention is to use the boldface letter corresponding to the elements in the syntactic domain. Thus the value function from the syntactic domain Digit to the integers is written as follows:

$$\mathbf{D} : \text{Digit} \longrightarrow \text{Integer}$$

The value of a semantic function is specified recursively on the trees of the syntactic domains using the structure of the grammar rules. This is done by giving a **semantic equation** corresponding to each grammar rule.

For example, the grammar rules for digits

$$D ::= \text{`0'} \mid \text{`1'} \mid \ldots \mid \text{`9'}$$

give rise to the syntax tree nodes

$$
\begin{array}{cccc}
D & D & \ldots & D \\
| & | & & | \\
\text{`0'} & \text{`1'} & \ldots & \text{`9'}
\end{array}
$$

and the semantic function $\mathbf{D}$ is defined by the following semantic equations,

$$
\begin{array}{ccc}
D & D & D \\
\mathbf{D}(\,|\,) = 0, & \mathbf{D}\,(\,|\,) = 1, \ldots, & \mathbf{D}\,(\,|\,) = 9 \\
\text{`0'} & \text{`1'} & \text{`9'}
\end{array}
$$

representing the value of each leaf.

This cumbersome notation is shortened to the following:

$$\mathbf{D}[[\text{`0'}]] = 0, \quad \mathbf{D}[[\text{`1'}]] = 1, \ldots, \quad \mathbf{D}[[\text{`9'}]] = 9$$

The double brackets [[…]] indicate that the argument is a syntactic entity consisting of a syntax tree node with the listed arguments as children.

As another example, the semantic function

$$\mathbf{N}: \text{Number} \longrightarrow \text{Integer}$$

from numbers to integers is based on the syntax

$$N ::= N\,D \mid D$$

and is given by the following equations:

$$N[[ND]] = 10 \cdot N[[N]] + N[[D]]$$
$$N[[D]] = D[[D]]$$

Here [[ND]] refers to the tree node $\begin{array}{c} N \\ / \backslash \\ N \quad D \end{array}$ and [[D]] to the node $\begin{array}{c} N \\ | \\ D \end{array}$. We

are now ready to give a complete denotational definition for the expression
language of Section 12.1.

12.3.4   Denotational Semantics of Integer Arithmetic Expressions

Here is the denotational definition according to the conventions just
described.

Syntactic Domains

E: Expression
N: Number
D: Digit

$$E ::= E_1 \; '+' \; E_2 \mid E_1 \; '-' \; E_2 \mid E_1 \; '\cdot' \; E_2$$
$$\mid \; '(' \; E \; ')' \mid N$$
$$N ::= N\,D \mid D$$
$$D ::= '0' \mid '1' \mid . \; . \; .\mid '9'$$

Semantic Domains

Domain v: Integer $= \{. \; . \; .,-2,-1,0,1,2,. \; . \; .\}$
Operations

$$+ : \text{Integer} \times \text{Integer} \longrightarrow \text{Integer}$$
$$- : \text{Integer} \times \text{Integer} \longrightarrow \text{Integer}$$
$$\cdot : \text{Integer} \times \text{Integer} \longrightarrow \text{Integer}$$

Semantic Functions

$$\mathbf{E} : \text{Expression} \longrightarrow \text{Integer}$$

$$E[[E_1 \; '+' \; E_2]] = E[[E_1]] + E[[E_2]]$$
$$E[[E_1 \; '-' \; E_2]] = E[[E_1]] - E[[E_2]]$$
$$E[[E_1 \; '\cdot' \; E_2]] = E[[E_1]] \cdot E[[E_2]]$$
$$E[['(' \; E \; ')']] = E[[E]]$$
$$E[[N]] = N[[N]]$$

$$\mathbf{N} : \text{Number} \longrightarrow \text{Integer}$$

$$N[[ND]] = 10 \cdot N[[N]] + N[[D]]$$
$$N[[D]] = D[[D]]$$

$$D : \text{Digit} \longrightarrow \text{Integer}$$

$$D[['0']] = 0, D[['1']] = 1, \ldots, D[['9']] = 9$$

In this denotational description we have retained the use of quotes to distinguish syntactic from semantic entities. In denotational semantics this is not as necessary as in other semantic descriptions, since arguments to semantic functions are always syntactic entities. Thus we could drop the quotes and write $D[[0]] = 0$, and so on. For clarity, we will generally continue to use the quotes, however.

To see how these equations can be used to obtain the semantic value of an expression we compute $E[[(2 + 3) \cdot 4]]$ or, more precisely, $E[['(' '2' '+' '3' ')' '\cdot' '4']]$:

$$
\begin{aligned}
E&[['(' '2' '+' '3' ')' '\cdot' '4']] \\
&= E[['(' '2' '+' '3' ')']] \cdot E[['4']] \\
&= E[['2' '+' '3']] \cdot N[['4']] \\
&= (E[['2']] + E[['3']]) \cdot D[['4']] \\
&= (N[['2']] + N[['3']]) \cdot 4 \\
&= (D[['2']] + D[['3']]) \cdot 4 \\
&= (2 + 3) \cdot 4 = 5 \cdot 4 = 20
\end{aligned}
$$

12.3.5   Environments and Assignment

The first extension to our basic sample language adds identifiers, assignment statements, and environments to the semantics. Environments are functions from identifiers to integers (or undefined), and the set of environments becomes a new semantic domain:

Domain *Env*: Environment = Identifier $\longrightarrow$ Integer $\cup$ {undef}

In denotational semantics the value undef is given a special name, *bottom*, taken from the theory of partial orders, and is denoted by a special symbol, "$\perp$." Semantic domains with this special value added are called **lifted domains** and are subscripted with the symbol "$\perp$." Thus Integer $\cup$ {$\perp$} is written as Integer$_\perp$. The initial environment Env_0 defined in Section 12.1, in which all identifiers have undefined values, can now be defined as $Env_0(I) = \perp$ for all identifiers I.

The evaluation of expressions in the presence of an environment must include an environment as a parameter, so that identifiers may be associated to integer values. Thus the semantic value of an expression becomes a function from environments to integers:

$$E : \text{Expression} \longrightarrow \text{Environment} \longrightarrow \text{Integer}_\perp$$

In particular, the value of an identifier is its value in the environment provided as a parameter:

$$E[[I]](Env) = Env(I)$$

In the case of a number the environment is immaterial:

$$E[[N]](Env) = N[[N]]$$

In other expression cases the environment is simply passed on to sub-expressions.

To extend the semantics to statements and statement lists, we note that the semantic values of these constructs are functions from environments to environments. An assignment statement changes the environment to add the new value assigned to the identifier; in this case we will use the same "&" notation for adding values to functions that we have used in previous sections. Now a statement-list is simply the composition of the functions of its individual statements (recall that the composition $f \circ g$ of two functions f and g is defined by $(f \circ g)(x) = f(g(x))$. A complete denotational definition of the extended language is given in Figure 12-4.

Syntactic Domains

> P: Program
> L: Statement-list
> S: Statement
> E: Expression
> N: Number
> D: Digit
> I: Identifier
> A: Letter

> $P ::= L$
> $L ::= L_1 \text{ ';' } L_2 \mid S$
> $S ::= I \text{ ':=' } E$
> $E ::= E_1 \text{ '+' } E_2 \mid E_1 \text{ '−' } E_2 \mid E_1 \text{ '•' } E_2$
> $\quad\quad \mid \text{ '(' } E \text{ ')' } \mid I \mid N$
> $N ::= N D \mid D$
> $D ::= \text{ '0' } \mid \text{ '1' } \mid . . . \mid \text{ '9' }$
> $I ::= I A \mid A$
> $A ::= \text{ 'a' } \mid \text{ 'b' } \mid . . . \mid \text{ 'z' }$

Semantic Domains

Domain v: Integer $= \{. . ., -2, -1, 0, 1, 2, . . .\}$
Operations
> $+$: Integer $\times$ Integer $\longrightarrow$ Integer
> $-$: Integer $\times$ Integer $\longrightarrow$ Integer
> $\bullet$: Integer $\times$ Integer $\longrightarrow$ Integer

Domain Env : Environment $=$ Identifier $\longrightarrow$ Integer$_\bot$ *continues*

Figure 12-4   A Denotational Definition for the Sample Language
Extended with Assignment Statements
and Environments

Semantic Functions

P : Program $\longrightarrow$ Environment
$$P[[P]] = L[[L]](Env_0)$$

L : Statement-list $\longrightarrow$ Environment $\longrightarrow$ Environment
$$L[[L_1 \;';'\; L_2]] = L[[L_2]] \circ L[[L_1]]$$
$$L[[S]] = S[[S]]$$

S : Statement $\longrightarrow$ Environment $\longrightarrow$ Environment
$$S[[\; I \;':='\; E \;]](Env) = Env \;\&\; \{I = E[[E]](Env)\}$$

E : Expression $\longrightarrow$ Environment $\longrightarrow$ Integer$_\perp$

$$E[[E_1 \;'+'\; E_2]](Env) = E[[E_1]](Env) + E[[E_2]](Env)$$
$$E[[E_1 \;'-'\; E_2]](Env) = E[[E_1]](Env) - E[[E_2]](Env)$$
$$E[[E_1 \;'\cdot'\; E_2]](Env) = E[[E_1]](Env) \cdot E[[E_2]](Env)$$
$$E[['('\; E \;')']](Env) = E[[E]](Env)$$
$$E[[N]](Env) = N[[N]]$$

N : Number $\longrightarrow$ Integer

$$N[[ND]] = 10 \cdot N[[N]]] + N[[D]]$$
$$N[[D]] = D[[D]]$$

D : Digit $\longrightarrow$ Integer

$$D[['0']] = 0, \; D[['1']] = 1, \; . \; . \; ., \; D[['9']] = 9$$

Figure 12-4   (continued)

12.3.6   Denotational Semantics of Control Statements

To complete our discussion of denotational semantics, we need to extend the denotational definition of Figure 12-1 to if- and while-statements, with the following abstract syntax:

$$S: \text{Statement}$$
$$S ::= I \;':='\; E$$
$$\quad | \; \text{'if'}\; E \;\text{'then'}\; L_1 \;\text{'else'}\; L_2 \;\text{'fi'}$$
$$\quad | \; \text{'while'}\; E \;\text{'do'}\; L \;\text{'od'}$$

As before, the denotational semantics of these statements must be given by a function from environments to environments:

$$S : \text{Statement} \longrightarrow \text{Environment} \longrightarrow \text{Environment}$$

We define the semantic function of the if-statement as follows:

$S[[\text{'if'}\ E\ \text{'then'}\ L_1\ \text{'else'}\ L_2\ \text{'fi'}]](Env) =$
$$\text{if}\ E[[E]](Env) > 0\ \text{then}\ L[[L_1]](Env)\ \text{else}\ L[[L_2]](Env)$$

Note that we are using the if-then-else construct on the right-hand side to express the construction of a function. Indeed, given F: Environment $\rightarrow$ Integer, G: Environment $\rightarrow$ Environment, and H: Environment $\rightarrow$ Environment, then the function if F then G else H: Environment $\rightarrow$ Environment is given as follows:

$$(\text{if}\ F\ \text{then}\ G\ \text{else}\ H)(Env) = \begin{cases} G(Env), & \text{if}\ F(Env) > 0 \\ H(Env), & \text{if}\ F(Env) \le 0 \end{cases}$$

The semantic function for the while-statement is more difficult. In fact, if we let $F = S[[\text{'while'}\ E\ \text{'do'}\ L\ \text{'od'}]]$, so that F is a function from environments to environments, then F satisfies the following equation:

$$F(Env) = \text{if}\ E[[E]](Env) \le 0\ \text{then}\ Env\ \text{else}\ F(L[[L]](Env))$$

This is a recursive equation for F. To use this equation as a specification for the semantics of F, we need to know that this equation has a unique solution in some sense among the functions Environment $\rightarrow$ Environment. We saw a very similar situation in Section 10.6, where the definition of the factorial function also led to a recursive equation for the function. In that case we were able to construct the function as a set by successively extending it to a so-called **least-fixed-point solution,** that is, the "smallest" solution satisfying the equation. A similar approach will indeed work here too, and the solution is referred to as the least-fixed-point semantics of the while-loop. The situation here is more complicated, however, in that F is a function on the semantic domain of environments rather than the integers. The study of such equations and their solutions is a major topic of domain theory. For more information, see the references at the end of the chapter.

Note that there is an additional problem associated with loops: nontermination. For example, in our sample language the loop

```
i := 1;
while i do i := i + 1 od
```

does not terminate. Such a loop does not define any function at all from environments to environments, but we still need to be able to associate a semantic interpretation to it. One does so by assigning it the "undefined" value $\bot$ similar to the value of an undefined identifier in an environment. In this case the domain of environments becomes a lifted domain,

$$\text{Environment}_\bot = (\text{Identifier} \longrightarrow \text{Integer}_\bot)_\bot$$

and the semantic function for statements must be defined as follows:

$$S : \text{Statement} \longrightarrow \text{Environment}_\bot \longrightarrow \text{Environment}_\bot$$

We shall not discuss such complications further.

12.4 AXIOMATIC SEMANTICS

Axiomatic semantics define the semantics of a program, statement, or language construct by describing the effect its execution has on assertions about the data manipulated by the program. The term "axiomatic" is used because elements of mathematical logic are used to specify the semantics of programming languages, including logical axioms. We discussed logic and assertions in the introduction to logic programming in Chapter 11. For our purposes, however, it suffices to consider logical assertions to be statements about the behavior of a program that are true or false at any moment during execution.

Assertions associated with language constructs are of two kinds: assertions about things that are true just before execution of the construct and assertions about things that are true just after the execution of the construct. Assertions about the situation just before execution are called **preconditions,** and assertions about the situation just after execution are called **postconditions.** For example, given the assignment statement

```
x  :=  x  +  1
```

we would expect that, whatever value x has just before execution of the statement, its value just after the execution of the assignment is one more than its previous value. This can be stated as the precondition that $x = A$ before execution and the postcondition that $x = A + 1$ after execution. Standard notation for this is to write the precondition inside curly brackets just before the construct and to write the postcondition similarly just after the construct:

$$\{x = A\} \; x \; := \; x \; + \; 1 \; \{x = A + 1\}$$

or

$$\{x = A\}$$
```
x  :=  x  +  1
```
$$\{x = A + 1\}$$

As a second example of the use of precondition and postcondition to describe the action of a language construct, consider the following assignment:

```
x  :=  1 / y
```

Clearly a precondition for the successful execution of the statement is that $y \neq 0$, and then x becomes equal to $1/y$. Thus we have

$$\{y \neq 0\}$$
```
x  :=  1 / y
```
$$\{x = 1/y\}$$

Note that in this example the precondition establishes a restriction that is a requirement for successful execution, while in the first example the precondition x = A merely establishes a name for the value of x prior to execution, without making any restriction whatever on that value.

Precondition/postcondition pairs can be useful in specifying the expected behavior of programs—the programmer simply writes down the conditions he or she expects to be true at each step in a program. For example, a program that sorts the array a [1] . . a [n] could be specified as follows:

$\{n \geq 1$ and for all i, $1 \leq i \leq n$, a[i] = A[i]$\}$
sort-program
$\{$sorted(a) and permutation(a , A)$\}$

Here the assertions sorted(a) and permutation(a , A) mean that the elements of a are sorted and that the elements of a are the same, except for order, as the original elements of the array A.

Such preconditions and postconditions are often capable of being tested for validity during execution of the program, as a kind of error checking, since the conditions are usually Boolean expressions that can be evaluated as expressions in the language itself. Indeed, a few languages such as Eiffel and Euclid have language constructs that allow assertions to be written directly into programs.

An **axiomatic specification** of the semantics of the language construct S is of the form

$$\{P\}\ S\ \{Q\}$$

where P and Q are assertions and that has the meaning that, if P is true just before the execution of S, then Q is true just after the execution of S.

Unfortunately, such a representation of the action of S is not unique and may not completely specify all the actions of S. In the second example, for instance, we did not include in the postcondition the fact that $y \neq 0$ continues to be true after the execution of the assignment. To specify completely the semantics of the assignment to x, we must somehow indicate that x is the only variable that changes under the assignment (unless it has aliases). Also, $y \neq 0$ is not the only condition that will guarantee the correct evaluation of the expression $1/y$: $y > 0$ or $y < 0$ will do as well. Thus writing an expected precondition and an expected postcondition will not always precisely determine the semantics of a language construct.

What is needed is a way of associating to the construct S a general relation between precondition P and postcondition Q. The way to do this is to use the property that programming is a **goal-oriented activity:** we usually know what we want to be true *after* the execution of a statement or program, and the question is whether the known conditions before the execution will guarantee that this becomes true. Thus postcondition Q is assumed to be given, and a specification of the semantics of S

becomes a statement of which preconditions P of S have the property that $\{P\}\ S\ \{Q\}$. To the uninitiated this may seem backward, but it is a consequence of working backward from the goal (the postcondition) to the initial requirements (the precondition).

In general, given an assertion Q, there are many assertions P with the property that $\{P\}\ S\ \{Q\}$. One example has been given: for $1/y$ to be evaluated, we may require that $y \neq 0$, or $y > 0$, or $y < 0$. There is one precondition P, however, that is the **most general** or **weakest** assertion with the property that $\{P\}\ S\ \{Q\}$. This is called the **weakest precondition** of postcondition Q and construct S and is written $wp(S,Q)$.

In our example, $y \neq 0$ is clearly the weakest precondition such that $1/y$ can be evaluated. Both $y > 0$ and $y < 0$ are stronger than $y \neq 0$ since they both imply $y \neq 0$. Indeed, P is by definition weaker than R if R implies P (written in logical form as $R \rightarrow P$). Using these definitions we have the following restatement of the property $\{P\}\ S\ \{Q\}$:

$$\{P\}\ S\ \{Q\} \quad \text{if and only if} \quad P \rightarrow wp(S,Q)$$

Finally, we define the axiomatic semantics of the language construct S as the function $wp(S,\_)$ from assertions to assertions. This function is a **predicate transformer** in that it takes a predicate as argument and returns a predicate result. It also appears to work backward, in that it computes the weakest precondition from any postcondition. This is a result of the goal-oriented behavior of programs as described earlier.

Our running example of the assignment can now be restated as follows:

$$wp(\text{x} := 1/\text{y},\ \text{x} = 1/y) = \{y \neq 0\}$$

As another example, consider the assignment $\text{x} := \text{x} + 1$ and the postcondition $\text{x} > 0$:

$$wp(\text{x} := \text{x} + 1,\ \text{x} > 0) = \{\text{x} > -1\}$$

In other words, for x to be greater than or equal to 0 after the execution of $\text{x} := \text{x} + 1$, x must be greater than -1 just prior to execution. On the other hand, if we have no condition on x but simply want to state its value, we have

$$wp(\text{x} := \text{x} + 1,\ \text{x} = A) = \{\text{x} = A - 1\}$$

Again, this may seem backward, but a little reflection should convince you of its correctness. Of course, to determine completely the semantics of an assignment such as $\text{x} := E$, where x is a variable and e is an expression, we need to compute $wp(\text{x} := E, Q)$ for *any* postcondition Q. This is done in Section 12.4.2, where the general rule for assignment is stated in terms of substitution. First, we will study wp a little further.

12.4.1   General Properties of *wp*

The predicate transformer $wp(S,Q)$ has certain properties that are true for almost all language constructs S, and we discuss these first, before giving axiomatic semantics for the sample language. The first of these is the following:

Law of the Excluded Miracle

$wp(S,\text{false}) = \text{false}.$

This states that nothing a programming construct S can do will make false into true—if it did it would be a miracle!

The second property concerns the behavior of *wp* with regard to the "and" operator of logic (also called conjunction):

Distributivity of Conjunction

$wp(S,P \text{ and } Q) = wp(S,P) \text{ and } wp(S,Q)$

Two more properties regard the implication operator "$->$" and the "or" operator (also called disjunction):

Law of Monotonicity

if $Q \rightarrow R$ then $wp(S,Q) \rightarrow wp(S,R)$

Distributivity of Disjunction

$wp(S,P \text{ or } Q) \rightarrow wp(S,P) \text{ or } wp(S,Q)$

with equality if S is deterministic.

The question of determinism adds a complicating technicality to the last law. Recall that some language constructs can be nondeterministic, such as the guarded commands discussed in Chapter 7. An example of the need for a weaker property in the presence of nondeterminism is discussed in Exercise 34. However, the existence of this exception serves to emphasize that, when one is talking about *any* language construct S, one must be extremely careful. Indeed, it is possible to invent situations in which all of the foregoing properties are questionable.

12.4.2   Axiomatic Semantics of the Sample Language

We are now ready to give an axiomatic specification for our sample language.

We note first that the specification of the semantics of expressions alone is not something that is commonly included in an axiomatic specification. In fact, the assertions involved in an axiomatic specification are primarily statements about the side effects of language constructs; that is, they are statements involving identifiers and environments. For example, the assertion $Q = \{x > 0\}$ is an assertion about the value of x in an environment. Logically, we could think of Q as being represented by the set of all environments for which Q is true. Then logical operations can be represented by set theoretic operations. For example, $P \rightarrow Q$ is the same as saying that every environment for which P is true is in the set of environments for which Q is true—in other words, that P is contained in Q as sets.

We will not pursue this translation of logic into set theory. We will also skip over the specification of expression evaluation in terms of weakest preconditions and proceed directly to statements, environments, and control.

The abstract syntax for which we will define the wp operator is the following:

$$P ::= L$$
$$L ::= L_1 \text{ ';' } L_2 \mid S$$
$$S ::= I \text{ ':=' } E$$
$$\mid \text{ 'if' } E \text{ 'then' } L_1 \text{ 'else' } L_2 \text{ 'fi'}$$
$$\mid \text{ 'while' } E \text{ 'do' } L \text{ 'od'}$$

Syntax rules such as $P ::= L$ and $L ::= S$ do not need separate specifications, since these grammar rules simply state that the wp operator for a program P is the same as for its associated statement-list L, and similarly, if a statement-list L is a single statement S, then L has the same axiomatic semantics as S. The remaining four cases are treated in order. To simplify the description we will suppress the use of quotes; code will be distinguished from assertions by the use of a different type.

Statement-lists.   For lists of statements separated by a semicolon, we have

$$wp(S_1 \text{ ; } S_2 \text{ ; } Q) = wp(S_1, wp(S_2, Q))$$

This states that the weakest precondition of a series of statements is essentially the composition of the weakest preconditions of its parts. Note that since wp works "backward" the positions of S_1 and S_2 are not interchanged, as they are in denotational semantics.

Assignment Statements.   The definition of wp for the assignment statement is as follows:

$$wp(I := E, Q) = Q[E/I]$$

This rule involves a new notation: $Q[E/I]$. $Q[E/I]$ is defined to be the assertion Q, with E replacing all free occurrences of the identifier I in Q. The notion of "free occurrences" was discussed in Chapter 11; it also arose in Section 10.6 in connection with reducing lambda calculus expressions. An identifier x is **free** in a logical assertion Q if it is not **bound** by either the existential quantifier "there exists" or the universal quantifier "for all." Thus, in the following assertion, j is free, but i is bound (and thus not free):

$$Q = (\text{for all } i,\ a[i] > a[j])$$

In this case $Q[1/j] = (\text{for all } i,\ a[i] > a[1])$, but $Q[1/i] = Q$. In commonly occurring assertions, this should not become a problem, and in the absence of quantifiers, one can simply read $Q[E/I]$ as replacing *all* occurrences of I by E.

The axiomatic semantics $wp(I := E, Q) = Q[E/I]$ simply says that, for Q to be true after the assignment $I := E$, whatever Q says about I must be true about E *before* the assignment is executed.

A couple of examples will help to explain the semantics for assignment.

First, consider the previous example $wp(x := x + 1,\ x > 0)$. Here $Q = (x > 0)$ and $Q[(x + 1)/x] = (x + 1 > 0)$. Thus

$$wp(x := x + 1, x > 0) = (x + 1 > 0) = (x > -1)$$

which is what we obtained before. Similarly,

$$wp(x := x + 1, x = A) = (x = A)[(x+1)/x]$$
$$= (x + 1 = A)$$
$$= (x = A - 1)$$

If-statements.   Recall that the semantics of the if-statement in our sample language were somewhat unusual: i f E t h e n L_1 e l s e L_2 f i means that L_1 is executed if the value of $E > 0$, and L_2 is executed if the value of $E \le 0$. The weakest precondition of this statement is defined as follows:

$$wp(\text{i f } E \text{ t h e n } L_1 \text{ e l s e } L_2 \text{ f i},\ Q) =$$
$$(E > 0 \rightarrow wp(L_1, Q)) \text{ and } (E \le 0 \rightarrow wp(L_2, Q))$$

As an example, we compute

$$wp(\text{i f } x \text{ t h e n } x := 1 \text{ e l s e } x := -1 \text{ f i},\ x = 1) =$$
$$(x>0 \rightarrow wp(x:=1, x=1)) \text{ and } (x\le 0 \rightarrow wp(x:=-1, x=1)) =$$
$$(x>0 \rightarrow 1=1) \text{ and } (x\le 0 \rightarrow -1=1)$$

Recalling that $(P \rightarrow Q)$ is the same as $(Q \text{ or not } P)$ (see Exercise 11.1), we get

$$(x>0 \rightarrow 1=1) = ((1=1) \text{ or not}(x>0)) = \text{true}$$

and

$$(x\le 0 \rightarrow -1=1) = (-1=1) \text{ or not}(x\le 0) =$$
$$\text{not}(x\le 0) = (x>0)$$

so

$$wp(\text{i f } x \text{ t h e n } x := 1 \text{ e l s e } x := -1 \text{ f i},\ x = 1) = (x > 0)$$

as we expect.

While-statements. The while-statement while E do L od, as defined in Section 12.1, executes as long as $E > 0$. As before, the semantics of the while-loop present particular problems. We must give an inductive definition based on the number of times the loop executes. Let H_i(while E do L od, Q) be the statement that the loop executes i times and terminates in a state satisfying Q. Then clearly

$$H_0(\text{while } E \text{ do } L \text{ od}, Q) = E \leq 0 \text{ and } Q$$

and

$$H_1(\text{while } B \text{ do } L \text{ od}, Q) = E > 0 \text{ and } wp(L, Q \text{ and } E \leq 0)$$
$$= E > 0 \text{ and } wp(S, H_0(\text{while } E \text{ do } L \text{ od}, Q))$$

Continuing in this fashion we have in general that

$$H_{i+1}(\text{while } E \text{ do } L \text{ od}, Q) =$$
$$E > 0 \text{ and } wp(L, H_i(\text{while } E \text{ do } L \text{ od}, Q))$$

Now we define

$$wp(\text{while } E \text{ do } L \text{ od}, Q)$$
$$= \text{ there exists } i \text{ such that } H_i(\text{while } E \text{ do } L \text{ od}, Q)$$

Note that this definition of the semantics of the while requires the while-loop to terminate. Thus a nonterminating loop always has false as its weakest precondition; that is, it can never make a postcondition true. For example,

$$wp(\text{while } 1 \text{ do } L \text{ od}, Q) = \text{false, for all } L \text{ and } Q$$

The semantics we have just given for loops has the drawback that it is very difficult to use in the main application area for axiomatic semantics, namely, the proof of correctness of programs. In the next section we will describe an approximation of the semantics of a loop that is more usable in practice.

12.5 PROOFS OF PROGRAM CORRECTNESS

The theory of axiomatic semantics was developed as a tool for proving the correctness of programs and program fragments, and this continues to be its major application. In this section we will use the axiomatic semantics of the last section to prove properties of programs written in our sample language.

We have already mentioned in the last section that a specification for a program S can be written as $\{P\}$ S $\{Q\}$, where P represents the set of conditions that are expected to hold at the beginning of a program and Q represents the set of conditions one wishes to have true after execution of the code S. As an example, we gave the following specification for a program that sorts the array a[1]..a[n]:

{n >= 1 and for all i, 1 <= i <= n, a[i] = A[i]}
sort-program
{sorted(a) and permutation(a, A)}

Two easier examples of specifications for programs that can be written in our sample language are the following:

1. A program that swaps the value of x and y:

    {x = X and y = Y}
    swapxy
    {x = Y and y = X}

2. A program that computes the sum of integers less than or equal to a positive integer n:

    {n > 0}
    sum_to_n
    {sum = 1 + 2 + · · · + n}

We will give correctness proofs that the two programs we provide satisfy the specifications of (1) and (2).

Recall from the last section that S satisfies a specification $\{P\} \; S \; \{Q\}$ provided $P \rightarrow wp(S,Q)$. Thus to prove that S satisfies a specification we need two steps: first, we must compute $wp(S,Q)$ from the axiomatic semantics and general properties of wp, and, second, we must show that $P \rightarrow wp(S,Q)$.

1. We claim that the following program is correct:

    {x = X and y = Y}
    t := x;
    x := y;
    y := t
    {x = Y and y = X}

We first compute $wp(S,Q)$ as follows:

$wp(\,t := x \,; x := y \,; y := t \,, x = Y \text{ and } y = X)$
$\qquad = wp(\,t := x, wp(x := y \,; y := t, x = Y \text{ and } y = X))$
$\qquad = wp(\,t := x, wp(x := y, wp(y := t \,, x = Y \text{ and } y = X)))$
$\qquad = wp(\,t := x, wp(x := y, wp(y := t \,, x = Y)$
$\qquad\qquad\qquad\qquad\qquad \text{and } wp(y := t \,, y = X)))$
$\qquad = wp(\,t := x, wp(x := y, wp(y := t \,, x = Y))$
$\qquad\qquad\qquad\qquad\qquad \text{and } wp(x := y, wp(y := t \,, y = X)))$
$\qquad = wp(\,t := x, wp(x := y, wp(y := t \,, x = Y)))$
$\qquad\qquad\qquad \text{and } wp(\,t := x, wp(x := y, wp(y := t \,, y = X)))$

by distributivity of conjunction and the axiomatic semantics of statement-lists. Now

$wp(\,t := x, wp(x := y, \; wp(y := t \,, x = Y))) =$
$\qquad wp(\,t := x, wp(x := y \,, x = Y)) \; = \; wp(\,t := x \,, y = Y) \; = \; (y = Y)$

and

$$wp(\,t := x, wp(\,x := y,\ wp(\,y := t, y = X)\,)\,) =$$
$$wp(\,t := x, wp(\,x := y, t = X)\,) = wp(\,t := x, t = X) = (x = X)$$

by the rule of substitution for assignments. Thus

$$wp(\,t := x\,;\,x := y\,;\,y := t, x = Y \text{ and } y = X) = (y = Y \text{ and } x = X)$$

The second step is to show that $P \rightarrow wp(S,Q)$. But in this case P actually equals the weakest precondition, since $P = (x = X$ and $y = Y)$. Since $P = wp(S,Q)$, clearly also $P \rightarrow wp(S,Q)$. The proof of correctness is complete.

2. We claim that the following program is correct:

```
{n > 0}
i := n;
sum := 0;
while i do
   sum := sum + i;
   i := i - 1
od
{sum = 1 + 2 + ··· + n}
```

The problem is now that our semantics for while-statements are too difficult to use to prove correctness. To show that a while-statement is correct, we really do not need to derive completely its weakest precondition $wp(\text{while}\ldots,Q)$, but only an **approximation,** that is, some assertion W such that $W \rightarrow wp(\text{while}\ldots,Q)$. Then if we can show that $P \rightarrow W$, we have also shown the correctness of $\{P\}$ while ... $\{Q\}$, since $P \rightarrow W$ and $W \rightarrow wp(\text{while}\ldots,Q)$ imply that $P \rightarrow wp(\text{while}\ldots,Q)$.

We do this in the following way. Given the loop while E do L od, suppose we find an assertion W such that the following three conditions are true:

(a) W and $(E{>}0) \rightarrow wp(L,W)$

(b) W and $(E{\leq}0) \rightarrow Q$

(c) $P \rightarrow W$

Then if we know that the loop while E do L od terminates, we must have $W \rightarrow wp(\text{while } E \text{ do } L \text{ od}, Q)$. This is because every time the loop executes, W continues to be true, by condition (a), and when the loop terminates, condition (b) says Q must be true. Finally, condition (c) implies that W is the required approximation for $wp(\text{while}\ldots,Q)$.

An assertion W satisfying condition (a) is said to be a **loop invariant** for the loop while E do L od, since a repetition of the loop leaves W true. In general, loops have many invariants W, and to prove the correctness of a loop, it sometimes takes a little skill to find an appropriate W, namely, one that also satisfies conditions (b) and (c).

In the case of our example program, however, a loop invariant is not too difficult to find:

$$W = (\text{sum} = (i + 1) + \cdots + n \text{ and } i \geq 0)$$

is an appropriate one. We show conditions (a) and (b) in turn:

(a) We must show that W and $i > 0 \rightarrow wp(\text{sum}:=\text{sum}+i\ ;\ i:=i-1, W)$. First, we have

$$
\begin{aligned}
wp(\text{sum}&:=\text{sum}+i\ ;\ i:=i-1, W) \\
&= wp(\text{sum}:=\text{sum}+i\ ;\ i:=i-1, \text{sum}=(i+1) + \cdots + n \text{ and} \\
&\qquad\qquad\qquad\qquad\qquad\qquad\qquad\qquad\qquad i\geq 0) \\
&= wp(\text{sum}:=\text{sum}+i, wp(i:=i-1, \text{sum}=(i+1) + \cdots + n \\
&\qquad\qquad\qquad\qquad\qquad\qquad\qquad\qquad\text{and } i\geq 0)) \\
&= wp(\text{sum}:=\text{sum}+i, \text{sum}=((i-1)+1) + \cdots + n \text{ and} \\
&\qquad\qquad\qquad\qquad\qquad\qquad\qquad\qquad i-1\geq 0) \\
&= wp(\text{sum}:=\text{sum}+i, \text{sum} = i + \cdots + n \text{ and } i-1\geq 0) \\
&= (\text{sum}+i = i + \cdots + n \text{ and } i-1\geq 0) \\
&= (\text{sum} = (i+1) + \cdots + n \text{ and } i-1\geq 0)
\end{aligned}
$$

Now $(W$ and $i > 0) \rightarrow (W$ and $i - 1 \geq 0)$, since

$$
\begin{aligned}
W \text{ and } i > 0 &= (\text{sum}=(i+1)+ \cdots +n \text{ and } i\geq 0 \text{ and } i>0) \\
&= (\text{sum}=(i+1)+ \cdots +n \text{ and } i>0) \\
&\rightarrow (W \text{ and } i-1 \geq 0)
\end{aligned}
$$

Thus W is a loop invariant.

(b) We must show that $(W$ and $(i \leq 0)) \rightarrow (\text{sum} = 1 + \cdots + n)$. But this is clear:

$$
\begin{aligned}
W \text{ and } (i\leq 0) &= (\text{sum}=(i+1) + \cdots + n \text{ and } i\geq 0 \text{ and } i\leq 0) \\
&= (\text{sum}=(i+1) + \cdots + n \text{ and } i=0) \\
&= (\text{sum}=1+ \cdots + n \text{ and } i=0)
\end{aligned}
$$

It remains to show that conditions just prior to the execution of the loop imply the truth of W. We do this by showing that $n > 0 \rightarrow wp(i:=n\ ;\ \text{sum}:=0, W)$. We have

$$
\begin{aligned}
wp(i&:=n\ ;\ \text{sum}:=0, W) \\
&= wp(i:=n, wp(\text{sum}:=0, \text{sum}=(i+1) + \cdots + n \text{ and } i\geq 0)) \\
&= wp(i:=n, 0=(i+1) + \cdots + n \text{ and } i\geq 0) \\
&= (0=(n+1) + \cdots + n \text{ and } n\geq 0) \\
&= (0=0 \text{ and } n\geq 0) \\
&= (n\geq 0)
\end{aligned}
$$

and of course $n > 0 \rightarrow n \geq 0$. In this computation we used the property that the sum $(i+1) + \cdots + n$ with $i \geq n$ is 0. This is a general mathematical property: empty sums are always assumed to be 0. We also note that this proof uncovered an additional property of our code: it doesn't work only for $n > 0$, but for $n \geq 0$ as well.

This concludes our discussion of proofs of programs. A few more examples will be discussed in the exercises.

Exercises

1. Our sample language used the bracketing keywords "fi" and "od" for if-statements and while-statements, similar to Algol68. Was this necessary? Why?

2. Add unary minuses to the arithmetic expressions of the sample language, and add its semantics to (a) the operational semantics and (b) the denotational semantics.

3. Add division to the arithmetic expressions of the sample language, and add its semantics to (a) the operational semantics and (b) the denotational semantics. Try to include a specification of what happens when division by 0 occurs.

4. The operational semantics of identifiers was skipped in the discussion in the text. Add the semantics of identifiers to the operational semantics of the sample language.

5. The denotational semantics of identifiers was also (silently) skipped. What we did was to use the set Identifier as both a syntactic domain (the set of syntax trees of identifiers) and as a semantic domain (the set of strings with the concatenation operator). Call the latter set Name, and develop a denotational definition of the semantic function I: Identifier $\longrightarrow$ Name. Revise the denotational semantics of the sample language to include this correction.

6. A problem that exists with any formal description of a language is that the description itself must be written in some "language," which we could call the **defining language,** to distinguish it from the defined language. For example, the defining language in each of the formal methods studied in this chapter are as follows:

> operational semantics: reduction rules
>
> denotational semantics: functions
>
> axiomatic semantics: logic

For a formal semantic method to be successful, the defining language needs to have a precise description itself, and it must also be understandable. Discuss and compare the defining languages of the three semantic methods in terms of your perception of their precision and understandability.

7. One formal semantic method not discussed in this chapter but mentioned in Chapter 10 is the use of the defined language itself as the defining language. Such a method could be called **metacircular,** and metacircular interpreters are a common method of defining LISP-like languages. Discuss the advantages and disadvantages of this method in comparison with the methods discussed in this chapter.

8. The grammar of the sample language included a complete description of identifiers and numbers. However, a language translator usually recognizes such constructs in the scanner. Our view of semantics thus implies that the scanner is performing semantic functions. Wouldn't it be better simply to make numbers and identifiers into tokens in the grammar, thus making it unnecessary to describe something done by the scanner as "semantics"? Why or why not?

9. The axiomatic semantics of Section 12.4 did not include a description of the semantics of expressions. Can you think of a way to include expressions in the axiomatic description?

10. Show how the operational semantics of the sample language describes the reduction of the expression $23 \cdot 5 - 34$ to its value.

11. Compute $E[[23 \cdot 5 - 34]]$ using the denotational definition of the sample language.

12. Show how the operational semantics of the sample language describes the reduction of the program $a := 2; b := a+1; a := b*b$ to its environment.

13. Compute the value $Env(a)$ for the environment Env at the end of the program $a := 2; b := a+1; a := b*b$ using the denotational definition of the sample language.

14. Repeat Exercise 12 for the program

```
a := 0 - 11;
if a then a := a else a := 0 - a fi
```

15. Repeat Exercise 13 for the program of Exercise 14.

16. The sample language did not include any input or output statements. We could add these to the grammar as follows:

$$<stmt> ::= \ldots \mid \text{'input'} <identifier> \mid \text{'output'} <exp>$$

Add input and output statements to the (a) operational semantics and (b) denotational semantics. (Hint for denotational semantics: Consider a new semantic domain IntSequence to be the set of sequences of integers. Then statement sequences act on states that are environments plus an input sequence and an output sequence.)

17. The sample language has unusual semantics for if- and while-statements, due to the absence of Boolean expressions. Add Boolean expressions such as x = 0, true, y > 2 to the sample language, and describe their semantics in (a) operational and (b) denotational terms.

18. Revise the axiomatic description of the sample language to include the Boolean expressions of Exercise 17.

19. Find $wp($a := 2; b := a+1; a := b*b , a=9$)$.

20. Find $wp($if x then x:=x else x:= 0−x fi, x≤0$)$.

21. Show the following program is correct with respect to the given specification:

```
{true}
if x then x := x else x := 0−x fi
{x ≥ 0}
```

22. Which of the following are loop invariants of the loop while i do sum := sum+i; i := i−1 od:
    (a) sum = i + · · · + n
    (b) sum = (i + 1) + · · · + n and i > 0
    (c) sum ≥ 0 and i ≥ 0

23. Prove the correctness of the following program:

```
{n > 0}
i := n;
fact := 1;
while i do
   fact := fact*i;
   i := i − 1
od
{fact = 1·2·. . .·n}
```

24. Write a program in the sample language that computes the product of two numbers n and m by repeatedly adding n m-times. Prove your program is correct.

25. In Section 12.4 and 12.5 we used the following example of a program specification using preconditions and postconditions:

{n ≥ 1 and for all i, 1 ≤ i ≤ n, a[i] = A[i]}
sort-program
{sorted(a) and permutation(a , A)}

Write out the details of the assertions sorted(a) and permutation (a , A).

26. Use operational semantics to reduce the following program to its environment:

```
n := 2;
while n do n := n−1 od
```

27. Show the correctness of the following program using axiomatic semantics:

```
{n > 0}
while n do n := n−1 od
{n = 0}
```

28. Show using general properties of *wp* that $wp(S, \text{not } Q) \rightarrow \text{not } wp(S,Q)$ for any language construct S and any assertion Q.

29. Show that the law of monotonicity follows from the distributivity of conjunction. (Hint: Use the equivalence of $(P \rightarrow Q)$ and $(Q \text{ or not } P)$.)

30. We did not describe how operations might be extended to lifted domains (domains with an undefined value) such as $\text{Integer}_\perp$. Give a definition for " + ", " − ", and " • " that includes the undefined value " $\perp$ ".

31. Sometimes operations can ignore undefined values and still return a defined value. Give an example where the " • " operation can do this. (Such operations are called nonstrict. Strictness was discussed in Chapter 10.)

32. The formal semantic descriptions of the sample language in this chapter did not include a description of the semantics in the presence of undefined values (such as the use of an identifier without an assigned value or a loop that never terminates). Try to extend the semantic descriptions of each of the three methods discussed in this chapter to include a description of the effect of undefined values.

33. We might be tempted to define an environment in denotational terms as a semantic function from identifiers to integers (ignoring undefined values):

$$\textbf{\textit{Env}}: \text{Identifier} \rightarrow \text{Integer}$$

Would this be wrong? Why or why not?

34. The text mentions that in the presence of nondeterminism it is not true that $wp(S,P \text{ or } Q) = wp(S,P) \text{ or } wp(S,Q)$. Let S be the following guarded if, in which either statement might be executed,

```
if
     true => x := x+1
     true => x := x−1
fi
```

Show that $wp(S, (x>0)\text{or}(x<0))$ is not equal to $wp(S,x>0)$ or $wp(S,x<0)$.

35. The operational semantics in Section 12.2 specified a left-to-right evaluation for expressions. Rewrite the reduction rules so that no particular evaluation order is specified.

36. The rule for reducing parentheses in operational semantics was written as the axiom '(' V ')' $=>V$, where V stands for a numeric value. Why is it wrong to write the more general rule '(' E ')' $=>E$, where E can be any expression?

37. In Section 12.2 we wrote three reduction rules for if-statements, but only two for while-statements.
    (a) Rewrite the rules for if-statements as only two rules.
    (b) Can one write three rules for the while-statement? Why?

38. Is it possible to express the evaluation order of expressions in denotational semantics? Explain.

39. In operational semantics, an environment must be given before an abstract machine can perform any reductions. Thus one (extremely abstract) view of operational semantics is as a function Φ: Program $\times$ Environment $\rightarrow$ Environment. In this sense, denotational semantics can be viewed as a curried version (see Section 10.6) of operational semantics. Explain what is meant by this statement.

Notes and References

Formal semantic methods are surveyed in Meyer [1990] and Pagan [1981]. Operational semantics, in essentially the form we have used, appears in Wikström [1987]. A different operational method is the Vienna definition language, which is surveyed in Wegner [1972]. A more detailed account can be found in Ollongren [1974] and a simple example in Marcotty and Ledgard [1986]. An outgrowth of VDL is the Vienna development method, or VDM, which is denotational in approach. A description of this method appears in Bjørner and Jones [1982] and Jones [1986]. Denotational semantics as they are presented here began with the early work of Scott and Strachey (see Stoy [1977]). An in-depth coverage of denotational semantics, including domain theory and fixed-point semantics, is given in Schmidt [1986].

Axiomatic semantics began with a seminal paper by Hoare [1969]. Weakest preconditions were introduced by Dijkstra [1975, 1976]. An in-depth coverage is given in Gries [1981]. For a perspective on nondeterminism and the law of the excluded miracle, see Nelson [1989].

13 PARALLEL PROGRAMMING

The idea of **parallel processing,** or executing many computations in parallel, has been around at least since the 1960s, when the first **multiprogramming** or **pseudoparallel systems** became available: systems in which many processes share a single processor and appear to execute simultaneously. Pseudoparallelism represented a considerable advance in computer technology, and it is still the standard way most larger machines operate today. It has also long been clear that **true parallelism,** in which many processors are connected together to run in concert, either as a single system incorporating all the processors (a **multiprocessor system**) or as a group of stand-alone processors connected together by high-speed links (a **distributed system**), would represent an even greater advance in computer technology, since this would be one way of solving the problem of the von Neumann bottleneck (see Chapter 1).

However, this seemingly simple idea has not been simple to put into practice, and truly parallel systems have only recently become widely available, despite extensive study of the issues involved. Thus a comprehensive study of parallel processing is beyond the scope of this text.

Nevertheless, programming languages have been intimately involved in the implementation of parallelism in at least three ways. First, programming languages have been used to express algorithms to solve the problems presented by parallel processing systems. Second, programming languages have been used to write operating systems that have implemented these solutions on various architectures. And, third, programming languages have been used to harness the capabilities of multiple processors to solve application problems efficiently.

A survey of the principles and practice of programming language design would therefore not be complete without a study of the basic approaches that programming languages have taken to expressing parallelism. In this study we must also distinguish between the parallelism as expressed in a programming language and the parallelism that actually exists in the underlying hardware. Programs that are written with parallel programming constructs do not necessarily result in actual parallel processing, but could simply be implemented by pseudoparallelism, even in a system with multiple processors. Thus parallel programming is sometimes referred to as **concurrent programming** to emphasize the fact that parallel constructs express only the **potential** for parallelism, not that parallel processing actually occurs (which is decided by the architecture of the particular system, the operating system, and the pragmatics of the translator interface). However, we will suppress this distinction and will refer to concurrent programming as parallel programming, without implying that parallel processing must occur.

In this chapter we briefly survey the basic concepts of parallelism, without which an understanding of language issues is impossible. We then survey basic language issues and introduce the standard approaches to parallelism taken by programming language designers. These include coroutines, a standard way of introducing pseudoparallelism; semaphores and their structured alternative, the monitor; and message passing. Languages used as examples include Modula-2, Ada, CSP, and Concurrent Pascal. Finally, a brief look is taken at some proposed ways of expressing parallelism in functional and logic programming languages.

13.1   INTRODUCTION TO PARALLEL PROCESSING

The fundamental notion of parallel processing is that of the **process:** it is the basic unit of code executed by a processor. Processes have been variously defined in the literature, but a simple definition is the following:

A process is a program in execution.

This is not quite accurate, since processes can consist of parts of programs as well as whole programs, more than one process can correspond to the same program, and processes do not need to be currently executing to retain their status as processes. A better definition might be the following.

> A process is an instance of a program or program part that has been scheduled for independent execution.

Processes used to be called **jobs,** and in the early days of computing, jobs were executed in purely sequential, or **batch** fashion. Thus there was only one process in existence at a time, and there was no need to distinguish between processes and programs.

With the advent of pseudoparallelism, several processes could exist simultaneously. A process now could be in one of several **states:** it could be **executing,** that is, in possession of the processor; it could be **blocked,** waiting for some activity such as input-output to finish, or some event such as a keypress to occur; or it could be **waiting** for execution by the processor.[1] In such a system the operating system needs to apply some algorithm to schedule processes for execution, and to manage a data structure, usually a queue, to maintain waiting and blocked processes. It also needs a method to cause processes to relinquish the processor, or timeout. The principal method for accomplishing this is the **hardware interrupt.**

In a true parallel processing system, where several processors are available, the notion of process and process state is retained much as in the pseudoparallel system. The complication is that each processor may individually be assigned to a process, and a clear distinction must be made between process and processor. Each processor may or may not be assigned its own queues for maintaining blocked and waiting processes.

The organization of the different processors is a critical issue to the operation of processes in a parallel processing system. Two primary requirements for the organization of the processors are

1. There must be a way for processors to synchronize their activities.
2. There must be a way for processors to communicate data among themselves.

For example, in a typical situation, one processor will be handling the input and sorting of data, while a second processor performs computations on the data. The second processor must not begin processing data before it is sorted by the first processor. This is a synchronization problem. Also, the first processor needs to communicate the actual sorted data to the second processor. This is a communication problem.

In some machines one processor is designated as a controller, which manages the operation of the other processors. In some cases this central control extends even to the selection of instructions, and all the processors

---

[1]This is a simplified description. Actual operating systems have a more complex state structure.

must execute the same instructions on their respective registers or data sets. Such systems are called **single-instruction, multiple-data or SIMD systems** and are by their nature multiprocessing rather than distributed systems. Such systems are also often **synchronous,** in that all the processors operate at the same speed and the controlling processor determines precisely when each instruction is executed by each processor. This implicitly solves the synchronization problem.

In other architectures all the processors act independently. Such systems are called **multiple-instruction, multiple-data or MIMD systems** and may be either multiprocessor or distributed processor systems. In an MIMD system the processors may operate at different speeds, and therefore such systems are **asynchronous.** Thus the synchronization of the processors in an MIMD system becomes a critical problem.

Hybrid systems are also possible, with each processor retaining some but not complete independence from the other processors. The difference between an SIMD and an MIMD system is illustrated in Figure 13-1.

In a similar way to the sharing of instructions in an SIMD system, memory may be shared. A system in which one central memory is shared by all the processors is called a **shared-memory system** and is also by nature a multiprocessor rather than a distributed system, while a system

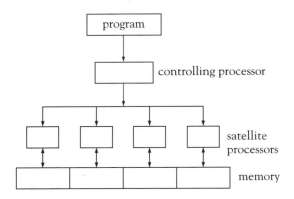

Figure 13-1a   Schematic of an SIMD Processor

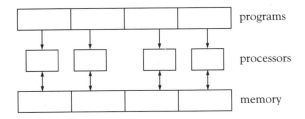

Figure 13-1b   Schematic of an MIMD Processor

in which each processor has its own independent memory is called a **distributed-memory system** (and may be either an actual distributed system or a multiprocessor system).

In a shared-memory system the processors communicate through the changes each makes to the shared memory. If the processors operate asynchronously, they may also use the shared memory to synchronize their activities. For this to work properly, each processor must have exclusive access to those parts of memory that it is changing. This is the **mutual exclusion problem.** Distributed-memory systems do not have to worry about mutual exclusion, since each processor has its own memory inaccessible to the other processors. On the other hand, distributed processors have a **communication problem,** in that each processor must be able to send messages to and receive messages from all the other processors asynchronously. Communication between processors depends on the configuration of links between the processors. Sometimes processors are connected in sequence, and processors may need to forward information to other processors farther along the link. If the number of processors is small, each processor may be fully linked to every other processor.

Again, it is possible for a system to be a hybrid between a shared-memory and a distributed-memory system, with each processor maintaining some private memory in addition to the shared memory and the processors having some communication links separate from the shared memory. Figure 13-2 illustrates the difference between a shared-memory system and a fully linked distributed-memory system.[2]

Regardless of organization of the underlying machine, it is the task of the operating system to integrate the operation of the processors and to shield the user from needing to know too much about the particular configuration. The operating system can also change the view the user has of the hardware, depending on the utilities it makes available. For example, the operating system could assign distinct parts of memory in a shared-memory system for exclusive use by each processor and use other parts of memory to simulate communications channels, thus making a shared-memory system appear to be a distributed-memory system. The operating system can even shield the user entirely from the fact that there is more than one processor and schedule users or processes on different processors automatically, according to an internal algorithm that attempts to allocate resources in an efficient way. However, automatic allocation of multiple processors is almost always less than optimal, and there is usually a need for operating systems to provide facilities for users to manage processes and processors manually. In general, an operating system will need to provide

1. A means of creating and destroying processes.

2. A means of managing the number of processors used by processes (for

---

[2]Figures adapted from Karp [1987], p. 44. Copyright 1987, IEEE. Used by permission.

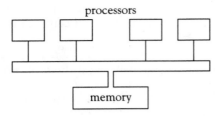

Figure 13-2a   Schematic of a Shared-Memory System

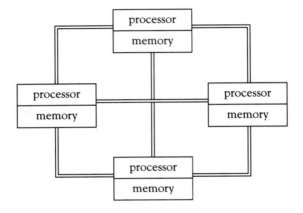

Figure 13-2b   Schematic of a Fully Linked Distributed-Memory System

example, a method of assigning processes to processors or a method for reserving a number of processors for use by a program).

3. On a shared-memory system, a mechanism for ensuring mutual exclusion of processes to shared memory. Mutual exclusion is used for both process synchronization and communication.

4. On a distributed-memory system, a mechanism for creating and maintaining communication channels between processors. These channels are used both for interprocess communication and for synchronization.

In the next section, we will see how similar facilities must be provided by programming languages to make parallel processing available to programmers.

13.2   PARALLEL PROCESSING AND PROGRAMMING LANGUAGES

Programming languages are like operating systems in that they need to provide programmers with mechanisms for process creation, synchronization, and communication. However, a programming language has stricter requirements than an operating system: its facilities must be machine independent and must adhere to language design principles such as readability, writability, and maintainability. Nevertheless, most programming languages have adopted a particular model of parallel organization in providing parallel facilities. Thus some languages use the shared-memory model and provide facilities for mutual exclusion, while others assume the distributed model and provide communication facilities. A few languages have included both models, the designers arguing that sometimes one model and sometimes the other will be preferable in particular situations.

A language designer can also adopt the view that parallel mechanisms should not be included in a language definition at all. If this is done, there are still ways that parallel facilities can be provided. Since this is the easiest approach to parallelism (from the point of view of the language designer), we will study this first. Also in this section, we will consider some approaches to process creation and destruction, since these are (more or less) common to both the shared-memory and the distributed models of parallelism. Model-specific facilities will be left to later sections. In particular, Section 13.3 will discuss **coroutines,** which are a standard way of providing facilities for pseudoparallelism (still the most common situation today). Sections 13.4 and 13.5 will discuss **semaphores** and **monitors,** two approaches to the shared-memory model. Section 13.6 will study **message passing,** a mechanism that follows the distributed model.

We will also need a number of standard problems in parallel processing to demonstrate the use of particular mechanisms. We will use the following two problems throughout the remainder of this chapter (other problems are discussed in the exercises):

1. *The bounded buffer problem.* This problem assumes that two processes are cooperating in a computational or input-output situation. One process produces values that are consumed by the second process. An intermediate buffer, or buffer process, stores produced values until they are consumed. A solution to this problem must ensure that no value is produced until there is room to store it and that a value is consumed only after it has been produced. This involves both communication and synchronization.

2. *Parallel matrix multiplication.* This problem is different from the previous one in that it is an example of an algorithmic application in which the use of parallelism can cause significant speedups. Matrices are essentially two-dimensional arrays, as in the following declaration of integer matrices (we consider only the case where the size of both dimensions is the same, given by the positive integer n):

```
VAR a,b,c: ARRAY [n,n] OF INTEGER;
```

The standard way of multiplying two matrices a and b to form a third matrix c is given by the following nested loops:

```
FOR i := 1 TO n DO
  FOR j := 1 TO n DO
    c[i,j] := 0;
    FOR k := 1 TO n DO
      c[i,j] := c[i,j] + a[i,k]*b[k,j];
    END; (* for k *)
  END; (* for j *)
END; (* for i *)
```

This computation, if performed sequentially, takes n^3 steps. If, however, we assign a process to compute each c[i,j], and if each process executes on a separate processor, then the computation can be performed in the equivalent of n steps. Algorithms such as this are studied extensively in courses on parallel algorithms. In fact, this is the simplest form of such an algorithm, since there are no write conflicts caused by the computation of the c[i,j] by separate processes. Thus there is no need to enforce mutual exclusion in accessing the matrices as shared memory. There is, however, a synchronization problem in that the product c cannot be used until all the processes that compute it have finished. A programming language, if it is to provide useful parallelism, must provide facilities for implementing such algorithms with a minimum of overhead.

13.2.1   Parallel Programming Without Explicit Language Facilities

As we have noted, one possible approach to parallelism is simply not to express it explicitly at all in the language. This is especially possible in functional, logic, and object-oriented languages, which have a certain amount of inherent parallelism implicit in the language constructs. (We have mentioned this before, but we will review it again in Section 13.7.)

In theory it is possible for language translators, using optimization techniques, to make use automatically of operating system utilities to assign different processors to different parts of a program. However, as with operating systems, the automatic assignment of processors is likely to be suboptimal, and manual facilities are needed to make full use of parallel processors. In addition, a programming language may be used for purposes that require explicitly indicating the parallelism, such as the writing of operating systems themselves or the implementation of intricate parallel algorithms.

A second alternative to defining parallel constructs in a programming language is for the translator to offer the programmer **compiler options** to allow the explicit indicating of areas where parallelism is called for. This is usually better than automatic parallelization. One of the places where this is most effective is in the use of nested loops, where each repetition of the inner loop is relatively independent of the others. Such a situation is the matrix multiplication problem just discussed.

Figure 13-3 shows an example of a parallel loop compiler option in

```
      integer a(100,100), b(100,100), c(100,100)
      integer i,j,k, numprocs, err
      numprocs = 10
C code to read in a and b goes here
      err = m_set_procs(numprocs)
C$doacross share(a,b,c), local(j,k)
      do 10 i = 1,100
        do 10 j = 1,100
          c(i,j) = 0
          do 10 k = 1,100
            c(i,j) = c(i,j) + a(i,k)*b(k,j)
   10 continue
      call m_kill_procs
C code to write out c goes here
      end
```

Figure 13-3   FORTRAN Compiler Options for Parallelism

FORTRAN code for the matrix multiplication problem. The example is for a FORTRAN compiler on a Sequent parallel computer. The compiler option is

```
C$doacross share(a,b,c), local(j,k)
```

that causes a preprocessor to insert code that parallelizes the outer loop. The share and local declarations indicate that a, b, and c are to be accessed by all processes, but that j and k are local variables to each process. The call to m_set_procs sets the number of processes (and processors) that are to be used, returning an error code if not enough processors are available. (Note that in the example the number of processes is ten, far below the number needed to compute optimally the matrix product; see Exercise 5.) The call to m_kill_procs synchronizes the processes, so that all processes wait for the entire loop to finish and that only one process continues to execute after the loop.

A third way of making parallel facilities available without explicit mechanisms in the language design is to provide a library of functions to perform parallel processing. This is a way of passing the facilities provided by an operating system directly to the programmer. This way, different libraries can be provided, depending on what facilities an operating system or parallel machine offers. Of course, if a standard parallel library is required by a language, then this is the same as including parallel facilities in the language definition.

Figure 13-4 is an example in C where library functions are used to provide parallel processing for the matrix multiplication problem. (C itself has no parallel mechanisms.) We note that the example of the use of a translator option to indicate parallelism (Figure 13-3) also used some of

```
#include <parallel/parallel.h>
#define SIZE 100
#define NUMPROCS 10

shared int a[SIZE][SIZE],b[SIZE][SIZE],
  c[SIZE][SIZE];

void main(void)
{int err;
 int multiply();
/* code to read in the matrices a and b goes
   here */
 m_set_procs(NUMPROCS);
 m_fork(multiply);
 m_kill_procs();
/* code to write out the matrix c goes here */
}
void multiply(void)
{int i,j,k;
   for (i = m_get_myid(); i < SIZE; i += NUMPROCS)
     for (j = 0; j < SIZE; ++j)
       for (k = 0; k < SIZE; ++k)
         c[i][j] += a[i][k] * b[k][j];
}
```

Figure 13-4   Use of a Library to Provide Parallel Processing

the same library procedures. (This example is also for a Sequent computer, for comparison purposes.)

In Figure 13-4 the four procedures m_set_procs, m_fork, m_kill_procs, and m_get_myid are imported from a library (the parallel/parallel library). m_set_procs and m_kill_procs are as in the previous example. m_fork creates the ten processes, which are all instances of the procedure multiply (the name fork comes from the Unix operating system, discussed shortly). In procedure multiply, m_get_myid gets the number of the process instance (from 0 to 9). The remainder of the code then divides the work among the processes, so that process 0 calculates c[0][i], c[11][i], . . ., c[91][i] for all i, process 2 calculates c[2][i], c[12][i], . . ., c[92][i], and so on.

13.2.2   Process Creation and Destruction

A programming language that contains explicit mechanisms for parallel processing must have a construct for creating new processes. We have seen this informally already in Figure 13-4, where calls to the library procedures m_set_procs and m_fork together created a fixed number of processes.

There are two basic ways that new processes can be created. One is to split the current process into two or more processes that continue to execute copies of the same program. In this case, one of the processes is usually distinguished as the **parent** while the others become the **children.** The processes can execute different code by a test of process identifiers or some other condition, but the basic program is the same for all processes. This method of process creation resembles the SIMD organization of Section 13.1 and is therefore called SPMD programming (for single program multiple data). Note, however, that SPMD programs may execute different segments of their common code and so do not necessarily operate synchronously. Thus there is a need for process synchronization.

In the second method of process creation, a segment of code (commonly a procedure) is explicitly associated with each new process. Thus different processes have different code, and we can call this method MPMD programming. A typical case of this is the so-called **fork-join** model, where a process creates several child processes, each with its own code (a fork), and then waits for the children to complete their execution (a join). Unfortunately, the name is confusing, because the Unix system call fork() (studied shortly) is really an SPMD process creator, not a fork-join creator. We will therefore refer to MPMD process creation rather than a fork-join creation. Note that Figure 13-4 is an example of MPMD programming (with m_kill_procs taking the place of the join).

An alternative view of process creation is to focus on the size of the code that can become a separate process. In some designs, individual statements can become processes and be executed in parallel. A second possibility is for procedures to be assigned to processes. This was the case in Figure 13-4, where the procedure multiply was assigned to processes via the call m_fork(multiply). A third possibility is for processes to represent whole programs only. Sometimes the different size of the code assignable to separate processes is referred to as the **granularity** of processes. The three choices of constructs for parallel execution that we have just listed could be described as follows:

1. statement-level parallelism: fine-grained

2. procedure-level parallelism: medium-grained

3. program-level parallelism: large-grained

Granularity can be an issue in program efficiency: depending on the kind of machine, many small-grained processes can incur significant overhead in their creation and management, thus executing more slowly than fewer larger processes. On the other hand, large-grained processes may have difficulty in exploiting all opportunities for parallelism within a program.

Regardless of the method of process creation, it is possible to distinguish between process creator (the parent process) and process created (the child process), and for every process creation mechanism, the following two questions must be answered:

1. Does the parent process suspend execution while its child processes are executing, or does it continue to execute alongside them?

2. What memory, if any, does a parent share with its children or the children share among themselves?

In Figure 13-4 the assumption was that the parent process suspends execution while the child processes compute. It was also necessary to indicate explicitly that the global variables a, b, and c are to be shared by all processes, using the keyword shared.

In addition to process creation, a parallel programming language needs a method for process termination. In the simplest case, a process will simply execute its code to completion and then cease to exist. But in more complex situations, a process may need to continue executing until a certain condition is met and then terminate. It may also be necessary to select a particular process to continue execution.

We will briefly study process creation and destruction mechanisms for each kind of granularity.

13.2.3 Statement-Level Parallelism

A typical construct for indicating that a number of statements can be executed in parallel is the **parbegin-parend** block:

```
parbegin
  S1;
  S2;
   . . .
  Sn;
parend;
```

In this statement the statements S1, . . ., Sn are executed in parallel. It is assumed that the main process is suspended during their execution, and that all the processes of the Si's share all variables not locally declared within an Si.

An extension of this mechanism is the parallel loop, or **doparallel** construct, which indicates the parallel execution of each iteration of a loop, as in

```
for i := 1 to n doparallel begin
  for j := 1 to n do begin
    c[i,j] := 0;
    for k := 1 to n do begin
      c[i,j] := c[i,j] + a[i,k]*b[k,j];
    end; (*for k*)
  end; (*for j*)
end; (*for i*)
```

This is similar to the $doacross compiler option of Figure 13-3.

13.2.4   Procedure-Level Parallelism

In this form of process creation/destruction, a procedure is associated with
a process, and the process executes the code of the procedure. Schematically, such a mechanism has the form

```
x := newprocess(p);
    . . .
    . . .
killprocess(x);
```

where p is a declared procedure and x is process designator—either a
numeric process number or a variable of type process. Figure 13-4 uses
library procedures that create processes essentially this way. An alternative
to this is to use declarations to associate procedures to processes:

```
var x: process(p);
```

Then the scope of x can be used as the region where x is active: x
begins execution when the scope of its declaration is entered, and x is
terminated on exit from its scope (if it has not already executed to completion). This is the method used by Ada in the declaration of tasks and
task types, which is discussed more fully in Section 13.5 (the **task** is
Ada's term for a process).

13.2.5   Program-Level Parallelism

In this method of process creation only whole programs can become
processes. Typically, this occurs in MPMD style, where a program creates
a new process by creating a complete copy of itself. The typical example
of this method is the fork call of the Unix operating system. A call to
fork causes a second child process to be created that is an exact copy
of the calling process, including all variables and environment data at
the moment of the fork. Processes can tell which is the child and which
is the parent by the returned value of the call to fork: a zero value
indicates that the process is the child, while a nonzero value indicates
the process is the parent (the value itself is the process number of the
child just created). By testing this value the parent and child processes
can be made to execute different code:

```
if (fork() == 0)
   {/*... child executes this part ...*/}
else
   {/*... parent executes this part ...*/}
```

After a call to fork, a process can be terminated by a call to exit.
Process synchronization can be achieved by calls to wait, which causes
a parent to suspend its execution until a child terminates.
Figure 13-5 gives sample C code for parallel matrix multiplication

```
#define SIZE 100
#define NUMPROCS 10
int a[SIZE][SIZE],b[SIZE][SIZE],c[SIZE][SIZE];

void main(void)
{int myid;
/* code to input a,b goes here */
  for (myid = 0; myid < NUMPROCS; ++myid)
    if (fork() == 0)
      {multiply(myid);
       exit(0);}
  for (myid = 0; myid < NUMPROCS; ++myid)
    wait(0);
/* code to output c goes here */
}
void multiply(int myid)
{int i,j,k;
  for (i = myid; i < SIZE; i+= NUMPROCS)
    for (j = 0; j < SIZE; ++j)
      {c[i][j] = 0;
       for (k = 0; k < SIZE; ++k)
         c[i][j] += a[i][k] * b[k][j];}
}
```

Figure 13-5   Sample C Code for the Fork Construct

using fork, exit, and wait. In this code, a fork is performed for each of the NUMPROCS child processes, and a wait is performed for each of the child processes as well. For simplicity, this code assumes that global variables are shared by all processes. (Warning! This is *not* true of processes in a standard Unix implementation. See Exercises 15 and 16 for a discussion.)

13.3   PSEUDOPARALLELISM AND COROUTINES

Coroutines were invented to model a pseudoparallel single-processor system and to enable the use of a high-level language to write pseudoparallel operating systems. Thus with coroutines there are no questions of mutual exclusion or synchronization. The primary questions are those of scheduling and transfer of control.

A **coroutine** is a program unit that can execute independently in pseudoparallel fashion. A coroutine is like a procedure in that it is activated from the main program, but unlike a procedure, a coroutine can **transfer** control at arbitrary points to other coroutines, and when control is transferred back to the coroutine, it **resumes** execution at the point from which it suspended its previous execution. Coroutines are symmetric in that no one of a group of coroutines is the parent, and none is the child. Coroutines execute sequentially, since there can only be one coroutine active at any particular moment, and a coroutine ceases to execute only when it transfers control to another coroutine.

This described behavior implies that each coroutine must have its own local runtime environment that remains in memory while the coroutine is inactive. This environment generally must include all activations of calls made from within the coroutine, plus a pointer to the location in the coroutine where execution is to resume, and a pointer to the environment of the creator of the coroutine.

As an example of the transfer of control among coroutines, consider the following pseudocode, with three coroutines:

```
coroutine A;
begin
  S₁;
  transfer B;
  S₂;
  transfer C;
  S₃;
end;

coroutine B;
begin
  S₄;
  transfer A;
  S₅;
end;

coroutine C;
begin
  S₆;
  transfer B;
  S₇;
end;
```

The following is the execution sequence for the code segments S_i in A, B, and C, assuming A begins executing first:

$$S_1 \quad S_4 \quad S_2 \quad S_6 \quad S_5$$
$$A \rightarrow B \rightarrow A \rightarrow C \rightarrow B$$

Notice that after control is transferred to B from C, B resumes execution with S_5 and then completes its code. Unless control is transferred again to A or C, their final code segments S_3 and S_7 will never be executed.

Questions that need to be answered about a coroutine mechanism are the following:

1. Is control immediately transferred to a coroutine when it is created?

2. Must both source and destination be named in a transfer of control between coroutines?

3. How is the creator of a coroutine distinguished from the coroutines it creates? In particular, is the main program viewed also as a coroutine?

4. When a coroutine executes to completion, does control automatically return to the creator of the coroutine, or does execution of the creator (and all its coroutines) terminate?

5. Is the management of the separate coroutine environments automatic, or does it require programmer intervention?

We shall study the coroutine mechanism of Modula-2 in some detail shortly, and in the process answer the foregoing questions for that language. Other languages that have significantly different coroutine facilities are Simula67 and BLISS, but we shall not study them here.

13.3.1   Coroutines in Modula-2

In Modula-2 coroutines are called processes, even though they do not execute truly in parallel. Process facilities in Modula-2 are part of the SYSTEM standard library. These facilities include

A NEWPROCESS procedure that creates a new coroutine and assigns it memory to be used to retain its local environment.

A TRANSFER procedure that transfers control from one process to another.

In Modula-2, NEWPROCESS creates a coroutine, but does not begin its execution. NEWPROCESS assigns a procedure and a **workspace** for the environment to a process variable. It is declared as

```
PROCEDURE NEWPROCESS (P: PROC; A: ADDRESS;
                      n: CARDINAL; VAR p1:
                                        PROCESS);
```

where P is any parameterless procedure (TYPE PROC = PROCEDURE), A is the starting address of the workspace, n is the size of the workspace, and p1 is the process variable to be created.

How workspace is allocated depends on the application and the particular implementation. A typical method is to allocate global ARRAY [1..m] OF WORD variables for each coroutine and use the ADR and SIZE functions to pass the starting address and size to NEWPROCESS. How big to make the array depends on the implementation and the coroutines involved.

The procedure TRANSFER has the following declaration:

```
PROCEDURE TRANSFER (VAR p1,p2: PROCESS);
```

Thus both the current process to be suspended and the next process to resume execution must be named in a transfer. The first call to TRANSFER in the main program has the effect of naming the main program as a coroutine equivalent to the coroutines it has created, but a call to NEWPROCESS is not required. Thus

```
VAR p,q,main: PROCESS;

BEGIN
  NEWPROCESS(...,p);
  NEWPROCESS(...,q);
  TRANSFER(main,p);
  ...
END...
```

creates coroutines p and q and names the main program process main. Transfers then can be made back to main from within p and q. Indeed, if any coroutine should execute to completion, the entire program will terminate, so if further processing is required, the procedure code for a coroutine should end in a transfer back to the main program. Automatic transfers are never performed.

13.3.2   A Bounded Buffer Coroutine Example in Modula-2

Since coroutines cannot execute in parallel, the examples given in the last section as test problems for parallel programming will seem rather trivial when written as coroutines. Indeed, matrix multiplication as a coroutine is no different from matrix multiplication as a procedure. The bounded buffer problem also seems trivial, since a producer coroutine would simply fill the buffer up before suspending and a consumer would empty it. However, there are situations where transfers may need to occur under conditions that change during execution, and situations like these are good ones for the use of coroutines. We will therefore modify the bounded buffer problem and then present a complete Modula-2 solution. Other variations are given in the exercises.

We assume that the producer wishes to read one line of input at a time, that is, any number of characters up to an end of line. The consumer, on the other hand, wishes to output characters with a specific fixed size to each line, say, twenty characters. A transfer from the producer to the consumer occurs when an end of line is encountered or if the buffer becomes full. A transfer from the consumer to the producer occurs when the number of characters in the buffer drops below the number needed to output a complete line.

Figure 13-6 shows a complete Modula-2 solution to this problem, where the buffer size is 50.

Another variation on the bounded buffer problem would be for the producer to test for input and transfer immediately if none exists, while the consumer would output one or more characters and then transfer back to the producer. See Exercise 14.

```
MODULE Coroutines;

FROM SYSTEM IMPORT ADDRESS, PROCESS, NEWPROCESS,
    TRANSFER, WORD, ADR, SIZE;

FROM InOut IMPORT Read, Write, WriteLn, EOL;

CONST WorkSpaceSize = 500;
      MaxBufferSize = 50;

VAR
      workspace1,workspace2:
                   ARRAY[1..WorkSpaceSize] OF WORD;
      main, producer, consumer: PROCESS;
      Buffer: ARRAY [1..MaxBufferSize] OF CHAR;
      BufferStart,BufferEnd,BufferSize: INTEGER;

PROCEDURE ReadChars;
VAR ch: CHAR;
BEGIN
  LOOP
    LOOP
      IF BufferSize = MaxBufferSize THEN
        WriteLn;
        EXIT;
      ELSE
        Read(ch);
        IF ch = EOL THEN
          EXIT
        ELSE
          INC(BufferSize);
          BufferEnd :=
                  BufferEnd MOD MaxBufferSize + 1;
          Buffer[BufferEnd] := ch;
        END;
      END;
    END;
    TRANSFER(producer,consumer);
  END;
END ReadChars;
```

Figure 13-6a   Modula-2 Code for a Bounded Buffer Problem

```
PROCEDURE WriteChars;
CONST OutputSize = 20;
VAR i: INTEGER;
BEGIN
  LOOP
    LOOP
      IF BufferSize < OutputSize THEN
        EXIT
      ELSE
        FOR i := 1 TO OutputSize DO
          Write(Buffer[BufferStart]);
          BufferStart :=
              BufferStart MOD MaxBufferSize + 1;
          DEC(BufferSize);
        END;
        WriteLn;
      END;
    END;
    TRANSFER(consumer,producer);
  END;
END WriteChars;

BEGIN (* main program *)

  NEWPROCESS(ReadChars,ADR(workspace1),
            SIZE(workspace1), producer);
  NEWPROCESS(WriteChars,ADR(workspace2),
            SIZE(workspace2), consumer);
  BufferSize := 0;
  BufferStart := 1;
  BufferEnd := 0;
  TRANSFER(main,producer);
END Coroutines.
```

Figure 13-6b   Modula-2 Code for a Bounded Buffer Problem—
Concluded

13.4   SEMAPHORES

A **semaphore** is a mechanism to provide mutual exclusion and synchronization in a shared-memory model. It was first developed by E. W. Dijkstra in the mid-1960s and included in the languages Algol68 and PL/I. A semaphore is a shared integer variable that may be accessed only via three operations: **InitSem, Signal,** and **Wait.** The *Wait* operation tests the semaphore for a positive value, decrementing it if it is positive and suspending the calling process if it is zero or negative. The *Signal* operation tests whether processes are waiting, causing one of them to continue if so and incrementing the semaphore if not. (These operations were originally called *P* and *V* by Dijkstra, but we will use the more descriptive names given earlier.)

Given a semaphore *S*, the *Signal* and *Wait* operations can be defined in terms of the following pseudocode:

Wait(S): if $S > 0$ then $S := S - 1$ else suspend calling process

Signal(S): if processes are waiting then wake up process

$$\text{else } S := S + 1$$

Unlike ordinary code, however, the system must ensure that each of these operations executes **atomically,** that is, by only one process at a time. (If two processes were to try to increment *S* at the same time, the actual final value of *S* would be unpredictable; see Exercise 61.)

Given a semaphore *S*, we can ensure mutual exclusion by defining a **critical region,** that is, a region of code that can be executed by only one process at a time. If *S* is initialized to 1, then the following code defines such a critical region:

> *Wait*(S);
> {critical region}
> *Signal*(S);

A typical critical region is code where shared data is read and/or updated. Sometimes semaphores are referred to as **locks,** since they lock out processes from critical regions.

Semaphores can also be used to synchronize processes. If, for example, process *p* must wait for process *q* to finish, then we can initialize a semaphore *S* to 0, call *Wait*(S) in *p* to suspend its execution, and call *Signal*(S) at the end of *q* to resume the execution of *p*.

An important question to be addressed when defining semaphores is the method used to choose a suspended process for continued execution when a call to *Signal* is made. Possibilities include making a random choice, using a first-in, first-out strategy, or using some sort of priority system. This choice has a major effect on the behavior of concurrent programs using semaphores.

As defined, a semaphore can be thought of as an abstract data type, with some added requirements. Indeed, semaphores can be defined using a Modula-2 definition module as follows (we also include means for process creation and destruction):

```
DEFINITION MODULE SemProcs;

TYPE Semaphore;

PROCEDURE CreateProcess(p:PROC;
                        workspacesize: CARDINAL);
```

```
PROCEDURE StartProcesses;

PROCEDURE Terminate;

PROCEDURE InitSem(VAR S: Semaphore; value:
    INTEGER);

PROCEDURE Wait(VAR S: Semaphore);

PROCEDURE Signal(VAR S: Semaphore);

END SemProcs.
```

The semantics of these procedures are as follows. Calls to CreateProcess associate processes with the code for the procedures passed as parameters. These processes do not begin to execute until StartProcesses is called. (We assume that all calls to CreateProcess occur before a single call to StartProcesses.) When StartProcesses is called, the caller is suspended until all created processes have called Terminate. If any created process finishes execution without calling Terminate, the whole program terminates. We also assume that the processes created by this module share all variables that are in the combined scope of their procedures.

Although Modula-2 does not actually provide this module, similar facilities are often provided. It is also possible to implement this module in pseudoparallel fashion using coroutines. See the exercises.

We will now solve the bounded buffer problem and the matrix multiplication problem in Modula-2 code using this module. After this, we will briefly discuss difficulties with semaphores, as well as implementation issues.

13.4.1   The Bounded Buffer Problem

The code in Figure 13-7 gives a Modula-2 solution for the bounded buffer problem using the SemProcs definition given earlier.

We note a number of things about this solution. It arbitrarily creates two producer and two consumer processes. We could in fact create as many of these as we wished. These processes all loop forever, so there are no calls to Terminate, and the main program is never resumed. Each producer process reads characters from the standard input, and each consumer process writes characters to the standard output.

This solution uses three semaphores. MutEx provides mutual exclusion to the global variables Buffer, BufferStart, and BufferEnd, which are shared since they are in the scope of all the process procedures. The semaphores NonEmpty and NonFull maintain the status of the number of stored items available. It would also be possible to keep a BufferSize shared variable and provide mutual exclusion to it instead of using NonEmpty and NonFull. The details are left to an exercise.

```
MODULE ProdCon;

FROM SemProcs IMPORT Semaphore, CreateProcess,
                     StartProcesses, InitSem,
                     Wait, Signal;
FROM InOut IMPORT Read, Write;

CONST WorkSpaceSize = 500;
      MaxBufferSize = 50;
VAR
    Buffer: ARRAY [1..MaxBufferSize] OF CHAR;
    BufferStart,BufferEnd: INTEGER;
    NonFull,NonEmpty,MutEx: Semaphore;

PROCEDURE Producer;
VAR ch: CHAR;
BEGIN
  LOOP
    Read(ch);
    Wait(NonFull);
    Wait(MutEx);
    BufferEnd := BufferEnd MOD MaxBufferSize + 1;
    Buffer[BufferEnd] := ch;
    Signal(MutEx);
    Signal(NonEmpty);
  END;
END Producer;

PROCEDURE Consumer;
VAR ch: CHAR;
BEGIN
  LOOP
    Wait(NonEmpty);
    Wait(MutEx);
    ch := Buffer[BufferStart];
    BufferStart :=
               BufferStart MOD MaxBufferSize + 1;
    Signal(MutEx);
    Signal(NonFull);
    Write(ch);
  END;
END Consumer;                            continues
```

Figure 13-7   The Bounded Buffer Problem Using Semaphores

```
BEGIN (* main program *)
  CreateProcess(Producer,WorkSpaceSize);
  CreateProcess(Producer,WorkSpaceSize);
  CreateProcess(Consumer,WorkSpaceSize);
  CreateProcess(Consumer,WorkSpaceSize);
  BufferStart := 1; BufferEnd := 0;
  InitSem(NonEmpty,0);
  InitSem(NonFull,MaxBufferSize);
  InitSem(MutEx,1);
  StartProcesses;
END ProdCon.
```

Figure 13-7   (continued)

13.4.2   Matrix Multiplication

A solution to parallel matrix multiplication is given by the Modula-2 code in Figure 13-8, again using the SemProcs module.

This code for matrix multiplication is different from that in Section 13.2 in that the processes do not operate on a set of fixed rows determined in advance, but select the next row to be computed by reading and incrementing the CurrentRow shared variable, which is protected by the MutEx semaphore. This represents a more dynamic (and possibly more efficient) solution. An arbitrary number of processes can be accommodated by this solution (we specified seventeen for no particular reason).

13.4.3   Difficulties with Semaphores

The basic difficulty with semaphores is that, even though the semaphores themselves are protected, there is no protection from their incorrect use or misuse by programmers. For example, if a programmer incorrectly writes

Signal(S);
...
Wait(S);

then the surrounded code is not a critical region and can be entered at will by any process. On the other hand, if a programmer writes

Wait(S);
...
Wait(S);

then it is likely that the process will block at the second wait, never to resume execution. It is also possible for the use of semaphores to cause **deadlock,** a situation where two or more processes are waiting for the other(s) to perform some operation (which will never occur because they are all waiting). A typical example is represented by the following code in two processes, with two semaphores S_1 and S_2 as on page 521:

```
MODULE MatrixMult;

FROM SemProcs IMPORT Semaphore, CreateProcess,
                     StartProcesses, Terminate,
                     InitSem, Wait, Signal;

CONST WorkSpaceSize = 500;
      MatrixSize = 100;
      NumProcs = 17;

TYPE Matrix = ARRAY [1..MatrixSize],
                    [1..MatrixSize] OF INTEGER;

VAR a,b,c: Matrix;
    CurrentRow, i: INTEGER;
    MutEx: Semaphore;

PROCEDURE Multiply;
VAR i,j,k: INTEGER;
BEGIN
  LOOP
    Wait(MutEx);
    i := CurrentRow;
    INC(CurrentRow);
    Signal(MutEx);
    IF i > MatrixSize THEN Terminate
    ELSE
      FOR j := 1 TO MatrixSize DO
        c[i,j] := 0;
        FOR k := 1 TO MatrixSize DO
          c[i,j] := c[i,j] + a[i,k]*b[k,j]
        END;
      END;
    END;
  END;
END Multiply;

BEGIN (* main program *)
  (* code to read in a and b goes here *)
  CurrentRow := 1;
  FOR i := 1 TO NumProcs DO
    CreateProcess(Multiply,WorkSpaceSize);
  END;
  InitSem(MutEx,1);
  StartProcesses;
  (* code to output c goes here *)
END MatrixMult.
```

Figure 13-8   Matrix Multiplication Using Semaphores

Process 1: $Wait(S_1)$;
   $Wait(S_2)$;
   ...
   $Signal(S_2)$;
   $Signal(S_1)$;
Process 2: $Wait(S_2)$;
   $Wait(S_1)$;
   ...
   $Signal(S_1)$;
   $Signal(S_2)$;

If Process 1 executes $Wait(S_1)$ at the same time that Process 2 executes $Wait(S_2)$, then each will block waiting for the other to issue a $Signal$. Deadlock has occurred.

To remove some of the insecurities in the use of semaphores, the monitor was invented (see Section 13.5).

13.4.4 Implementation of Semaphores

Generally, semaphores are implemented with some form of hardware support. Even on single-processor systems this is not an entirely trivial proposition, since an operating system may possibly interrupt a process between any two machine instructions. One common method for implementing semaphores on a single-processor system is the **TestAndSet** machine instruction, which is a single machine instruction that tests a memory location and simultaneously increments or decrements the location if the test succeeds. Assuming that such a $TestAndSet$ operation returns the value of its location parameter and decrements its location parameter if it is > 0, we can implement $Signal$ and $Wait$ with the following code schemas:

$Wait(S)$: while $TestAndSet(S) < = 0$ do {nothing};
$Signal(S) : S := S + 1$;

This implementation causes a blocked process to **busy-wait** or **spin** in a while-loop until S becomes positive again through a call to $Signal$ by another process. (Semaphores implemented this way are sometimes called **spin-locks.**) It also leaves unresolved the order in which waiting processes are reactivated: it may be random or in some order imposed by the operating system. In the worst case, a waiting process may be preempted by many incoming calls to $Wait$ from new processes and never get to execute despite a sufficient number of calls to $Signal$. Such a situation is called **starvation.** Starvation is prevented by the use of a scheduling system that is **fair,** that is, guarantees that every process will execute within a finite period of time.

Modern shared-memory systems usually provide facilities for semaphores that do not require busy-waiting. Semaphores are special memory locations that can be accessed by only one processor at a time, and a queue is provided for each semaphore to store the processes that are waiting for it.

13.5   MONITORS

A monitor is a language construct that attempts to encapsulate the mutual exclusion and synchronization mechanisms of semaphores. The idea is that a more structured construct will reduce programming errors and improve the readability and correctness of code. Originally designed by Per Brinch-Hansen and C. A. R. Hoare in the early 1970s, it has been used in the languages Concurrent Pascal and Mesa.

A **monitor** is an abstract data type mechanism with the added property of mutual exclusion. It encapsulates shared data and operations on this data. At most one process at a time can be "inside" the monitor, that is, using any of the monitor's operations. To keep track of processes waiting to use its operations, a monitor has an associated queue, which is operated in a first-in, first-out fashion.

A monitor therefore can be viewed as a language entity with the following schematic structure:

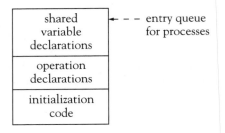

This organization of a monitor provides for mutual exclusion in accessing shared data, but it is not adequate by itself to synchronize processes that must wait for certain conditions before continuing to execute. For example, in the bounded buffer problem, a consumer process must wait if no items are in the buffer, and a producer must wait if the buffer is full.

For this reason a monitor must also provide **condition variables,** which are shared variables within the monitor resembling semaphores: each has an associated queue with processes waiting for the condition, and each has associated **suspend** and **continue** operations, which have the effect of enqueuing and dequeuing processes from the associated queue (as well as suspending and continuing execution). Sometimes (unfortunately) these operations are also called signal and wait as for semaphores, but their operation is different. If a condition queue is empty, a call to *continue* will have no effect, and a call to *suspend* will **always** suspend the current process.

One question that must be answered to describe the behavior of a monitor completely is what happens when a *continue* call is issued to a waiting process by a process in the monitor. There are now potentially two processes active in the monitor, a situation that is forbidden. Two possibilities exist: either the suspended process that has just been awakened by the *continue* call must wait further until the calling process has left the monitor or the process that issued the *continue* call must suspend until the awakened process has left the monitor.

We will illustrate the use of a monitor with a solution to the bounded buffer problem in Concurrent Pascal. Matrix multiplication and other questions are left to the exercises.

13.5.1   Concurrent Pascal

Concurrent Pascal has a monitor construct similar to that just described. Condition variables are called **queues**, and the operations on a queue are called d e l a y and c o n t i n u e. There are two simplifications to the operation of a queue variable, however:

1. A call to c o n t i n u e by a process in the monitor causes that process to exit the monitor immediately, so that the awakened process can resume execution immediately.

2. Each queue is limited to contain only one suspended process at a time. Thus, if two d e l a y calls are made in a row on the same queue variable, an error occurs.

We now write a solution for the bounded buffer problem in Concurrent Pascal. We encapsulate the buffer in the monitor declaration of Figure 13-9 on page 524.

In the code of Figure 13-9, a buffer is declared as a monitor type, with two callable procedures indicated by the keyword e n t r y. (Procedures without the keyword e n t r y are internal to the monitor.) Code that makes use of the buffer monitor of Figure 13-9 is given in Figure 13-10 on page 525.

In Figure 13-10, process types p r o d u c e r and c o n s u m e r are declared, and processes p and q are declared variables of type p r o d u c e r and c o n s u m e r. A variable b of monitor type b u f f e r is also declared. The i n i t b , p (b) , q (b) statement in the main program has the effect of allocating space for all the variables of b and executing the initialization part of b. It also begins execution of p and q. Note that p and q call the entry procedures of b using the dot notation b . i n s e r t and b . d e l e t e familiar to us from records and modules.

As another example of the use of monitors, we show in Figure 13-11 on page 526 how to imitate a semaphore using a monitor in Concurrent Pascal.

It is also possible to imitate the behavior of a monitor using semaphores (see Exercise 28). Thus monitors and semaphores are equivalent in terms of the kinds of parallelism they can express. But monitors provide a more structured mechanism for concurrency than semaphores, and they ensure mutual exclusion. Monitors cannot guarantee the absence of deadlock, however (see Exercise 29).

```
type buffer =
monitor
var store: array [1..MaxBufferSize] of char;
    BufferStart,BufferEnd,BufferSize: integer;
    nonfull,nonempty: queue;

procedure entry insert(ch: char);
begin
  if BufferSize = MaxBufferSize then
    delay(nonfull);
  BufferEnd := BufferEnd mod MaxBufferSize + 1;
  store[BufferEnd] := ch;
  BufferSize := BufferSize + 1;
  continue(nonempty);
end;

procedure entry delete(var ch: char);
begin
  if BufferSize = 0 then delay(nonempty);
  ch := store[BufferStart];
  BufferStart := BufferStart mod MaxBufferSize+1;

  BufferSize := BufferSize - 1;
  continue(nonfull);
end;

begin (* initialization *)
  BufferEnd := 0;
  BufferStart := 1;
  BufferSize := 0;
end;
```

Figure 13-9   A Bounded Buffer Monitor in Concurrent Pascal

13.6 MESSAGE PASSING

Message passing is a mechanism for process synchronization and communication using the distributed model of a parallel processor. It was introduced around 1970 by Brinch-Hansen and others.

In its most basic form, a message passing mechanism in a language consists of two operations, *send* and *receive,* which may be defined as follows:

```
PROCEDURE send(To: Process; M: Message);

PROCEDURE receive(From: Process; M: Message);
```

```
const MaxBufferSize = 50;
type buffer =
monitor
   . . .
   (as above)
   . . .
end;

type producer =
process (b: buffer);
var ch: char;
begin
  while true do begin
    read(ch);
    b.insert(ch);
  end;
end;

type consumer =
process (b:buffer);
var ch: char;
begin
  while true do begin
    b.delete(ch);
    write(ch);
  end;
end;

var p: producer;
    q: consumer;
    b: buffer;
begin
  init b, p(b), q(b);
end.
```

Figure 13-10   A Producer and Consumer in Concurrent Pascal

In this form, both the sending process and the receiving process must be named. This implies that every sender must know its receiver, and vice versa. In particular, the sending and receiving processes must have names within the scope of each other. A less restrictive form of *send* and *receive* removes the requirement of naming sender and receiver:

```
PROCEDURE send(M: Message);

PROCEDURE receive(M: Message);
```

```
type semaphore =
monitor (n : integer);
var i: integer;
    q: queue;

procedure entry wait;
begin
  if i > 0 then i := i - 1
  else delay(q);
end;

procedure entry signal;
begin
  continue(q);
  i := i + 1;
end;

begin
  i := n;
end;
```

Figure 13-11   A Semaphore as a Concurrent Pascal Monitor

In this case, a sent message will go to any process willing to receive it, and a message will be received from any sender. More commonly, a message passing mechanism will require *send* to name a receiver, but allow *receive* to receive from any process. This is asymmetrical, but it mimics the situation in a procedure call, where only the caller must know the name of the called procedure, while the called procedure has in general no knowledge of its caller.

Other questions that must be answered about the *send* and *receive* operations revolve around the synchronization of processes that wish to communicate via *send* and *receive*:

1. Must a sender wait for a receiver to be ready before a message can be sent, or can a sender continue to execute even if there is no available receiver? If so, are messages stored in a buffer for later receipt?

2. Must a receiver wait until a message is available to be sent, or can a receiver receive a null message and continue to execute?

In the case where both sender and receiver must wait until each other is ready, the message passing mechanism is sometimes called **rendezvous.** When messages are buffered, additional questions arise. For example, is there a size limit on the number of messages that can be buffered? And what process manages the buffer? If a separate process manages the buffer, then sometimes the buffer (or its managing process) is named in the *send* and *receive* calls, instead of the sending and receiving processes. In this case, we have a **mailbox** mechanism, where processes "drop off" and "retrieve" messages from named (or numbered) mailboxes. Sometimes mailboxes are assigned **owners** (for example, a process that creates a mailbox can become its owner). In this case the mailbox may be managed by its owner instead of a separate process. See Exercise 53 for an example of the use of mailboxes.

Essential to any message passing mechanism are **control facilities** to permit processes to test for the existence of messages, to accept messages only on certain conditions, and to select from among several possible messages. Often these control structures are influenced by or are based on Dijkstra's **guarded if** and **guarded do** commands (see Chapter 7).

In the following, we will discuss two language implementations of message passing: Hoare's communicating sequential processes and Ada.

13.6.1   Communicating Sequential Processes

This language mechanism, called **CSP** for short, is really a language schema rather than a language in itself. It was introduced by Hoare [1978] as a suitable mechanism for distributed processing in a microcomputer network.

CSP has the following notation for the *send* and *receive* operations. Let the sending process have name s e n d e r and the receiving process have name r e c e i v e r. Then s e n d e r sends a message m to r e c e i v e r by executing an **output command** of the form

    r e c e i v e r ! m

while r e c e i v e r receives message n from s e n d e r by executing an **input command** of the form

    s e n d e r ? n

The exclamation mark indicates "send" and the question mark indicates "receive." Note that both s e n d e r and r e c e i v e r must be named in this mechanism.

The semantics of the input and output commands are as follows. The processes must rendezvous at the two commands; that is, if r e c e i v e r ! m is executed first, s e n d e r must suspend execution until s e n d e r ? n is executed by r e c e i v e r, and vice versa. At the rendezvous the message transfer has the effect of the assignment n : = m. For this to occur, type compatibility rules for assignment must be satisfied. If either process has terminated when the other requests a message transfer, that process will also terminate with an exception.

CSP has two control constructs based on Dijkstra's guarded commands. The first is an alternative command like the guarded if and is written

    [G1 - > C1 ‖ G2 - > C2 ‖ . . . ‖ Gn - > Cn]

In this command, each G_i is a **guard** consisting of (optional) declarations, Boolean expressions, and an input command. The C_i's are command lists. A guard **fails** if any of its Boolean expressions or its input command fails. An input command fails if the process it is requesting input from has terminated. If all the guards of an alternative command fail, the process terminates. If any guards succeed, one is chosen arbitrarily, and its associated command list is executed. Note that an input command may cause the alternative command (and its process) to suspend execution until an associated output command is executed.

The second control structure for concurrency in CSP is the **repetitive command,** corresponding to Dijkstra's guarded do command:

```
*[G1 -> C1 || G2 -> C2 || ... || Gn -> Cn]
```

The syntax of this command is exactly that of the alternative command, but with an asterisk in front to represent repetition. The semantics are as with the alternative command, except that the command is executed repeatedly until all guards fail, at which point the repetitive command fails and control is transferred to the command following the repetitive command.

CSP uses a similar construct to create parallel processes. The command

```
[p :: command-list || q :: command-list]
```

defines processes p and q and begins executing their associated commands in parallel.

As an example of the use of CSP, we give in Figure 13-12 a solution to the bounded buffer problem with one consumer and one producer process. (Since CSP is not a language, but a language scheme, we ignore programming niceties such as constant declarations.)

Note in the code the need for synchronization between the consumer process and the buffer process using the call more(). This is necessary, since output statements cannot be part of a guard in CSP.

13.6.2 Concurrency in Ada

Ada has a concurrency mechanism that combines some of the features of message passing and monitors. A process in Ada is called a **task,** and a task is declared using specification and body declarations similar to the package mechanism (see Chapter 8):

```
task T is
    entry P...
    entry Q...        task specification
    ...
end;
```

```
[producer :: *[ ch: char -> read(ch); buffer!ch] ||

 consumer ::
   buffer!more();
     *[ch: char; buffer?ch ->
                write(ch); buffer!more()] ||

buffer ::
store: (1..50) char;
bufferend,bufferstart,buffersize: integer;
bufferend := 0;
bufferstart := 1;
buffersize := 0;
*[buffersize < 50; ch: char; producer?ch ->
      bufferend := bufferend mod 50 + 1;
      store(bufferend) := ch;
      buffersize := buffersize + 1 ||
 buffersize > 0; consumer?more() ->
      consumer!store(bufferstart);
      bufferstart := bufferstart mod 50 + 1;
      buffersize := buffersize -1]
]
```

Figure 13-12   A Bounded Buffer Solution in CSP

```
task body T is  ⎫
-- declarations  ⎪
begin            ⎬ task body
-- code          ⎪
end T;           ⎭
```

A task exports entry names to the outside world in a similar way to a monitor. These entries can be "called" by another task using the usual dot notation T.P, T.Q, and so on. Entries have code associated to them in the task body (again like monitors). Entries can also have parameters. Calling and accepting a task entry operate as a rendezvous in message passing, with the parameters acting as the message. Each entry has an associated queue to maintain processes that are waiting for an accept statement to be executed. This queue is managed in a first-in, first-out fashion.

A task begins to execute as soon as the scope of its declaration is entered. It executes the code of its body in sequential fashion. When the end of the scope of the task declaration is reached, the program waits for the task to terminate before continuing execution. A task terminates by reaching the end of its code or by executing a terminate statement (discussed shortly). It is also possible to declare task types and variables to get more than one task of a particular type or to get dynamic control over task execution. For example,

```
task type T is
    . . .
end;

task body T is
    . . .
begin
    . . .
end T;

P,Q: T;
```

declares a task type T and two tasks P and Q of type T.

A task determines when to accept an entry call and associates code to the entry using the **accept-statement,** which has the following form (in EBNF notation):

> accept <entry-name> [<formal-parameter-list>]
> [do <statements> end];

When an accept-statement is executed, the caller remains suspended while the code in the accept body is executed (the statements between the **do** and the **end**). An accept-statement does not need to name the caller of the entry. Thus Ada's message passing mechanism is asymmetric, like procedure calls (and unlike CSP). The entry/accept mechanism can be used entirely for synchronization, in which case a body of code for the entry is unnecessary.

A choice among entries in an Ada task can be made using the **select-statement,** which is the equivalent of the alternative command in CSP. The EBNF for a select statement is

> select
> [when <condition> = >] <select-alternative>
> {or [when <condition> = >] <select-alternative>}
> [else <statements>]
> end select;

where a select alternative is an accept-statement followed by a sequence of statements, or a delay-statement (not described here) followed by a sequence of statements, or a terminate statement.

The semantics of the select-statement are as follows. All the conditions in the select-statement are evaluated, and those that evaluate to true have their corresponding select-alternatives tagged as **open.** An open accept-statement is selected for execution if another task has executed an entry call for its entry. If several accepts are available, one is chosen arbitrarily. If no open accepts are available and there is an else part, the statement sequence of the else part is executed. If there is no else part, the task waits for an entry call for one of the open accepts. If there are no open accepts, then the else part is executed if it exists. If there is no else part, an exception condition is raised (see Chapter 7).

There is no Ada statement corresponding to the CSP repetitive command. However, repetition can easily be achieved by surrounding a select-statement with a loop-statement.

As an example of these mechanisms, Figure 13-13 shows a solution to the bounded buffer problem using a task to encapsulate the buffer.

Using the buffer task, producer and consumer task types can be

```
task Buffer is
   entry insert(ch: in CHARACTER);
   entry delete(ch: out CHARACTER);
end;

task body Buffer is
   MaxBufferSize: constant INTEGER := 50;
   Store: array (1..MaxBufferSize) of CHARACTER;
   BufferStart: INTEGER := 1;
   BufferEnd: INTEGER := 0;
   BufferSize: INTEGER := 0;
begin
   loop
     select
       when BufferSize < MaxBufferSize =>
         accept insert(ch: in CHARACTER) do
           BufferEnd :=
                   BufferEnd mod MaxBufferSize + 1;
           Store(BufferEnd) := ch;
         end;
         BufferSize := BufferSize + 1;
       or when BufferSize > 0 =>
         accept delete(ch: out CHARACTER) do
           ch := Store(BufferStart);
         end;
         BufferStart :=
                 BufferStart mod MaxBufferSize + 1;
         BufferSize := BufferSize - 1;
     end select;
   end loop;
end Buffer;
```

Figure 13-13   A Bounded Buffer as an Ada Task

declared as in Figure 13-14, and then any number of variables of these task types declared. Note that in Figure 13-14 neither a producer nor a consumer has any entries. These tasks execute in parallel without any synchronization or communication: all the synchronization is within the buffer task, which acts as a monitor surrounding the buffer operations.

The programs in Figures 13-13 and 13-14 have the property that they never terminate but continue to execute their loops indefinitely. Termination of tasks in Ada can occur in one of two ways. Either the task executes to completion and has not created any dependent tasks (i.e., child processes) that are still executing, or the task is waiting with an open **terminate** alternative in a select-statement, and its **master** (the block of its parent task in which it was created) has executed to completion. In that case, all the other tasks created by the same master must also have terminated or are waiting at a terminate alternative, in which case they all terminate simultaneously. This avoids the necessity of writing explicit synchronizing statements (such as *join* or *wait*) in a parent task that must wait for the completion of its children.

We offer two more examples of the use of tasks in Ada. The first example (Figure 13-15) is an implementation of a semaphore type as a task type, in which we have included a terminate alternative in the select-statement, indicating termination when its scope is exited. The second (Figure 13-16 on page 534) is an Ada package using tasks for parallel matrix multiplication.

```
task type Producer;
task body Producer is
  ch: CHARACTER;
begin
  loop
    TEXT_IO.GET(ch);
    Buffer.insert(ch);
  end loop;
end Producer;

task type Consumer;
task body Consumer is
  ch: CHARACTER;
begin
  loop
    Buffer.delete(ch);
    TEXT_IO.PUT(ch);
  end loop;
end Consumer;
```

Figure 13-14   Producer and Consumer Task Types in Ada

```
task type Semaphore is
  entry InitSem (n: in INTEGER);
  entry Wait;
  entry Signal;
end;
task body Semaphore is
  count : INTEGER;
begin
  accept InitSem (n: in INTEGER) do
    count := n;
  end;
  loop
    select
      when count > 0 =>
        accept Wait;
        count := count - 1 ;
      or
        accept Signal;
        count := count + 1;
      or
        terminate;
    end select;
  end loop;
end Semaphore;
```

Figure 13-15   A Semaphore Task Type in Ada

13.7   PARALLELISM IN NONPROCEDURAL LANGUAGES

Parallel processing using functional or logic programming languages is even more in its infancy than that of procedural languages. The study of nonprocedural parallel processing began in the early 1980s and is still very much in a stage of experimentation. Nevertheless, a number of good proposals have been made, including MultiLisp, QLisp, SpurLisp, Parlog, Aurora Prolog, and FGHC. In the following only the barest overview of this new field is provided. The reader is encouraged to consult the references at the end of the chapter for more information.

In earlier chapters we have mentioned that nonprocedural languages such as LISP and Prolog offer more opportunities for automatic parallelization by a translator than do procedural languages. The opportunities for parallel execution in such languages fall into two basic classes:

1. And-parallelism.   In this form of parallelism, a number of values can be computed in parallel by child processes, while the parent process

```
generic Size: INTEGER;
package IntMatrices is
  type IntMatrix is array (1..Size,1..Size) OF
                                       INTEGER;
  function ParMult(a,b: in IntMatrix) return
                                       IntMatrix;
end;
package body IntMatrices is
  function ParMult(a,b: in IntMatrix) return
                                       IntMatrix is

    c: IntMatrix;
    task type Mult is
      entry DoRow (i: in INTEGER);
    end;
    task body Mult is
      iloc: INTEGER;
    begin
      accept DoRow (i: in INTEGER) do
        iloc := i;
      end;
      for j in 1..Size loop
        c(iloc,j) := 0;
        for k in 1..Size loop
          c(iloc,j) :=
                      c(iloc,j) + a(iloc,k)*b(k,j);
        end loop;
      end loop;
    end Mult;
  begin -- ParMult
    declare m: array (1..Size) of Mult;
    begin
      for i in 1..Size loop
        m(i).DoRow(i);
      end loop;
    end;
    return c;
  end ParMult;
end IntMatrices;
```

Figure 13-16   Parallel Matrix Multiplication in an Ada Package

waits for the children to finish and return their values. This type of parallelism can be exploited in a functional language in the computation of parameters in a function call. For example, in LISP, if a process executes a function call

```
(f   a   b   c   d   e)
```

it can create six parallel processes to compute the values f, a, ..., e. It then suspends its own execution until all values are computed, and then calls the (function) value of f with the returned values of a through e as parameters. Similarly, in a let-binding such as

```
(let  ((a  e1)  (b  e2)  (c  e3))  (...))
```

the values of e1, e2, and e3 can be computed in parallel.

In Prolog a similar and-parallel opportunity exists in executing the clause

```
q  :-  p1,p2,...,pn.
```

The p1 through pn can be executed in parallel, and q succeeds if all the pi succeed.

Implicit in this description is that the computations done in parallel do not interfere. In a purely functional language, the evaluation of parameters and let-bindings causes no side effects, so noninterference is guaranteed. However, most functional languages are not pure, and side effects or state changes require that and-parallelism be synchronized. In Prolog, the instantiation of variables is a typical and necessary side effect that can affect the behavior of and-parallelism. For example, in the clause

```
process(N,Data)  :-
            M  is  N-1,
            Data  =  [X|Data1],
            process(M,Data1).
```

the three goals on the right-hand side cannot in general be executed in parallel, since each of the first two contribute instantiations to the last. Thus synchronization is also necessary here.

2. Or-parallelism. In this type of parallelism, execution of several alternatives can occur in parallel, with the first alternative to finish (or succeed) causing all other alternative processes to be ignored (and to terminate). In LISP, an example of such parallelism can occur in the evaluation of a cond expression:

```
(cond  (p1  e1)  (p2  e2)  ...  (pn  en))
```

In this situation it may be possible for the ei that correspond to true pi conditions to be evaluated in parallel, with the first value to be computed becoming the value of the cond expression. (It may also be possible to compute the pi themselves in parallel.) In this case it may also be necessary to synchronize the computations. But there is another problem as well: or-parallel computation makes the cond into a non-deterministic construct (similar to Dijkstra's guarded if), which may change the overall behavior of the program if the order of evaluation is significant. For example, an else-part in a cond should not be evaluated in parallel with the other cases.

In Prolog, or-parallelism is also possible in that a system may try to satisfy alternative clauses for a goal simultaneously. For example, if there are two or more clauses for the same predicate,

```
p(X) :- q(X).
p(X) :- r(X).
```

a system may try to satisfy q and r in parallel, with p succeeding with X instantiated according to the one that finishes first (or perhaps even saving other instantiations in a queue). In fact, this is consistent with the semantics of pure logic programming, since alternative goals are satisfied nondeterministically. However, in common Prolog implementations, the correct execution of a program may depend on the order in which alternatives are tried. In this case, a strict ordering may need to be applied. For example, in a common program for factorial in Prolog,

```
fact(X,Y) :- X = 0,!, Y = 1.
fact(X,Y) :- Z is X-1, fact(Z,Y1), Y is X * Y1.
```

the first clause needs to be tried before the second (or reaching the cut in the first should terminate the second).

The synchronization and order problems we have mentioned for both and-parallelism and or-parallelism are difficult to solve automatically by a translator. For this reason, language designers have experimented with the inclusion of a number of manual parallel constructs in nonprocedural languages. In some cases these are traditional constructs like semaphores or mailboxes, with modified semantics to provide better integration into the language. In other cases more language-specific means are used to indicate explicit parallelism.

There is, however, another argument for the inclusion of explicit parallelism in nonprocedural languages. In many situations one may wish to suppress the creation of small (i.e., fine-grained) processes when the computational overhead to create the process is greater than the advantage of computing the result in parallel. This may be the case, for example, in highly recursive processes, where as one approaches the base case, one may not want to create new processes, but switch to ordinary computation. Or one may wish to suppress parallel computation altogether when the values to be computed have a small computational overhead.

In the following we will briefly indicate a few of the explicit parallel mechanisms employed in some of the parallel LISPs and Prologs mentioned at the beginning of this section.

13.7.1 LISP Parallelism

The more natural form of parallelism for LISP seems to be and-parallelism, and this is the kind most often implemented. In the language Multilisp, which like Scheme (see Chapter 10) has static scoping and first-class function values, parallel evaluation of function calls is indicated by the syntax

```
(pcall f a b c ...)
```

which is equivalent to the evaluation of (f a b c ...) but with parallel evaluation of its subexpressions. Even more parallelism can be achieved in Multilisp by the use of a "future": if f has already been computed in the function call (f a b c), then the execution of f can proceed even before the values of a, b, and c have been computed, at least up to the point in f where those values are used. For example, in an f defined by

```
(define (f a b) (cond ((= a 0) ...)
                      ((> b 0) ...) ...))
```

the value of b is never used if a evaluates to 0, so the computation can proceed regardless of how long it takes to compute b.

A **future** is a construct that returns a pointer to the value of a not yet finished parallel computation. A future resembles (but is not identical to) delayed evaluation, as represented in the delay primitive of Scheme, studied in Section 10.5. In Multilisp a call

```
(pcall f (future a) (future b) ...)
```

allows the execution of f to proceed before the values of a and b have been computed. When the execution of f reaches a point where the value of a is needed, it suspends execution until that value is available. Futures have been included in other parallel LISPs besides Multilisp, for example, Qlisp and Spur Lisp.

Qlisp includes a parallel let-construct called **qlet** to indicate and-parallelism in let-bindings:

```
(qlet p (bindings) exp)
```

This construct will evaluate the bindings in parallel under the control of the predicate p. If p evaluates to nil, ordinary evaluation occurs. If p evaluates to a non-nil value, then the bindings will be computed in parallel. If p evaluates to the special keyword :eager, then futures will be constructed for the values to be bound.

Spur Lisp includes more traditional process creation, destruction, and synchronization facilities. The primitive make-process creates a new process via the call

```
(make-process E)
```

It immediately begins executing E and returns a reference to the new process. There are also primitives suspend-process, resume-process, and kill-process. Typically for LISP, processes are first-class values: they can be parameters to and returned values from procedures and processes. Synchronization is performed by mailboxes, which in Spur Lisp are just queues of messages (of arbitrary types), with primitives make-mailbox, send, and receive. See Exercise 53 for an example of the use of mailboxes in Spur Lisp.

13.7.2   Prolog Parallelism

The more natural form of parallelism for Prolog appears to be or-parallelism, although both forms have been implemented. In an or-parallel Prolog, one can manually indicate which goals are to be unified in parallel. For example, in Aurora Prolog, the ":− parallel" indicator is used to specify parallel execution, as in

```
:- parallel delete/3
delete([H|T],H,T).
delete([H|T],X,[H|R]) :- delete(T,X,R).
```

(The /3 indicates that the delete clauses involved have three parameters.) A call to delete([1,2,3],X,T) will now create three solutions in parallel, namely, (X=1,T=[2,3]), (X=2,T=[1,3]), and (X=3, T=[1,2]).

And-parallelism is more difficult in Prolog because of the interactions of instantiations mentioned earlier, and because there is no natural return point for backtracking. One version of and-parallelism uses **guarded Horn clauses** to eliminate backtracking. A guarded Horn clause is one of the form

```
h :- g1,...,gn | p1,...,pm.
```

The g1,...,gn are **guards,** which are executed first and which are prohibited from establishing instantiations not already provided. If the guards succeed, the system **commits** to this clause for h (no backtracking to other clauses occurs), and the p1, . . ., pm are executed in parallel. Such a system is FGHC (for flat guarded horn clauses). A sample FGHC program is the following, which generates lists of integers:

```
generate(N,X) :- N = 0 | X = [].
generate(N,X) :- N > 0 | X = [N|T], M is N-1,
                                generate(M,T).
```

The problem with FGHC is that it places severe constraints on variable instantiation, and hence on unification. This results in a significant reduction in the expressiveness of the language. An alternative is to provide **variable annotations** that specify the kind of instantiations allowed and when they may take place. A language that does this is **Parlog.** In Chapters 10 and 11 we discussed the difference between input variables and output variables to a procedure: input variables are like value parameters; that is, they have incoming values but no outgoing values. Output variables, on the other hand, have only outgoing values. In Prolog this means that input variables may be instantiated when initiating a goal, but may not be instantiated during the process of satisfying the goal, and similarly for output variables. Parlog distinguishes input variables from output variables in a so-called **mode declaration** by writing input variables with a "?" and output variables with a "^." If during the process of satisfying a goal, an uninstantiated input variable must be unified, the process suspends until such time as the variable becomes instantiated. A further tool for controlling instantiations is "directional" unification: the goal X = Y has a variant X <= Y, which only allows X to be instantiated, not Y.

As an example of and-parallelism in Parlog, consider the following quicksort program:

```
mode qsort(P?,S^).
qsort([],[]).
qsort([H|T],S) :- partition(H,T,L,R),
                   qsort(L,L1),
                   qsort(R,R1),
                   append(L1,[H|R1],S).
mode partition(P?,Q?,R^,S^).
partition(P,[A|X],[A|Y],Z) :- A < P:
                              partition(P,X,Y,Z).
partition(P,[A|X],Y,[A|Z]) :- A >= P:
                              partition(P,X,Y,Z).
partition(P,[],[],[]).
```

Parlog selects an alternative from among clauses by the usual unification process and also by using guards. It then commits to one alternative. In the foregoing qsort, the partition predicate has guards to prevent incorrect choices. After selecting a clause, Parlog creates a process for each goal on the right-hand side. Thus Parlog will execute the four goals on the right-hand side of qsort in parallel. Since L and R are input variables to the two right-hand calls to qsort, their associated processes will suspend as soon as these are needed for unification, until the first partition process produces them. The append process (whose definition is not shown) will also suspend until its first two arguments become available.

This concludes our brief survey of nonprocedural parallelism.

Exercises

1. Describe the differences between a process and a coroutine.

2. How many links does a fully linked distributed system with n processors need? How do you think this affects the design of fully linked systems with many processors?

3. Some parallel processors limit the number of processes that a user can create in a program to one less than the number of processors available. Why do you think this restriction is made? Is such a restriction more or less likely on an SIMD or MIMD system? Might there be a reason to create more processes than processors? Explain.

4. It is possible to compute the sum of n integers in fewer than n steps. Describe how you could use k processors to do this, where $k < n$. Would there be any advantage to having $k \geq n$?

5. The text mentioned that matrix multiplication can be done in n steps using n^2 processors. Can it be done in fewer steps using more processors?

6. Describe the difference between SPMD and MPMD programming. Would you characterize the program of Figure 13-3 as SPMD or MPMD? Why?

7. Why did the text prefer to use the term MPMD instead of fork-join?

8. Explain why both large-grained and small-grained parallelism can be less efficient than medium grained. Try to give programming examples to support your argument.

9. The C code of Figure 13-4 assumes that NUMPROCS is less than SIZE. What happens if NUMPROCS > SIZE? Rewrite the code of Figure 13-4 to take advantage of the extra processors if NUMPROCS > SIZE.

10. A typical process synchronization problem is that of resource allocation. For example, if a system has three printers, then at most three processes can be scheduled to print simultaneously. Write a program to allocate three printers to processes in
    (a) Modula-2 using the SemProcs module of Section 13.4.
    (b) Concurrent Pascal using monitors.
    (c) CSP using message passing.
    (d) Ada using tasks.

11. A standard problem (like the bounded buffer problem) that is used to test a concurrent language mechanism is the **readers-writers** problem. In this problem stored data is continuously accessed (read) and updated (written) by a number of processes. A solution to this problem must allow access to the data by any number of readers, but by only one writer

at a time. Write a solution to this problem using any of the four languages of the previous exercise.

12. Another standard concurrency problem is the **dining philosophers problem** of Dijkstra. In this problem five philosophers spend their time eating and thinking. When a philosopher is ready to eat, she sits at one of five places at a table heaped with spaghetti. Unfortunately, there are only five forks, one between every two plates, and a philosopher needs two forks to eat. A philosopher will attempt to pick up the two forks next to her, and if she succeeds, she will eat for a while, leave the table, and go back to thinking. For this problem,
    (a) Describe how deadlock and starvation can occur.
    (b) Why are there five philosophers and not four or three?
    (c) Write deadlock-free solutions to this problem in the four languages indicated in Exercise 10. (Hint: Allow only four philosophers to sit at the table.)
    (d) Is it possible to guarantee no starvation in your solution to (c)? Explain.

13. The bounded buffer coroutine program of Figure 13-6 doesn't work if $Outputsize > MaxBufferSize$. Rewrite the code of Figure 13-6 so that it will work for all buffer and output sizes.

14. Write a Modula-2 coroutine solution for a bounded buffer problem in which a producer tests for input (for example, with a KeyPressed function), reading it if it exists, writing it to the buffer (but not to the screen), and transferring immediately to a consumer that outputs one or more characters (to the screen) if they exist and then transfers back to the producer. Is it possible for your program to miss input?

15. The C code for matrix multiplication in Figure 13-5 doesn't work in a typical Unix implementation, since a fork does not cause memory to be shared. This problem can be solved using files, since forked processes continue to share files. Rewrite the code to compute the matrix c correctly using files. Comment on the efficiency of your solution.

16. Can Figure 13-5 be corrected by using pointer variables to share the addresses of the arrays among several processes? Explain why or why not.

17. Write an implementation for the Modula-2 SemProcs module of Section 13.4 using coroutines. Describe how this implementation makes the solution to the bounded buffer problem in Section 13.4 behave.

18. Use a protected counter variable to replace the semaphores NonEmpty and NonFull in the bounded buffer solution of Figure 13-7.

19. Compare the probable efficiency of the semaphore matrix multiplication solution of Figure 13-8 with the solution of Figure 13-4 as a function of the number of processors/processes. What are the issues involved?

20. Given two processes p and q, and a semaphore S initialized to 1, suppose p and q make the following calls:

p: wait(S);

...

wait(S);

q: wait(S);

...

signal(S);

Describe what will happen for all possible orders of these operations on S.

21. Describe how the busy-wait implementation of a semaphore can cause starvation.

22. Here is an alternative to the code for the semaphore operations:

$Wait(S)$: $S := S - 1$;
       if $S < 0$ then suspend the calling process;

$Signal(S)$: $S := S + 1$;
       if $S >= 0$ then wake up a waiting process;

Compare this to the code in Section 13.4. Is there any difference in behavior?

23. Does it make any sense to initialize a semaphore to a negative value?

24. Sometimes a language will provide only a **binary semaphore** mechanism, in which the stored value is Boolean instead of integer. Then the operations wait and signal become

$Wait(S)$: if S = true then S := false
       else delay the calling process

$Signal(S)$: if processes are waiting then wake up a process

       else S := true;

(To distinguish them from binary semaphores, the semaphores described in the text are sometimes called **counting semaphores.**) Show how a counting semaphore can be implemented using binary semaphores.

25. Wirth [1988] includes the following Processes module, which is similar but not identical to the SemProcs module described earlier (semantics of the operations are given in comments):

```
DEFINITION MODULE Processes;

TYPE SIGNAL;

PROCEDURE StartProcess(P: PROC; n: CARDINAL);
(* starts a process with code P and workspace
   size n *)
```

```
PROCEDURE SEND(VAR s: SIGNAL);
(* allows a waiting process to resume execution;
   has no effect if no process is waiting *)

PROCEDURE WAIT(VAR s: SIGNAL);
(* always waits until another process executes a
   SEND on s *)

PROCEDURE Awaited(s: SIGNAL): BOOLEAN;
(* returns TRUE if a process is waiting for s,
   otherwise FALSE *)

PROCEDURE Init (VAR s: SIGNAL);
(* initializes s *)

END Processes.
```

Describe the similarities and differences between this module and the SemProcs module of the text. Rewrite the bounded buffer solution of Figure 13-7 using this module. Does the code need significant revision?

26. A lock is sometimes distinguished from a semaphore by being nonblocking: only one process can acquire a lock at a time, but if a process fails to acquire a lock, it can continue execution. Suppose that a lock L has two operations, a Boolean function **lock-lock(L)** that returns true if the lock has been acquired, false otherwise and **unlock-lock(L)** that unlocks the lock (having no effect if the lock is already unlocked). Write an implementation for a lock in Modula-2, Concurrent Pascal, CSP, and Ada.

27. (a) Discuss the limitations of Concurrent Pascal monitors from the point of view of ease of implementation of the language.
    (b) Discuss the limitations of Concurrent Pascal monitors from the point of view of ease of programming in the language.

28. Show how semaphores can be used to imitate the behavior of a monitor in Concurrent Pascal.

29. If one monitor entry calls another monitor entry, deadlock may result. Construct an example to show how this can happen.

30. Describe why, in Figure 13-11, the implementation of the signal semaphore operation in Concurrent Pascal using the code

```
continue(q);
i := i + 1;
```

is correct.

31. In CSP an input command fails only if its source is terminated, and an output command fails only if its destination is terminated or its expression

(i.e., message) is undefined. However, the types of the messages in successful corresponding input and output commands must also match. What happens if there is a type mismatch, if not failure? (There is essentially only one other possibility.) Why do you think this choice was made?

32. In CSP and Ada the bounded buffer was represented by a process/task, while in Concurrent Pascal and Modula-2 (with semaphores) the buffer was a passive data structure with mutual exclusion. Is it characteristic of message-passing systems to represent shared data by processes? Discuss.

33. A shared-memory system can imitate the mailbox version of message passing by defining a mailbox utility using mutual exclusion. Write a Modula-2 library module to implement mailboxes (i.e., queues of data with *send* and *receive* primitives).

34. A shared memory system can imitate a distributed system by implementing message passing between processes using a generic mailbox with messages tagged by the sending (and possibly the receiving) process. Write a Modula-2 library module to imitate the message passing of CSP.

35. Describe in detail the reasons for the `more()` synchronization call in the bounded buffer solution in CSP of Figure 13-12. What would happen if it were left out?

36. Are there situations in which it would be preferable to have a fixed order for the selection of alternatives in CSP? Is nondeterminism preferable in other cases? Discuss.

37. Parameters are not allowed in Modula-2 coroutines, CSP processes, or Ada tasks, but parameters are allowed in Concurrent Pascal monitors. Why is this the case? What difficulties would you foresee in adding parameters to Modula-2 coroutines? To Ada tasks? Are there situations where this would be useful?

38. Write an implementation of a semaphore in CSP.

39. Write a solution to parallel matrix multiplication in CSP and Concurrent Pascal.

40. In CSP a guard in an alternative command has the following syntax:

    <guard> ::= <guard-list> | <guard-list> ; <input-command>
                | <input-command>
    <guard-list> ::= <guard-element> { ; <guard-element> }
    <guard-element> ::= <boolean-expression> | <declaration>

    Describe the order in which Boolean expressions, declarations, and input commands can occur. Is there a reason for this order?

41. In Ada the caller of an entry must suspend execution during the execution of the corresponding accept-statement. Why is this necessary?

42. In an Ada select alternative, an accept-statement can be followed by more statements. For example, in the bounded buffer solution in Ada, we wrote

```
accept insert(ch: in CHARACTER) do
  BufferEnd := BufferEnd mod MaxBufferSize + 1;
  Store[BufferEnd] := ch;
end;
BufferSize := BufferSize + 1;
```

Note that `BufferSize` is incremented outside the accept-statement. Is there a reason for this? Could the statement be put inside the accept? Could the statement `Store[BufferEnd] := ch` be moved out of the accept-statement? Why?

43. In Ada a task type can be used in the declaration of other types. In particular, pointer (or access) types to task types can be declared, as in

```
task type T is ... end;
type A is access T;
...
x: A;
```

The variable x now represents a pointer to a task. When does the associated task begin executing? When might it terminate?

44. In Ada a task is not automatically terminated when the end of the scope of its declaration is reached in its parent task. Instead, the parent suspends until the task completes. Why do you think this choice was made in the design of Ada?

45. In the Ada implementation of a semaphore, the `Signal` entry always incremented the semaphore value. Is this correct? Why?

46. An alternative for the Ada implementation of semaphores is to test for the existence of a waiting task using the attribute `COUNT`, which is predefined for entries. The code inside the loop would then read as follows:

```
select
  when count > 0 =>
    accept Wait;
    count := count - 1;
  or
    accept Signal;
    if Wait'COUNT > 0 then
      accept Wait;
    else
      count := count + 1;
    end if;                                          continues
```

continued

```
    or
        terminate;
end select;
```

Is this implementation preferable to the one given? Why or why not?

47. In Figure 13-16 (parallel matrix multiplication in Ada), we used a local variable i l o c inside task Mu l t to store the current row index of matrix multiplication for use outside the accept-statement. We could have avoided the need for i l o c by writing the whole body of Mu l t inside the accept-statement, as follows:

```
task body Mult is
begin
   accept DoRow ( i: in INTEGER ) do
      for j in 1..Size loop
         c(i,j) := 0;
         for k in 1..Size loop
            c(i,j) := c(i,j) + a(i,k)*b(k,j);
         end loop;
      end loop;
   end;
end Mult;
```

What is wrong with this solution?

48. This chapter ignored the question of formal semantics for concurrent programs. (Some studies are mentioned in the references.) Can you think of problems that may be encountered in applying axiomatic semantics to concurrent programs? What about denotational semantics?

49. The matrix multiplication solution in Ada of Figure 13-16 uses the size of the matrix to determine the number of tasks. Rewrite the solution to use a number of tasks specified as an input parameter to the Pa rMu l t function.

50. Or-parallelism in Prolog can be viewed as a parallel search of the tree of alternatives (see Chapter 11), where at each node a new process is created to search each child. Describe how these processes can coordinate their activities to allow backtracking.

51. Write an (Ada or Modula-2) procedure to perform a parallel search of an unordered binary tree.

52. In Spur Lisp a distinction is made between a process and a future. Is there a reason for this?

53. In Spur Lisp the following is an implementation of a semaphore using a mailbox (using the syntax of Scheme from Chapter 10):

```
(define (inc-sem s n)
    (cond ((= n 0) s)
          (T (send () s) (inc-sem s (- n 1))))))

(define (init-sem n)
    (let ((sem (make-mailbox)))
         (inc-sem sem n)))

(define (wait s)
    (receive s))

(define (signal s)
    (send () s))
```

Describe the operation of this implementation.

54. Discuss the claim made in the text that or-parallelism is more natural for Prolog, whereas and-parallelism is more natural for LISP.

55. Describe in detail the way or-parallel Prolog computes the three solutions to delete([1,2,3],X,T) in parallel. What time savings would you expect (in terms of numbers of steps)?

56. How much actual parallelism is performed in the and-parallel Prolog example of generate on page 538?

57. In and-parallel Prolog, if a guard encounters an uninstantiated variable, execution is suspended until the variable is instantiated (by another process). Why is this necessary? Are there any problems with this requirement?

58. Explain why backtracking is difficult in and-parallel Prolog.

59. In Figures 13-4 and 13-5 the main process creates new child processes to compute the matrix product and then suspends until all the child processes have finished. This is wasteful. Rewrite these programs so that the main process also performs some computations in parallel with its children.

60. Compare the notion of mailbox to that of a buffer.

61. Suppose two processes both attempt to increment a shared variable S that is unprotected by a mutual exclusion mechanism. Suppose the assignment

$$S := S + 1$$

consists within each process of three machine instructions:

> Load S into a *reg*
> Increment the *reg*
> Store the *reg* to S

What values might S have after both processes complete their increment operations? Show how each value can be obtained.

Notes and References

Recent surveys of parallel programming languages are the September 1989 issue of ACM *Computing Surveys* (Vol. 21, no. 3) and the July 1989 issue of *IEEE Software*. Some individual articles from these issues are also mentioned in the following. Another survey article is Andrews and Schneider [1983].

A survey of parallel architectures appears in Duncan [1990]. The diagrams in Section 13.1 are adapted from Karp [1987], where several methods of adding parallelism to FORTRAN are also studied. See also Karp and Babb [1988] for examples similar to those of Section 13.2. A method of providing language-independent parallelism through the use of a standard interface to a shared-memory area called "tuple space" is studied in Carriero and Gelernter [1989a,b; 1990]; the method itself is called **Linda.**

Coroutines and concurrency mechanisms in Modula-2 are studied in King [1988]. Simula67 also has coroutines, where they are represented by classes. For an introduction to Simula coroutines, see Birtwistle et al. [1973]. Grune [1977] contains an interesting example of a Simula coroutine.

Semaphores were introduced by Dijkstra [1968b]. See Silbershatz, Peterson, and Galvin [1990] for a study of their use in operating systems. Monitors were introduced by Hoare [1974] and made part of the Concurrent Pascal language designed by Brinch-Hansen [1975]. A successor to Concurrent Pascal is the **Edison** language, described in Brinch-Hansen [1981]. CSP was introduced by Hoare [1978]. CSP became the foundation for the programming language **Occam,** designed to run on a proprietary parallel system called the **transputer.** See Jones and Goldsmith [1988]. The Ada task mechanism is studied in Wegner and Smolka [1983] and Gehani [1984]. Some examples also appear in Horowitz [1984].

A description of Multilisp is in Halstead [1985]. QLisp is described in Goldman and Gabriel [1989] and SpurLisp in Zorn et al. [1989]. The examples of parallel LISP programs in Section 13.7 and the exercises are adapted primarily from these latter two references. Surveys of parallel Prologs include Ciancarini [1992], Shapiro [1989], and Tick [1991]. Parlog is studied in Conlon [1989], Gregory [1987], and Ringwood [1988]. FGHC is described in Ueda [1987], and Aurora Prolog in Lusk et al. [1988].

BIBLIOGRAPHY

Abelson, H. and G. J. Sussman with Julie Sussman. 1985. *Structure and Interpretation of Computer Programs.* Cambridge, Mass.: MIT Press.

Aho, A. V., J. E. Hopcroft, and J. D. Ullman. 1983. *Data Structures and Algorithms.* Reading, Mass.: Addison-Wesley.

Aho, A. V., B. W. Kernighan, and P. J. Weinberger. 1988. *The AWK Programming Language.* Reading, Mass.: Addison-Wesley.

Aho, A. V., R. Sethi, and J. D. Ullman. 1986. *Compilers: Principles, Techniques and Tools.* Reading, Mass.: Addison-Wesley.

Andrews, G. R. and F. B. Schneider. 1983. "Concepts and notations for concurrent programming." *Computing Surveys* **15(1),** 3–43.

ANSI-1815A. 1983. *Military Standard: Ada Programming Language.* Washington, D.C.: American National Standards Institute.

Ashley, R. 1980. *Structured COBOL: A Self-teaching Guide.* New York: John Wiley & Sons.

Baase, S. 1988. *Computer Algorithms: Introduction to Design and Analysis,* 2nd ed. Reading, Mass.: Addison-Wesley.

Backus, J. W. 1981. "The history of FORTRAN I, II, and III." In Wexelblat [1981], pp. 25–45.

Backus, J. W. 1978. "Can programming be liberated from the von Neumann style? A functional style and its algebra of programs." *Comm. ACM* **21(8),** 613–641.

Backus, J. W. et al. 1957. "The FORTRAN automatic coding system." *Proceedings of the Western Joint Computing Conference,* pp. 188–198. Reprinted in Rosen [1967], pp. 29–47.

Barnes, J. G. P. 1982. *Programming in Ada.* Reading, Mass.: Addison-Wesley.

Barnes, J. G. P. 1980. "An overview of Ada." *Software Practice and Experience* **10,** 851–887. Also reprinted in Horowitz [1987].

Barron, D. W. 1977. *An Introduction to the Study of Programming Languages.* Cambridge: Cambridge University Press.

Bird, R. and P. Wadler. 1988. *Introduction to Functional Programming.* Englewood Cliffs, N.J.: Prentice-Hall.

Birnes, W. J. (ed.). 1989. *High-Level Languages and Software Applications.* New York: McGraw-Hill.

Birtwistle, G. M., O.-J. Dahl, B. Myhrhaug, and K. Nygaard. 1973. *Simula Begin*. Philadelphia: Auerbach.

Bishop, J. 1986. *Data Abstraction in Programming Languages*. Reading, Mass.: Addison-Wesley.

Bjørner, D. and C. B. Jones. 1982. *Formal Specification and Software Development*. Englewood Cliffs, N.J.: Prentice-Hall.

Bobrow, D. G., L. G. DeMichiel, R. P. Gabriel, S. Keene, G. Kiczales, and D. A. Moon. 1988. "The Common Lisp object system specification." *ACM SIGPLAN Notices* **23(9)** (special issue).

Bobrow, D. G. and M. Stefik. 1983. *The LOOPS Manual*. Palo Alto, Calif.: Xerox Palo Alto Research Center.

Böhm, C. and G. Jacopini. 1966. "Flow diagrams, Turing machines and languages with only two formation rules." *Comm. ACM* **29(6),** 471–483.

Booch, G. 1986. *Software Engineering with Ada*, 2nd ed. Menlo Park, Calif.: Benjamin/Cummings.

Bridges, D. and F. Richman. 1987. *Varieties of Constructive Mathematics*, London Mathematical Society Lecture Note Series #97. Cambridge: Cambridge University Press.

Brinch-Hansen, P. 1981. "The design of Edison." *Software Practice and Experience* **11,** 363–396.

Brinch-Hansen, P. 1975. "The programming language Concurrent Pascal." *IEEE Transactions on Software Engineering* **SE-1(2),** 199–207.

Brodie, L. 1981. *Starting FORTH: An Introduction to the FORTH Language*. Englewood Cliffs, N.J.: Prentice-Hall.

Budd, T. 1987. *A Little Smalltalk*. Reading, Mass.: Addison-Wesley.

Burks, A. W., H. H. Goldstine, and J. von Neumann. 1947. "Preliminary discussion of the logical design of an electronic computing instrument." In *John von Neumann: Collected Works*, Vol. V, pp. 34–79. New York: Macmillan, 1973.

Burstall, R., D. MacQueen, and D. Sanella. 1980. *HOPE: An Experimental Applicative Language*. Report CSR-62-80, Computer Science Dept., Edinburgh University, Scotland.

Cardelli, L., J. Donahue, L. Glassman, M. Jordan, B. Kaslow, and G. Nelson. 1989a. "Modula-3 Report (revised)," DEC Systems Research Center Report No. 52. Digital Equipment Corp., Palo Alto, Calif.

Cardelli, L., J. Donahue, L. Glassman, M. Jordan, B. Kaslow, and G. Nelson. 1992. "Modula-3 Language Definition," *SIGPLAN Notices* **27(8),** 15–42.

Cardelli, L., J. Donahue, M. Jordan, B. Kaslow, and G. Nelson. 1989b.

"The Modula-3 type system." *Sixteenth Annual ACM Symposium on Principles of Programming Languages*, pp. 202–212.

Cardelli, L. and P. Wegner. 1985. "On understanding types, data abstraction, and polymorphism." *ACM Computing Surveys* **17(4)**, 471–522.

Carriero, N. and D. Gelernter. 1990. *How to Write Parallel Programs: A First Course.* Cambridge, Mass.: MIT Press.

Carriero, N. and D. Gelernter. 1989a. "How to write Parallel Programs: A guide to the perplexed." *ACM Computing Surveys* **21(3)**, 323–357.

Carriero, N. and D. Gelernter. 1989b. "Linda in context." *Comm. ACM* **32(4)**, 444–458.

Chomski, N. A. 1956. "Three models for the description of language." *I.R.E. Transactions on Information Theory* **IT-2(3)**, 113–124.

Church, A. 1941. *The Calculi of Lambda Conversion.* Princeton, N.J.: Princeton University Press.

Ciancarini, P. 1992. "Parallel programming with logic languages." *Computer Languages* **17(4)**, 213–239.

Clark, R. L. 1973. "A linguistic contribution to GOTO-less programming." *Datamation* **19(12)**, 62–63. Reprinted in *Comm. ACM* **27(4)**, April 1984.

Clark, K. L. and S. Å. Tärnlund (eds.) 1982. *Logic Programming.* New York: Academic Press.

Cleaveland, J. C. 1986. *An Introduction to Data Types.* Reading, Mass.: Addison-Wesley.

Clocksin, W. F. and C. S. Mellish. 1987. *Programming in Prolog*, 3rd ed. Berlin: Springer-Verlag.

Cohen, J. 1988. "A view of the origins and development of Prolog." *Comm. ACM* **31(1)**, 26–37.

Cohen, J. 1981. "Garbage collection of linked data structures." *Computing Surveys* **13(3)**, 341–367.

Colmerauer, A. 1982. "Prolog and infinite trees." In Clark and Tärnlund [1982].

Conlon, T. 1989. *Programming in PARLOG.* Reading, Mass.: Addison-Wesley.

Cooper, D. 1983. *Standard Pascal User Reference Manual.* New York: W. W. Norton.

Cox, B. 1986. *Object-Oriented Programming: An Evolutionary Approach.* Reading, Mass.: Addison-Wesley.

Cox, B. 1984. "Message/object programming: An evolutionary change in programming technology." *IEEE Software* **1(1)**, 50–69.

Curry, H. B. and R. Feys. 1958. *Combinatory Logic*, Vol. 1. Amsterdam: North-Holland.

Dahl, O.-J., E. W. Dijkstra, and C. A. R. Hoare. 1972. *Structured Programming*. New York: Academic Press.

Dahl, O.-J. and K. Nygaard. 1966. "SIMULA—An Algol-based simulation language." *Comm. ACM* **9(9)**, 671–678.

Dane, A. 1992. "Birth of an old machine." *Popular Mechanics*, March 1992, 99–100.

Davis, R. E. 1982. "Runnable specifications as a design tool." In Clark and Tärnlund [1982].

Demers, A. J., J. E. Donahue, and G. Skinner. 1978. "Data types as values: Polymorphism, type-checking, encapsulation." *Conference Record of the Fifth Annual ACM Symposium on Principles of Programming Languages*, pp. 23–30. New York: ACM Press.

Dijkstra, E. W. 1976. *A Discipline of Programming*. Englewood Cliffs, N.J.: Prentice-Hall.

Dijkstra, E. W. 1975. "Guarded commands, nondeterminacy, and the formal derivation of programs." *Comm. ACM* **18(8)**, 453–457.

Dijkstra, E. W. 1968a. "Goto statement considered harmful" (letter to the editor). *Comm. ACM* **11(3)**, 147–148.

Dijkstra, E. W. 1968b. "Co-operating sequential processes." In F. Genuys (ed.), *Programming Languages: NATO Advanced Study Institute*. New York: Academic Press.

Donahue, J. E. and A. J. Demers. 1985. "Data types are values." *ACM Transactions on Programming Languages and Systems* **7(3)**, 436–445.

Duncan, R. 1990. "A survey of parallel computer architectures." *IEEE Computer* **23(2)**, 5–16.

Ellis, M. A. and B. Stroustrup. 1990. *The Annotated C++ Reference Manual*. Reading, Mass.: Addison-Wesley.

Falkoff, A. D. and K. Iverson. 1981. "The evolution of APL." In Wexelblat [1981], pp. 661–674.

Friedman, D. P., C. T. Haynes, and E. Kohlbecker. 1985. "Programming with continuations." In P. Pepper (ed.), *Program Transformations and Programming Environments*. New York: Springer-Verlag.

Futatsugi, K., J. Goguen, J.-P. Jouannaud, and J. Meseguer. 1985. "Principles of OBJ2." In *Proceedings of the ACM Symposium on Principles of Programming Languages*, pp. 52–66.

Gabriel, R. P. 1985. *Performance and Evaluation of Lisp Systems*. Cambridge, Mass.: MIT Press.

Gabriel, R. P., J. L. White, and D. G. Bobrow. 1991. "CLOS: Integrating object-oriented and functional programming." *Comm. ACM* **34(9)**, 29–38.

Gehani, N. H. 1984. *Ada: Concurrent Programming.* Englewood Cliffs, N.J.: Prentice-Hall.

Gelernter, D. and S. Jagannathan. 1990. *Programming Linguistics.* Cambridge, Mass.: MIT Press.

Geschke, C., J. Morris, and E. Satterthwaite. 1977. "Early experience with Mesa." *Comm. ACM* **20(8)**, 540–553.

Ghezzi, C. and M. Jazayeri. 1987. *Programming Language Concepts.* New York: John Wiley & Sons.

Ginsberg, M. L. (ed.). 1987. *Readings in Nonmonotonic Reasoning.* Los Altos, Calif.: Morgan Kaufmann.

Gleaves, R. 1984. *Modula-2 for Pascal Programmers.* Berlin: Springer-Verlag.

Goguen, J., C. Kirchner, J. Meseguer, H. Kirchner, T. Winkler, and A. Megrelis. 1988. "An introduction to OBJ3." In S. Kaplan and J.-P. Jouannaud (eds.), *Conditional Term Rewriting Systems First International Workshop (Orsay).* Berlin: Springer-Verlag.

Goguen, J. A. and J. Meseguer. 1987. "Remarks on remarks on many-sorted equational logic." *ACM SIGPLAN Notices* **22(4)**, 41–48.

Goguen, J. A., J. W. Thatcher, and E. G. Wagner. 1978. "An initial algebra approach to the specification, correctness, and implementation of abstract data types." In Yeh [1978], pp. 80–149.

Goldberg, A. 1984. *Smalltalk-80: The Interactive Programming Environment.* Reading, Mass.: Addison-Wesley.

Goldberg, A. and D. Robson. 1989. *Smalltalk-80: The Language.* Reading, Mass.: Addison-Wesley.

Goldman, R. and R. P. Gabriel. 1989. "Qlisp: Parallel processing in Lisp." *IEEE Software,* July 1989, 51–59.

Goodenough, J. B. 1975. "Exception handling: Issues and a proposed notation." *Comm. ACM* **16(7)**, 683–696.

Gregory, S. 1987. *Parallel Logic Programming in PARLOG: The Language and Its Implementation.* Reading, Mass.: Addison-Wesley.

Gries, D. 1981. *The Science of Programming.* New York: Springer-Verlag.

Griswold, R. E. 1981. "A history of the SNOBOL programming languages." In Wexelblat [1981], pp. 601–645.

Griswold, R. E. and M. Griswold. 1983. *The Icon Programming Language.* Englewood Cliffs, N.J.: Prentice-Hall.

Griswold, R. E. and M. Griswold. 1973. *A SNOBOL4 Primer*. Englewood Cliffs, N.J.: Prentice-Hall.

Griswold, R. E., J. F. Poage, and I. P. Polonsky. 1971. *The SNOBOL4 Programming Language*, 2nd ed. Englewood Cliffs, N.J.: Prentice-Hall.

Grune, D. 1977. "A view of coroutines." *ACM SIGPLAN Notices*, July 1977, 75–81.

Guttag, J. V. 1977. "Abstract data types and the development of data structures." *Comm. ACM* **20(6)**, 396–404.

Halstead, R. H., Jr. 1985. "Multilisp: A language for concurrent symbolic computation." *ACM Transactions on Programming Languages and Systems* **7(4)**, 501–538.

Hanson, D. R. 1981. "Is block structure necessary?" *Software Practice and Experience* **11(8)**, 853–866.

Henderson, P. 1980. *Functional Programming: Application and Implementation*. Englewood Cliffs, N.J.: Prentice-Hall.

Hindley, J. R. 1969. "The principal type-scheme of an object in combinatory logic." *Trans. Amer. Math. Soc.* **146(12)**, 29–60.

Hoare, C. A. R. 1981. "The emperor's old clothes." *Comm. ACM* **24(2)**, 75–83.

Hoare, C. A. R. 1978. "Communicating sequential processes." *Comm. ACM* **21(8)**, 666–677.

Hoare, C. A. R. 1974. "Monitors: An operating system structuring concept." *Comm. ACM* **17(10)**, 549–557.

Hoare, C. A. R. 1973. "Hints on programming language design." *ACM SIGACT/SIGPLAN Symposium on Principles of Programming Languages*. Reprinted in Horowitz [1987], pp. 31–40.

Hoare, C. A. R. 1969. "An axiomatic basis for computer programming." *Comm. ACM* **12(10)**, 576–580, 583.

Hoare, C. A. R. and N. Wirth. 1966. "A contribution to the development of ALGOL." *Comm. ACM* **9(6)**, 413–431.

Hopcroft, J. E. and J. D. Ullman. 1979. *Introduction to Automata Theory, Languages, and Computation*. Reading, Mass.: Addison-Wesley.

Horn, A. 1951. "On sentences which are true of direct unions of algebras." *J. Symbolic Logic* **16**, 14–21.

Horowitz, E. 1987. *Programming Languages: A Grand Tour*, 3rd ed. Rockville, Md.: Computer Science Press.

Horowitz, E. 1984. *Fundamentals of Programming Languages*, 2nd ed. Rockville, Md.: Computer Science Press.

Horowitz, E. and S. Sahni. 1984. *Fundamentals of Data Structures in Pascal.* Rockville, Md.: Computer Science Press.

Hudak, P. 1989. "Conception, Evolution, and Application of Functional Programming Languages." ACM *Computing Surveys* **21(3)**, 359–411.

Ichbiah, J. D., J. G. P. Barnes, J. C. Heliard, B. Krieg-Brueckner, O. Roubine, and B. A. Wichmann. 1979. "Rationale for the design of the Ada programming language." ACM *SIGPLAN Notices* **14(6)**, Part B.

IEEE. 1985. ANSI/IEEE Std 754-1985: Standard for Binary Floating-Point Arithmetic. Reprinted in ACM *SIGPLAN Notices* **22(2)**, 9–25.

Iverson, K. 1962. *A Programming Language.* New York: John Wiley & Sons.

Johnson, S. C. 1975. "Yacc—Yet another compiler compiler," Computing Science Technical Report No. 32. AT&T Bell Laboratories, Murray Hill, N.J.

Jones, C. B. 1986. *Systematic Software Development Using VDM.* Englewood Cliffs, N.J.: Prentice-Hall.

Jones, G. and M. Goldsmith. 1988. *Programming in Occam 2.* Englewood Cliffs, N.J.: Prentice-Hall.

Kaehler, T. and D. Patterson. 1986. *A Taste of Smalltalk.* New York: W. W. Norton.

Kamin, S. 1983. "Final data types and their specification." ACM *Trans. on Programming Languages and Systems* **5(1)**, 97–123.

Karp, A. H. 1987. "Programming for parallelism." *IEEE Computer* **21(5)**, 43–57.

Karp, A. H. and R. G. Babb II. 1988. "A comparison of 12 parallel Fortran dialects." *IEEE Software,* September 1988, 52–67.

Kernighan, B. W. and D. M. Ritchie. 1988. *The C Programming Language* (ANSI Standard C), 2nd ed. Englewood Cliffs, N.J.: Prentice-Hall.

Kernighan, B. W. and D. M. Ritchie. 1978. *The C Programming Language.* Englewood Cliffs, N.J.: Prentice-Hall.

King, K. N. 1988. *Modula-2: A Complete Guide.* Lexington, Mass.: D. C. Heath.

Knuth, D. E. 1974. "Structured programming with GOTO statements." ACM *Computing Surveys* **6(4)**, 261–301.

Knuth, D. E. 1972. "Ancient Babylonian algorithms." *Comm.* ACM **15(7)**, 671–677.

Knuth, D. E. 1967. "The remaining trouble spots in Algol60." *Comm.* ACM **10(10)**, 611–617. Also reprinted in Horowitz [1987], pp. 61–68.

Knuth, D. E. and L. Trabb Pardo. 1977. "Early development of programming languages." In *Encyclopedia of Computer Science and Technology*, Vol. 7, pp. 419–493. New York: Marcel Dekker.

Koffman, E. B. and F. L. Friedman. 1990. *Problem Solving and Structured Programming in FORTRAN 77*, 4th ed. Reading, Mass.: Addison-Wesley.

Kowalski, R. A. 1988. "The early years of logic programming." *Comm.* ACM **31(1)**, 38–43.

Kowalski, R. A. 1979a. "Algorithm = Logic + Control." *Comm.* ACM **22(7)**, 424–436.

Kowalski, R. A. 1979b. *Logic for Problem Solving*. New York: Elsevier/North-Holland.

Kurtz, T. E. 1981. "BASIC." In Wexelblat [1981], pp. 515–537.

Lamprecht, G. 1983. *Introduction to Simula 67*. Braunschweig, Germany: Vieweg.

Lampson, B. W. 1983. "A Description of the Cedar Language," Technical Report CSL-83-15. Xerox Palo Alto Research Center, Palo Alto, Calif.

Lampson, B. W., J. J. Horning, R. L. London, J. G. Mitchell, and G. J. Popek. 1981. "Report on the programming language Euclid," Technical Report CSL-81-12. Xerox Palo Alto Research Center, Palo Alto, Calif.

Lampson, B. W. and D. Redell. 1980. "Experience with processes and monitors in Mesa." *Comm.* ACM **23(2)**, 105–117.

Landin, P. J. 1966. "The next 700 programming languages." *Comm.* ACM **9(3)**, 157–165.

Lesk, M. E. 1975. "Lex—A lexical analyzer generator," Computing Science Technical Report No. 39. AT&T Bell Laboratories, Murray Hill, N.J.

Lewis, H. and K. Papadimitriou. 1981. *Elements of the Theory of Computation*. Englewood Cliffs, N.J.: Prentice-Hall.

Lippman, S. B. 1989. *C++ Primer*. Reading, Mass.: Addison-Wesley.

Liskov, B., R. Atkinson, T. Bloom, E. Moss, J. C. Schaffert, R. Scheifler, and A. Snyder. 1984. *CLU Reference Manual*. New York: Springer-Verlag.

Liskov, B. and A. Snyder. 1979. "Exception Handling in CLU." *IEEE Transactions on Software Engineering* **SE-5(6)**, 546–558. Also reprinted in Horowitz [1987], pp. 254–266.

Liskov, B., A. Snyder, R. Atkinson, and C. Schaffert. 1977. "Abstraction mechanisms in CLU." *Comm.* ACM **20(8)**, 564–576. Also reprinted in Horowitz [1987], pp. 267–279.

Lloyd, J. W. 1984. *Foundations of Logic Programming*. New York: Springer-Verlag.

Louden, K. 1987. "Recursion versus non-recursion in Pascal: Recursion can be faster." ACM SIGPLAN Notices 22(2), 62–67.

Luckam, D. C. and W. Polak. 1980. "Ada exception handling: An axiomatic approach." ACM Transactions on Programming Languages and Systems 2(2), 225–233.

Lukaszewicz, W. 1990. Non-monotonic Reasoning: Formalization of Common-sense Reasoning. New York: Ellis Horwood.

Lusk, E. et al. 1988. "The Aurora or-parallel Prolog system." In Proceedings of the International Conference on Fifth Generation Computer Systems, ICOT, Tokyo, pp. 819–830.

MacLaren, D. M. 1977. "Exception handling in PL/I." ACM SIGPLAN Notices 12(3), 101–104.

Mandrioli, D. and C. Ghezzi. 1987. Theoretical Foundations of Computer Science. New York: John Wiley & Sons.

Marcotty, M. and H. Ledgard. 1986. Programming Language Landscape, 2nd ed. Chicago: SRA.

Martin-Löf, P. 1979. "Constructive mathematics and computer programming." In L. J. Cohen et al. (eds.), Logic, Methodology and the Philosophy of Science, Vol. VI. New York: North-Holland. 1982.

McCarthy, J. 1981. "History of LISP." In Wexelblat [1981], pp. 173–185.

Meyer, B. 1992. Eiffel: The Language. Englewood Cliffs, N.J.: Prentice-Hall.

Meyer, B. 1990. Introduction to the Theory of Programming Languages. Englewood Cliffs, N.J.: Prentice-Hall.

Meyer, B. 1988. Object-Oriented Software Construction. Englewood Cliffs, N.J.: Prentice-Hall.

Milner, R. 1978. "A theory of type polymorphism in programming." J. Computer and System Sciences 17(3), 348–375.

Milner, R. and M. Tofte. 1991. Commentary on Standard ML. Cambridge, Mass.: MIT Press.

Milner, R., M. Tofte, and R. Harper. 1990. The Definition of Standard ML. Cambridge, Mass.: MIT Press.

Mitchell, J. C. and R. Harper. 1988. "The essence of ML." Fifteenth ACM Symposium on Principles of Programming Languages, pp. 28–46. New York: ACM Press.

Mitchell, J. G., W. Maybury, and R. Sweet. 1979. "Mesa Language Manual, Version 5.0," Technical Report CSL-79-3. Xerox Palo Alto Research Center, Palo Alto, Calif.

Moon, D. A. 1986. "Object-oriented programming with Flavors." OOPSLA 1986, ACM SIGPLAN Notices 21(11), 1–8.

Moon, D. A. 1984. "Garbage collection in large Lisp systems." *Proceedings of the 1984 ACM Symposium on Lisp and Functional Programming*, pp. 235–246. New York: ACM Press.

Moore, D. L. 1977. *Ada, Countess of Lovelace: Byron's Legitimate Daughter.* London: Murray.

Morrison, P. and E. Morrison (eds.). 1961. *Charles Babbage and His Calculating Engines.* New York: Dover.

Naur, P. 1981. "The European side of the last phase of the development of Algol 60." In Wexelblat [1981], pp. 92–139.

Naur, P. (ed.). 1963a. "Revised report on the algorithmic language Algol 60." *Comm. ACM* **6(1)**, 1–17. Also reprinted in Horowitz [1987], pp. 44–60.

Naur, P. 1963b. "GOTO statements and good Algol style." *BIT* **3(3)**, 204–208.

Nelson, G. (ed.). 1991. *Systems Programming with Modula-3.* Englewood Cliffs, N.J.: Prentice-Hall.

Nelson, G. 1989. "A generalization of Dijkstra's calculus." *ACM Transactions on Programming Languages and Systems* **11(4)**, 517–561.

Nygaard, K. and O.-J. Dahl. 1981. "The development of the SIMULA languages." In Wexelblat [1981], pp. 439–480.

O'Donnell, M. J. 1985. *Equational Logic as a Programming Language.* Cambridge, Mass.: MIT Press.

Ollongren, A. 1974. *Definition of Programming Languages by Interpreting Automata.* New York: Academic Press.

OOPSLA. 1986ff. ACM Conference on Object-Oriented Programming Systems and Languages. Also published as various issues of *ACM SIGPLAN Notices*.

Pagan, F. G. 1981. *Semantics of Programming Languages: A Panoramic Primer.* Englewood Cliffs, N.J.: Prentice-Hall.

Parnas, D. L. 1985. "Software aspects of strategic defense systems." *Comm. ACM* **28(12)**, 1326–1335. Reprinted from the *American Scientist* **73(5)**, 432–440.

Perlis, A. J. 1981. "The American side of the development of Algol." In Wexelblat [1981], pp. 75–91.

Peyton Jones, S. L. 1987. *The Implementation of Functional Programming Languages.* Englewood Cliffs, N.J.: Prentice-Hall.

Popek, G. J., J. J. Horning, B. W. Lampson, J. G. Mitchell, and R. L. London. 1977. "Notes on the design of Euclid." *ACM SIGPLAN Notices* **12(3)**, 11–19.

Radin, G. 1981. "The early history and characteristics of PL/I." In Wexelblat [1981], pp. 551–575.

Randell, B. and L. J. Russell. 1964. *Algol 60 Implementation.* New York: Academic Press.

Rees, J. and W. Clinger (eds.). 1986. "The revised[3] report on the algorithmic language Scheme." *ACM SIGPLAN Notices* **21(12)**, 37–79.

Richards, M. and C. Whitby-Strevens. 1979. *BCPL—The Language and Its Compiler.* Cambridge: Cambridge University Press.

Ringwood, G. A. 1988. "Parlog86 and the dining logicians." *Comm.* ACM **31(1)**, 10–25.

Ripley, G. D. and F. C. Druseikis. 1978. "A statistical analysis of syntax errors." *Computer Languages* **3(4)**, 227–240.

Robinson, J. A. 1965. "A machine-oriented logic based on the resolution principle." *Journal of the ACM* **12(1)**, 23–41.

Rosen, S. 1972. "Programming systems and languages 1965–1975." *Comm.* ACM **15(7)**, 591–600.

Rosen, S. (ed.). 1967. *Programming Systems and Languages.* New York: McGraw-Hill.

Rosser, J. B. 1982. "Highlights of the history of the lambda calculus." *Proceedings of the ACM Symposium on Lisp and Functional Programming*, pp. 216–225. New York: ACM Press.

Rubin, F. 1987. ' "GOTO statement considered harmful' considered harmful" (letter to the editor). *Comm.* ACM **30(3)**, 195–196. Replies in the June, July, August, November, and December 1987 issues.

Sammet, J. E. 1981. "The early history of COBOL." In Wexelblat [1981], pp. 199–243.

Sammet, J. E. 1976. "Roster of programming languages for 1974– 75." *Comm.* ACM **19(12)**, 655–699.

Sammet, J. E. 1972. "Programming languages: History and future." *Comm.* ACM **15(7)**, 601–610.

Sammet, J. E. 1969. J. E. 1969. *Programming Languages: History and Fundamentals.* Englewood Cliffs, N.J.: Prentice-Hall.

Schmidt, D. A. 1986. *Denotational Semantics: A Methodology for Language Development.* Dubuque, Iowa: Wm. C. Brown.

Schneiderman, B. 1985. "The relationship between COBOL and computer science." *Annals of the History of Computing* **7(4)**, 348–352. Also reprinted in Horowitz [1987], pp. 417–421.

Schönfinkel, M. 1924. "Über die Bausteine der mathematischen Logik." *Mathematische Annalen* **92(3/4)**, 305–316.

Schwartz, J. T., R. B. K. Dewar, E. Dubinsky, and E. Schonberg. 1986. *Programming with Sets: An Introduction to SETL.* New York: Springer-Verlag.

Sebesta, R. W. 1989. *Concepts of Programming Languages.* Redwood City, Calif.: Benjamin/Cummings.

Sethi, R. 1989. *Programming Languages Concepts and Constructs.* Reading, Mass.: Addison-Wesley.

Shapiro, E. 1989. "The family of concurrent logic programming languages." *ACM Computing Surveys* **21(3)**, 412–510.

Shaw, C. J. 1963. "A specification of JOVIAL." *Comm. ACM* **6(12)**, 721–736.

Shaw, Mary (ed.). 1981. *Alphard Form and Content.* New York: Springer-Verlag.

Silbershatz, A., S. Peterson, and P. Galvin. 1990. *Operating System Concepts.* Reading, Mass.: Addison-Wesley.

Snyder, A. 1986. "Encapsulation and inheritance in object-oriented languages." *ACM SIGPLAN Notices* **21(11)**, 38–45.

Springer, G. and D. P. Friedman. 1989. *Scheme and the Art of Programming.* Cambridge, Mass.: The MIT Press.

Steele, G. 1984. *Common Lisp: The Language.* Burlington, Mass.: Digital Press.

Steele, G. 1982. "An overview of Common Lisp." *Proceedings of the ACM Symposium on Lisp and Functional Programming,* pp. 98–107. New York: ACM Press.

Steele, G. 1977. "Debunking the 'expensive procedure call' myth." *Proceedings of the National Conference of the ACM,* pp. 153–162. New York: ACM Press.

Stein, D. 1985. Ada: *A Life and Legacy.* Cambridge, Mass.: MIT Press.

Sterling, L. and E. Shapiro. 1986. *The Art of Prolog.* Cambridge, Mass.: MIT Press.

Stoy, J. E. 1977. *Denotational Semantics: The Scott-Strachey Approach to Programming Language Semantics.* Cambridge, Mass.: MIT Press.

Stroustrup, B. 1986. *The C++ Programming Language.* Reading, Mass.: Addison-Wesley.

Swinehart, D. C., P. T. Zellweger, R. J. Beach, and R. B. Hagmann. 1986. "A structural view of the Cedar programming environment." *ACM Transactions on Programming Languages and Systems* **8(4)**, 419–490.

Tanenbaum, A. S. 1976. "A tutorial on Algol68." *Computing Surveys* **8(2)**, 155–190. Also reprinted in Horowitz [1987], pp. 69–104.

Teitelman, W. 1984. "A Tour Through Cedar." *IEEE Software*, April 1984, 44–73.

Tesler, L. 1985. "Object Pascal report." *Structured Language World* **9(3)**, 10–14.

Tick, E. 1991. *Parallel Logic Programming*. Cambridge, Mass.: MIT Press.

Turbo. 1988. *Turbo Pascal 5.5 Object-Oriented Programming Guide*. Scotts Valley, Calif.: Borland International.

Turner, D. A. 1986. "An overview of Miranda." *ACM SIGPLAN Notices* **21(12)**, 158–166.

Turner, D. A. 1982. "Recursion equations as a programming language." In Darlington J. et al. (eds.), *Functional Programming and Its Applications*. Cambridge: Cambridge University Press.

Ueda, K. 1987. "Guarded Horn clauses." In E. Y. Shapiro (ed.), *Concurrent Prolog: Collected Papers*, pp. 140–156. Cambridge, Mass.: MIT Press.

Ungar, D. 1984. "Generation scavenging: A non-disruptive high performance storage reclamation algorithm." Proceedings of the ACM SIGSOFT/SIGPLAN Symposium on Practical Software Development Environments, *ACM SIGPLAN Notices* **19(5)**, 157–167.

Ungar, D. and R. Smith. 1987. "SELF: The power of simplicity." *OOPLSA* 1987.

Warren, D. H. D. 1980. "Logic programming and compiler writing." *Software Practice and Experience* **10(2)**, 97–125.

Wegner, P. 1976. "Programming languages—The first 25 years." *IEEE Transactions on Computers* **C-25(12)**, 1207–1225. Also reprinted in Horowitz [1987], pp. 4–22.

Wegner, P. 1972. "The Vienna definition language." *ACM Computing Surveys* **4(1)**, 5–63.

Wegner, P. and S. A. Smolka. 1983. "Processes, tasks, and monitors: A comparative study of concurrent programming primitives." *IEEE Transactions on Software Engineering* **SE-9(4)**, 446–462. Also reprinted in Horowitz [1987], pp. 360–376.

Wexelblat, R. L. 1984. "Nth generation languages." *Datamation*, September 1, 111–117.

Wexelblat, R. L. (ed.). 1981. *History of Programming Languages*. New York: Academic Press.

Whitehead, A. N. 1911. *An Introduction to Mathematics*. Oxford: Oxford University Press.

Wikström, Å. 1987. *Functional Programming Using Standard ML*. Englewood Cliffs, N.J.: Prentice-Hall.

Winograd, T. 1979. "Beyond programming languages." *Comm. ACM* **22(7)**, 391–401.

Wirth, N. 1988a. *Programming in Modula-2*, 4th ed. Berlin: Springer-Verlag.

Wirth, N. 1988b. "From Modula to Oberon." *Software Practice and Experience* **18(7)**, 661–670.

Wirth, N. 1988c. "The programming language Oberon." *Software Practice and Experience* **18(7)**, 671–690.

Wirth, N. 1976. *Algorithms + Data Structures = Programs*. Englewood Cliffs, N.J.: Prentice-Hall.

Wirth, N. 1974. "On the design of programming languages." *Proc. IFIP Congress* **74**, 386–393. Amsterdam: North-Holland. Reprinted in Horowitz [1987], pp. 23–30.

Wirth, N. and H. Weber. 1966a. "Euler: A generalization of Algol, and its formal definition," Part I. *Comm. ACM* **9(1)**, 13–23.

Wirth, N. and H. Weber. 1966b. "Euler: A generalization of Algol, and its formal definition," Part II. *Comm. ACM* **9(2)**, 89–99.

Wulf, W. A., R. L. London, and M. Shaw. 1976. "An introduction to the construction and verification of Alphard programs." *IEEE Transactions on Software Engineering* **2(4)**, 253–265.

Wulf, W. A., D. B. Russell, and A. N. Habermann. 1971. "BLISS: A language for systems programming." *Comm. ACM* **14(12)**, 780–790.

Yeh, R. T. (ed.). 1978. *Current Trends in Programming Methodology*, Vol. IV, *Data Structuring*. Englewood Cliffs, N.J.: Prentice-Hall.

Zorn, B., K. Ho, J. Larus, L. Semenzato, and P. Hilfinger. 1989. "Multi-processing extension in Spur Lisp." *IEEE Software*, July, 41–49.

Zuse, K. 1972. "Der Plankalkül." *Berichte der Gesellschaft für Mathematik und Datenverarbeitung*, No. 63, Part 3, Bonn.

ANSWERS TO SELECTED EXERCISES

Chapter 1

2.

```
function numdigits(x: integer): integer;
begin
  if x < 10 then
    numdigits := 1
  else
    numdigits := numdigits(x div 10) + 1 ;
end;
```

5. The problem is in defining the g c d of u and v when v is negative. The procedural version tests for negative v the first time through its loop and returns u if v < 0. This is incorrect, but it does protect against a possible infinite loop. The functional version tests only for v = 0. The behavior of the recursion depends on the behavior of u MOD v when v is negative, and this behavior is unspecified (although in this case it is usually just a question of the sign of the result). Choosing which is correct depends on your point of view: Is it better to have a well-defined but wrong result or an undefined result?

9. The Pascal standard defines overflow as an error that may not be detected during execution. Different translators reflect different approaches to this problem. Some translators cause a runtime error to occur, halting execution. Others let overflow occur undetected, which allows program execution to continue but with incorrect results (for example, the factorial function may return a negative result). In general, overflow is difficult to test for in a high-level language *before* it occurs. In Pascal, the predefined constant m a x i n t can be used to establish a test, as follows:

```
function fact (n: integer): integer;
var temp: integer;
begin
  if n < 2 then fact := 1
  else begin
    temp := fact(n−1);
```
continues

continued

```
        if maxint div n < temp then fact := -1
        else fact := temp * n;
    end;
end;
```

This code uses -1 as a return value indicating that overflow has occurred, but program execution is not halted. (It may appear that the test `maxint div n < temp` is not a precise one, since (`maxint div n`) `* n` is less than `maxint` if n does not divide `maxint`. Properties of integers guarantee, however, that we cannot have both `maxint div n < temp` and `temp * n <= maxint`.)

11. Some readers might assume that this question asks whether a language contains an actual predefined string type. With this interpretation, only the language standards for Ada and Scheme provide a predefined string type, and in Ada, it is given by the following declarations:

```
subtype POSITIVE is INTEGER range
    1..INTEGER'LAST;
type STRING is array(POSITIVE range <>) of
    CHARACTER;
```

That is, strings in Ada are equivalent to an unconstrained array of characters. However, the question really asks only if string types are available in a language, not if they are predefined, and all the listed languages do have available string types.

In Standard Pascal all types `packed array [1..n] of char` are considered string types, while in Modula-2 string types are all types `ARRAY [0..n] OF CHAR`. In FORTRAN77 string types are declared as `CHARACTER*N`, where N is a positive integer constant, as in

```
CHARACTER*80 LINE
```

which declares the variable `LINE` to be a string of 80 characters.

In C strings are pointers to characters, as in

```
char * line
```

which makes them closer to the Ada strings in that they do not have a predefined length, as in Pascal, Modula-2, and FORTRAN.

The predefined operations that come with the string data types are as follows, by language.

Pascal: None, except for the usual operations of assignment and comparison. Lexicographic ordering is used for the comparison operators "<," "<=," ">," ">=." String constants, or literals, are given using single quotes, as in `'This is a string'`.

Modula-2: None, except for the usual operations, similar to those of Pascal. (Some relaxation of the "same-length" requirement of Pascal are provided.) String constants can be given using either single or double quotes, as in `'This is a string'` or `"This is a string"`.

Ada: In addition to assignment and comparison, as in Pascal, Ada provides concatenation with notation "&", as in

```
"This is a" & "string"
```

C: C provides no operations that give the desired behavior for strings (note that usual comparison "= =" of two strings tests for identity of pointers, not equality of strings). However, C provides a standard library of string functions, including `strcat` (concatenation), `strcmp` (comparison), `strlen` (length, or number of characters), and other memory-oriented utilities (C does not automatically allocate memory for strings as do Pascal, Modula-2, and Ada).

FORTRAN: The FORTRAN77 standard provides for the usual comparisons and assignment (with truncation and blank padding for different-sized strings) and also for concatenation and substring operations. Concatenation is given by two forward slashes "//." Substrings are indicated by parenthesized constants separated by a colon, as in `LINE(10:20)`. The predefined `LEN` function returns the length of a string.

Scheme: Scheme has a range of predefined string functions, including `string-length`, `string-append` (concatenation), `string-substring`, `string=?` (string comparison for equality), and `string<?` (string less than comparison).

15. The errors are as follows:

Line 1: The question mark in `ModSample?` is a lexical error; the legal characters in Modula-2 programs do not include the "?" character.

Line 5: The declaration of the returned type as `BOOLEAN` cannot be determined by the compiler to be an error, since the function does not always supply a returned value in the subsequent code. Thus this must be classified as a logic error.

Line 7: This line contains two errors. The first is the test `v > 0`. This differs from the `v = 0` test of the original and can result in an infinite recursive loop. This is a logical error. The second error is the missing `RETURN` statement after the `THEN`. This is not a syntax error, since empty statements are legal. It is also not a static semantic error, since the compiler cannot in general tell whether every path through a function has a return-statement. However, when the function is executed a return value is necessary, and so this is a dynamic semantic error.

Line 9: There is a missing semicolon after the identifier g c d. This is a syntax error.

Line 10: There is a missing declaration of x and y here, a static semantic error.

Last Line: An identifier is missing after the END and before the period. Syntax error. (A static semantic error would result if the identifier were there but did not agree with the original name of the module.)

18. The question really is one of whether a goto-statement exists and can be used to override the structuring of the if-statement, as in

```
program testgoto;
label 10;
begin
  goto 10;
  if 2 < 1 then
    10: writeln('ack!')
  else writeln('ok.');
end.
```

In Modula-2 no goto is available, so this is impossible. In Standard Pascal and Ada, it is also impossible, since a goto cannot jump inside a structured construct. In C and FORTRAN (permissive languages both), this is permitted.

20. (a) The value of a variable is dynamic since it can change during execution.
   (b) The data type of a variable cannot change during execution; it is fixed during translation by its declaration.
   (c) The name of a variable is also fixed by its declaration and cannot change during execution, except in the following ways:
      (1) A var parameter can become an alias for another variable during execution, as for example in

```
var y: integer;

procedure p(var x: integer);
begin
  . . .
end;

begin
  . . .
  p(y);
  . . .
end.
```

During the call p(y), the name x becomes temporarily another name for y.

(2) A variable pointed to by another variable can be accessed using different names, as in

```
var p,q: ^integer;

begin
  new(p);
  p^ := 2;
  q := p;
  q^ := 1;
end.
```

After the assignment q := p, the same (dynamically allocated) variable can be accessed using the names p^ and q^. (An alternative view would say that the variable *accessed* using the *operations* p^ and q^ has in fact no name of its own, so we cannot say that its name has changed.)

Chapter 2

1. (a) The cistern is assumed to be a rectangular solid with volume $=$ length $\times$ width $\times$ height. Let $L =$ length and $W =$ width. Since height $=$ length, the volume V is given by $V = L^2W$. The cross-sectional area $A = LW$, and $A + V = 120$. Substituting gives

$$LW + L^2W = 120$$

and solving for W gives

$$W = \frac{120}{(L + L^2)}$$

or

$$W = \frac{120}{L(1 + L)}$$

The algorithm performs the division of 120 by $1 + L$ first, and then the division by L, so the precise steps of the algorithm are specified by a left-to-right evaluation of the formula

$$W = 120/(1 + L)/L$$

(b) A Pascal function that returns the width given the length and area plus volume is as follows:

```
function Bab (length, sum: real) : real;
var temp: real;
begin
  temp := sum / (length + 1.0);
  Bab := temp / length;
end;
```

Whether this is really easier to understand than the Babylonian description depends on the reader. Those knowledgeable about computers and Pascal may find the procedure easier to read, while others may find the Babylonian version preferable. Note that the steps described are the same, however.

5. JOVIAL—Jules' Own Version of the International Algorithmic Language: Developed by Jules Schwartz at SDC Corporation, based on Algol58, a predecessor to Algol60. Used by the U.S. Air Force as its standard language for many years, only to be replaced by Ada. See Shaw [1963].

Euler: A language designed by Niklaus Wirth in the 1960s in which he developed some of his ideas on simplicity in language design; a predecessor of both Algol-W and Pascal. See Wirth and Weber [1966a,b].

BCPL: A systems programming language developed in England in the late 1960s, it was a strong influence on the C language. See Richards and Whitby-Stevens [1979].

Alphard: A language developed at Carnegie Mellon University in the late 1970s incorporating ideas on abstract data types similar to Euclid and CLU. See Wulf, London, and Shaw [1976] and Shaw [1981].

HOPE: An experimental functional language developed at Edinburgh University in the late 1970s. Many of its ideas were incorporated into ML. See Burstall, MacQueen, and Sanella [1980].

7. Here are a few ways of determining dates of origin:

1. Date language development began
2. Date of first publication about the language
3. Date first translator became available outside the development team
4. Date of publication of first language definition
5. Date of first use of the language outside the development team
6. Date of first commercially available translator

The criterion for date of origin is important for the existence question posed in Exercise 6 in at least two ways. First, a language can exist only after its date of origin, so the criterion for date of origin must be satisfied by the criterion for existence. Second, the disappearance of a language can be judged by the same conditions. For example, if there are no more commercially available translators, or the language is no longer in use outside the development team, the language can be said to no longer exist.

13. **(a)** The difference is that the mathematical definition is not an algorithm, in the sense that it provides no direct construction of the gcd, but is just a property that the gcd must satisfy, which may require the checking of a possibly infinite set of numbers.

    (b) Since the given definition is not an algorithm, it cannot be used directly to program a computation of the gcd. Certain additional properties of numbers can, however, be used to reduce the computation involved in the definition to a manageable size. For example, if we use the property that any divisor of both u and v must be between 1 and the min of u and v, we can check the given property for every number between 1 and $\min(u,v)$, until success is reached, as for example, in the following Pascal procedure:

```
function gcd(u,v: integer) : integer;
var min, i, j : integer;
    done, found: boolean;
begin
  if u <= v then min := u else min := v;
  i := min; found := false;
  while not found and (i > 1) do
    if (u mod i = 0) and (v mod i = 0) then
    begin
      j := min; done := false;
      while (j > 1) and not done do begin
        if (u mod j = 0) and (v mod j = 0) then
          if i mod j <> 0 then done := true
          else j := j-1
        else j := j-1
      end;
      if j = 1 then found := true
      else i := i - 1;
    end else i := i - 1;
  gcd := i;
end;
```

Of course, this algorithm searches for the gcd in a particular order, namely, from min (u,v) down to 1 (indeed, by using the further property that the gcd is in fact the largest number that divides both u and v, we could eliminate the inner while-loop altogether). Thus it cannot be said to "implement" the definition, even though it is closer to the spirit of the definition than Euclid's algorithm (it is also enormously less efficient than Euclid's algorithm).

(c) Mathematics is not always concerned with the **construction** of things, but sometimes only with their existence. And even when a possible construction is given (as with constructions of the real numbers), the processes used take potentially infinitely many steps (as with limits). Programs can express only those aspects of mathematics that are concerned with finite constructive quantities and properties. (See the mention of **constructive mathematics** in the text.)

Chapter 3

3. The principle of uniformity says that things that are similar should look similar. Using the carat in the expression f ∧ makes the file variable f look like a pointer and f ∧ its dereferenced value. So the question is: Are pointers and files sufficiently similar? Indeed, there are similarities: the declaration "file of *t*" is somewhat similar to "pointer to *t*", and in both cases the type of the dereferenced value is *t*. Also a pointer p cannot be used until it is initialized with a call new(p), and similarly a file f cannot be used unless a call reset(f) or rewrite(f) precedes its use. The variable f ∧ can also be treated just like a regular variable, as can p∧. There are differences, however. A file has many more attributes than a pointer: it has a name in the execution environment; it has a status (closed, open, read only, etc.); it has a current position in the file, from which the next piece of data is moved into the file buffer; it has a location on the storage medium (disk, tape, RAM, etc.). There are also restrictions on file variables in Pascal that do not apply to pointer variables, for example, that file variables cannot be value parameters to procedures or that file variables cannot be components of other files (contrary to the usual use of pointers).

   The question here is whether the differences overwhelm the similarities, and to a certain extent this is a matter of opinion. In the author's opinion, files are sufficiently unlike pointers that the reuse of the "∧" notation for file buffers can be called a nonuniformity.

4. The author has not seen any statements by Niklaus Wirth on the rationale for Pascal's lack of the LOOP/EXIT construct, or why he decided to include it in Modula-2. However, there are at least two possible reasons for its absence in Pascal. The first is simplicity: with three repetition constructs already (while-loops, for-loops, and repeat-loops), Pascal was already "loop heavy," and it could be hard to justify adding yet another loop construct to a language that is designed with the explicit goal of simplicity. The second possible reason for excluding the LOOP/EXIT is that Pascal has only *single-entry, single-exit* constructs; that is, control must always pass through all intermediate statements in a control statement before exiting. For example, in an if-statement, all statements on each side of the if must be executed, depending on the value of the

condition. Similarly, if a while-loop or repeat-loop is entered, all statements in its body must be executed before the loop can be exited. This is not true for the LOOP/EXIT construct, and indeed, there can be more than one EXIT for a single LOOP. (This may also be why Pascal does not include a RETURN statement, which creates multiple exit paths within functions and procedures.) Thus we could interpret this as a uniformity issue: in Pascal all control structures are uniformly single entry, single exit (as long as gotos are not used).

8. One possibility would be to separate the declaration of variants from the record declaration, as is done in C using the u n i o n keyword (see Chapter 6). For example, in C a variant data structure that can be either integer or char can be declared as follows:

```
union {int x; char c;}
```

In C there are no discriminant fields, however, but they could be introduced as parenthesized parameters to the declaration (as they are in Ada), as follows (in Modula-2-style syntax):

```
UNION (b: BOOLEAN) OF
   TRUE: x: INTEGER |
   FALSE: c: CHAR
END;
```

In this example we have retained most of the syntax of the case-statement in Modula-2, except for the use of UNION and the parenthesized discriminant.

12. In C an attempt was made to make the semicolon consistently a terminator for both declarations and statements. This removes the problem in Pascal of interrupting the else part of an if-statement by accidentally using a semicolon:

Pascal:

```
if x = 0 then y := 2;   ← incorrect use of semicolon
else y := 3;
```

C:

```
if (x == 0) y = 2;   ← semicolon required here
else y = 3;
```

The insistence on semicolons following statements in C also prevents an additional problem in Pascal:

Pascal:

```
if x = 0 then begin
   y := 2;
   z := 3  ← adding a new statement after this one
end;         will cause a syntax error
```

C:

```
if (x == 0)
{y = 2;
   z = 3;}  ← this semicolon required; adding
              statements not a problem
```

On the other hand, there are a few variations on the use of semicolon in C that one could view as slight inconsistencies. One is the use of the semicolon as a separator for the control expressions of a for-statement:

```
for (i = 0 ; i < n-1 ; ++i)
          ↑          ↑
```

(semicolon used as separator here)

Also, semicolons follow all statements *except* the compound statement {. . .}. This makes function declarations (or definitions as they are called in C) look different too, since a function declaration includes the compound statement giving its body:

```
int gcd (int u, int v)
{if (v == 0) return u;
  else return gcd (v, u % v);}
                              ↑ no semicolon here
```

16. Readability: Ada's comment notation is difficult to confuse with other constructs, and the comment indicators are always present on each comment line. By contrast, a Modula-2 comment may have widely separated comment symbols, so it may not be easy to determine what is a comment and what is not (especially noticeable if a comment extends over more than one video screen). Embedded Modula-2 comments may also be confusing, since parentheses are used for so many things:

```
PROCEDURE p ((* this is a comment*)): INTEGER;
PROCEDURE p ((* this is an error *): INTEGER;
```

Nested comments can also present readability problems in Modula-2:

```
(* A comment
      (* a nested comment
  . . .
but only one comment closer *)
```

Thus Ada comments may be judged more readable than Modula-2's.

Writability: Ada's comments require extra characters for each new line of comments. This makes it more difficult to write an Ada comment, if only from a count of the number of extra characters required. Modula-2's comments, on the other hand, can be written more easily with a single opening and closing character sequence. In Modula-2 it is also unnecessary to know whether a comment has already been opened to add a new comment, since comments can be nested (unlike Pascal).

Reliability: A more readable comment convention is likely to be more reliable, since the reader can more easily determine errors, so Ada is likely to be more reliable in its comment convention. The main feature of Ada comments that perhaps increases their reliability is their *locality of reference*: all comments are clearly indicated locally, without the need for a proper matching symbol farther on.

19. Ripley and Druseikis [1978] collected statistics on programming errors in Pascal made by graduate students. They concentrated only on syntax errors and found that these broke down into categories as follows:

Missing token errors	41.4%
Wrong token errors	38.7%
Multiple token errors	12.1%
Extra token errors	8.0%

By far the most common missing token was the semicolon, followed by missing end and begin tokens. Wrong token errors were led by confusion between commas and semicolons and assignment and equality. Multiple token errors were led by out-of-order declarations such as

```
var x: integer;
type t = array[1..10] of char;
```

Extra token errors were led by extra var, type, and semicolon tokens, such as the following:

```
var x: integer;
var b: boolean;
```

Suggestions for changes to the syntax of Pascal could include the following, based on their analysis:

1. Allow extra var and type tokens in declarations.
2. Allow declarations to occur in any order.
3. Make semicolon a terminator.
4. Use commas instead of semicolons to separate parameters in a procedure declaration, as in

```
procedure p(x:integer, var y:boolean);
```

5. Let end of lines function as semicolons, if the semicolon is missing.

6. Let structured constructs open blocks, so `begin` is unnecessary.

7. Introduce new tokens for assignment and equality, such as "$< -$" for assignment and "$= =$" for equality.

Indeed, many Pascal compilers have relaxed the language to include suggestions 1 and 2 here. Modula-2 has included suggestion 6. One language that uses suggestion 5 is Miranda. C uses suggestions 3 and 4. Suggestion 7 is made necessary only because of continuing confusion among languages of the use of "$=$." (C and FORTRAN use it for assignment; Pascal, Modula-2, and Ada use it for equality.)

23. An obvious advantage of arbitrary-precision integers is that it frees the behavior of integers from any dependence on the (implementation-dependent) representation of the integers, including elimination of the need for considering overflow in the language definition (see Exercise 1-9). The disadvantage is that the size of memory needed for an integer is not static (fixed prior to execution), and therefore memory for an integer must be dynamically allocated. This has serious consequences for a language like Pascal. For example, in the following code,

```
var x: record i: integer; b: boolean end;
    . . .
x.i := 100;
x.b := true;
    . . .
x.i := 10000000000000000;
    . . .
```

the allocation of new storage for x on the second assignment to x.i means x.b must also be reallocated and copied, unless indirection is used. Indeed, a reasonable approach would be to make integer variables into pointers and automatically allocate and deallocate them on assignment. This means that the runtime system must become "fully dynamic," substantially complicating the implementation of the language. The arithmetic operators, such as addition and multiplication, also become much less efficient, since a software algorithm must be used in place of hardware operations.

In principle, a real number with arbitrary precision can be represented in the same way as an arbitrary-precision integer, with the addition of a distinguished position (the position of the decimal point). For example, 33.256 could be represented as (33256,2), the 2 expressing the fact that the decimal point is after the second digit. (Note that this is like scientific notation, with the 2 representing a power of 10: $33.256 = .33256 \cdot 10^2$.) The same comments hold for such reals as for arbitrary-precision integers. However, there is a further complication: while integer operations *always* result in a finite number of digits, real operations can result in infinitely many digits! (Consider the result of 1.0/3.0 or sqrt(2.0).) How many digits should these results get? Any answer is going to have to be arbitrary. For this reason, even systems with arbitrary-precision integers often place restrictions on the precision of real numbers. (Scheme calls any number with a decimal point *inexact,* and any time an integer—which is exact—is converted to a real, it becomes inexact, and some of its digits may be lost.)

Chapter 4

2. A sample test in Pascal would insert a comment in the middle of a reserved word, such as in

```
program ex;
be(*a comment*)gin
end.
```

In all languages mentioned, this produces an error, transforming "begin" into the two identifiers "be" and "gin". Thus comments are considered white space in all these languages.

7. We use "−" for subtraction and "/" for division (since this is integer division, the "/" corresponds to the div operation of Pascal and Modula-2). We add these operations to the BNF and EBNF, leaving the modification of the syntax diagrams of Figure 4.5 to the reader:

BNF:

<exp>   ::= <exp> + <term> | <exp> − <term> | <term>
<term>   ::= <term> • <factor> | <term> / <factor> |
                                                      <factor>
<factor>   ::= (<exp>) | <number>
<number>   ::= <number> <digit> | <digit>
<digit>   ::= 0 | 1 | 2 | 3 | 4 | 5 | 6 | 7 | 8 | 9

EBNF:

<exp>   ::= <term> {(+ | −) <term>}
<term>   ::= <factor> {(• | /) <factor>}
<factor>   ::= '('<exp>')' | <number>
<number>   ::= <digit> {<digit>}
<digit>   ::= 0 | 1 | 2 | 3 | 4 | 5 | 6 | 7 | 8 | 9

Note: In the EBNF we have used parentheses to group operations within pairs of brackets in the first two rules. This makes parentheses into new metasymbols. An alternative is to write

<exp>   ::= <term> {<addop> <term>}
<addop>   ::= + | −

<term>   ::= <factor> {<mulop> <factor>}
<mulop>   ::= • | /

Note that writing the first rule in the following form is incorrect (why?):

<exp>   ::= <term> {+ <term>} | <term> {− <term>}

9. We add unary minuses to the grammar of Exercise 7 in case (a) of this exercise.

BNF:
<exp>   ::= <exp> + <term> | <exp> − <term> |
                                    − <term> | <term>
<term>   ::= <term> • <factor> | <term> / <factor> |
                                    <factor>

. . . etc.

EBNF:
<exp>   ::= [−] <term> {(+|−) <term>}
<term>   ::= <factor> {(• | /) <factor>}

10. (c)

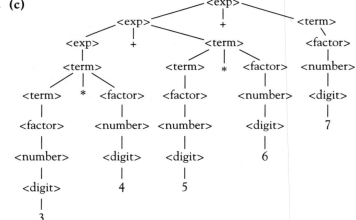

14. Figure 4.7 is almost a working Pascal program. Here is a working C version:

```
#include <stdio.h>
#include <ctype.h>
char Token;

void exp(void);
void term(void);
void factor(void);

void GetToken(void)
{while ((((Token = getchar()) ==' ') ||
        (Token == '\t'));}
```

```
void Error(void)
{printf("Error!\n");
 exit(0);}

void number(void)
{if isdigit(Token)
   {while (isdigit(Token)) Token = getchar();
     /* Don't call GetToken here, since non-digits
         should end a number */
    if ((Token == ' ') || (Token == '\t'))
      GetToken();
    /* Make sure Token is non-white-space */}
  else Error();
}

void factor(void)
{if (Token == '(')
   {GetToken'(');
    exp();
    if (Token == ')') GetToken();
    else Error();}
  else number();
}

void term(void)
{factor();
 while (Token == '*')
 {GetToken();
   factor();}
}

void exp(void)
{term();
 while (Token == '+')
 {GetToken();
   term();}
}

void parse(void)
{GetToken();
 exp();}

void main(void)
{parse();
  /* insist on seeing end of line to eliminate
      widows */
  if (Token == '\n') printf("success\n");
  else Error();
}
```

18. Writing the rule as <exp> ::= <term> + <term> allows only one
    "+" operation per expression, so that, for example, 3 + 4 + 5 would
    become illegal. This is not fatal to writing more than one "+" operation
    in an expression, since parentheses can be used: the expression (3 + 4)
    + 5 remains legal. But it does remove the ambiguity by changing the
    language recognized rather than by changing the grammar but not the
    language.

22. Suppose a declaration has the form **var** __;, where "__" stands for the
    strings usable for variable identifiers. Suppose further that only two
    letters, say, a and b, are usable as variable identifiers. Then the possible
    declarations without redeclaration are {var a;, var b; , var a; var b; , var
    b; var a;}. These could be generated by EBNF rules

    <declaration> ::= ε | var a; [var b;] | var b; [var a;]

    Now suppose that c is also a legal identifier. Then instead of six
    legal declaration sequences there are fifteen, and EBNF rules look as
    follows:

    <declaration> ::= ε | var a; <no-a> | var b; <no-b> |
                        var c; <no-c>
    <no-a> ::= ε | var b; [var c;] | var c; [var b;]
    <no-b> ::= ε | var a; [var c;] | var c; [var a;]
    <no-c> ::= ε | var a; [var b;] | var b; [var a;]

    There are now four grammar rules instead of one. The grammar is growing
    exponentially with the number of variables. Thus, even in a language
    where variables can be only two characters long, there are nearly a
    thousand possible variables, and perhaps millions of grammar rules. Writing a parser for such a grammar would be a waste of time.

25. We give here the BNF and EBNF rules. Translating the EBNF into
    syntax diagrams is left to the reader. If a statement sequence must have
    at least one statement, the grammar rule is easily stated as the following.

    BNF: <stmt-seq> ::= <stmt-seq> ; <stmt> | <stmt>
    EBNF: <stmt-seq> ::= <stmt> {; <stmt>}

    However, statement sequences usually are allowed to be empty, which
    complicates the problem. One answer is to use the previous solution
    and a helper rule, as follows.

    BNF:

    <stmt-seq> ::= ε | <stmt-seq1>
    <stmt-seq1> ::= <stmt-seq1> ; <stmt> | <stmt>

    (Similarly for EBNF.)

29. (a) Here are the number of reserved words in each language:

C:	32
Pascal:	35
Modula-2:	40
Ada:	63

(b) In Pascal predefined identifiers not only include the standard data types, such as i n t e g e r, that correspond to reserved words in C, but also include functions such as s i n, c o s, a b s, c h r, o r d, and so on. These correspond to standard library functions in C. Modula-2 also has (more or less) standard library functions, as well as predefined identifiers, and in Ada predefined identifiers are the same as those identifiers defined in standard libraries. Thus just adding predefined identifiers alone is still misleading. Perhaps one should add all predefined identifiers *and* standard library identifiers to have a fair comparison. But if one wishes to get an idea only of the complexity of a language parser, rather than the language as a whole, counting reserved words does do that.

31. Indeed, FORTRAN is a language without reserved words, so it is certainly possible for a language to have no reserved words. The problem is that all language constructs become essentially context dependent, and a parser cannot decide which construct is applicable without help from the symbol table and semantic analyzer. This enormously complicates the parsing process, and context-free grammar techniques cannot be used. For this reason, the trend has been toward greater use of reserved words and less use of predefined identifiers.

33. The difference is immaterial in terms of recognizing numbers. The parse tree becomes significant only if the tree itself is used for further translation or computation. In the case of a number, the main "further translation" that is needed is to compute its value. If we try to compute its value recursively, based on the structure of the tree, we notice a difference in complexity between the two tree structures. Consider, for example, the number 234. It has the two possible parse trees

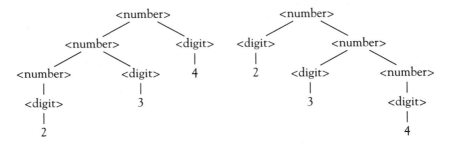

In the left-hand tree, at a number node with two children, its value can be computed by multiplying the value of its left child by 10 (in base 10) and adding the value of its right child. In the right-hand tree, a more complex computation is required, namely, the number of digits in

each value must also be computed. For example, to compute the value of the root of the right-hand tree, the value of its left child (2) must be multiplied by $100 = 10^2$ (the exponent $2 =$ the number of digits of its right child), and then added to the value of its right child (34). Thus the left-hand tree, which resulted from the left-recursive rule, is to be preferred. This is an example of the principle of syntax-directed semantics (see Section 4.3).

38. **(a)** The first condition of predictive parsing is satisfied by the grammar, since the first grammar rule is the only one with an alternative, and

$$\text{First}('(' <\text{list}> ')') \cap \text{First}('a') = \{'('\} \cap \{'a'\} = \phi$$

To show that the second condition for predictive parsing is satisfied, we must show that $\text{First}(<\text{list}>) \cap \text{Follow}(<\text{list}>) = \phi$, since $<\text{list}>$ is optional in the second grammar rule. We first compute $\text{First}(<\text{list}>)$. By the second grammar rule, $\text{First}(<\text{list}>)$ contains $\text{First}(<\text{exp}>)$. Since this is the only contribution to $\text{First}(<\text{list}>)$, we have $\text{First}(<\text{list}>) = \text{First}(<\text{exp}>)$, and from the first grammar rule we have $\text{First}(<\text{exp}>) = \{'(' \ 'a'\}$, so $\text{First}(<\text{list}>) = \{'(' \ 'a'\}$. To compute $\text{Follow}(<\text{list}>)$, we note that the first grammar rule shows that ')' can follow a list. The second grammar rule gives us no additional information (it tells us only that $\text{Follow}(<\text{list}>)$ contains $\text{Follow}(<\text{list}>)$), so $\text{Follow}(<\text{list}>) = \{')'\}$. Then

$$\text{First}(<\text{list}>) \cap \text{Follow}(<\text{list}>) = \\ \{'(' \ 'a'\} \cap \{')'\} = \phi$$

so the second condition for predictive parsing is satisfied.

(b) Pseudocode for expression and list are as follows:

```
procedure exp;
begin
  if Token = '(' then begin
    GetToken;
    list;
    if Token = ')' then GetToken
    else Error;
  end else if Token = 'a' then GetToken
  else Error;
end;

procedure list;
begin
  exp;
  if (Token = '(') or (Token = 'a') then list;
end;
```

Note that in the code for list we used First($<$list$>$) to decide whether to make the optional recursive call to list. We could just as well have used the Follow set (which will, however, give a slightly different behavior in the presence of errors):

```
procedure list;
begin
  exp;
  if (Token <> ')') then list;
end;
```

Chapter 5

3. **(a)** In Pascal, a global variable is a variable associated to the main program block and is declared at the beginning of the program. A global variable is visible to all procedures in the program. In C, a global variable is declared external to any function (including the main program function) and need not be declared at the beginning of the program. It is visible to all functions that follow its declaration. The FORTRAN COMMON declaration has the advantage of appearing in every procedure that has access to global variables; that is, procedures do not automatically gain access to globals (so COMMON is a little like an IMPORT statement in Modula-2). It has the added flexibility of allowing a name change or alias, but aliasing can be confusing. Additionally, if the position of the variable in the COMMON block is changed in the main program, it needs to be changed everywhere else as well. Thus the declaration of a global variable is essentially spread over all COMMON declarations, violating the principle of locality and creating the opportunity for serious errors, since variables are identified by position only. In addition, COMMON declarations can subvert the type system, since no check on type equivalence is performed on COMMON variables. Thus a CHAR variable can be declared COMMON with a REAL variable.

   (b) The EQUIVALENCE statement is used to identify variables within the same procedure or function rather than across procedures. Its primary use was to reuse memory allocated to different variables when the uses of the variables did not overlap. This reuse of memory was necessary because of the restricted size of memory in early computers. In modern systems it is much less important, and translators are also able to determine such "overlay" possibilities automatically, which is preferable, because it avoids the problems with aliasing and type subversion that EQUIVALENCE shares with COMMON.

6. Pascal forward declarations of procedures/functions are necessary in algorithms that are heavily recursive, such as recursive-descent parsing, where two procedures might call each other, as in

```
procedure A;
begin
   . . .
   B;
   . . .
end;

procedure B;
begin
   . . .
   A;
   . . .
end;
```

Since Pascal requires declaration before use, there is no order in which A and B can be declared without causing an error. The solution is to use a forward declaration:

```
procedure B;  forward;

procedure A;
begin
   . . .
   B;
   . . .
end;

procedure B;
begin
   . . .
   A;
   . . .
end;
```

A forward declaration binds a name to a procedure type, including the types of all its parameters (and its return type if it is a function). It also binds a scope to the procedure name by the declaration before use principle (i.e., it functions as a normal declaration with respect to scope). Finally, a forward declaration binds the names of the parameters to data types (and scopes), since Pascal requires that parameter lists and return types of procedures declared forward not be repeated in the actual declaration:

```
function f (x: integer) : boolean; forward;

   . . .
```

```
function f; (* no declaration of parameters
                and return type here ! *)
begin
  . . .
end;
```

8. **(a)** A declaration. It binds a new name to a datatype.
   (b) A declaration. It binds a name to a new datatype.
   (c) A definition, since allocation during execution is implied by a Pascal variable declaration.
   (d) A declaration, since the actual allocation of the code for the procedure does not occur when a forward declaration is processed.

11. The declaration of a and b external to any function has global scope, except for the scope hole for a inside p and the scope hole for b inside q. The declaration of function p has global scope (following its declaration), except for p itself, where the local declaration of p creates a scope hole. The local declarations of a and p inside function p have scope equal to the block of the function p. The declaration of print, q, and main all have global scope, beginning with each declaration. The declaration of b inside function q has scope equal to the block of q. Using dynamic scope, the major change is that, since print is called from inside q, q's local declaration extends over print. Thus the local b inside q creates a scope hole for the global b during the execution of print when called from q. This results in a different output. Using static scoping (the actual rule in C), this program prints 3 and 1, whereas if dynamic scope were used the program would print 3 and 4.

14. The problem is that, if dynamic scoping is used, type checking cannot be performed until execution since a particular name can mean different variables at different times during execution. Thus a static type is of no use, since references cannot be resolved statically. A simple example of this problem is given by the following program (in Pascal syntax):

```
program ugly;
var x: integer;

procedure p;
begin
  if x = 'a' then writeln('ok')
  else writeln('oops');
end;
procedure q;
var x: char;
begin
  x := 'b';
  p;
end;                                        continues
```

continued

```
begin (* main *)
  q;
end.
```

Statically, there is a type error in procedure p, in that the only declaration of x known when p is processed is the global one of x as an integer. However, p is called only from q, so the global declaration of x does not extend over p during execution. Instead, the local declaration of x within q, which declares x to be a char, extends to p during execution, and the code of p turns out to be type correct after all. Thus the use of dynamic scope requires that dynamic typing also be used.

There is no similar problem with static scoping and dynamic typing, since type checking can use the static scope structure, and every variable must have its type computed prior to any references to it whether it is statically or dynamically typed. For example, the Scheme language uses static scoping and dynamic typing.

17. No. For instance the scope hole problem exists for dynamic scope as it does for static scope (see the answer to Exercise 11). In that exercise, global b remains allocated through the execution of q and print, and so has extent equal to the duration of program execution (it is statically allocated), even though the (dynamic) scope of global b does not extend to q or print.

20. It is possible that a translator will allocate the same location to x and y, since they are the first variables declared in successive blocks. If this is the case, then the program will print garbage for x (since x has not been assigned prior to the first printf) and 1 for y. It is also possible that garbage is printed for y also, which means that the compiler assigns new space to y instead of reusing the space of x.

24. The call new(x) allocates x^, and the call new(x^) allocates x^^. The calls are needed in that order, since x^ must be allocated before the call new(x^) assigns the address of x^^ to the location of x^. We would also need a call new(y) if not for the fact that the assignment y := x^ provides an allocation for y^ by sharing with the location of x^^.

30. (a)   <exp> ::= <exp> <exp> <op> | <number>
          <op> ::= + | ·
          <number> ::= <number> <digit> | <digit>
          <digit> ::= 0 | 1 | 2 | 3 | 4 | 5 | 6 | 7 | 8 | 9

32. The problem is that the arithmetic operations can take more than two operands, so two interpretations of the expression are

    (+ 3 (* 4 5 6))

and

```
(+ 3 (* 4 5) 6)
```

with values 123 and 29, respectively.

39. **(a)** This doesn't work because in Pascal the parameters a and b are evaluated when the c a n d function is called, so both a and b are always evaluated.

   (b) Yes. Normal order evaluation delays the evaluation of a and b until those values are required in the computation. Thus b is evaluated only if the statement c a n d : = b is reached, that is, if a is true. If a is false, b is never evaluated, so the resultant effect is indeed a c a n d function.

Chapter 6

4. The order is false $<$ true. The reason is that the boolean type is considered to be a predefined enumeration type equivalent to the following type declaration,

   ```
   type boolean = (false,true);
   ```

   so that $ord(false) = 0$, $ord(true) = 1$, $succ(false) = true$, and $pred(true) = false$. If f a l s e and t r u e were made incomparable, the boolean type would represent a special addition to the type structure, like integer and real. Interpreting b o o l e a n as an ordinal type allows such expressions as the following to be written:

   ```
   if (x <= y) < (x <= z) then writeln('ok')
   else writeln('ack');
   ```

   which is equivalent to the following:

   ```
   if (x <= z) and (x > y) then writeln('ok')
   else writeln('ack');
   ```

   Indeed, a $<$ b is equivalent to b and n o t a, and a $<=$ b is equivalent to b o r n o t a. This is probably more confusing than helpful, however, so there doesn't seem to be a real gain in making b o o l e a n into an ordinary type.

8. **(a)** Suppose X is finite, with n elements. Then the set $X \times$ CHAR is also finite and has more elements than X does (if CHAR has 128 elements, typical for ASCII character sets, then $X \times$ CHAR has n times 128 elements). But this contradicts the equation $X \times$ CHAR $= X$. So X must be infinite.

(b) Consider an element x in the set X, and suppose X satisfies the equation $X = X \times$ CHAR. Then $x = (x',c)$ for some x' in X and character c. Now the same can be said of x': $x' = (x'',c')$, where x'' is an element of X. Continuing in this way, we get an infinite number of characters c, c', c'', . . ., which must be part of x.

(c) Consider the infinite Cartesian product

$$P = \text{CHAR} \times \text{CHAR} \times \text{CHAR} \times \ldots$$

The set P consists of all infinite tuples $(c_1,c_2,c_3,\ldots)$ where each c_i is in CHAR. This certainly satisfies the equation, since $P \times$ CHAR consists of the set $((c_1,c_2,c_3,\ldots), c_0)$, which is the same as $(c_0,c_1,c_2,c_3,\ldots)$, which is the same as P itself (just add one to all the indices). There is also a sense in which the set P is the smallest such set. We omit the details.

11. (a) A subtype in Ada is not a new type, but is always considered to be part of its base type. Instead, a subtype is an indication to a compiler to perform range checking on its value during execution. By contrast, a derived type is a completely new type that is incompatible with its base type and other types without explicit type conversion.

(b) Pascal uses declaration equivalence, so the declaration

```
type newint = integer;
```

does not create a new type, but the type newint is equivalent to integer. Thus this declaration is equivalent to the Ada subtype declaration.

(c) The Ada declaration creates a new type New_Int, which cannot be achieved in Pascal through simple renaming. Thus there is no declaration that is completely equivalent to the Ada declaration. It is possible to imitate it, however, using a type constructor, such as

```
type newint = record i: integer end;
```

or

```
type newint = array [1..1] of integer;
```

These are not equivalent to the Ada declaration since one must write x.i or x[1] to access the value of a variable of type newint.

14. Given the expression if e_1 then e_2 else e_3, a reasonable type correctness rule would require that e_1 have Boolean type and that e_2 and e_3 be type equivalent. The inferred type of the whole expression would then be the (common) type of e_2 and e_3. Given an optional else-part, where e_3 may be absent, one could still use the type of e_2 as the inferred type of the expression, but this leaves undefined what value the expression might have if the Boolean condition evaluates to false during execution. Algol68 does allow this to happen, in which case the returned value is undefined (which may result in a runtime error). LISP has a similar behavior. For the purposes of strong typing, it is preferable to require the else-part to be present in an if-expression. This is the case with the C if-expression (Exercise 15).

19. (a) The problem is that integers usually occupy more than one byte, while Booleans are only one byte long. Thus the following allocation occurs for x:

address of x

Thus assigning the value TRUE to x . b will be placing the internal representation of TRUE somewhere into the middle of the memory allocated for x . i, resulting in some value, but not the value of x . b.

(b) In the case where the lowest-order byte of the value of x . i is the leftmost byte in the memory allocated for x . i, it is possible to print the correct value for x . b by first initializing x . i to zero, as follows:

```
x . i  := 0 ;
x . b  := TRUE ;
WriteInt(x . i , 1) ;
```

This depends on the style of architecture of the machine—those having the lowest-order byte at the lowest memory location are called **little-endian,** while others are called **big-endian.** This dependency on the style of architecture cannot be removed.

23. (a) x, y, z, and w are all equivalent under structural equivalence. Similarly, i and j are equivalent under structural equivalence.

(b) x and y are possibly equivalent under name equivalence (this is an ambiguity; in Ada they would not be). Otherwise, none of the variables are equivalent.

(c) x and y are equivalent under declaration equivalence. z and w are also equivalent, but not to x and y. i and j are also not equivalent (but are fully compatible in Pascal, so there is no operation that will distinguish them; see Exercise 24).

27. The basic differences of syntax between Pascal and Modula-2 can be seen in the following examples:

Pascal:

```
record
  x : integer ;
  y : real ;
```

continues

continued

```
case b: boolean of
  true: (c: char;
         z: real);
  false: (w: integer)
end;
```

Modula-2:

```
RECORD
  x: INTEGER;
  y: REAL;
  CASE b: BOOLEAN OF
    TRUE: c: CHAR;
          z: REAL |
    FALSE: w: INTEGER
  END;
END;
```

Note the use of the vertical bar "|" in Modula-2 to separate the field lists in a variant part, while Pascal uses parentheses to group them. Note further the fact that the Modula-2 declaration has two END keywords, one ending the variant part and one ending the record declaration itself, while Pascal has only one end, which ends both the variant part and the record as a whole. It is for this reason that the variant part in Pascal must come at the end of the declaration and that there can be only one variant part (but see Exercise 28). For completeness, we also note that Modula-2 allows ranges as case labels while Pascal does not, and Modula-2 has an optional ELSE part at the end of a case, while Pascal requires that all cases be listed.

30. The difficulty is that a union declaration is most commonly used within a struct declaration, and in C this creates a new level for accessing the fields of the union, while in Pascal and Modula-2 the field access is at the same level as the surrounding record. For example, given the following declaration in Pascal,

```
var x: record
         i: integer;
         case b: boolean of
           true: (r: real);
           false: (c: char)
       end;
```

the fields of x would be referenced as x.i, x.b, x.r, and x.c. By contrast, in C we would write the declaration as

```
struct {int  i;
        int  b;
        union {double  r;
               char  c;} u;
      } x;
```

and the fields of x would be accessed as x . i, x . b, x . u . r, and x . u . c. Note that accessing union members requires the use of two field references. This makes the use of unions cumbersome and often results in practice in a struct such as the foregoing being written without the union.

32. The declaration

```
var  f:  file  of  t;
```

automatically declares implicitly a file buffer variable of type t, and the expression f ^ refers to the file buffer variable. In addition to this file buffer reference operation, f has a number of predefined functions that are automatically defined for it, including reset (f), rewrite (f), get (f), put (f), read (f , x), write (f , x), and eof (f) (the variable x is of type t). (The functions eoln (f), readln (f , x), and writeln (f , x) are only available for text files and so are not defined for all files.)

38. It is consistent for C to treat array and pointer types similarly in its type equivalence algorithm, since arrays are viewed as being essentially pointers to the first element. Indeed, given the declaration

```
int  x[10];
```

the first element of x can be accessed as either x [0] or ∗ x.

Similarly, in a parameter declaration x [ ] and ∗ x have the same meaning. Now the reason that structural equivalence is used for pointers is related to the fact that all pointers are viewed as essentially equivalent. Moreover, in a recursive declaration such as

```
struct  charrec {char data;
                 charrec * next;} * x;
```

using declaration equivalence it would be impossible to write

```
x = x->next;
```

(see Exercise 6), and thus list operations (among others) could not be written without typedefs:

```
typedef struct charrec * charlist;
typedef struct charrec
              {char data;
               charlist next;};
charlist x;
```

However, typedefs are not actually part of the type equivalence algorithm—they were an addition to the original language, and do not create new types, only synonyms for existing types. By contrast, structures and unions have names created by declarations independent of typedefs (for example, struct charrec in the foregoing declarations). Thus declaration equivalence can apply to these declarations, but not to pointers or arrays.

42. Typical operations for strings include length, assignment (or copy), comparison (both "=" and "<" using lexicographic order), concatenation, substring extraction, the position of a character, the character at a particular position, and replacement of characters within a string. Arrays of characters in a language like Modula-2 (or packed arrays of characters in Pascal) support assignment, comparison, character extraction, and character replacement well (at least within the size constraints provided for in the language). The other operations are not supported directly. Concatenation and substring extraction are particularly problematic because of the restriction that arrays have fixed sizes. In a language with dynamically sized arrays, such as C or Algol60 there are fewer problems with size restrictions, but most of the given operations are not supported (including assignment and comparison in C). C has a standard string function library that removes most of these problems. Modula-2 usually has a string library module, and the language has open array parameters, which allows for more flexibility in dealing with variable-length strings (in particular, allowing the definition of a string function module that can handle strings of arbitrary size). Ada has a predefined string type that is equivalent to an unconstrained (or open-sized) array of characters. Ada directly supports assignment, comparison, concatenation, and substring extraction (through slicing).

45. The assignment i := VAL(INTEGER,c) causes a runtime error because the value of c is 50000, which is out of range of the integer i (type conversion functions such as VAL always imply range checking). The assignment i := INTEGER(c), on the other hand, will not generate a runtime error, since this represents a cast, and casts always reinterpret values without applying range checks (indeed, i usually gets the value -15536 because of the reinterpretation of 50000 as a two's complement number). By contrast, the assignment i := c has unspecified behavior, since it represents an automatic conversion provided by the assignment compatibility of integer and cardinal types. Some translators may provide a runtime range check, and others may not (in practice most translators treat this in the same way as the VAL conversion).

Chapter 7

2. The issue is whether a new reserved word o t h e r w i s e should be added to the language, or whether the existing keyword e l s e should be reused. Adding a reserved word compromises the simplicity of the language a little, while reusing another reserved word brings up uniformity issues. In this case the use of e l s e for a "catch-all" case is similar but not identical to its use in an if-statement. Which principle wins is a matter of judgment by the language designer. For example, in C, which also strives for simplicity, the switch-statement (equivalent to the Pascal case-statement) uses the new reserved word d e f a u l t. Apparently, the de-signers considered this situation to be enough different to deserve a new reserved word.

5. **(a)** We might try to view w h i l e e 1 d o e 2 as an expression by giving it the data type of e 2 and having it return the last computed value of e 2 before e 1 becomes false. The problem is that if e 1 evaluates to false the first time, e 2 is never evaluated, and so no value can be returned. We could avoid this problem in one of two ways. The first possibility is for the expression to return an undefined result if e 1 evaluates to false the first time. The second possibility is to give the expression the data type and last value of e 1 (that is, Boolean), since e 1 is always evaluated. The problem with this second possi-bility is that every while-expression (or at least every one that terminates) will evaluate to false, so its returned value is of little use.

   (b) The construct r e p e a t e 1 u n t i l e 2 does not have the same problem as the while-expression, since the body is always evaluated. Thus the data type and value can be that of (the last evaluation of) e 1.

   (c) C has no repeat- or while-expressions; it has only while-statements and do-while-statements (the equivalent of a repeat-statement). Algol68, on the other hand, is an expression language, so the while construct is an expression and returns a value. (As with the if-expression, Algol68 uses the first solution described in part (a), returning an undefined value if the Boolean condition evaluates to false.) Algol68 has no repeat construct.

9. **(a)** The standard example of an if-statement with an ambiguous parse is one with two ifs and one else:

   ```
   if c1 then if c2 then s1 else s2
   ```

   This statement does have a unique parse using this new grammar, since if we try to match the e l s e to the outermost i f, we must match i f c 2 t h e n s 1 to a <matched-statement>, which it isn't. However, a slightly more complex example still results in an am-biguity:

```
if c1 then if c2 then s1 else if c3 then s2
  else s3
```

It is possible to parse this either as

```
if c1 then (if c2 then s1 else (if c3 then s2))
  else s3
```

or

```
if c1 then (if c2 then s1 else (if c3 then s2
  else s3))
```

(We have used parentheses to indicate association of the elses. The translation into parse trees should be immediate.) The first parse is, of course, incorrect.

(b) Here is an unambiguous grammar:

<stmt>   ::= <matched-stmt> | <unmatched-stmt>
<matched-stmt>   ::= if <cond> then <matched-stmt>
                                        else <matched-stmt>
                       | <other-stmt>
<unmatched-stmt> ::= if <cond> then <matched-stmt>
                                        else <unmatched-stmt>
                       | if <cond> then <stmt>

14. The output of the program using each parameter passing mechanism is as follows:

pass by value:	1	1
pass by reference:	3	1
pass by value-result:	2	1
pass by name:	2	2

16. (a) In the case of an expression like X+Y or 2, a temporary memory location can be allocated during load time. Then code is generated to compute the value of the expression into this location, and the address of the temporary location is passed to the subroutine. Thus CALL P(X,X+Y,2) has the same effect as

```
TEMP1 = X+Y
TEMP2 = 2
CALL P(X,TEMP1,TEMP2)
```

(b) If, for example, we wished to pass X by value in the preceding call, we could write CALL(X+0,X+Y,2).

(c) Since 1 is a constant in the call P(1), there are two possibilities. The first is to use the method just described, with a temporary location being allocated and 1 stored into it. Then on the second call, 1 is not stored again (since it is a constant), with the result that 2 gets printed. The other possibility is that 1 is stored with the program code, and its address is passed to the subroutine. Now an attempt to change a location in the code segment will result in a runtime error, since the code segment is usually read only.

19. An example is the following program:

```
program text;
var i: integer;

function p(y:integer): integer;
var j: integer;
begin
  j := 1;
  p := y;
end; (* p *)

procedure q;
var j: integer;
begin
  i := 2;
  j := 2;
  writeln(p(i+j));
end; (* q *)

begin (* main *)
  q;
end.
```

This program prints 3 using pass by text (it would print 4 using pass by name). Note that programming languages using pass by text must also use dynamic scoping, since otherwise it is possible to pass an expression outside the scope of one of its component variables (consider the case where i is also local to q in the preceding example).

24.

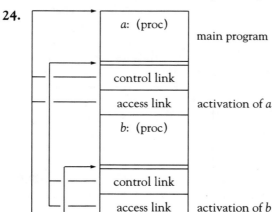

continues

continued

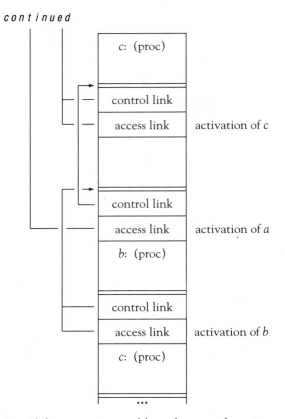

28. If the array is passed by reference, there is no problem, since the array need not be stored locally, but only its address (and perhaps size, which in any case is computed dynamically). In C all arrays are addresses, so there is also no problem in C (and size is never an issue, since C does no range checking on indices). The problem occurs with open array parameters passed by value. In this case, the array may be assigned to locally, in which case a local copy must be made (some optimizing compilers check for local assignments before generating code to make a copy). The problem is that if the array is copied directly into the activation record, the offsets of the parameters and local variables that are allocated after the array are unknown prior to execution, which inhibits efficient access, since local variables can no longer be found by fixed offset from the top of the activation record using the environment pointer. The solution is to introduce a further level of indirection, where arrays are stored in an area of the activation just below the fixed part, and are referenced by an address stored in the fixed part. For example, suppose a procedure p is declared as follows in Modula-2:

```
PROCEDURE p(a: ARRAY OF INTEGER; b: CHAR;
    c: ARRAY OF REAL);
```

Then a call to p would result in the following structure of its activation record:

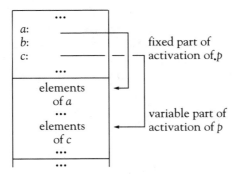

The cost of the extra level of indirection is less than the cost of dynamically computing all offsets.

32. **(a)** If procedures are never parameters, they must always be called from an environment that is enclosed in the environment where they are defined. That means that when a procedure is called, its location can be found by the usual access chaining, and the environment pointer to the activation where the procedure is found is now the environment pointer of the procedure closure, since the procedure must be defined in the environment in which it is found.

(b) In Modula-2 the following restriction is stated in the language definition:

> If a formal parameter specifies a procedure type, then the corresponding actual parameter must be either a procedure declared at level 0 or a variable (or parameter) of that procedure type. It cannot be a standard procedure.

Thus, in Modula-2, only global procedures can be passed as procedure parameters. Thus any procedure that is assigned to a parameter can be assumed to have global environment, and the environment pointer of its closure need not be computed in advance.

36. An exception handler often will print an error message along with taking corrective action, indicating what went wrong. If several different things can go wrong, a parameter can indicate the precise nature of the failure. For example, if a bounds check fails, it would be helpful to know the exact value of the index that caused the failure. If a parameter cannot be passed during the raising of an exception, this means that the information must be printed before the exception is raised. If this exception occurs in many different places, this increases the code size and the burden on the programmer (this is precisely the reason parameters were introduced for procedures). In some cases where the needed information varies only over a small set of possibilities, the information can be provided by declaring an exception for each possibility. Of course, this

greatly increases the number of exceptions. Clearly, parameters in exception handlers is a great convenience, although not an absolute necessity.

41. Since exceptions in Ada are propagated dynamically up the call chain using control links, it is possible to propagate an exception outside its scope, since static scoping is used. If this happens, the name of the exception is not known in the activation that must handle it, and the exception cannot be named explicitly in an e x c e p t i o n part. However, Ada provides the possibility of a catch-all o t h e r s choice in an exception part, and this will handle even those exceptions that have been propagated beyond their scopes.

Chapter 8

2. (a) $\text{realpart}(x{\cdot}y) = \text{realpart}(x){\cdot}\text{realpart}(y)$
$- \text{imaginarypart}(x){\cdot}\text{imaginarypart}(y)$
$\text{imaginarypart}(x{\cdot}y) = \text{realpart}(x){\cdot}\text{imaginarypart}(y)$
$+ \text{imaginarypart}(x){\cdot}\text{realpart}(y)$

(b) $\text{realpart}(x/y) = (\text{realpart}(x){\cdot}\text{realpart}(y)$
$+ \text{imaginarypart}(x){\cdot}\text{imaginarypart}(y)) \,/\, L$
$\text{imaginarypart}(x/y) = (\text{imaginarypart}(x){\cdot}\text{realpart}(y)$
$- \text{realpart}(x){\cdot}\text{imaginarypart}(y)) \,/\, L$

where $L = \text{realpart}(y)^2 + \text{imaginarypart}(y)^2$.

8. type deque(element) **imports** boolean

operations:
create:	$\rightarrow$ deque
empty:	deque $\rightarrow$ boolean
front:	deque $\rightarrow$ element
rear:	deque $\rightarrow$ element
addfront:	deque X element $\rightarrow$ deque
addrear:	deque X element $\rightarrow$ deque
deletefront:	deque $\rightarrow$ deque
deleterear:	deque $\rightarrow$ deque

variables: q: deque; x: element

axioms:

empty(create) = true
empty(addfront(q,x)) = false
empty(addrear(q,x)) = false
front(create) = error

rear(create) = error
front(addfront(q,x)) = x
front(addrear(q,x)) = if empty(q) then x else front(q)
rear(addrear(q,x)) = x
rear(addfront(q,x)) = if empty(q) then x else rear(q)
deletefront(create) = error
deleterear(create) = error
deletefront(addfront(q,x)) = q
deletefront(addrear(q,x)) = if empty(q) then q else
$$addrear(deletefront(q),x)$$
deleterear(addrear(q,x)) = q
deleterear(addfront(q,x)) = if empty(q) then q else
$$addfront(deleterear(q),x)$$

9. All the arithmetic operations are constructors, as well as the makecomplex operation. The operations realpart and imaginarypart are selectors, both of which are inspectors. There are no destructors or predicates. Thus there are two inspectors and six nondestructive constructors, and so the total number of axioms should be 12.

15. Mathematically, every function has a value that depends only on the value of its parameters (such functions in programs are called **referentially transparent**—see Chapter 10). Thus a function with no parameters that is referentially transparent must always return the same value; that is, it is a constant function. The assumption in algebraic specifications that operations are referentially transparent is problematic for nonfunctional languages because some of the operations may involve memory changes, such as allocation, deallocation, or assignment. For example, in an implementation of a queue, a call to create may allocate and initialize a header record for a queue and return a pointer to this header. Then another call to create will return a different pointer. Similarly, a call to enqueue may not actually return a different value, but return the same pointer, only with an extra element added in memory. This can make the interpretation of the axioms problematic. For example, instead of the queue axiom

dequeue(enqueue(q,x)) = if empty(q) then q else
$$enqueue(dequeue(q),x)$$

we could have written

dequeue(enqueue(q,x)) = if empty(q) then create else
$$enqueue(dequeue(q),x)$$

In this case, the dequeue operation on the left may not actually return the same pointer value as the create operation on the right. The problem is not with the axioms, but with their interpretation in actual implementations. What is needed is a reinterpretation of the equal sign between the two sides of the equations. For example, if empty(q) = true, is q = create? We could say "yes" by simply rewriting the " = " operation to return true whenever two queues are empty, regardless of their actual allocation status. Indeed, in an actual abstract data type implementation, it may be necessary to write new equal and assign operations to cover the anomalies introduced by allocation and assignment.

17. (a) We refer to the six axioms by position 1 through 6 and write the numbers of the axioms used after each equality:

front(enqueue(enqueue(create,x),y))
    = front(enqueue(create,x))   [by (2) and (4)]
    = x   [by (1) and (4)]

19. One possibility is efficiency, particularly with regard to object code reuse. Although, in principle, it would be nice if all instantiations of a generic package could reuse the same code for the package operations, in practice it is difficult to generate code that can handle data with different sizes and behavior, and such code is liable to execute less efficiently than code that is tailored for a particular data type (the reason for developing static data typing in the first place). Thus it is likely that a compiler will generate new code for each instantiation of a generic type. If the instantiation is delayed to the actual declaration of a variable from the package, then the compiler may be forced to generate a new instantiation for each declaration, instead of being able to share code among all instantiations that use the same data type. Another problem is primarily syntactic, but also presents translation difficulties: a STACK is not itself a package in Ada, but is a data type exported by the STACKS package. Thus making the ELEMENT type a parameter to the STACK type makes it unavailable for use by the operations of the package, unless it is also made a parameter to them. Ada's solution is to make ELEMENT a parameter to the whole package, which implies that supplying it cannot be delayed to an actual declaration using the exported STACK type. Alternatively, the designers could have made packages into types (the way tasks are types; see Chapter 13), but this would introduce the problem of dynamically allocating packages (indeed, tasks, which may be types, are not permitted to have parameters).

22. Two possibilities are that dequeue(create) and pop(create) could simply return create instead of error:

dequeue(create) = create

pop(create) = create

Problems arise, however, with the return values of front(create) and top(create). To return an actual value, the imported type **element** must have a distinguished value (perhaps called **nil** or **undefined**) that can become the returned value. This places an added restriction on what data types can be used as elements, something that is difficult to represent in the specification method described in this chapter (Ada does have a way of specifying such restrictions as generic formal subprograms; see the example on page 273). An alternative would be simply to specify these rules with the keyword **undefined** and leave it to the implementor whether this should be an actual error or whether an undefined or distinguished value is returned.

25. The C language has a separate compilation facility. To facilitate this, C has an e x t e r n declaration, which can be used (among other things) to indicate that a variable or function is defined in a separate file (that is, allocated or provided with a function body), and C also has a textual inclusion facility that allows a file to be directly included in another file by giving its name in an # i n c l u d e directive. The use of these facilities has evolved in a direction similar to that of abstract data type interface and implementation parts by putting e x t e r n declarations in a **header file** (with a .h extension) and putting the actual definitions and code in an associated code file (with a .c extension). The data types and operations in the header file can now be made available to another program by including the header file in the program file, and then linking the two code files together. However, C translators make no attempt to check data types, parameters, or correct usage across separately compiled files, so the use of these conventions, while simulating abstract data types, cannot be said to be an actual ADT mechanism, since the conventions are not enforced by the language.

28. No. Consider the picture on page 281. The compilation of either implementation module requires the existence of only the two definition modules, while the circular dependency at link time depends on the imports within both implementation modules.

31. Since the initial algebra is the image of members of the free algebra, every member of the initial algebra can be represented by a series of constructor operations, that is, enqueue, dequeue, and create. Thus every initial algebra member q has the form enqueue(q',x), dequeue(q'), or create, where q' is another initial algebra member. Now consider the number of operations in the representation of the algebra member q, and pick a representation that has the smallest number of operations. We show that this representation must be in canonical form. Suppose not, so that one of the operations is a dequeue operation:

$$q = . . .(\text{dequeue}(. . .)$$

Pick the innermost dequeue operation, so that

$$q = . . .(\text{dequeue}(\text{enqueue}(. . .(\text{enqueue}. . . .)$$

and let q' be the subpart that begins with the dequeue:

$$q' = \text{dequeue}(\text{enqueue}(\text{enqueue}(. . .)))$$

Then by the last axiom of the algebraic specification of the queue ADT, the dequeue can be interchanged with all the enqueue operations except the last:

$$q' = \text{enqueue}(\text{enqueue}(. . .(\text{deque}(\text{enqueue}(\text{create},x)), . . .)))$$

Now by the same rule dequeue(enqueue(create,x)) = create, and

$$q' = \text{enqueue(enqueue(. . .(create), . . .))}$$

Thus the representation of q' has had the number of operations reduced by two, and so q itself has a shorter representation, which is a contradiction to the choice of representation. Thus the shortest representation can contain no dequeue operations and so must be in canonical form.

It remains now to show that the initial and final semantics of a queue are the same. Suppose not, so that two different elements q and q' of the initial algebra are equal in the final algebra. Write q and q' in canonical form. These canonical forms must be different. Suppose they differ for the first time at some interior point:

$$q = \text{enqueue(enqueue(…enqueue(}q1,…)))$$
$$q' = \text{enqueue(enqueue(…enqueue(}q2,…)))$$

with $q1$ = enqueue($q3,x$) and $q2$ = either create or enqueue($q4,y$) with $y \neq x$. In either case we have $q1 \neq q2$ in the final algebra, since front($q1$) = x and front($q2$) = error or y. But then $q \neq q'$ in the final algebra, since each enqueue with the same element must preserve equality (and inequality) in the final algebra. This finishes the proof.

34. The type REAL in Modula-2 does not need to be imported since it is a predefined type (and therefore implicitly "imported" into every module). On the other hand, modules in Modula-2 cannot have parameters, so the type e l e m e n t, which is a parameter in the algebraic specification, must be imported to be available. (In a sense it becomes a "constant parameter" to the module.)

Chapter 9

2. In Chapter 5 an object was defined as an area of storage that is allocated in the environment as a result of the processing of a declaration. In Chapter 9 an object was defined to be an instance of a class that can respond to messages. The primary difference in concept is the passive nature of an object according to the first definition and the active nature of the object according to the second. Thus, in object-oriented languages, objects are viewed as controlling their own internal state, while in ordinary imperative languages, objects are acted upon by operations from "outside." In this view even named constants and values can be viewed as objects in an object-oriented language (as indeed t r u e and f a l s e are objects of class True and False in Smalltalk), while these are not objects in the sense of Chapter 5, since they are not allocated their own space in the environment.

5. An example is the extension of a queue to a deque, given in the chapter. If operations are to be added, access is needed to the internal implementation of a queue, but this makes derived class deque dependent on internal details. If the internal implementation of queue is really hidden from all other classes, then deque must be implemented from scratch.

8. Since x is an object of class A, the fact that x might actually be an object of class B can only be checked during execution. Thus the validity of the call x . m cannot be checked statically. The subtype principle is in fact designed to facilitate static validity checks, and it states the opposite of the situation here, namely, that all the methods of class A are callable for derived object y.

11.   (a) The suggested **protected** mechanism is essentially the same as the C++ protected access specifier, and the suggested **hidden** mechanism is like the private specifier in C++. In C++, however, there is also **private derivation** in that a derived class can inherit as private all protected and public members from a base class, and then selectively make them protected/ public again:

```
class A
{private: int a;
 protected: int b;
 public: int c;};
class B : private A
{protected: A::b;
 ...};
```

In this example b and c become private members of B, and then the access of b is adjusted to protected within B.

(b),(c) Both questions involve increasing the protection of inherited features. As mentioned in the previous exercise, this creates a problem with the subtype principle. (For example, in the previous C++ declarations, public A::c becomes private in B. Now if in a client x is declared to be an A and y to be a B, after the assignment x :- y, should it be possible to access x . c?) Nevertheless, there are circumstances in which one might wish to protect inherited features from use by a client, as in the use of a dequeue to implement a stack. It makes less sense to allow inherited protected features to be made hidden from descendants, since the whole nature of inheritance is to allow for reuse and extension of existing code.

(d) Making a hidden feature protected or public is clearly impossible by the nature of the mechanism. Making a protected feature public is also questionable, and is also unnecessary, at least for methods, since a new public method can be defined that simply calls the protected method.

14. The keyword v i r t u a l is used in Simula in two senses: to create deferred methods whose actual implementation will be specified in a derived class and to apply dynamic binding to methods. This makes the use of dynamic binding somewhat clumsy, in that a method cannot be declared virtual and given an implementation at the same time.

18. If the order of initializations is not made explicit by the creation routine itself, an order must be inferred from the declarations. In the case of single inheritance, this does not present a problem, since there is one path from the current class to the root of the class hierarchy. Usually, initializations are scheduled in reverse order on this path. In the case of multiple inheritance, there may be multiple paths forming a *DAG*, and any schedule would have to represent a topological sort of the *DAG*. One way of scheduling (used by C++) is in left-to-right order of the declared base classes, so that given the *DAG*

the order of initialization would be A, B, A, C, D, and in the case

the order would be A, B, C, D. (Note that in this case A should not be initialized twice.) An alternative solution (Eiffel) is to require that all ancestor initializers be explicitly called.

22. (a) No. It is possible, and even necessary for efficiency, for a compiler to determine when a method is never redefined in a descendant class. Such methods can be made static and called directly, since there is no question of the meaning of such a method during execution. Only methods that are actually redefined in some descendant class need to obey dynamic binding and have their meanings determined at execution time.

(b) There is no specific way to obtain static binding for features that are redefined. (There is a way of *preventing* redefinition, by using the f r o z e n keyword, as in

```
frozen isEqual(y: ...) : BOOLEAN is ...
```

Now i s E q u a l cannot be redefined in a descendant class.)

26. A class method is a method of class C l a s s, and so responds to a message sent to a class viewed as an object of class C l a s s. Thus the message n e w is sent to a class name, as in

```
x <- LinkableObject new
```

29. **(a)** The message `whileTrue` should be sent to a block object (the condition to be evaluated). There are two possible forms, one without parameters and one with: (`B1 whileTrue`) simply evaluates block B1 until it returns false; (`B1 whileTrue: B2`) evaluates B1 and goes on to evaluate B2 if the result of B1 is true. These two methods could be defined as follows in the definition of a Block class:

```
whileTrue
    self value
       ifTrue: (self whileTrue)
       ifFalse: nil
whileTrue: aBlock
    self value
       ifTrue: [aBlock value.
                 self whileTrue: aBlock]
       ifFalse: nil
```

33. **(c)** Here is an Eiffel implementation:

```
class complex
creation
   makeComplex -- a nondefault creation feature
feature {NONE}
    re,im: REAL; -- not exported
feature
    makeComplex (x,y: REAL) is
       do
          re := x;
          im := y
       end; -- makeComplex
    realpart : REAL is
       do Result := re end;
    imaginarypart : REAL is
       do Result := im end;
    infix "+" (y: complex) : complex is
       do
          !!Result.makeComplex(re+y.realpart,
                                im+y.imaginarypart)
       end; -- "+"
    infix "-" (y: complex) : complex is
       do
          !!Result. makeComplex(re-y.realpart,
                                 im-y.imaginarypart)
       end; -- "-"
```

continues

continued

```
        prefix "−" : complex is
          do
            !!Result.makeComplex(−re,−im)
          end; −− "−"
        infix "∗" (y: complex) : complex is
          do
            !!Result.makeComplex(re∗y.realpart−
                                   im∗y.imaginarypart,
                       im∗y.realpart+re∗y.imaginarypart)
          end; −− "∗"
        infix "/" (y: complex) : complex is ...
      end; −−complex
```

34. (b)

```
        template<class T> class linkableObject
        {public:
           T data;
           linkableObject<T>∗ next;
           linkableObject (void) {next = 0;}
           linkableObject (linkableObject<T>∗ link)
             {next = link;}
        };

        template<class T> class queue
        {protected:
           linkableObject<T>∗ rear;
         public:
           queue (void) {rear = 0;}
           int empty (void) {return rear == 0;}
           void enqueue (T item);
           void dequeue (void);
           T front(void) {return (rear->next->data);}
           ~queue(void);
        };
```

36. (a) C++

```
        class gcd
        {private:
           int x,y;
         public:
           gcd(int u, int v)
             {x = u; y = v;}
           int value(void)
             {if (y==0) return x;
              else
```

```
            {gcd t(y,x % y);
              return t.value();}
         }
    };
```

(b) Eiffel

```
class gcd
creation make
feature {NONE}
  x,y: INTEGER;
feature
  make (u,v: INTEGER) is
     do
        x := u;
        y := v;
     end; -- make
   value : INTEGER is
     local t: gcd
     do
        if x = 0 then
          Result := y
        else
          !!t.make(y,x \\ y);
               -- \\ is mod in Eiffel
          Result := t.value;
        end
     end -- value
end -- class gcd
```

(c) Smalltalk

```
Class name: Gcd

Superclass: Object
Instance variables: x,y

Methods:
    make: u with: v
        x <- u.
        y <- v
    value
      | t |
      y == 0
      ifTrue: [↑ x]
      ifFalse: [t <- Gcd new.
               t make: y with: (x rem: y).
               ↑ t value]
```

39. There may be no virtual methods at all, and so always having a VMT pointer at the beginning of the allocated space is wasteful and unnecessary. In the diagrams, space for the VMT was allocated only when a virtual function declaration was encountered.

43. The problem is that indirect references to objects of the unspecified parameter must be used, since local allocation cannot occur. Thus every use of an object of the parameter class must be replaced by an indirect reference. In Eiffel and Simula objects of classes are always references anyway (except for Eiffel's expanded classes), so this requires no extra work. In C++, however, arbitrary classes are not pointers, so the compiler must provide the indirection.

Chapter 10

2.

```
PROCEDURE ReadMax1 (maxsofar,x: INTEGER) :
                                             INTEGER;
BEGIN
  IF x = 0 THEN RETURN maxsofar;
  ELSE
    IF x > maxsofar
    THEN maxsofar := x;
    END;
    ReadInt(x); WriteLn;
    RETURN ReadMax1(maxsofar,x);
  END;
END ReadMax1;

PROCEDURE ReadMax (): INTEGER;
VAR x: INTEGER;
BEGIN
  ReadInt(x); WriteLn;
  IF x = 0 THEN (* do nothing *)
  ELSE
    RETURN ReadMax1(x,x);
  END;
END ReadMax;
```

5. In Pascal,
   (a)

```
function B(n,k: integer): integer;
var t,i: integer;
begin
```

```
      if (n >= 0) and (k >= 0) and (n >= k) then
      begin
        t := 1;
        for i := 1 to k do
          t := t * (n-i+1) div i; (* exact division
                                              here *)
        B := t;
      end else B := 0; (* actually undefined
                                              here *)
  end;
```

(b)

```
  function B(n,k: integer): integer;
  begin
    if (n >= 0) and (k >= 0) and (n >= k) then
      if (k = 0) or (k = n) then B := 1
      else B := B(n-1,k-1)+B(n-1,k)
    else B := 0; (* actually undefined here *)
  end;
```

(c) If we use a global array to keep precomputed values of the function, we can reduce the number of calls significantly, since the recursive equation repeats certain calls (B(10,5) saves 16 calls):

```
  var Memo: array [0..20,0..20] of integer;
      (* only up to 20 *)
  function B(n,k: integer): integer;
  begin
    if (n >= 0) and (k >= 0) and (n >= k) then
      if (k = 0) or (k = n) then begin
        B := 1;
        Memo[n,k] := 1;
      end else if Memo[n,k] > 0 then
        B := Memo[n,k]
      else begin
        Memo[n,k] := B(n-1,k-1)+B(n-1,k);
        B := Memo[n,k];
      end
    else B := 0; (* actually undefined here *)
  end;
```

6. No. A function that is referentially transparent has a value that depends only on the value of its parameters. A function that has no side effects makes no change to memory or program state. It is possible for a function to make no changes to memory and still not be referentially transparent. For example, any function whose value depends on the value of a non-local variable is not referentially transparent, as in the following code:

```
program refex;

var x: integer;

function p(y: integer): integer;
begin
  p := x + y;
end;

begin
  x := 1;
  writeln(p(2));
  x := 3;
  writeln(p(2));
end.
```

If p were referentially transparent in the foregoing code, the same value should be printed twice. In fact, the program prints 3 and 5.

Similarly, a function can make changes to memory and still be referentially transparent, as in the following code:

```
program refex2;
var x : integer;

function q;
begin
  x := x+1;
  q := 0;
end;
begin
  . . .
end.
```

The function q changes x, but its value is always 0, regardless of the context from which it is called. (A referentially transparent function with no parameters is a constant function; that is, it always returns the same value.)

7. (c)

Scheme:

```
(define (collect)
  (let ((n (read)))
       (if (= n 0) ()
           (cons n (collect))))))
```

ML:

```
fun collect {} =
    let val n = getint (std_in)
      in
        if n = 0 then nil
        else n :: collect{};
      end;
```

Miranda:

```
collect = collectlist $+
```

|| $+ is the standard input stream

```
collectlist m = [ ], if hd m = 0
              = (hd m): (collectlist (tl m)),
                otherwise
```

j)

Scheme:

```
(define (twice f) (lambda (x) (f (f x))))
```

ML:

```
fun twice f n = f (f n);
```

Miranda:

```
twice f n = f (f n)
```

The function (twice (twice sqr)) is the function that computes the sixteenth power of its argument.

13.

```
(define (deep-reverse L)
        (cond ((null? L) ())
              ((atom? L) L)
              (T (append (deep-reverse (cdr L))
                 (list (deep-reverse (car L)))))))
```

19. (a) ((lambda (x y) E) 2 3)
  (b) No. The let evaluates all its bindings in the scope surrounding the let, as the foregoing interpretation of the let as a lambda shows. To allow letrec to handle recursive references within its

bindings, these bindings must be evaluated within the scope of the
l e t r e c itself; that is, the names established in the binding list are
assumed to already have meanings. This is impossible to imitate in
a function call unless delayed evaluation is used *and* the arguments
are evaluated using dynamic scope (this was called pass by text in
Exercise 19 of Chapter 7). Since Scheme does not use this evaluation rule (on either count), l e t r e c cannot be imitated by a
lambda.

(c) The value of b uses the value of a, which has not yet been bound.
(It would be legal if a had a value in the surrounding scope, but
this might not be what the user intended.)

(d) If a l e t could be interpreted as equivalent to a cascade of l e t s,
then this would be legal. For example, if the given l e t were equivalent to

```
(let ((a 2))
    (let ((b (+ 1 a)))
        ...))
```

then all would be well. Given the equivalence in part (a), this
would be equivalent to saying that lambda expressions are fully
curried. But this is not true (see Exercise 23).

23. **(a)** The following attempt will produce an error in Scheme:

```
(define (add x y) (+ x y))
> add
(add 2)
> #Error: not enough arguments to proc add
```

(b)

```
(define (curry f)
   (lambda (n) (lambda (m) (f n m))))
```

27. **(a)**

```
allsquares = [n | n <- [0..] ; issquare n]

where

issquare n = n = sqr (entier (sqrt x + 0.5))
sqr x = x * x
```

30. The problem is the ML f a c t function is written using an else-clause,
and the else-clause causes an infinite recursive regress. Clearly, it is
beyond the scope of a translator to know when a recursive call will never
return. On the other hand, given the Miranda definition (with guards),

```
fact n = 1, if n = 0
       n * fact (n−1), if n > 0
```

it is possible for a translator to realize that this is only a partial function, undefined for n < 0. In the case of ML, we can use an exception to indicate the partialness of f a c t :

```
fun fact n = if n < 0 then raise fact
             else if n = 0 then 1
                  else n * fact (n−1);
```

34.

```
(define (even? n) (= (remainder n 2) 0))
(define (intlist n) (cons n (delay (intlist
                                     (+ 1 n)))))
(define (evens L)
        (let ((a (car (force L))))
          (if (even? a)
              (delay (cons a (evens (cdr
                                      (force L)))))
              (evens (cdr (force L))))))
```

These two procedures can be put together as follows:

```
(take 10 (evens (delay (intlist 2))))
```

41. A lambda expression for the twice functions is $\lambda f.\lambda x.f\ (f\ x)$. Thus twice (twice sqr) has the following expression:

$$(\lambda f.\lambda x.f\ (f\ x))\ ((\lambda f.\lambda x.f\ (f\ x))\ (\lambda x.\ \cdot\ x\ x))$$

We reduce this stepwise in the following, using sqr to represent the sqr function:

Normal Order:

$$(\lambda f.\lambda x.f\ (f\ x))\ ((\lambda f.\lambda x.f\ (f\ x))\ sqr)\ =$$
$$(\lambda x.[(\lambda f.\lambda x.f\ (f\ x))\ sqr]([(\lambda f.\lambda x.f\ (f\ x))\ sqr]\ x)\ =$$
$$(\lambda x.(\lambda x.sqr\ (sqr\ x))((\lambda x.sqr\ (sqr\ x))\ x)\ =$$
$$(\lambda x.(sqr\ (sqr\ ((\lambda x.sqr\ (sqr\ x))\ x))))\ =$$
$$(\lambda x.(sqr\ (sqr\ (sqr\ (sqr\ x)))))$$

Applicative Order:

$$(\lambda f.\lambda x.f\ (f\ x))\ ((\lambda f.\lambda x.f\ (f\ x))\ sqr)\ =$$
$$(\lambda f.\lambda x.f\ (f\ x))\ (\lambda x.sqr\ (sqr\ x))\ =$$
$$(\lambda x.(\lambda x.sqr\ (sqr\ x))((\lambda x.sqr\ (sqr\ x))\ x))\ =$$
$$(\lambda x.(\lambda x.sqr\ (sqr\ x))(sqr\ (sqr\ x)))\ =$$
$$(\lambda x.(sqr\ (sqr\ (sqr\ (sqr\ x)))))$$

45. Since H = (λF.λn. (if (n=0) 1 ($\cdot$ n (F ($-$ n 1))))) and H fact = fact, we have

fact 1 = (H fact) 1 =
    [(λF.λn.(if (n=0) 1 ($\cdot$ n (F ($-$ n 1))))) fact] 1 =
    [λn.(if (n=0) 1 ($\cdot$ n (fact ($-$ n 1))))] 1 =
    (if (1=0) 1 ($\cdot$ 1 (fact ($-$ 1 1)))) = ($\cdot$ 1 (fact 0)) =
    ($\cdot$ 1 ((H fact) 0)) =
    ($\cdot$ 1 ([(λF.λn. (if (n=0) 1 ($\cdot$ n (F ($-$ n 1))))) fact] 0)) =
    ($\cdot$ 1 ([λn.(if (n=0) 1 ($\cdot$ n (fact ($-$ n 1))))] 0)) =
    ($\cdot$ 1 (if (0=0) 1 ($\cdot$ n (fact ($-$ 0 1))))) =
    ($\cdot$ 1 1) = 1

49. Since the unused half of available memory is immediately available for allocation, blocks in the used half of memory that are reached during garbage collection can be immediately moved to the unused half of memory on a first-come basis (we must maintain a pointer to the first unused location of the unused half as this process proceeds). The pointer that was used to reach the block currently being moved can then be updated to the new location. The remaining problem is when a previously moved block is again encountered during the further search for accessible blocks. The garbage collector must discover that the block has already been moved, and where its new location is. This can be done by storing a marker and reference pointer right in the memory of the block after it has been copied. This takes up no extra room, since the memory has already been copied. (Of course, the marker must be distinguishable from any actual data that may occur at its location in the block.)

Chapter 11

3. We show $a \rightarrow$ false is logically equivalent to not(a) using a truth table. By Exercise 1, $a \rightarrow$ false is false if a is true, and true if a is false, so we have

a	not a	a → false
T	F	F
F	T	T

The equivalence follows.

7. As we mentioned in the answer to Exercise 13 of Chapter 2, the definition of the gcd is not an algorithm, so we must supply an order for the tests to be performed. We do this as in the solution to the previous exercise by working backward through the integers $1 <= n <= \min(u,v)$. For simplicity, we also use the property that the largest number in that range that divides both u and v is in fact the gcd:

```
gcd(U,V,X) :- min(U,V,M),
                greatestdivisor(U,V,M,X).
greatestdivisor(U,V,M,M) :- divides(U,M),
                              divides(V,M),
                              !.
greatestdivisor(U,V,M,X) :
          - N is M-1, greatestdivisor(U,V,N,X).
min(U,V,U) :- U < V.
min(U,V,V) :- U >= V.
divides(U,M) :- N is U mod M, N = 0 .
```

This implementation has linear time in the size of $\min(u,v)$, but it is still much less efficient than Euclid's algorithm (which has logarithmic time complexity).

11.

```
last([X],X).
last([X|Y],Z) :- not(Y = []), last(Y,Z).
```

14. The following solution uses append as defined on page 440:

```
merge([],X,X).
merge(X,[],X).
merge([X|Y],[Z|W],[X|V]) :-
          X < Z,
          merge(Y,[Z|W],V).
merge([X|Y],[Z|W],[Z|V]) :-
          X >= Z,
          merge([X|Y],W,V).
mergesort([],[]) :-!.
mergesort([X],[X]) :-!.
mergesort(X,Y) :-
          split(X,U,V),
          mergesort(U,W),
          mergesort(V,Z),
          merge(W,Z,Y).
split(X,U,V) :-
          size(X,N),
          M is N // 2, /* // = div */
          take(M,X,U),
          append(U,V,X).
size([],0).
size([X|Y],N) :-
          size(Y,M),
          N is M+1 .
take(0,X,[]).                    continues
```

continued

```
take(N,[X|Y],[X|Z]) :-
        N > 0,
        M is N-1,
        take(M,Y,Z).
```

17. Since control is expressed by backtracking in Prolog, without the cut it is possible that further alternatives remain to be computed and that the attempt to satisfy the last goal will not be the last computation performed. With the cut, however, the runtime system can throw away any alternatives and maintain a strictly linear (or stacklike) structure in its search to satisfy future goals. The attempt to satisfy the last goal can indeed be viewed as a tail-recursive call, since after it returns no further computation is made.

21. The solution for the factorial function is

```
fact(N,M) :- fact1(N,M,1).
fact1(0,SoFar,SoFar).
fact1(N,M,SoFar) :-
                N > 0,
                X is N-1,
                Y is N * SoFar,
                !,
                fact1(X,M,Y).
```

24. Consider the search tree as pictured on page 441. The cut applies to rule 2, which is only used to produce the rightmost branch from the root. Thus the cut is encountered only at the end of the search and therefore eliminates none of the search paths. Indeed, since the cut is in the last defining clause for ancestor, there will never be a case in which this cut will make the search for the first solution more efficient (although it will prevent a further search for more solutions). To improve the efficiency, the second rule should be written first rather than trying to use a cut.

27. The difference is caused by Prolog's treatment of not(X=Y). If X and Y are not both already instantiated when this goal is reached, the goal will succeed by unifying X and Y, and so the goal not(X=Y) will fail, thus causing the sibling1 goal to fail. This means that sibling1 is only useful for testing the sibling relationship for two already instantiated variables. On the other hand, sibling2 may also be used to find sibling pairs, since X and Y can be instantiated by the parent subgoals before reaching the not(X=Y). Thus sibling2 has more general application and therefore is better.

31. The goal not(human(X)) is interpreted as the failure of the goal human(X). But since X is not instantiated, human(X) will succeed if there are any humans at all, and so not(human(X)) will fail.

34. In the lambda calculus, variables are bound by being attached to a lambda symbol, and in logic, variables are bound by being attached to existential ("there exists") and universal ("for all") quantifiers. In a purely syntactic sense, then, they are equivalent notions, although lambda calculus is "simpler" in that it has only one symbol that binds variables, while "standard" logic (i.e., first-order predicate calculus) has two. In a slightly more semantic sense, the universal quantifier of logic is more suggestive of the role of the lambda in lambda calculus, in that, given a universal quantifier, a particular substitution for the bound variable can occur. For example, given the statement "for all x in S $p(x)$ is true," one can substitute a particular s from S for x to get the true statement $p(s)$, which is suggestive of beta-reduction (i.e., function application) in lambda calculus. The existential quantifier is less similar in behavior to any operation in the lambda calculus.

38. The point being made is that Prolog provides the control through the implementation algorithms, particularly the versions of resolution and unification algorithms that are implemented by the system. The programmer has no way of affecting the way the system responds to particular programs, so that the only way to change behavior is to change the logic of the program. However, Prolog does in fact provide some limited control mechanisms in two ways. First, the cut allows the user to change the control the system has over backtracking. Second, the deterministic nature of the search of the database in Prolog—usually sequential— allows the programmer to affect the control by rearranging the order of the program clauses. Neither of these is really a change in the logic of the program.

Chapter 12

1. The keywords f i and o d are necessary tokens for the parser to determine what statements are contained within the statement block and to disambiguate the dangling else problem. Thus they represent "concrete" syntax used to construct the syntax tree. If we are interested only in abstract syntax, that is, we assume that the syntax tree has already been constructed, then these tokens are unnecessary, and the semantics of a language can be specified without regard to the precise concrete syntax used to express the structure of the syntax tree.

4. This question is about the difference between strings as they are constructed by the syntax rules for identifiers and the identifiers themselves. This is similar to the distinction between '0' and 0, and we will write 'a' for the character and a for the identifier. We also write $id + a$ for the identifier id with the letter a appended. The reduction rules for identifiers are as follows:

$$‘a’ => a$$
$$‘b’ => b$$
$$\cdots$$
$$‘z’ => z$$

$$id\ ‘a’ => id + a$$
$$id\ ‘b’ => id + b$$
$$\cdots$$
$$id\ ‘z’ => id + z$$

Now our use of I in the operational semantics should be changed to id to refer to identifiers constructed by the given reduction rules rather than strings representing the syntactic representation of identifiers. (Perhaps even better would be to use IV, for identifier value, instead of id, just as reduced numbers were indicated by V.) There is one more inference rule needed that allows for the reduction of a string to an identifier on the left of an assignment:

$$\frac{<I := E \mid Env>,\ I => id}{<id := E \mid Env>}$$

8. Even if we make numbers and identifiers into tokens, if a scanner just produces the token and does not save the actual string representing an identifier (or the value of a number), then the necessary information to determine the meaning of the identifier or number will be lost. Thus the scanner cannot escape making these semantic constructions unless we decide to make each character of an identifier or number into a token, and this would be hopelessly inefficient. Indeed, the actual semantic content of the construction of the name of an identifier, or the value of a number, is relatively trivial, and, once we have understood the distinction between syntax and semantics, there is a practical advantage to ignoring these scanner constructions in the formal semantics as well (the complexity of the specification is reduced). See Exercises 4 and 5.

12. We sketch the reductions, listing the number(s) of the rules used in each reduction on the right:

$$a := 2;\ b := a + 1;\ a := b \cdot b$$
$$=> \quad <a := 2;\ b := a + 1;\ a := b \cdot b \mid Env_0> \qquad (19)$$
$$=> \quad <b := a + 1;\ a := b \cdot b \mid \{a = 2\}> \qquad (16, 18)$$
$$=> \quad <a := b \cdot b \mid \{a = 2, b = 3\}> \qquad (15, 7, 3, 17, 16, 18)$$
$$=> \quad \{a = 9, b = 3\} \qquad (15, 9, 5, 17, 16)$$

15. Label the statements of the program as follows:

```
S1:  a  := 0-11;
S2:  if a then a := a else a := 0-a fi
```

Then we have

$P[[P]](a) = L[[L]](Env_0)(a) = L[[S1;S2]](Env_0)(a) =$
$(L[[S2]]{\circ}L\,[[S1]])(Env_0)(a) = (L[[S2]](L[[S1]](Env_0))(a) =$
$S[[S2]](S[[S1]](Env_0))(a) = (S[[S2]](S[[a:=0-11]](Env_0))(a) =$
$(S[[S2]](Env_0\&\{a=E[[0-11]](Env_0)\}))(a) =$
$(S[[S2]](Env_0\&\{a=(E[[0]](Env_0)-E[[11]](Env_0))\}))(a) =$
$(S[[S2]](Env_0\&\{a=(N[[0]]-N[[11]])\}))(a) =$
$(S[[S2]](Env_0\&\{a=(D[[0]]-(10{\cdot}N[[1]]+N[[1]])\})))(a) =$
$(S[[S2]](Env_0\&\{a=(0-(10{\cdot}D[[1]]+D[[1]])\})))(a) =$
$(S[[S2]](Env_0\&\{a=(0-(10{\cdot}1+1))\}))(a) =$
$(S[[S2]](Env_0\&\{a=(0-11)\}))(a) =$
$(S[[S2]](Env_0\&\{a=-11\}))(a) =$
$(S[[S2]](\{a=-11\}))(a) =$
$(S[[\text{if a then a}:=\text{a else a}:=0-a\text{ fi}]](\{a=-11\}))(a) =$
$(L[[a:=0-a]](\{a=-11\}))(a) =$
$(S[[a:=0-a]](\{a=-11\}))(a) =$
$(\{a=-11\}\&\{a=E[[0-a]](\{a=-11\})\})(a) =$
$(\{a=-11\}\&\{a=(E[[0]](\{a=-11\})-E[[a]](\{a=-11\})\})(a) =$
$(\{a=-11\}\&\{a=0-(-11)\})(a) = (\{a=-11\}\&\{a=11\})(a) =$
$(\{a=11\})(a) = 11$

19. $wp(\,a:=2\,;\quad b:=a+1\,;\quad a:=b*b,\ a=9) =$
    $wp(a:=2\,;\quad b:=a+1,\ 9=b*b) =$

    $wp(a:=2\,;\quad b:=a+1,\ b=3\text{ or }b=-3) =$
    $wp(a:=2,\ a+1=3\text{ or }a+1=-3) =$

    $wp(a:=2,\ a=2\text{ or }a=-4) = (2=2)\text{ or }(2=-4) = \text{true}.$

22. (a) and (b) are not invariant; (c) is invariant.

25. sorted(a) = for all i, $1\le i\le n-1$, $a[i]\le a[i+1]$
    permutation(a,A) =
          there exists a function $f:\{1,\ldots,n\}\to\{1,\ldots,n\}$
          such that for all i,j, $1\le i<j\le n$, $f(i)\ne f(j)$
          and such that for all i, $1\le i\le n$, $a[i] = A[f(i)]$.

28. By the distributivity of conjunction and the law of the excluded miracle,
    $wp(S,Q)$ and $wp(S,\text{not }Q) = wp(S,Q\text{ and not }Q) = wp(S,F) = F$.
    Negating, we get

    not$(wp(S,Q)$ and $wp(S,\text{not }Q)) =$ not $wp(S,Q)$ or not $wp(S,\text{not }Q)$
                                            $= T$

    By the equivalence of $P\to Q$ with $(Q$ or not $P)$, this says that $wp(S,\text{not } Q)\to$ not $wp(S,Q)$.

31. We could define $0\cdot\text{anything} = 0$, meaning that if the first operand is 0, the second may be undefined, and the result is still 0. Similarly, we could also define anything $\cdot\,0 = 0$. (Notice that for both these definitions to hold, the computation must be nondeterministic.)

33. In a typical semantic definition, identifiers have undefined values until they are assigned a value. If we wanted to eliminate u n d e f as a value,

we could try to initialize all variables to 0. This will work as long as the result of all operations in the language are defined for all values. In the sample small language of this chapter, there is no division, so this approach would work in this case. In a more realistic language, however, division by zero will result in an undefined value (or possibly a "halt"), and the definition of the environment must allow for this to happen.

37. **(a)** Here are two rules for the if-statement:

$$\frac{<E|Env> => <V|Env>, \ V > 0}{<\text{'if' } E \text{ 'then' } L_1 \text{ 'else' } L_2 \text{ 'fi' } | \ Env> \ => \ <L_1 | \ Env>}$$

$$\frac{<E|Env> => <V|Env>, \ V \le 0}{<\text{'if' } E \text{ 'then' } L_1 \text{ 'else' } L_2 \text{ 'fi' } | \ Env> \ => \ <L_2 | \ Env>}$$

(b) One might be tempted to try to rewrite the "while" rules as three rules like the original "if" rules, including a general condition reduction similar to rule 20. But this is incorrect, since this would imply that the condition of the "while" is evaluated only once, whereas it must be reevaluated if it evaluates to a $V > 0$.

Chapter 13

1. A coroutine is like a process in that it executes in an independent manner. Unlike a process, however, it cannot be executed simultaneously with other coroutines, and it retains control until it explicitly transfers control to another coroutine.

4. To sum n integers using k processors, with $k < n$, we could divide the n integers into k groups and assign each processor to sum a group in parallel. Then assign one processor to sum the sums of the k groups. This takes approximately n div $k + k$ steps, which is less than n if $2 \le k \le n$ div 2. A better method is to use the so-called **binary fan-in** technique, where n div 2 processors are assigned the task of adding two adjacent numbers (the ith processor adds the $2i$th and $(2i + 1)$th number) in parallel. Then the results of these additions are added two at a time by n div 4 processors (these can be some of the same processors that performed the first set of additions). The cascade continues until there is only a single value, which is the sum of all the integers. This computes the sum in $\log_2(n)$ time using at most n processors (even if each level is scheduled on different processors). This is the best speedup that can be achieved on standard kinds of machines, so there is no advantage to using more than n processors. See, for example, Baase [1988], Chapter 10.

7. There is confusion between the use of the term fork-join to describe the creation of satellite processes that execute different code (MPMD) and the use of fork and join calls in Unix, where a forked process continues to exit (a copy of) the same code.

10. **(a)** The following Modula-2 solution uses a "buffer" of printers, a binary semaphore to provide mutually exclusive buffer access, and a counting semaphore to determine availability of a printer. The code for ReleasePrinter also tests for the release of an already-free printer, but it cannot keep track of which process owns a particular printer (so it is possible for a process to release a printer it hasn't acquired). To solve this problem, we would need to introduce a process identifier mechanism and attach to each acquired printer the identifier of the process that acquired it. (Similar comments hold for the other sections of this problem.)

```
DEFINITION MODULE Printers;
FROM ... IMPORT PrinterType;
(* PrinterType assumed defined elsewhere -it
        may be a device name or memory address *)
PROCEDURE AcquirePrinter(VAR Printer:
                                    PrinterType);
PROCEDURE ReleasePrinter(VAR Printer:
                                    PrinterType);
END Printers.

IMPLEMENTATION MODULE Printers;
FROM ... IMPORT PrinterType;
FROM SemProcs IMPORT Semaphore, InitSem,
                            Signal, Wait;
CONST NoPrinters = 3;
VAR Available,MutEx: Semaphore;
    PrinterBuffer: ARRAY[1..NoPrinters] OF
                                    PrinterType;
    NextPrinter,LastPrinter: INTEGER;

PROCEDURE AcquirePrinter(VAR Printer:
                                    PrinterType);
BEGIN
  Wait(Available);
  Wait(MutEx);
  Printer := PrinterBuffer[NextPrinter];
  NextPrinter := NextPrinter MOD NoPrinters + 1;
  Signal(MutEx);
END AcquirePrinter;

PROCEDURE InUse(Printer: PrinterType): BOOLEAN;
VAR I: INTEGER;
BEGIN
  FOR I := NextPrinter TO
```

continues

continued

```
            LastPrinter+NoPrinters DO
              IF PrinterBuffer[I MOD NoPrinters] = Printer
              THEN
                RETURN FALSE;
              END;
            END; (* for *)
            RETURN TRUE;
          END InUse;

          PROCEDURE ReleasePrinter(VAR Printer:
                                              PrinterType);
          BEGIN
            IF NOT InUse(Printer) THEN
              RETURN;
            END;
            Wait(MutEx);
            LastPrinter := LastPrinter MOD NoPrinters + 1;
            PrinterBuffer[LastPrinter] := Printer;
            Signal(MutEx);
            Signal(Available);
            Printer := (* a null value *);
          END ReleasePrinter;


          BEGIN (* initializations *)
            InitSem(Available,NoPrinters);
            InitSem(MutEx,1);
            NextPrinter := 1; LastPrinter := NoPrinters;
            . . .
            (* Initialization of PrinterBuffer *)
            . . .
          END Printers.
```

(b)

```
          type Printers = monitor;
          const NoPrinters= 3;
          var
          (* PrinterType assumed defined elsewhere — it
                may be a device name or memory address *)
            PrinterBuffer: array[1..NoPrinters] of
                                              PrinterType;
            NextPrinter,LastPrinter,Count: integer;
            requester: queue;

          procedure entry AcquirePrinter(var Printer:
                                              PrinterType);
```

```
begin
  if Count = 0 then delay(requester);
  Printer := PrinterBuffer[NextPrinter];
  NextPrinter := NextPrinter mod NoPrinters + 1;
  Count := Count −1;
  continue(requester);
end ;

function InUse(Printer: PrinterType) : boolean;
var i: integer;
begin
  InUse := true;
  for i := NextPrinter to
                        LastPrinter +NoPrinters
  do
    if PrinterBuffer[I mod NoPrinters] = Printer
    then InUse := false;
end ;


procedure entry ReleasePrinter(var Printer:
                                    PrinterType);
begin
  if InUse(Printer) then begin
    LastPrinter :=
                  LastPrinter mod NoPrinters + 1;
    PrinterBuffer[LastPrinter] := Printer;
    Printer := (* a null value *);
    Count := Count + 1;
  end;
end ;

begin (* initializations *)
  NextPrinter := 1; LastPrinter := NoPrinters;
  Count := NoPrinters;
  . . .
  (* Initialization of PrinterBuffer *)
  . . .
end
```

(c) CSP requires that the printer allocator know the names of the processes that will be requesting a printer, so in the following program we can actually test accurately for the validity of a printer release. As before, we note that CSP is not a complete language, so we use Pascal-like syntax when necessary and ignore programming niceties. We assume an array P of 100 processes that can request a printer.

```
printers ::
     assigned: (1..100) printertype;
     printerbuffer: (1..3) printertype;
     nextprinter,lastprinter,count: integer;
     nextprinter := 1;
     lastprinter := 3;
     count := 3;
        ...
     (* initialization of printerbuffer to
        available printers and assigned to
                            null printer values *)
        ...
     *[(i:1..100) count > 0;
          P(i)?aquireprinter() ->
          P(i)!printerbuffer(nextprinter);
          assigned(i) :=
                    printerbuffer(nextprinter);
          nextprinter :=
                         nextprinter mod 3 + 1;
          count := count - 1
     || (i:1..100) printer: printertype;
        P(i)?printer ->
          [assigned(i) = printer ->
             lastprinter :=
                         lastprinter mod 3 + 1;
             printerbuffer(lastprinter) :=
                                     printer;
             assigned(i) := ... ;  (* a null
                                     value *)
             count := count + 1
          ]
     ]
```

(d)

```
task Printers is
--PrinterType assumed defined elsewhere - it
--may be a device name or memory address
entry AcquirePrinter(Printer: out PrinterType);
entry ReleasePrinter(Printer: in out
                                  PrinterType);
end;
task body Printers is
  NoPrinters: constant INTEGER := 3;
  PrinterBuffer: array(1..NoPrinters) of
                                  PrinterType
          := (...); -- initialization
  NextPrinter: INTEGER := 1;
```

```
      LastPrinter: INTEGER := NoPrinters;
      Count: INTEGER := NoPrinters;
      tempPrinter: PrinterType;
      function InUse(Printer: in PrinterType)
                                    return BOOLEAN is
    begin
      for i in NextPrinter..LastPrinter+NoPrinters

      loop
        if PrinterBuffer(i mod NoPrinters) =
                                        Printer
        then
          return FALSE;
        end if;
      end loop;
      return TRUE;
    end InUse;
  begin
    loop
      select
        when Count > 0 =>
          accept AcquirePrinter(Printer: out
                                PrinterType)
          do
            Printer := PrinterBuffer(NextPrinter);
          end;
          NextPrinter :=
                  NextPrinter mod NoPrinters + 1;
          Count := Count - 1;
        or
          accept ReleasePrinter(Printer: in out
                                PrinterType)
          do
            tempPrinter := Printer;
            Printer := ...; -- a null value
          end;
          if InUse(tempPrinter) then
            LastPrinter :=
                  LastPrinter mod NoPrinters + 1;
            PrinterBuffer(LastPrinter) :=
                                    tempPrinter;
            Count := Count + 1;
          end if;
        or terminate;
      end select;
    end loop;
  end Printers;
```

16. No. When a process forks in Unix a copy is made of all allocated memory, including dynamically allocated pointers. The pointers refer to memory local to each forked process only. (This is facilitated by the fact that all pointers are relative to the starting address of memory allocated to each process.)

19. The code of Figure 13.8 has each process choosing the row it works on dynamically as computation proceeds, so faster processes can compensate for slower ones. The code of Figure 13.4, on the other hand, allocates the work evenly to all processes at the beginning, so if one process is slower, it will hold up the entire program. Thus we expect the Figure 13.8 program to work faster if processes are scheduled on different processors, some of which are faster than others, or if processes may be suspended by the system for any reason. In particular, if there are more processes than processors, the program of Figure 13.8 should run faster, since those processes that do get assigned processors will get to do as much work as they can before they are suspended. However, in a system where all processes can be scheduled on separate processors operating at the same speed, then the program of Figure 13.4 will run faster because there is no need for synchronization during the computation and its associated overhead. In particular, the program of Figure 13.4 is preferable for SPMD systems.

23. Not really. Initializing a counting semaphore to a negative value means that a number of processes will need to call Signal before any process can be unblocked from a call to Wait. This does not make sense either for mutual exclusion or for access to resources.

30. The question is whether i can be safely incremented after the calling process is allowed to continue. Such a process is signaling that it is releasing a resource or leaving a critical section, so it can continue without waiting for i to be incremented. Processes that are waiting for the semaphore will still wait for i to be incremented, so no error can result.

35. If the consumer?more() test is not there, then the guard for sending a character to the consumer will succeed, and whenever the buffer is not empty, it will block waiting for the consumer to respond to the output command consumer!store(bufferstart). This means that the buffer will not process new incoming characters from the producer, and the producer will block waiting for the buffer to respond. Now both the buffer and the producer are waiting for action from the consumer. This is contrary to the intended behavior of the buffer, which should only block if the buffer is full. Indeed, if the buffer always waits for the consumer to request a character when it is nonempty, it will tend to behave like a one-character buffer, that is, not a buffer at all.

38. In CSP a semaphore needs to know the names of the processes that will be using it. An example in Hoare [1978] implements a counting semaphore S shared among an array P(i:1..100) of processes as follows:

```
S:: count: integer;
    count:= 0;
    *[(i:1..100) P(i)?signal()
                            -> count := count + 1 ||
      (i:1..100) count > 0; P(i)?wait()
                            -> count := count - 1]
```

41. The accept statement is within the scope of the parameters of the entry. Since some of the parameters may be out parameters, these can be assigned at any time during the accept statement, and the caller cannot resume execution until the values of all the out parameters are specified.

44. A task cannot automatically be terminated before it completes its processing, even if the end of its scope in its parent task is reached. For example, in the matrix multiplication of Figure 13.16 (or the solution to Exercise 50 that follows), the ParMult procedure must wait for the completion of the Mult tasks, since the result will not be available until all these tasks finish. On the other hand, it would be possible to write specific synchronizing statements (entry calls) that would force a parent to wait for such completion. The designers probably considered that explicitly writing these synchronizing statements was likely to be forgotten by programmers. The alternative is that child processes that loop indefinitely must be explicitly terminated by a terminate statement in a select alternative, or the parent process will suspend indefinitely when it reaches the end of that child's scope. Thus the designers have opted for indefinite suspension as a less serious error than abrupt termination.

47. This Ada code is actually closer to the pseudocode description of the operation of Signal and Wait in Section 13.4. It will execute slightly more efficiently than the original code, since the original code will always increment count when accepting a Signal, only to have it immediately decremented again if a process is suspended on Wait. However, this code is also slightly more complex. Nevertheless, its closer approximation to the definition and its slightly improved speed make it preferable to the original code.

50. The following program uses dynamic scheduling of row computations as found in Figure 13.8. An alternative strategy is the fixed partitioning of row computations of Figure 13.4. See Exercise 19.

```
generic Size: INTEGER;
package IntMatrices is
    type IntMatrix is array (1..Size,1..Size) OF
                                            INTEGER;
    function ParMult(a,b: in IntMatrix;
            numProcs: in INTEGER)
                                return IntMatrix;
                                            continues
```

continued

```
      end;
      package body IntMatrices is
        function ParMult(a,b: in IntMatrix;
                                   numProcs: in INTEGER)
                                   return IntMatrix is

    c: IntMatrix;
    nextRow: INTEGER := 1;

    task Semaphore is
      entry Signal;
      entry Wait;
    end;
    task body Semaphore is
      acquired: BOOLEAN := FALSE;
    begin
      loop
        select
          when not acquired =>
            accept Wait do
              acquired := TRUE;
            end;
          or
            accept Signal;
            acquired := FALSE;
          or
            terminate;
        end select;
      end loop;
    end Semaphore;

    task type Mult is
    end;
    task body Mult is
      iloc: INTEGER;
    begin
      loop
        Semaphore.Wait;
        iloc := nextRow;
        nextRow := nextRow + 1;
        Semaphore.Signal;
        exit when iloc > Size;
        for j in 1..Size loop
          c(iloc,j) := 0;
          for k in 1..Size loop
            c(iloc,j) :=
                    c(iloc,j) + a(iloc,k)*b(k,j);
```

```
            end loop;
          end loop;
        end loop;
      end Mult;
    begin -- procedure ParMult
      declare m: array (1..numProcs) of Mult;
      begin
        null;
      end;
      return c;
    end ParMult;
  end IntMatrices;
```

53. A process is an independently executing section of code, while a future represents the return value of a still-executing process to another process. Processes can exist without futures: if processes are independent of each other, no futures are required. Similarly, futures can exist without processes or parallel computation: pass by name "thunks" can be thought of as futures in a nonparallel setting. (Spur Lisp actually places some restrictions on futures as opposed to ordinary processes. Futures are processes that execute essentially only to produce values—the underlying process of a future cannot be accessed or modified by process functions such as kill-process or suspend-process.)

56. The search tree of the Prolog program is displayed here. Since alternatives at the same level are executed in parallel, we can get a sense of how much parallel computational payoff there is by comparing the height of the tree to the number of nodes in the tree. In this case there are seven nodes, but the height of the tree is four. Thus we expect a savings of about three steps, or as much as three sevenths of the execution time. (Because of unification and process overhead, this is not likely to be achieved.)

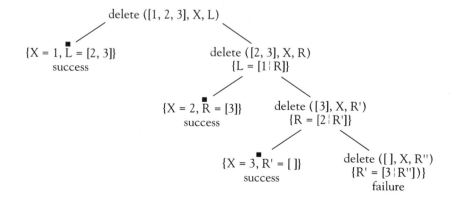

Index

628